COLLECTIVE BARGAINING

COLLECTIVE BARGAINING

THIRD EDITION

Neil W. Chamberlain

Armand G. Erpf Emeritus Professor
Graduate School of Business
Columbia University

James W. Kuhn

Courtney C. Brown Professor of Organization and Management
Graduate School of Business
Columbia University

McGRAW-HILL BOOK COMPANY

New York   St. Louis   San Francisco   Auckland   Bogotá
Hamburg   Johannesburg   London   Madrid   Mexico   Montreal   New Delhi
Panama   Paris   São Paulo   Singapore   Sydney   Tokyo   Toronto

This book was set in Times Roman by University Graphics, Inc. (ECU).
The editors were Patricia A. Mitchell, Ellen W. MacElree, and Laura D. Warner;
the cover was designed by Scott Chelius;
the production supervisor was Marietta Breitwieser.
R. R. Donnelley & Sons Company was printer and binder.

COLLECTIVE BARGAINING

1 2 3 4 5 6 7 8 9 0   DOC DOC   8 9 8 7 6 5

ISBN 0-07-010441-7

Library of Congress Cataloging in Publication Data

Chamberlain, Neil W.
    Collective bargaining.

    Includes bibliographical references and index.
    1. Collective bargaining.   2. Industrial relations.
3. Collective bargaining—United States.   I. Kuhn,
James W.   II. Title.
HD6971.5.C43   1986   331.89   85-7814
ISBN 0-07-010441-7

CONTENTS

PREFACE

Collective bargaining has developed in recent years in ways quite different from those that were assumed only a decade ago. While it has spread to the public sector and is widely used there, it has actually declined in the private sector. Fewer workers in business firms are now covered by collective bargaining agreements today than at any time in the past generation. There is a continuing, pervasive skepticism about the worth of collective bargaining among both the public and management. It meets with no great opposition where it is already well established; but except for unionists few are convinced that it should be more widely practiced than it is at present. Dissatisfaction continues to be expressed with procedural anachronisms that linger on, and many labor advocates raise concerns over the failure of collective bargaining to win a more commanding place in the relationships of employers and employees.

This third edition of *Collective Bargaining* has been revised to reflect both recent research and the changes in labor institutions and industrial relations. It still considers the history, nature, problems, and potential of collective bargaining, stressing the evolutionary nature of the bargaining process, the mixture of styles, both primitive and sophisticated, that continue to manifest themselves, and the ongoing changes in procedures, and even in conception, of bargaining. These emphases seem as appropriate today as they did when the first edition appeared.

Popular commentators and many labor scholars believe that both unions and managements need to consider new approaches to old needs in a time of spreading industrialization throughout the world and consequent increases in world competition. The needs are compounded by rapidly changing technologies that are increasing service occupations and industries much faster than manufacturing, long the bastion of unions and collective bargaining. Both union and management negotiators have so concentrated upon the daily issues and narrow concerns of their immediate responsibilities that there has been all too little experimentation in new forms of collective bargaining. Only out of the difficulties of plant closures, threatened bankruptcies, and declining markets have both parties realized that cooperation may be more than an ideal—it may be a necessity.

Policy with respect to the appropriate role of government in labor relations is also undergoing change. Attitudes toward public authority and responsibility on the strike and wage fronts have been subjected to critical review. Some labor leaders have become so disenchanted with the federal government's role through the National Labor Relations Board that they have suggested at least a partial repeal of the basic statutes, and the de facto breaking of a national union by the federal administration in 1981 indicated a greatly altered relationship between government and unions. If attitudes and trends are highly inconclusive, this too reflects a continued questioning of whether old problems, now arising in changed contexts, do not present the need for fresh solutions.

We have attempted to incorporate more the attitude of quest than of conclusion in these pages, and more the need for analysis to modify policies than for analysis to explain existing practices.

Finally, we wish to acknowledge our intellectual debt to the innumerable scholars and researchers who have created many of the materials out of which these pages have been spun. Many lively minds have reflected on the issues of collective bargaining, to our benefit. We have enjoyed and profited from discussions and exchanges with our colleagues, not only at the Graduate School of Business, Columbia University, but also in the profession at large. In acknowledgment of this debt, rather than as an assertion of accomplishment, this book can properly be said to be a collaboration of many more than two people.

Neil W. Chamberlain
James W. Kuhn

COLLECTIVE BARGAINING

INTRODUCTION

THE DIVERSITY OF COLLECTIVE BARGAINING

"Collective bargaining" is the term Americans use to describe the activity of employers and representatives of organized employees through which the two parties establish and administer rules and conditions of work as well as hours and wages. Narrowly construed, it refers only to the periodic negotiating of agreements that define specific terms and provisions; more widely defined, it includes all the processes through which employers (or employing organizations) and unions interact.

In the United States, collective bargaining has displayed various forms and reveals even today, in careful examination, several natures. Workers and employers—union leaders and managers—have not developed collective bargaining according to any theoretical model or even a well-structured notion of how it should proceed. They pragmatically adopted one form or another and discovered its particular nature as they responded to their successes and failures of the moment. Experience more than theory has molded collective bargaining, producing an untidy variety that can be neither easily described nor succinctly analyzed. Scholars have not always agreed upon the features that best characterize American unionism and its collective bargaining. Some have argued that the essence of unions is their variety, whereas others have stressed common features within their variety.

Representative of the former point of view is Professor Robert F. Hoxie, of the University of Chicago. Writing before 1917, he found the differences among unions and their collective bargaining to be more significant than their similarities. He described five major types and several lesser types of union-

1

ism.[1] Professor Selig Perlman, of the University of Wisconsin, represents the second point of view. In his *A Theory of the Labor Movement,* first published in 1929, he defended the thesis that American unionism tended toward a typical kind of collective bargaining. Through it unionists pursued limited goals of winning control of wages and jobs. Convinced that opportunities were scarce, workers organized to protect their job interests, bargaining to establish the rules and conditions that define their "collective ownership over the whole amount of [job] opportunity."[2] In thus describing unions and collective bargaining, he emphasized their common elements in different settings and played down their differences. The analyses and descriptions of both Hoxie and Perlman, and of those who follow their respective leads, have much validity and can be applied usefully today, more than half a century after they were offered. In American collective bargaining one can find central tendencies and make reasonable generalizations; one would be well advised to note, however, the wide and sometimes amazing diversity within which they occur.

Much of the diversity arises from the fact that collective bargaining is at once old and new, and it has manifested this dual characteristic over a long time span. In every decade over the past century or more, some workers and employees have only begun to practice it, exploring its potential and adapting its forms. Yet others, at least 175 years ago, carried on in a fashion suggestive of modern, well-established union-management relationships. The term itself belongs to the twentieth century, though Beatrice Webb coined it in 1881.[3] More than a decade later, in 1902, the Industrial Commission, created by an act of Congress in 1898, noted the slow spread of the term "collective bargaining": "It is not often employed in common speech in the United States, but is gradually coming into use among employers and employees in Great Britain. It evidently describes quite accurately the practice by which employers and employees in conference, from time to time, agree upon the terms under which labor shall be performed."[4]

What are the reasons for the mixture of both old and new use of this process that only slowly gained recognition and a name? They are several; the most important at first was discontinuity in the use of bargaining methods and bargaining organizations through most of the nineteenth century. For many years bargaining was so intermittent and negotiated outcomes were so ephemeral

---

[1]Business unionism; friendly, or uplife unionism; revolutionary unionism, of socialist and quasi-anarchistic kinds; predatory unionism, of holdup and guerilla forms; and dependent, or company unionism. See Robert F. Hoxie, *Trade Unionism in the United States,* New York: D. Appleton & Company, Inc., 1917.

[2]Selig Perlman, *A Theory of the Labor Movement,* New York: Augustus M. Kelley, 1949, p. 242.

[3]Beatrice Potter (Mrs. Sidney Webb), *The Cooperative Movement in Great Britain,* London: George Allen & Unwin, Ltd., 1891, p. 217. However, Terence Powderly, who served as General Master Wordman in the Knights of Labor, says in his autobiography that Andrew Roy, a student of and participant in coal miners' organizations, wrote as early as 1874 of the "right of the miners to bargain collectively." [Terence V. Powderly, *The Path I Trod,* Harry J. Carman, Henry David, and Paul N. Guthrie (eds.), New York: Columbia University Press, 1940, p. 310.]

[4]*Final Report of the Industrial Commission,* Reports of the Industrial Commission, vol. 19 (1902), p. 834.

that observers—and even participants—hardly recognized the elements of continuity and similarity among their activities. Furthermore, bargaining practices varied considerably from place to place and industry to industry; negotiations also changed as the structures of business enterprise and unions altered with the coming and flowering of industrialization.

Neither workers nor employees at first had any clear notion of what form of collective bargaining might best serve their interests. A unilateral determination and imposition of terms appeared to promise the greatest advantage. Employers favored unilateral bargaining. First, they were used to setting the terms of work and insisted that they continue to do so, except when forced by unions' superior bargaining power to agree to other terms. Second, employers saw bargaining as an intermittent and opportunistic activity, required only when economic conditions favored unions and worked against themselves. If now and then they had to put up with unions' unilateral imposition of terms, they could be assured that times would soon change and they could resume their own imposition.

Both parties were thus able to make the most of whatever short-term advantages came their ways. Their flexible and immediate responses sacrificed opportunities for nurturing much stability in their relationships, but the costs involved seemed slight. Unions appeared and vanished quickly in any case; most business firms were small, usually but enlarged images of a single entrepreneur, and almost as subject as unions to the uncertainties of economic vicissitudes. Business conditions through most of the nineteenth century did not encourage considerations of long-term dealings with a group of employees.

Gradually unions found ways of establishing themselves as continuing organizations, and many employing firms grew large and durable enough to value the benefits of attaching workers to their jobs. Both managers and union leaders came to realize the value of stability, as well as of flexibility, in negotiating wages and conditions of work. Managerial acceptance of unions and collective bargaining has seldom been wholehearted or unreserved, however. As a result, unorganized employers have continued to resist efforts to organize unions, and a pervasive adversarial approach to industrial relations prevails even where unions established themselves long ago. Only in recent years, confronted by previously unknown competitive pressures from abroad, have managers in some firms and industries begun seriously to explore the promise of partnership with unions and cooperation at the workplace: creative problem solving, to their mutual gain.

CHANGE AND VARIATION IN COLLECTIVE BARGAINING

The instabilities of unions through most of the nineteenth century contributed to the uncertainties of collective bargaining. As unions gained members and strength, bargaining advanced, only to wane or disappear when unions weakened and lost members. Prior to the Civil War, workers found they could usually organize successfully during business upturns, in the prosperity phase of business cycles. In the downturns that followed, however, the unions collapsed. Unable to cope with the unemployment and low wages of depression, workers again and again saw their labor movements virtually die out.

The discontinuity of many unions and the uncertain strength of those that survived significantly affected collective bargaining. An early development of a bargaining technique might be killed before it could take root and spread. Neither workers nor employers could learn to effectively use a system that depended for its existence upon unions whose own existence was uncertain. Hard experience taught the validity of this lesson over and over as workers in various industries sought the benefits of collective bargaining.

Thus for a century collective bargaining had developed a history, even if tenuous, and in this sense was old; workers in a few industries and occupations had experimented with one or another form of bargaining for several generations. At the same time, with little or no continuous organization, they often had to invent anew union forms and rediscover union activities. By the end of the nineteenth century, however, a number of craft unions, such as those of the carpenters, miners, cigar makers, and printers, had firmly established themselves and collective bargaining in their limited industrial sectors. Workers, employers, and the public became more accustomed to and accepting of collective bargaining in these restricted sectors; but in the economy at large many people still perceived unions as new and dangerous organizations and saw collective bargaining as a novel, untried, and radical process.

In the twentieth century collective bargaining has remained a curious mixture of old and new, no longer because of its discontinuity, but rather because it has spread unevenly, surging into full development in one place, occupation, or industry while still completely absent in others. It did not take hold among the skilled workers and then spread uniformly and steadily among the rest of the work force. Although it no longer disappeared and unions seldom dissolved during depressions and hard times, workers in whole industries and in many occupations did not attempt to organize even in prosperity and booms.

THE STRUGGLE TO ESTABLISH COLLECTIVE BARGAINING

In the early nineteenth century, during the germinal phase of the process that much later came to be known as collective bargaining, both parties concerned themselves first of all with flexibility. The unions of that period were not even called unions. What we call a union was then known among its members as a "society" or as "the body," and sometimes employers referred to it opprobriously as a "combination." A society, body, or combination seldom had continuity of organization. It existed most of the time in a quiescent state, rising to life only for particular occasions. At such times the members would hold meetings at one another's homes, elect temporary officers, and decide programs of action.

The method of seeking wage change seems to have been simple and direct. The members of the trade association—the cordwainers (leatherworkers), for example—would gather and agree among themselves on the "price list," or piece rates that were to be sought. They then took an oath that none were to work for less or work alongside any journeyman who worked for less. Committees appointed from among their number then visited the masters at their shops to inform them of the actions taken. The masters were advised that their employees would not report for work until the demands had been met.

Local Unilateral Bargaining

In such a unilateral campaign the members would call a strike ("turn out" or "stand out," in the language of the day) against those employers who refused to accept the revised "bill of wages." Since all employers seldom conceded on the initial notice, a strike was a necessary and integral part of the process of increasing wages. The demands that they had drawn up as the body were not bargaining proposals, set two or three times higher than the expected settlement price. They did not intend or expect compromise. The campaign was not a process of negotiation, but rather a trial of economic strength to determine whose wage decisions would prevail—the body's (union's) or the employer's.

As the contests of strength between the organized employees and disorganized employers became more frequent and the employers began better to recognize the pattern, they consulted among themselves to reach a common understanding, either to accept or to reject the worker's terms. Those employers who refused to go along with the body's demands might be subject to its punitive action, usually blacklisting. In general, the informal employers' associations aimed to put down the strike, not by any process of reaching an agreement, but simply by wearing down the strikers. On neither side, therefore, was there any thought of compromise; each approached the other with only the possibility of winning or losing. That possibility was greatly influenced by general economic conditions and the state of the market.

Well past the middle of the century, unilateral imposition of terms continued to mark the typical union-employer relationship. Each party set wages if and when it could maximize a tactical advantage. Unionists, on the one hand, struck when they believed that economic circumstances so favored them that they could obtain the whole of their demand, without countenancing concession. Such a time was usually one of rising prices. On the other hand, employers reduced wages when they believed the economic occasion was propitious for securing the whole of a reduction. In such a time of depression and high unemployment they did not need to worry about placating their workers with any compromise. It is obvious that such a system of wage setting allowed greater flexibility to both parties and provided little stability. As long as unions appeared only spasmodically and their wins were few, employers suffered few inconveniences from the instabilities; the benefits of flexibility were far greater and more important to them. Most employers continued to oppose unionism and any say by workers in the setting of wages;[1] more important, only a few found they had to deal with unions in any case.

A few union leaders and business spokespersons had begun to question the wisdom of unilateral imposition of terms. Although it offered flexibility to employers, it also imposed high costs. More regular and stable, controllable procedures for fixing wages could provide attractive benefits. Horace Greeley,

---

[1]Probably representative of employer sentiments were the strong comments by the editor of the *New York Journal of Commerce*. With respect to union wage demands in 1850 and 1851, he wrote on February 6, 1851: "Quite recently the combination have raised the price of week hands to our price ($14), and have added 2 cents a thousand to the price of piecework, making 32 cents a thousand. They have enacted various other rules for the government of employers, which we shall adopt when we make up our minds to yield our independence, our self-respect, and the control of our own business, to the dictation of a self-constituted power outside of the office." And on February 7, the *Journal* continued the attack as follows: "Who but the miserable, craven-hearted man, would permit himself to be subjected to such rules, extending even to the number of apprentices he may employ and the manner in which they shall be bound to him, to the kind of work which shall be performed in his own office at particular hours of the day, and to the sex of the persons employed, however, separated into different apartments of buildings? For ourselves, we never employed a female as a compositor, and have no great opinion of apprentices, but sooner than be restricted on these points, or any other, by a self-constituted tribunal outside of the office, we would go back to the employment of our boyhood, and dig potatoes, pull flax, and do everything else that a plain, honest farmer may properly do on his own territory. It is marvelous to us how any employer, having the soul of a man within him, can submit to such degradation." [From George A. Stevens, *New York Typographical Union No. 6*, New York State Department of Labor, Annual Report of the Bureau of Labor Statistics (1911), part I, pp. 239, 240–241.]

onetime president of the New York printers' union and later reformer-politician and publisher of the *New York Daily Tribune,* argued strongly against unilateral imposition. It was but a kind of "unregulated, unrestricted competition—the free trade principle of 'every man for himself' and 'buy where you can the cheapest'—[that] tends everywhere and necessarily to the depression of wages and the concentration of wealth." He pointed out that unilateral action imposed the heavy losses and wastes of strikes:

> We believe that strikes, or refusals of journeymen to work at such wages as they can command, are seldom necessary—that proper representations and conciliatory action on the part of journeymen would secure all requisite modifications of wages without striking—and that the aggregate of wasted time, misdirected energy, embittered feeling and social anarchy which a strike creates is seldom compensated by any permanent enhancement of wages thus obtained.[2]

National union leaders, too, found unilateral action costly, as well as a threat to union stability and even existence. In the post-Civil War period, when national unions experienced a mushrooming growth in their respective trades, the officers of the new organizations soon found that unilateral action by their constituent local unions was an embarassment at best and an unbearable drain on limited resources at worst. Such action provoked adverse public reaction at a time when they were seeking to expand their influence in the national arena; it also encouraged irresponsible locals to demand support from their national treasuries, threatening the financial stability of the struggling national organizations.

The Gradual Spread of Bilateral Bargaining

The Moulders, as early as 1865, required their local unions to follow specified bargaining procedures before striking. Perhaps even more significant was the development of agreements whose life did not depend solely on economic exigencies. In the iron industry the United Sons of Vulcan and employers, meeting in conference, reached an agreement on February 13, 1865. It was described a decade and a half later as "probably the first important attempt at conciliation[3] in this country."[4] After the first year's experience under the agreement, the parties made some changes in the terms, which then remained in force for seven years! Similar stability in collective bargaining was developing

---

[2]*New York Daily Tribune,* April 13, 1853. The full statement can be found in Stevens, *New York Typographical Union No. 6,* pp. 621–622.

[3]The term "conciliation" was then commonly used to indicate the process of fixing wages, indicating it was primarily a contest between incompatible demands and not the horse trading or bargaining that now prevails.

[4]Joseph D. Weeks, *Report to the Governor of Pennsylvania on the Practical Operation of Arbitration and Conciliation in the Settlement of Differences Between Employers and Employees in England,* Harrisburg, Penn.: Lane S. Hart, 1879, p. 111; quoted in John R. Commons et al., *History of Labour in the United States,* vol. 2, New York: The MacMillan Company, 1921, p. 80.

in the anthracite coal region of Pennsylvania at about the same time, in the early 1870s. The Knights of St. Crispin (shoemmakers) in Massachusetts also succeeded in winning negotiated agreements that were continued with adjustments and changes over a period of years.[5]

Gradually, in one negotiation after another, collective bargaining made headway and gained acceptance during the closing years of the nineteenth century. The national agreement negotiated in the stove-foundry industry in 1891 provided a major impetus. It brought to a close some thirty years of bickering and warfare between employer and employee groups. Under the new system, committees consisting of three representatives from the union and three from the employers were to meet annually to draft terms covering the organized portion of the industry. Local disputes, affecting only a single plant and its workers, were to be settled by the immediate parties if possible. In the event of continued disagreement the controversy was to be referred to the national presidents of both organizations; failing their agreement, a joint conference committee similar to the original negotiating committee was to serve as final referee. Stable agreements had been negotiated before, but none matched this epochal agreement for scope or stability. Coming as it did as a climax to years of friction, it served as an incentive and guide to the relatively few employers who recognized and regularly negotiated with unions.

At the turn of the century, collective bargaining was still a relatively unimportant part of the industrial scene. In 1901 union membership totaled just over 1 million in a nonagricultural work force of over 16 million. Fewer than 7 percent of industrial workers enjoyed collective bargaining, and more than a third of them were in mining and building trades. Only a tiny minority of employers were willing to recognize unions for the purpose of negotiations. In some cases managers or employer associations negotiated only if the circumstances of union strength or public demands of a rare kind made it expedient. They steadily threw over the union and resumed an independent course whenever the situation permitted. Until the passage of federal legislation in the thirties that outlawed such activities, corporate managers and employers often combated unions with industrial espionage, blacklisting, and strikebreakers.[6] Even in recent years, as will shortly be described, some managers have used such tactics to defeat or resist union-organizing drives.

Employers Challenge Collective Bargaining

The steel industry, with its large-scale structure and basic contribution to the national economy at the turn of the century, might have provided a stability beneficial to collective bargaining. Instead, in the formation of gigantic business corporations, particularly that of the United States Steel Corporation in

---

[5] *Eighth Annual Report of the Bureau of Labor Statistics,* Massachusetts, 1877, pp. 41–43.

[6] The three practices "to which workingmen most frequently object," according to the Industrial Commission in 1898 in *Final Report of the Industrial Commission,* p. 890.

1901, it offered managers the power and ability to stamp out unionism and to discard labor negotiations. In the same year, the employers undertook in earnest an antiunion offensive. The National Metal Trades Association adopted a policy frankly opposed to collective bargaining through unions. In 1903, the National Association of Manufacturers followed suit in its "Declaration of Labor Principles." Also in 1903, more than 100 employers' associations joined to establish the Citizens' Industrial Association as a spearhead for the "open shop" drive, as the antiunion movement came generally to be known. If the collective bargaining movement had gained ground, it had also solidified its opposition.[7]

The scientific management movement posed another threat to collective bargaining. It had begun in the post-Civil War period but did not attract widespread attention in this country until about 1910. Through job standardization and time and motion study it promised to remove all disputes over a fair day's work. It was argued that the increased production resulting from greater efficiency as well as the new incentive systems, which were presumed to be psychologically founded, would permit workers to earn higher wages. By this two-pronged approach, all the traditional disputes between workers and managers would be solved scientifically. There was little room for collective bargaining, since it could only disturb the "scientific" conclusions. The decisions in those areas in which labor had for so long been fighting for a voice were to be removed to an impartial, objective set of judges—the efficiency engineers. Although the movement was not explicitly antiunion, unionists nevertheless perceived in it a danger to the collective bargaining movement.

The fight that unions waged against this new philosophy constitutes one of

---

[7]Where certain unions acquired a power greater than that of the employers they faced, the system of negotiations was sometimes abandoned for unilateral imposition of terms. The report in 1915 of the second industrial commission appointed by Congress (the Commisssion on Industrial Relations) described a well-defined system of union control in the San Francisco building trades at that time which duplicated the system employed more generally almost a hundred years earlier. All decisions of individual unions on wages and working conditions required the approval of the San Francisco Building Trades Council before they could be imposed. Upon such approval, the union would inform the employers when the new scale or revised conditions would go into effect.

The president of the Building Trades Employer's Association described the system before the Industrial Commission: "There is no collective bargaining in this city, as I understand the term. The system in vogue in this city is: The unions pass a so-called law raising the scale of wages or changing the working conditions; that is referred to the Building Trades Council for their approval; if approved by the Building Trades Council, it is put in force; sometimes notice is given and again no notice is given in spite of the fact that the Building Trades Council say that one of their laws is that a ninety days' notice must be given before a change in wages or working conditions is put into effect. The employer has no voice whatever in making the above-stated rules; the employer's part consists in making what resistance he can; this resistance has met with no degree of success, excepting cases of housesmiths' trouble in the matter of eight-hour day in structural shops. Collective bargaining, as I understand the term, presumes discussion and consultation by the parties concerned before agreements are made. Here there is no such discussion. The so-called agreement is the ultimatum of one party which the other party has no choice but to accept." [Ira B. Cross, "The San Francisco Building Trades," in John R. Commons (ed.), *Trade Unionism and Labor Problems,* Boston: Ginn and Company, 1921, p. 484.]

the most absorbing chapters in the history of the American labor movement.[8] For our present interest, however, it is sufficient to note that this threat to union security spurred intensive union organization, increased efforts on behalf of collective bargaining, and stimulated preliminary explorations into the field of union-management cooperation for production improvement. The promise of union injury was thus not fulfilled, and the problem posed was partly solved in later years when unions won the right to question the findings of a company's efficiency engineers and even to introduce their own engineers to check on the company's experts. As scientific management became better understood, those who applied it realized that broad areas of its subject matter required value judgment rather than scientific objectivism, so the need for consultation, negotiations, and agreement had not, after all, been removed.

Employee Representation as an Alternative

The employee-representation movement limited the spread of unions and collective bargaining more than did the scientific management movement. Its support came from employers who rebelled at the notion of dealing with their workers through "outside" representatives. Variations of employee representation have regularly appeared and are still used as a method of blocking unionization. The first plan placed in effect is sometimes said to have been that in a Pittsburgh lamp company in the winter of 1903–1904, although Filene's of Boston sponsored certain employee representation activities as early as 1898. The first use of employee representation in a company with a large work force came in 1915, when managers of the Colorado Fuel and Iron Company, with 12,000 employees, instituted one such plan.

Although there were many variations between representation plans, the basic elements were the same. They offered a "constitutional" system under which the employees in an individual company or plant, shop by shop or department by department, selected representatives to a "legislature," in which management was also represented. Representation plans usually did not allow separate meetings of the parties—indeed, the concept of "parties" was sometimes disavowed by substituting for it the concept of workers and management as constituting together the citizens of an industrial community. Nevertheless, workers' representatives were permitted to raise questions concerning wages and working conditions in assembly. The final decision, though, rested with management. The whole plan thus resembled a large complaint committee through which managers could learn the complaints of the workers and, in turn, convey to them what was being done on their behalf. It was more a communication system than a means of joint decision making. Leaders in the movement stressed the latter aspect, nevertheless, and employee representa-

---

[8]A succinct statement of the opposing views is found in Hoxie, *Trade Unionism in the United States,* chaps, 12, 13.

tion was made to appear preferable to collective bargaining. They argued that it allowed both workers and employers to avoid the costs of strikes, lockouts, iolence, picketing, and other such unsavory activities.

Some of those in the representation movement sought to spread the idea that employee representation was a form of collective bargaining, despite certain basic and evident differences. A comparison of the differences can be made when they are presented as follows:

Employee representation	Collective bargaining
Employees can be represented only by fellow employees in the same company.	Employees can be represented by anyone they choose, whether or not in employ of the company.
Committee represents the employees of only one plant or company.	Local union commonly joins with other local unions for greater strength.
No provision for appeal over management decision. Independent action by employees not contemplated.	Management decision may be contested by strike action.
Usually initiated by management.	Usually initiated by employees.

Such differences have led those making special studies of representation plans to conclude that employee-representation systems and collective bargaining are "distinct and conflicting systems" diametrically opposed in principle.[9] Certainly this was the view of trade-union leaders, since employee representation by its very nature operated independent of them. In some respects, employee representation seemed to constitute a more effective, if less direct, threat to the collective bargaining movement than the blunt, warlike forms of opposition—espionage, blacklisting, and strikebreaking pools. Employee-representation systems preempted any role for collective bargaining and employers insisted they were good substitutes, promising the same benefits.

Advance during World War I

The preemption of the role of collective bargaining was a serious matter for unionists; collective bargaining was still a relatively unimportant industrial phenomenon and any challenge was a serious threat to its existence. At the beginning of World War I only a small segment of the work force had organized, and few employers were willing to recognize unions and bargain or negotiate with them. Despite their limited numbers, the small group of unionists and the minority of employers with whom they dealt were gradually developing, through trial and error, the general features of today's typical collective

---

[9]Carroll E. French, *The Shop Committee in the United States,* Baltimore: The John Hopkins Press, 1923, pp. 12–15. Paul H. Douglas also discusses the differences in "Shop Committees: Substitutes for or Supplement to Trade Unions?" *Journal of Political Economy,* vol. 29, 1921, p. 89.

bargaining. To secure stability in the relationship they came to depend upon written agreements, whose general terms continued in force until appropriately changed through negotiations. Day-to-day problems and issues of application of the terms under specific conditions increasingly came to be treated separately through "grievance procedures." Such treatment offered opportunity for adjustments over the life of the agreement, and periodic, often annual, renegotiation of the whole agreement permitted alterations and flexibility to meet changing economic conditions. Strikes might still occur, but the parties increasingly became wary of using them to gain a short-term advantage with any dip or rise in the economy. Both union leaders and employers came to appreciate the benefits of a given set of rules governing their dealings over the period of the agreement. Rules allowed stability and permitted both parties to turn more attention to other matters of importance.

Federal control of labor relations during World War I led to an expansion of the unions' influence, but at the same time it stimulated the employee-representation movement. The National War Labor Board ordered managers to negotiate with their employees, but except in those companies that previously had established relations with "outside" unions, managers were not required to deal with other than their own employees. For all practical purposes the board endorsed employee representation, and in fact it encouraged and even ordered the establishment of such systems as a means of solving local disputes and relieving itself of a potentially greater caseload.[10]

Though the board had supported employee representation as well as unions, collective bargaining made its greatest gains to date. By the end of the war, union membership had surged to unprecedented numbers, nearly 3½ million—not quite 9 percent of the civilian labor force and less than half its relative size today. Railroad and other transportation workers had enrolled three-quarters of a million, the building trades had recruited almost as many, and a quarter of a million clothing workers and nearly half a million miners had joined unions. Unions represented a large group and collective bargaining was an important process in industrial America; the president sought to regularize their role in the economy. President Wilson assembled a National Industrial Conference after the war, composed of representatives of management, organized labor, and the public, to work out a tripartite code of industrial relations to facilitate the transition from war to peace. Managers sponsored their employee-representation plans and sharply clashed with union leaders who favored collective bargaining. The points of view are illustrated by the resolutions proposed by the two groups. Management representatives suggested the following:

> . . . that without in any way limiting the right of a wage earner to refrain from joining any association or to deal directly with his employer as he chooses, the right of wage

---

[10]A comprehensive summary of the board's position is contained in *Report of the National War Labor Board* (1920), pp. 56–67.

earners in private as distinguished from government employment to organize in trade and labor unions, in shop industrial councils, or other lawful form of association, to bargain collectively, to be represented by representatives of their own choosing in negotiations and adjustments with employers in respect to wages, hours of labor, and other conditions of employment, is recognized; *and the right of the employer to deal or not to deal with men or groups of men who are not his employees and chosen by and from among them is recognized;* and no denial is intended of the right of an employer and his workers voluntarily to agree upon the form of their representative relations. [Italics supplied.]

Neither the public nor the unions' representatives were willing to accept this proposal, which would have favored the employee-representation system over the collective bargaining system. It permitted the employer to insist on the former and to deny the latter.

The union conferees offered a counterproposal:

The right of wage earners to organize without discrimination, to bargain collectively, to be represented by representatives of their own choosing in negotiations and adjustments with employers in respect to wages, hours of labor, and relations and conditions of employment is recognized.

Management representatives would not entertain this proposal, for it would have required them to recognize outside unions. The president's conference broke on this issue and adjourned without accomplishment.[11]

But if the struggle between these two systems remained unresolved during this period, the drama of that contest should not be allowed to blind us to a significant change. In a sense, the end of World War I marked also the end of an era of industrial relations. Wartime compulsory negotiation had stimulated the employee-representation movement. The postwar drive by organized labor to substitute collective bargaining for representation had motivated a spirited defense of the latter by the employers as a group. Having thus espoused a process of *collective* representation, even though not the process sought by the unions, many employers found it difficult to retrace their steps to individual bargaining. Some found it even undesirable. From this point on, labor relations would remain largely a collective matter. The only issue was the nature

[11]The public group was willing to accept the union proposal, but only after it had entered a resolution of its own that sought to harmonize the two views: "The right of wage earners in trade and labor unions to bargain collectively, to be represented by representatives of their own choosing in negotiations and adjustments with employers in respect to wages, hours of labor, and relations and conditions of employment is recognized. This must not be understood as limiting the right of any wage earner to refrain from joining any organization or to deal directly with his employer if he so chooses." The management group refused to support this resolution since it would have required their acceptance of collective bargaining whenever employees preferred this to representation. On the other hand, the union group refused to accept it since it would have forbidden the closed shop. See the account given by Judge Elbert H. Gary, appointed as a public representative to the conference, in *Review of Reviews,* vol. 60, 1920, p. 487; also *Monthly Labor Review,* vol. 9, 1919, p. 1342.

of the collective agency. The situation was neatly summarized in a statement in 1920 by Royal Meeker, commissioner of the U.S Bureau of Labor Statistics:

> The huge majority of employers in this country are, and always have been, opposed to labor organizations. The President's First Industrial Congress came to a deadlock on the question of the right of employees to organize and to choose representatives to deal with management. The employer group in the conference must be taken as representing the majority of employers the country over. The speeches made by these representative employers were often difficult to understand, but their attitude of mind was never for a moment in doubt. They had been driven by hard experience to abandon individual bargaining, but they vigorously maintained their right to dictate the terms of the collective bargain. These employers conceded the right of workers to organize in a given plant and to be represented by representatives chosen from among the employees of that plant, provided the representatives so chosen were agreeable to the management of said plant.[12]

The Twenties: Union Decline and Doldrums for Collective Bargaining

Throughout the twenties, employee representation remained a serious threat to collective bargaining. Union membership had risen to over 5 million by 1920, but thereafter declined throughout the decade, ending in 1929 at less than 3½ million, a 32-percent drop. Even as unions shrank and collective bargaining disappeared from many plants and factories, the employee-representation movement thrived. It added as many as 1 million employees and acquired a "firm hold" in iron and steel, machine manufacturing, coal and iron mining, textiles, food products, and public service corporations, and was making its entry into railroads and meat-packing.[13]

Even where unions received federal legislative protection for collective bargaining, as in the case of the railroad workers in 1926, they could no more than hold their own. They began the decade with 1¼ million members and ended it with fewer than 900,000, a 28-percent decline. Railroads have long attracted a special public interest and their workers had received special treatment in labor relations since 1888. The failure of the Railroad Labor Board, established under the Transportation Act of 1920, to satisfy either the carriers or the railway brotherhoods led to the Railway Labor Act of 1926, which was further strengthened by amendments in 1934. The government recognized the right of the railroad workers to negotiate through representatives chosen at their own discretion. It imposed on railroad managers the duty to negotiate exclusively with the employees' representatives on matters of "rates of pay, rules and working conditions."

Not only did railroad workers enjoy a strategic economic position in the

---

[12]Royal Meeker, "Employees' Representation in Management of Industry," *Monthly Labor Review*, vol. 10, 1920, p. 7.

[13]French, *The Shop Committee in the United States*, p. 29.

nation, but they also were clearly engaged in interstate commerce, an activity under the exclusive authority of the federal government.[14] Under the Supreme Court's then narrow definition of interstate commerce, almost no other groups of workers could look to the federal government for aid in organizing or encouragement in bargaining. As in the past, all except railroad employees secured collective agreements only if they were strong enough to get recognition of their unions and to force bargaining. In most states, the law created further obstacles to union organization, providing the injunction as a device by which employers might stop strikes and break up union efforts to organize or to support economic demands. The Supreme Court in a number of cases between the turn of the century and 1927 also had greatly restricted union use of boycotts and strikes, holding them to be in violation of the Antitrust Act of 1890.[15]

The Thirties and World War II: Federal Encouragement of Collective Bargaining

The first attempt to extend benefits enjoyed by the railworkers to employees generally came in 1933 with passage of the National Industrial Recovery Act (NIRA), which sought to organize business along lines of "fair competition." Its supporters hoped that it would stimulate recovery from the deep depression. Section 7(a) of that act simply required that every code of fair competition contain a guarantee of the right of the employees to organize and select representatives for collective bargaining. It asserted no obligation on the part of the employers to *recognize* unions, however, or to bargain with them, though a labor board created to administer this vague provision, after temporizing for some months, eventually read such obligations into it. Meanwhile, employee-representation plans mushroomed. They were not forbidden by the act, and managements attempted by using them to head off workers' own union organization.

After Supreme Court invalidation of the whole NIRA machinery and the subsequent passage of separate legislation expressly and exclusively for collective bargaining, employees in all businesses affecting interstate commerce finally received rights matching those accorded railroad employees in 1926. The National Labor Relations Act of 1935 (also known as the Wagner Act), the constitutionality of which the Supreme Court upheld in 1937, contained

---

[14]It should also be remembered that the brotherhoods were among the oldest labor organizations in the country and were practiced in the art of legislative lobbying. Their strategic economic position would have meant little in the absence of effective political organization. The potential strength of this combination of bargaining power and strategic position is exemplified in the events leading to the passage in 1916 of the Adamson Act, which established an eight-hour day on the railroads. See *Wilson v. New,* 243 U.S. 332, 1917; and Thomas Reed Powell, "The Supreme Court and the Adamson Law," *University of Pennsylvania Law Review,* vol. 65, 1917, p. 607.

[15]For a summary treatment of the restrictions applied to unions from 1900 to 1930, see Charles O. Gregory and Harold A. Katz, *Labor and the Law,* 3d ed., New York: W. W. Norton & Company, Inc., 1979, chap. 7.

unequivocal guarantees of the right of employees to form into unions and engage in concerted activity, including strike action, without fear of employer reprisal. It also contained uneqivocal prohibitions against interfering with union activity or refusing to recognize and bargain with unions.

The net implication of the National Labor Relations Act was that employee organization was primarily a matter of concern to employees only; employers were required to accept and work with whatever organization their employees established. Consequently the old employee-representation plans were outlawed. Such plans were established by the employer, not by the employees, and hence did not meet the new prohibition against employer control. Thus, by legislative action, what had begun as a major threat to collective bargaining in this country was now transformed into an aid to the unions; for in the organizing campaigns that swept the country after 1937, employee-representation plans, now rendered illegal, were sometimes found by the unions to constitute effective nuclei for new unions.

In 1932 only about 2½ million employees—10 to 12 percent of industrial workers—were employed under collective agreements; between 7 and 8 percent came under employee-representation plans; and approximately 80 percent of all industrial workers were employed under individual contracts.[16] By 1944, with the encouragement of federal labor laws and the high employment and labor shortages during World War II, union membership climbed to its highest point up to that time: over 14 million. So large a membership meant that collective bargaining covered almost a third of the economy's nonagricultural employees. The greatest change had come in the mass-production industries—automobiles, steel, rubber, glass, and electrical equipment—where great concentrations of semiskilled workers had joined with the craft workers to form new industrial unions and to bargain collectively.

When unions spread throughout the mass-production industries in the 1930s and early 1940s, collective bargaining followed the patterns developed by two generations of negotiators. They had experimented with many procedures and processes, but they had found a generally satisfactory balance of stability and flexibility in a fixed-term agreement with grievance procedures to handle disputes arising under it. The parties usually renegotiated their agreements each year. Both sides still commonly appealed to economic tests of strength—strikes or lockouts—for a resolution of disputes either over the terms of the agreement or arising under the agreement. During World War II the government sought peaceful alternatives to such appeals, and under the aegis of the National War Labor Board it introduced many employers and managers, as well as union leaders, to arbitration by outside neutrals and to intervention and mediation by third parties.

Neither the new union members nor their inexperienced and often young leaders were much interested in promoting stable collective bargaining. They were more concerned with the problems of consolidating their own positions

---

[16]*Collective Agreements,* International Labour Office (1936), p. 221.

within the growing organizations and appealing to the unorganized to join them. Union negotiators sought ways of demonstrating their militancy and their devotion to industrial democracy through quick and ready "direct action." They perceived few gains from responsible unionism, preferring to make the most of any circumstances that lent advantage to them.

The managers of many large corporations, learning to deal with unions for the first time, also did not yet appreciate the need for more stability than that provided by annual agreements and an open-ended grievance procedure, even though disputes often ended in strikes and walkouts before the parties reached final settlement. Most managers still rejected the notion of arbitration as a final grievance step, finding repugnant to their putative prerogatives the acceptance of an outsider as a final authority in settling disputes. The regular expiration of the agreement, with its renegotiation, also offered the illusion that the relationship between company and union was a temporary arrangement, depending upon voluntary choice and decision. As both parties learned from experience, however, they were inextricably tied to each other for long terms; they came to realize they dared not treat the needs and demands of each other in temporarily convenient ways. Such treatment offered too little stability upon which to build what was clearly now a necessary and enduring relationship.

The widespread acceptance by industrial managers of collective representation in the twenties—though they still rejected *union* representation—and the swift enrollment of workers in unions in the early thirties finally affected the courts' interpretation of the law of contract and group action. The doctrine of individual freedom of contract had in previous years been raised by the Supreme Court as a barrier to union activity:[17] employment contracts executed by individual employees were considered superior to any collective agreement that sought to supersede them. Now, however, the law gave *collective* contracts primacy. "Individual contracts, no matter what the circumstances that justify their execution or what their terms, may not be availed of to defeat or delay the procedures prescribed by the National Labor Relations Act looking to collective bargaining, nor to exclude the contracting employee from a duly ascertained bargaining unit; nor may they be used to forestall bargaining or to limit or condition the terms of the collective agreement."[18]

We will review in Chapter 11 the various effects of the decisions of the National Labor Relations Board (NLRB) on the bargaining process. Here we note that the board and the courts, from the beginning in 1935, have insisted first that the organization chosen by a majority of employees in a defined unit or jurisdiction is the exclusive representative of *all* employees in that unit;[19]

---

[17]For example, see *Adair v. United States,* 208 U.S. 161, 28 Sup. Ct. 277 (1908); and *Hitchman Coal Co. v. Mitchell,* 245 U.S. 229, 38 Sup. Ct. 65 (1917).

[18]*J.I. Case Co. v. NLRB,* 321 U.S. 332, 337 (1944).

[19]For a brief examination of this doctrine of majority representation, see the Denver Tramway case, *Decisions of the National Labor Board* (NRA), August 1933–March 1934, p. 64; *National Labor Relations Board,* Sen. Rep. 573, 74th Cong., 1st Sess. (1935), pp. 13–14, and H.R. Rep. 1147, 74th Cong., 1st Sess., 1935, pp. 20–22; and Lewis L. Lorwin and Arthur Wubnig, *Labor Relations Boards,* Washington D.C.: The Brookings Institution, 1935, pp. 191–195.

and second that the parties are obligated to negotiate in good faith with the intent of arriving at an agreement which, at the request of either party, must be reduced to a written contract. The old practice of unilateral imposition of terms has been declared contrary to public policy.[20]

With the ending of World War II, collective bargaining emerged as a dominant process of industrial relations in the manufacturing, construction, transportation, and utilities industries. The government's loosening of wage and price controls encouraged a wave of strikes in major industries the like of which was never seen before or since. In 1946 alone, more than 10 percent of the employed workers were involved in work stoppages, and the time lost to strikes in the private nonfarm economy was more than six times greater than the average time lost through strikes in any of the previous nineteen years! Many Americans believed collective bargaining was not working well. Unions and collective bargaining had not fulfilled Congress's expressed hopes of "substantially minimizing" industrial strife. They appeared to be increasing it.

Congress passed the Labor-Management Relations Act of 1947 (also known as the Taft-Hartley Act) to remedy some of the defects collective bargaining had displayed. However, the act's chief significance lay in its confirmation of the policy first endorsed in the National Labor Relations Act of 1935. It made unmistakable the public's continued commitment to collective bargaining and to the protection of workers' rights to organize "for the purpose of negotiating the terms and conditions of their employment." Furthermore, through the act the federal government assumed almost full responsibility for regulating unions' activities and collective bargaining except where these related to purely local affairs. The Supreme Court decided that the federal government had largely preempted the area of labor-management relations, having excluded state regulation in the detailed and often intricate provisions of the laws regulating collective bargaining and other union activities in any company whose business extends beyond a state's boundaries. Congress made some attempt to enlarge the area of state jurisdiction over labor matters, but collective bargaining had become largely an activity of national regard.

THE SEARCH FOR STABILITY: THE CASE OF THE AUTOMOBILE INDUSTRY

The negotiations between the United Automobile Workers (UAW) and General Motors Corporation (GM) from 1937 to 1955 illustrate well the develop-

---

[20]For a comprehensive examination of the National Labor Relations Board's rulings, see its annual reports. The Labor-Management Relations Act of 1947 added obligations resting upon the union as well as upon the employer, established certain restrictions upon strikes affecting the national health and welfare, and revised the use of injunctions and the status of damage suits for breach of collective contract; but, with only minor exceptions, it did not modify the board's interpretation of the meaning of the duty to bargain collectively as developed over a twelve-year period. The act did specify, however, that the duty to bargain involved the union as well as the employer; previously it ran only against the employer, although the board had in 1947 ruled that refusal of a union to bargain in good faith relieved the employer of any obligation to bargain. See *In the Matter of the Times Publishing Co.,* 72 NLRB 676 (1947).

ment and acceptance of collective bargaining as well as increasing appreciation of leaders of both unions and companies for the need to reconcile flexibility and stability in collective bargaining. They began in 1937 only a step away from the unilateral action common a century before. After a series of skirmishes and struggles that ended in a three-month sit-down strike, the UAW won company recognition as bargaining agent only for its members. Only in 1939, after a five-week strike by 7000 skilled workers, did GM recognize the UAW as the exclusive bargaining agent for *all* production and maintenance employees in its organized plants. GM and UAW negotiators then worked out the first agreement in the industry. The next year, 1940, the parties set up an office of impartial umpire, or arbitrator, to help resolve disputes arising under the agreement. It, too, was the first in the industry. Before the parties could voluntarily work out further bargaining relationships, the nation entered World War II, and both had to negotiate under the eye of government agencies for almost 4 years. Wage and price controls and production for government procurement dominated all industrial relations.

With the ending of the war in August 1945, the UAW and GM entered a stormy period of negotiations and strikes. It began with a long strike that lasted from November 1945 to March 1946. Company officials sought more stability than they previously had known, through an agreement whose terms extended beyond a single year; but union leaders feared economic conditions would change too much to risk a longer term, and they wanted to ensure continued flexibility. The parties compromised on a two-year agreement, but with a provision that it could be opened for renegotiations of "economic issues" in the spring of 1947. They had begun to experiment with ways of combining the conflicting desires for stability and flexibility.

They reopened the agreement in 1947, negotiating a wage increase and adding various fringe benefits. General Motors officials continued to be dissatisfied with the yearly negotiations; their frequency was troublesome and the uncertainty they projected costly. Managing so large a corporation required careful planning and well-integrated scheduling. Neither could be reliably carried out as long as labor costs were unpredictable and strikes or interruptions of work were regular annual threats. As important as the managers' dissatisfactions with the annual negotiations was the maturing of the union. The union leadership had consolidated itself after many years of bitter rivalry and intraorganizational fighting. At the 1947 convention Walter Reuther won reelection as union president, and by routing his left-wing opponents he became undisputed leader in the UAW.

Automatic Wage Increases and Multiyear Agreements

As the 1948 negotiations proceeded, the UAW prepared for a strike. Reuther was a strong, imaginative bargainer, but his members were not united in favor of a strike. The Buick workers voted against a strike, as did those in the tool-and-die unit at the Fisher No. 23 plant. With the workers indicating a less than wholehearted support of a walkout, company negotiators pushed their proposals for stabilizing relationships while allowing flexibility in wage setting. They proposed quarterly cost-of-living wage adjustments and "improvement factor" increases on the basis of anticipated increases in productivity. With an extended agreement, these changes promised to end the annual bargaining over wages. Management explained its offer:

> The suggestions we have to offer for a realistic and practical approach to the problem as it affects our employees take into account both the need for stability and the desirability of future progress. . . . [They will] *improve the buying power of an hour of work* so that over a period of years the worker is assured of an improved standard of living; . . . the relations between management and labor [will] be stabilized over a substantial period of time. What we propose can only succeed if we can be assured of stable and cooperative relations with our employees. For this reason our proposals must hinge upon your willingness to enter into an agreement to remain in force for a long-term period.[21]

The union accepted GM's proposals, though it agreed to only a two-year term. The automatic wage features proved to be attractive, serving the busy union leaders' interests as well as those of the company managers. The UAW officers, too, managed a large, far-flung organization. In negotiating literally thousands of agreements, they found GM's proposed provisions a welcome development. The 1948 agreement proved itself over the two years of its existence.

The next general negotiations opened in the spring of 1950 and concluded peacefully, with the parties announcing a five-year agreement. The cost-of-living adjustment continued and the annual improvement factor was increased. Ford and Chrysler also agreed to five-year terms for their agreements. Five years turned out to be too long a period to go without renegotiating wages and fringes, however. The unexpected outbreak of the Korean war drastically changed the economy; prices rose rapidly and war production increased. The government imposed various forms of wage and price controls. In February 1953, UAW and GM negotiators opened formal meetings at which they amended the agreement to take into account the altered and unexpected conditions. In announcing the outcome, both union and management expressed approval. In a joint conference, Reuther remarked in part:

> We are pleased that the General Motors Corporation has accepted the principle that a collective bargaining agreement must be a living document under which the workers' equity is maintained in the case of circumstances impossible for the parties to forsee when the contract was originally negotiated.

Harlow H. Curtice, the new president of GM, described the agreement as a

practical solution to problems created by the Korean war.

---

[21]Benjamin M. Selekman, Stephen H. Fuller, Thomas Kennedy, and John M. Baitsell, *Problems in Labor Relations,* 3d ed., New York: McGraw-Hill Book Company, 1964, pp. 513–514.

He noted that the 1950 contract had had a stabilizing influence on labor-management relations and added:

> We expect the understanding reached today will contribute even more to stabilizing relations among our employees for the remaining two years of the contract.[22]

Two years later, during the 1955 negotiations, GM and UAW agreed to a three-year term, and most succeeding agreements have been for three years; other major automobile producers followed suit.

The Spread of Stability

The growth of the UAW, the spread of collective bargaining in GM, and the developing stability of relationships in the auto industry mirrored what was happening elsewhere. Nationally, union membership continued to grow after World War II; and collective bargaining's coverage spread over more and more blue-collar workers in industries in which they already had secured bases among the largest employers. With the outbreak of the Korean war in 1950, total union membership sharply jumped to a new level of about 17 million. In the years 1950 to 1955, a larger share of the labor force was covered by collective bargaining agreements than at any period before or since. Even so, the spread of collective bargaining occurred chiefly in industries long accustomed to bargaining and negotiations. Few white-collar workers looked to collective bargaining as a method of determining wages and working conditions, and the number of white-collar workers was increasing rapidly even in manufacturing. Workers and employers in the large trade, service, and government sectors, which accounted for 47 percent of all wage and salary workers, hardly knew collective bargaining at all. Few workers in nonprofit organizations or on farms had had an opportunity to join a union, either.

Employer opposition in unorganized sectors and industries continued to be strong, though only occasionally mounted with the vehemence and determination shown by managers in the first quarter of the century and before. Union growth and collective bargaining's spread would surge in one location, only to stagnate or fall back at another place. Over the decade from 1953 to 1963, union membership stabilized at between 16 million and 17 million; in the next decade, it added about 3½ million new members. A number of employee organizations and associations—of teachers, nurses, police, and engineers, among others—began to involve themselves in collective bargaining. They often avoided national affiliation with labor unions, but in almost every other way became a part of the collective bargaining system.

The Long-term Agreement throughout Industry

As collective bargaining spread, so did the recognition that it would thrive best with the kind of stability that the UAW and GM had sought. They had not

---

[22]Ibid., p. 521.

been the first, only the most prominent, to negotiate a long-term agreement. The Department of Labor reported in early 1956 that at least 2¾ million workers were covered by "long-term labor-management terms that specified the size of wage increases" to be received that year.[23] Since the department reviewed only agreements that covered 1000 or more workers, the figure indicates that perhaps as many as 30 percent of union members already had secured long-term agreements. At that time and for some years afterwards, however, labor economists did not note any trend toward longer-term agreements; their future appeared highly uncertain. By 1961, when more complete data became available, the trend was evident. Nearly 40 percent of agreements showed a duration of three or more years; fewer than 4 percent were for a year or less. (See Table 1.) In manufacturing, 43 percent of agreements had durations of three or more years. This was no doubt an increase since the early post-World War II period, but the proportion was noticeably smaller than that of long-term agreements in such nonmanufacturing industries as mining, railroads, airlines, and construction. In these, unions and employers had typically bargained collectively for many more years than had the parties in manufacturing, and they had already opted for more stability and less (or at least other kinds of) flexibility in their relationships. In 1961, for example, nearly 90 percent of mining agreements and 65 percent of construction agreements lasted three or more years; in railroads and airlines 95 percent lasted four or more years.

A 1980 survey showed that the trend toward long-term agreements continued, with only 10 percent in all industries as short as two or fewer years. In manufacturing, agreements with terms of three or more years accounted for more than 75 percent of the total, up from 43 percent nineteen years earlier. Almost every industry within the sector showed the same trend, with the proportion of agreements lasting two years or less down sharply. The three-year agreement had become typical. In the textile industry, a quarter of the workers was covered by agreements of one year or shorter, and more than half were covered by agreements of two years or less; yet the single largest group of workers was covered by three-year agreements. This peculiar pattern is probably the result of the industry's having two distinct parts—in the north a longtime and stable relationship between union and management; but in the south an unstable, adversarial relationship in which management fights union organizing and resists collective bargaining. In the former, agreements probably tend toward long duration, and in the latter, they are probably short-term.

Curiously, the data reveal as well a reverse trend away from long-term agreements of four or more years and toward the three-year agreements. This trend is most marked in nonmanufacturing industries, particularly in mining, transportation, services, and construction. Only in hotels and restaurants, utilities, and communications was there evidence of an increased use of long-term agreements. Most surprising of all, the duration of agreements in the auto

---

[23]See H. M. Douty, "Post-War Wage Bargaining in the United States," in Walter Galenson and Seymour Martin Lipset (eds.), *Labor and Trade Unionism,* New York: John Wiley & Sons, Inc., 1960, pp. 197 & 201.

TABLE 1
DURATION OF AGREEMENTS COVERING 1000 OR MORE WORKERS, BY INDUSTRY

Industry	12 mos. or less		13–24 mos.		25–35 mos.		36 mos.		37–47 mos.		48 mos. and over	
	1961	1980	1961	1980	1961	1980	1961	1980	1961	1980	1961	1980
All	3.7*	0.7	27.1	9.2	12.6	10.7	36.5	64.4	0.7	11.1	0.7	3.8
Manufacturing	3.7	0.5	33.3	5.9	19.9	15.9	39.6	53.9	0.6	22.0	1.3	1.8
Food, kindred	2.4	0.9	73.8	13.5	5.7	5.7	17.3	75.7	0	3.2	0.4	1.0
Tobacco	17.1	0	83.3	0	0	0	0	100	0	0	0	0
Textile mills	13.9	26.0	44.7	29.3	11.1	6.2	27.2	38.5	1.4	0	0	0
Apparel	2.3	0	11.5	0	2.6	1.7	74.4	57.3	0	41.0	3.3	0
Lumber, wood	4.2	0	62.5	0	0	0	18.0	90.4	0	9.6	15.3	0
Furniture	3.0	0	30.7	11.5	21.4	11.3	38.0	67.3	7.0	0	0	0
Paper	30.7	0	63.7	31.0	0	0	5.6	62.8	0	1.5	0	10.0
Printing, publishing	1.4	0	72.5	60.4	15.3	3.8	5.2	19.3	0	0	0	4.6
Chemicals	6.3	0	45.7	25.2	2.6	0	38.3	55.3	2.2	0	5.8	16.5
Petroleum†	17.9	0	66.7	89.4	0	10.6	11.0	0	0	0	0	19.5
Rubber, plastic‡	3.2	0	88.9	0	3.2	78.1	0	19.9	4.0	2.0	0.8	0
Leather	0	4.8	78.0	32.0	3.7	0	18.4	53.7	0	9.5	0	0

24

Stone, clay, glass	11.2	0	77.0	2.5	0.9	0	9.2	97.5	0	0	1.8	0
Primary metals	0.6	0.2	10.0	0.2	79.0	3.0	9.0	94.6	0.8	2.0	0	0
Fabricated metals	4.0	0	29.4	4.7	23.8	14.6	42.8	44.7	0	33.1	0	2.9
Machinery	2.1	0	19.8	1.7	51.1	45.9	21.2	42.2	0.9	10.1	2.2	0
Electrical machinery	3.8	0	26.5	4.6	4.8	1.8	60.0	68.4	0.3	23.4	2.5	1.7
Transportation equipment	0.4	0.5	21.9	2.1	7.5	26.1	69.0	25.0	0.8	44.2	0.1	2.2
Instruments	9.2	0	48.2	17.4	2.1	18.8	17.2	63.8	0	0	17.8	0
Nonmanufacturing	3.8	0.9	20.3	12.0	4.5	6.3	33.1	73.4	0.7	2.0	8.7	5.5
Mining	0	0	2.8	0.8	8.2	4.4	0.7	94.8	0	0	0.7	0
Transportation§	1.0	0	20.7	0.3	2.3	1.2	68.2	98.6	0.4	0	3.3	0
Communications	7.4	0	18.8	1.5	0	6.3	7.4	91.6	0	0.2	0.2	0.3
Utilities	24.0	7.5	63.1	39.9	2.2	6.6	7.0	44.9	0	0.6	0.8	0.5
Wholesale trade	11.9	0	21.4	0	6.0	21.3	76.6	69.9	0	0	0	2.1
Retail trade	2.2	0	49.1	5.0	14.6	10.1	10.3	78.6	1.7	5.8	21.2	0.4
Hotels, restaurants	0.6	0	16.3	2.4	1.2	0	36.7	28.4	0	5.2	23.1	64.1
Services	1.4	0	33.0	32.8	5.2	5.6	31.1	55.2	8.1	3.5	11.6	2.9
Construction	5.7	0.1	20.3	16.9	9.4	7.8	37.1	64.9	0.5	1.9	24.5	7.2

*Percentage of workers covered. For 1961, agreements of indefinite length not included, so totals do not sum to 100.

†In 1961, products of petroleum and coal.

‡In 1961, rubber products.

§Excludes railroads and airlines.

Source: "Major Union Contracts in the United States," *Monthly Labor Review,* vol. 85, October 1962, pp. 1142–1143; and *Characteristics of Major Collective Bargaining Agreements, January 1, 1980,* Bureau of Labor Statistics Bulletin 2095, May 1981, table 1.4, pp. 14–15.

industry (transportation equipment) both increased and decreased. The shares of workers covered by agreements of either less or more than three years increased markedly.

Apparently UAW and company negotiators have found that although the three-year agreement was appropriate for the large companies, more flexibility was needed in dealing with smaller ones. They have evidently reduced the duration of the agreements somewhat to meet the more changeable needs and demands of smaller firms in the industry. The data also suggest that negotiators in several of the nonmanufacturing industries have found that many long-term agreements of four or more years' duration provided too little flexibility, particularly in a time of inflation. But there appears to be little inclination among negotiators in either manufacturing or nonmanufacturing industries to return to the earlier prevalence of the twelve-month agreement, with its annual hassle of bargaining. Both union and management prefer more stability than that.

THE OLD AND THE NEW IN COLLECTIVE BARGAINING

Collective bargaining has changed over the last forty to fifty years, but it still displays a mixture of old and new. In some industries it has a history more than a century old, whereas in other industries it is still so new that the parties have not yet negotiated their first agreement, processed a single grievance, or experimented with needed or desired stability of relationship. Even among those parties who have long bargained, some still do not use arbitration to settle grievance disputes, and only a few have tried systematic joint efforts to increase productivity or even to improve so basic and useful an item as a safety program.

The differences between the early efforts of workers to participate in a determination of the conditions under which they were employed and workers' efforts today should be neither exaggerated nor minimized; then and now workers have persisted in a basic drive to organize for an effective voice in the manner and terms of their employment. Our brief review does not support the notion that workers generally have been led to organize only on the basis of false promises or coercion. They have sought collective bargaining as a way of gaining some participation in the control of their work lives. This inevitably raises difficulties in harmonizing the interests, rights, and duties of organized employees, management, and the public. The problems we face today in these respects are not new ones, though they come in different settings and with varying degrees of urgency.

The changes over the years in the duration of agreements among industries are one indication of how the parties have experimented, adapting collective bargaining to needs and experiences. They suggest that collective bargaining will continue to register significant differences over time and among the various unions and employers. In some occupations, industries, or areas, unions and bargaining have firmly established themselves, becoming regular, recognized parts of industrial affairs. In others, their advocates are still seeking rec-

TABLE 2
MEMBERSHIP OF LABOR ORGANIZATIONS IN THE UNITED STATES AND
SHARE OF TOTAL LABOR FORCE (THOUSANDS)

	Membership		Total labor force	Percent union members	
	Unions	Unions and associations			
1956	17,490		70,387	24.8	
1960	17,049		73,126	23.3	
1964	16,841		76,971	21.9	
1968	18,916	20,721	82,272	23.0	25.2
1972		21,657	85,903		25.2
1976		22,662	96,917		23.4
1980		22,366	106,821		20.9

Source: 1956–64 data from *Directory of National and International Labor Unions in the United States, 1965,* Bureau of Labor Statistics Bulletin 1493, 1966, p. 51; *Director of National Unions and Employee Associations, 1971,* Bureau of Labor Statistics Bulletin 1750, 1972, table 6, p. 72; and Courtney D. Gifford, *Directory of U.S. Labor Organizations,* 1982–83 ed., (Washington, D.C.: Bureau of National Affairs) 1982, table 2, p. 1.

ognition and acceptance, struggling to gain bargaining rights. Forms of bargaining fully developed in one industry or region may still be experimentally or hesitantly approached or even ignored in another. These great differences color the views and affect the values of even the experienced, assured participants in the collective bargaining process. For good reason unionists are defensive; they are well aware that they represent only the smaller part and a declining share of the labor force. (See Table 2.) Unions in the goods-producing sector have experienced a generation of relative decline and more than a decade of absolute loss. (See Table 3.) It is little wonder that their leaders seek to enhance their unions' security with provisions unique to the American scene—the dues checkoff and the union shop and its variations.[24]

Union Membership by Occupation and Industry

Managers are also affected by their awareness of the large number of unorganized employees, not covered by collective bargaining. They are aware that not all their colleagues in other firms in the same or different industries have to bargain collectively with union representatives. American managers are especially sensitive about their reserved rights—their claimed prerogatives—to direct the work force and exercise authority within the firm. Managers typically argue that any right not explicitly limited by the agreement can be exercised at

[24]These arrangements are usually lumped under the rubric of union security provisions. The dues checkoff allows management to deduct union dues from a member's paycheck when authorized by the member; the union shop is a requirement that all workers in a bargaining unit join the certified union (or at least pay dues) after thirty days on the job.

TABLE 3
MEMBERSHIP IN LABOR ORGANIZATIONS, 1970 AND 1980, AND CHANGES BY INDUSTRY (THOUSANDS)

	1970	1980	Absolute change, 1970 to 1980	Percentage change, 1970 to 1980
Goods producing	11,948	8,612	−3,336	−27.9
Durable manufacturing	5,269*	4,284*	− 985	−18.7
Nondurable manufacturing	3,710*	2,405	−1,305	−35.2
Construction	2,576	1,574	−1,002	−38.9
Mining	369	286	−83	−22.5
Agriculture, foresting, fisheries	24	63	39	162.5
Service producing	9,884	12,785	2,901	29.4
Government	4,080	5,554†	1,474	36.1
Transportation, communications, public utilities	2,806	2,903	97	3.5
Trade	1,549	1,753	204	13.2
Services	1,394	2,385‡	991	71.1
Finance, insurance, real estate	55	190	135	245.5

*Omits members in miscellaneous manufacturing.
†Includes medical, hospital, and educational service professionals as well as public administration employees.
‡Excludes all medical, hospital, and educational service professionals.
Source: Directory of National Unions and Employee Associations, 1971, Bureau of Labor Statistics Bulletin 1750, 1972, table 16, p. 80; and Gifford, *Directory of U.S. Labor Organizations,* table 14, pp. 57–8.

their discretion. The defensiveness and suspiciousness that infuse the attitudes of both parties are not apt to disappear as long as unions continue to confront large numbers of unorganized workers and as long as managers regularly meet and deal with colleagues who do not have to recognize unions and bargain collectively.

Despite the minority position of union members in the labor force, they have established themselves in a wide array of key industries and occupations. They are found in every manufacturing industry, among both blue- and white-collar employees. They also include actors; musicians; baseball, football, and hockey players; movie directors; salesclerks; security guards; nurses; news reporters; truck drivers; and veterinarians. In addition, such workers as teachers, professors, postal employees, insurance agents, meat cutters, and engineers use collective bargaining to their advantage; so do such surprising groups as union organizers, union clerical staff members, employees of Internal Revenue Service, and professionals who work for the National Labor Relations Board.

Although the diversity of occupations among union members is great, in 1980 more than half of all members still worked in blue-collar jobs. Semiskilled operators accounted for a little over a quarter of the total membership, and workers in the skilled crafts contributed about a fifth. More than a third of union members held white-collar occupations, with teachers alone accounting for one out of twelve union members. (See Table 4.) The organization of the teaching occupations is remarkable, with more than half of all employed workers being union members. Only truck drivers (transportation-equipment operators) come close, with 45 percent of those employed being in unions. Among white-collar workers a significantly larger portion of professionals and technical workers than of the lesser-ranked clerical and sales workers have joined unions. Unionism has proved popular among the more highly skilled, usually better-paid white-collar workers, much as it proved more successful among craft workers than among the semiskilled and unskilled workers in the nineteenth century.

Collective bargaining has popularly been associated primarily with manufacturing; at least, newsworthy negotiations and strikes have occured in the automobile industry (in which 61 percent of the employed workers were union members in 1980) and the steel industry (in which 58 percent were in unions). The unions in these industries have been large and the leaders often colorful. The drama of collective bargaining in some manufacturing industries can mislead casual observers, however, for the share of union members is highest in industries historically subjected to government regulation—railroads, airlines, shipping, communications, and utilities. Furthermore, the share of union

TABLE 4
EMPLOYED WAGE AND SALARY WORKERS IN LABOR ORGANIZATIONS
BY OCCUPATION, MAY 1980

Occupation	Number (thousands)	Percentage of total union membership	Percentage of all employed W&S workers
White collar	7,017	34.9	15.3
Professional, technical, kindred	3,272	16.3	22.7
Teachers, except college	1,688	8.4	51.6
Managers and administrators, except farm	681	3.4	7.6
Clerical, kindred	2,857	14.2	16.3
Sales	207	1.0	4.1
Blue collar	11,101	55.2	39.1
Craft, kindred	4,308	21.4	38.9
Operatives, except transportation	3,990	19.9	40.0
Transportation equipment operatives	1,439	7.2	44.6
Nonfarm laborers	1,365	6.8	33.1
Service workers	1,954	9.7	16.2
Total	20,095	100	23.0

Source: *Earnings and other Characteristics of Organized Workers,* Bureau of Labor Statistics Bulletin 2105, May 1980, table 2, pp. 8–10.

TABLE 5
PERCENTAGE OF EMPLOYED WAGE AND SALARY WORKERS
IN LABOR ORGANIZATIONS, BY MAJOR INDUSTRY, MAY 1980

Industry	Percentage union members
Transportation, communications, public utilities	48.0
Durable manufacturing	34.8
Government	34.2*
Mining	32.1
Construction	31.6
Nondurable manufacturing	28.5
Foresting, fisheries	13.5
Trade	10.1
Services (excludes government employees)	4.0
Finance, insurance, real estate	3.7
Agriculture	3.5

*Includes members in public administration and all members in medical, hospital, and educational professional services.
Source: Gifford, *Directory of U.S. Labor Organizations,* table 14, pp. 59–60.

members among government employees is almost as high as that in durable manufacturing. (See Table 5.) In 1980, almost 75 percent of postal workers and 37 percent of local government workers, 26 percent of state employees, and 19 percent of federal workers were in unions.

The Shift to Services

In recent years union membership has shifted markedly, decreasing rapidly over the decade of the seventies in goods-producing industries and increasing in the services sector. (See Table 3.) The loss of members was particularly large in nondurable manufacturing, 1.3 million; but construction unions lost 1 million members and unions in durable manufacturing saw almost as many members disappear. The losses were so large that even sizable increases in union membership in the service sector could not offset them. The gains among government employees, particularly teachers, were also impressive. The recession of the early 1980s sped up the decline of membership in manufacturing unions, with the AFL-CIO estimating that it had lost 18 percent of its members between 1980 and early 1983. Over this period the Steelworkers declined by 39 percent, losing nearly half a million members, and the Auto Workers by 19 percent, a loss of a quarter of a million.[25]

The relative decline in employment of the goods-producing sector, from 33 percent of total wage and salary employment in 1970 to 27 percent in 1982, has not provided much opportunity for unions in manufacturing industries to

[25]William Serrin, "Union Membership Falls Sharply," *The New York Times,* May 31, 1983.

TABLE 6
MEMBERSHIP IN LABOR ORGANIZATIONS AS PERCENT OF
NONAGRICULTURAL EMPLOYMENT, BY STATE, 1980

Ten highest states		Ten lowest states	
1 New York	38.7%	41 Arkansas	16.0%
2 Michigan	32.4%	42 Arizona	15.8%
3 Pennsylvania	34.6%	43 Kansas	15.5%
4 West Virginia	34.4%	44 Oklahoma	15.3%
5 Washington	34.4%	45 South Dakota	14.7%
6 Alaska	33.6%	46 Virginia	14.7%
7 Ohio	31.5%	47 Florida	11.7%
8 Illinois	30.6%	48 Texas	11.4%
9 Montana	29.2%	49 North Carolina	9.6%
10 Wisconsin	28.6%	50 South Carolina	7.8%

Source: Bureau of the Census, U.S. Department of Commerce, *Statistical Abstract of the United States,* 1984, Washington, D.C.: U.S. Government Printing Office, 1983, Table No. 728, p. 440.

increase membership and extend the coverage of collective bargaining. Not only have they had to deal with a lack of growth in the number of potential members, but they have also confronted a movement of jobs from regions with long-established union organizations to areas where unions are relatively rare. Geography has a definite effect on collective bargaining coverage. In the mid-Atlantic, northeastern, and Pacific states, the extent of bargaining is two to four times greater than in the south and some of the midwestern states. (See Table 6.) It is not uncommon for a company that has unionized plants in the northeast to operate nonunion factories in the south or southeast. Company closing of organized plants in the north and opening of new unorganized plants elsewhere, usually the Sunbelt, became a matter of dispute and heated bargaining in the auto industry in 1976 and 1979.

General Motors, for example, had opened eleven new plants, all in the south, and the UAW succeeded in winning representational elections in only two of them. The union leaders charged the company with fiercely opposing their organizing efforts and sought "preferential consideration" for GM workers seeking jobs in the new plants, as well as a promise of "neutrality" from the company in the union campaigns to organize the new plants. The matter was eventually resolved quietly, but the fact that such an issue could roil negotiations between two parties that have long bargained together indicates the sensitivities involved.

EMPLOYER RESISTENCE TO COLLECTIVE BARGAINING

Unions have good reason to be sensitive about representational elections, for over the years they have won a decreasing share. (See Table 7.) The downward

TABLE 7

SHARES OF REPRESENTATION ELECTIONS* WON BY
UNIONS, 1962–1981

	Percentage of union wins	Percentage of union losses
1962–1966	59.5	40.5
1967–1971	56.2	43.8
1972–1976	50.9	49.1
1977–1981†	46.9	53.1

*Excludes decertification elections.
†Data for 1981, year ended September 30; other years ended June 30.

Source: National Labor Relations Board, *Annual Reports.*

trend has been evidenced at least since World War II, suggesting a basic and long-term cause at work. By the late 1970s almost two-thirds of the workers eligible to vote—400,000 to 500,000—chose "no union"; unions won less than half of the elections. Union leaders know, as do managers, that the odds are against any organizing effort to extend collective bargaining, even in a new plant of a company long organized elsewhere. Though managers may not often move a plant or production simply to escape collective bargaining, they cannot be unaware that a move may provide such a result; and union leaders suspect that managers' awareness may influence their decision—and their behavior at the bargaining table.

In addition, union leaders have seen the number of decertification elections increase significantly since the late forties. While the absolute number of workers involved each year is small compared to total union membership, the upward trend is troubling to unionists. The number of decertification elections increased fivefold, and the proportion lost by unions increased from about two-thirds in the period 1948–52 to three-quarters by 1980.[26]

Even without the present threats to stable collective bargaining from outside and surrounding influences, union leaders have discovered that just maintaining their membership within a given bargaining unit is a continual, demanding task. Not only may firms move plants and production to new areas, but firms experience a high turnover of employees. In 1977 turnover in durable manufacturing for each month averaged 3.7 accessions and 3.4 separations for every 100 employees. Of course, most of the workers continued on their jobs and in their positions, but the yearly flow of people into and out of a particular work

[26]John C. Anderson, Charles A. O'Reilly III, and Gloria Busman, "Union Decertification in the U.S.: 1947–77," *Industrial Relations,* vol. 19, Winter 1980, pp. 100–107. See also I. Chafetz and C. R. P. Fraser, "Union Decertification: An Exploratory Analysis," *Industrial Relations,* vol. 18, Winter 1979, pp. 59–69. On the basis of a study of cases in British Columbia, the researchers found that decertification typically occurred in smaller units of unskilled workers employed by owner-operators.

force is very large, equal to 40 percent of the total work force. In some high-turnover industries, such as lumber and furniture, the flow may be equal to two-thirds of the work force. With such large and easy movement into and out of a bargaining unit, union-organizing efforts cannot let up.[27]

Added to these forces and influences, which hinder or at least do not favor the spread of collective bargaining, are outright business opposition and publicly announced antiunion campaigns; it is little wonder that even unions and managements with histories of long, regular dealings often find their negotiators under strain and tension as they bargain. These influences tend to encourage adversarial stances and erode the possibilities for cooperation. Particularly irritating to the process of collective bargaining is such action as that taken by the National Association of Manufacturers in the late 1970s with its creation of a Council on Union-Free Environment. The group's 450 member companies joined together to discourage unionization and collective bargaining; the purpose of such avoidance was, the council announced, to benefit themselves and their employees.[28]

Antiunion Campaigns to Counter Organizing Drives

An additional irritant to business-union relationships has been the emergence of numerous consultants who help company managers formulate antiunion tactics and develop techniques that allegedly persuade employees to vote non-union. The AFL-CIO reported in 1983 that 401 such consulting firms had promoted antiunion programs in the preceding three years; an additional 126 firms had conducted seminars on union avoidance. To keep all member unions informed about such activities, the AFL-CIO began publication of a regular "Report on Union Busters."[29]

The contrast is very great between the collective bargaining experience in firms such as those that joined the council, or otherwise find collective bargaining distasteful, and those that have long engaged in it, developing fully and well their relationships with their unions. Since such contrasting experiences exist almost side by side in the United States, we briefly present two of them, one in textiles, the other in steel. They illustrate the diversity of form that collective bargaining can take. The contrast may also suggest how the differential growth and spread of collective bargaining can generate tensions and fears when parts of the labor movement and business community deal with each

---

[27]In 1980 the Bureau of Labor Statistics expanded coverage of turnover in industries other than manufacturing. Preliminary analysis indicated that this turnover generally may be higher than in manufacturing. "On an annual basis . . . the average firm hired almost as many workers as its average employment. . ." See Malcolm S. Cohen and Arthur R. Schwartz, "U.S. Labor Turnover: Analysis of a New Measure," *Monthly Labor Review,* vol. 103, Nov. 1980, p. 9. A few years later, in an economy move, the government cut collection of all turnover data.

[28]"Taking Aim at 'Union-Busters'," *Business Week,* Nov. 12, 1979, p. 98.

[29]Carey W. English, "Business Is Booming for 'Union Busters'," *U.S. News & World Report,* vol. 94, May 16, 1983, p. 61.

other in ways and through forms diametrically opposed to those used elsewhere.

Employer Opposition to Unionism: The Case of J. P. Stevens

J. P. Stevens is not a typical American industrial firm, but it is the second-largest publicly owned textile company in the country. In its militant antiunion stand it was atypical of a sizable minority of businesses only in the publicity and notoriety it gained. Its managers fought union-organizing attempts for many years, at least since the company had begun its move to the south. Between 1951 and 1975 they closed twenty-one textile mills in the north, which had employed 11,700 workers. Having left unionization behind, they did not intend to see it follow them. In 1963, when the Textile Workers Union of America first approached its workers in the south, the company announced its stand:

> Our positive intention is to oppose this union and by every proper means to keep it from coming in here. It is our sincere belief that if the union gets in here, it would operate to . . . [our employees'] serious disadvantage.[30]

Fourteen years later, in 1977, company officials declared that:

> . . . there are many reasons why both employers and employees may sensibly believe, in their relations with each other, the intervention of a Union is not to the best interests of either. There are likewise many facts of human history and experience which strongly reinforce the view that unopposed and inordinate growth of power in collective organizations, whether labor unions or others, constitutes a fundamental danger to individual liberty and human rights.[31]

The officials apparently wrote without irony, innocently ignoring their own *collective* power exercised through a company of 44,000 workers in eighty-five plants, sixty-three of them in the South.

The union secured twelve representation elections at Stevens plants in the south between 1965 and 1975, but won only one of them, at Roanoke Rapids, North Carolina. Murray Finley, the president of the Amalgamated Clothing and Textile Workers Union (ACTWU), argued that Stevens managers fought the union so bitterly and resisted collective bargaining so tenaciously that the workers could not vote freely and fairly. Indeed, the attitudes and behavior of Stevens managers appear to have been lifted from the nineteenth and early twentieth centuries. How they may have influenced Stevens workers' voting is a matter of opinion and dispute, but the court record is replete with descriptions of antiunion tactics. Foremen and supervisors harassed union sympathizers and fired them, violating the rights of at least 289 workers, whom courts

---

[130]Walter Guzzardi, Jr., "How the Union got the Upper Hand on J. P. Stevens," *Fortune,* June 19, 1978, p. 88.

[231]Statement of J. P. Stevens & Co., Inc., filed with the Labor Subcommittee, Committee on Human Resources, U.S. Senate, Nov. 7, 1977, p. 2.

ordered reimbursed an average of almost $4500 apiece. They were found guilty of "bugging" the private rooms of union organizers in the search for intelligence. So often did the unions seek redress and charge illegal company acts that a judge of the second circuit court noted that in the 1977 contempt proceedings before him was Stevens case XVIII!

Union and company negotiators bargained over an agreement at Roanoke Rapids after the union won the representation election, but to no avail. By 1979—five years later—they had not yet reached a conclusion, for most of the time the company refused to consider the inclusion of either an arbitration clause or a dues checkoff in the agreement. When company officials finally did offer to accept these two provisions, union negotiators found other reasons for continuing the impasse. Meantime, the union had sought public and political support for its attempts to organize Stevens.

The union attempted to organize a consumer boycott of Stevens products, though they appeared under so many name brands that buyers could not easily identify them. In 1977 the leaders persuaded the mayor of Atlanta, then running for reelection, to cut off any city purchases of Stevens products. The procurement cutoff was shortlived but indicated clearly the animosity between union leaders and Stevens managers. A year later the union called public attention to the membership of Stevens' chief executive officer, James D. Finley, on the board of the Manufacturers Hanover Trust Company in New York. The publicity and subtle threats of a boycott against the bank persuaded Finley to resign from the board, apparently with the blessing of the bank officials. The union then used similar tactics to encourage Stevens directors from outside companies to sever their Stevens positions.

With an even more daring tactic the union pressured Stevens managers through their largest source of funds, Metropolitan Life Insurance Company, which held $97 million, or 43 percent of Stevens' long-term debt. The union proposed to contest the 1980 election of two members to Metropolitan's board of directors. Metropolitan estimated the cost of a contest would add some $5 to $7 million to its expenses. As a consequence, the chairman of Metropolitan acted behind the scenes to persuade—or encourage—Stevens managers to reach a prompt settlement with the union. Later, in October 1980, Stevens and the union reached an agreement; the company recognized the union as the exclusive representative of about 10 percent of its employees and granted a modest wage increase. The union promised to stop harassing the company.

Union Response: New Tactics against Management

Collective bargaining has operated at such a minimal level between Stevens and the ACTWU that it has hardly existed. As long as the parties consider themselves to be wary adversaries, little of benefit can accrue to either. Not only do they deny themselves the richer rewards that collective bargaining can offer, but the relationship produces spillover, or external costs, enlarging the fears of other unionists and deepening the suspicions of managers elsewhere.

Each sees what injuries the other is capable of inflicting and wonders if the laws, practices, or rules should not be changed to prevent such action. Managers are alarmed by what appears the growing strength and pugnacious power of unions when they may force board members to resign, secure cancellation of government procurement contracts, mount nationwide boycotts, and interfere in board elections. Such efforts appear to take collective bargaining far in directions antithetical to business interests. Such activities may confirm managerial nightmares that collective bargaining could become an exceedingly dangerous, troublesome procedure.

From a labor perspective, one may draw an opposite lesson. Despite a variety of laws, successful court suits, and favorable rulings by the National Labor Relations Board, the union has made only slight gains at Stevens; it has hardly succeeded more in the rest of the south. Probably no more than 10 percent of southern textile workers had joined unions as late as 1984. The long Stevens campaign against organization of its workers and its reluctant agreement with the ACTWU suggest the fierce passions and strong opposition to both unions and collective bargaining that still exist in the United States. They produce an unease among unionists throughout the nation and contribute to their feeling that even in its strongholds, collective bargaining can be threatened or besieged.

WHERE IS COLLECTIVE BARGAINING GOING?

Union advocates are already familiar with the melancholy statistics that show a decline in the share of workers in the country covered by collective bargaining to the level recorded before the *beginning* of World War II. Over the past twenty years unions have brought only one new worker under collective bargaining coverage for every 10 who filled jobs added to the labor force. Furthermore, the largest number of those organized has been in the public rather than the private sector. In fact, union membership is declining in manufacturing. (See Table 3.) Such a decline is important because ever since the vigorous drives in the mass-production industries during the 1930s, the public, and no doubt labor leaders themselves, have considered manufacturing the bastion of organized labor and the typical setting for collective bargaining.

Despite the continuing existence of antiunion sentiment among some American managers and resistance to collective bargaining in some companies and industries, the J. P. Stevens is more the exception than the rule. Many managers may prefer not to bargain collectively with union representatives, but if their employees choose bargaining, most accept it and negotiate in good faith; that is, they meet at reasonable times and places to discuss wages, hours, and conditions of work, setting down in writing such understandings as may be reached. Managerial acceptance of collective bargaining and willingness to experiment with it to help solve pressing industry problems of lagging productivity is illustrated in steel. Although the major firms and the United Steel Workers of America (USW) had been involved in many industrywide strikes in the past, and some firms fought organizing efforts in the 1930s, there has been no large strike in steel since the 116-day work stoppage of 1959–1960.

As a result of that long strike, in which complex, intractable local issues delayed settlement, the parties recognized the need to maintain a continuing relationship during the times between the industrywide negotiations, in order to deal with issues that did not lend themselves to periodic consideration. They established a Human Relations Research Committee in 1960 "to plan and oversee studies and recommend solutions of mutual problems" involving the determination of equitable wage and benefit adjustments, job classification, wage incentives, seniority, and "such other overall problems as the parties, by mutual agreement, may from time to time refer to the Committee."[32] In 1962 they changed the name to the Human Relations Committee (HRC), recognizing that its function went beyond fact-finding to include attempts to negotiate acceptable solutions to the various problems addressed. Though it was hailed by outside observers, local steel-union leaders denounced the HRC for downgrading their role in negotiations and elevating that of staff technicians. In 1965 a new union president, who had run against the HRC, eliminated any reference to it in the renegotiated agreement. However, both he and industry leaders wanted to eliminate crisis bargaining and strikes or strike threats, with their attendant problems of steel users' stockpiling and increasing their reliance upon imports. Steelworkers as well as the companies lost in such situations.

After carefully examining a number of proposals for a new bargaining approach, company and union representatives adopted in early 1973 an experimental negotiating agreement (ENA). The parties agreed that there would be no strike or lockout at the expiration of the agreement; they would submit all national issues not resolved through collective bargaining to a panel of impartial arbitrators for final and binding decision. They thereby assured steel users that there would be no interruption of supplies. In return for this assurance the steel companies paid an economic price, providing a bonus of $150 to each steel employee; guaranteeing a minimum wage increase of 3 percent annually, subject to additional increases that might be later negotiated; and ensuring a cost-of-living provision. In addition, local unions could still strike over local issues. The union and the big companies negotiated the three succeeding agreements under the ENA, in 1974, 1977, and 1980. As they concluded the 1980 agreement, they decided to postpone a decision on continuing the ENA. Some company leaders complained that the wage costs of the ENA had been very high—since they still had to contend with outbreaks of local strikes over shop and plant issues, the benefits were too low compared to the costs. During early negotiations, in 1982, company officials refused to consider a renewal of ENA when the agreement expired in mid-1983. Inflation had raised the cost-of-living adjustments rapidly and under the conditions of high unemployment and slumping sales, the union was not apt to strike in any case.

---

[32]James J. Healy (ed.), *Creative Collective Bargaining,* Englewood Cliffs, N.J.: Prentice-Hall, Inc., 1965, p. 7.

Rather than wrangle over the costs and benefits of the ENA, however, the negotiators recognized they needed to supplement their existing collective bargaining with new and more imaginative procedures. Admitting the industry problems of high labor costs, declining productivity, and a myriad of local disputes, the negotiators proposed to experiment with new methods of cooperation in designated plants. They established labor-management participation committees to work outside the usual existing shop grievance and safety procedures. The committee members, who were rank-and-file workers and departmental supervisors, were charged to explore ways of giving workers a voice in improving job environment, work schedules, and production processes, while at the same time helping to cut costs.

Neither union militants nor conservative managers, who believe in the value of old-line, hierarchical order of bosses and workers, showed enthusiasm for the plan. The negotiators who had established the new committees hoped they would help. One negotiator said, "Steel has so damn many problems we realized that unless we replace the adversarial relationship with a cooperative attitude, we're both in trouble." The Steelworkers' vice president, Joseph Odorcich, commented, "The managers have got to listen to the workers because they know more about the plant than any industrial engineer or boss. This [experiment] goes way beyond improving productivity. I'm talking about people having confidence in one another."[33]

Experiments do not always succeed, of course. In the early 1970s the major steel companies attempted to get workers' productivity committees to help them cut cost; workers interpreted the attempt as a speedup, and many local managers refused to share problem solving with their employees. The efforts of the early 1980s may be no more successful than those that preceded them, but they indicate that the parties to collective bargaining are using the process with more flexibility than in the past to grapple with their mutual problems. They show a willingness to consider extending collective bargaining beyond what had become its usual and traditional role of setting wages and fixing the conditions of work. Their efforts remind outside observers that collective bargaining not only can be, but also actually is, more than the hostile sparring of a J. P. Stevens and an ACTWU. The parties know very well that company and union or workers' interests do not always coincide in steel, but they have learned what Stevens managers have not yet perceived: that their interests do not always diverge. While they remain adversaries in some respects, they may be partners in others.

Collective bargaining in the steel industry does not provide the most extreme example of cooperative relationships between business managers and union leaders. In 1980 the chairman of the ailing, nearly bankrupt Chrysler Corporation nominated the president of the UAW for election to the board of directors, as a quid pro quo for union concessions.

---

[33]John Hoerr, "Beyond Bargaining: Unions and Bosses Try Trust," *Business Week,* May 5, 1980, p. 43. See also "A Try At Steel-Mill Harmony," *Business Week,* June 29, 1981, pp. 132–133.

In April 1984, Eastern Airlines elected four union representatives to its 19-member board of directors. One of the labor members commended the election: "It's not just tokenism. . . . It's a change in the way Eastern is running its business." That business appeared to improve after the change. Workers or labor representatives are on the boards of at least 15 large, publicly held American companies.[34] Meanwhile, Americans contemplate the oddity of bitter business opposition to unions and collective bargaining in some industries and regions of the country, while in other industries and localities, business managers deal harmoniously and peacefully with union leaders and find collective bargaining a useful way of handling industrial problems at the place of work.

CONCLUSION

Collective bargaining in the United States today appears in many different forms; it may manifest one characteristic in one place or industry and contradictory features in another. These forms develop out of the mixing of old and new unionism; from the bargaining of inexperienced negotiators and that of lifetime professionals; and from the expedient, necessary adjustments made by practitioners in routines, procedures, and organizations to fit a changing economy and a transforming society. Industries, trades, and occupations rise and fall. As state and local government employment rose over the last two decades, union leaders saw opportunities for expanding organization that their peers in manufacturing unions did not enjoy. Public employees had to learn how to bargain with diffused government authorities when public sentiment and law disapproved of strikes. They could not expect much helpful guidance from, say, the leaders in the coal-mining union or the UAW's officials. The organizing efforts of the miners and autoworkers were one or two generations away, and in any case the economy, the social setting, and the politics of collective bargaining in government were greatly different. For the same kinds of reasons, the miners and autoworkers had not been able to copy the experience of the earliest unionists, the cordwainers and printers; the world changes so much that current organizing efforts and the collective bargaining that develops out of it inevitably will be shaped to somewhat different forms, decade by decade. New unions and managers who are collective bargaining novices do not have to start completely afresh if they examine the lessons of history; but either or both may ignore history, as in the case of J.P. Stevens, where management insists on an older pattern, a throwback to methods of the late nineteenth century. Unions and managers may borrow from procedures and policies widely adopted and followed, but will almost surely have to adapt them to fit their special needs. Consider the development of collective bargaining in the new area of public service. Government officials have often viewed negotiating over wages, hours, and conditions of work as distastefully as did mid-nineteenth

---

[34]Gary Cohn, "Labor's Big New Role Inside Eastern Airlines Seems to be Succeeding," *The Wall Street Journal,* Oct. 31, 1984.

century employers. They and many public commentators have sometimes sounded as echoes of the past in denouncing the use of the strike and of any negotiated limitations of their managerial functions. In the unions' and governments' general acceptance of fixed-term written agreements and grievance procedures, though, they have benefited from the experience and lessons of collective bargaining in the private sector. In some states and cities, leaders of public employees' unions and their government counterparts have gone beyond traditional and common collective bargaining procedures to experiment with new ways to resolve disputes, to define bargaining units, and even to specify subject matters.

Various national and local influences, acting with varying effect over time, help to explain why collective bargaining "arrived" earlier in some places than others. These influences also help to explain why bargaining has taken some of its diverse forms. For example, sometimes a particularly forceful union leader or a flamboyant manager—a John L. Lewis of the miners, a James Hoffa of the Teamsters, or a Lemuel Boulware of General Electric—dominated his fellows in a particular industry. At times, public opinion favored unions, as in the depression of the 1930s; but at other times, as in the early sixties after the revelation of shocking corruption among unions, public sentiment was antiunion. The attitudes of the judiciary and the press also varied. Politicians might bid for labor support in a city like New York or ignore its presence in a state like Nebraska.

Furthermore, union and management negotiators have had to modify their conduct of collective bargaining as the structures of their various organizations have changed. Leaders of a craft union negotiating with many small employers will conduct their bargaining quite differently from the way the negotiators of a mass-industry union deal with professional managers of a large company. The bargaining style of local plant officers negotiating the terms of a local agreement will not be the same as that of national union officers responsible for working out the terms of a companywide agreement affecting workers in many plants scattered over a number of regions. Negotiators for District Council 37 of the American Federation of State, County, and Municipal Employees (AFSCME), cannot approach bargaining with the public officials of New York City in the same way the leaders of the United Automobile Workers deal with managers of General Motors; the procedures and outcomes may also be different when union negotiators deal with managers of nonprofit organizations such as hospitals, private colleges, or museums rather than with managers of a business enterprise.

The collective bargaining with which we are concerned consists primarily of those activities of employers or managers and union leaders who negotiate agreements defining the general terms under which employees will consent to work. In the early days of the nineteenth century, such terms covered little more than a scale of wage rates. By the turn of the century, negotiators in several industries had considerably elaborated their agreements. By this time they were also distinguishing between disputes over the terms of employment and those arising out of application of those terms. The latter came to be known as grievances. The distinction between the two kinds of disputes led negotiators to devise different processes to handle them. Whereas negotiators originally treated all disputes, whatever the kind, in the same way, they began to handle grievances—the day-to-day disputes *under* the agreement—through regular, specially recognized procedures.

This kind of collective bargaining is common and typical today, but as the explanations in this chapter indicate, great variations exist. Given the mixture of both old and new unionism and the conditions under which bargaining has developed, these variations are both understandable and explainable. More difficult to explain is the lag in both collective bargaining's acceptability and its spread among the work force. A generation ago, in the fifties, so many workers had endorsed and sought union membership that it spread rapidly. It appeared to be sweeping all blue-collar workers under its coverage and soon was expected to include white-collar employees as well. Collective bargaining had enlisted at least some workers in almost every occupation from janitors to engineers and in every industry; negotiators on both sides of the bargaining table spoke with power and authority. By the 1960s the increase in numbers of workers under collective bargaining began to drop behind the growth of the work force. Absolute union membership continues to rise in the eighties, but more slowly than in the immediately preceding decades.

Apparently, the aggregating force of the unions' common rule has been weakened or deflected by more and stronger forces than labor scholars—and labor leaders—expected two decades ago. The common rule, first enunciated by Sidney and Beatrice Webb before the turn of the century,[35] was unionists' demand that minimum wages and conditions of work be established and applied to all workers within an establishment. Only with the enforcement of such a rule did workers believe they could protect themselves from a worsening of conditions and a low wage level. Certainly early unionists in the United States who sought to impose wage terms unilaterally upon their employees believed that there was a sound economic need for and usefulness in the common rule.

Today, and for some time past, however, national legislation imposing various minima in wages and working conditions has changed attitudes and practices of professional managers, particularly in the large corporations; and a rapidly shifting occupational structure within the labor force may have changed the attractiveness and general applicability of unions' common rule. It may be that collective bargaining and unions have come close to their limits of growth in this country; they may continue to expand in one place but shrink in another. Nevertheless, both unions and the collectively bargained common rule have demonstrated their usefulness and their staying power. Neither is apt to wither away to insignificance. They will long be important institutions whose natures and operations we need to understand deeply and well.

---

[35]Sidney Webb and Beatrice Webb, *Industrial Democracy,* New York: Longmans, Green & Co., Ltd., 1926, pp. 560–561.

THE NATURE OF COLLECTIVE BARGAINING

Efforts to define the nature of a thing often lead to sterile argument. Concepts necessarily reflect points of view, and in the social sciences there is usually limited opportunity to test their reliability. Many economists, for example, have written at length but inconclusively on the meaning or nature of "capital," "rent," "interest," "value," "money," and similar terms. Such writings reflect more than mere academic interest, for definitions serve practical needs. One is not as good as another. How people define collective bargaining—that is, how they regard it—will in part determine how they practice it.[1]

We are not concerned here with all the purposes or functions that collective bargaining *might* serve. Rather we are concerned with its *general* nature as it is found in the United States. We are not interested at the moment, for example, in the fact that some unionists at times have made collective bargaining an instrument of political-party advancement or that some political creeds advocate its use for this purpose. Communists have long insisted that under their regime, trade unions and thus collective bargaining are instruments of the state; and they believe that in a noncommunist country, party leaders should use both to further the interests of the party. A few American unionists have from time to time espoused this definition of collective bargaining, but they have not won many adherents. It is not commonly understood as a method of gaining political control and has seldom been used for such purpose in the United States.

---

[1] In this sense, definition need not require actual verbalization. Managers of union officials may entertain a particular definition of collective bargaining even though they have never reduced it to words.

COLLECTIVE BARGAINING AND THE COMMON RULE

Through collective bargaining, the parties involved determine the general terms under which all members of the bargaining unit will work. They allow for some variations, of course, such as wage differentials among workers with different seniority ranks; in different occupations; or even performing the same job but possessing different skills, working different shifts, or sharing greater or lesser preference for overtime. Variations continue to exist because (1) they may be of too little importance to require general regulation; (2) they allow differences above some minimum or below some maximum standard that is generally applicable; or (3) as in the examples just given, the general standard itself defines the rule under which the variations are permissible.

Collective bargaining negotiations, then, seek agreements whose terms not only prescribe uniformity of treatment for those covered but also allow diversity and permit variation of treatment. Some terms may set uniform standards of disciplinary action, applicable to all, while others, such as those prescribing layoffs, allow diverse treatment according to length of service. Still other terms permit managers to vary their rewards to workers within certain discretionary limits, as in the case of promotions. They may be free to promote as long as they do not discriminate on the basis of union activity, race, sex, age, religion, or politics.

Theoretically, agreements recognize certain areas wherein employees may be treated individually, without regard for uniformity. The recognition arises under the so-called management's rights clauses and out of the nation's basic labor law. Section 9(a), of the Labor-Management Relations Act of 1947 allows managers to bargain individually with any worker over grievances as long as the settlement does not conflict with the collective agreement. In practice, however, managers seldom exercise their right to make rules for individuals; the practical force of the common rule greatly restricts managerial freedom. Furthermore, an individual settlement, made on a managerial initiative, is almost always more favorable to the employee than that provided by the terms of the agreement. Without very good and convincing reasons for the settlement, the manager may find other workers using it as a precedent, thus pushing up general standards at the firm's expense. The realities of the agreement and the workplace thus impose discretionary boundaries upon managers, even though these realities may not much hamper managers' freedom in the particular areas listed in the management's rights clause. In addition, both parties negotiate within legal constraints. The law, as applied by government agencies and interpreted by the courts, requires bargaining over some issues, permits negotiations over others, and forbids some issues to be the subjects of agreements. Chapter 4 explores in detail the legal constraints on the subjects of collective bargaining.

The collective agreement is a collection of common rules. It is the result of a collective bargaining effort, within legal limits, whereby unionists participate in the determination of work rules that help eliminate competition among workers; it is also a result of management's efforts to ensure stability in labor matters and increase employee acceptance of the necessary web of rules that permit and promote cooperation at the place of work.

Workers, Unions, and the Common Rule

Whenever work was scarce and workers lacked a union to protect them, the neediest and most desperate were likely to underbid their competitors simply to obtain *some* job and *some* income. Employers did not need to be ruthless (though some were), nor did they even bring about the situation; it developed out of the individual worker's struggle to survive at a time when there was no such thing as unemployment compensation. The downward pressure on wages affected all workers, of course, not just those who bid lower. To meet this threat, workers tried to agree among themselves on the minimum terms that *any* worker would accept. Other workers would refuse to work alongside a worker who broke the agreement. An earlier labor economist explained:

> The competition of master with master for labor is not so keen that it is not neutralized and more than neutralized by the competition of laborer with laborer for work; and by combination the laborer tries to do away with the suicidal competition of laborers with each other.[2]

This was the common rule, which gradually evolved into the collective agreement. The early unionists developed their common rule through collective action, not by negotiating an agreement with the employer but simply by agreeing among themselves on minimum acceptable terms. Suffering from some grievance or believing themselves entitled to an increase in wages, they would come together to set their terms. They then would swear an oath, sometimes with hand upon the Bible, that they would not work for wages lower than those decided on among themselves.

The weakness of this procedure for establishing the common rule was its dependence on general acceptance. If new or migrant workers came into the community, the union members had to persuade or coerce them to join in the oath. Masters sought to exploit the weakness, advertising for workers in newspapers in nearby communities. Imported workers owed no allegiance to the local common rule and often proved effective in reducing wages and serving as strikebreakers. Even if no outsiders underbid wages, the hardest-pressed workers would sometimes feel compelled, despite their oaths, to accept their master's terms. Such acceptance might precipitate a general abandonment of the common rule. To guard against defections by the weak, American labor unions very early tried to build up and provide strike benefits. As long as they were small and available for only a short time, the common rule remained in danger.

Union's need for greater protection of their common rule encouraged their

[2]John Davidson, *The Bargain Theory of Wages,* New York: G.P. Putnam's Sons, 1898, pp. 167–168.

leaders to demand the "closed shop." If they could force an employer to hire only those who were union members, they could safeguard their common rules. If workers underbid the union terms, they could be threatened by being expelled from or refused admission to the union. If employers hired only through the union, the isolated worker would have no chance at a job. Employers generally have opposed the closed shop as the primary support of any common rules, consenting to it only under severe pressure, since it all too easily denied them any voice in the making of those rules. They finally succeeded in formally outlawing the closed shop in the Labor-Management Relations Act of 1947, though other forms of union security such as the union shop and dues checkoff remained available.

Because of the difficulties in enforcing uniform terms unilaterally and because of employer resistance to the closed shop, many organized workers began to turn to collective bargaining. When *both* union and employer had worked out the terms of employment, there was less of a threat from needy unemployed or competing workers. Moreover, the process of joint negotiations that produced the collective agreement gave both parties—employer and union—a chance to talk with each other as well as confront each other. Collective bargaining thus expanded the common rule's simple function of protection to a principle of participation as well.

Workers or their representatives usually participate in collective bargaining directly and explicitly. This form of bargaining is the most easily recognized and is commonly the only form described in texts and studies or reported in newspapers. An indirect, implicit form of collective bargaining has emerged in recent years, however; it faintly resembles the bargaining in which unions engaged in the early 1800s, when they typically promulgated their common rule unilaterally. With experience and growing sophistication, union leaders began to anticipate the needs and attitudes of employers as well as employees, and their demands were then tolerable to an employer and might be won without much of a struggle; a demand perceived by employers as outrageous could provoke strong and sustained resistance. Union demands were thus shaped by implicit or expected employer responses even before explicit collective bargaining developed.

Managers and the Common Rule

Managements' establishment of work rules and setting of wages and conditions of work in unorganized plants and offices are also shaped in part by the implicit and presumed demands of unions. Managers of even small organizations of only a few hundred employees can find themselves confronted with union-organizing drives; their employees may choose union representation and then by right of law can insist upon bargaining collectively under government protection. To forestall unionization, managers have reason to offer terms not unlike those gained by nearly or similarly situated unionized workers. Managers or their trade associations monitor collective bargaining in these cases, though the result has the appearance of an employer-imposed common rule. By implicit bargaining, then, we mean the formulation of general terms of employment by union or management with conscious attention to the other's needs but without direct negotiation.

The appearance and use of the employer-imposed common rule is clear in the way managers of nonunion firms have followed the lead of unionized firms in providing nonwage benefits such as pensions, health plans, vacations, and leaves. In some cases, nonunion firms may even provide benefits better than those won by unions. The general occurence of the employer-imposed common rule is also indicated by the prevelance of employee complaint systems[3] for unorganized workers. A common rule, by definition, must apply to all, with similarly situated employees receiving similar treatment. Thus the introduction of a common rule requires the development of a system of adjudication and enforcement. Such development is exactly what has taken place, even among nonunion employers.

The Nonunion Common Rule

In 1954, the National Industrial Conference Board reported that only 21.5 percent of companies studied offered a formal complaint system for their nonunion hourly personnel.[4] Less than a decade later, in 1962, another study found that 54 percent of nonunion firms in the south had established formal complaint systems, suggesting that "unions may be exercising a real, though indirect, influence on the use of grievance systems in nonunion plants."[5] In 1978, the Conference Board took another look at nonunion employee complaint systems and found them widespread; the report indicated that managers clearly offered them in response to unionization and had borrowed procedures from unions:

> Employee morale among nonunionized work forces is being addressed by management in 326 companies by taking a page from the union book of services: formal complaint or grievance systems. These exist in 45 percent of the responding *unionized* companies.
>
> They are more common among companies that are entirely nonunion—69 percent of these respondents had formal complaint systems. Furthermore, it appears that the less unionized company favoring union containment is likely to have instituted a nonunion complaint system (62 percent of the cases). Only 37 percent of the highly unionized, bargaining-emphasis group had formal systems for their remaining unorganized employees.[6]

---

[3]Few nonunion complaint systems provide arbitration and final decisons by an outside neutral. Usually grievants can only appeal complaints from one level of management to a higher one. By union standards such a system provides both incomplete and inadequate protection for workers.

[4]P. Selznick, *Law, Society, and Industrial Justice,* New York: Russell Sage Foundation, 1969.

[5]H. Ellsworth Steele and Homer Fisher, Jr., "Effects of Unionism in Southern Plants," *Monthly Labor Review,* vol. 87, 1964, pp. 258, 265.

[6]Audrey Freeman, *Managing Labor Relations,* research report no. 765, New York: The Conference Board, 1979, p. 60.

The development is significant because the nonunion complaint system indicates the degree to which all parties have accepted the notion of the common rule. Not only may it be negotiated jointly, but it may also be imposed by either union or employer, through implicit bargaining.

A kind of implicit bargaining is involved in the development of the formal complaint systems, although managers initiate it to avoid union organizing. Another Conference Board report pointed out that:

> Virtually all executives who were interviewed saw the complaint procedure as an important part of union avoidance. One of them summarized these views: "We did not develop this procedure because we are nice, but because we want the nonunion employees to stay that way. We put the system in under the threat of a union organizing drive. We know that we have provided employees with a vehicle because the union organizers say the system is good. . . . Furthermore, companies that resort to the specialized assistance of consulting or industry groups in the development of union avoidance policy are much more likely to have such systems than companies that do not. Of 89 companies that use a consulting firm for union prevention, 61 percent have a complaint system.[7]

Since a significantly bigger share of large rather than small firms have nonunion employee complaint systems, it would seem that bureaucratic necessities as well as antiunion sentiments play a role in the development of the system. (See Table 8.) Managers in large firms probably enjoy fewer personal relationships with their employees, governing the organization with more rules, regulations, and complicating procedures than are used in small firms. The larger the firm, the more specialized the various staffs are apt to be, and thus the more likely they are to formalize the work and relationships they oversee.

[7]Ronald Berenbeim, *Nonunion Complaint Systems: A Corporate Appraisal,* research report no. 770, New York: The Conference Board, 1980, p. 5.

TABLE 8
PERCENTAGE OF COMPANIES WITH
NONUNION EMPLOYEE COMPLAINT SYSTEMS,
BY SIZE AND UNIONIZATION

	Nonexempt employees	
	Under 5000	Over 5000
Nonunion employees	67	88
Some union employees	42	54

Source: Adapted from Ronald Berenbeim, *Nonunion Complaint Systems: A Corporate Appraisal,* research report no. 77a, New York: The Conference Board, 1980, chart 1, p. 4.

THE COLLECTIVE AGREEMENT AND
THE GRIEVANCE PROCESS

Workers' collective action early gave rise to the common rule and then to collective bargaining. Now it appears that the existence of collective agreements has helped influence managers of unorganized work forces also to adopt a common rule. What is the relationship of the resulting general or common rules (collectively negotiated or unilaterally imposed) to the individual interests of the employees? We are now concerned with the collective as against the private, with the group as against the individual, and with the general as against the specific. In our examination we shall necessarily be led to consider the grievance process as well as the common rule. The former involves, among other things, the application of the rule to particular situations and cases. We shall have a good deal more to say about the grievance procedure in Chapter 5, but for the moment we shall focus on this one important role it plays in the collective bargaining relationship whether explicit or implicit. It is a mechanism used by the parties to determine whether the established rules have been properly applied in a given situation, usually involving one or a small number of workers.

The problem with which we are now dealing can be set forth more concretely. It is sometimes said that the grievance process is a means of meeting individual needs and resolving the tensions of particular employees. Such means and resolutions transcend the collective agreement and extend collective bargaining, for they must take into account the entire range of human emotions and sentiments evoked in the industrial community no less than in any other. Since no set of rules can be foresighted and comprehensive enough to provide for all contingencies giving rise to grievances, the adjustment procedure must fill the breach by seeking solutions to these problems. Such problems "cannot be exorcised by pronouncing them out of . . . bounds."[8]

The soundness of this line of thought should not, however, blind us to the question it raises but does not answer. Individual grievances may have an important effect upon harmony in a shop and the rules cannot anticipate all situations likely to provoke grievance; it is also true that the process does not always *successfully* solve the grievance that it embraces. If "the sense of injustice of aggrieved workers runs deeply to the very center of their being,"[9] the same reasoning that suggests the advisability of seeking solutions to personnel problems even if not covered by an agreement also favors formal settlement of complaints by nonunion employees under nonunion common rules.

Union representatives frequently ask arbitrators to disregard the technicalities of a contract and meet the human and production problems involved in grievances; managers in nonunion plants find such disregard sensible under

---

[8]Isadore Katz, "Minimizing Disputes through the Adjustment of Grievance," *Law and Contemporary Problems,* vol. 12, 1947, p. 259. This article presents a well-reasoned version of the above problem.
[9]Ibid.

their own common rule. One outstanding arbitrator declared that "the quality and success of the administration of the agreement is not measured by the degree of compliance with it, but rather by the degree to which it aids the achievement of just and harmonious production. . . . The labor agreement [and common rule, however devised] looks to continuous performance . . . and continuous association in a common enterprise from which both parties must derive their shares."[10]

What then becomes of the common rule? What is the nature of collective bargaining when the forms of its agreements may be abandoned or applied from case to case? Here we encounter the issue of the relationship of the collective to the individuals composing it. In analyzing this problem, we shall discover that the way in which both judges and the parties involved view the collective agreement is tied closely to their views of the bargaining process. One may examine the nature of collective bargaining and the agreement from three conflicting viewpoints, which focus upon different aspects of and suggest divergent answers to union-management problems and public policy conclusions. These viewpoints are that collective bargaining is (1) a means of contracting for the sale of labor, (2) a form of industrial government, and (3) a system of industrial relations. We shall discuss each of these in turn.

THE MARKETING CONCEPT AND THE AGREEMENT AS A CONTRACT

The collective agreement historically has been a statement of the terms under which a company's employees collectively are willing to work. Courts have distinguished it from the labor contract, under which an individual *commits* him- or herself to perform service for a period (sometimes of indefinite duration) for a specified remuneration. Failure to honor this commitment may render the person liable to a damage suit for breach of contract. The collective agreement commits no one to give service but merely provides for the terms under which services are rendered. Even this legal distinction, however, does not attempt to disguise the fact that for most practical purposes, the collective agreement has replaced the individual labor contract.[11] One may view collective bargaining as a process that determines the terms under which employees will continue to supply their labor to a company, and which newly hired workers will accept. Both parties generally tend to emphasize this view by the attention they give to wage scales and their negotiated changes. This attentiveness suggests that the money exchange is the most important basis of the agreement. Union negotiators ask on behalf of their members that managers agree to raise

---

[10]Harry Shulman, *Conference on Training of Law Students in Labor Relations,* vol. 3, 1947, pp. 663–664. See also Morris L. Ernest, "The Development of Industrial Jurisprudence," *Columbia Law Review,* vol. 21 1921, p. 155.

[11]For a discussion of employees' individual rights under a collective agreement see David E. Feller's detailed examination of relevant court cases up to the early seventies, "General Theory of the Collective Bargaining Agreement," *California Law Review,* vol. 61, May 1973, pp. 663–718.

wages by a certain percentage or by a certain amount per hour. If the parties do not reach agreement on the price of labor, no sale is made; the employees sell their individual labor only on terms collectively determined.

If the money basis for the collective contract suggests most strongly a sale of labor, it does not exclude the possiblity that other terms may also be insisted upon and granted. Union leaders may ask not only for a given wage scale but also for shorter hours, longer lunch periods, a seniority system, a vacation plan, and sundry other items, all as the price of the labor of its members. Regardless of the variety of such demands and their nonmonetary nature, they still constitute the terms of sale of the labor that is collectively determined through the union. Collective bargaining remains a means for employees to sell their labor through a common agent.

The Legal Background

As already noted, collective bargaining originated as a means of enforcing a union-formulated, and then a union-influenced common bill of wages. The forerunner of the modern trade agreement was a simple price list setting forth the amounts to be paid to every worker for a particular job. (Such a list today would be called a schedule of "piece rates," though this is much less common than hourly rates.) At least as early as 1827 in this country, courts suggested that a bill of prices setting forth an agreed-upon schedule of piece rates in the tailoring trade might contain the necessary elements of a contract. A Philadelphia judge, during a trial alleging conspiracy on the part of the journeymen tailors, referred to such a schedule as an implied contract and intimated that its violation might be made the basis for a civil action. For a variety of reasons, however, courts delayed their recognition of a legal status for such agreements. For one thing, there was considerable doubt about the legal status of the union, one of the contracting parties. At first, the conspiracy doctrine in its extreme interpretation cast suspicion upon the union's very right to existence. In a later period there was considerable legal confusion over the status of an unincorporated association. Again, courts decided that union-employer agreements were best regarded as simply understandings, statements of intention, or memoranda. As such they were no more enforceable than the minutes of a meeting. Futhermore, the fact that the terms of employment might be accepted only after unilateral action by one of the parties colored the whole process with coercion, quite contrary to the voluntarism presumed to accompany bilateral contracting.

As negotiated and written collective agreements became more common, labor experts increasingly recognized their close kinship to contracts. Some began to argue that the alleged coercion that earlier had tainted its character, should, on the contrary, be considered a safeguard of its voluntary nature. They pointed out that privileges of strike and lockout were alternative to a contract settlement; after all, the exercise of bargaining power did not necessarily lead to or require the acceptance of the other's proffered terms. With the passage of time, managers began to realize that the common rules incorporated in agreements had their genesis as much in the nature of modern, large-scale industrial enterprise as they did in collective bargaining. There were substantial reasons apart from union pressure for managers to find them acceptable. The voluntary bargaining that preceded or accompanied any rule setting, more and more influenced the whole process.

There is no indication that the written labor agreement originated as a contract. In time, however, it borrowed the form of the contract, and as its use spread people came to view it as at least a relative of the contract. Those who argued for its legal enforceability stressed its likeness to the contract. The final report of the Industrial Commission in 1902 was quite explicit in its identification of the mechanics, if not the end result, of collective bargaining and contracting: "It should be clearly understood that the process by which employers and employees, directly and without the intervention of outside parties, agree upon the terms of the labor contract is precisely similar in nature to the process of bargaining between two parties regarding any other contract.[12] The report went on to deplore the fact that collective agreements were not given the legal standing of "other" contracts.[13]

Its peculiar nature became the subject of legal analysis.[14] In 1931, after a survey of reported decisions, one specialist reached the conclusion that a collective agreement was "something more than a custom yet something different from a contract for the breach of which damages is the normal remedy.[15] Increasingly, collective bargaining was being accepted as a marketing process that resulted in a contract. In 1935, a leading labor economist testified before the Senate Committee on Education and Labor: "Now, collective bargaining has a well-defined meaning, the basis of which is cooperative marketing of labor. That is all it is. This is the basis of it." To elaborate, he compared that

---

[12]*Final Report of the Industrial Commission,* p. 832

[13]Ibid., p. 856: "Not a few persons believe that the system of collective bargaining would become much more effective if the terms of trade agreements were made legally binding in the same way as the terms of other contracts."

[14]Among articles in law journals of the time dealing specifically with this subject were the following: William Gotham Rice, Jr., "Collective Labor Agreement in American Law," *Harvard Law Review,* vol. 44, 1931, pp. 572–608; J. Blumberg, "Nature, Validity and Enforcement of Collective Bargaining Agreements," *New York University Law Quarterly Review,* vol. 11, 1933, pp. 262–269; H. C. Johnson, "An Analysis of the Present Legal Status of the Collective Bargaining Agreement," *Notre Dame Law Review,* vol. 10, 1935, pp. 413–443; G. T. Anderson, "Collective Bargaining Agreements," *Oregon Law Review,* vol. 15, 1936, pp. 229—253; T. R. Witmer, "Collective Labor Agreements in the Courts," *Yale Law Journal,* vol. 48, 1938, pp. 195–239; and M. A. Pipin, "Enforcement of Rights under Collective Bargaining Agreements, *University of Chicago Law Review,* vol. 6, 1939, pp. 651–672.

[15]Rice, "Collective Labor Agreement in American Law," p. 604. Rice's judgment was based on his inability to uncover any case in which damages had been awarded for a breach of the agreement except as the agreement was considered to form part of an individual contract, for the breach of which or fortuitous interference with which suit had been brought.

marketing of labor to the marketing of eggs, likening the grading of eggs for market to the grading of skills by the unions.[16]

A study made in the office of the solicitor of the U.S. Department of Labor revealed that by 1941, despite variations in state judicial practice, it was "possible to make a collective bargaining agreement that will be enforceable in the courts just as other contracts.[17] The contractual elements of voluntary agreement, a consideration for both parties, and means of enforcement were all presumed to be present. Finally, the Labor-Management Relations Act of 1947 threw open the federal courts to damage suits for violation of collective agreements, thus guaranteeing a judicial form for such suits regardless of variations in state practices. The contractual status of the agreement was thus assured.

Marketing and Bargaining Power

The marketing theory of bargaining is intimately connected with the notion of the collective agreement as a contract. The same or a similar ethical mode shapes both. Collective bargaining as a marketing process assumes that individual workers possess too little bargaining power separately to be able adequately to protect themselves. The philosophy of individualism, which pervaded the political and economic theory of the nineteenth century, asserted that two or more people would voluntarily enter into a bargain or contract only if it served their maximum mutual advantage. That principle was undermined, however, if the bargain was based on dire necessity. To many observers of the labor scene, it seemed apparent that in most instances individual workers bargained under the whip of need to conclude a wage agreement; all too many workers agreed to employers' terms simply to survive. Only a casuist would consider a worker's acceptance of an employment contract to be voluntary under such circumstances.

The American economy was always volatile, providing an unstable foundation for both workers and employers; it created a general sense of uncertainty, particularly for less skilled workers. Business cycles occurred irregularly but surely, typically lasting about forty months from peak to peak. (Over the history of the United States up to 1984, at least forty-six cycles can be traced.) Unemployment was the inevitable accompaniment of the downturns and troughs. In the first third of the twentieth century, the nonfarm unemployed

---

[16]*National Labor Relations Board, Hearings on S. 1958,* 74th Cong., 1st Sess., 1935, pp. 873–875. In 1947, an attorney specializing in labor law testified at the House hearings on the Taft-Hartley bill: "I define bargaining as a process by which one person, if he wants something, approaches the man who has got it, and offers a price for it, and they use all of the arts of bargaining to reach an agreement. We had the process in this country in the old days when we did horse trading. We do it now when we trade in the old jalopy on a new car. We go to the dealer. We do some bargaining. And people, when they bargain, they use all sorts of wiles and arts and devices and techinques to get what they want. *Amendments to the National Labor Relations Act, Hearings on H.R. 8,* 80th Cong., 1st Sess., 1947, vol. 4, p. 2733.

[17]David Ziskind, *The Law behind Union Agreements,* U.S. Department of Labor, 1941, p. 2 (Mimeographed.)

numbered on average over 2 million annually. Before the great depression of the thirties, the rate of nonfarm unemployment ranged from a high of 19.5 percent in 1921 to a low of 2.4 percent in 1918 and 1919, during World War I; but it averaged more than 9 percent over the period, 1900 to 1930.

Intensifying the problems of unemployment and contributing to the competition for jobs were the hundreds of thousands of migrants permanently leaving the farms for the cities and the even larger flows of immigrants from abroad. At least half a million people from farms left for city work each year and immigration saw more than 1 million people added to the U.S. population in six of the years from 1900 to 1914, with an average of almost three-quarters of a million in the other years. From 1915 to 1929 immigration averaged 364,000 annually. Though nonagricultural employment increased rapidly, at about half a million additional jobs each year over the first third of the century, the rise was not fast enough to easily absorb all who sought work in the new industries and expanding established factories. Except in the boom years of World War I, most workers with no, few, or modest skills confronted an intensely competitive labor market.

With little or no savings, individual workers had scant means for sustaining a search for alternatives to proffered employment at however low a wage. Each individual competed with innumerable others and individual workers took what employers offered. Many observers and certainly labor leaders argued that the bargain was not between equals; it was forced by circumstances that seemed always to weigh upon the employee to the advantage of the employer. The unbalanced situation could be summed up in the phrase "labor's disadvantages."[18]

It was this perceived imbalance that collective action sought to right. "The province of trade-union action is the strengthening of the position of the laborer as a bargainer, the enabling him, in particular, to resist that pressure of circumstances of which employers might be ready to take advantage."[19] By common action workers could prevent themselves from being played off against each other. For this reason union members bitterly condemned noncomformers and nonunionists from the very inception of the labor movement. Any independence, coupled with their individual bargaining weakness, threat-

[18]W. H. Hutt, *Theory of Collective Bargaining,* London: P. S. King & Staples, Ltd., 1930, pp. 5–8. John Mitchell, an oustanding union leader and president of the United Mine Workers, set forth the principle of labor's disadvantage in "The Economic Necessity of Trade-unionism," *The Atlantic Monthly,* vol. 113, 1914, pp. 161–170, reprinted in the *University of North Carolina Record,* Extension series 40, no. 182, 1929, p. 22: "Since the workingman has little or no money in reserve and must sell his labor immediately; since, moreover, he has no knowledge of the market and no skill in bargaining; since, finally, he has only his own labor to sell while the employer engages hundreds or even thousands of men and can easily do without the services of any one of them, the workingman, if bargaining on his own account and for himself alone, is at an enormous disadvantage."
[19]Davidson, *The Bargain Theory of Wages,* p. 268. John Mitchell similarly declared: "Trade unionism starts from the recognition of the fact that under normal conditions the individual, unorganized workman cannot bargain advantageously with the employer for the sale of his labor." John Davidson, *Organized Labor,* American Book and Bible House, 1903, pp. 2–3.

ened the position of all who had banded together. By using the device of the common rule, employees collectively could insist that an employer who hired any of their number must offer no less than a standard minimum. While employers might dispense with the services of any single employee, few could dispense with the services of all. Most employers were faced with the necessity of complying, of compromising, or of temporarily suspending operations in an effort to wear down the resistance of the employees.

Limitations of the Marketing Concept

Workers' collective action did not create additional employment alternatives, of course. It indicated their acceptance of a limited number of jobs, even as they tried to restrict employers' ability to profit from it.[20] They could impose that restriction by increasing the bargaining power of the workers relative to that of the employers. "The object of trade-union policy, through all the maze of conflicting and obscure regulations, has been to give to each individual worker something of the indispensability of labor as a whole."[21]

Perhaps the theory of collective bargaining as a marketing process assumes too easily that the collective action of unions can *restore* some original equality of bargaining between worker and employers—an equality that was presumed to characterize their relationship under the philosophy of individualism. Aside from the tenuousness of this assumption, there is little to suggest that collective bargaining established (or reestablished) an equality of advantage between management and workers. It has done so only in the sense that it is as difficult for one as for the other to dispense with some bargain if both continue to exist. To the extent that employers find it a hardship to replace an entire staff of employees, they must reach some collective bargain with the union. Under individual bargaining, an agreement was necessary only to the particular employee. Under collective bargaining, however, the questions of who occupies the more strategic position and who possesses the greater bargaining power remain to be answered.

Not only does the marketing concept of collective bargaining fail to focus attention upon these questions, but it also takes an overly narrow view of the agreement. It suggests that the agreement is strictly and definably limited, constituting the sum total of obligations of all parties. Running for a specified period of time, it does not require anyone to make further concessions or mod-

---

[20]Collective bargaining is not the only program sponsored by the labor movement. Unions have used other devices to attack the lack of employment alternatives. In earlier years, organized workers unable to wrest from their employers terms which they felt juistified founded cooperative workshops of their own. These efforts at self-employment, with only a few exceptions, proved ephemeral. More recently unions have turned to a political program for governmental provision of the number of jobs necessary to full employment when private industry fails to do so.

[21]Davidson, *The Bargain Theory of Wages*, p. 267.

ify its terms during that period.[22] In the bargaining conference the union has marketed the labor of its members; the terms secured are set forth in a binding contract.

The contracct is now enforceable in courts of law,[23] though as a matter of practice the negotiating parties seldom call upon the courts for enforcement; most agreements contain within them their own means of enforcement—the grievance procedure. Only in the event that grievance settlement fails to dispose of a dispute over the contractual obligation of the parties may the courts intervene. When they do, it is apt to be on the petition of an individual worker who charges that neither union nor management has protected his or her rights under the contract.[24] This kind of troubling issue aside, if one regards the agreement as a contract then the grievance procedure is best viewed as a means of enforcing the contract. The procedure may serve other functions as well—a communications channel or a means of administering local rules—but its judicial function is clear.

Construction of the agreement as a contract leads naturally to its strict interpretation and application. Its terms represent the bargain struck. Pressure for deviation from its provisions to accommodate what are claimed as special circumstances is likely to be looked upon as only a scarcely concealed and inadmissible continuation of the same power tactics that led to its signing as a term settlement. To permit departure from the agreed provisions would be to encourage a constant rebargaining of the agreement throughout its lifetime. As a legal instrument, its clauses are expected to be honored for their period of effectiveness. Modification by mutual agreement, while possible, is frowned upon for the same reason.

There is the further danger that to permit a loose construction of the bargain will set a precedent. What was intended only as an exception may become the

---

[22]As early as 1954, the National Labor Relations Board held, however, that during the life of the agreement bargaining may be required with respect to matters *which had not been discussed before* or included in the agreement. For an early decision on this point see *California Cotton Cooperative Association,* 110 NLRB 1494.

[23](a) Suits for violation of contracts between an employer and a labor organization representing employees in an industry affecting commerce as defined in this Act, or between any such labor organizations, may be brought in any district court of the United States having jurisdiction of the parties, without respect to the amount in controversy or without regard to the citizenship of the parties.

(b) Any labor organization which represents employees in an industry affecting commerce as defined in this Act and any employer whose activities affect commerce as defined in this act shall be sound by the acts of its agents. Any such labor organization may sue or be sued as an entity and in behalf of the employees whom it represents in the courts of the United States. Any money judgment against a labor organization in a district court of the United States shall be enforceable only against the organization as an entity and against its assets, and shall not be enforceable against any individual member or his assets. [Section 301 (a) and (b) of the Labor-Management Relations Act of 1947, 61 Stat. 56, 29 U.S.C. 185.]

[24]See, for example, *Figueroa de Arroya v. Sindicato de Trabajadores Packinghouse, AFL -CIO,* 425 F. 2d 281 (1st Cir. 1970), *cert. denied,* 400 U.S. 877 (1970); and *Vaca v. Sipes,* 386 U.S. 171 (1967).

rule. Moreover, if in the course of applying the terms some unanticipated consequence should create a problem for one party or the other, there is opportunity to amend the offending provision upon expiration of the agreement, at the time of renegotiation.

Considered in this light, the common rules become more or less rigid commandments. Grievance settlement is not governed by the circumstances peculiar to an individual's situation or common to a class of cases. It depends exclusively upon the rule as spelled out in the agreement, and the rule is to be applied without discrimination to all who come within its terms. The occasional injustice that may result is to be more compensated by assurance of performance and stable employee-management relations. Stability comes when all concerned know what can be expected. The primary purpose of the *common* rule is thus preserved by its even and sure application.

The parties can always agree, of course, to consider grievances not covered by the agreement's terms. They may settle such grievances without benefit of common rule. Nevertheless, to treat the agreement as a contract presumes that its terms describe *all* the obligations within the union-management relationship; many agreements acknowledge that presumption by limiting the grievance process only to alleged violations of the agreement.

Is the Marketing Concept Useful for the Future?

The marketing concept of collective bargaining may have been more appropriate and useful in earlier times—at the turn of the century, for example—than today. Then unskilled laborers and farm workers made up half the labor force. Many of them supplied more muscle power than skill for the employer's use; and most could be considered interchangeable and were easily replaceable. Both workers and employers were used to discontinuous employment relationships, the former able to quit at will and the other to fire at will. Selling one's labor often was not markedly different from commercial sales.

As employers have come to use more highly trained and skilled workers in complex industrial technologies, the employment relationship cannot easily be broken without inflicting heavy costs upon both parties. Today's unskilled labor is relatively far more knowledgable about and skilled in use of machines tools, and equipment than was the unskilled worker of eighty years ago. The marketing concept of collective bargaining thus increasingly becomes only of historical interest. It implies more discontinuity in employment than is usually practical and less interdependence of employer and employee than in fact exists in most situations today.

THE GOVERNMENTAL CONCEPT AND THE AGREEMENT AS LAW

Primarily because the marketing theory of collective bargaining seems to deny continuity in the bargaining relationship, some scholars and lawyers suggested a different theory. While they could admit the contractual nature of the bargaining relationship, they preferred to view the agreement as a constitution that sets forth the principles by which the parties govern their relationships. On the basis of it, the parties erect an industrial government, a system of rules and authority at the place of work for the occupational group, office, agency, company, or industry—whichever is the designated bargaining unit. The parties need some balance of bargaining power, but this rests first of all on the mutual dependency of the two parties. Only secondly and derivatively does it rest on the power of each to veto the acts of the other through concerted economic pressure.

Union and management representatives in joint conference write the industrial constitution and convene periodically to endorse it and rewrite parts: "[T]he results of those conferences is always the same, an agreement of some kind, verbal or written, which, because of the mutual power to veto, must necessarily be a comprmise."[25] The principal function of the labor constitution (or labor agreement) is to "set up organs of government, define and limit them, [and to] provide agencies for making, executing, and interpreting laws for the industry, and means for their enforcement."[26]

Later, Professor Sumner Slichter of Harvard University expressed this concept in words that were to be widely accepted in the field of industrial relations:

> Through the institution of the state, men devise schemes of positive law, construct administrative procedures for carrying them out, and complement both statute law and administrative rule with a system of judicial review. Similarly, laboring men, through unions, formulate policies to which they give expression in the form of shop rules and practices which are embodied in agreements with employers or are accorded less formal recognition and assent by management; shop committees, grievance procedures, and other means are evolved for applying these rules and policies; and rights and duties are claimed and recognized. When labor and management deal with labor relations analytically and systematically after such a fashion, it is proper to refer to the system as "industrial jurisprudence."[27]

A Three-Branched Government

In common with other governments, the industrial polity has its legislature, executive branch, and judiciary. The legislature consists of the bargaining committees, which meet as often as needed to negotiate the basic laws in the trade agreement which they—or their predecessors—have also written. Because it is basic, the agreement cannot, however, be expected to provide for all contin-

---

[25]William M. Leiserson, "Constitutional Government in American Industries," *American Economic Review,* vol. 12, supplement, 1922, p. 61. This article remains perhaps the most systematic exposition of the governmental approach to collective bargaining and has been chiefly relied on here to present that view.

[26]Ibid.

[27]Sumner Slichter, *Union Policies and Industrial Management,* Washington, D.C.: The Brookings Institution, 1941, p. 1.

gencies in the day-to-day operations of a business. New problems often arise that must be met before the parties can amend the labor agreement or industrial constitution. Local union committees meet with management to solve these problems, but such legislation as they enact of course must not conflict with the fundamental law of the agreement.

The agreement applies only to the particular bargaining unit for which it has been drafted; within that unit it supersedes all other regulations and requirements. A subsidiary or supplementary agreement conflicting with its terms has no standing, just as courts may strike down government actions if they do not conform to the Constitution. Any injury sustained as a result of a violation of the basic agreement is customarily redressed, and faulty applications of the agreement are similarly treated.

The right of initiative, within the framework of the agreement, characterizes the executive branch. This authority is typically vested in management.[28] Changes in methods of production; introduction of new machinery; determination of the products to be manufactured; scale and timing of production; standards of quality; and organization of personnel in such matters as assignments to jobs, transfers, and promotions—these are typical areas in which the agreement either specifically or tacitly recognizes management as the executive office. Management must accord with all the rules; it must act within the boundaries jointly defined. Management may initiate a layoff but it must proceed in line with any agreed requirements concerning notice, designation of the employees to be laid off on the basis of seniority, part-timing of remaining employees, and so on. Management may discharge an employee for disciplinary reasons, but only after meeting jointly determined standards such as adequate warning, timely action, and a fair hearing.

But the agreement is a two-party bargain, and employees may feel that managers have sometimes not complied with the provisions of the agreement. Or managers themselves may be uncertain about the precise nature of the standards to which they must conform. As a check on unwarranted executive behavior or as a means of resolving uncertainties, the parties need judicial procedures. They are provided in the form of the grievance process, culminating in arbitration. Grievance arbitration should not be confused with arbitration of the actual terms of the agreement (commonly known as interest arbitration), which properly is a legislative, not a judicial, activity. Questions of rights claimed under the agreement, but denied in practice, can be appealed to joint

[28]In some industries, particularly construction, union officers carry out many employment functions and perform various personnel activities. They often administer the rules by which workers are transferred, assigned, and promoted. Union officers may select workers for hiring in the first instance, sending them to a constuction site to work for a contractor. As a result grievance in construction go to arbitration less frequently than in other industries. If the job steward and employer's work superintendent fail to settle a job dispute, the local union's business agent intervenes. Either the union agent works out a resolution or a strike will be called and the matter then settled. See D. Quinn Mills, "Construction," in Gerald G. Somers, (ed.), *Collective Bargaining: Contemporary American Experience,* Industrial Relations Research Association, 1980, pp. 86–89.

tribunals with equal numbers of union and management members. The members review the procedural requirements and the merits of the case. If they discover injury, redress can be ordered. In some instances they sit as judicial officials in a court of equity, determining whether generally accepted conventions of fair dealing have been followed. In other instances they interpret the meaning of the agreement for the guidance of the parties. Their ruling stands unless it is appealed to a higher tribunal (or unless some future joint conference overrules it by amending the agreement).

An early study of collective bargaining in the Chicago clothing industry pointed out the close analogy between the decisions of impartial umpires (final arbitrators in the judicial chain) and the federal Supreme Court. Decisions of the former could be sorted into categories labeled "scope of the government," "jurisdiction of the industrial courts," "special immunities of the workers' representatives," "general immunities of industrial citizenship," and so on, in the same way as those of the latter.[29] The details of the grievance process are explored in Chapter 5.

The Requirements for Industrial Governance

The founding organizations cannot establish and maintain the kind of industrial government described above unless they have assured their own continuity. The industrial government they establish rests upon both union and management jointly, and the passing of either ends the government. Continuity is far more significant under this approach to collective bargaining than under the marketing theory. The marketing theory implies that a union, only selling labor, may negotiate the collective terms periodically, allowing its organizational activities to lapse between sales. There might be no harmful effect for the union as long as it can ready itself for the next negotiations; the employer should not suffer either, assuming that grievances and other worker complaints are resolved by management fiat or disgruntled workers leaving. Under the governmental approach, however, the lapse of industrial government between bargaining sessions to renegotiate the agreement (that is, constitutional conventions) would prove ruinous. There would then be no process of joint conferral on problems of mutual interest as they arise in the shop. It is this joint, continuing process that gives life and meaning to the bare bones of constitutionalism—industrial democracy—in industry.

The governmental theory also stresses, as the marketing theory does not, the need for an exclusive representative of the employees in the bargaining unit. If the agreement is a contract, the union may easily negotiate terms for its members only, leaving nonmember workers to work out their own contractual terms. The existence of competing sellers of labor, whether collective or individual, might be undesirable in the union view, but it would not be an anom-

---

[29]Leiserson, "Constitutional Government in American Industries," pp. 66–75.

aly. To have competing governments—industrial or otherwise—with the same jurisdiction would be unworkable. Two parties may compete for control of a government, but government is not duplicated except in a state of rebellion.

To fulfill its function, a government must have power to discipline its citizens to assure compliance with its laws. Such a power is negated if constituents may escape such discipline by the simple act of renouncing citizenship (this is, membership in the union) while remaining within the same jurisdiction as either unattached employees or members of a rival union. The concept of joint government in industry moves one inexorably to accept the need for a single exclusive agency whose laws and judicial enforcement are uniform throughout the bargaining unit, affecting all employees in that unit whether they are members of the union or not.[30] That is to say, the sovereignty of the industrial government must not be impaired.

Indeed, it is the emphasis on an exclusive government within a single bargaining unit that suggests the ethical principle underlying the governmental approach to collective bargaining. That principle may be stated as the sharing of industrial sovereignty. It has two facets. The first involves a sharing by management and the union of *power* over those who are governed, the employees. The second involves a joint defense of the *autonomy* of the government established to exercise such power, a defense primarily against interference by the state. Both stem from a desire of the parties to control their own affairs through their joint activities.

Union leaders, as representatives of the employees, insist on sharing with managers the power to direct the working lives of the employees. They seek to establish and administer rules, regulations, or "laws" that are mutually acceptable. The latter must have the approval of the employees (through their representatives) and the employer. Managers, then, no longer claim a prerogative to promulgate such laws and to exercise such control—sovereignty in one sense; the power and control are jointly shared through the collective bargaining conference. "Government by discussion enters into industry (as it did in the state) when the ruler can no longer arbitrarily force obedience to his laws, and must get the consent of those who are to obey the regulations."[31]

Sovereignty and Outside Interference

The sharing of sovereignty involves joint participation of union and management but not intervention or control by others. Both management and union

---

[30]In American society, founded as it is upon democratic principles, this need for an exclusive rule-making agency in industry has found its expression, through labor legislation, in the doctrine of majority representation. Under this doctrine all employees in the bargaining unit may press for their preferences among competing unions. The union receiving the largest vote, provided it receives a majority of the votes cast, is then designated as the exclusive representative of *all* the workers, whether they are members of the union or not; and it then joins with management to negotiate terms and conditions of work. The resulting provision of the collective agreement are binding upon all employees in the bargaining unit.

[31]Leiserson, "Constitutional Government in American Industries," p. 60.

oppose third-party intervention in the settlement of their own industrial (governmental) problems:

> Organized groups may be regarded as having political attributes: they exercise a kind of private government over their members. In this relationship they have generally proved very impatient of any interference by the courts and have tried, in many instances, to establish in practice a more or less complete immunity from legal actions. The bylaws of trade unions, cooperatives, trade associations, and fraternal societies often prescribe limitations which prevent the appeal of domestic controversies to external agencies, and the courts will not interfere in intra-corporate affairs, for example, with the same readiness that they will adjudicate disputes between unorganized persons. Group autonomy is impossible where government intervenes continually in these domestic disputes.[32]

Union and management antipathy to outside interference has lessened only slightly over the years. The parties now have come to tolerate, though not always appreciate, the intervention of government mediators in negotiations that threaten to break down. Such mediators do not possess authority to impose a settlement. Voluntary arbitration of the terms of a new or renewing agreement is still uncommon. Suggestions that compulsory arbitration be adopted, even in such restricted areas as public utilities, is fiercely opposed by union officials and industrial leaders alike.

When managers possess undisputed sovereignty in their industrial sphere, they consider their freedom to act as they deem best an essential ingredient of a classical, individualistic liberal society. Unions have now joined with managers in claiming that the ethical principle of self-determination bars outside intervention into their private decisions. The parties jointly assert an autonomy over their group affairs. They share sovereignty over internal matters, and they defend it against external interference. Managers' claims to industrial autonomy and even the joint union-management demands of self-determination are based on notions of a nineteenth-century liberal society. The needs of a complex, interdependent industrial economy today, in which nine out of ten workers are employed by and serve organizations, hardly allow government to validate the full reach of managerial claims or to respect the joint demands for self-determination in "free" collective bargaining. The federal government not only limits the subject matter of bargaining, forbidding negotiations on some subjects and requiring negotiations on others, but also influences the parties' decisions by determining the workers covered by the negotiated terms. Increasingly in recent years government has also intervened, in both union and non-union relationships, to establish certain terms and conditions of work, particularly those affecting safety on the job; discrimination in hiring, promotion, and pay; and pension funding. It is possible that government will go further than simply establishing such terms; it has already provided cumbersome

---

[32]James J. Robbins and Gunnar Hecksher, "The Constitutional Theory of Autonomous Groups," *Journal of Politics,* vol. 3, 1941, pp. 12–13.

appeals procedures for those employees who seek enforcement of their legislature. With nearly 80 percent of the work force unorgainzed and thus bereft of a truly independent complaint system—and easily accessible neutral arbitrators—it is not surprising that public policy has moved, even if hesitantly, to provide such a system.

In the unionized sector both management and unionists have learned the usefulness—perhaps even the necessity—of asking outsiders to sit as judges (arbitrators) of disputes that arise under the industrial constitution. Although the parties customarily attempt to limit the arbitrator's jurisdiction, it is not often limited in fact. Complex, poorly drafted, or ambiguous contract provisions and the myriad unforeseen industrial situations that arise at the place of work result in the need for much interpretation and discretion. Justice Douglas wrote in a famous decision:

> The collective agreement . . . calls into being a new common law—the common law of a particular industry or of a particular plant . . . and arbitration is the means of solving the unforeseeable by molding a system of private law for all the problems which may arise and to provide for their solutions in a way which will generally accord with the variant needs and desires of the parties.[33]

Industrial Common Law

We may recall that common law is often referred to as "judge-made law." It is the application of principles that find their source elsewhere than in the written law of constitution or legislative statute. It develops by force of cumulation and precedent and can be stated with a logic and vitality that no other form of law has in greater degree. While the source of such law may be the courts, it may be traced—in Justice Oliver Wendell Holmes's famous words—to "the felt necessities of time, the prevalent moral and political theories, intuitions of public policy,"[34] which find their expression through the courts.

The common law thus has an underlying basis of social morality that in time courts translated into objective standards carrying a normative rather than a moral quality. "In other words, the standards of the law are external standards, and, however much it may take moral considerations into account, it does so only for the purpose of drawing a line. . . . What the law really forbids, and the only thing it forbids, is the act on the wrong side of the line, be that act blameworthy or otherwise."[35] This objectification may be overstated, for the line is not sharply drawn. It is perhaps more like a strip, on each side of which an act is objectively either legal or illegal. Within the strip, though, an act may be either, depending upon whether there is a more subjective appraisal of morality than of normality.

---

[33] *United Steelworkers of America v. Warriors and Gulf Navigation Co.,* 40 LC 66, 629 (1960), 70, 813–70,814.

[34] Oliver Wendell Holmes, Jr., *The Common Law,* Boston: Little, Brown and Company, 1881, p. 1.

[35] Ibid., p. 110.

Nevertheless, for a number of situations to which the principle applies, the strip is no different from a line, for the matter will fall on one side or another in any event. Moreover, precedent narrows the strip, in some cases by specifying exceptions to the principle or special classes of cases. The more judges can use external standards, the more they can avoid probing intent and instead ascertain compliance on the basis of facts. However slippery facts may be, they can probably be grasped more surely than can intent. Thus it does not matter if a person intended well when injuring another; nor is it significant that a person sought to inflict harm when acting within the bounds of allowable behavior. In the absence of written standards for permissible action, the concept of "prudent" or "average" conduct may be used. In Holmes's time, more than today, the jury of average citizens was able to offer content to that concept in specific situations.

Now, in the same manner in which a body of common law accumulated in our courts of law, so has a body of industrial common law developed among our various employing organizations. Grievances not susceptible to settlement by application of agreements' terms may be resolved by referring them to some other base of morality. It may be that of felt necessities of organizational operations, of prevailing industrial ethical standards, or of culturally determined standards of justice. Justice Douglas suggested such a base in his 1960 decision on arbitrability:

> [The] labor arbitrator's source of law is not confined to the express provision of the contract, as the industrial common law—the practices of the industry and the ship—is equally a part of the collective bargaining agreement although not expressed in it. The labor arbitrator is usually chosen because of the parties' confidence in his knowledge of the common law of the shop and their trust in his personal judgment to bring to bear considerations which are not expressed in the contract criteria for judgment.[36]

The origin of the term "common law"[37] goes back to the days when in England the royal courts established a judicial superiority over the numerous lesser jurisdictions of a previously decentralized kingdom. They thus permitted the universalizing of legal principles and the consequent elimination of variant doctrines. In the same way, the development of industrial common law through joint grievance procedures has encouraged the use of standard principles for worker-management relations throughout all employing organizations. The universalizing process has not stopped at company, firm, or agency boundaries; it is spreading throughout all organizations. This result should not be surprising when we recall the nature of common law. It originated in the prevailing ethical concepts and the requirements of daily community life. The former are sufficiently similar throughout society to provide a common basis for the standards governing employer-management relations generally; the lat-

---

[36]Majority opinion, *United Steelworkers of America v. Warrior and Gulf Navigation Co.,* 40 LC 66,629, (1960), 70,813.

[37]Not to be confused with the notion of the unions' common rule, discussed earlier in this chapter.

ter are not equally applicable in all work situations, but they tend toward similarity over many different industries.

Interpretation and Application of the Law

The matter of industrial discipline provides perhaps the most favorable example of a common ethical approach in many different situations, union or nonunion, public or private, and profit or nonprofit. A look at a collection of grievance-arbitration decisions reveals the common prinicples used to judge just penalty for employees. A precise formulation of them may not be possible, but one can recognize the widespread acceptance of such objective standards of discipline as the following:

• The formulation of work rules which, even if not posted, employees may reasonably be expected to know and understand
• Specification of the offense and due process that allows discussion, investigation, and a fair hearing, with the accused permitted counsel of a chosen representative
• A ban on double jeopardy and something akin to a statute of limitations
• Evidential requirements as to weight and burden of proof
• A penalty that fits the offense

Employees, whether union members or not, increasingly expect managers to abide by such principles, and in unionized organizations, union agents will almost always insist upon their observance. Furthermore, arbitrators or umpires will ordinarily enforce such principles, whether or not they find expression in any agreement.

We have made a distinction between the constitutional or statutory law of industry and its common law. In the former, the agreement establishes the terms of the employee-management relationship, and individual cases are governed by those terms. In the area of common law, where no written standards control, it is the mutual recognition of prevailing ethical concepts and the needs of production that provide the basis of decision and ultimately the norms of action. In the case of the written rule, bargaining power—the superior withholding power of one contestant over the other, management in one instance and the union in another—determines the nature of the particular relationship. In the case of the unwritten rule, the relationship is less localized and takes its roots in prevalent *social* customs, outlooks, and folkways. Deviation from terms of the written rule may be difficult, but deviation from the unwritten code is less difficult if that code is founded on an expectancy of reasonable behavior under given circumstances. We repeat, after Holmes, that the life of such a system of prescribed conduct stems not from logic but from experience.

The sharpness of such a distinction becomes blunted upon reflection, however. In practice there is less difference between the two systems of law than may at first appear. The *interpretation* and *application* of the statute (or the agreement) must proceed from the same individuals who look to the institutional setting—even though sometimes tardily—for guidance in construing what actions may reasonably be required of people in their relations with each other. The same ethical forces that help determine the common law continue to operate even when standards of behavior have been reduced to writing. These serve to mold the law in operation. As Holmes has suggested, the primary function of the statute is to induce judges to lay down a rule of law; it serves to influence, and it becomes a "matter of fact" to be weighed along with all the other facts in a case.[38] However, the statute does not often furnish ready-made answers to specific problems, except perhaps in those cases where such an answer would probably have been reached anyway. In applying a seniority clause that recognizes greater merit and ability over length of service, the arbitrator's determination of greater merit and ability and of whose judgment is final may be based less on logical derivatives from the seniority clause of the agreement than on the experience and morality of the time and place. In time such moral judgment becomes normative judgment, leading to objective standards which in fact replace the written rule of the agreement.

If there is a tendency toward such replacement as seen by those who hold the governmental or jurisprudential view of collective bargaining, the reliance upon experience as one of the bases of judgment means that the drive to universalize is held in check. There are two influences at work, seemingly contradictory in nature: one, the effort to establish the *common* rule, or standards that establish the same liabililty for reasonable behavior on the part of all within the social unit; and the other, the reliance upon the logic of the situation rather than the logic of the rule to determine cases that seem to warrant special treatment even though falling within the rule. This is the universalizing as opposed to the individualizing principle, with sufficient recognition of the latter—the *extraordinary* justice that was the basis for the early system of equity—to make the former more acceptable.

Those who accept this view of the collective agreement do not feel the same urgency to adhere strictly to its provisions as do those who consider it a contract. Deviations are permissible and at times even desirable; there is more emphasis upon reasonable conduct and less upon logical consistency, without at the same time belittling that virtue. Departures from the common rule, if founded in the requirements of experience and morality, are looked upon as preserving rather than destroying the common rule; the rule becomes less brittle as it is made more flexible.

THE INDUSTRIAL RELATIONS CONCEPT AND THE AGREEMENT AS JOINT DECISIONS

The governmental concept of collective bargaining proceeds by analogy. It likens the systems of union-management relations to the constitutional forms

---

[38]Holmes, *The Common Law,* pp. 150–151.

well known in modern states. There is, however, no need for such analogy. The nature of the bargaining process is explainable in terms appropriate to its own organizational setting. It is a method of conducting industrial relations, a procedure for jointly making decisions on matters affecting labor. This view is not antithetical to the governmental approach, but it discards the analogy to *state* government and builds upon the fact of *group* government. It recognizes that in every institution or organization some governmental form is necessary. The presence of the union allows the workers, through their union representatives, to participate in the determination of the policies that guide and rule their work lives.[39] The expressed willingness or unwillingness of union leaders to participate in making business decisions and administering shop rules is entirely irrelevant. The fact that time and again union leaders have disavowed any interest in becoming decision makers is immaterial. Collective bargaining *by its very nature* involves union representatives in decision-making roles.

The bargainers who negotiate the agreement exercise final and binding authority in those areas with which they concern themselves. Union representatives meet with owner representatives to reach joint decisions and incorporate them in a written agreement. The decisions cannot be overruled or rescinded for the period of agreement, except by another joint conference possessing similar authority. Union representatives alone are powerless to modify the terms; owner representatives (those whom we designate as directors and managers) are equally without authority to alter the joint agreement. It is subject to change only by *mutual* agreement of these two groups or representatives.

The agreement thus becomes a set of directive orders, a guide for administrative action within the firm. It provides a framework bounding the discretion of managers and unionists alike.[40] At lower levels of company and union there may be further negotiations, carried on within the framework of the collective agreement; plant officials and a local union leader, for example, often negotiate subsidiary agreements within the permissible discretionary limits of the master agreement covering all the plants of a company. At the other extreme, a shop supervisor may collaborate informally with a union steward by working out a shop understanding as to how they will handle recommendations for promotions, within the terms set forth in the collective agreement. In some instances a local union leader may join with lower-level managers to establish and carry

---

[39]Even if employees have not joined a union, managers may respond to union policies and adhere to union standards, as mentioned earlier in the discussion of nonunion grievance procedures. Nonunion employees may thus enjoy a kind of indirect union representation and participation.

[40]When an agreement requires management to promote on the basis of seniority unless there is a significant difference in ability between the workers involved, it limits managers' rights and should be seen as such. Seniority in such a case does not allocate job rights among employees but restricts managers' rights to fill a vacancy at will. Managers may choose to promote on the basis of ability, but they may ignore it and promote by seniority. In neither case would they violate the agreement. A junior employee who claimed superior ability to a promoted senior worker would not ordinarily receive any recognition.

out policies on which the master agreement is silent. For example, an agreement may say nothing about transfers, but an office superintendent—within the limits of discretion allowed—may locally negotiate a transfer policy with the workers' representatives. In these and other transactions where the union leaders participate in making managerial policy, they must be responsible to their superior union officials and mindful of their rights and duties under the agreement if they are not to threaten the whole structure of functional organization within the company.

Union leaders and workers want some means of assuring the enforcement of the decisions in which they participate. They want to be able to question managerial decisions that they feel are unsatisfactory. The grievance procedure is the instrument with which the union and workers can test the limitations on managerial discretion. It may be used as well to continue bargaining, binding management further or loosening the bonds stipulated in the agreement. The agreement may, for example, establish the policy that in scheduling vacations, the employees' wishes shall be considered. Those applying this policy are not forced to acquiesce in the employees' desire. They retain discretion in the final scheduling, but they are obligated procedurally to entertain the requests of the workers and substantively to accommodate such expressed preferences where feasible. Failure to give consideration to employees' wishes can be made the basis for complaint, and the union may force compliance with the agreement, appealing to arbitration as a last resort. An appeal to the strike is sometimes permitted, but usually both union and management have found arbitration to be a better method of settling disputes over compliance with the explicit and assumed provisions of the agreement.

Operating within the Interstices of the Agreement

In every organization there are, however, numerous implied directives that take their place alongside those which have been made specific. An eminent labor scholar, Archibald Cox, long ago pointed out:

> There are too many people, too many problems, too many unforseeable contingencies to make the works of the contract the exclusive source of rights and duties. One cannot reduce all the rules governing a community like an industrial plant to fifteen or even fifty pages. Within the sphere of collective bargaining the institutional characteristics and the governmental nature of the collective-bargaining process demand a common law of the ship which implements and furnishes the context of the agreement. We must assume that intelligent negotiators acknowledged so plain a need unless they stated a contrary rule in plain words.[41]

If an organization is to function, persons in administrative positions must often deduce or infer the policies that they invoke. They must do so because their superiors and standard operating procedures may give no clear directive

---

[41]A. Cox, "Reflections on Labor Arbitration," *Harvard Law Review,* vol. 72, 1959, p. 1402.

and no firm limits to their discretion. Though they do not possess final authority, they must proceed on the basis of what they believe is expected of them by those who do possess such authority. Sometimes the inference is easy to make and unlikely of error. Other times it may not be so clear and may be more likely to contain error or, at a minimum, to result in disparate administrative policies throughout the company. Despite this danger, the process of administrative interpolation cannot be eliminated. The agreement does not—cannot—spell out all the rules and provisions that the union and employer jointly expect to be observed in daily operations. All aspects of the organized employee-employer relationship cannot possibly be anticipated. After outlining the most important provisions, the best that can be done is to suggest the general principles of fairness and cooperation that are intended to guide all decisions. Decisions may be in accordance with what seem like reasonable assumptions to the manager (or less commonly the union official) who makes them, but they may nevertheless be challenged in the grievance procedure. They may be questioned just as in the case of decisions made in accordance with the more definite standards of the agreement. Settling these questions through the grievance procedure assists in clarifying intentions that may otherwise remain vague and uncertain.

Where the union is involved, there are thus two kinds of provisions for management to observe—the known, written provisions of the agreement and the assumed guides or standards in which union interest is implicit but not always actively expressed. The difference between these two sets of guides results primarily from the greater precision and universality of the one over the other and only secondarily from any delimitation of the union's fields of interest. Their purpose is the same: to supply a basis for action and decisions that is acceptable to both the union and the employer in those matters where mutuality is admitted and discretion required.

Once we recognize the sameness in purpose of the explicit provisions set forth in the agreement and of the rules that are assumed, we can see the agreement in its proper perspective. It becomes not a binding legal document, but rather a rule for workers, union leaders, and managers. As such they may apply it flexibly to ensure that they accomplish its intended objective. They need to continue production and serve their mutual interests at the same time; their pragmatic application of the agreement provides its significance and reveals its nature.

Deviations from the provisions of the agreement are permissible if the parties agree they are necessary to gain the objectives of the crafted provisions. One may also defend deviations if they pose no threat to the agreement standards. In effectively performing their administrative activities, both managers and union leaders must depend upon reasonably continuous guides and understandings. Their decisions must be more or less consistent in application. If deviations are so frequent or so important as to threaten a desired provision or if they raise doubt about the standard itself, they vitiate the function of the agreement. Departures are sometimes desirable for operational reasons, though, and they can be countenanced as long as they do not create such a danger. In the terms we have previously used, operational requirements determine application of the common rule. The presumption in favor of the common rule may be rebutted by special circumstances that indicate that a special solution is preferable.

We are indebted to Professor Harry Shulman, onetime umpire for the Ford Motor Company and the United Automobile Workers, for an elaboration of the place of arbitration in the grievance procedure under such a conception of the nature of the collective agreement:

> Unlike litigants in a court, the parties in a collective labor agreement must continue to live with each other both during the dispute and thereafter. While they are antagonists in some respects, they are also participants in a joint enterprise with mutual problems and mutual interests. The smooth and successful operation of the enterprise is important to the welfare of both. A labor dispute submitted to arbitration is not a controversy as to a past transaction, like the typical law suit in which each litigant desires to win, and, win or lose, to wind up the litigation and have nothing more to do with the matter. A labor dispute submitted to arbitration is a mutual problem which affects the future relations of the parties and the smooth operation of their enterprise. The objective of the parties, notwithstanding their contentions in advocacy, must be, not to win the immediate contentions, but to achieve the best solution of the problem under the circumstances. An apparent victory, if it does not achieve such a solution, may boomerang into an actual defeat. An award which does not solve the problem and with which the parties must nevertheless live, may become an additional irritant rather than a cure.
>
> This means that the parties' approach must be radically different from that of litigants. A litigant does not care whether he wins his law suit because the tribunal understood the problem, and made a wise judgment or because the tribunal was actually confused or was influenced by wooden technicality or irrelevant or emotional considerations. But the parties in a labor dispute submitted to arbitration, seeking an award with which they must both live harmoniously in the future must seek not merely a victory but a wise and enlightened award based on relevant factors and full understanding of the problem. And they must, therefore, seek to have the arbitrator know as much as possible about their enterprise, their interests in it, and the problem involved.[42]

The Principle of Mutuality

The ethical principle underlying the concept of collective bargaining as a process of joint decision making is that those who are integral to the conduct of an enterprise should have a voice in decisions of concern to them. We may

---

[42]Quoted in *United States Steelworkers of America v. Warrior and Gulf Navigation Co.,* 40 LC 66,629 (1960), 70,813. Justice Douglas took judicial notice of the difference between labor agreements and the usual contract in this landmark case: "When most parties enter into a contractual relationship they do so voluntarily, in the sense that there is no real compulsion to deal with one another as opposed to dealing with other parties. This is not true of the labor agreement. The choice is generally not between entering or refusing to enter into the relationship, for that in all probability pre-exists the negotiations."

call this the "principle of mutuality." It is a correlate of political democracy; as Brandeis pointed out, "collective bargaining is today the means of establishing industrial democracy—the means of providing for workers in industry the sense of work, of freedom, and of participation that democratic government promises them as citizens."[43]

Mutuality recognizes that property is the basis for authority only over property. Authority over people requires consent. Defining authority within an organization thus involves defining areas of joint concern within which the parties seek decisions by agreement. As conceptions of workers' interests and the area of joint concern expand, so too does the participation of the union in management.

The principle of mutuality is often misunderstood. It is sometimes suggested that meeting with union leaders before managers make decisions is primarily a sop to the leaders rather than a benefit to the workers. If a managerial decision is advantageous to employees, it is argued, why should consultation be necessary?[44]

If owner-appointed managers on their own initiative wish to grant paid vacations to the workers, why should they not be free to do so without bargaining with the union? The answer lies in the mutuality of concern with such a policy. On what basis shall vacations be granted? To what extent, if at all, should employees with long-term service benefit over those with short-term service? On what basis should compensation be granted—average earnings (if so, over what period?); straight rates, with overtime included; with extra pay if holidays fall in the vacation period? Is it possible that employees would prefer less vacation time if more paid holidays were granted, or would they prefer a less liberal vacation plan if a more liberal retirement policy were provided? On what basis shall vacations be scheduled? What if the company cannot spare key workers when their planned vacation period arrives? Should employees be required to take their vacations during periods of layoff, whenever those may occur? Can vacations be split? Workers could raise all these and numerous other questions upon the introduction of a vacation system. Owner-appointed managers acting alone, of course, could answer them, but whether such answers best meet the desires of the employees, balanced against the needs of the organization, cannot be assured unless there is opportunity for the workers to discuss such matters through their representatives. This means a process in which the workers, by representation, join in managing the affairs of concern to them.

The principle of mutuality does not compel agreement before action may be undertaken. It constitutes no injunctive process operating against continuity

---

[43]Louis D. Brandeis, *The Curse of Bigness,* Osmond K. Fraenkel (ed.) as quoted by Clarence M. Lewis, New York: Viking Press, Inc., 1934, pp. 70–95.

[44]This is the viewpoint of those managers who espouse or practice "Boulwarism," a management approach developed in the 1950s by Lemuel. R. Boulware of General Electric. The company's slogan which accompanied the approach was "Do right voluntarily in the unified best interests of all."

of the business. It requires only acceptance of each other's legitimate rules and reasonable meetings and discussions with an intention to reach agreement if at all possible. If there is no meeting of minds, however, solution must come, under existing institutional arrangements, through a contest of economic power. "Absent a contractual waiver of [the right to strike] mutuality requires, and collective agreements are to be construed as contemplating, . . . if the employer is left free [after negotiations] to impose revisions in employment terms without regard to the desires of the employees, the latter are entitled to a comparable degree of freedom of action, namely, the peaceable withholding of their service, in order to protest, or to secure the nullification of the employer's action."[45] The fact that managers' decisions may be reached through such pressure devices, as an accepted method and procedure, is one of the phenomena distinguishing our economic society from most others, both historically and to a lesser degree contemporaneously.

Finally, the determination of the areas of joint concern, within which the bargaining process operates, involves a process of progressive definition. In part that definition may be supplied by law, through labor legislation, and through administrative rulings and court decisions. Much more important, however, it is provided by agreement between the parties themselves. The same process by which agreement is reached in areas of mutual concern also decides the boundaries of those areas. Definition may not be easy, and it may be forthcoming only after strike or lockout. But this process of defining the areas wherein joint agreement shall be sought is itself a matter for joint agreement, and it is subject to the same procedures.

CONCLUSION

We may briefly summarize these three views of collective bargaining as follows:

The marketing concept looks upon collective bargaining as a means of contracting for the sale of labor. It is an exchange relationship. Its justification is its assurance of some voice on the part of the organized workers in the terms of sale. The same objective rules that apply to the construction of all commercial contracts are invoked, since the union-management relationship is a commercial one. If a situation is covered by the terms of the agreement, one derives an answer to a specific problem logically from the agreement.

The governmental concept views collective bargaining as a constitutional system in industry. It is a political relationship. Union leaders share sovereignty with managers over the workers and, as their representatives, use that power in their interests. Both parties apply the agreement by weighing the relation of the agreement's terms to the needs and ethics of the particular case. Interpretation of the terms follows from the logic of experience and morality,

---

[45]*In the matter of Massey Gin and Machine Workers,* 78 NLRB 189 (1948).

so that the parties mold the agreement to the dominant operational needs of both, rather than the reverse.

The industrial relations concept views collective bargaining as the systemization of a functional relationship. Union leaders join with company officials in reaching decisions on matters in which both have vital interests. When the terms of the agreement fail to provide the expected guidance, the parties look to the joint objectives.

As has already been suggested, it would be erroneous to consider these three approaches to be sharply distinguished from one another or mutually exclusive. We may profitably inquire into the relationship among them.

1 To some extent, they represent stages of development of the bargaining process itself. Early negotiations were a matter of simple contracting for the terms of sale of labor. This characteristic predominated until the establishment, in the first part of this century, of systematic relationships in the clothing industry, with pathbreaking use made of the office of impartial arbitrator. These developments led to elaboration of the governmental theory. The industrial relations approach was foreshadowed by the union-management cooperation programs after World War I. Its later statement can be traced to the National Labor Relations Act of 1935, which established a legal basis for union participation in the decision-making process; to the subsequent sudden organization of mass-production industries along industrial lines; and more recently to the organization of government employees. Even as they have wrestled with these profound organizational developments, managers and unionists have had to hammer out a conception of union-management relations that defined their relative authorities and responsibilities. Theories of the nature of collective bargaining thus mirror the evolution of the bargaining process.

2 To some extent the three approaches constitute different stages in the recognition of collective bargaining. Collective bargaining as government existed long before the statement of the governmental theory. Joint industrial governence was evident very early in collective bargaining's history in this country, for employers were not slow to complain of unions usurping their powers. However, it took students and practitioners of labor relations a longer time to recognize the various aspects of the bargaining process, which existed almost from its inception. Some still refuse to accept collective bargaining as actually contstituting a system of joint governance in areas of mutual concern. This delayed acceptance is traceable to the existence of larger institutional patterns and our conception of the social structure as a whole; these condition us to assign to certain groups particular, stable roles. As a result we may not adjust our thinking to changing situations.

3 To some extent, the three natures of collective bargaining are different conceptions of what the bargaining process should be. They express normative judgments. Some person even today believe that the contract system provides the greatest freedom in relationships. Others accept the governmental system as establishing law and order in industry. Still others regard the industrial relations system as suggesting a means of integrating union and business activities in a way congenial to both organizations. Whatever one's motive, acceptance of a theory does not affect its validity or invalidity.

4 To some extent the three natures suggest different emphasis of various aspects of collective bargaining. In the usual bargaining relationship today, a contract does link two parties together and establishes the terms on which that link shall be maintained. In certain circumstances courts may give legal force to an agreement. The bargaining process is a species of government suggestively analogous to that of the modern state; the use of grievance procedures for juridical purposes assuredly makes a valuable contribution to collective bargaining. Union leaders do join with company officials in making certain decisions. One can simultaneously maintain all three natures of collective bargaining, with each providing a different emphasis; each stresses a different guiding principle and can influence the kinds of actions taken by the parties. In part, society at large supplies the emphasis through its govenmental instruments. In larger part, the parties themselves in their bargaining supply an interpretation of their practices and policies. Which approach one chooses to stress will be determined by the view one adopts of the nature of the bargaining process and the bargaining agreement.

There is profit in differentiating among the three natures. In examining industrial relations problems one will find each can serve as a useful tool for analysis, suggesting different possible solutions to the same problem. Moreover, each provides guides in the study of union-management relationships. The marketing approach suggests that a study of contract law and the principles of price-oriented economics can be fruitfully applied in limited ways to bargaining systems. The governmental approach suggests a study of government, political-party relationships, and the nature of authority as most pertinent to the bargaining process. The industrial relations concept suggests the study of business processes and industrial organization as means of getting to the roots of problems of collective bargaining.

The distinctions made in this chapter are not simply abstract issues of academic interest alone. They lead to differences of procedures that may be vitally significant in determining the degree of success or failure of the bargaining relationship. Only a few of these differences are mentioned below; others will be developed in greater detail in later chapters.

The marketing approach stresses the presence of alternatives, however limited, to any given union-management relationship. If the parties reach no agreement on terms, there is no sale of labor. Futhermore, those who see the agreement as a marketing contract are generally reluctant to allow unions the right to arbitrate grievance falling outside the agreement's scope. For them, the contract represents the whole of the bargain struck, and the manager retains undiluted discretion in and control over all other matters. Thus the grievance procedure must adhere rather rigidly to the clauses of the agreement. Under the marketing approach, grievances must be judged on the basis of what is required by the contract. To submit under union pressure to arbitration on issues other than those embraced in the agreement surrenders more than the bargain calls for.

Under the governmental and industrial relations approaches, the parties in the grievance procedure can freely modify the terms as the occasions warrant, though with due care not to destroy the intent of the agreement and the standards it provides. The parties resolve grievances on the basis of what is required by the circumstances, of which the agreement is only one part— although a very important part.

The governmental and industrial relations approaches stress the continuity of a given relationship. They regard collective bargaining as a continuous process. The distinction between grievances covered and those not covered becomes blurred. For the former, there is a system of law to cover each contingency; for the latter, the parties recognize that union interest in all rules and regulations affecting workers may not be exhausted by the requirements of the agreement. All contingencies simply cannot be anticipated. As a result the grievance procedure is available for disputes over issues not mentioned in the agreement.

Under the marketing concept, withholding of data, distortion of fact, or capitalizing on information unknown to the other party may be shrewd bargaining or a good sales technique. Under the governmental concept, it may be difficult to determine whether particular data should be considered to be part of the "government's" official records, accessible to both parties, or to be campaign material, a matter of party politics. Under the industrial relations concept, all relevant data become necessary to an informed joint decision; while this approach does not assume automatic harmony between the two parties, it emphasizes the need for cooperation.

The marketing approach contemplates relationships based on two-party voluntary contract, with the courts as the final arbiter of the agreement's meaning. It accepts the possibility of judicial intervention as desirable for the preservation of collective bargaining. The governmental approach looks to the autonomy of the industrial government, presuming nonintervention by others. The general availability of the courts for enforcement of the terms is regarded as a detriment rather than an advantage, not only because it invades the sovereignty of the enterprise, but also because it leaves judgment to those to whom the experience of the enterprise may be unintelligible. A permanent umpire selected by the parties may be able to overcome the latter objection.

Because of these and other significant differences in results, it would appear worthwhile when appraising the industrial relations issues of our times to remember that the nature of the bargaining process is neither simple nor fixed and unchanging. Its characteristics and functions may be difficult to place, since these, as well as the institutional setting, are subject to continual adaptation. Of one thing we may be fairly certain: The legal, economic, and political significance of collective bargaining as it has evolved and is evolving will be obscured if we treat it as though its nature were not—or should not be—substantially different from that of the collective bargaining of previous generations.

In later chapters we will explore how the various natures of collective bargaining can affect the role of collective bargaining in society at large. We now turn our attention to collective bargaining as the parties carry it out in the shop and at the place of work.

THE FORMS AND CONTENT OF COLLECTIVE BARGAINING

Baseball players and actors confront work and job problems different from those of miners and longshoring workers; teachers and nurses hardly relate to their managers in the same manner in which farm workers or bricklayers approach their employers. It is thus not surprising that unions and managers of such diverse groups conduct collective bargaining in various ways. Yet there is enough similarity between the variety of periodic negotiations over the terms of an agreement and the several kinds of grievance procedures to allow one to generalize, describing with considerable accuracy the American style of collective bargaining.

It manifests three general characteristics. The first is its decentralized nature, with negotiations typically taking place on a company-by-company basis. Even when employers, most commonly in nonmanufacturing, form associations for joint bargaining, they seldom include all firms and workers in the industry. There are few, if any, agreements that cover all industry employees as in some European countries; and seldom does an agreement even cover all the employees, white- as well as blue-collar, in a company or plant. The second characteristic is the general adversarial stance of both parties. Managers have traditionally guarded their asserted prerogatives—their right to manage. Union leaders have only sporadically and opportunistically challenged such assertions. Both parties have been quite comfortable to have managers retain the initiative in administering the agreement and applying its term, as long as the union can question decisions and actions after the fact, winning redress when appropriate. Now and then, typically at managers' initiative and at a time of crisis, some have experimented with joint problem-solving processes, less adversarial and more cooperative than those traditionally relied upon. The public usually applauds such experimentation and scholars are always ready to discover a new trend or a significant change in collective bargaining in such developments. As we shall see later, adversarial relationships between management and unions have diminished considerably since World War II, but the change has been gradual and, as noted in the last section, uneven.

The third characteristic of the forms and content of collective bargaining is their pragmatic origins. The parties usually regard each other warily from their adversarial positions, but they are quite ready to deal with each other in practical ways with the factual subject matters they bring to the bargaining table. They seldom engage in ideological or political debate when bargaining. As pensions and complicated health issues became important bargaining issues, both parties recognized the need for experts to help analyze their various proposals and to work out the details. As collective bargaining spread in the public sector, unionists recognized the reluctance of the public to wholeheartedly endorse strikes. Unionists accepted arbitration as a means of reaching final settlement even though historically American unions and management have strongly rejected interest arbitration—that is, third-party determination of the terms of agreements.

THE NEGOTIATING PROCESS

Union and management negotiators conduct their bargaining in a variety of ways. Those participating may range from national officers and rank-and-file workers on the union side to chief executive officers and staff experts on dental plans on the company side. The procedures they follow to discuss, explore, and debate proposals range from formal to informal and from simple to complex. Whatever procedures the parties use to conduct their negotiations, they negotiate some of the nation's most important economic decisions. One agreement, for example, may change the labor costs of a single company by millions of dollars. Changes that encourage technological improvements or otherwise improve productivity may lower costs significantly; and those that add fringe benefits, raise hourly rates, or impose restrictive work rules may add greatly to costs. One agreement may affect thousands of workers in a large firm of a major industry; its terms may also set a pattern and affect the whole economy.

PROPOSAL AND COUNTERPROPOSAL

Negotiations do not catch union leaders or company managers by surprise. Most agreements specify a date when they will expire;[1] and in any case, by law one or another of the parties must serve a sixty-day notice upon the other that an agreement will be terminated or modified.[2] Thus the negotiators have time

---

[1] Only 5 out of 1550 agreements covering 1000 workers or more, as of 1980, did *not* specify a termination date. See *Characteristics of Major Collective Bargaining Agreements, January 1, 1980,* Bureau of Labor Statistics, Bulletin 2095, May 1981, table 1.2, p. 12.

[2] Labor-Management Relations Act, 1947, Sec. 8d(1)–(4).

to prepare themselves for the discussion of new terms and the modification of old ones.

Experienced negotiators, but not necessarily union members or the public, know the approximate economic limits of likely settlements before they sit down at the bargaining table. The existing terms, comparable earlier settlements, and general industry conditions indicate the most probable overall range within the limits. But any agreement is a package of many different items, each of which can be defined or specified in a variety of ways; the parties may trade off an increase in pension benefits for a limit on a cost-of-living adjustment, for example, or make seniority rules more flexible in return for an extra holiday. Even the participants cannot forecast the exact mix of adjustments and details that they will find mutually acceptable. Furthermore, in many negotiating situations neither party can know for sure if a strike or lockout will take place if no agreement is reached by the expiration date of the old agreement. Such an occurence almost always complicates negotiations. Its possibility adds to the other, common and usual uncertainties.

Experimental Negotiations in Steel

To reduce the uncertainty that a strike threat carries with it, the United Steel Workers (USW) and the largest steel makers, including U.S. Steel, Bethlehem, Jones & Laughlin, Republic, National, and Inland, in 1973 approved an experimental negotiating agreement (ENA).[3] The union promised not to call a nationwide strike in steel, even if the parties had not reached a new settlement by the expiration date, and the companies promised a bonus and at least a 3 percent settlement. They thus guaranteed themselves and, more importantly, their customers that production would not be interrupted during negotiating years.

The president of the United Steel Workers, I. W. Abel, wrote shortly after the initiation of the ENA, "We believe this unprecedented experiment will prove there is a better way for labor and management to negotiate contracts. The new procedure will not only relieve both sides of the pressure of a potential shutdown, but will also offer us a genuine opportunity to achieve results equal to those obtainable when the threat of a strike exists."[4] The parties extended the ENA from one negotiation to the next. Before they began bargaining in 1980, Lloyd McBride, then USW president, endorsed it strongly, with the overwhelming backing of the union's Basic Steel Industry Conference. "[It] will enable both sides to conduct 'cohesive' bargaining and that it 'leaves us free to join hands on problems, such as trade, that affect both industry and the workers.'"[5]

Not all steel managers were sure that the gain in production certainty was

[3]See Chapter 1 for the background of the agreement.
[4]I. W. Abel, "Steel: Experiment in Bargaining," *AFL-CIO Federationist,* July 1973, p. 6.
[5]"Edgy Steelworkers Set their Goals High," *Business Week,* Dec. 24, 1979, p. 46.

worth the costs imposed by the ENA. It lessened consumers' "hedge buying" in anticipation of a strike and reduced incentives to import steel, but the costs were so high that managers of the largest companies warned that continuation of the ENA into the eighties would have to be examined carefully indeed. More notable is the fact that in no other industry have major firms or unions chosen to try an ENA approach. Outside the steel industry, negotiating parties apparently found the uncertainties of a strike threat useful,[6] or at least not as costly as the alternative to which the USW and the large steel companies agreed. The costs of the ENA to the steel companies appear to have been high indeed. In 1973, average hourly earnings in basic steel were 23 percent above those in manufacturing generally. By 1982, they had climbed higher, to 65 percent, the highest wages in the economy for production workers. Moreover, the rapid rise took place at a time of increasing foreign competition and significant restructuring of steel markets domestically. In July of that year the steel employers announced that they would agree to no further extensions of the ENA.

The union also discovered that the ENA raised its organizational costs and created other problems. Union dissidents did not have to face up to the consequences of their proposals and thus left unresolved some internal conflicts. Within the Steel Workers, dissidents denounced the ENA and tried to discredit the incumbent leadership. They argued that the members could have gained more by at least threatening to strike. Their effort did not win a majority of votes but may have intensified internal union conflict.

Preparations for Negotiations

In most organizations both parties come to the bargaining table with many uncertainties, not only about the specifics of a settlement each hopes to achieve but also how each can achieve it. The negotiators must sensitively recognize and understand the influences and pressures that play upon them if they are to cope with these uncertainties; furthermore, they have to be ready to take an active role in shaping the negotiations to fit within overall constraints which they cannot control. Union leaders, as democratically elected officials, must be responsive to their members' needs. They must carefully and continually balance diverse political interests, particularly if rank-and-file ratification of the settlement is required, as is the case in many unions.

To prepare for negotiations—to ready members and officers for bargaining—a large union, such as the USW, has its research staff update basic information about past settlements, present terms, and variations among their hundreds of local agreements and their several national agreements such as those in steel, aluminum, containers, and copper. The members of the USW's

---

[16]Another part of the ENA was the submission to arbitration of all unresolved disputes over the terms of a new agreement. Although neither the steel companies nor the Steel Workers used this provision, other managers and union leaders may have been hesitant to copy a proposal that might involve outsiders in the bargaining process.

contract administration department solicit from local union leaders "gripe letters" about noneconomic issues and follow up with visits to plants to examine first hand the problems involved. The national staff also receives formal resolutions submitted by district conferences and local unions. From their own findings, the formal resolutions, and suggestions of the top national officers, the union researchers prepare a statement of proposals and goals for the forthcoming negotiations. This is submitted to a Wage Policy Board (WPB) that meets some months before negotiations are to begin. It consists of the national officers, district directors,[7] and about 145 local delegates elected on the basis of membership. The WPB formulates the bargaining goals and submits them to local union representatives, usually presidents, who make up the Basic Steel Industry Conference, for approval. The Conference provides opportunity for wide discussion and approval of the goals. If there is serious opposition to some proposals or unhappiness over the absence of others, the union negotiators need to learn about it early. They also use the meetings as opportunities to educate the local and district leaders about realistic and probable estimates of the goals that can be won. In 1982 and 1983 the Conference twice voted down recommendations submitted by the union negotiators. The WPB then dropped 90 nonsteel representatives from membership and on the third try secured approval.

In the meantime, the industrial relations staffs of the steel companies are also preparing for the upcoming negotiations. They may solicit comments and suggestions about problems arising out of the existing agreement from foremen, supervisors, and plant managers; they examine the grievance records, looking for issues that arise repeatedly and might be better dealt with under a change of terms; they examine other settlements in the industry or community, especially those believed to be comparable and relevant to their own labor market.[8] Typically in large firms the corporate vice president of industrial relations prepares the proposals, which are then reviewed by the chief executives.[9] The process of development of a company's initial proposals is not as democratic in form as that in the unions, since the underlying structure of the two organizations is different. In both, however, the central staff and top officers play key roles in formulation.

One should be aware that typical procedures do not reflect the wide variation in the ways unions and managers in many industries develop their proposals. In construction, for example, most firms are relatively small and are members of multiemployer associations. They negotiate on a craft basis, usu-

[7]The country is divided into major districts, each with a director and staff to help Steel Workers locals deal with problems peculiar to their geographic locations and to help the national officers in Pittsburgh keep in touch with the locals.

[8]See "Bargaining Outline for Management," *Collective Bargaining Negotiations and Contracts,* vol. 14, no. 939, Bureau of National Affairs, May 25, 1981, pp. 11–19. It is a recommendation for managers that was first offered in 1956 and has since "become a classic negotiators continue to follow."

[9]See Thomas A. Kochan, *Collective Bargaining and Industrial Relations: From Theory to Policy and Practice,* Homewood, Illinois: Richard D. Irwin, Inc., 1980, Table 6-5, p. 197.

ally with either a local union or a district council, whose procedures for defining proposals are much simpler and less formal than those of a union such as the Steel Workers. The national building-trades unions usually offer only general supervision of local bargaining and settlements.

Where firms are many or small, their managers may find it difficult or impossible to develop proposals on which they can all agree. Such is the case in the trucking industry, where time and again one or another group of employers has pursued its own interests, ignoring its initial endorsement of a common front, to settle with the Teamsters on such terms as it can get.[10] In other cases there may be several unions bargaining with a number of employers, as was well illustrated in the New York newspaper negotiations in recent years. In 1964 confusion reigned when ten unions and seven publishers of eight newspapers negotiated with each other. Rivalries and distrust added to the complexity of the negotiations and contributed to a 140-day strike in 1964. By 1978 the number of publishers had declined to three, though the same number of unions were involved; confusion and distrust continued.

Not infrequently the parties seek to influence each other even before formal bargaining begins. The managers of the New York City newspapers attempted such influence in their 1978 negotiations. They both offered a carrot and threatened a stick in hope of inducing the Pressmen to change their restrictive staffing rules. The year before the agreements were to expire, *The New York Times* told stockholders that it has to reduce the ruinously costly overmanning, but the senior vice president for industrial relations assured the president of the Pressmen that all the publishers wanted to resolve the issue "with honor for both sides." The publishers of the *New York Daily News* and the *New York Post,* however, flew nonunion managers and technicians to Texas and Oklahoma on weekends, where they demonstrated their ability to put out a paper without union workers. The publishers apparently were telling the union members that they meant to change the manning assignments on the presses, peacefully if they could but forcefully if necessary. The union leaders heard the pre-negotiating threat more clearly than they did the promise of an honorable settlement. They became convinced that they were facing a determined attack upon their conditions of work, one so serious that they would have to resist it fiercely. A strike that lasted from two to three months resulted before the parties reached a settlement, with the publishers going separate ways.[11]

The parties often do not make their messages or meaning clear to each other, sometimes unintentionally but sometimes for tactical reasons. One writer on the subject of negotiations has warned that "Negotiation isn't always neat. And it is often not nice."[12] Negotiations are not neat because the bargainers must

---

[10]Harold Levinson, "Trucking," in Somers, *Collective Bargaining: Contemporary American Experience,* p. 105.

[11]For the full story of these negotiations see A. H. Raskin, "A Reporter at Large: The Negotiation," *The New Yorker,* January 22, 1979, pp. 41–87; January 29, 1979, pp. 56–85.

[12]Gerard I. Nierenberg, *Fundamentals of Negotiating,* New York: Hawthorn Books, Inc., 1973, p. 6.

juggle many complex variables over which they enjoy but limited control. They must be ready to seize any advantage that is offered and must be ready to cope with changing situations as they unfold. Thus participants will be wary of making detailed, specific proposals until well into the negotiations, waiting to gauge both their own side's willingness to live with a set of particulars and to test the limits of acceptability to the other side.

Negotiations in Autos

The 1970 auto negotiations illustrate the uses of generalities and ambiguity by both sides in making proposals. The agreement was to expire September 14 at midnight. About two months before, the chief union negotiator presented a "package" to the General Motors managers, asking first for a series of nonwage demands such as voluntary overtime, a paid dental plan, an unbroken holiday between Christmas and New Year's Day, discounts on company products (a benefit white-collar workers had long enjoyed), and a paid leave at the birth of a child, for workers with more than thirty days' service. He also asked for a "harmony clause" in which GM would pledge not to intervene in union attempts to organize white-collar workers; he challenged the company to reveal how much it spent on pollution control; and he demanded an end to time clocks. (The UAW still required its own clerical and janitorial employees to punch time clocks at Solidarity House, the union headquarters.) This nonwage request was only pro forma and both sides knew it. It served the purpose, though, of responding to demands from members and local unions. It was probably referred to a subcommittee for further discussion, offering opportunity for both endless discussion and the draining of emotion. The request did not surface again and it did not impede or impair consideration of the larger and more important proposals.

The next day the chief union negotiator presented the economic requests— a substantial wage increase, an unlimited cost-of-living adjustment, retirement after thirty years' work, and some smaller items. He had not specified the wage increase, but the managers on the opposite side of the table replied that the size of the demand stunned them. It was, said the top negotiator, "more far-reaching and extensive than anything we had read or heard about."[13]

Neither side made any specific wage proposal for the next six weeks while both sides explored various aspects of the economic package and listened carefully to the arguments presented, trying to gauge the relative importance of the various items under consideration. Was there general agreement on the overall size of the package? How high would GM go? How low would be too low for the union? Under pressure from the rank-and-file, would the union leaders feel they would have to reject management's last offer before expiration? If so, the company would almost surely have to come up with a better package to end the strike. How good an offer dared the managers make at first? General

---

[13]William Serrin, *The Company and the Union,* New York: Alfred A. Knopf, Inc., 1973, p. 38.

Motors decided to play a cautious game: offer some, but be ready to go higher. Two weeks before expiration the company made a specific offer, but its top negotiator complained, "We had to make [this] offer in total darkness because . . . [the union] wouldn't tell us anything. So we were sure we weren't going to put anything in it that wasn't essential and necessary. It wasn't a small offer, but we made it clear at the time that this was not the last word."[14] The union finally presented its specific wage demands almost a week later, on September 5.

Neither party made its proposal public, though news reporters sought details. On the television show *Meet the Press,* the UAW president would only say that the union sought a settlement within the framework of recent settlements by the Printers in New York City and by the Teamsters in a national accord. Both sides adjusted their proposals, the union down and the company up, over the next few days as the expiration date approached, but not until just before the old agreement came to an end did the union leaders publicly announce the specifics of their wage proposals. For two months the parties had retained considerable flexibility for themselves, making the offers and counteroffers more freely than would have been the case had all been public.

The 1970 auto negotiations also offer some examples of how managers and union leaders may signal information to each other indirectly during negotiations. The union leaders believed that there was strong worker sentiment to "uncap the cost-of-living adjustments (COLA)." In the previous negotiations the union had agreed to a ceiling on COLA of eight cents per year, only to see inflation spurt afterwards. The president, Leonard Woodcock, publicly announced the union's determination to take off the cap, or failing that, to seek wage increases large enough to more than keep up with the price level. He thus had warned GM that the cap was serious business indeed. To increase pressure on GM to uncap COLA and to find out how the management might respond, the UAW used the Caterpillar gambit.

The UAW was negotiating with the Caterpillar Tractor Company at the same time that it was bargaining with GM; it secured from the smaller, less profitable company an uncapped COLA and argued that GM could not refuse to follow suit. General Motor's chief negotiator insisted that "Caterpillar bargains for Caterpillar. GM bargains for GM." What Caterpillar did would have no influence on GM's position, he asserted. But the UAW president heard an implication in GM's statement: Although the company was not simply going to follow Caterpillar, "the way he said it, it made it clear to me that *this* we were going to get. It was just a question of time."[15] Reading meaning into statements according to the way they are said or seeking out intentions indicated only implicitly can be a trying task, subject to many errors. It is easier if the negotiators are experienced and well acquainted with each other's style and mode of expression. They can listen to and watch for suitable clues that may

[14]Ibid., p. 48.
[15]Ibid., pp. 185–186.

suggest the areas open to adjustment or those on which there can be no give. In the 1970 negotiations, when the UAW president wanted to indicate that he and the union were ready to settle and that they had offered their final proposal, for example, he changed the mode of communication by appealing directly to GM's chief executive officer, over the head of the chief company negotiator. Significantly, he laid out for the chairman only those demands that the chief negotiator had already received. The company negotiators read this as a sign that the unionists believed a settlement on the terms described by the president was both possible and needed. The company quickly responded with a final offer and the parties soon reached a settlement.

Rituals and Tactics in Negotiations

Even these few illustrations of the way unions and managements prepare their proposals and counterproposals suggest the tactical use to which they lend themselves. We may recall from our historical review that in earlier years the terms drafted by the parties were not proposals, tentatively and cautiously specified, but demands, to be enforced by unilateral action; they were thus adopted only after those concerned—the union members or the employers— were convinced that they were feasible. Only with the development of bilateral negotiation and collective bargaining as we know it today did unions and employers begin to veil their initial proposals, asking more or offering less than they expected finally to accept. Since one can "cost out" a proposal package using a variety of financing assumptions—the size of the work force, productivity changes, and future capacity utilization—there is seldom a fixed, objective, factual price that can be attached to it. (Both managers and union leaders are tempted to overestimate costs publicly; the former to justify price increases, and the latter to convince members of their bargaining prowess.) The negotiating parties therefore enter into bargaining with great uncertainty on both sides, confronting schedules of possibilities that range from the more to the less desirable. Each party seeks a schedule of items as desirable for itself as the other will tolerate. Little wonder that they fence and feint with each other; they seek clues about the other's irreducible needs while hiding their own as well as they can. As they thrust and parry, they must keep one eye on the clock that indicates the time before the old agreement ends, when they will have to consider the added uncertainties of a strike or lockout. Negotiations are not just a process of ritualized exaggeration and lying, as some observers and even practitioners have suggested,[16] but a difficult, complex game of discovering the

---

[16]Professors Carson, Wokutch, and Murrmann have argued that although many forms of bluffing in labor negotiations are legal and also economically advantageous, they nevertheless typically constitute lying. They can reach such a conclusion only by assuming that each party knows its own settlement position. In fact, parties may know their own preferences but can assign only probabilities to possible settlements. They can lie about their estimation of probabilities, but they probably usually avoid doing so. The purpose of negotiations is to transmit signals and provide information; the more trust that can be developed, the easier the purposes are served. Only through negotiations can the parties improve their estimate of the strength of commitment each has to various possible

terms on which both parties can continue their relationship. It requires high art as well as careful calculation and thus can best be played by those who know it well and have developed their negotiating skills through both study and practice. Experienced negotiators also insist that an important ingredient of negotiations is the personal characteristics of the bargainers—the "interacting chemistry" of those in charge.

THE NEGOTIATING COMMITTEES

National or industrywide bargaining is usually conducted by the top officials of the national union in collaboration with representatives of local unions. The presence of local officials creates a problem to which unions have applied a variety of solutions. Shall local representatives come instructed by their members regarding their course of conduct in negotiations, or shall they be left to resolve matters as they find best under the prevailing and immediate conditions?

After some experimentation, most American unions have adopted the view that local instruction of delegates to national conferences leads to inflexibility and may sacrifice the good of the whole to the special interests of a small group. Furthermore, most union leaders have come to realize that effective negotiations can be carried on best by a relatively small number of bargainers at any one time. Rather than wide representation at the bargaining table, unions tend to use officers at the highest appropriate level, who are experienced negotiators, while increasing the breadth of representation in the formulation of general proposals and ratification of the settlements. The newer the union, the wider the representation is likely to be at the bargaining table.

For example, the United Farm Workers, which grew to strength only in the seventies, still emphasizes extremely democratic procedures in negotiations. The negotiating committee is headed, as is common in other industries, by the union president or by seconds, along with the necessary legal and research support staff. In addition, the committee includes direct representatives from the ranch or farm locals involved or generally elected rank-and-file members. Since multiemployer bargaining units are common, a bargaining team can consist of 100 or more members! So large a group has sometimes proved to be distracting to employer representatives, though most of the members take little part in the sessions; they serve primarily as observers, loyal unionists who can assure local members that their leaders fought hard for them and secured the best settlement possible.[17]

---

settlements and thus help themselves decide what settlement, at what cost, is available. They can hardly lie about a settlement that is unknown to either as negotiations start and that is discovered only as negotiations continue. See Thomas L. Carson, Richard E. Wokutch, and Kent F. Murrmann, "Bluffing In Labor Negotiations: Legal and Ethical Issues," *Journal of Business Ethics,* vol. 1, Feb. 1982, p. 13.

[17]See Karen S. Koziara, "Agriculture," in Somers, *Collective Bargaining: Contemporary American Experience,* pp. 263–314.

The Complications of Democracy: The Case of the Coal Miners

Such assurance is important, for without it the members may not accept a hard-bargained settlement. A rejection is dangerous for the union leaders particularly if they recommended acceptance. It is a repudiation of their presumed best efforts. It may also be costly for employers. They will have to return to the bargaining table with the realization that only a strike or an improved settlement or both must follow. In 1981 the leaders of the United Mine Workers (UMW) and the Bituminous Coal Operators Association (BCOA) suffered such a rebuff when the underground coal miners voted down the initial settlement. From 1950 to 1973, only officers of the two organizations had been involved in negotiations. John L. Lewis, the former powerful and legendary union president, had dispensed with democratic procedures in negotiating as in other areas of union activities. His immediate (and corrupt) successor Tony Boyle continued the Lewis way.

After 1973, under a democratically elected president, the UMW established new, more representative procedures for bargaining. The actual negotiations were still conducted by the union's principal officers—president, vice president, and secretary-treasurer, with the assistance of staff specialists. Helping to formulate union demands, ratify the agreed terms, and assist in selling the completed settlement was a newly established contract bargaining council consisting of board members and presidents of the eighteen districts covered by the agreement. When the president and the bargaining committee reached a tentative settlement in 1981, just four days before the old agreement was to expire, the council examined the terms of the settlement and approved it, but unfortunately with a split vote, 21 to 14. (Nevertheless, this was the first time in its eight-year existence that the council had approved a settlement without previously sending it back for renegotiation.)

Reflecting the council's close vote, the selling of the settlement was as difficult as its negotiating—but less successful. Many local union leaders and rank-and-file members roundly criticized the union president when he appeared before them to urge ratification. When the votes were counted, 67 percent had been cast against the settlement. The union constitution obligated district leaders (and council members) "to use their best efforts to secure approval by the members," but with local and district elections continuing through the whole period, dissidents saw opportunities to win both office and militant reputations. The president had no choice but to accept the verdict of his members. He explained, "I said I thought the tentative contract we worked out with the industry was a good one. That was my honest opinion but the only opinion in this union that really matters is that of the membership."[18] After more than two months of strike, industry and union negotiators gingerly worked out terms more favorable to the workers than the first settlement. During the sec-

---

[18]Carol Hymowitz and Thomas Petzinger, Jr., "Talks in Coal Strike Unlikely to Resume for At Least a Week; Union Digs for Unity," *The Wall Street Journal,* April 10, 1981.

ond round of negotiations, the UMW president improved the bargaining committee's communications with the union members by means of the council. In the first round, he convened the council only after settlement had been reached. In the second round, he summoned it to Washington, where he and the top leaders were meeting with the BCOA representatives. He reported to the council daily and thoroughly discussed ongoing bargaining moves and the matters over which the parties were bargaining.

The union leadership also showed more sophistication in dealing with news media after the second round. Instead of beginning his local promotion of the settlement in a district known to be hostile to him and the agreement, the second time the president started his tour, as the newspapers reported:

> in Alabama, where he expected a relatively friendly reception instead of Pennsylvania or Ohio. "Last time all we saw on TV was people mad and hollering at Sam Church, [the UMW president] but last night they showed all these miners in Alabama clapping for him," says Willie Vance, a local union president from Logan County, West Virginia. "That's got to have some effect on miners here."[19]

The improved selling of the second settlement, as well as its better terms, and the pressure of the long strike had their effect. The members approved the new agreement.

There can be too much democratic participation in the negotiating committee, making agreement among the negotiators difficult, with trade-offs to secure compromises all but impossible. As long as the public favors democratic unions, with substantial member influence in major decisions, negotiators will have to bargain with due attention to rank-and-file expectations. If members are unrealistic, they will have to be made aware of the constraints on the settlement, and in any case they need a full explanation of the terms and their implications.

Rejection as a General Problem

The appeal to the rank-and-file for approval of settlements is time-honored. It goes back to the earliest organized efforts of workers in this country. This democratic custom of an earlier day perhaps carried greater meaning then, when the workers involved were few in number and easily assembled. In negotiations today in which these same circumstances obtain—in small locals—the old arguments in favor of membership approval retain their validity. But in negotiations involving large numbers of employees, especially when they are scattered in many plants of the same company or among many companies within the country, membership approval, while desirable, tests the ability of leaders of both parties to be responsive to employees and strains the capability of union officers to keep their members informed about bargaining develop-

---

[19]Carol Hymowitz and Thomas Petzinger, Jr., "After 1st Loss, UMW Leaders are Confident," *The Wall Street Journal,* June 5, 1981.

ments and knowledgeable about the conditions under which union gain can be made.

A generation ago hardly more than three-fifths of the work force had completed high school, but today high school graduates and those with more advanced schooling make up 90 percent of the work force aged 25 to 34 years. The better-schooled workers not only have the educational background to understand the issues involved in negotiations and settlements, but are well aware of industry and national economic conditions through television and the other ubiquitous news media. Both union leaders and managers therefore will need to learn how to use modern means of communication more effectively than most of them have to date. The coal-mining negotiators learned that lesson the hard way in 1981.

From time to time managers, arbitrators, and even union leaders have complained that the rate at which workers refuse to ratify hard-bargained agreements is too high.[20] It is not clear what standard they use to measure the rate, however. Through the 1970s refusals to ratify averaged between 9 and 12 percent of those presumably difficult cases that involved the Federal Mediation and Conciliation Service. This would be only one out of eleven or twelve agreements, surely not too high for so important a matter as the setting of wages and terms of work. William Simkin, a former director of the service, found that unsatisfactory wage settlements occasioned most rejections. Furthermore, divided, disputed leadership also appears to be an important source of rejection.

In a study of forty-one cases in which workers rejected settlements, the leading associated factors were a lack of consensus among the negotiating committee and the absence of a recommendation by the committee. Observers have noted for many years that union leaders have expediently used membership rejection of a proposed agreement to stiffen the demands of the negotiating committee and to increase pressure on management.[21] If this is used frequently, of course, company negotiators allow for initial rejection and wait until later negotiations to make their final offers. The tactic then contributes to delay and probably makes resolution of issues more difficult. Even a unanimous recommendation does not assure membership approval, however; in more than a quarter of the cases the rank and file rejected settlement despite unified committee support.[22]

National and Local Negotiations

Forming a representative and experienced, able committee that can work together effectively is a continuing problem for both management and unions.

---

[20]See, for example, William E. Simkin, "Refusals to Ratify Contracts," *Industrial and Labor Relations Review,* vol. 21, July 1968, pp. 518–540.

[21]See Neil W. Chamberlain, *Collective Bargaining Procedures,* Washington, D.C.: American Council on Public Affairs, 1944, pp. 40–41.

[22]Donald R. Burke and Lester Rubin, "Is Contract Rejection a Major Collective Bargaining Problem?" *Industrial and Labor Relations Review,* vol. 26, Jan. 1973, p. 827.

Many unions now divide local and national issues, allowing local negotiating teams to bargain at their places of work concurrently with the national efforts. The local negotiations deal with such subjects as wage differentials between job classifications, seniority arrangements, work sharing, administration of layoffs, scheduling of hours and vacations, and time-study procedures. This practice has the merit of allowing those union leaders and managers who are best informed about particular issues to resolve them. It also helps assure locals that their problems will not be ignored or swept aside in the rush and trouble of settling the large, overall issue.

The meshing of local and national negotiations does not always proceed smoothly. National negotiators have to be careful to keep the local bargainers informed and to prepare them for likely outcomes. The Steel Workers' officials learned this lesson during the industry bargaining of 1982–83. The twenty-nine member executive board had monitored the top-level negotiations through November 1982, and its members were well aware that depressed sales and high unemployment made significant concessions inevitable. Production was down to 40 percent of capacity and almost a third of steelworkers, roughly 135,000, had been laid off. The board unanimously approved a concession package on Thursday, November 18; it was presented to the Basic Steel Industry Conference the next day. The conference, whose 375 members were local union officials, had been negotiating over local issues, and as the final union ratifying body it rejected the package by a 2 to 1 vote. Many members had learned of the scope of its concessions only on Friday morning, the day they voted, and had been shocked at their size. A staff official commented, "Everyone was so busy negotiating that no one was out there talking to the locals, finding out how much they'd give up and communicating how bad things were."[23] Not until after another three months of negotiations did the parties finally win approval of another negotiated concession package. This time its size and rationale were well explained to the conference members.

Local negotiations, even if well meshed with those at the national level, have proved to have some serious drawbacks. A settlement at the national level, for example, does not necessarily mean that strikes will be avoided at the local plant level. In both the automobile and steel industries, companies have been plagued with local strikes for weeks after the general master agreement has been ratified. The UAW, for example, conducted 155 local negotiations in 1971 while its national leaders were striving for a settlement with the top managers of GM. Each local was free to strike if it did not secure a local settlement.

Multiunion and Multiemployer Problems

Among government workers, negotiations and union negotiating committees have been especially complex for those involving the U.S. Postal Service. Bargaining has been conducted at three levels: first, nationwide for all mail-pro-

---

[23]Carl Hymowitz and J. Ernest Beazley, "Steel's Recovery Is Seen Set Back By Union's Vote," *The Wall Street Journal*, Nov. 23, 1982.

cessing employees; second, nationwide for each group of craft employees; and third, locally for employees in each installation. The craft settlements are appended to the national agreement and those of the local negotiators supplement the national terms. The four largest unions[24] at first joined together in negotiating with the Postal Service, but they did not find joint action easy. Unable to reach a consensus on a spokesperson from among the leaders of the four unions, they hired an outside negotiator to represent them on issues that cut across craft lines. In 1978 even this unusual arrangement fell apart when the Rural Letter Carriers withdrew to negotiate separately. The other three unions continued their complicated coordination.[25]

Employers also sometimes have difficulty in putting together a stable and unified bargaining committee. After the tumultuous negotiations and 111-day strike in the bituminous coal industry of 1977–78, managers of the largest coal-mining firms insisted changes had to be made in the membership and procedures of the producers' bargaining committees. For many years, small as well as large producers had selected representatives to sit on the negotiating team, and BCOA staff members also participated. Particularly during the difficult negotiations of 1977–78, the larger firms objected to the quibbling and dithering of the smaller firms during the difficult bargaining with weak and indecisive union leaders. Producers' unity had splintered so often that they had had to appoint four different chief negotiators.

In disgust, the nation's largest coal-mining employer, Consolidated Coal Company, a wholly owned subsidiary of Conoco, withdrew from BCOA. Conoco's chairman vowed not to return until the largest companies were offered greater control of negotiations. United States Steel's managers demanded similar changes if their company was to continue as a member. After several months of meetings and tough bargaining among the employing companies, the 130 members of BCOA, through their 40-member board, approved a new negotiating committee for 1981. It was to consist of three members from the largest companies, halving its size, and to report to a nine-member committee of chief executive officers of the other major coal producers. The managers of the large producers believed that the new procedures would reduce industry factionalism by imposing tighter control and discipline at the bargaining table.

Some small producers complained that the new committee represented oil and steel companies whose managers did not know the philosophy or understand the language of the men in the mines.[26] Many of the new negotiators had not gained their labor relations experience in coal. But when the vote came to

---

[24]American Postal Workers Union, 251,000 members; National Association of Letter Carriers, 230,000 members; National Rural Letter Carriers Association, 63,000 active members; and National Post Office Mail Handlers Division of the Laborers' International Union, at least 28,000 members.

[25]J. Joseph Lowenberg, "The U.S. Postal Service," in Somers, *Collective Bargaining: Contemporary American Experience,* pp. 456–457.

[26]Thomas Petzinger, Jr. and Carol Hymowitz, "Anxiety is Growing in the Coal Industry over Conoco Unit's Tough Labor Stance," *The Wall Street Journal,* March 27, 1980.

reorganize the bargaining committee, the small producers could muster less than a quarter of the BCOA votes, which were based on each producer's output. This was because oil, steel, and utility companies had doubled their control of coal production between 1965 and 1980, raising it to nearly half. Since the reorganized committee still involved the industry in a long strike, the second-longest in history, managers of both small and larger producers wondered if multiemployer bargaining was possible any longer. A more democratic union, a younger, better-schooled work force, and a greatly changed pattern of company ownership may have made old procedures unworkable.

In some associations, the negotiated agreement becomes binding upon members only if they individually sign it. Under such an arrangement, the membership may elect to accept or reject the terms reached in conference; the association representing it has no power to compel its acceptance of the agreement reached with the union, and any compulsion to force the member's adherence to its terms must be brought by the union itself. In contrast, a number of associations delegate full binding authority to their bargaining representatives so that members are automatically committed to any conference agreement, as does the BCOA. In between these extremes, there are various degrees of authority: limitation of discretion on certain vital issues; limitation of discretion within a broad framework; or requirement of ratification by a majority vote of the membership or the board of directors or—in rare instances—by a unanimous membership vote.

Division of managerial authority or failure to clarify the limits of authority of management's negotiators has sometimes been as annoying to union representatives as the latter's lack of binding authority has at times been to management. Not only is any agreement delayed, but the union may find itself in the position of shadowboxing, not knowing whether its views are reaching those who have the power to say "yes," and even reduced to the necessity of calling a strike to secure consideration.

CONFERENCE ORGANIZATION

In a conference between representatives of a local union and plant managers, the drafting of terms for an agreement may not be particularly complicated. The parties can conduct negotiations, especially in small companies, without formal organization. Almost all other bargaining sessions have to be organized more systematically, usually with recognized spokespersons on each side who order discussion and direct the main affairs of the negotiations. Without procedural order discussion can break down into a series of undirected and irrelevant arguments. Not infrequently the chief management negotiator may tend to act as overall chairperson, to the extent that function is performed at all, or the chair may alternate between the parties from session to session.

On occasion, usually in negotiations between smaller companies and local unions, the parties, relatively inexperienced in industrial relations, may call upon an impartial chairperson, most likely a professional conciliator supplied by the Federal Mediation and Conciliation Service or a state mediation agency. Unfortunately, they tend to do this only after reaching an impasse, thus placing the mediator at a disadvantage. The latter must not only perform the customary duties of the chair in preserving order and encouraging agreement through procedural devices, but must also attempt to provide a solution to the impasse.

Mediators almost unanimously agree that the earlier they participate in negotiations, the more likely they are to succeed in helping the parties reach agreement. They become more familiar with the issues and thus better prepared to suggest compromises or more acceptable formulations. Also, an outside neutral, capable of exercising to the greatest advantage the authority of the chair, may steer negotiations toward an agreement by using procedures that avert argument and give priority to issues on which agreement can be reached, creating an atmosphere of mutual accommodation. Procedures may include the appointment of a subcommittee to investigate a knotty question and report back to the full conference, the supplying to negotiators of information on others' experiences with which they may not be familiar, or the calling in of expert opinion to settle factual disputes.

In addition to a head negotiator on each side and a conference chairperson, the parties sometimes appoint a conference secretary, or at least each side will have a member take notes or make a record. But in smaller, informal meetings no record may be kept at all. In major conferences a court recorder may make a verbatim transcript of proceedings. Parties sometimes find this useful in later disputes over the meaning of terms and provisions in the final agreement, referring to the transcript just as federal courts turn to the *Congressional Record* to interpret the intent behind legislation. Verbatim records have drawbacks, however. If one party insists upon them, the other may interpret this as a sign of distrust and even antagonism. Such fears do not ease negotiations. Some negotiators object that recording every statement inhibits frankness; furthermore, they argue that if interpretation of the agreement is needed, the record of negotiating discussions is more likely to cloud and confuse rather than to clarify matters. Arguments and debates at the bargaining table are seldom models of careful analysis and closely reasoned examination.

Subcommittees and Side Agreements

The use of joint conference subcommittees for a variety of purposes is one organizational device that has proved particularly helpful. Some experienced negotiators assert that its importance and usefulness is hard to overemphasize. Where the parties negotiate changes in complex employee benefit plans, for example, they need to give special and expert attention to the consequences. In particular, subcommittees examine the technical issues in pensions, insurance, health and medical plans, and supplemental unemployment benefits. Subcommittees may also study the special needs and demands of skilled workers or the extraordinary safety problems of workers assigned to certain dangerous jobs. Other kinds of issues arise from time to time that require the specialized attention a subcommittee can provide: the employment of women in positions heretofore closed to them, the problem of drug abuse among employees in a high-speed steel-rolling mill, the assignment of work in a parts depot, or the seniority issues arising from the merger or two plants and the integration of their work forces. The subcommittees do not always agree on the issues, but they can, through their findings and reports, clarify and narrow down the problems, enabling the main body of negotiators to resolve them more easily than otherwise. Occasionally, though not often, if a subcommittee finds its assignments more complex than expected, the parties may defer final action on the issue to a date subsequent to the general agreement.

The parties also deal less formally with some matters than with those treated by subcommittees. An issue may arise that they agree to handle on the side and even unilaterally, in good faith. In the 1976 negotiations with GM, the UAW complained that union representatives at some plants were not provided a place to meet employees for the purpose of explaining their health benefits and helping them fill out forms and make applications. The company spokesman agreed to remedy the matter and in a letter attached as an appendix to the agreement wrote:

> We understand that there are problems at some locations involving the office area available and the furnishings needed. We are interested as you are in providing facilities which enable the union benefit plan representatives to carry out their responsibilities. We will work with you and our divisions on any problems in this regard brought to our attention.

There were 64 such additions, statements, and clarifications appended to the national agreement—153 pages, more than those of the main body of the agreement. The matters ranged from special "short shift" problems to noise abatement and expeditious grievance handling.

Conference Procedure

In the actual negotiations between bargaining parties, there may be no ordered procedure or only a very informal procedure. This is particularly true of local negotiations. Describing his own experience, one union representative remarked: "There is no order at a conference. If the boss wants to go fishing, the union goes fishing with him. If he wants to talk about baseball, you talk about baseball. If the union is strong, the reverse may be true." This lack of procedural plan is in part due to a belief by some that any semblance of parliamentary order makes the conference stilted, puts every participant on guard, and renders agreement more difficult. Nevertheless, most bargainers have developed certain broad patterns of negotiating to which they adhere.

Bargaining parties sometimes meet informally in preliminary discussions to establish the order and scope of their proceedings. More informally, they may only agree upon certain important issues and their general priority. Especially in negotiations between two experienced parties, such as a major electrical equipment producer and the International Union of Electrical Workers or one of the national airlines and the International Association of the Machinists, they proceed almost as if by ritual. Each makes an opening statement and then the parties adjourn for study of the initial proposals by subcommittees or by general discussion.[27] They often accuse each other of following a script, so usual and routine become some of the presentations and responses.[28] The opening presentations may take several days, however, not merely a brief few hours of summary. General Motors negotiators characterized the UAW's presentation as "the *Perils of Pauline* approach," since it was often stretched over many days. The chief negotiator offered and explained only a few of the changes and proposals each day, however, so that the union could publish and distribute them to all the locals.[29] Keeping the members well informed about how their representatives are pushing the workers' interests is an important and necessary part of negotiations. Whatever the length of the presentations or their content, it is not uncommon for one party or the other—or both—to express dismay and register shock, amazement, and surprise at the proposals offered.

The ritualized presentations can present opportunity for the parties to disconcert each other, if they believe such an action will serve a useful tactical purpose. In 1973 negotiation between the General Electric Company (GE) and a coordinated bargaining committee of unions, the unions temporarily disrupted the company's plans for publicizing its offer to the employees and its proposals for a new agreement. Usually the managers carefully timed the release of GE's offer—pamphlets, broadsides, and handbills at all their plants across the country for all their tens of thousands of employees, and detailed information packets for local newspapers and radio, and television stations—to coincide with the presentation made to the union negotiators across the table. It amounted to a blitz, effectively swamping union responses and answers, which necessarily followed by many hours, if not days. The company's proposals and supporting data usually overshadowed the union's more modest news effort.

In this particular negotiation, when the union members sensed the company was about ready to make its presentation they asked for a caucus meeting, left the room, and promptly disappeared for several days. Unwilling to publicize the company proposals before presenting them officially to the unions, the GE managers had to cancel all releases, sending hold orders to all the plants and

---

[27]Abe Raskin, long the labor reporter for the *New York Times,* has described the regular process of opening negotiations between John L. Lewis, powerful president of the UMW from the 1920s to 1960, and the BCOA. Lewis always began by magniloquently describing the wretched conditions of the miners and ended by asserting that the employers *should, could,* and *would* agree to the terms which he would reveal in his own good time. The Association chair responded in as grand a speech as he could muster, explaining the plight of the coal producers who *should not, could not,* and *would not* agree to whatever demands the miners would try to impose on them. Thereupon, the time having arrived for lunch, the parties would adjourn to eat.

[28]Serrin, *The Company and The Union,* pp. 26, 38.

[29]Ibid.

all their public relations offices. The tactic proved to be only a minor annoyance to GE, but it gave considerable satisfaction to many of the union negotiators who resented what they described as the determined arrogance of the company in dealing with them. They believed that their action revealed to management how they felt better than any arguments and discussions had done.

The Caucus, Where the Work Is Done

The caucus is probably the most necessary of all conference procedures, accounting for more bargaining time than across-the-table negotiating. The AFL-CIO Labor Studies Center drafted a statement on its use and distributes it widely; its title, "The Caucus—An Important Bargaining Tool," suggests the great value unions give to the caucus. As the statement points out, the parties do not spend most of their time in give-and-take across the table from each other:

> Most of the time what really takes place at the bargaining table is the announcement of a position by one side accompanied by some words of justification. The other side responds, sometimes with questions, sometimes with a general comment and questions. Often, particularly during the latter stages of negotiations, one side will leave the room for a caucus. This is particularly true of the union side. During the caucus, the union reviews its positions and proposals. . . . The union prepares its answers to a management proposal. *It is in the caucus that the real give-and-take discussion takes place in bargaining.* That's why caucusing is so important to the bargaining process.[30]

In caucus meetings the various members of the bargaining team can review their interests and examine any proposal or decision as it affects them and their constituencies. The members can discuss among themselves the significance and meaning of a management offer: is it the final one, is it sometimes less than can be secured, or is it an alternative to a union proposal? In a caucus, members can "blow their stacks" and relieve their emotions in a safe way; they can work out intramural disagreements, slow down the pace of negotiations, review progress, or devise new tactics and strategy in light of incoming information and late developments.

In some cases, the major action takes place for long periods in caucus meetings, with informal negotiations conducted by the principals if and as needed. In the 1981 bargaining between the UMW and the BCOA negotiators, a stalemate was reached about two weeks before the expiration of the old agreement. The parties could not agree upon a pension settlement, changes in work rules, the purchase and use of nonunion coal by signatories to the agreement, an absenteeism policy, and the dismantling of the arbitration review board. While

---

[30]"Union Caucus: Important Bargaining Tool," *Collective Bargaining Negotiations and Contracts,* no. 824, Bureau of National Affairs, Dec. 30, 1976, pp. 41,311–41,312.

they were unable to resolve these matters, the overall issue of wage increase and cost-of-living adjustment could not be approached. The negotiators agreed to separate and to meet with the councils to whom each reported, the union's in Washington, D.C. and the BCOA's in Pittsburgh. When the bargaining committees returned after a weekend away, neither side offered a way to break the stalemate and they returned again to their home bases.

Negotiations had apparently broken down, but in fact they continued—by phone, with each side caucusing in cities several hundred miles away. The chief negotiators kept each other informed of developments and proposals by telephone, bargaining by long distance. Within a few days they had worked through enough of the troublesome issues to enable them to meet again to specify the final details of a settlement. It was clear that much of the bargaining involved was within the caucuses of the two parties, particularly within the union caucus; the bargaining was not limited to that between the union's and the employers' committees. Since the union members rejected the settlement, as noted earlier, the example may caution an observer, however, that long-distance communication by phone may not be the best supplement to the necessary and useful caucus.

In the coal-mining negotiations the parties could agree on so few issues that their efforts to proceed to other, unexplored ones were stymied. If after initial discussion the parties cannot reach agreement on a particular issue, they usually table it. Later, in light of the tentative agreements reached on other issues and in light of later concessions and compromises, the tabled issue may be examined again and more easily resolved.

As agreement is reached clause by clause, some negotiators begin the construction of the new contract; thus the progress of the conference is clearly indicated. Until the conclusion of the entire contract and its approval in its entirety by both parties, however, an agreement to each issue is only tentative, for the clauses of a contract may be interrelated. The settlement of one may affect the determination of another, and a concession on one clause won early in the conference may be traded for a concession on another, more important issue sometime later.

USE OF ECONOMIC DATA

The negotiating proposals and their formulation, presentation, and defense usually involve the use of a wide array of factual information, including economic data of various kinds, from price indexes and company earnings to wage rates, pension costs, and injury rates. The abandonment of unilateral imposition of terms and the resort to bilateral negotiations introduced elements of horse trading and uncertainty into the bargaining process. Bilateral negotiation does not require gross exaggeration, but prudent bargainers carefully hedge the specifics of their proposals as long as possible and also support them with as solid an economic base as available information allows. We may now inquire to what degree and in what ways company, industry, and national economic data help the parties arrive at their collective agreements.

The Contribution of Economic Data

Some economic data inevitably get introduced into collective bargaining, such as the average wage paid to workers in a classification, plant, or firm; changes in the cost of living (at least as imperfectly measured by the consumer price index); the total additional cost of a new dental plan; the labor costs per unit of production; the cents-per-hour increase in straight-time earnings of a percentage wage raise; the effect of a total package upon prices of the company's products; the comparative wage structure of competing companies; the profit position of the company; or the dollar amount of imports in the company's market. Our question, though, is the extent to which this or other information plays a role in the settlement. Are economic data controlling factors in reaching an agreement, or are they merely rhetorical and irrelevant filigree, ignored when the parties get down to their serious bargaining?

Experienced negotiators offer varying answers to this question, some a strong no and others a decided yes; the consensus falls somewhere between. There are those who from their experience contend, as one industrial relations manager did, that economic fact "doesn't amount to a damn in helping to reach an agreement. The real basis for agreement is the fear that there will be trouble otherwise." Similarly, an international representative of one union declared, "High wages and better working conditions are not won by argument, but by the only weapon workers have—the right to strike. All the data and arguments presented don't convince the employer. The union is willing to show why it makes certain demands, but the basic question is not how strong a case the union presents in argument, but, will my plant operate or will it not?"

Other negotiators, although unwilling to deny that factual data have some significance in collective bargaining, stress their limitations. A coal-mining employer who long had observed the BCOA conferences believed that they serve a valuable purpose in keeping union wage demands within competitive limits—"in preventing the union from making such excessive demands that substitute fuels will be given a boost." But in helping the union to determine just *what* wage increase shall be sought or *what* increase employers should offer, he considered factual data of no value. The executive vice president of an eastern manufacturing corporation, in somewhat the same vein, said, "The statistical facts of the case may not warrant the terms of the final agreement, for there are many points that influence the final results. Nevertheless, without factual information, the results may easily be less satisfactory to all."

Despite doubts about the relevance of economic data to many of the specifics in agreements, the parties undoubtedly have increased their use of them in recent years. As the reliability, detail, and volume of available statistics increase, they become more useful. Furthermore, the sensible, informed administrator knows that analyses of improvements in pension, health, welfare, and unemployment programs as well as productivity factors and COLA require arrays of statistics and much factual information. As important is the fact that such programs generate statistics that can be, and are, used elsewhere and at other times in bargaining.

The Limits of Economic Data

Insofar as economic data provide the basis for an objective understanding of workers' and a firm's situations, they deserve an important place in negotiations. The adequate collection of pertinent information might well encourage greater reliance on it in bargaining. If some negotiators find economic data helpful in reaching agreement, why have not all those involved in bargaining used them as readily? Why are economic data not relied upon even more than they are at present? The answers appear to be in the nature of data and in the manner in which the parties are tempted to employ them in collective bargaining.

First of all, economic data measure variables along certain dimensions, but not all; they thus may be incomplete for the purpose at hand. Furthermore, they may reveal themselves as inherently ambiguous; various dimensions may be shown to change at rates quite different from each other. For example, skilled workers receiving a higher hourly wage than average production-line employees may wish to maintain their differential. Which differential is to be kept—the relative one, which implies at least the same percent increase for both, or the absolute differential, implying the same cents-per-hour raise for each? In choosing one kind of increase, the negotiator also has to choose to preserve one differential and let the other change. There is simply no other solution indicated by the data. Data can reveal the nature of the choice to be made, and they very likely will also provide the basis for a complaint once it is made. The problem of relative and absolute measurements and comparisons is ever present in the use of economic data and is typical of many other problems that data create in and of themselves.

When the parties negotiate wage changes, which data are most appropriate? Workers may be interested most in real take-home pay—what is recorded on the paycheck after all withholding taxes, social security taxes, and other deductions are taken out and corrections are made for the effects of inflation. They may calculate their earnings on a daily basis, though, using base hourly rates, adjusted for shift differential and overtime. Managers may be most concerned over the long run with labor cost per unit of output, which is an important element in price determination and thus profits. They may focus in the short run on total compensation, including wage payments and fringe costs (such expenses as pensions, unemployment pay, medical benefits, subsidized lunches, company-provided clothes, and washup on travel time). Out of these various earnings or costs the parties can almost always pick those that will prove their case; in fact, several good cases may offer themselves to be made in all honesty. Workers' real take-home pay may have declined even as a company's overall unit labor costs have increased. Both may legitimately propose a change in wages and support their proposals with objective data. Only with forebearance, understanding, and some goodwill can data be useful in illuminating the issues and helping to resolve problems.

Knowing full well the ambiguities in, and problems with, economic data, it is not surprising that parties seldom view them as the sole basis for an argument. After deciding on its bargaining position, each side will make selective use from the available data to justify its proposals to its own supporters and constituencies and the public. Seldom do they consider a procedure whereby each may contribute relevant information that can be integrated into a meaningful description of the situation both face and on which a joint decision can be made. Facts are regarded as "bargaining cards" to be played or withheld as tactical considerations warrant. One company negotiator stated:

> As nearly as I can tell, both sides are making much more use of objective materials, statistics, and survey information. At the same time, however, it is my impression that such materials appear less and less at the table. Each side is better prepared and the other side knows he is. Each holds its own data to itself. They are reluctant to use data jointly, or any other objective materials, for they may not support the positions that they have already taken.

Even were the parties to avoid using economic data argumentatively, the data alone would not indicate the basis for agreement. Often legitimate arguments can arise, as already noted, about which facts are relevant. And even with complete agreement on the facts, disagreement may emerge over their interpretation. However, if parties were more intent on using data to understand more thoroughly the effects of their proposals and to explore more fully the consequences of their decisions, the range and intensity of disagreement could be narrowed.

Economic Data as Argument, Not Analysis

Some of the obvious—and important—consequences of the policy of using facts as arguments (as in a debate) rather than as a basis for agreement (as in a government commission) have been the following: (1) discouragement of the development of adequate research facilities by both employers and unions, since factual argument—however unreliable—may be secured simply by resort to the many partisan sources available to both groups; (2) development of an attitude of disrespect toward all economic data, since they are regarded only as arguments to be supported if they turn in favor of the bargainers or rebutted or ignored if they weigh against them; and (3) placement of the bargaining relationship primarily upon the basis of crude economic strengths in antagonism, thus postponing a more mature union-management relationship.

The economic data developed by union and management research organizations and presented at the conference table have usually been intended less as a basis of agreement than as a point of attack. This "factual argumentation" in collective bargaining has resulted not only in the destruction of much of the value of such data as are obtainable but also in the denial to the other party, where this is possible, of pertinent data that may support its case. Unions have often maintained that they have a moral right to secure from a company information, generally of an accounting nature, concerning its financial position, although this has frequently been denied by management.[31] The denial of this information may be viewed as a negative form of factual argumentation; managers may find the data all too helpful to the union's claims. Another reason why managers may decline to submit company data to union representatives is their fear that union negotiators will distort the data to provide material for factual argument rather than use them in a genuine effort to arrive at demands which are economically justified.

The long-run economic effects of the argumentative use of economic data may be disadvantageous to both parties involved and to the bargaining process itself. It injects into negotiations disputes over facts in addition to the disputes over interests with which collective bargaining is primarily concerned. Negotiations can thus become weighted down with lengthy and meaningless arguments over the validity or invalidity of several conflicting sets of figures purporting to explain the same situation. On occasion, such debate has actually descended to the level of a juvenile street argument. Moreover, it is fully as pointless, since each party is interested not in eliciting the facts of the situation but only in destroying the other's position to support its own.

Although in a few rare instances economic studies made by one of the bargaining parties independently of the other have been accepted by both as a valid basis of negotiations, the net result of treating fact as argument has been to discredit independent studies. Each party lacks confidence in the data supplied by the other. Even when union representatives complain that companies deny them access to the books, they will sometimes add that the figures they do obtain are usually untrustworthy. It is not surprising, then, that there are those who maintain that in arriving at agreement, factual considerations are of little significance.

The disadvantages of such misuse of economic data have not gone entirely unnoticed by those immediately involved. Because the need for facts as a basis for negotiation and agreement is great and because it cannot be satisfied by independent collection of information of unquestioned validity, attempts occasionally have been made to secure an agreement on the pertinent facts of a situation. By a process of factual accord, both bargaining parties reduce the area of conflict, expediting and facilitating agreement on issues of interest. Such determinations of fact may take the form of attempts to reconcile conflicting sets of data prepared by the bargaining parties independently; agree-

---

[31]A spokesman of the Ford Motor Company replied as follows when asked about the use of cost data in labor negotiations: "While Ford attempts to place costs on union demands wherever possible, these costs do not form the sole basis for Company positions inasmuch as it is felt that the answers to be bargained over are the wages and benefits to be provided to employees represented by the union in light of sound business judgments and economic and public policy. Discussions purely on the basis of costs can result in management abdicating its responsibilities to its employees by allowing the union to dictate benefits, provided the costs are not too high. Managements' responsibility goes far beyond determining how much it will pay for its work force.

Since internal studies often appear self-serving, reference is often made to studies conducted by governmental agencies and other natural sources. It is questionable except as they support the general philosophy of the parties, how much of a role such studies play in resolution of the issues involved."

ment on a source of data to be accepted by both groups as authoritative; establishment of joint fact-finding commissions, either permanent or ad hoc in nature; or joint employment of impartial third-party investigators.

Opening the Books to the Union

The sharp recession of the early 1980s and the resulting economic pressure upon many business corporations convinced managers in a number of firms that more freely than ever in the past they should open their books to union officials and share factual information with their employees. Uniroyal agreed to give the United Rubber Workers the right to audit the company's books and the union president was granted the right to appear before the Uniroyal board twice a year. In 1981 United Airlines agreed that two members of the Air Line Pilots Association could verify the company's problem, using confidential financial data. International Harvester agreed to a similar union inspection. At the *New York Daily News,* the Allied Printing Trades Council won the right to have independent accountants and a management consulting firm analyze the company's finances and submit to it a report of them.[32]

There is no doubt that a number of negotiators, both union and employer, are exploring the possibilities of an increased factual approach to collective bargaining. Although encouraging such an approach, however, some employers have not recognized that their attitude involves a moral obligation to supply the unions with such company records as will permit the drafting of factually based proposals, provided, of course, that the union has established its own good faith. Little can be done by either party without a sympathetic response from the other.

A factual basis for collective bargaining probably offers some hope for a more smoothly functioning employer-union relationship, but it does not eliminate differences between union and management over interpretation of the facts or conflicts over which are germane to the issues at hand. As has been noted, divergent views of jointly determined fact will provide conflict, and disagreement will arise over the relative weights to be accorded various economic considerations. Moreover, it is apparent that data are useful only insofar as the parties devise and accept procedures for making use of them. As yet such devices as the joint conference for exploring and agreeing upon the relevant data are not common. Perhaps the basic impediment to the use of economic facts in reaching agreement lies in the conception held by the parties of the nature of the bargaining process itself, a topic explored in Chapter 2.

RESOLUTION OF DEADLOCKS

Despite the most earnest efforts to reach agreement, there may come a time in any bargaining conference when each party feels that it has compromised as

---

[32]Richard A. Beaumont, "The Risks of Opening Corporate Books to Unions," *The Wall Street Journal,* Oct. 18, 1982.

much as is feasible, and deadlock may ensue. In an attempt to get negotiations off dead center, the conferees may resort to mediation. In mediation, a neutral third party enters the negotiations, listening to each party and seeking to discover the circumstances under which each may be willing to make further concessions. To the neutral agent the negotiators may be willing to confide an inclination to yield ground provided the other party gives way too. Learning the true resistance point of each, the mediator may be given the key to agreement. In other conferences one or both groups may have maneuvered themselves into positions from which they can retreat only with loss of prestige, and the intervention of the mediator provides an opportunity for each to give ground in response to the suggestion of a disinterested outsider, without seeming to yield to the other.

Some union leaders feel that an appeal to a mediator to intervene is a sign of weakness, indicating a willingness to make further concessions and an inability to rely on one's own strength. A number of employers also believe that government conciliators are biased in favor of organized labor. Despite such attitudes, enough parties accept mediation so that a mediator's intervention is not at all unusual. Some international unions now require their chartered locals to use the Federal Mediation and Conciliation Service before dissolving the bargaining conference, and some collective agreements provide for the calling in of a mediator should a deadlock be reached in negotiations for the subsequent agreement.

If mediation fails or if the issues in dispute are so sharply drawn that the negotiators feel a resort to mediation would be fruitless,[33] the two parties may sometimes agree to arbitrate their differences. This method, however, is still uncommon. A few unions maintain a staff of experts whose chief function is to assist local unions in the preparation and presentation of their cases before arbitration boards, and some industries have established their own arbitration councils.

Many negotiators, probably a majority, still frown on the arbitration of contract terms. Some union representatives claim that arbitration boards consciously or unconsciously are usually biased against labor; some employers believe that the arbiter customarily settles disputes by "splitting the difference," so that the union must always win concessions and the employer must always lose. Companies sometimes oppose arbitration on the grounds that it grants control of company policy to an outside agency, thus improperly delegating management's responsibilities. Both groups have charged that arbitrators are not always well versed in the economic and technical aspects of the company or industry, so their decisions may be ill-advised. Some have claimed that agreement upon an arbiter is as difficult as agreement upon the issue in dispute and that the cost of arbitration proceedings is an impediment to their

---

[33]Mediation performs least well when the parties' economic demands most sharply diverge. See Thomas A. Kochan and Todd Jick, "The Public Sector Mediation Process: A Theory and Empirical Examination," *The Journal of Conflict Resolution,* vol. 22, 1978, p. 214.

use. A frequent criticism by union representatives is that the delay involved sometimes postpones settlement for such a length of time that the morale of the union membership may be broken.

If all possible efforts at agreement through direct negotiation or mediation have failed and if the parties are unwilling to accept settlement by arbitration, the resolution of the deadlock usually comes through strike or lockout. This exercise of bargaining power is examined in Chapter 15.

CONCLUSION

Our brief examination of the development of collective bargaining in the United States reveals that most early agreements were oral. Unions whose membership numbered only a few dozen to a few hundred members, negotiating with small employers or proprietors in the early part of the nineteenth century, could get along with such informal agreements. As employers began to hire hundreds and then thousands and even tens of thousands of workers and with the rise of large unions enrolling members not only in one location but in many plants of a single firm, as well as members in many different firms, the terms and provisions became too complex to be treated informally. They had to be written down.

The growth in the size of unions brought with it a multiplicity of groups and factions *within* the organization that needed to be reconciled if effective collective bargaining were to be maintained. The increase in the size of firms also created many managerial interests that had to be brought together and unified. The coordination of the various interests on both sides of the bargaining table required a negotiating process that was not at all simple. In preparing for bargaining, and in conducting the negotiating sessions, those involved always had to keep in mind the variety of interests and values they represented. The wide range of issues typically incorporated into the final agreement make side agreements and specialized negotiating procedures useful. As the interests and issues changed over time, the negotiating process has changed and will continue to adjust to the emerging needs of the parties.

The widespread employment of collective bargaining after 1937, aside from legal requirements growing out of a Supreme Court decision[34] and the Labor-Management Relations Act of 1947,[35] inevitably led to the greater use of the written agreement. Once the parties had reached an accommodation with each other, given the complex issues that each had resolved, both had a stake in maintaining the stability of relationship reached through the negotiating effort. They also recognized that their understandings often involved matters so comprehensive and technical in nature that their preservation depended upon writ-

---

[34]*H. J. Heinz Co. v. NLRB,* 311 U.S. 514 (1941).
[35]Section 8(d) of the National Labor-Management Relations Act of 1947 requires both employers and union to execute "a written contract incorporating any agreement reached if requested by either party. . . ."

ten descriptions. Similarly, if the terms and provisions were to be applied efficiently and understood throughout both organizations, the parties needed reasonably precise statements of the terms to be applied over the duration of the agreement.

We now turn our attention to the nature of those terms and the extent of those provisions. We have examined the practice of negotiating the collective agreement, and now we consider the issues about which union leaders and managers negotiate—the subject matter of collective bargaining.

THE SUBJECT MATTER OF COLLECTIVE BARGAINING

Legislatures, government labor agencies, and the courts over the years have sought to define the appropriate subjects for collective bargaining. At first they were concerned especially with bargaining in the private sector, but in the last decade they have also dealt with government negotiations. Their decisions have almost always been based on pragmatic responses to partisan and public pressures and needs; seldom have they grounded their actions in a particular notion of what collective bargaining should be.

GOVERNMENT INFLUENCE ON THE CONTENT OF THE AGREEMENT

When Congress passed the National Labor Relations Act of 1935 (also known as the Wagner Act), no one saw much need to regulate the content of labor agreements or to determine what the parties should or should not have to bargain about. The then chairman of the Senate Committee on Education and Labor expressed a nearly universal viewpoint: "All the bill proposes to do is to escort them [the union negotiators] to the door of their employer and say, 'Here they are, the legal representatives of your employees.' What happens behind those doors is not inquired into, and the bill does not seek to inquire into it."[1]

By 1947, when Congress enacted the Taft-Hartley proposals, many lawmakers and citizens had come to believe the government should do more. Not only was it time to inquire into bargaining matters beyond the door, but it was nec-

---

[1]Senator David I. Walsh, *Congressional Record,* 74th Cong., 1st Sess., May 16, 1935, p. 7660.

essary to impose some regulations and limits on those matters. Union membership had increased greatly in the meantime and union influence had grown even more. Union leaders had used collective bargaining to win significant benefits for workers, and they had also learned how to use it to protect and build the strength of the union organization. Many people feared powerful unions might use their strong bargaining position in ways that would impair the effectiveness of management and the efficiency of the economy.

A popular focus of attention was union security provisions—attempts by unionists to protect their organizations by requiring employers to hire only union members (closed shop) or at least making membership necessary once hired (union shop). These provisions, along with hiring halls and the involuntary checkoff, had long been a part of American collective bargaining. The relatively small number of workers affected, however, had left most people unaware of them. The rapid spread of unions in the late thirties and the forties acquainted a wide public for the first time with these time-tested provisions, convincing a sizable portion that they were threats not just to business institutions but also to American ideals. Only a minority of the electorate became alarmed, but many expressed doubts that collective bargaining could be left merely to the interested parties; they favored some restrictions upon the content of agreements.

The Labor-Management Relations Act of 1947, approved by Congress over the president's veto, attempted to limit the spread of the union shop and prohibited outright the closed shop. The act made "featherbedding" illegal, but in 1953 the Supreme Court greatly diluted the force of this prohibition by declaring that although a union could not lawfully bargain for pay for work not performed, it was not unlawful to bargain for pay for unnecessary work.[2] The act also limited the purpose for which joint welfare funds could be used and the method of their administration. The act also required ample notification be given any termination of an agreement. Later, in the Labor-Management Reporting and Disclosure Act of 1959 (also known as the Landrum-Griffin Act), Congress made "hot-cargo" agreements illegal. (If the managers of another firm agree not to handle the goods of a struck firm, that is, treats them as hot cargo, it thereby applies indirect pressure on the struck firm, reinforcing the union's direct pressure.) These specific prohibitions and regulations of the subject matter of collective bargaining indicate the sensitivity of public policy to particular issues and the willingness of the legislature to declare certain subjects out-of-bounds.

While labor scholars debate the merits of legislative restrictions on the subject matter of collective bargaining, the issue that arouses practitioners most is the freedom of unions to bargain over what are considered managerial activities. Managers often discuss the appropriateness of subject matter in terms of invasion of management prerogatives or encroachment on the right to manage. The courts and the government agencies usually eschew such a philosophical

---

[2]*American Newspaper Publisher's Association v. NLRB,* 345 U.S. 100 (1953).

approach, dealing with each case on its own merits. Following this common-law approach, they have ruled at various times that managers must bargain with union representatives over such topics as Christmas bonuses, stock-sharing plans, and the relocation of a plant. The National Labor Relations Board has also ruled that bargaining may look to matters of safety rules, work clothing, retirement and pension plans, profit sharing, merit rating systems, and the subcontracting of specialized operations previously performed by the company's own employees. Despite its many rulings, however, the NLRB has not set forth any principle or standards to guide either union or management negotiations. Its reluctance to do so is not surprising, for not even the parties involved in negotiations have been able to agree on any line dividing appropriate and inappropriate subject matters, although they have tried.

Management Attitudes

At one time business managers argued that the determination even of wage rates should be left to market forces, personified in the individual employer. For example, in 1853 the editors of the *New York Journal of Commerce* asserted:

> Suppose the Printers' Union should succeed by a forced violation of the law of demand and supply in driving the price of composition up to a figure beyond what the profits of the business would bear, what would be the consequences? One consequence would be that it would crush weak establishments and throw the hands employed in them out of business. Establishments which do but just live at the old prices would die at the new. The men thus discharged would seek employment where they could find it; and might perchance be glad to take "$2 a day and roast beef," if they could not get $2.87½ as demanded by the union. If, however, a reaction were not produced in this way it would be in another. For, if such enormous prices could be realized by typesetting, thousands would think it just the business for their boys to learn and in a few years the market would be glutted with an over-supply of hands. Men who violate the laws of nature, even in a matter of trade, are sure to be punished for it sooner or later by the operation of these laws, if no other way.[3]

Nearly a century later the president of General Motors expressed himself in very much the same way. At a time when the United Automobile Workers were seeking to bargain over a pension plan which the company had earlier unilaterally instituted, he remarked:

> If we consider the ultimate result of this tendency to stretch collective bargaining to comprehend any subject that a union leader may desire to bargain over, we come out with the union leaders really running the economy of the country; but with no legal or public responsibility and with no private employment except as they may permit. . . .
>   Only by defining and restricting collective bargaining to its proper sphere can we hope to save what we have come to know as our American system. . . . Until this is

[3]Stevens, *New York Typographical Union No. 6*, p. 251.

done the border area of collective bargaining will be a constant battleground into the area of managerial functions.[4]

As the courts and NLRB had recognized, the issue had to be treated pragmatically case by case, for there could be no ideological agreement on general standards. Unionists and their supporters would not commit themselves to definite limits on the subject matter of collective bargaining.

In asking union leaders to restrict the subject matter of negotiations, the president of GM was sentimentally harkening back to an earlier and simpler day when the manager's word had been the law of the shop. His longing was understandable, but his sense of realism was distorted. Unions had long interested themselves in and bargained over virtually all the subjects that managers such as GM's president would have liked to exclude. As early as 1869, the miners' union had concerned itself with the price of coal, for price fluctuations affected their earnings. In more recent times, the United Mine Workers had experimented with various devices, including support of federal legislation, to secure some measure of control over the industry's price policy and thereby protect the wage rate. Other examples abound. Unions in the printing trades had organized foremen since at least 1889; clothing workers had for years assisted in setting production standards; and building-trades unions had long acted as their industry's employment agency. During the great depression of the thirties, the hosiery workers had even helped determine the investment policies of firms with which they negotiated.

Management Rights

Unable to secure labor's general agreement to a definition of—and limits on—the appropriate subject matter of collective bargaining, managers sought piecemeal agreement. They began increasingly to insist upon a management rights clause in their negotiated agreements; increasingly, they won them! (See Table 8.) Whether measured by the share of agreements or of workers affected, there was a decided increase in the management's rights clauses in the decade and a half from 1963 to 1978, across almost all industries. In 1963–64 less than half the agreements contained management's rights provisions, but by 1980 more than three-fifths did. Although union leaders were unwilling a generation earlier to agree to general limits on the subjects of collective bargaining, most have agreed piecemeal, on a company-by-company basis, to a declaration of management's rights.

Many such clauses are very brief and remain unchanged and unchallenged from negotiation to negotiation. A typical clause is as follows:

The corporation has the exclusive right to manage its plants and offices and direct its affairs and working forces subject only to such regulations and restrictions governing the exercise of these rights as are expressly provided in this agreement.

[4]*The New York Times,* March 24, 1948.

TABLE 8
MANAGEMENT'S RIGHTS CLAUSES IN AGREEMENTS COVERING 1000 WORKERS OR MORE, 1963–64 AND 1980

Industry	Percentage of agreements (with clauses)		Percentage of workers covered under clauses	
	1963–64	1980	1963–64	1980
All	48	62	47	60
Manufacturing	63	76	68	79
Primary metals	89	90	96	95
Transportation equipment	87	88	85	95
Electrical machinery	75	88	86	93
Textiles	50	55	39	59
Stone, clay, glass	80	91	82	89
Fabricated metals	79	85	76	87
Machinery	77	86	71	77
Rubber, plastic	83	79	73	84
Furniture, fixtures	60	71	64	68
Tobacco	27	62	22	66
Paper	48	76	36	76
Leather	54	64	48	71
Petroleum refining	56	60	64	51
Chemicals	66	69	70	63
Lumber, wood	25	36	23	50
Food, kindred	32	49	32	37
Printing, publishing	14	40	7	25
Apparel	15	26	5	11
Nonmanufacturing	29	48	21	45
Mining, crude petroleum	70	88	11	96
Utilities	84	90	79	95
Retail trade	32	62	30	56
Transportation (excluding railroads and airlines)	16	39	17	44
Services	35	58	45	55
Hotels, restaurants	26	52	20	53
Wholesale trade	20	58	14	54
Construction	10	32	9	29
Communications	20	40	17	28

Source: *Major Collective Bargaining Agreements: Management Rights and Union-Management Cooperation,* Bureau of Labor Statistics Bulletin 1425–5, April 1966, table 1, p. 4; and *Characteristics of Major Collective Bargaining Agreements, Jan. 1, 1980,* Bureau of Labor Statistics Bulletin 2095, May 1981, table 2-4, p. 28.

Others are longer and more detailed, specifying a number of matters about which the union will not attempt to bargain. These may include the type of product, its design and research; selling, marketing, and advertising, including pricing policy; financial decisions about the use of capital; and the structure of managerial organization.

Though labor and management could not settle their ideological differences over limits to collective bargaining, they resolved the practical problems without great difficulty. They increasingly accepted management's rights provisions and at the same time extended the areas covered by their agreements. But the more detailed coverage, particularly in the area of fringe benefits, did not appear to push unions farther and farther into the area of managerial functions. They proceeded in paradoxical ways: unions refused to limit the subject matter of collective bargaining but increasingly agreed to define management's rights; managers sought explicit statements of their rights but regularly agreed to an ever expanding scope of collective bargaining. Thus, the paradox is more shadow than substance; each formally insisted upon its ideology but in practice pursued settlements pragmatically.

Managerial Prerogatives

American managerial ideology of employer rights draws its form and terminology from an age when the law of master and servant provided it substance. The relationship implies antidemocratic values and is congenial to so medieval a term as "prerogatives." Unfortunately, many managers have stoutly defended managerial prerogatives, apparently insensitive to the objections most Americans would raise to any such claim, particularly as an ideology. Using an obsolete terminology, managers may have misled themselves as well as unionists in the debate over managerial rights. They seemed to be defending a special position rather than a unique role in any organization. That role is to coordinate the many bargains that an enterprise must make with all kinds of groups and interests—such as suppliers, customers, workers, regulators, investors, and lenders—so that the firm enjoys an inflow of revenues greater than the outflow of expenditures.[5] The groups and interests with whom managers bargain may make the coordination difficult or easy, depending upon the pressure applied, but unless those pressuring management assume the coordinating role themselves, managers will continue to manage. Their role is defined not ideologically but rather functionally: the carrying out of a necessary and inescapable procedural activity.

Practical Limits to Management Rights

The changes in union agreements made jointly and voluntarily by the parties over recent years suggest that neither the formal declarations of management's rights nor the actual extensions of collective bargaining much affect the managers' pragmatic functional role. We find an increase in the number and coverage of rights clauses *and* also in practical restrictions on management's rights. For example, consider limits on subcontracting, an activity once considered by managers as necessarily and exclusively their province. One com-

[5]See Neil W. Chamberlain, *A General Theory of Economic Process,* New York: Harper & Brothers, 1955, chaps. 12, 18.

pany, with wide support from business generally, took its refusal to bargain over subcontracting to the Supreme Court. In a landmark decision the Court ruled in 1964 that subcontracting was a mandatory topic of negotiations.[6] By 1980 nearly 60 percent of major agreements contained limits on subcontracting, the share having increased steadily over time.[7] Managers have been reluctant, however, to agree to advance notice, particularly for technological change and plant closing or relocation. Only about 10 percent of major agreements call for advance notice in the latter case, which was a matter of greatly heightened concern during the early 1980s when hundreds of manufacturing plants closed their gates. Unable to win advance notice through collective bargaining, unions turned to legislation, securing in a few states notice of as long as a month.

Negotiations and the resulting agreement may limit managerial rights in three ways. First, as noted above, the parties may agree to restrictions, regardless of the managements' rights clause. Indeed the clause itself is subject to renegotiation, though once included in an agreement it tends to remain unaltered in form. Second, the intent of a management's rights clause depends on the intent of the entire agreement. Managers may insist that they retain in writing an unfettered right to schedule production, for example, but in scheduling they will still have to bargain with the union over hours of work, starting time, overtime, shift changes, transfer of employees, seniority arrangements, and pace of work. After such bargaining, the claim to a unilateral right to schedule production may be rather empty. Moreover, some authorities see in the recognition clause, which acknowledges the right of the union to represent the employees, a commitment entitled to equal consideration with a management's rights clause; the two may be viewed as complementary. Such acknowledgement sometimes limits authority which managers believe they have protected by "specific wording."

Third, as long as there is a no-strike pledge in the agreement, it is hard to prevent any worker complaint from being processed through the grievance procedure, right up to arbitration. Grievances are of course subject to the terms of the agreement—workers complaining that they have been unfairly treated are unlikely to secure remedial action unless there is something in the agreement to support their cases—but it is through the grievance process (in which arbitration is almost always used in the final stage) that judgment is made as to whether grievances are covered by the agreement. That determination is

---

[6]*Fibreboard Paper Prods. Corp. v. NLRB,* 279 U.S. 203 (1964).

[7]Although the Supreme Court has long held that an employer must bargain over a decision to subcontract work, it has not been willing to require bargaining over a decision to change a part of the business or to terminate a contract with a customer. (See *First National Maintenance Corporation v. NLRB,* 452 U.S. 666 (1981). The National Labor Relations Board and the courts have often disagreed over employers' duty to bargain when reductions or changes in business will result in loss of jobs for employees. Generally the board has asked, "Did the plant closing or partial shutdown adversely affect the employment status of employees?" Since the answer is usually yes, the board requires bargaining. The courts, however, have asked if bargaining would adversely affect employers' ability to manage. Answering yes, they usually rule that employers need not bargain.

partly a matter of interpretation and—as we shall see in examining the grievance process later—also to some extent a continuation of the bargaining power
relationship between the two parties. For these three reasons a management's
rights clause can scarcely be considered to resolve the question of what issues
are bargainable, even at a given point in time and certainly over time.

Why do managers insist on including management's rights provisions, and
why despite their apparent ineffectiveness do they continue to add these
clauses to agreements? Professor Paul Prasow suggests the following answer:

> [I]t is done for educational, for psychological reasons, to remind union officers, shop
> stewards, employees—and arbitrators too—that management never relinquishes its
> administrative initiative, its right to establish the status quo. The management rights
> clause reaffirms that the procedural relationship between the parties remains unal-
> tered; it underscores that its right of administrative initiative is unimpaired by the
> collective bargaining relationship.[8]

Another, more prosaic reason may be that as industrial relations becomes
more professionalized, management negotiators feel they must produce a
"good-looking," tidy document. Managerial sentiment, served by professional
expertise, favors the inclusion of a provision on management's rights, no matter what the practical effect may be. It is a showpiece, but one of honor, rather
like a decorative coat of arms a family may hang in the front hall to proclaim
its pretensions and status.

THE RIGHT TO MANAGE AND THE SCOPE OF THE AGREEMENT

Managers commonly assert that property rights undergrid their claims to make
business decisions free from the constraints of collective bargaining. Acting as
trustees or delegated representatives of property owners (i.e., stockholders),
they have the right and, indeed, the duty to organize and direct machinery,
materials, and money. A union which seeks to force management's agreement
to increase output, modify price policy, adopt different accounting conventions, or make a different line of products is said to be trespassing upon the
legal rights of private property. Such a line of argument, while possessing surface plausibility, overlooks the important fact that the property basis of management carries no duty on the part of others to *be* managed.

The trouble with property ownership as a conferer of authority is that it
gives command only over *things*. This involves no special difficulties in a society of small property holders and individual proprietorships, for control over
things is all that is needed to produce for and sell in the market. But when
business enterprise assumes a corporate form and requires the cooperation of
large numbers of people performing specialized functions, control over things
ceases to be sufficient.

[8]Paul Prasow, "The Theory of Management Reserved Rights—Revisited," *Proceedings* of the
26th Annual Winter Meeting, Industrial Relations Research Association, Dec. 28–29, 1973, p. 78.

Except in the case of authoritarian relationships (for example, in the military services in this country and in totalitarian societies), people can be managed and directed only with their own consent. While property rights carry with them a power of disposition of goods, they do not carry an equal power to use those goods *if* the cooperation of others is necessary to that use. Cooperation, without which the property right is reduced to a power of disposition, cannot be commanded. It can be won only by consent. And there is no legal compulsion upon workers to cooperate. There is no legal statement of the terms on which cooperation must take place. The definition of those terms is left directly to the parties involved, and there is nothing in the law to stop the union from demanding, as the price of its members' cooperation, a voice in some matter previously determined independently by management. Since property rights do not mean that one has command over others, management *may* find it essential to share its authority as a means of inducing cooperation if it is to maintain the value of a going business. Over time, it becomes customary to share authority, in order to win cooperation, in certain recognized areas of business decisions—wages, for example, or hours, or perhaps the speed of assembly lines.

Thus the right to manage and direct others does not flow out of legal rights but must be granted by those very people who are managed and directed; the price of the grant may be that management must yield its independence in certain matters of business operation. Which matters? *Potentially* none would seem to be excluded—whatever matters are deemed important to those whose cooperation is being sought.

The determination of the appropriate subject matter of collective bargaining is clearly not a matter of fixed principle. The inclusion of new matters in collective agreements is simply evidence of changing social relationships. Even when the NLRB and the courts require bargaining over certain issues, management does not have to surrender functions or areas of control to unions. The electrical workers' unions bargaining with General Electric, for example, have never secured company agreement to the union shop. They have pressed for it regularly and included it as part of their demands to be met before settling strikes, but company negotiators have refused to consider it. The case illustrates the harsh reality that managers do not get their way or maintain their claimed rights by wishing. They must bargain forcefully with unions, realistically measuring the benefit of maintaining their stand against the willingness and ability of unions to insist upon their proposals.

Over time the union's views—and management's—concerning what is or is not of direct interest to employees undergo change, not solely because of "enlightenment" or the shift of political influence, but because social and economic conditions, social institutions, and public values change. The work force today is significantly better schooled and more knowledgeable about the world than it was a generation ago; it is more heterogenous, with a large share of women, minorities, the handicapped, and others now participating. Our industrial and production complexes are bigger and more interdependent than ever before, relying increasingly upon the processing of information. Competition from around the world is a new challenge to both managers and workers and thus to unions.

Emerging Legal Limits on Managerial Rights

In such a changing environment, an observer can hardly be surprised if public evaluation of managerial rights also changes. Under the common law prevailing in all states until very recently, managers could exercise the ancient right to fire for any or no reason; that is, they could fire at will. Noting the social and economic changes, judges have confronted this unfettered right and found it increasingly questionable in the modern economy. A New Hampshire court found a company had acted in "bad faith or malice" when it fired a woman who had refused to date her foreman.[9] A federal district court ruled against a company's dismissal of an employee with thirteen years' service who claimed he was fired to avoid payment to him of a pension.[10] The California Supreme Court reversed the two-lower court decisions and ruled that an employee with fifteen years' service, who claimed he was fired because he refused to participate in an alleged price-fixing scheme, could proceed with his suit.[11] These cases indicate that courts are questioning managerial rights as traditionally exercised and suggesting that due process is in order. The questioning is important, for it arises not from union demands—the employees in recent cases have not been union members—but from a changing public sense of right and fairness. It reminds us that the subject matter of collective bargaining may change because the environment changes as well as because unions demand change.

UNION INTERESTS AND THE SCOPE OF AGREEMENT

Collective bargaining has extended its range of subjects over the last fifty years, but most of this extended coverage took place in the buoyant years of union growth through the thirties and forties. Consider just two subjects that have received much public notice: supplemental unemployment benefits (SUB) and severance pay. Over the period from 1962 to 1980, SUB coverage increased very little overall, though the number of manufacturing workers under SUB provisions increased from 43 to 51 percent. (See Table 9.) Provision for severance pay declined slightly in the proportion of workers covered, though it increased in the relative number of agreements; it increased modestly in nonmanufacturing and declined a bit in manufacturing. The two provisions are found most commonly in transportation equipment (autos, trucks, and airplanes) and primary metals (steel, copper, and aluminum), and are only scattered elsewhere. Despite the attractiveness of the provisions and the publicity

---

[9]*Olga Monge v. Beebe Rubber Company,* 316 A. 2d 549 (New Hampshire) (1974).
[10]*Morton Savodnik v. Korvettes, Inc.,* 488 Fed. Supp. 822 (1980).
[11]*Gordon Tamney v. Atlantic Richfield Co.,* 27 Cal. 3d 839 (1980).

TABLE 9
PROVISIONS FOR SUPPLEMENTAL UNEMPLOYMENT BENEFITS AND
SEVERANCE PAY, BY SHARES OF AGREEMENTS AND WORKERS AND BY
INDUSTRY, 1962–63 AND 1980 (IN AGREEMENTS COVERING 1000
WORKERS OR MORE)

| | Supplemental unemployment benefits | | | |
| | Percentage of agreements | | Percentage of workers covered | |
	1962–63	1980	1962–63	1980
All industry	14	14	25	26
Manufacturing	22	25	43	51
Nonmanufacturing	2	4	3	4

| | Severance pay | | | |
| | Percentage of agreements | | Percentage of workers covered | |
	1963	1980	1963	1980
All industry	30	34	41	39
Manufacturing	37	43	56	54
Nonmanufacturing	20	25	22	27

Source: For 1962–1963 data see *Major Collective Bargaining Agreements: Supplemental Unemployment Benefit Plans and Wage-Employment Guarantees,* Bureau of Labor Statistics Bulletin No. 1425-3, June 1965, table 1, p. 78; and *Severance Pay and Layoff Benefit Plans,* Bureau of Labor Statistics Bulletin No. 1425-2, March 1965, table 1, p. 13. For 1980 data see footnote, table 8.

they have received, only a minority of workers covered by agreements enjoy them, and they are spreading very slowly indeed to other industries and workers. These data indicate that a union's introduction of a new and even desirable subject matter to collective bargaining does not ensure its wide adoption.

Do Union Leaders Always Favor Broader Scope?

One need not conclude that managerial resistance is the only reason more unions have not sought and won SUBs or severance pay, thus enlarging their scope of bargaining. Unions are political bodies, operating within the constraints of an economic environment; their leaders thus respond in varying degrees and in continuously changing ways to the demands of the members. While the SUB and severance pay may be issues of vital concern to steelworkers and autoworkers, they may be so costly in effort and in alternative demands foregone that workers in printing, furniture, or textiles do not seek them. The union members in the latter industries have chosen to pursue other goals; or their leaders, at any rate, do not perceive a widespread demand for such benefits.

Union officials prefer to avoid issues that can give rise to intraunion disputes and that force them to take sides against any members. This is an important reason why union leaders prefer promotions, transfers, layoffs, and recalls on the basis of seniority. It is a clear, objective standard that can operate impersonally and almost automatically. Union negotiators might find that attempting to influence the location of a new plant would be politically unwise. Members in one existing local might want the new plant located near them, while another union local might argue for a place closer to it. The same kind of difficulty could arise if union officers helped decide the product mix; some members would be hurt, and some would gain. How could an elected officer choose among members without incurring more disfavor than favor?

Because involvement in managerial functions can create serious political problems for union leaders, the limited use made of the collective bargaining provisions listed in Table 10 is hardly surprising. Less than half of the workers are covered by the roughly one-third of agreements that provide labor-management committees for safety or specify how workers are to share "slack work," yet both involve matters that one might think of considerable concern to almost all workers and unions. Provisions for safeguarding the rights of older workers are quite scarce, as are those establishing industrial relations committees. In these areas, as in the daily responsibilities of job assignment, skill classification, production standards, and maintenance of discipline, union

TABLE 10
SELECTED PROVISIONS PERTINENT TO MANAGEMENT RIGHTS, 1980
(IN AGREEMENTS COVERING 1000 WORKERS OR MORE)

	Percentage of agreements	Percentage of workers
Safety, labor-management committee for	37	43
Slack work, total	28	41
Division of work	6	6
Reduction in hours	18	29
Regulation of overtime	4	6
Applicability of testing*	19	30
Testing	19	30
Crew size, limitations on	22	22
Environmental†	11	21
Hazardous work differential	17	17
Productivity, labor-management committee for	5	17
Worker protection‡	4	7
Retention of older workers	10	7
Industrial relations, committee for	4	4
Hiring of older workers	5	3

*Includes those that provide testing as a part of training and in layoff procedures.
†Designed to safeguard workers and the in-plant environment from health and safety hazards.
‡Protection of employees from hostile environment or criminal hazards at, or traveling to, work.
Source: See footnote, Table 8.

officers show little desire to join in managing and in initiating action; they prefer to retain their freedom to protest management's decisions and to stay out of the cross fire of criticism and avoid the wounding resentments of their own members.

Unions have not pushed massively and inexorably into vital policy areas. They have pushed when they could and when it was in their clear interest to do so, advancing when management was careless or weak and retreating when management aggressively resisted them. When unions do enlarge their powers, it is almost always in those areas where they have long been established: wages, hours, and conditions of employment.

Managers Sometimes Favor Broader Scope

Examples of how union investment in vital issues can expand appeared during the recession of the early 1980s. Some of the largest, unionized manufacturing and transportation companies found themselves under severe economic pressure; the unions with which they negotiated suffered greatly reduced membership as layoffs thinned the ranks of employees. Both parties in a number of cases sought and won concessions from each other, the unions agreeing to freeze or cut wages and give up work rules and management conceding direct union participation in decision making to a degree seldom considered before.

For example, Goodyear agreed to build a tire plant near Akron and to expand its Topeka plant in return for work-rule changes and wage concessions. Uniroyal agreed to set up a joint council to discuss company finance and performance with outside directors; it also allowed union officers to make annual presentations to the board of directors. For these changes the union gave up wage benefits estimated to be worth about $35 million over the term of the agreement. In the steel industry, two small companies—Colt Industries and McLouth—opened their books to the union in return for wage concessions. A number of airlines—Pan Am, Braniff, Continental, Republic, United, and Western—were pressed by the competition developed under deregulation and the recession; these also opened their books to their unions as a quid pro quo for pay cuts, wage freezes, and changes in work rules. Many of the large trucking companies promised not to establish nonunion subsidiaries if the Teamsters accepted a three-year wage freeze and concessions on the cost-of-living adjustments.[12]

The number of firms that have accepted the union as a closer partner in management is still relatively few, but it is nevertheless significant. It includes a number of very large and influential companies. Professor D. Quinn Mills argued that once companies have agreed to open their books to unions, to listen to union leaders on issues beyond traditional collective bargaining topics, and even to give workers stock options, they may have to embrace a new strat-

---

[12]A. H. Raskin, "The Cooperative Economy," *The New York Times,* Feb. 14, 1982.

egy of employee relations and accept a loss of long-claimed prerogatives. He concludes that managers must make union leaders a:

> part of a broadened management team, in a way successfully practiced in Japan and Germany. U.S. managers find this idea distasteful and have not, in the past, worked at it. If they realize what is occurring and try to strengthen joint labor-management efforts to build sound businesses, concession bargaining can make a long-term contribution to the U.S. economy.[13]

Not all observers are as sanguine in their forecasts. Douglas H. Soutar, senior vice president of industrial relations of ASARCO and an experienced negotiator, believed that management was making a serious mistake in embracing what he called "togetherness programs currently in high fashion." He said that the decision-making rights agreed to:

> very likely will remain in the collective bargaining contracts, perhaps forever, setting precedents internally and for other employers, and probably requiring new rounds of efforts, under unknown future conditions, to bargain them back as concessions tended for some new invested quid pro quos. The box score on the impact [of these recent agreements] in the early 80's will not really be in much before the end of this decade, when we may repent at our leisure![14]

Mills believed the range of subject matter collective bargaining can be expanded to the benefit of both parties and to the economy as well; Soutar was skeptical that managers will find such expansion in their interests and believed that they will be able to cut it back at a later time only at considerable cost. Readers may want to compare current developments with these two predictions about the future of American industrial relations and reach their own conclusions about the appropriate scope of bargaining and the rights of managers.

THE SUBJECT MATTER OF COLLECTIVE BARGAINING IN THE PUBLIC SECTOR

Managements and unions have extended the area of collective bargaining where it served their mutual interests. Managers have not resisted every extension, even when it limited their management activities, and union leaders have sought extensions only in certain areas of particular interest to their members. The issue of general limits is ideologically controversial, but resolving the practical problems is much less so. Neither party has found that it needed or desired as extreme a position as its ideology implies.

Given the experience in the private sector, one would not expect an analogous dispute over the limits of collective bargaining to arise in the public sec-

---

[13]Quinn Mills, "When Employees Make Concessions," *Harvard Business Review,* vol. 61, May–June 1983, pp. 103–113.
[14]Douglas H. Soutar, "Institutional Problems in Collective Bargaining and Problem Solving," speech delivered at Carnegie-Mellon University, Oct. 28, 1982, p. 15. (Mimeographed.)

tor. Both observers and the parties involved might have noted the practical resolution, realizing that ideological differences are more difficult to reconcile than actual problems that come to the bargaining table. However, when public employees in significant numbers secured the right in the sixties to bargain collectively through representatives of their own choosing, many, including legislators and public managers, saw dangers ahead.

The first issue was the sovereignty of government as the final and determinate authority. For elected officials or their appointed managers to delegate or share that authority with union negotiators would contradict and undermine government sovereignty. Second, public sector industrial relations intimately affect public interests vital to the order, health, and safety of society. The interests are too important to be subject to negotiations by a union. Third, even if the law forbids strikes by public employees, public employees can exercise significant political power and thus affect not only their unions' side of the table but management's side as well.

After considering these conditions, the federal government and most states formally have limited the subject matter of collective bargaining in the public sector. The Advisory Commission on Intergovernmental Relations recommended strict limits:

> [The] Commission believes statutory descriptions of management rights is necessary if well defined parameters to discussion are to be established. In a democratic political system dealings between public employers and public employee organizations . . . must necessarily be limited by legislatively determined policies and goals. This may involve merely a restatement of basic management prerogatives and civil service percepts.[15]

Subject Matter for the Federal Government

The federal government established its limits through three laws. Executive Order 11491, issued in 1970, first constrains the scope of bargaining within the limits described in all applicable laws and regulations, including the personnel policies published by the Civil Service Commission in the *Federal Personnel Manual* and by agency personnel policies. It further excludes from negotiations a long list of specified management rights. Under Title VII of the Civil Service Reform Act of 1978, the subject matter of collective bargaining is similarly restricted. Both the executive order and the act exclude an agency's mission, budget, organization, number of employees, and internal security practices from bargaining. Furthermore, they state that managers' right to hire, assign, direct, lay off, retain, or take disciplinary action against employees is not bargainable. However, an agency may, at its option, negotiate provisions that

---

[15]Advisory Commission on Intergovernmental Relations, *Labor-Management Policies for State and Local Government,* 1969, pp. 102–103, quoted in Harry T. Edwards, R. Theodore Clark, Jr., and Charles B. Craver, *Labor Relations Law in the Public Sector,* 2d ed., New York: The Bobbs-Merrill Company, Inc., 1979, p. 282.

affect the numbers, types, and grades of employees or positions assigned to work projects or subdivisions; it may also establish provisions affecting technology, work performance, the procedures for exercising managerial authority, and the appeals procedures for workers adversely affected by managerial actions. Of course, only Congress and the president determine wage increases and fringe benefits, with the pay scales fixed in accordance with the standards of the Federal Pay Comparability Act.

Postal service employees bargain under the constraints of the Postal Reorganization Act of 1978. It allows a wider scope of bargaining than either the executive order or the Civil Service Reform Act. Postal workers can negotiate wages, hours, and other terms and conditions of employment unless specifically reserved to management, and in general they are subject to the provisions of the Labor-Management Relations Act of 1947.

Subject Matter among the States

The Committee on Economic Development, a study/research group of corporate managers from the largest business firms, strongly recommended to the states the federal approach to the subject matter of collective bargaining. They still favored the obsolete term "prerogative," casting back memories to business arguments of thirty years ago:

> [I]n enacting or revising public sector collective bargaining legislation, states should identify the topics subject to collective bargaining and should also stipulate those management prerogatives not subject to bargaining.[16]

The two largest teachers' organizations opted for a far wider scope of collective bargaining. The National Education Association declared that "negotiations should include all matters which affect the quality of the educational system."[17] The president of the American Federation of Teachers took his stand with the union leaders of 1948: "We would place no limit on the scope of negotiations—the items which are subject to the bargaining process. Anything on which the two parties can agree should become a part of the agreement . . . in fact anything having to do with the operation of the school is a matter for professional concern and should thus be subject to collective bargaining."[18] The California Assembly Advisory Council, chaired by Professor Benjamin Aaron, an experienced arbitrator and well-known expert in labor law, merely suggested that its members did "not see any compelling distinction between

---

[16]*Improving Management of the Public Work Force,* New York: Committee for Economic Development, 1978, pp. 76–77.

[17]National Education Association, *Guidelines for Professional Negotiation,* Washington, D.C.: National Education Association, 1965, pp. 21–22, printed in Myron Lieberman and Michael Moskow, *Collective Negotiations for Teachers,* Chicago: Rand McNally & Company, 1966, p. 225.

[18]Charles Cogen, "Collective Bargaining: The AFT Way," speech given at National Institute on Collective Negotiations in Public Education, Rhode Island College, Providence, R.I., July 8, 1965, pp. 2, 7. Printed in Lieberman and Moskow, *Collective Negotiations for Teachers,* p. 226.

the public and private sector that would justify the inclusion of management-rights clauses in public employee relations statutes."[19]

The states have dealt with limits on collective bargaining in various ways. Some simply require agencies to bargain over wages, hours, and other terms and conditions of employment, but others have imposed specific limitations. In almost all states the scope of bargaining is limited, of course, by the rules and regulations of the civil service systems, by the prevailing rate systems for establishing wages, and by the various salary ordinances and legislated fringe benefits frequently found in cities.

On the basis of experience in the private sector one may confidently predict that public employees' unions will extend the subject matter of collective bargaining sufficiently to satisfy their interests. Moreover, we can expect agency managers to discuss and agree to provisions that affect or even limit their specified managerial rights without making them any less managers. We need not fear that public sector unions, any more than private sector unions, aspire to take over the responsibilities of management or that they have the power to do so in any case.[20]

PERSONNEL AND RELATED PROVISIONS

We shall now turn our attention to some of the matters that have found their way into collective agreements. To write of these in detail would require a lengthy volume in itself. We shall be content here to survey in the most summary fashion some of the ways in which the union, through the bargaining process, has affected the conduct of management in the United States. It goes without saying that not all the provisions mentioned are to be found in every agreement, and indeed it would be the unusual agreement which covered all the topics listed. The matters discussed below are to be regarded as taken from a composite of many agreements from many industries.[21]

In light of the above discussion, one should expect that the matters in which unions have most successfully gained the right of participation are those which bear a direct and immediate relationship to the work environment and economic security of employees. In a thorough canvass, one could uncover instances where a particular union, in specific circumstances, has negotiated with a company even on such issues as depreciation policy, the quality of the product or service, capital financing, and the location of the company. But

---

[19]*Final Report of the Assembly Advisory Council on Public Employee Relations,* California, 1973, p. 139, quoted in Edwards et al., *Labor Relations Law in the Public Sector,* p. 282.

[20]See Donald H. Wollett, "The Bargaining Process in the Public Sector," *Oregon Law Review,* vol. 51, 1971, pp. 177–182.

[21]Those who wish to examine in greater detail the subject matter of collective bargaining may consult *Collective Bargaining Negotiations and Contracts* and *Labor Arbitration Reports,* reporting services of the Bureau of National Affairs. Also see the various bulletins periodically published by the Bureau of Labor Statistics under various titles such as those mentioned in the sources for tables 8, 9, and 10.

these represent unusual situations and we shall not mention them further. Our interest at the moment runs simply to the customary and usual subjects of collective bargaining.

Hiring, Seniority, and Job Assignment

For the most part, these are matters normally considered to be of a pesonnel nature—employment, transfers, promotions, discipline, and the broader issues of wages and hours. What should be of interest, however, is the scope of the union's interest in these matters. We shall discover that unions deal effectively with problems directly connected with the production process where these have been demonstrated to have a substantial impact upon the security and job satisfaction of the employees—problems such as the content or require-ment of a job, methods of operation, and rates of operation and workloads. Finally, some of the concessions won by unions and incorporated into collec-tive bargaining agreements may appear to be minor victories. They may do nothing more than codify company practices. The significance of these conces-sions, however, is that practices become a matter of agreement, no longer sub-ject to exclusive management control. The union wins a right to be consulted before changes in practice are made.

Let us examine first the manner in which unions have affected hiring and employment policies. Industrial unions in the mass-production industries early bargained for and won provisions banning discrimination on the basis of race, color, creed, and national origin. Later they added sex and age. But by 1965 only 28 percent of the sample of agreements examined by the Bureau of National Affairs (BNA) had banned such discrimination. In response to the Civil Rights Act of 1964 and the Age Discrimination in Employment Act of 1967, both unions and management decided to incorporate the bans into their agreements. The percentage incorporating these provisions had risen to 46, by 1975 to 74, and by 1979 to 84.[22]

In addition to an interest in the personal characteristics of job applicants, now powerfully supported and encouraged by federal law, unions have also been concerned with applicants' professional qualifications, a concern power-fully stimulated by a desire to reduce job competition as well as to enhance employee quality. By weeding out those who cannot surmount certain hurdles, unions can help maintain the prestige, status, and pay differentials of their skilled members. They also provide advancement opportunities for their mem-bers. In the automobile, steel, and construction industries unions have estab-lished the largest numbers of jointly administered apprenticeship programs. In construction 78 percent, in steel (primary metals) 69 percent, and in autos (transportation equipment) 56 percent of all agreements have apprenticeship provisions. General Motors and the UAW, for example are joint members of

---

[22]Editors of Collective Bargaining Negotiations and Contracts, *Basic Patterns in Union Con-tracts,* 9th ed., Washington, D.C.: Bureau of National Affairs, May 1979, p. 111. The Bureau of Labor Statistics reported almost the same figure for major agreements in 1980.

a Skilled Trades and Apprenticeship Committee that meets monthly in Detroit and oversees the work of local apprenticeship committees in each plant employing apprentices. The national agreement also sets the ratio of apprentices to journeymen and the standard work week, wage rates, and seniority status of apprentices.

Collective agreements sometimes place other limitations on managers' freedom to hire employees in the labor market. This is obviously the case when unions serve virtually as an employment office for companies, as in the building trades, the maritime trade, and longshoring.[23] Some agreements proscribe new hirings before certain provisions have been met. Most important are the seniority provisions. Seniority is a ranking based on hiring date, maintained through continuous service with a company and usually beginning after some trial period. Roughly 90 percent of manufacturing workers covered by large agreements maintain their seniority through a layoff and are called back to work in order of seniority. In some industries work is so seasonal and unsteady that unions do not rely heavily upon seniority to apportion jobs, however. In apparel almost two-thirds of the workers covered by collective bargaining do not enjoy seniority rights during layoffs, and in construction only a handful do, fewer than one in twenty.

One difficulty in applying the seniority principle when laying off employees has concerned the question of whether employees displaced from a regular job should "bump" the junior workers next below or be given the job of the worker with least seniority in the department. The first alternate leads to a series of bumps in a falling-domino fashion, whereas the second obviates the disturbance of employees in the intermediate classifications. The BNA study of agreements in 1979 found that a small portion allow bumping throughout the company and a larger portion allow bumping only within a plant. Neither union nor management is apt to favor companywide bumping among a number of geographically dispersed plants. Within a single location, though, managers understandably favor shorter over longer bumping chains, restricting them to employees' classifications and work groups in about one-third of the cases. Many of the provisions agreed to by managers of big, multiplant firms specify that employees cannot bump unless they are qualified to perform the new job.[24] In any event, a layoff may require many transfers. To smooth this difficult period, agreements sometimes provide for joint conferences of union and management representatives, at which both parties review the schedule of transfers in advance of its effective date.

In filling vacancies in new plants or even in old plants, managers may be

---

[23]The Supreme Court held that hiring halls, as such employment offices are called, are not illegal if they do not require employees to join the union before securing a job. It quoted Senator Taft, one of the authors of the Labor-Management Relations Act of 1947; "The employer should be able to make a contract with the union as an employment agency. The employer should be able to give notice of vacancies, and in the normal course of events to accept men sent to him by the hiring hall." [*Local 357, Teamsters v. NRLB,* 365 U.S. 667 (1961).]

[24]Editors of Collective Bargaining Negotiations and Contracts, *Basic Patterns in Union Contracts,* p. 53.

obligated to give preference to employees who wish to transfer from existing jobs. Almost half of workers covered by large agreements enjoy transfer rights. Provisions for transfers and preferential hiring are found primarily in the agreements made with large firms, where multiplant operations are common. Unionists are interested in protecting the employment rights of their fellow members, as these provisions indicate, even at the expense of other and new employees.

After workers are hired, they must be assigned to some job. Unions usually take no special interest in an employee's original assignment (unless it involves the placement of a new worker without special qualifications in a position superior to qualified employees with seniority); however, questions of worker reassignments are sometimes subject to joint decision in important particulars. A particular move may be prohibited, foreclosing managers from certain action, or prescribed in various details. In addition there are some clauses that leave discretion with the employee.

Prohibitive provisions may declare that no employee can be reassigned without consent; that employees with specified company seniority may not be transferred against their wishes from one plant or locality to another; that employees of one major department of the company shall not be assigned to jobs in another department except for temporary periods—such as two weeks—in an emergency or when arranged with the local shop committee; or that temporary assignments of employees that carry them outside their locality may not exceed some specified period.

In the provisions that prescribe how transfers are to be made, seniority is the commonly accepted factor, sometimes modified to preserve some discretion on the basis of a worker's ability. The rule unions seek is that for "good" jobs the employee with the greatest seniority shall be chosen; for "bad" jobs the one with the least seniority shall be selected. Of course, jobs are not always so easily labeled. For example, an unpleasant job in a paint shop, exposing workers to both heat and fumes, may also carry an attractive hourly rate.

The assignment of employees to particular shifts (day, afternoon, or night); to particular machines (as in the garment industry, where sewing machine operators are responsible for the care of their machines and resent being moved from one to which they have given their attention); or to particular runs (as in the case of truck or bus drivers) may also be a matter of joint concern. Sometimes written clauses cover the matter, and at other times the parties rely upon unwritten understandings that can be interpreted and applied through the grievance procedure.

Promotions and Discipline

Another subject of collective bargaining that is of direct and immediate interest to employees is promotion. Promotions may be considered a form of hiring, the recruiting being from among the present employees. Some managers have retained the discretion to determine whether a particular job shall be filled by hiring from outside or by promotion from within, but many unions have successfully urged the latter policy. Once managers have decided that a vacancy is to be filled by promotion, a "bidding" procedure is called for by some agreements. Thus a common arrangement in the electrical utility field is the provision that vacancies within the bargaining unit be posted by management for a specified period of time, during which interested employees may bid for the job. This procedure ensures that no interested employee is overlooked and that uninterested employees are not considered.

Whether or not an agreement calls for a bidding arrangement, there remains the necessity of determining which of a number of employees is most deserving of the promotion. In general, it may be said that unions have consistently sought to have this question answered on the basis of objectively measured seniority, while managers have attempted to make the primary determinant their appraisals of relative ability. In the sample of 400 agreements studied by the BNA, seniority was assigned a role in determining promotions in two-thirds; it was the sole factor in one-tenth of the agreements and a determining factor in one-third. In less than a quarter of the agreements, seniority was a secondary factor in promotions.[25]

Despite the wording of those provisions that place primary emphasis on relative abilities, in actual operation seniority frequently becomes the controlling consideration. Such control does not necessarily imply that ability is ignored. Jobs are usually structured so that the incumbent learns a portion of the tasks in the next-higher-rated position and is at least minimally qualified for promotion. Unions have also been able to emphasize seniority by their appeal to grievance arbitrators that managers demonstrate *by objective standards* that a junior employee is more qualified for promotion than one with greater seniority. Devising a practical system that provides objective measurements is a problem; it will not take much consideration to convince oneself of the difficulties involved. It is the objectivity of seniority that commends it to unions as the principal guide in such matters as promotions.

In the matter of discipline, unions have been especially successful in establishing a joint interest with management. In the BNA sample of agreements 90 percent provide for discharge, either for cause (or "just cause") or for specified offenses such as contract violation (primarily unauthorized strikes), violation of leaves or company rules, intoxication, dishonesty or theft, incompetence, insurbordination, failure to obey safety rules, or misconduct. About two-thirds of the agreements set forth discharge procedures; warnings are required in about a quarter, predischarge hearings are permitted in 17 percent, and written notice is required in 36 percent. Under more than three-quarters of the agreements an employee may appeal a discharge. Reinstatement with back pay for employees improperly discharged is required in 43 percent of the agreements.[26]

In general, management retains the right to impose penalties for proper

---

[25]Ibid., p. 74.
[26]Ibid., p. 6–9.

cause, while the union has the right to protest through the grievance procedure. The two parties have built up a body of disciplinary doctrine through decisions in the grievance procedure. As a consequence of arbitrators' decisions, there has grown up the closest approximation to common law to be found in industry. The analogy should not be pressed too far, but it does not involve much distortion.

In matters of discipline, perhaps the first question customarily raised by unionists is whether just cause exists for imposing penalty. Here it is important to ascertain whether the employee knew that the conduct was improper and subject to penalty. Knowledge on the part of the offending employee of the standards of conduct being enforced may be shown in several ways. Management may have posted rules covering the conduct in question. In some cases, certain standards are considered to be understood or implied, even in the absence of general promulgation, such as prohibition of assault upon a fellow worker or theft of company property. In other instances, an employee might know that the conduct was improper, having received an individual warning on a prior occasion.

Other subsidiary questions may have to be answered. Was the language of the notice, warning, or order clear and free from ambiguity? Has the particular standard been required of all employees, or have some been discriminatorily treated, held to standards that were overlooked in the cases of others? Have rules been systematically enforced so that employees could reasonably expect them to be effective? We all know of the existence of certain municipal ordinances that remain on the books even though they are never observed; similarly, sometimes plant rules–such as "no smoking"—are commonly disregarded, so that an employee, without warning, could not reasonably be expected to believe that they would be enforced.

These are just some of the questions asked in appraising the just-cause basis for discipline. In answering them, general rules are hammered out in arbitration; these rules become as important a part of the collective bargaining relationship as if they were spelled out in the agreement itself.

Certain procedural requirements customarily have to be observed in the meting out of discipline, though there is no uniformity among companies. Some of the contractual provisions or arbitration decisions require specification of the offense for which an employee is being punished. Only then may an employee properly prepare a defense. In more than a fifth of the BNA's sample agreements there must be notice not only to the employee but also to the union representative (the counterpart in industry of the accused's right to counsel), followed by a hearing. Findings must conform to the charges made, of course, and discipline cannot be justified by evidence unrelated to the original charge. If an employee has been charged with theft, for example, but the findings do not substantiate the charge, discipline will not be upheld even though the evidence also indicates excessive absenteeism. Occasionally arbitration decisions have upheld the principle that an employee may not be punished twice for the same offense—the substantial equivalent in industry of the rule against "double jeopardy" to be found in our civil courts—as well as the principle that an offense committed sufficiently remotely in time cannot be used as the basis for later punishment—the industrial equivalent of a statute of limitation. A "statute of limitations" appears in 28 percent of the sample agreements.

Finally, there is the question of the reasonableness of the penalty. Even if there is cause for discipline, it may be that the penalty invoked is excessive—discharge for a first-time, minor infraction, for instance. Of course, if an employee repeatedly commits offenses within a short period, the penalties may be increased. In general an arbitrator is free to determine whether a penalty "fits the crime." Sometimes the question of the nature of permissible penalties is raised. The customary punishment is discharge or suspension for a specified period of time. Other penalties are available, however, such as demotion or fines. In some situations the former may conflict with the seniority provisions of the agreement, while in other cases legislation may prevent levying against workers of fines to be paid to the company.

Quality of Working Life

The provisions affecting personnel policy so far discussed are the usual and traditional ones. In general the parties jointly establish them in their periodic negotiations; management executes or administers them; and employees process complaints arising under them through the grievance procedures. Thus they are established, administered, and validated within the bounds of normal union-management adversarial relations. In recent years a few managements have introduced new kinds of provisions that do not fit easily within the old boundaries of collective bargaining. They involve joint procedures, often from top management down to the place of work, through which the parties seek solutions to a variety of work-related problems that hold down productivity gains and make work less satisfying to employees than it might be. The new provisions are most widely known under the terms "quality of work life" (QWL) or "work innovation." These were selected to avoid controversial alternatives such as "productivity improvement," which suggested a speedup to many unionists, or "worker participation," which implied more sharing of control than most managers would accept.

Quality of work life and work innovation provisions take many forms and cover a wide range.

> The unifying theme of work innovations is the attempt [jointly] to design into jobs of all employees those characteristics which have hitherto been reserved for professional and management jobs—variety, relative autonomy, identifiable product, scope for creativity, and judgment. Work innovation discards the "scientific management" concept of one-man/one-motion. There is no one best form of innovation; each organization must tailor a solution to its own unique requirements.[27]

[27] *Productivity Through Work Innovation*, Executive Summary, A Work in America Institute Policy Study, New York: Pergamon Press, 1982, p. 4.

Advocates of QWL or work innovation programs often claim more for their introduction and use than evidence reveals. Consultants who have helped introduce the programs and early observers usually indicate that they provide benefits of various kinds, but the data are not hard nor are the standards against which performance is measured specified ahead of time.[28] The Ford Motor Company and the UAW agreed to a joint Employee Involvement (EI) process in October, 1979 and proceeded gradually and voluntarily, carefully avoiding unlikely promises and attempting to safeguard their existing collective bargaining. They set up committees at all levels to increase the involvement of employees in matters affecting their work. They recognized that the committees' work was outside of collective bargaining, that it did not preempt issues that the parties should bargain about, and that it was not a substitute grievance procedure. In a handbook distributed to all employees they asserted that:

> It's not a gimmick to spur productivity, although increased job satisfaction and employee contributions may result in better products. While it has great promise, Employee Involvement can't be an answer to all the problems of employees, the Union, or the Company.

The Employee Involvement program has continued for a number of years, and enough support both within management and in the union has developed that it may be termed successful, at least at some Ford plants. Informed observers are skeptical, though, that such joint labor-management programs will flourish and spread widely. They point out that programs usually arise out of crisis; for example, the drastic loss of auto sales to foreign imports in the 1970s shook the automobile industry, and the recession of the early 1980s produced the highest levels of unemployment among autoworkers in forty years. If there is a recovery, however, the EI may languish and fade as such programs have in the past. Under aegis of the National War Labor Board during World War II management and unions set up thousands of joint committees similar to those under QWL and work innovation. Most disappeared within a few years.

Nevertheless, if managements become less sensitive about their prerogatives to direct the work force and if unions discover they can accommodate their work rules to increased job flexibility, the blurring of worker and supervisory roles, and new promotion patterns, QWL-type programs may help lessen, though not eliminate the adversarial nature of relationships of management and unions.[29]

---

[28]See, for example, a report on work innovation in the federal government: James E. Martin, "Union-Management Committees in the Federal Sector," *Monthly Labor Review,* vol. 99, Oct. 1976, p. 30.

[29]For a skeptical evaluation of QWL's long-term contributions to industrial relations see George Strauss, "Quality of Worklife and Participation as Bargaining Issues," no 434, Institute of Industrial Relations, Berkeley, Calif.: University of California, 1980.

WAGE AND HOUR PROVISIONS

Wages represent one of the more traditional fields of collective bargaining, and it is to be expected that the impact of unions here has been an important one. Again it should be held in mind that the variety of provisions in agreements makes it difficult to speak of general practices. We shall describe arrangements which are prevalent and which give a fair approximation of what is to be expected. The system (or lack of system) under which each individual was paid an individual rate has largely disappeared; now industrial workers are likely to be grouped together under particular classifications to which wages or wage brackets are attached. In an automobile plant, for example, despite the fact that employees on an assembly line perform varied operations, workers may all bear the designation "assemblers" and receive the same rate. In some plants the number of such classifications runs high, and each classification is paid its particular rate. The union may challenge the classification of a particular job through the grievance procedure, claiming, for instance, the worker who is operating on a subassembly line and who is therefore classified as "assembly—minor" is actually so closely integrated with the main assembly process that the classification should be "assembly—major" and paid a higher rate. In some companies questions about appropriate rates or rate ranges for a particular classification are grievable, whereas in others they may be considered only when negotiating a new agreement.

The management of any sizable work force finds that it must use job evaluation in the setting of wage rates. The purpose is to rationalize the wage structure, paying similar jobs similar rates to avoid invidious comparisons and to still worker discontent. Each job or classification evaluated is weighted on the basis of a number of factors such as the amount of training or experience necessary to learn the job, the hazard involved, the pleasantness of the working conditions, the responsibility entailed, and so on. On the basis of such factors, a score is given to each classification; and depending on its score, each classification is placed in a "labor grade." The number of grades in any company varies; one company may have nine such grades, another fifteen or thirty. Each grade embraces a numerical range, so that all job classifications scored between 80 and 90 points, for example, are placed in labor grade 3. All jobs falling within a particular labor grade are paid the same basic wage rate.

Where management has introduced job evaluation systems, unions can usually raise grievances about the procedures or the outcomes. In only 16 percent of all large agreements (but 27 percent of large agreements in manufacturing) are the systems specified or mentioned. The most common provision requires managers to consult with union representatives or to notify them before putting a new rate or classification into effect. A number of agreements require negotiations with the union; and rarely managements agree to implement changes only with union consent. During the negotiations over the general agreement, of course, unions may seek changes in rates and classifications.

The relationship of occupational wage rates to one another is generally referred to as the "wage structure" of a plant. For the most part, the wage structure is taken as given. It is subject to alteration if workers can show that one rate is inequitable in the light of other rates (the factor of equitable comparison, discussed in Chapter 12) or that the content of a job has been changed. Despite grievances concerning such inequities, the wage structure, on the whole, retains a certain fixity from year to year. The wage question with which unions and management are most concerned is the wage *level*. Each has a definite interest in the size of any increase or decrease that is to be applied to all the rates making up a wage structure.

We have been speaking of hourly or time rates, but it is also true that firms may pay workers on an incentive or piece-rate basis, in which earnings fluctuate with output. More than half of all large manufacturing agreements (but 72 percent of all the workers covered) provide for incentive wage systems. They are exceedingly rare in nonmanufacturing industries, where only about 5 percent of agreements include them (and about 5 percent of workers are covered). A fair earning rate is customarily determined on the basis of company experience or time studies. The union may enter a plea on behalf of a worker that the incentive or piece rate is too "tight" and that the output standard is excessive for the earnings. An incentive system usually offers a base rate, a guarantee to the worker that when output falls for reasons other than effort a minimum will be paid.

Most agreements contain a number of other wage provisions that we will only touch on here. In many cases where a rate range is attached to a classification, a worker's progression from the minimum rate to the maximum is dependent upon a demonstration of increasing productivity. This is the system known as "merit rating." If a worker is passed over when merit increases are awarded, the action can be grieved, charging unfairness. Differentials and bonuses are sometimes given for night-shift workers; or a bonus may be paid for work considered hazardous, such as handling toxic chemicals or entering areas of heavy radioactivity (see Table 10). Some agreements spell out in considerable detail the rate to be paid to workers who are temporarily transferred to jobs carrying a different rate. In such cases an agreement may provide, for example, that if the transfer does not exceed three days, workers shall continue to be paid their regular rate but that after three days they shall be paid the higher of the two rates involved.

The subject of hours is also important in any collective agreement. Uniformly, the normal hours of work per week are a negotiated matter. In some companies the normal hours, perhaps 35 or 40 per week, apply to all employees. In other companies the number of hours varies with classification, so an employee in a special classification may have a normal work week either longer or shorter than other workers. In most contracts the union has established restrictions on the scheduling of the workweek. These may range from the binding commitment that regular manufacturing operations shall be confined to five consecutive days, Monday to Friday, inclusive, except for certain operations designated as continuous, to a provision which simply states that the employee's workweek shall be a calendar week beginning at the start of the Monday shift. Hours or days worked outside of those so specified are paid at penalty rates. Changes in shift hours may sometimes be made only after advance notice to or discussion with the union.

Equalization of hours among employees is a principle which has become widely established in one form or another. Provisions requiring the equalization of overtime among employees, for example, are found in about 60 percent of large manufacturing agreements and in a considerable portion of nonmanufacturing agreements. Approximately 40 percent of manufacturing workers enjoy the right to refuse overtime, but fewer than 10 percent in nonmanufacturing possess that right under agreements. Mandatory overtime is a troublesome issue among workers, particularly if managers give little or no prior notice. When the supervisor comes around an hour before the end of the shift and announces, "late work this evening," many workers find their personal lives disarranged. Voluntary overtime, however, increases the need for careful scheduling by management—and a degree of control over production that many smaller firms simply do not possess. Since many unions make overtime both expensive and difficult to use effectively, managers confronted with strong provisions have to learn to use less overtime than they otherwise would find helpful.

Unions have also been concerned with the question of what constitutes hours of work for purposes of pay. Among the items for which an employee may receive pay, by agreement, are "call-in" time, when workers report for duty without previous notification that work is not available; rest periods; lunch hour; time spent preparing tools and equipment; time spent changing clothes; time involved in returning from distant assignments; and time occupied in receiving instructions at the commencement of the working day.

Determination of the hours or days for which employees will be paid special penalty rates is a matter which has received considerable attention from unions. The Fair Labor Standards Act has supplemented their efforts by requiring the payment of overtime rates under specified circumstances. Collective agreements often go beyond this legislation, however, requiring penalty rates not only when more than eight hours in a day or forty hours in a week have been worked but also, in a number of companies, for work performed on Saturdays, Sundays, or holidays, regardless of the number of hours worked during that week. This has at times given rise to the arrangement known as "overtime on overtime," in which a worker may be paid 1½ times the special, overtime Saturday or Sunday rate.

Just as there is a question as to what are to be considered hours worked for purposes of pay, so is there a question as to what are to be considered days worked for purposes of overtime. Some agreements require that a holiday falling within the regular workweek be counted as a day regularly worked; similarly, a day of illness or an absence otherwise excused may occasionally be included.

SUPPLEMENTAL BENEFITS

Union interest in and influence on supplemental benefits is well known. The wide provision of pensions, holidays and vacation time, insurance, and health care for union workers has spurred most managements to provide the same benefits for all their workers. Supplemental benefits as a share of payrolls have shown an upward trend for a long time. The share was less than 25 percent in 1957 and was over 40 percent by 1978.[30] Government policy also affects employers' supplemental costs in no small way. The employers' part of the social security tax made up just over 3 percent of payroll in 1957; it was almost 8 percent in 1978, a larger relative increase than for any of the other fringes.

Recent studies suggest that union effects on supplemental benefits exceed those on wages, emphasizing how important union negotiations have found them.[31] Those benefits that favor senior and older workers receive union negotiators' greatest attention. Such workers tend to dominate union political life, as the largest, most active interest group. Ninety percent of large manufacturing agreements contain provisions for vacations, as do over half those in non-manufacturing. (Few agreements in construction provide for vacations at all. The work is so seasonal and irregular that few workers would qualify for vacations if at least a year's full-time employment had to be shown.) In almost all cases the length of vacation is linked to length of service. In 1957 few agreements allowed vacations longer than four weeks, and three weeks was typical. In 1978 six weeks had become not uncommon, with many agreements offering more than three weeks. Provisions for paid holidays have also become widespread. Eighty-four percent of all large agreements offer holidays; more than half provide nine to eleven days, and twelve percent provide from twelve to twenty days per year. A generation ago fewer than seven holidays per year was typical. There are sometimes special rules concerning eligibility for payment, governing who can take holidays off with pay and under what circumstances. Under some agreements, an employee must report to work on the working days before and after the holiday to receive pay for it.

Pension and various insurance provisions account for the single largest share of supplemental benefits costs to management—37 percent in 1978. (It was 34 percent in 1957.) They have increased greatly in number, variety, and coverage over the past twenty years. By 1979 more than 80 percent of BNA's sample agreements provided sickness and accident, hospitalization, and surgical insurance benefits; 95 percent offered life insurance coverage. More than half the agreements provided major medical insurance and maternity care as well as accidental death and dismemberment benefits.[32] In the late seventies and early eighties dental coverage increased rapidly. By 1979 more than 40

---

[30]*Employee Benefits, 1978,* Washington, D.C.: Chamber of Commerce of the United States, 1979, table 19, p. 27. Data from 159 companies.

[31]Richard B. Freeman, "The Effect of Unionism On Fringe Benefits," *Industrial and Labor Relations Review,* vol. 34, July 1981, pp. 489–509.

[32]Editors of Collective Bargaining Negotiations and Contracts, *Basic Patterns in Union Contracts,* p. 41.

percent had dental insurance, up from 15 percent in 1975. Unions also have pushed urgently for coverage of prescription drug costs, and agreements with provisions for them rose from 16 percent in 1975 to 24 percent in 1979.

So popular are supplemental benefits that offer pay for time when an employee is not at work, not able to work, or retired that we may expect them to be extended to almost all unionized employees. They are a "positive good," one that is increasingly attractive as income rises. Furthermore, in these years of rising tax rates, most fringes are nontaxable, no small matter to increasingly large numbers of employees. Spillover to nonunion employees can be expected, for managers are not apt to offer such attractive benefits to only their unionized workers. Nonunion employers, particularly large companies, often already provide supplemental benefits that match or outrank those gained by unions.

THE EFFECTS ON PRODUCTION POLICIES

In a sense, a system of classification of business decisions that draws a line between personnel administration and production policies makes an artificial distinction. The two are inseparably related. The assignment of employees, the selection of individuals for promotion or layoff, the system of discipline, and the effect of wages and other forms of remuneration as incentives are all inextricably tied up with the production process. Nevertheless, by custom we have come to think of production as related to the mechanics of the process. It determines the specific job requirements, the functional relation of jobs in a sequence leading to an end product, the determination of machine and material requirements, and so on.

Managers at times are tempted to treat production matters as routine engineering problems and neglect their effect on workers. The temptation is dangerous, for it ignores a fundamental reality of all production processes: they are founded on the continuing need for massive cooperation among all the people involved. That cooperation can easily be withdrawn by workers—blue-or white-collar—who feel aggrieved. The close relations between personnel and production matters will become apparent as we now turn briefly to issues that have generally been considered to belong to the latter category.

In general, collective agreements contemplate, in the words of one impartial arbitrator, "that management shall instruct the employees as to the work to be performed, and that . . . the employees shall perform the work which they are instructed to do." Despite this principle, the question frequently arises of whether workers may properly be called upon to perform certain operations as part of their jobs. The concept of division of labor has a firm hold upon union philosophy. As long as duties required fall within the description of the classification covering the workers, there is only infrequent and spasmodic resistance by employees to work assignments. There is often opposition, however, to the performance of duties that employees conceive to be outside the requirements of their job classifications. This is an issue to which variant solutions have been offered, both in collective bargaining and during arbitration. In most situations in which managers change the content of an employee's job or rearrange work duties—actions frequently necessary in the production process—the only basis for employee protests is classification. It may be, for example, that new duties warrant reclassification at a different rate, even though a supervisor disagrees.

Unions may take a firm stand against rearrangement of job duties if it should involve loss of work. An example is the reduction of the printing-press crews on newspapers, where technological change reduced manning by half or more. Airline pilots argued that three pilots were required in big planes for security and safety. The airlines countered that two pilots satisfactorily performed all necessary functions. Some electrical workers' unions have also insisted—at times successfully—that a line crew be composed of a specified number of workers, for the sake of safety. And finally, the question of crew size in turn often leads to the further issues of workload or rate of operation. At times the content of a job, the number of workers, and the rate of operation are so interrelated as to become a single problem.

Standards or rates of operation constitute one of the areas of production control in which unions have militantly affirmed their interests. In most companies, they have won the right to protest production standards, customarily resulting in a retiming of the process involved. Managements have not always been willing to submit disputes in this area to arbitration, however. Fifteen percent of all large agreements exclude wage adjustments from any arbitration, and only in the exceptional company do unions participate in the original determination of workloads or operating speeds. They nevertheless continue to press for such participation.

Much has been written in the popular press of unions' opposition to technological changes. Contest over the introduction of improved machinery and methods has never been widespread, however. Although unions retain their concern for the immediate unemployment effects, they have usually sought to meet the problem not by opposing change but by controlling its timing. Occasional arrangements have been made for new technological processes to be accompanied by provisions that allow reabsorption of displaced workers. For example, they may be carried on the payroll for some specified period of time or even until retirement, as in the case of the New York typographers. Unions have also sought retraining of displaced workers or severance pay to ease the transition between jobs.

CONCLUSION

We have hardly explored the various approaches taken by unions and managements to different situations. Such an exploration can best be undertaken not simply by referring to agreement provisions but by studying grievances as they appear in arbitration reports. Arbitrators customarily summarize and evaluate the positions of the respective parties, relating them to daily problems, thus providing an expanded view of the agreement. One becomes aware, too, in such a study, of the exceptional provisions embracing an area of managerial activity not often covered by collective bargaining, which in some particular instance has become an issue vitally affecting the welfare of the workers. We do not generally think of collective bargaining as being concerned with the location of a plant or office, for example, and yet under some circumstances unions have reached agreement with employers binding the latter not to change the location of their operations during the lifetime of the agreement.[33]

If any conclusion can be reached as to the appropriate subject matter of collective bargaining, then, it is that one cannot label certain matters as bargainable and exclude others as beyond the union's interest. Such labels do not often stick. With changing economic, social, and political relationships, issues that were once of no concern to the workers may become of direct interest, with the possibility of union control discovered or created. One may question whether the impact of a union on any given sphere of an organization's operation is desirable or undesirable, just as one may wonder whether the influence of a trade association is beneficial or not. This is a question to which the answer cannot be readily found simply by dividing all matters into the two classifications: those bargainable and those not bargainable.

The difficulty some people encounter in accepting the possible expanding influence of unions is the insistent question: Where will it all end? To this no answer can be supplied, despite the dogmas of conservative despair and radical determinism. We may be sure, however, that the efforts to make the process of change *end now* are foredoomed to failure. Energy may be more effectively expended in directing the course of changes that are prompted by evolving social relationships than in seeking to halt them. The issue becomes less one of *whether* the unions should be heard on certain matters than one of how well considered their proposals are. Managers cannot defend their interests simply by turning a deaf ear to particular topics and repeating "no." Unions' bargaining power will at times permit such a rude reply to be overridden. Nor are unions likely to insist on joint control if they thereby neglect other vital interests of their own. It is through discussion and mutual persuasion that the best chances lie for determining workers' proper interest in the conduct of the organization upon which, in varying degrees, they and others depend for their livelihoods.

---

[33]This has been true of unions dealing with employers operating small shops with a low capital investment, who have sometimes in the past removed almost overnight to a location outside a unionized area in hope of escaping the union's scale of wages.

THE GRIEVANCE PROCESS

After agreeing to the general terms that are to govern their relationships, managers and union officers do not break off collective bargaining. The signing of the agreement and its acceptance by both parties is but the beginning of collective bargaining. By far the most important activity, as measured by time, effort, and personnel involved, is that of the grievance process. It continues on a daily basis at the place of work. First, the two parties must settle any differences of opinion about the meaning and interpretation of various provisions of the agreement. Second, they must agree on how to apply the general terms to changed, unforeseen, and specific situations. Third, as the time period of agreements has lengthened and the coverage has been extended, in some cases, to include tens of thousands of workers in many different locations, union officers and managers have had to deal realistically with workers' and supervisors' demands for local adjustments and modifications of the basic agreement.

THE GROWTH OF ADJUDICATION UNDER THE AGREEMENT

In the early years of collective bargaining in this country, union leaders and employers did not differentiate the process of formulating a basic agreement from that of adjudication, administration, and adjustment under the agreement. As we have seen, on occasions negotitations would begin with a problem arising under an agreement and lead to a strike over the agreement itself. Though these problems might arise frequently and each was a potential dispute, the parties made little attempt to establish any procedure by which they might regularly and peacefully settle them. Employers dealt with their unions only as long as they were negotiating the basic agreement; they recognized no continuing relationship.

The reason is easy to understand. As long as the general terms were fixed by unilateral action and were respected only while the other party was on the upper end of the economic seesaw, there was no mutual interest in the continuity of those terms. At least one party always looked forward to modifying them when its bargaining power and strategic position permitted. The process of modification might proceed on a day-to-day basis, by a nibbling away at the application of the general terms. If union members believed that an employer was not complying with the terms of employment as they understood them, they could support their contention only by the same show of strength that had won those terms in the first place. Moreover, the establishment of any regular, continuous relationship would have implied acceptance of the union, an affirmation many employers were unwilling to make.

A major step in the development of collective bargaining occurred when some trade unionists and employers agreed to abide by their jointly negotiated agreements for a fixed period of time. As this development proceeded they began to appreciate that the process of adjudication and adjustment under the agreement was fundamentally different from the process of making the agreement itself. The threat or use of a strike by the union or of a lockout by the employer might be necessary to reach the basic agreement, but a show of strength to enforce or interpret it was redundant as long as the parties dealt with each other in good faith. The earlier agreements, which were often only oral understandings or demands imposed by one party, were too unstable to permit any regular handling of disputes. The existence of a jointly written, fixed-period agreement, however, allowed the parties to set up a regular procedure for dispute settlement. It consisted simply of a meeting of union and employer representatives in conference when a dispute arose about some provision of the agreement. They then settled the dispute on the basis of the rules already laid down in the agreement, not on the basis of the relative bargaining advantage enjoyed at the moment by the employer or the union.

In some instances, union and employer representatives were able to agree on the way to apply a general provision of the agreement to a particular situation. In other instances, however, the two parties would find themselves in serious disagreement. This appeared to leave each party with only the unhappy alternatives of either enforcing its own view with the threat of strike or lockout or else giving in. For practical people, a third choice existed, and by the end of the nineteenth century, union leaders and employers often chose it: to arbitrate their disputes. They learned through experience that when they selected an arbitrator to judge their disparate views, settlement of day-to-day shop disputes could be achieved with neither party sacrificing too much. Arbitrators were expected not to impose an independent judgment but to attempt to construe the intent of the parties. They were to be stict constructionists who would refer to, and were limited by, the terms of the agreement.

All parties benefited from the special procedure for interpreting and applying a collective agreement. Previously, if workers claimed that they were not being paid the wage called for by the schedule of rates while their employer insisted they were, and if enough fellow workers felt the employer was unjustly depriving one or more of them of their due, the controversy was likely to boil up into a strike involving the entire shop and the whole union. In one of the earliest grievances recorded, such a case is described.

The Case of the Journeymen Tailors

A group of journeymen tailors working in Philadelphia in 1826 walked out in protest when their employers, Messrs. Robb and Winebrener, discharged six of their tailors for insisting upon a job rate for a lady's pongee riding habit. The tailors believed they were entitled to the rate under a bill of prices that the union had drawn up and to which the employers had agreed.[1]

Under procedures developed much later, the parties could have settled the dispute according to the rules of the agreement, and such a strike could have been averted. If the union members and the employer had not been able to agree upon the appropriate wage rate for the job, the matter could have been referred to arbitration. The workers would have continued in their jobs even though receiving a rate they considered less than their due, secure in the knowledge that if an impartial arbitrator upheld their view after reviewing the facts, they would be fully recompensed. The settlement procedure, including arbitration, assured continuity of production for the employer and uninterrupted work for the workers. At the same time, neither party stands in danger of material loss if the arbitrator's decision goes against it, for that decision is limited by the arbitrator's understanding of the parties' original intentions.

Disputes over General Terms and under the Agreement

It took a good many years for these benefits to become generally understood, but in the meantime some union members and employers were encouraged to

---

[1]"We come now to the origin of this difficulty, and the occurrences in the shop of Messrs. Robb and Winebrener. Early in late August, these gentlemen received an order to make a pongee riding habit; the notice being short, it was put in the hands of six of the men ... It was finished and delivered. On pay night, when these men went to receive their wages, they were surprised at an offer made by Mr. Winebrener of six dollars for what their bill of prices secured them at least seven dollars. They however distinctly declined receiving the six dollars, as not being the compensation they were entitled to, and their employers as distinctly refused to give them more. Both parties immediately instituted inquiries as to the practice in other establishments, and each, it appears, returned equally satisfied with the propriety of their original determination. Messrs. Robb and Winebrener at last yielded, paid the seven dollars, and as a punishment for asserting their undoubted rights, dismissed the six men from their service.

On the dismission of these workers, the others, fourteen in number, without premeditation or preconcert, influenced by no other motive than indignation at what they considered an act of oppression, only desirous to express their diapprobation of the treatment which their fellows had received, merely for refusing to submit to a wanton invasion of their rights, immediately threw up their work, and on the refusal of Robb and Winebrener to re-employ the men, quit their services." John R. Commons et al. (eds.), *Documentary History of American Industrial Society,* vol. 4, Glendale, Calif: The Arthur H. Clark Company, 1910–1911, pp. 143–144.

extend the settlement procedure. They began to use it where individual work-ers were involved in disputes that could not be resolved by reference to the agreement but which involved more general and commonly recognized prin-ciples of equity. If a manager were to discharge a worker for faulty performance or improper conduct, for example, the workers might protest. The worker involved and members of the work team might protest the penalty as unrea-sonable or even claim the worker innocent of the alleged offense. Though the agreement might be silent on the subject of the worker's or the union's right, the issue could be referred on its own merits to a conference between union and employer representatives and, if necessary, to arbitration. The referral could be made without risking strike, lockout, material cost of interrupted work and production, or loss of principle.

As people began to better understand the distinction between disputes over the general terms of a collective agreement and those arising after an agreement was made, the means used to settle the latter came to be known as the griev-ance procedure.[2] Through it employers and union officials sought to solve the problems of individual workers as well as to settle disputes over the application and interpretation of an agreement's general terms. When the parties employed the grievance procedure for judicial and administrative purposes, each disa-vowed the use of their organization's bargaining power or strategic position to force a decision favorable to itself. In effect, they agreed to seek solutions to particular problems on the basis of standards already jointly recognized, such as those spelled out in their agreement, or on the basis of equity values bor-rowed from a commonly shared legal and social heritage.

In contrast, when they approached their negotiations of the basic agreement, they had no mutually accepted standards or principles available to guide their decisions. Each party then tried to wrest concessions from the other on the basis of its economic strength. If agreement was reached at all, it was more the result of relative power than of common principles.

Arbitration under the Agreement

Arbitration was not and is not a necessary part of the grievance procedure. Even without it employers and union leaders could approach disputes under an agreement with a sense of mutuality that differs from the adversarial spirit of negotiating the basic terms. The epochal national agreement in the stove industry in 1891 did not include arbitration as a step in its explicitly devised grievance machinery.[3] Indeed, most grievances have always been adjusted directly by union and employer representatives. But even if it is not essential,

---

[2] The origin of this term seems to be at least as recent as that of the term "collective bargaining." The expression was not used in the 1902 report of the Industrial Commission, but by 1911 it had gained currency, probably through establishment of such boards of grievances as those in the cloth-ing industry, to be mentioned shortly.

[3] It brought to a close some thirty years of bickering and warfare between employer and employee groups. Professor Selig Perlman hailed it as inaugurating the era of trade agreements. *A History of Trade Unionism in the United States,* New York: Augustus M. Kelley, Inc., 1950, pp. 142–145.

both parties have found through experience that arbitration is the only effective means of *ensuring* some mutually acceptable disposition of grievances and at the same time of promoting continuity of production and work for the life of the agreement. Union and employer agreement to use arbitration is almost the sine qua non of their acceptance of a formal, explicit grievance system; the spread of such systems can almost be measured by the use of grievance arbitration.

Some indication of the gradual resort to arbitration following its late start is provided by the Industrial Commission in its final report of 1902:

> While thus local collective bargaining as to the general conditions of labor is seldom carried on by any very formal system, a large proportion of the local agreements themselves provide more or less formal methods of conciliation and arbitration, as regards minor disputes concerning the interpretation of their terms, usually by joint arbitration committees. Such committees are either temporary—being chosen by the parties to a particular dispute—or, somewhat less commonly, they are permanent, being chosen by the parties to the agreements as such, and having authority to settle all disputes arising during their term of office. Such permanent committees are found especially in those trades where both employers and employees are strongly organized.[4]

In its study of collective bargaining in the United States, the commissson reported that although employers and unionists differentiated between disputes over the terms of agreement and disputes arising under the agreement, with few exceptions they had not established any special procedures for dealing with the latter. Grievances were handled locally, though "such local machinery does not usually rest upon definite agreements between employers and employees but is either a matter of custom or governed by the rules of the separate organization."[5] Certain regional agreements made special provisions. A noteworthy example occurred in the Illinois bituminous mines, where the state coal operators' association had hired a special commissioner whose sole duty was to assist in the settlement of disputes under the agreement. However, the agreement did not permit arbitration, and if the parties could not peacefully come to a settlement themselves, they were free to use the strike or lockout.

There was acceptance and use of a grievance procedure "in those trades where both employers and employees [were] strongly organized," as the commission reported, but one must remember that total membership of all unions in 1902 was only about 10 percent of the workforce. Few trades were completely organized, and in many important industries, such as coal mining, steel, railroads, textiles, shipping, and meat-packing, employers had defeated union-organizing attempts, were fighting unions, or had scarcely recognized a union's right to represent workers. Where employers and managers resisted and resented a union's existence they were unlikely to agree to any terms, let alone establish permanent consultative machinery, with or without arbitration as its

---

[4]*Final Report of the Industrial Commission,* p. 838.
[5]Ibid., p. 842.

capstone. Even after the National Labor Relations Act of 1935 required recognition of unions and bargaining in good faith, many employers for a time refused to accept arbitration of grievances. They contended that vesting final judgment in an outsider deprived managers of their right to make their own decision. By 1945, however, when union membership had greatly increased both absolutely and relatively since 1902, management representatives were able to give general endorsement to the full grievance procedure. The president's Labor-Management Conference of 1945 unanimously recommended that all labor agreements specify a complete procedure for settlement of grievances, including arbitration.[6]

GRIEVANCE HANDLING AT THE PLACE OF WORK

During World War II, both managers and union leaders developed their grievance systems and learned to use arbitration of grievances at the insistence of the National War Labor Board. The procedures insisted upon by the board had been distilled from "the best practices of employers and unions developed through years of collective bargaining and of trial and error."[7] It was this cumulative experience of almost half a century that emphasized the desirability not only of third-party arbitration but also of immediate initial attention to grievances by those at the place of work. Shop managers and local union leaders had the intimate knowledge of the complaints necessary to provide prompt and equitable settlement and thus to ensure workers a practical enjoyment of their rights under the agreement.

Early grievance procedures had grown out of the demands of workers and union representatives that employers live up to the terms of the agreement. The roving business agent of the building-trade union, the walking delegate on the docks, and the shop steward of the craft union thus came to assume the informal roles of police.[8] The importance to the union and to collective bargaining of local policing and of prompt settlement of most grievances at the place of work was at first not widely appreciated by either unions or employers and certainly not by the public. By 1912, grievance procedures were established in two major industries—anthracite coal and clothing—but the feature publicized as most exemplary was arbitration.

As a consequence of the Coal Strike Commission's award in the famous strike of 1902, the anthracite industry established procedures for the adjustment of disputes. Since the mine operators had bitterly opposed and fiercely fought recognition of the United Mine Workers as the miners' representative, it is not surprising that their opposition should have carried over to the newly

---

[6]*The New York Times,* Nov. 30, 1945, p. 17.

[7]From a statement of the National War Labor Board issued July 1, 1943, quoted in *The Termination Report of the National War Labor Board,* vol. I, 1947–48, pp. 65–66.

[8]Sidney Webb and Beatrice Webb, *The History of Trade Unionism,* London: Longmans, Green & Co., Ltd. 1950 pp. 304–306, 489; and H. A. Millis and R. E. Montgomery, *Organized Labor,* New York: McGraw-Hill Book Company, 1945, p. 251.

devised grievance procedure. The procedure applied to all anthracite mines and provided a top board to settle disputes under the agreement award, but it did not provide for bilateral grievance adjustment in the mines themselves. This was a serious weakness, for the operators could easily evade local compliance with the agreement. They denied the union any right to police their performance, insisting upon direct settlement with the individual employee who voiced an issue.

Not until 1912 was this flaw remedied and a comprehensive five-stage procedure set up. A miner who had a grievance was first to discuss the matter with his foreman in the mine. Failing a satisfactory settlement there, a local grievance committee of three fellow employees (commonly local union officials) met with company representatives. If still no agreement was reached, the two district members of the top board of conciliation—one for the union and one for the company—sought resolution of the dispute; and if unsuccessful they referred the matter to the full board of conciliation, consisting of three members each for the union and the company, elected by districts. In all these steps the attempt was to settle the issue by bilateral discussion, which of course did not guarantee settlement. Such an assurance was provided, however, in the final stage—decision by an umpire chosen for each case as needed.[9]

Union's and employers' recognition and use of a grievance procedure offered a reasonable hope for, and encouraged the practice of, prompt and equitable settlement of disputes. Collective bargaining increasingly came to be a more readily available process. Not only the union leaders and top managers but also the lowest union member, the shop steward, and the foreman could participate daily in its operation.

Trial and Error in Coal Mining

The impact on miner-operator relationships has been reported by one who made a study of the system after its first ten years of operation. Noting that the extended series of stages of discussion were designed to encourage settlement by the parties themselves and "to eliminate as far as possible the element of arbitration," this investigator commented:

> At the same time it must be remembered that the average individual mine worker naturally looks upon the enterprise process of settling disputes as a series of appeals from the decisions of his employer or of his employer's representatives. He has been accustomed to look for compulsion from his employer, and at one time his only method of appeal from his employer's decision was the strike. The new method of

[9]In practice, however, the parties so frequently selected one of three men (Carroll D. Wright and Charles P. Neill, both former United State Commissioners of Labor, and former United States Circuit Judge George Grey) that it may almost be said that they made use of permanent umpires. Edgar Sydenstricker, *Collective Bargaining in the Anthracite Coal Industry,* Bureau of Labor Statistics Bulletin 191 (1916), p. 97.

"conciliation" is to him a means by which he can refer his employer's decision to some other authority.[10]

No figures are available on the number of grievance discussed prior to inauguration of the formal system of 1903, but it is clear that they were rarely aired.[11] And although the number of grievances processed is not a sufficient indication of the health and vitality of employee-employer relationships, the large increase in the number of grievances occurring after 1903 suggests that complaints miners previously would have nursed silently were now being brought into the open, talked about, and settled. In the ten-year period ending in 1913, two hundred fifty-three cases were presented to the board of conciliation. Of these, the board refused to entertain five; thirty-two were settled by the parties themselves before the board proceeded to a hearing; and another eighty-nine were withdrawn by the complainant, often indicating informal agreement. Seventy-eight decisions were rendered by the board, and forty-nine disputes had to be submitted to an umpire. Wage issues predominated throughout the period. The unwillingness of the employers to accept the union is indicated by the fact that charges of discrimination against workers for the union activity made up the second-largest grievance category.

Developments in the Clothing Industry

Perhaps even more publicized than the procedures for dispute settlement instituted by the anthracite coal award was the permanent grievance system adopted in the clothing industry in the years before World War I. A formal adjustment procedure was established in the Hart, Schaffner and Marx Company in Chicago following a strike in 1910; and it is sometimes said to be the first successful experience in working out a "comprehensive plan for the adjustment of labor disputes in an individual business concern.[12] A marketwide strike in the cloak, suit, and skirt industry of New York City in the same year was terminated with the protocol,[13] a landmark in the history of union-management relations; among its provisions it contained the plan for a board of grievances and a board of arbitration. This elaborate system covered an employers' association (the Cloak, Suit, and Skirt Manufacturers' Protective Association, whose membership was made up of numerous small-scale shop owners) and nine locals of the International Ladies' Garment Workers Union, known collectively by the name of their central body, the Joint Board of the

---

[10]Ibid., p. 89.

[11]Ibid.

[12]Thomas Tongue, "The Development of Industrial Conciliation and Arbitration under Trade Agreements," *Oregon Law Review,* vol. 17, 1938, p. 270.

[13]A most interesting account of the strike and subsequent negotiations is contained in Alpheus T. Mason, *Brandeis: A Free Man's Life,* New York: The Viking Press, Inc., 1946, chap. 19. Louis D. Brandeis, later an associate justice of the United States Supreme Court, was largely instrumental in the acceptance by both parties of the terms of the Protocol.

Cloak and Skirt Makers' Unions. The four-step grievance procedure gave the individual worker or shop owner the opportunity to present complaints to immediately available grievance representatives and to appeal the grievance through the succeeding steps if dissatisfied with the disposition of the case. If the case was important enough, it might finally be taken to the three-member board of arbitration, of whom one was a neutral representative.

By their example in using a grievance procedure, employers and union leaders in the clothing and anthracite coal industries greatly influenced the American approach to dispute settlement under collective agreements. The older unions in the twenties and the mass-production unions in the thirties sought to establish the same basic grievance procedure—several successive steps through which the worker and a representative might appeal a grievance if necessary to a final hearing and decision by an outside party. The nature of the typical appeals procedure can perhaps be better appreciated by tracing through the various steps of an actual case.

A TYPICAL GRIEVANCE AND ITS SETTLEMENT

Believing that she had unjustifiably been denied the opportunity to work on a regular day, Jo Parcy informally complained to her supervisor, Lee Madison. Madison told her that nothing could be done. It was a tough break, but there was no violation of the agreement and thus no remedy. Dissatisfied with the answer, Parcy sought out her shop steward, J. D. Nettler, and together they drafted a formal grievance:

> On January 4, I came to work on my regular shift. But for reasons beyond my control, due to icy streets, the city buses which are my only means of transportation made it impossible for me to get here before 7:50 A.M., fifty minutes after starting time. My home was contacted by supervision, and was informed that I was on my way. When I arrived I was not admitted to the plant for they had called somebody to replace me. I feel the whole thing is unjustified and am asking to be compensated for 8 hours lost time at the rates provided for in Article 8(d)(l) [the reporting pay provision][14] of the agreement.

> Representative of Local No. 2   Complainant
> s/J. D. Nettler   s/Josephine Parcy

Three days after Nettler filed the grievance with Madison, he and Madison and Parcy met to discuss the matter. Although he was sympathetic to Parcy's loss, Madison pointed out that he could not run the packaging department shorthanded, storm or no storm. After waiting nearly forty-five minutes, he had called in another employee who lived across the street from the plant. By

---

[14]Article 8, "Reporting for Work Pay": "When an employee reports for work at the regular shift time without having been notified to the contrary by his or her supervisor . . . and is not assigned work, the employee shall be paid for one-half the normal shift at the rate of 75 units per hour at the base rate or at the hourly rate customarily paid."

waiting for Parcy, the company had lost money, and he could not see that it was right for it to pay out more. Though he did not discuss his underlying concern at the meeting, Madison knew that any pay awarded to Parcy would put him over his allotted budget for the final packaging-inspection job. He was anxious not to incur any extra labor costs in his department, for the company had been pressing its supervisors to keep within their budgets and offering bonuses to those who trimmed costs below the budgets. Nettler replied that if Madison was going to take such a hardnosed stand, they would turn the grievance over to the chief steward and take it to Mr. Coppers, the department superintendent.

Several days later, Parcy, Nettler, and Madison met with the chief steward and Coppers in the latter's office. They reexamined the matter carefully, arguing at length about the exact times when Parcy reported in and when her replacement was called, but agreeing in general on the facts of the case. Coppers said that he had gone over the matter with Meyers, an assistant in the industrial relations department, and that neither of them could find any violation of the agreement in the way the supervisor had handled the matter. "It is admitted that transportation was difficult on the morning involved," he wrote in his answer after the meeting, "but this has no bearing on the fact that jobs must be covered. I feel there is no justification for this request for lost time, and it is therefore rejected." In order to be fair, he suggested that he would be willing to let Parcy work to make up the hours she had lost, but not at overtime; Coppers, too, did not want to add any extra labor costs in his department. After some heated discussion, the chief steward and Nettler rejected the suggestion. They pointed out that Parcy could legally work the hours only as a fill-in over the next few months during weeks when, because of layoffs, she would work fewer than forty hours. Furthermore, there would be seniority complication and no end of trouble.

Parcy and Nettler appealed the grievance to the third step, in which the plant grievance committee and the director of industrial relations and two of his aides considered the matter at their next regularly scheduled meeting. They called in Parcy and Madison and questioned them carefully. After Parcy and Madison had left the meeting, the grievance chairman argued that Parcy had acted in good faith and that the company ought to show its good faith. Simply to dismiss the grievance would be shoddy treatment of a loyal, long-service employee. He pointed out that other employees knew about the case and would take careful note of the company's decision. "We think it is a question of whether you think penny-pinching or a loyal work force is more important to the company. We've always said room 313 [the accounting office] really runs this place. If you turn Parcy down, it'll prove it."

The director granted that the situation was "rather unusual, where Parcy, through no fault of her own, arrived after a replacement had been arranged to take her place. There is no contract violation in denying her work, though, under the circumstances of this particular day.... However, considering the worker and her efforts to meet the shift schedule, the company feels that she should not be unduly penalized." The director proposed that if the union would agree that the case was an unusual one and in no way established a precedent, the company would agree to compensate Parcy with four hours of reporting pay, the allowance due employees who are called to work on days when no work is available.

Parcy was still dissatisfied, but the chairman told her that the grievance committee did not feel it would make sense for the union to spend $500 to take the case to arbitration on the chances of winning only one worker's pay for a day. Parcy felt she had no choice but to accept the settlement.

This case illustrates the most conspicuous elements of a typical grievance procedure. At each of several succeeding steps, the grievance may be appealed to higher-ranking officers who are less likely to be personally involved in the case and are more likely to be able to judge it on its merits. In the first step a single union representative (usually called the steward, committeeman, or representative) meets with the supervisor to try to settle the problem at its source. The final bilateral discussions commonly take place between the union's plant grievance committee and the company's industrial relations officers, who meet regularly in an effort to solve problems before grievances arise and also to settle grievances appealed to them. The activity of the bilateral meetings might be likened to that of a professional fire department, which not only helps put out fires but also seeks to prevent fires before they start. The lower steps are more like those in a volunteer fire department, which is available only when called.

VARIATIONS IN PROCEDURES

Agreements generally provide for three to four steps, though a few may list as many as five.[15] The number does not increase proportionally with the size of the company, for promptness is an essential characteristic of successful grievance settlement. A multiplication of steps in a large company, where employees may file thousands of grievances each year, would lead to an intolerably expensive procedure if delay is to be avoided.

Variations in grievance procedures are common as union and management negotiators seek to adapt to special circumstances and experiences. One agreement may require answers to grievances within twenty-four hours, and another may require answers within ten days. About half of the sample agreements in the BNA study specify how grievances must be presented; fewer than 55 percent of these require grievances to be in writing, and the remainder allow them to be made orally.[16] About the same proportions specify management's response in like fashion. Some agreements define grievances widely and others define them narrowly. Roughly three-fifths of the BNA's sample of agreements

[15]Editors of Collective Bargaining Negotiations and Contracts, *Basic Patterns in Union Contracts,* pp. 11–17.

[16]Editors of Collective Bargaining Negotiations and Contracts, *Basic Patterns in Union Contracts,* p. 12.

permit grievances over any interpretation or application of their provisions; about one-fifth describe only certain disputes as grievable; and somewhat fewer than one-fifth exclude various complaints. Some grievances, such as those involving a large number of workers or discharge cases, may skip initial steps. Two-thirds of the BNA's sample provide for such special handling.

Small Union Locals

Small union locals may bring in a representative from the national union at an early step to give expert guidance and help; large locals often use expert grievance representatives in disputes over health and welfare compensation, unemployment benefits, time study, apprenticeship, or job classification. These experts meet with appropriate company representatives, specialists who try to settle, outside regular procedures, the knotty grievances arising from particularly complex provisions. Almost half of all agreements in manufacturing and about a fifth in nonmanufacturing have provision for joint committees to investigate and resolve safety issues.[17]

The Farm Workers

In some industries, because of peculiar circumstances, grievance procedures vary considerably from the typical. The United Farm Workers, for example, do not have local unions and thus have no stable leadership at the place of work to process grievances. Its members migrate from one ranch to another as the seasons and harvests change; when a rancher hires a work force at harvest time, union members elect at least one ranch committee that performs many of the functions for which local union officers and shop stewards are responsible in work places of more stable employment. The seasonality of work and the continual turnover among those elected to the ranch committees creates considerable inefficiency in the administration of the agreement and often frustrates quick settlement of grievances.[18] Seasonal work and a constantly changing place of work pose special problems for grievance handling in the building trades as well. In addition, construction foremen are usually union members, and several employers and unions will almost always be involved at each building site. Standard grievance procedures do not meet the needs of either workers or employers in such a situation. The unions' appointed business agents have responsibility for members scattered in sites over wide geographic areas, and they, rather than employers or supervisors, are apt to be the key decision makers in grievance settlement. With unsteady work and continual turnover, the workers seldom raise grievances about promotions or discharges; but they regularly challenge management about hiring, particularly hires not

---

[17]Bureau of Labor Statistics, *Characteristics of Major Collective Bargaining Agreements,* January 1, 1978, Bulletin 2065, Washington: Government Printing Office, 1980, table 2.7, p. 25.
[18]Koziara, "Agriculture," p. 288.

made through the union. Overtime payments and fringe-benefit contributions are also frequent issues of dispute.

Construction and Trucking

In neither construction nor trucking have employers and unions made much use of arbitration as a final grievance step. The pace of work moves so quickly in construction and the moving of workers from site to site is so frequent there is no time for a multistep, long procedure. Both parties have settled for "instant justice." Professor D. Quinn explains:

> When the job steward and the employer's superintendent fail to settle a[n informal] grievance, the business agent of the local union intervenes. If he is also unsuccessful, a strike is likely to be called on the spot. The grievance, and the strike, are then settled in some manner.[19]

In trucking the formal grievance procedures resemble those found in most unionized manufacturing plants, but in fact the system operates quite differently. At least since the time of James Hoffa as national president, the Teamsters have pressed for informal and open-ended procedures. There is no arbitration, except for discharge cases, and that only at local option. With no formal explanation for particular settlements and no body of precedents created, union officials retain a high degree of flexibility in the resolution of grievances. Of course, such informality and avoidance of legalisms lends itself to abuse—favoritism among employees and discriminatory treatment among workers.[20]

Public Employees

The development of union-management grievance procedures for public employees has been complicated by existing civil service complaint systems. Traditionally, civil service commissions have protected workers within their jurisdiction from arbitrary treatment, establishing detailed rules for hiring, transfers, promotion, and dismissal. In the sixties and seventies the federal government and a majority of state governments established grievance procedures through which employees could appeal complaints arising under the labor-management agreement. They were modeled on grievance procedures in the private sector.[21] With their introduction, confusion has sometimes arisen about which procedures to use for various worker complaints or job disputes.

---

[19]Mills, "Construction," pp. 88–89.
[20]See Levinson, "Trucking," pp. 128–129.
[21]See James P. Begin, "The Private Grievance Model in the Public Sector," *Industrial Relations,* vol. 10, February 1971, pp. 21–35; James E. Martin, "Application of a Model From the Private Sector to Federal Sector Labor Relations," *The Quarterly Journal of Economics and Business,* vol. 16, Winter 1976, pp. 69–78; and "Summary of State Labor Laws," *Government Employees Relations Report,* Washington, D.C.: Bureau of National Affairs, June 26, 1978, Ref. File 51: 501–531.

Union leaders are tempted to use the two procedures selectively, choosing the one that proves most efficacious for a particular kind of grievance.[22] Understandably, public managers find such a union choice disadvantageous to themselves; they have recommended or secured changes that require employees to use one or the other procedures, but not both. In 1977 the Los Angeles County Board of Supervisors proposed to eliminate civil service protection for all public employees in bargaining units, except in matters of hiring and promotion. The federal government chose an alternative solution. Under Executive Order 11616, which sets the terms for union-manangement bargaining in federal agencies, workers cannot appeal discharges through their unions' negotiated grievance procedures. They must continue to use the civil service's statutory procedures, though they are entitled to union representation if they desire it.

The conflict and confusion over the dual grievance procedures will not be eliminated until legislators change the laws that mandate the provisions for civil service appeals. Until that time, public employees and their union representatives and public managers will have to make the best of their two, often parallel, systems.

THE SIGNIFICANCE OF THE PROCEDURE FOR WORKERS

The grievance steps specified in agreements serve different purposes in the settling of various grievances. As in other appeals procedures, the parties process fewer cases in each succeeding step, with the less contentious and more routine being settled first. By far the largest portion of grievances never progress beyond the first step, and probably even more complaints are never even formalized in writing. Despite the importance in fact of these early stages of the grievance process, union and management officials alike frequently belittle their importance in principle. Union officers often complain that the steps below the industrial relations level are mere formalities; and company managers admit that lower supervisors rely upon precedents in answering grievances, usually consulting with the top office before answering other grievances of whose import they are not sure.

The bulk of grievance settlement may look like mere formality to the union and company officers who deal with grievances at the higher levels. The grievances that engage their skill and interest often involve complex and novel matters of policy and interpretation of past settlements. But just because the chief company and union grievance handlers emphasize those issues (and the top-level procedural steps where they are resolved), the other and routine grievances are not therefore insignificant. They are not necessarily unimportant to the workers who originate them, nor do they prove to be unimportant in the whole grievance process. Focusing attention and concern on grievance arbitration and the step immediately preceding it tends to distort one's understanding

[22]See Alan E. Bent and T. Zane Reeves, *Collective Bargaining in the Public Sector,* Menlof Park, Calif.: The Benjamin/Cummings Publishing Co., 1978, pp. 35–37.

of the grievance process. It demeans the work carried on in the lower steps and magnifies unduly that performed in the higher, so that the whole grievance process appears to be dominatingly judicial in nature.

Adjudication

Adjudication is indeed an important function of the grievance process. While workers can expect a measure of impartiality in the upper stages of the grievance process, which are removed from the conflicts and tempers of the shop, arbitration by a neutral carries even greater assurance of equity. Workers value its results: protection against arbitrary managerial action, the opportunity for a full hearing, and recompense if they demonstrate that management infringed upon or denied their rights.

The advantage of judicial judgment is also its limitation; it protects workers' rights *after* management has acted—not before. The compensation provided by a grievance award may not be at all appropriate to the injury done. That supervisors should ignore the interests and rights of workers and give only tardy recognition to them can be an affront to the workers' dignity and self-respect. Workers thus seek through the grievance process not just compliance and compensation after the act but consultation before it.

Union members have shown themselves to have high expectations of their grievance process. Almost four-fifths of a random sample indicated that their union leaders should put a lot of effort into the handling of grievances. Fewer than one in twenty, however, thought the union was doing a very good job with grievances, and almost a quarter indicated performance was "not too good" or "not good at all."[23] The survey suggested that both unions and management need to work harder than they have to improve the system and thereby contribute to an important element in workers' quality of work life.

A Means of Communication and Administration

Many of the written grievances on record in company and union files indicate not so much dissatisfaction with specific management decisions as workers' frustration at being ignored in what they can contribute. They desire to have a hearing and a chance to express their feelings and opinions and to offer their knowledge. The complaints are often vague and unrelated to the agreement; but however complaints are written, supervisors are required to meet with the grievers and their stewards to consider the matters at issue respectfully and carefully. The consideration that supervisors and company officers must give to grievances probably helps explain why workers do not look upon the grievance process as a failure even though management rejects by far the largest

---

[23]Thomas A. Kochan, "How American Workers View Labor UNion," *Monthly Labor Review,* vol. 102, Apr. 1979, pp. 29–30.

ortion of all complaints. Even when grievance answers are less than
artial, as is the case sometimes at the lower levels, workers may be reason-
y satisfied just to have had an opportunity to express their views, to be lis-
ned to, and to hear directly and immediately the supervisors' arguments. The
iscussion may range far afield from the official complaints, giving the grievers
i chance to bring up other matters not properly arising in a formal complaint.
Thus the formal procedures merge into informal methods of treating work
problems.

General Motors' management found in the late seventies that its grievance
procedures were too formal. Over the decade it had received an average of well
over a quarter of a million written grievances per year—two grievances for
every three workers in the bargaining unit. In the 1979 negotiations the company proposed that the union join with it in encouraging stewards and supervisors to meet informally and attempt resolution of complaints before writing
them down.[24] Too much formality can certainly overload the procedures, making settlement slower and more distant from the workers involved. But without the formal procedures in place, there would be less reason to resolve disputes informally. A mix of both formal and informal approaches to grievances
will almost always produce better results than will one or the other by itself.

The formal grievance procedure ensures workers and their representatives
a chance to approach managers if informal relationships break down. Workers
are able informally to advise supervisors and company officers and to consult
with them. Union representatives and managers need to consider jointly the
problem of applying and interpreting customs, precedents, shop rules, and general provisions of the agreement. One probably cannot separate in fact the
administrative function from that of adjudication. The former is performed
through, and under the cover of, the judicial grievance procedure. Nevertheless, one may usefully and formally make the distinction.

Union representatives at the place of work can become highly competent in
and knowledgeable about industrial relations and the administration of the collective agreement. In some situations they play roles very similar to those of
management. Such is the case in both construction and trucking, as mentioned
above. In other cases in which management is diffused or fractured, as in city
and local governments, the full-time union grievance handlers find themselves
pushed by circumstances to assume managerial responsibilities. For example,
District Council 37 of the American Federation of State, County and Municipal Workers, in New York City, enrolls over 10,000 members in many different mayoral offices, semi-independent city agencies, and special administration bodies, from hospitals to museums, schools to parks, and jails to license
bureaus. The District Council provides a more centralized and coherent system for interpreting personnel policies and processing grievances than the city
itself does. In order to prevent disputes and conflicts between different groups

---

[24]Berenbeim, *Nonunion Complaint Systems: A Corporate Appraisal*, p. 9.

of workers within its membership, the Council officers must often coordinate grievance settlements and work out administration details, the implication of which local managers may be able to ignore or overlook.[25]

The Role of the Shop Steward

In most companies that recognize unions, key union stewards work full-time at handling grievances. Only a small minority of companies either do not pay such full-time union officials or strictly limit the time they may spend on grievance work. The pay, in total, can reach impressive sums. General Motors in 1970 complained that in the previous year "it had paid in its plants more than 13 million [32 million in 1981] dollars to union committeemen who do not work on assembly lines or at machines, but who represent union members in disputes with management.[26] Although they do not work at the regular jobs for which they were originally hired, the member-elected stewards do work, and usually long and hard, at handling grievances. They become familiar with all parts of the plant, meeting managers and workers at every level and getting to know the individuals of importance in the company bureaucracy. They can aid managers or hinder them no little bit. Whether they are originally intended to or not, union representatives at the place of work participate to a surprising degree in activities that managers publicly insist are strictly their concern.[27]

Union representatives help administer such matters as training programs, subcontracting arrangements, programs for improving use of machines and installing equipment, job classification plans, and incentive pay systems. They typically help administer seniority provisions: bumping rise in layoffs; seniority claims to preferred jobs, shifts, and location; priorities in transfers; and order of recall as work picks up. These often extremely complex problems are well suited for joint administration, as many managers recognize. At the same time, to join managers in resolving any issue that discriminates among workers on the basis of personal judgment, not objective criteria, puts union representatives in an uncomfortable position. In such instances they often prefer to offer their advice informally; it is politically safer to serve on those administrative committees that deal with relatively uncontroversial issues such as safety, apprenticeship, absenteeism, and community fund drives.

By assuming administrative duties, unions have extended their influence beyond the compliance and judicial purposes of the grievance process, but they have kept within its original spirit. When properly carried out, both functions

---

[25]For more detais see David Lewin, Raymond D. Horton, and James W. Kuhn, *Collective Bargaining and Manpower Utilization in Big City Governments,* Montclair, N.J.: Allanheld, Osmun, 1979, Chap. 5, pp. 97–121.

[26]William Serrin, *The Company and the Union,* New York: Alfred A. Knopf, 1973, p. 156.

[27]The Supreme Court has ruled that union representatives must be involved in disciplinary matters as soon as managers talk to the employee. Previously, when an employee was suspected of an action that could lead to suspension or discharge, managers could question that employee privately, not having to notify the steward or local union officers until after they had acted. See *NLRB v. Weingarten, Inc.,* 420 U.S. 251 (1975).

contribute to stable, peaceful relationships between unions and management during the life of an agreement.

A news reporter well described the vital work a shop steward performs to the benefit of the workers, union, and management. He wrote about a district committeeman at a Ford Motor Company assembly plant in Wixom, Michigan.

> [He was] elected by the 287 people in his department to serve as the full-time representative with management. . . . But unofficially [he] *is* the union to his people. He is the first and often the only union representative they deal with, and is every bit as important to them as is . . . the UAW president. . . . [He] seems to spend much of his time roaming around, slapping people on the back, chit-chatting and poking his head into unfinished cars to check things out. But it's all done for a purpose: finding problems. "The main function of a committeeman is to settle problems right on the floor," [he] says. "I'm a mediator, a foot-soldier out there. Without the committeemen, Ford couldn't run the plant." Ford might dispute this assertion, but there is no denying that [his] meanderings uncover problems—or that he is the man on the spot.[28]

The role of such a steward, with the power to contribute to the smooth running of the plant's operations, does not just happen; a successful grievance system makes large demands upon the effort, honesty, patience, and understanding of both managers and union leaders. Supervisors must be willing to admit their mistakes; stewards cannot push grievances simply to enhance their political reputations, nor can they push worthless grievances out of weakness. Industrial relations officers and members of plant grievance committees must not duck the tough decisions unfavorable to their side by passing the buck to an arbitrator. Neither can they concentrate all settlements in their own hands, stifling lower-level settlement. To do so militates against prompt action and can lead to settlements that show little understanding of conditions at the place of work.

Problems in Grievance Handling

At times and under some circumstances company and union officers are not able to meet the requirements of an effective grievance process discussed above. First, the more centralized a company's administration, the more grievances get pushed to higher levels of authority and the more workers grieve. Presumably, workers find both delays involved in distant settlement and centralized managerial control, in itself, less satisfactory.[29] Second, supervisory styles greatly influence both the number of grievances and the level of settlement. Supervisors who act arbitrarily, emphasizing their formal authority at the

---

[28]Walter Morsberg, "As Union Man at Ford, Charlie Bragg Deals with Problems, Gripes," *The Wall Street Journal,* July 26, 1973.

[29]David A. Peach and E. Robert Livernash, *Grievance Initiation and Resolution: A Study in Basic Steel,* Cambridge; Harvard University Press, 1974, pp. 89–152.

expense of workers' trust and consideration, tend to stimulate grievances and find them difficult to settle in the early steps.[30]

The third reason centralized administration seems less satisfactory is that stewards and union officers handling grievances must regularly stand for election, and they often find politics looming large in their dealings. The more hotly contested the local elections, the more likely it is that those who handle grievances will find political considerations influencing the grievances filed and the level at which they are settled. Politics appear to affect disciplinary grievances in particular.[31] One manager in a large multiplant company explained:

> The grievance procedure is effective in cycles. . . . Number one, the union is a political animal; they are elected, have to satisfy their constituency, to *assume* the vote. . . . *Six* to seven months before election time they won't settle, won't give in in bargaining. It's very difficult to give in at these times. The number of grievances in process will grow.[32]

Moreover certain workers tend to grieve more than others. As work forces change, or if a department or plant employs a large number of "grieving" workers, grievance procedures can become strained and ineffective in resolving disputes. Among those most likely to grieve are the younger, better-schooled workers and union activists; grievers also tend to be workers who have more absences, take more sick leave, have poorer disciplinary records, earn less, and have won fewer wage increases than nongrievers.[33] The four influences upon the grievance process—the structure of management, the style of management, union politics, and the kind of work force—are only the most prominent among many. So large a number of diverse influences does not permit easy predictions of grievance outcomes or of the effectiveness of a particular grievance system. Neither can be evaluated without careful and detailed examination.

THE GRIEVANCE HANDLERS AND FRACTIONAL BARGAINING

Both union and management need to have informed representatives available at all times to handle grievances as they arise. For the system to work only occasionally and spasmodically would defeat its basic purpose. When complaints are unattended, workers become disgruntled and tension rises in the shop. Supervisors and stewards need to know the agreement reasonably well

---

[30]E. A. Fleishman and E. F. Harris, "Patterns of Leadership Behavior Related to Employee Grievances and Turnover," *Personnel Psychology,* vol. 15, 1972, pp. 43–56.

[31]Jeffrey Gandz, "Employee Grievances: Incidence and Patterns of Resolution," *Proceedings of the Thirty-first Annual Meeting,* Industrial Relations Research Association, Aug. 1978, pp. 167–168.

[32]Quoted by R. Herding, *Job Control and Union Structure,* Rotterdam: Rotterdam University, Press, 1972, p. 186.

[33]Philip Ash, "The Parties to the Grievance," *Personnel Psychology,* vol. 23, spring 1970, pp. 13–38; and John Prices et al., "Three Studies of Grievances," *Personnel Journal,* Jan. 1976, pp, 32–37.

and to be kept up to date on arbitration decisions and high-level settlements. They need to understand the procedures, supplying answers, conducting inquiries, and remedying errors in accordance with the rules and provisions of the agreement. Training is vital and experience helpful in providing representatives who can handle grievances in an informed way.

To ensure the availabiltity of grievance settlement, unions must provide an adequate number of representives at the place of work. (At General Motors, the UAW elects one district representative for each 250 employees covered by the agreement. In plants with 500 or fewer workers, the members may elect 3; in plants with 500 to 1000 workers, 5; and in plants of 1000 to 1500, 7 representatives.) Typically, the workers elect from among the ranks of their own department or work group. If a representative should quit or be discharged or promoted, the workers select a replacement at a new election. If a representative is laid off in slack times, with the probability that he or she will be called back in a few days or weeks, there is little point in calling a new election; yet without a representative the constituents would not be well served. The representative might also be absent during work because of low seniority standing. To meet the requirements of availability, many agreements provide superseniority for union officers who handle grievances. Of the BNA sample of agreements, 45 percent assure special job security to grievance representatives, with more than half the agreements in manufacturing but only a third in nonmanufacturing including such assurances.

Being at the place of work, however, does not help representatives to handle and investigate grievances unless they have some freedom to leave their workstations and move about appropriate areas of the plant to talk with workers, other union officers, and supervisors. Agreements almost always guarantee representatives the right to interrupt their jobs, after notifying their supervisors, to take care of grievance duties. For time spent off the job on legitimate grievance work, the union, the company, or both jointly reimburse representatives at their regular rates of pay.

Shop representatives must be more than merely available if they are to be effective. They must feel free to challenge management with no threat of retaliation. For this reason, union members fiercely defend their shop representatives, resisting any management attempts to limit their activities or to discriminate against them. As a result, workers and union leaders sometimes defend a representative's behavior even when it is of a kind that would receive little or no defense if engaged in by a rank-and-file employee. Although they are not immune from company discipline, able and active shop stewards can affirm a point of view more or less independently of management. Their independence, influence with the workers, and administrative duties (formal and informal) give them a position of importance in the shop. Often they become secondary or even equal centers of power in the shop, sometimes rivaling the supervisor and higher line managers. This development of shop representatives, when mixed with the democratic politics of the shop and the dynamics of work flows, production schedules, and shop technologies, significantly alters the basis and function of the grievance process.

Bargaining in the Grievance Process

Two assumptions underlie the premise that peaceful grievance settlement can be assured if union leaders and managers fulfill the prerequisite of continuous, responsible, and informal good-faith handling of grievances. The first is that the negotiators of the collective agreement are in fact as well as in law the representatives of all the workers and supervisors: the only two relevant organizations are the local union and the plant management. The second assumption is that in adjudicating, interpreting, and applying the terms of an agreement, the daily negotiators enjoy approximately the same relative bargaining power as did those who agreed to the overall terms of the agreement.

The assumptions are valid only as long as workers can expect, and are willing, to fulfill their job demands through the regular union organization and will accomplish their work goals in accordance with the regulations set forth or agreed to by the official negotiators. These assumptions are often invalidated by particular segments of the work force. The technology in many industries enables small groups of specialized or strategic workers to interface with the production of a whole plant or a complete assembly-line operation. Their bargaining power is thus often greater than that of the local union as a whole. Through job action they can inflict upon management losses greatly disproportionate to their numbers. Moreover, the cost of "buying off" their demands—even though their action is in violation of the agreement—is usually much smaller than the loss they can impose.

Likewise, some technologies and changing work conditions give supervisors an advantageous bargaining position from time to time, enabling them to get adjustments of work rules or to negotiate with the shop representatives for more freedom to assign, transfer, promote, or rate workers. Special conditions, therefore, sometimes put one or the other of the parties in the shop in a position to bargain for benefits not secured in the collective agreement.

Furthermore, members of work groups and shop supervisors often grasp this opportunity since they may feel a greater sense of responsibility to settle their own shop problems than to adhere to policies of the wider organizations. The centralization of personnel and industrial relations authority in staff groups tends to insulate supervisors from a sense of responsibility to company policy. And in large industrial unions where work groups of many different skills and varying work interests are enrolled, the diverse workers not infrequently develop a greater sense of loyalty to their own work groups than to the union. Thus it is that where once the grievance procedure seemed to promise peaceful settlement of disputes arising after the collective agreement was signed, in some situations the basis for the promise has been so undermined or weakened as to make the promise only conditional.

One finds throughout American industry, and particularly in the great mass-production plants, occasional and even frequent use of disruptive bargaining tactics, subtle sabotage of production, overtime bans, slowdowns, and unauthorized, "wildcat" strikes. A close study of the relationship between workers and supervisors at the place of work reveals that each party applies pressure on the other to force or to induce settlements favorable to itself. What was supposedly eliminated and made unnecessary by the grievance procedure in fact still exists or has reappeared in a different guise.

The Local Sources of Bargaining Power

Shop controversies conducive to bargaining in the grievance process arise from a number of sources. One source is the range of discretion that is permitted both by provisions of the agreement and by shop rules. For example, supervisors can discriminate through discipline and commendation of workers or through assignment of work among a crew. The line between allowable and improper discretion is a fine one, but workers and supervisors daily measure it so closely that even slight changes are significant to them. Under the agreement, supervisors are usually allowed in emergencies to perform work normally done by a member of the bargaining unit. Union representatives and supervisors may define an emergency quite differently in different cases and may bargain over the criteria to apply in different situations. Or an agreement may grant workers reasonable time for personal needs. When production schedules lag, supervisors may decide that a reasonable time is noticeably shorter than when work is slack. Workers may feel that a reasonable time should vary with their needs, not the supervisor's.

Another source of local shop bargaining is the agreement that fixes only the method or standard of settlement, but not specific terms. In the case of piecework rates, bargaining is essential since a rate of exchange is set between a subjective element and an output of a given product.[34] There is no reason to expect that a company time-study expert and the workers will automatically reach the same judgment as to the proper effort for a given output. Other bargaining issues arise if workers become dissatisfied with changes in their condition and see ways of exerting pressure to secure remedies. Under long-term agreements, workers probably feel the need for introducing a flexibility that allows them to adjust the agreement and its provisions. Technologies, employment opportunities, and economic conditions that change rapidly can quickly make fixed agreements intolerable if there is no chance for modification and adjustment.

The largely informal bargaining that is conducted under the cover of the grievance procedures should not be confused with the collective bargaining that produces the overall agreement. Rather than the whole of the local union, only groups of workers and their representatives—fractions of the plant work force—engage in grievance bargaining. For this reason, the term "fractional bargaining" is appropriately and usefully applied to it. Individual workers or single shop representatives do not typically conduct fractional bargaining, for

[34]More than half the major agreements, covering 70 percent of the workers, provide incentive wage systems in manufacturing; incentive systems are rare in nonmanufacturing, with only 3 percent of the agreements including them. See *Characteristics of Major Collective Bargaining Agreements,* Bureau of Labor Statistics Bulletin 2095, January 1, 1980, table 3.2. p. 41.

only under unusual circumstances would an individual be able to exert enough pressure upon supervisors to force them to bargain. An individual's grievance has a fair chance of being considered on its merits. The grievance of work group, however, is just as likely to be considered on the merits of the group's bargaining power as upon the merits of the grievance. Since the response of a group of workers to a settlement may be a matter of pressing concern to supervisors racing to meet a production deadline, expediency may, and often does, temper considerations of merit. Supervisors can ignore group demands only at risk. Their own advancements, bonuses, and job security depend more on getting production out or cutting unit costs than on following the provisions of the agreement. If a work group wishes to speed up management, hurry along a grievance hearing, or gain some special privileges for its members in terms of pay, seniority, hours, or workload, supervisors may well be tempted to agree in the face of a threatened walkout or slowdown if the cost to one or another of them is not too high. That the cost to the company in other departments may be high indeed may not weigh heavily. Professor Al Nash described such a situation in an auto plant where he once served as committeeman. His group had filed a grievance about a leaking roof over the assembly line, but management did not respond. As the grievance slowly wound its way through one level to another, he and the workers decided to apply some extra pressure. First, he donned a pith helmet at work as he walked the line to dramatize the need for protection from the rain. There was no result. He then brought in an umbrella and held it over the workers, pretending to shield them from the dripping rain.

> Finally, when these tactics failed to provide a solution, I discreetly encouraged the workers affected by the rain to go to the men's room in a body with a case of mass diarrhea. The roof was soon repaired.[35]

Individual and Group Grievances

Shop representatives, as well as supervisors, approach group grievances differently from the way they approach the grievances of individuals; when grievances affect more voters, they have a higher political potential for elected representatives. A shop steward may be a union officer and legally bound to act only in the interests of the whole union, but politically the position is held on the suffrance of the work group; the steward must be responsive to the work group before he or she can be responsible to the larger organization. Thus, only at the higher, less locally involved levels can union and management organizations afford the luxury of not recognizing work groups. Supervisors and shop stewards must contend with them. They do so not because they are irresponsible, but because they do not always have practical alternatives.

Work groups existed before there were grievance procedures and even before there were unions;[36] the flow of production and its technology have long

---

[35]Al Nash, "The Local Union: Center of Life in the UAW," *Dissent*, vol. 25, Fall 1978, p. 402.
[36]Stanley B. Mathewson, *Restriction of Output among Unorganized Workers*, New York: The Viking Press, Inc., 1931, pp. 15–127.

grouped workers of similar skills, fostering among them common interests and a sense of self-identification that may be stronger than identification with the union.[37] The rise of unionism and the development of the grievance procedure, however, have given work groups a protected position, continuity, and unity of action that they did not enjoy before. With no union to protest, managers could hire, fire, and discipline workers at will, without having to answer to anyone. Any workers or group of workers who withheld or who were suspected of withholding cooperation lost their jobs. Any continued, organized opposition or resistance to management was nearly impossible.

Problems and Benefits of Fractional Bargaining

Now that the collective agreement limits the authority of management, workers can more openly group themselves around the privileged shop representatives and collectively act in their own interests. Under the protection of the agreement, they can with greater immunity engage in activities that earlier would have brought penalties. Using organized tactics, they can now force supervisors and even higher managers to bargain with them, and sometimes they gain their narrow, parochial demands, uncompromised by the conflicting demands and needs of other groups just as deserving.

Paradoxically, then, collective bargaining and unions have helped to strengthen the identity and power of fractional groups, where such groups can form and maintain themselves. Grievance procedures and the presence of the protected shop steward sometimes favor the growth of a power center within, though not necessarily an integral part of, the local union. The procedures and the protection are not alone responsible for the power center, but they have given it new direction and strength. They have given some workers an opportunity to organize themselves into semiautonomous groups in the shop, to which they show more loyalty than they do to the union.

Understandably, neither top union leaders nor management officials have shown much enthusiasm for recognizing the autonomy of work groups and the legitimacy of their fractional bargaining. Such recognition might encourage a kind of anarchy within the union, corrupting the broader loyalties of the members and shop representatives and benefiting a few work groups in a strong bargaining position at the expense of others less advantageously situated. For managers, fractional bargaining has two obvious consequences. First, it may lead to interruption of production, for even where workers seldom engage in work stoppages and more overt tactics, they can subtly disrupt production as they apply pressure to supervisors. Second, fractional bargaining can bring about confusion and conflict in company policy if supervisors in different parts of a plant or company settle grievances in different ways. In time the integrity of the collective agreement itself can be destroyed, to the detriment of union and management.

---

[37]See Leonard R. Sayles, *Behavior of Industrial Work Groups,* New York: John Wiley & Sons, Inc., 1958.

Notwithstanding the undesirable consequences of fractional bargaining over grievances, the value of the grievance system is not destroyed. Many, if not most, grievances and problems arising during the life of an agreement can be, and usually are, settled peacefully and equitably. Furthermore, even fractional bargaining has advantages that should not be forgotten. Shop determination of such matters as worker rotation in jobs, overtime assignment, seniority in job placement, and local variation in other matters such as job classification and even pay rates can be advantageous, allowing large firms to adapt more expeditiously to local opportunities and immediate circumstances. When tools, machines, and techniques change rapidly, as they do in many American industries, managers and union leaders need to explore and consider more than one approach in coordinating the efforts of workers and the rhythm of machines. Stability and peace are not the only characteristics of good industrial relations. The industrial process presents us with so many variables and unknowns that flexibility and experimentation also commend themselves.

Besides the benefits that can accrue to the firm and union from fractional bargaining, there are benefits for workers too. In the daily informality of the work group, workers probably have a better chance to participate in decisions, to be heard, and to make their influence felt than in even the local union. If workers gain increased satisfaction from participation in the bargaining maneuvers and if a meaningful industrial democracy is thereby encouraged, the dimming of the utopian promise of peaceful settlement of all disputes may not be too high a price to pay. The grievance system in practice promises less, and yet at the same time more, than those who developed it foresaw.[38]

NONUNION COMPLAINT PROCEDURES

Although complaint procedures roughly comparable to those described above are found in some unorganized companies and appear to be spreading, most managements have introduced them reluctantly. No good surveys of nonunion complaint procedures have yet been made, but a few nonrandom samples of company systems suggest that it is the managements of large manufacturing firms that tend to adopt them. Both their size and their blue-collar work force make them favored union targets, of course. The National Industrial Conference Board found that the larger the proportion of nonunionized employees (legally free to join a union), the more likely a company is to have established a system. The board's researchers report that this relationship indicates:

> that "employee complaint systems are a significant element in union prevention strategy . . . [and] companies that resort to the specialized assistance of consulting or industry groups in the development of union avoidance policy are much more likely to have such systems than companies that do not."[39]

---

[38]The issues involved in fractional bargaining are explored at greater length in James W. Kuhn, *Bargaining in Grievance Settlement,* New York: Columbia University Press, 1961.

[39]Berenbeim, *Nonunion Complaint Systems: A Corporate Appraisal,* pp. 3–5. See also David W. Ewing, "What Business Thinks About Employee Rights," *Harvard Business Review,* Sep.–Oct. 1977, vol. 55, pp. 81–94.

A kind of implicit or unilateral bargaining appears to be involved. Perceiving a possible challenge or threat by union-organizing drives, managers respond by offering their employees terms and conditions equal or similar to those promised by union leaders. Along with comparable pay and fringes, they offer variations of a grievance procedure. The effectiveness and long-term success of these managerial complaint systems remain to be tested. Managers' ambivalence toward them suggests that they will not prove very satisfactory to workers with persistent complaints. While managers would like to encourage workers to bring forth complaints, they prefer not to define them carefully or to formalize the system. Furthermore, almost none has opted for a final step involving arbitration. Thus, establishing the systems' credibility with employees and persuading them to use them has seldom been easy.

Only a few managements have yet devised workable complaint systems, and others are challenged by unions with compelling pressure to develop more effective procedures. Legally, managers of nonunion employees have long been able to discipline and fire workers at will, as noted above. But legislatures have increasingly eroded that freedom by making illegal any firing that discriminates on the basis of race, color, religion, national origin, handicap, veteran status, sex, or age. Though not all employees are covered, thousands file complaints each year with enforcing agencies such as human rights and equal employment opportunity commissions. (Union as well as nonunion employees are covered, and none of them have to exhaust whatever internal remedies may be available before filing charges. Union members can thus bypass their own grievance procedures if they do not believe they will serve well or fairly.)[40]

In addition, Congress has included in a number of regulatory acts[41] provisions for protecting employees who complain about their working conditions. Though the number of workers asking for protection under these laws against employer reprisal is still small, the potential is large. The handling of complaints through state and federal agencies could increase dramatically if workers continue to find neither union grievance handling nor company complaint systems any more satisfactory than they appear to be at present.

State and federal courts also are reconsidering the desirability of public policy that allows employers to fire at will. Managers have sometimes exercised that right in an arbitrary, capricious way. With an ever better-schooled citizenry, more knowledgeable about the possiblility of due process, judges find it increasingly difficult to uphold a doctrine rooted in an earlier, mercantile age that governed the relationship of masters and servants. Some state courts have held that employer promises, made either orally or in employee handbooks, constitute contracts that preclude dismissals except for just cause.[42] They are reading into the usual list of employees rules and benefits, regularly provided

---

[40]See *Alexander v. Gardner-Denver Co.,* 415 U.S. 36 (1971).

[41]These include: Clean Air Act (42 USC 7622); Energy Reorganization Act (42 USC 5851); Federal Water Pollution Control Act (33 USC 1367); Safe Drinking Water Act (42 USC 300j-9); Solid Waste Disposal Act (42 USC 6971); and Toxic Substances Control Act (15 USC 2622).

[42]"The Growing Costs of Firing Nonunion Workers," *Business Week,* Apr. 6, 1981, p. 95.

to employees, a promise and right of due process—something very much like a complaint procedure or grievance system.

Both union leaders and corporate managers might wisely consider the implications for them and their grievance procedures of the recent legislation and court decisions affecting employee rights. Legislators have shown themselves more interested in democratic values and due process at the place of work than have either unions or managers. They perceive, as judges increasingly do, a widespread public desire for more fairness in the employment relationship, though they show no favor towards strengthening unions as a way to ensure fairness.

We have noted that union members highly value their grievance procedures, and at the top of the list of improvements desired they put improved use and administration of these procedures. In surveys of nonunion employees, *including managers themselves,* well over half indicate unhappiness with the fairness in, and lack of opportunity to contribute fully to, the employment relationship.[43] There thus appear to be a number of signs that management's traditional authoritarian style, with its denial of appeal and acceptance of arbitrary treatment of workers, is increasingly unacceptable to workers at all levels. The slow growth of unions and their relative decline raise a question, however, of whether unions have made their grievance procedures attractive alternatives to management's self-controlled but still unilateral discretion.

That neither of these two institutions has been able to satisfactorily meet the apparent wide and increasing demand for employee rights, protection on the job and due process at the place of work is itself significant. It suggests that broader public policy, such as contained in the Civil Rights Act, may be needed to provide an adequate bill of rights in the work environment generally.

CONCLUSION

Only gradually did management and unionists recognize the useful role of a grievance process. In their early encounters they both focused on their differences and seldom realized the potential benefits of a stable, ordered relationship. With such a focus, a grievance process did not offer much to either party. Employers presumed their rights to be limited only by the forces of the labor market, and workers sought primarily to limit market pressure upon their wages. As employers increasingly became professional managers, they came to appreciate the value of a stable work force. The maintenance of such a work force required at least a minimal fairness in the application of work rules and consistency in the administration of company policy. Once work rules were in place and effectively applied, managers found that they had established, even in the absence of a union, something akin to a grievance process. Union leaders also moved gradually toward a grievance process, at first not distinguishing conflicts over wages and other conditions of employment (disputes over inter-

---

[43]Berenbeim, *Nonunion Complaint Systems: A Corporate Appraisal,* p. 3.

ests) from controversy over interpreting the terms to which they had given their assent (disputes over rights). They, too, were interested in stability—but not so much stability of the work force as stability of the relationship with management.

For union members at the place of work, the grievance process quickly became a matter of significance, particularly in those large shops and bureaucratic offices where company rules, organizational policies, and contract provisions govern most of the activities at the place of work. Where managers and workers deal with each other more informally or where employees are relatively free to work at their own pace under little supervision, grievance handling is not as valuable or needed.

The grievance process incorporates much more than merely a judicial function, interpretation of the terms of the agreement; those who handle grievances and seek settlement, on both the management and union sides, find that the needs of their organizations and the demands of those they serve require them to fill other roles. They become administrators; communicators; and even negotiators for group interests at the place of work, particularly if the group is so positioned that it can win for itself better terms than the overall agreement provides.

The spread of the nonunion complaint procedure is a striking development of the last twenty years. Its continued elaboration and the increasing recognition that the courts give to employees' rights suggest that the grievance process may find far wider success than unions have. It is not unusual for nonunion employees to choose a fellow employee, particularly one who has developed some expertise in interpreting work rules, to represent them at hearings conducted within the firm; many managements may also submit the decisions and rulings of lower and middle managers to arbitration hearings. Employees appear to like a grievance process, in both union and nonunion work places. It is a means of protecting them against bureaucratic mistreatment and arbitrary managerial decisions; thus it is apt to become an increasingly important aspect of organization activities, whether unions are involved or not.

THREE

POWER AND POLITICS IN COLLECTIVE BARGAINING

A basic reality of American industrial life is cooperation. It is ubiquitous at places of work—workers cooperate with each other and with their managers. The high productivity of the work force and its continued effectiveness in adapting to new technologies are indicators of that cooperation. It is taken so much for granted that the public often forgets the intricate, sophisticated ways workers and managers interact to sustain it. It is so much a part of our world that even slight interruptions or temporary lapses alarm the public, generating pressure for resolution of problems and restoration of the usual levels of cooperation.

Within a basically cooperative relationship, unions and management—workers and managers—find that they seek divergent goals and pursue different interests. Management usually organizes itself formally as a unitary hierarchy; it sorts out conflicting interests and chooses among clashing goals in a more or less authoritarian manner. Unions operate more democratically and must settle their conflicts in relatively open debate and resolve their differences through majoritarian procedures. Both union leaders and managers must usually consider carefully how the members will evaluate the terms they negotiate. This consideration greatly complicates bargaining, injecting into it the uncertainities of poor communications, misunderstandings by members and by leaders, and the problems of political maneuver and play.

Both parties must work out complicated trade-offs among their own discordant preferences before they can even bargain with each other. Once they reach at least tentative agreements among themselves, they must then plot their strategy for dealing with the opposite party. The common need to maintain basic cooperation and the public expectation that it will be sustained allow union and management two key approaches to bargaining. Not only may they threaten to raise the cost of the relationship, but they may also promise to increase the return to it. While each may seek to force agreement by withholding cooperation, each may also attempt to induce agreement by offering increased cooperation. Intricate combinations of threats and promises are possible, which, along with the political complications confronting each side, make for great uncertainties in the negotiations. The task of each party is to find out as best it can what the other wants and needs and then decide what it can and must offer to reach a settlement. It is a task that requires a high degree of political skill and negotiating art as well as mastery of the facts and wide knowledge of the economic setting.

BARGAINING POWER

Bargaining power is a useful concept, but a tricky one. Observers of the labor scene widely use it as if it were self-explanatory, needing no further definition, but a little consideration will quickly convince one that what seems simple is in fact not. Many labor relations analysts regard bargaining power as the ability of one party to control the setting of wage rates, sometimes within given limits. Various scholars have offered approaches toward a theory of bargaining using this implied definition of bargaining power. One of the earliest was Professor A. C. Pigou. We can instructively consider his approach as an aid in exploring the nature and significance of the concept.[1]

BARGAINING WITHIN A RANGE OF INDETERMINATENESS

Pigou assumed that when union and management bargain about a change in wage scale, there is a certain wage above which the union will not want to go, fearing the resulting unemployment. He also assumed that there is a wage below which management will not want to go, believing that it would not attract or hold an adequate labor supply. Too high a wage will cut the demand for labor and too low a wage will lessen the supply; these wages set the boundaries to the wage bargain, enclosing a *range of indeterminateness*. A settlement is not likely to be reached outside the range, but one cannot specify where within the range the parties may actually reach settlement. However, the union will have a lower wage limit that it would just accept rather than strike. Man-

[1]The summary is taken from A. C. Pigou, *Economics of Welfare,* 4th ed., London: Macmillan & Co., Ltd., 1938, pp. 451–461.

agement will have an upper wage limit that it would barely accept rather than face a strike. These limits are the respective "sticking" or "resistance" points, above or below which one or the other of the parties will not move without first taking a stand. If management's upper limit lies above the union's lower limit, both confront a *range of practicable bargains,* within which it is possible for agreement to be reached by negotiations. The parties can reach an agreement because the union will accept any wage within the range rather than strike and management is prepared to accept any wage within the range rather than court a strike. If management's sticking point lies below the union's, a strike will be inevitable. (Table 11 shows these relationships.)

Given a range within which practicable bargains can be made, no strike need take place. Nevertheless, there remains the question of where within the range the concluding bargain will be struck. Each of the parties will seek to push toward the other's limit, and in the process of bluff and bluster by which this result is sought, they may find themselves involved in overt conflict that neither wants and that both may realize is unwarranted.

The range of indeterminateness thus sets voluntary limits to the exercise of the parties' bargaining power. It is relative bargaining that will determine the settlement point within the range. The parties will comprehend the limits of range of practicable bargains only through their estimates of relative bargaining powers. These include, of course, their respective evaluations of the costs of a strike.

Other writers besides Pigou have assumed such ranges of boundaries to the bargain. John R. Commons introduced the concept of "limits of coercion," a

TABLE 11*
BARGAINING WITHIN A RANGE OF INDETERMINATENESS

Rate/Hour	a	Rate/Hour	b
$9.35	Union's maximum (upper limit of range of indeterminateness)	$9.35	Union's maximum (upper limit of range of indeterminateness)
$8.50	Employer's maximum (upper limit of range of practicable bargains)	8.60	Union's minimum
8.00	Union's minimum (lower limit of range of practicable bargains)	8.00	Employer's maximum
6.00	Employer's minimum (lower limit of range of indeterminateness)	6.00	Employer's minimum (lower limit of range of indeterminateness)

*In column *a*, an agreement can be reached without strike between $8.00 and $8.50, since within this range both parties would prefer any settlement rather than accept a strike to secure a more advantageous rate. In column *b*, however, no such range of practicable bargains exists. The minimum wage which the union would accept without strike is above the maximum wage which the employer would grant rather than face a strike. What wage will actually be settled upon here depends on the outcome of an economic fight. All that can be said is that it will fall somewhere within the range of indeterminateness, as the union would not want any wage higher than the upper limit of this range, and the employer would not want a rate lower than the lower limit.

range of bargains bounded by the alternative bargains open to buyer (employer) and seller (union).[2] Richard E. Walton and Robert B. McKersie also used the notion of positive and negative settlement ranges.[3] (They are positive when the union's lowest acceptable point of settlement overlaps and is below management's highest acceptable settlement. They are negative if there is no overlap, when the union's lowest acceptable point is above management's lowest.) *Within* such limits or ranges there is room for the play of bargaining power and negotiating ability. Despite the authority of such scholars, though, the notion of a range of bargains is probably no more than a formal abstraction, not a matter of practical importance in bargaining. It obscures rather than clarifies the more important concepts of bargaining power.

First, the parties do not know what limits may be imposed by the impact of a given wage rate upon the demand for and supply of labor. If limits do exist, the parties can only "guesstimate" them on the basis of experience. The range of indeterminateness assumed by Pigou is itself indeterminate. Second, although the bargainers may approach each other with rough, tentative sticking or resistance points in mind, they realize that their function in negotiations— and one of the uses of bargaining power—is to give the gloss of acceptability to proposals that at first appear unreasonable.

In the mid-1960s many managements saw union proposals for dental insurance as outside the bounds of serious negotiations. But as unions pressed for their inclusion and became more specific in their negotiations such insurance seemed more reasonable and became increasingly possible. Management demands can also gain acceptance over the course of negotiations. When the airlines' managements found themselves hard-pressed by competition in the early eighties after deregulation of the industry, a number of the large, well-established companies proposed to change pilots' work rules and increase the number of their flying hours. The Air Line Pilots Association initially found such proposals outrageous, but after seven months of negotiations the pilots at United agreed: the proposals had become reasonable to them. If there existed in the minds of the parties such a notion as a range of reasonableness, a range of practicable bargains, or limits of coercion, it was established through negotiations and in the process of agreement. As will be noted shortly, the same forces that operate to set the wage *within* such a range, if one is assumed, must also operate to set the range itself. Since these are interlocking and often simultaneous processes, there is no point in—or method of—distinguishing between them.[4]

[2]John R. Commons, *Institutional Economics: Its Place in Political Economy,* New York: The Macmillan Company, 1934, p. 331.

[3]Richard E. Walton and Robert B. McKersie, *A Behavioral Theory of Labor Negotiations,* New York: McGraw-Hill Book Company, 1965, pp. 41–45.

[4]On the basis of an extensive survey of negotiating processes, Professor Thomas Kochan reports that "the vast majority of negotiations have some implicit or explicit target or bottom-line figures in mind either going into negotiations or after the early stages of negotiations are completed." He

BARGAINING POWER AS THE ABILITY TO EXPLOIT AND IMPOSE COSTS

Professor Commons, one of the great pioneers in the field of labor studies, concluded: "Bargaining power is the proprietary ability to withhold products or production pending the negotiations for transfer of ownership of wealth."[5] He offered the definition as a generic one, applicable to the determination of scarcity values throughout the economy. It bears the defect of Commons's preoccupation with the significance of property rights in capitalistic society, resting bargaining power solely on ownership without respect to the economic circumstances in which it is enjoyed. The *proprietary* ability to withhold production through strike or lockout may be unaccompanied by *actual* ability, that is, power. As Professor Frank H. Knight has pointed out, "freedom to perform an act [which embraces proprietary ability] is meaningless unless the subject is in possession of the requisite means of action, and . . . the practical question is one of power rather than formal freedom.[6]" The right to strike cannot be equated with bargaining power. At the very least, there are degrees of effectiveness in the use of the asserted right, a fact commonly conceived as material to bargaining power though without significance to proprietary ability.

Professor Henry Simons, a thoroughgoing libertarian, or more accurately an economic liberal in the older, classical sense, defined bargaining power as monopoly power and related it to organization.[7] For him, bargaining power was group restraint over individual action. As such it constituted a departure from the normative ideal of the perfectly competitive economy and had no rationale except intended abuse for group advancement. It was, therefore, the power to exploit, and an increase in bargaining power represents an increased capacity to exploit. This narrow approach may be maintained only on the premise of an atomistic society in which group action is considered antisocial. If we abandon such curious, if time-honored, assumptions, we may justifiably admit producers' organizations—business firms as well as unions. Both may be fully respectable and neither has to be exploitative.

If we admit the absence of perfect competition, bargaining power bears some relation to the ability to realize one's desires. Consequently, one may expand bargaining power by improving knowledge or increasing mobility, among other methods that can hardly be labeled monopolistic and exploita-

---

finds these targets, resistance points, or goals to be tenuous, subject to change as negotiations proceed, and based, above all. upon "the probability of achieving alternative targets in bargaining without a strike or an impasse, or otherwise, to estimate the costs and benefits of taking a strike to achieve the target." See Kochan, *Collective Bargaining and Industrial Relations: From Theory to Policy and Practice,* chap. 7, 8, especially pp. 204–205, 211–212.

[5]Ibid., p. 267.

[6]Frank H. Knight, *Freedom and Reform,* New York: Harper & Row, Publishers, Incorporated, 1947, p. 4.

[7]Henry C. Simons, *Economic Policy for a Free Society,* Chicago: The University of Chicago Press, 1948, pp. 129, 154.

tive. There is something inadequate about a definition of bargaining power that condemns all group activity for possessing such power in any degree.

The Possibility of Integrative Bargaining

Professor Sumner Slichter, an influential labor scholar a generation ago, wrote: "Bargaining power may be defined as the cost to A of imposing a loss upon B."[8] This description appears to be defective, however, in suggesting either that the objective of one party is to impose a loss upon the other (rather than secure an advantage to itself) or that a loss to B may be identified with advantage to A.[9]

Walton and McKersie pointed out the ways in which bargaining might serve productive or integrative as well as distributive purposes[10] thus bargaining power involves more than possible losses imposed upon one party or the other. As John Cross has emphasized, bargaining and the powers associated with it involve the joint explorations of the complexities of the matters at hand. The goal of negotiating in union-management relations is not to impose unfavorable, costly terms on the other, but to set the terms for future, ongoing cooperation.[11] Harold W. Davey also insists that a gain by one party in bargaining need not infer a corresponding loss to the other. "It overlooks the salient point," he writes, "that *living together under a written three-year contract . . .* requires that the agreement be *mutually acceptable.* The contract is the end product of *joint decision making.*"[12]

Concession and Resistance in Bargaining Power

Finally, special attention should be directed to the concept of bargaining power implicit in Professor Hicks' analysis of wage setting under collective bargaining his analysis or versions of it continue to be the starting place for many examinations and studies of bargaining power.[13] He starts with the proposition that

[8]Sumner Slichter, "Impact of Social Security Legislation upon Mobility and Enterprise," *American Economic Review,* vol. 30, suppl., 1940, p. 57. The idea is repeated in "Good Bargains and Bad Bargains," *Collective Bargaining Contracts,* Bureau of National Affairs, 1941, pp. 46–48. This same approach has been elaborated by Joseph Shister in "The Theory of Union Bargaining Power," *Southern Economic Journal,* vol. 10, 1943–1944, pp. 151–159.

[9]The criticism that this definition implies that bargaining power must always be exercised at a positive cost is hardly well taken, however. Cost may obviously be considered in a negative sense. Thus Pigou in his *Economics of Welfare,* p. 454, has pointed out that under given circumstances a strike would represent negative cost to a union or to an employer.

[10]Integrative bargaining is the joint solving of common problems where both parties gain; distributive bargaining is joint decision making by both parties to resolve conflicts of interest where one wins only if the other loses.

[11]John G. Cross, *The Economics of Bargaining,* New York: Basic Books, Inc., Publishers, 1969.

[12]Harold W. Davey, *Contemporary Collective Bargaining,* 3d ed., Englewood Cliffs, N. J.: Prentice-Hall, Inc., 1972, p. 99.

[13]The presentation here is taken from J. R. Hicks, *Theory of Wages,* New York: The Macmillan Company, 1932, chap. 7.

the willingness of employees to strike and of management to resist a strike depends upon what is to be gained by each through a strike. The *duration* of the strike, in particular, will be governed by the relative return.

The greater the wage increase sought by a union, the more willing management is to face a long strike; the more willing the union to undertake a long strike, the greater is its potential gain. On this assumption one may set up for management a schedule of wage changes which it would be willing to pay rather than face a strike of a given length; the wage changes and strike durations would vary directly. At each point on the schedule the anticipated cost of the strike and the anticipated cost of the wage concession balance. The schedule indicates that at any point on the curve management should be willing to grant any lower wage increase rather than face a strike of the associated duration. It would prefer a strike, however, rather than grant a wage higher than the schedule. Hicks calls it management's "concession schedule."

One may draw a similar schedule for the union, showing the length of time its members would remain on strike rather than allow their wage to fall below a particular rate. At any higher wage, they would forgo a strike; at any lower wage, they would strike. Such a schedule may be thought of as the union's "resistance curve" Hicks implies that management is better informed than the union officials so that it knows both its own concession schedule and the union's likely resistance schedule over the course of a strike. Union leaders know only their resistance schedule.

The Hicks Bargaining Schedule

These two curves are diagramed in Figure 1. *OE* represents the wage that management would have undertaken in the absence of union pressure; *EE'* is management's concession curve. At any point on the curve the costs of the given wage increase and the costs of the strike of the associated duration are equal. Management's curve levels off at some rate, since above this rate it would prefer to close down the business. *UU'* is the union's resistance curve, at any point on which the sacrifice of accepting a lower wage rate matches the costs of striking for the indicated length of time. The union's curve generally will join the wage axis on the left-hand side, since there is usually some rate above which it would not push for fear of employment repercussions; and on the right the curve will meet *EU'*, since there is some length of time beyond which the union would simply be unable to carry on a strike but would have to settle on management's terms, that is, wage *OE*.

At some point *P*, management's concession curve and the union's resistance curve will intersect each other. The associated wage rate *OP* represents the best possible bargain for both parties, for at any higher wage demand management would prefer to entertain a strike. This preference is based on the belief that the employees would not hold out for as long as would be necessary to make the strike as costly to it as the demanded increase in the wage bill. At any wage less than *OP,* the union would not have extracted its maximum bargaining

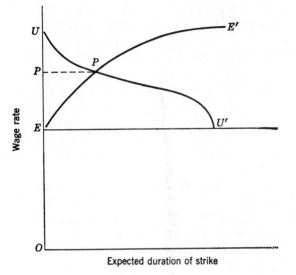

Expected duration of strike

FIGURE 1
Hicks' bargaining schedules.

advantage; management would have been willing to pay more, in the belief that the employees would have stayed out longer before accepting less. A prolonged strike caused by holding out for a lower wage would be more costly to it than settlement at the higher rate. *OP* is not necessarily a determinate wage for Hicks, since it is "the highest wage which skillful negotiations can extract from the employer."[14] Unless the union negotiators are in top form, they may not gain so high a wage.

Thus the task of the union negotiators is to identify point *P*. If the bargaining is skillfully conducted, a strike not only will be avoided but could not possibly do either party any good. Strikes represent a miscalculation by either party of its own or the other's bargaining power, on the strength of which the concession and resistance curves are drawn. "There is a general presumption that it will be possible to get more favorable terms by negotiating than by striking."[15] Moreover, time is on the side of management past some point in a strike. As the strike continues, management is interested only in the cost of the remainder of the strike, and since the union's staying power begins to decline from the first day of the strike, with the passage of time its resistance curve moves to the left, reducing the highest wage obtainable. That is to say, the concession and resistance curves are conceived as drawn at a moment in time. They do not last throughout the duration of the strike—they do not show that when the strike goes into its sixth week, for example, the union will be prepared to take a wage of so much and the employer will be prepared to grant a wage of so much. These curves represent the wage both parties will accept rather

[14]Ibid., p. 144.
[15]Ibid., pp. 144–145.

than face *future* strikes of given (i.e., anticipated) duration. They are thus presumably being redrawn throughout the period of the strike, as the parties' expectations change.

Of course, conditions may change to improve the union's bargaining position. Such an occurrence presumably would bring forth a new point *P,* which the union bargainers would strive to reach. Other things remaining equal, fighting it out to the bitter end *must* simply mean going back on management's terms. Except for occasional resort to the strike to keep management mindful of the power of the union or to improve the cohesion of the members, a strike "arises from the divergence of estimates [of management and union] and from no other cause."[16]

One criticism of the conception of bargaining power implicit in Professor Hicks' formulation is that it addresses only the influence of prices and the determination of wages. Hicksian bargaining power is hardly analytical; more variables are needed to provide an understanding of the complexities involved. Furthermore, more than wages are involved in bargaining; the importance of *all* the conditions under which the cooperation of economic partners takes place must not be slighted. We are concerned with group power in terms of both theory and policy, and bargaining power has its greatest relevance to groups. It concerns the whole of group relationships and *wage* determination as tastes, skills, and competitive forces is to say little about the total relationship between the parties that collective bargaining seeks to establish and maintain on the basis of relative bargaining power. Even for the economist, price is not the only matter of interest. The nature of economic organizations (including intergroup relationships) through which economic activity proceeds is at least as much a subject of interest to the economist as to the political scientist, and that interest cannot be satisfied by exclusive attention to price or wage issues. Bargaining power is relevant to all organized economic relationships; between management and union only one of its functions is the determination of prices and wages.

THE COSTS OF AGREEING AND DISAGREEING

We take the view that bargaining power is an effective force underlying the whole collective bargaining relationship and the process of union-management negotiations. Broadening Professor Hicks' implicit concept, we define bargaining power as the ability to secure another's agreement on one's own terms. A union's bargaining power at any point of time *is,* for example, management's willingness to agree to the union's terms. Management's willingness, in turn, depends upon the costs of disagreeing with the union terms relative to the costs of agreeing to them. Note that such a definition does not assume either party is *forced* to do something that it would not do if it could exercise complete discretion. A union may simply acquiesce in a layoff or plant closing because

[16]Ibid., p. 147.

the law and industrial legitimacy makes disagreeing with management's action too expensive relative to the costs of agreeing. Of course, most unions have sought and managements have granted provisions that lessen unions' cost of agreeing—special unemployment pay, rehire rights in the case of layoffs, and severance pay or transfers to other plants in the case of closings. Bargaining power is not at its highest level when one of the parties must force or coerce the other to terms—for example after a long strike or lockout; it is far more impressive, though undramatic because so effective, when one party simply accepts the terms offered it with no particular contemplation of disagreeing. In such cases the cost of disagreeing with the terms is so high relative to the cost of agreeing and the balance between them so plain that negotiations may be absent or short and agreement either implicit or barely acknowledged.

If the cost to management of disagreeing with the union is high relative to the cost of agreeing, the union's bargaining power is enhanced. If a strike is very costly to management and the union's terms are quite inexpensive, the union's chances of getting its demands are improved. If the cost to management of disagreeing with the union is low relative to the cost of agreeing to the union's terms, the union's bargaining power is diminished. If sales are off and production is being cut back anyway, a strike may be relatively inexpensive compared with the cost of the union's demand. In such a case the union's chance of getting its demands are not good.

These statements in themselves reveal nothing of the strength or weakness of the union relative to management since management might possess a strong or weak bargaining power to press its own terms Only if the cost to management of disagreeing with the union's terms is greater than the cost of agreeing to them and the cost to the union of disagreeing with management's terms is less than the cost of agreeing to them is the union's bargaining power greater than management's. More generally, only if the difference to management between the cost of disagreement and agreement on labor's terms is proportionately greater than the difference to labor between the cost of disagreement and agreement on management's terms can one say that labor's bargaining power is greater than management's.

The Relative Nature of Bargaining Power

Bargaining power as defined here is not an inherent attribute of the parties or some absolute amount of power available for any and all bargaining situations. The parties may change it as they use different tactics to influence each other.[17] The passage of time also may bring changes of bargaining power for unions and management as their costs change, economic conditions shift, or public opinion and government influence mobilize for or against one of the bargain-

---

[17]Professor Carl Stevens suggests that shifts and changes of tactics should be viewed as the use of existing bargaining power to gain objectives rather than as ways of changing the magnitude of bargaining power. See "On the Theory of Negotiations," *Quarterly Journal of Economics,* vol. 72, 1958, p. 93, footnote 2.

ers.[18] Bargaining power changes too with the nature of the demands made, the costs of agreement and disagreement being relative to the demands. In general the greater the demand the greater the resistance to it and therefore the less the bargaining power of the union.

The word "cost" is here being used in a broad sense, as disadvantage; thus it includes pecuniary and nonpecuniary costs. Not all costs can be reduced to a common denominator, of course, but in making decisions some sort of balance *must* be struck, even with respect to incommensurate matters, if decision is to be made and action undertaken. The very incommensurability of certain issues makes possible the changing of minds that might be unpersuaded if all significant issues could be reduced by an economic calculus to a numerical balance or imbalance.

There is some use in dwelling on this point briefly. Previously we said that a major difficulty with definitions of bargaining power has been the fact that they have dealt with only one issue in the bargaining process, wages, and that numerous other issues not reducible to a dollar scale of values are also involved. The sort of balancing costs contemplated in the definition of bargaining power just given does not require measurement of costs in any arithmetical sense, however. The balancing of incommensurable items may be accomplished in the same way that oranges may be balanced against apples on a consumer's demand indifference map. What these costs of agreement and disagreement may be to the bargainers cannot be known precisely enough to permit balancing, except through the exploratory process of negotiation. Through negotiating, the feasible and infeasible combinations become apparent.

Several points are to be noted about this definition of bargaining power:

1 It takes into account the total situation—not only the striking or resistance capacities of the parties, but the economic, political, and social circumstances insofar as these bear upon the cost of agreement or disagreement. In fact, there appears to be no meaningful way in which a union's striking power, for example, can be separated from surrounding economic and political forces.

2 It allows for the shifting of bargaining power over time. It is not static, but dynamic. Even within brief periods of time, relative positions may change considerably as the parties maneuver for advantage in the bargaining process or as time presses them against deadlines or imposes new and higher costs.

3 The concept of bargaining power, which is here oriented toward a group decision-making process, is not exclusively tied to two-party negotiations.

---

[18]Professor A. Cartter adds a "time term" to his bargaining model, adapted from J. Pen's model in "A General Theory of Bargaining," *American Economic Review.* vol. 42, 1952, pp. 24–42. He believes that "time automatically tends to bring about a settlement, for the passage of time gradually increases the [cost of disagreement] . . . for both parties." A. Cartter, *Theory of Wages and Employment,* Homewood, Ill.; Richard D. Irwin, Inc., 1959, pp. 123–126. John G. Cross argues that the bargaining process is fundamentally time-dependent. The passage of time imposes costs which motivate both parties to press for a resolution of their disagreement. See Cross, *The Economics of Bargaining,* pp. 12–14 and 45–48.

Although in this analysis we shall primarily be interested in the union-management relationship, the concept is equally applicable to situations involving joint decisions of more than two parties.

4 If agreement is reached, it must be on terms that for all the parties concerned represent a cost of agreement equal to, or less than, a cost of disagreement.

5 If disagreement persists, it must be because for at least one of the parties the costs of disagreement are less than the costs of agreement.[19]

6 Bargaining power for any party may be increased by anything that lowers the relative cost of agreement to the other party or raises the relative cost of disagreement.

The Subjective Element in Bargaining Power

In elaborating this concept of bargaining power, let us first turn our attention to the factors influencing the cost of disagreement; then we shall consider the determinants of the costs of agreement. In terms of a negotiating process, management's estimate of the costs to it of disagreeing with the union will be conclusive to it. The estimate may be wrong, of course, as management discovers for itself or as union negotiators persuade it. The same analysis applies to the union's evaluations of its costs and the influences that bear upon them. Consequently, bargaining power becomes in part of a matter of influencing the psychological reactions of the negotiators; the parties may use the tactics of bluff, but it is also possible to influence the other party's estimate of the costs of agreeing and disagreeing on proffered terms by a straight factual approach.

The latter is most helpful if one of the parties assumes an unwarrantably optimistic or unrealistic estimate. Both bluffing and factual presentations may be useful, for the parties usually make proposals, offers, and counteroffers sequentially, providing information to each other about the intentions, interests, and preferences of each. Each new piece of information may help the parties better to evaluate the costs of agreeing and disagreeing to the others' terms, thus possibly changing the balance of bargaining power.[20]

---

[19]Professor Stevens points out that two parties may fail to reach a settlement and will continue bargaining even though one may enjoy a greater coefficient of bargaining power than the other. The reason is, he explains, that there is not only a necessary condition for settlement, the *existence* of an acceptable settlement, but also a sufficient condition; i.e., the parties must be informed and aware of the possible settlement. Disagreement could thus persist because the parties are unaware of their available route to settlement. See Carl Stevens, *Strategy and Collective Bargaining Negotiation,* New York: McGraw-Hill Book Company, 1963, pp. 21–22, 169.

[20]John Cross, in his study of bargaining, concluded that bluffing in general works to the bluffer's disadvantage. Despite its adverse effects, experienced negotiators regularly use bluffing as an important bargaining tactic. He argues that bluffing may produce disadvantages to the bluffer, but it also offers a benefit in deemphasizing the competitive element and allowing the appearance of cooperation. Since the fundamental purpose of negotiations is to organize future cooperation, bluffing makes a worthwhile contribution. The apparent deception or misleading demands and bids are ways of softening the blunt differences to be resolved and easing difficult concessions that may have to be made. John G. Cross, *The Economics of Bargaining,* pp. 166–179.

UNION TACTICS AND THE COSTS OF DISAGREEING

The most widely publicized tactics are those by which one party seeks to raise the cost of disagreeing with its terms to the other. The union uses the strike, withholding labor until its terms are met; management may threaten to replace striking workers with nonunion labor.[21] Regardless of who initiates either action, both parties are subjected to costs, of course. When a union conducts a strike aimed at shutting down a business operation, the employees must also bear a cost—their loss of wages. Management's estimate of how long the employees will submit to a loss of wages will partly determine its estimate of the duration of the strike and consequently the cost to it of rejecting the union's terms. Similarly, in the event that management refuses to continue operations except on the old terms, it is itself equally subjected to some loss from reduction or cessation of operations. The losses may be those of present profits, for example, or perhaps even of future profits through loss of customers. The union's estimate of how long management will or can stand such a drain will affect, in part, its estimate of the cost to the management of refusing to agree to the union's terms.

As a result, each party makes efforts to increase the effectiveness of these tactics and to render itself immune to the tactics of the other. The efforts center primarily around the union's seeking to strengthen the strike weapon and management's seeking to weaken it. In some of the earliest recorded turnouts of journeymen, we find evidence of the use of strike benefits to lengthen the staying power of the workers and thus increase the cost to the masters of disagreeing with them. Strike benefits were used at least as early as 1805, in the strike of the Philadelphia shoemakers; and in the 1827 conspiracy trial of the Philadelphia journeymen tailors, there was even an attempt made to buy off strikebreakers with strike benefits. Of course, managements throughout the years have generally sought to limit union interference with members who sought to return to work or with nonunion workers who sought to replace the strikers.

Time of a Strike

Both union and management have carefully and thoroughly explored the tactical aspects of conducting strikes. Each attempts to conduct itself so that maximum costs fall upon the other party while only minimum costs are imposed upon itself. The timing of a strike, for example, can be a matter of considerable

---

[21]Such replacement can be viewed as a form of lockout, a characterization made by the air traffic controllers of the federal government's firing of those who struck in 1981 and replacing them with new employees. Since the lockout can be used to discriminate against union membership, the courts have insisted that several criteria be met before it can be legally used: the expiration of the agreement, a bargaining impasse, the serving of a legitimate economic or bargaining interest, and only temporary replacement of employees. (To replace employees permanently would discourage union members' rights to concerted activity.) The government discharged striking air traffic controllers because they had sworn not to strike and the law forbade strikes by government employees. Possessing no legal right to strike, the controllers could be replaced legally and permanently.

importance. A strike against an automobile firm just after it has invested in retooling for a model change and when it is ready to begin its competitive sales campaign for the new model would probably be more effective than at any other time of the year. The printing unions in New York for many years timed the expiration of their agreements with newspaper publishers to coincide with the beginning of the period of heaviest advertising, between Thanksgiving and Christmas. Also, a strike by baseball players during the summer inflicts heavier losses upon the team owners than one called in the winter.

Under some conditions striking workers may find that the money costs of a strike to them may moderate rather than steadily increase. For example, sixteen states, including New York, Massachusetts, and California permit strikers' families to receive Aid to Families with Dependent Children (AFDC). The amount of aid averaged only $250 per family per month in 1980, about a week's earnings after taxes. But if AFDC is supplemented by food stamps, and in New York and Rhode Island by unemployment pay (after a seven-week waiting period), a striker's family may receive a noticeable amount of assistance. Managers and many taxpayers object to such payments, believing that they place the government on one side of the bargaining table, favoring strikers. Even without government assistance some strikers may be able to find temporary or part-time work elsewhere and feel little pressure to agree to management's terms.

Workers in Key Positions

The very structure of unions is in part determined by strike effectiveness. One advantage of the craft-union structure is the key position that skilled workers frequently play in an enterprise, coupled with the relatively low wage bill which they entail. A strike of a handful of powerhouse employees may close down an entire plant, imposing upon management a substantial cost of disagreeing with their terms, whereas because of their small number the cost of agreement may be negligible in comparison, even if they demand a large pay increase. The cost of disagreement to management can be materially reduced, however, if striking craft workers can be replaced; and here enters one powerful incentive for craft unions to exercise control over *all* workers with given skills and training who might provide replacements for those striking.

Craft-union members have sometimes found that they do not occupy as key a position as they had assumed and thus their ability to impose a high cost of disagreement with their terms may be far more limited than expected. The 15,000-member Professional Air Traffic Controllers Organization (PATCO) in 1981 illegally struck the Federal Aviation Administration (FAA) during a dispute over the terms of an agreement it was negotiating. The leaders had expected to snarl air travel across the country, inflicting heavy costs upon the traveling public and airlines, thus pressuring the government agency. However, the FAA had found a way of safely controlling air traffic with a computerized metering technique called "flow control"; it required less than one-third the number of controllers usually on the job. The FAA fired the strikers and with supervisors, nonunion workers, and Air Force personnel it was able to maintain a reasonable level of service, greatly diminishing the effectiveness of the controllers' walkout. In many high-technology industries, such as petroleum refining and telephone communications, key or skilled workers also find themselves in the position of the air traffic controllers—replaceable.

In the case of unskilled or semiskilled workers, there is little possibility of gathering under one union all those who could substitute for striking employees. The very lack of skill increases the opportunity for substitution. But at the same time that it becomes easier for the employer to find substitutes for any given semiskilled worker, growth in the size of industrial establishments makes it more difficult to replace an entire body of employees. Here an industrial union shows great strike effectiveness by being able to take away from management virtually its whole working force in event of disagreement. Unsurprisingly, therefore, the industrial union has its greatest strength in large plants rather than small shops, since in the latter the possibility of management's replacing the whole staff of employees in event of strike still remains.

Recruiting Sympathizers

In addition to the strike as a bargaining weapon, the device of picketing has been developed to a high degree of usefulness by unions. This generally serves to support a strike, though it may be used independently. A picket line advertises a strike and strengthens it insofar as members of other unions refuse to cross it, whether they are engaged in their personal or their employer's business. The picket line has acquired an almost religious significance for many union members, so that its violation takes on aspects of sacrilege and taints the offender. In the presence of such dogma, it becomes possible for even a small group of employees to isolate the company from the economy, inflicting a cost of disagreement upon the company out of all proportion to their significance to its operations.[22]

The cost to the employer of disagreement with the union is thus in some instances dependent upon the union's ability to provoke sympathetic action by unionists in other establishments or other trades. Striking workers frequently seek the support of the powerful Teamsters union, which by reason of its strategic function of delivering supplies and removing finished products can sometimes bring enormous pressure upon an employer.

In addition to the picket line, a means by which unions in the past (less frequently today) sought to increase the cost to the employer of disagreeing with them by arousing outside support was the secondary boycott. It was outlawed by the Labor-Management Relations Act of 1947 and the Labor-Man-

---

[22]In some situations where customers or the public may be hostile to unions, a picket line may have no effect or even a favorable effect upon a firm's business. Union picketing of suburban shopping centers, for example, or expensive jewelry stores or dress shops in urban centers, have often attracted customers.

agement Reporting and Disclosure Act of 1959, though unions occasionally still resort to it covertly. The boycott itself is a time-honored tactic. Through the boycott, unions encourage others to have nothing to do with a struck company or its sympathizers. The "we do not patronize" list is the best-known example of such action. Since the primary boycott is virtually restricted to instances where the employer is selling directly to the public and since the effects of the boycott campaign can be slow in making themselves felt, unions often attempt to extend the boycott to secondary sources of influence.

The Secondary Boycott

Through the secondary boycott, the striking union brings pressure upon a sympathizing union in a related company to strike, too, even if the latter union has no dispute with its employer. The intent is to force the second company to seek a mediated settlement of the original dispute in order to solve its own difficulties. In some instances the union brings pressure directly upon a second employer, without going through the latter's union; it might throw a picket line around the premises and thus persuade the workers to refuse to enter the plant. The nature of the secondary boycott can perhaps be most easily grasped by referring to Figure 2, in which the arrows indicate directions of pressure.[23]

[23]The Teamsters sometimes use the tertiary boycott as a means of evading the legal restrictions on the secondary boycott. By applying direct pressure upon shippers to induce their organized truckers not to deal with unorganized truckers, the union can gain leverage. The line of coercion runs from organized to unorganized carrier via the shipper as a third party. See Ralph James and Estelle James, "Hoffa's Leverage Techniques in Bargaining," *Industrial Relations,* vol. 3, 1963, p. 79.

FIGURE 2
Secondary and primary boycotts.

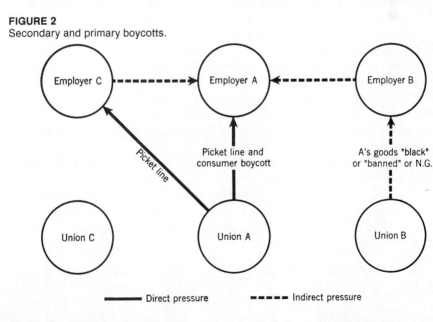

In not all cases is it or was it necessary for the second union actually to strike. The first union might declare the goods produced by the primary employer A "banned," "no go," or "black." By doing so, it might persuade union members at other plants working for other employers to refuse to handle them. Employer A would quickly find the usual markets cut off or reduced; or the primary union A might picket a secondary employer C, inducing C to apply indirect pressure to employer A. The following case was related in a Senate debate to illustrate its effectiveness and what the speaker believed was the unfairness of the technique:

> The Barbers Union in a dispute with the Terminal Barber Shops, Inc., located in the Waldorf-Astoria Hotel, picketed entrances to the Waldorf-Astoria Hotel. The evidence shows that for a few days business went on as usual, and then the Teamsters Union recognized the picket line and refused to deliver supplies to the Waldorf-Astoria. There were no linens brought in. There was no milk. There was no food. Supplies could not go out. The greatest hotel in the country was about to come to a standstill. . . . As a result, the management of the Waldorf-Astoria Hotel had to say to the concern which had leased the barbershop space, "You will have to yield. If you do not, we cannot renew your lease."[24]

New Techniques

More recently unions have innovatively attempted to adapt the secondary boycott to legal forms that will generate pressure upon management. One has already been mentioned in Chapter 1: the Amalgamated Clothing and Textile Workers Union sought to prevent outside directors from sitting on J. P. Stevens' board of directors and to prevent Stevens officers from serving on boards of other companies. The effort culminated in a union threat to contest the election of nominees to the board of the Metropolitan Life Insurance Company, a major lender of Stevens. A contest would have been expensive for Metropolitan, and the threat apparently persuaded its chairman to seek a resolution of the labor dispute, putting pressure on Stevens's managers to settle. Later, in 1981, the Air Line Pilots Association proposed to conduct a similar "corporate campaign" against Texas Air and its nonunion subsidiary, New York Airways, Inc., with whom it had a dispute. The union was soon confronted with larger problems, arising from the air traffic controllers' strike and the resulting government limitations on airline flights, and thus the campaign was sidetracked almost before it began.

The United Food and Commercial Workers, in 1979, attempted in a labor dispute to pressure the Seattle–First National Bank. It urged its members and all depositors sympathetic with it to withdraw funds from the bank, hoping to secure withdrawals of 25 percent or $1.6 billion of the bank's total deposits of $6.3 billion. The campaign was not a success, suggesting that indirect action

---

[24]Senator Curtis, *Congressional Record,* U.S. Senate, April 24, 1959, p. 5955, quoted in the *Legislative History of the Labor-Management Reporting and Disclosure Act of 1959,* vol. II, Washington: Government Printing Office, 1959, p. 1178.

through business ties, boards, and financial markets is not easy and is only rarely successful.

These new techniques of raising management's cost of disagreeing with union terms nevertheless show a marked increase in union sophistication. They are not unlike the tactics and pressures that business leaders themselves use in their dealings with each other, though business spokespersons do not appreciate their use by unions. The *Wall Street Journal* editorially condemned the Amalgamated Clothing and Textile Workers Union for its corporate campaign against Stevens:

> We can't sympathize with the union's last-ditch tactic. Because Stevens can't be beaten in a fair and square stand-up fight, [the union] has now resorted to terrorizing businessmen who do business with Stevens. The object is to starve Stevens into submission by isolating it from the rest of the business and financial community.[25]

A broader perspective allows one to appreciate the advance that these newer tactics represent. After all, in the past labor's concerted activities, such as strikes, picketing, and secondary boycotts, have on occasion been accompanied by violence. The history of industrial relations recites all too many bloody conflicts and deaths as employees and unionists have sought grimly to make good their efforts to keep the price of disagreement high for each other. Strikers have sought to stop back-to-work movements, and employers have sought to use strikebreakers.[26] More significant than the possibility of violence is the fact that the reliance on overt tactics for increasing bargaining power has had its repercussions on the very governmental form of the unions. Effective and efficient use of these tactics often necessitates a tightly held leadership operating on authoritarian and military principles. Democracy within unions can be afforded only in between contests with the employer. From the time the agreement is reached on the demands to be made upon the company until those demands are won or lost, union leaders argue that the actions of members must be firmly controlled to restrain the weakest of the individual strikers from capitulating or providing leverage for the employer to split the striking organization. Perhaps if union leaders become more expert and successful in using the newer, more indirect managerial techniques of manipulating funds and influencing boards, stockholders, and consumers, there will be a beneficial effect upon union organization and democracy, too.

Withdrawal of Cooperation

If the above tactics are the more dramatic methods by which a union attempts to impose upon management a high cost of disagreeing with it, more subtle

---

[25] *The Wall Street Journal,* March 24, 1978.

[26] A peculiarity of American labor law is the requirement that employers recognize and bargain collectively with a union certified by the NLRB only as long as there is no strike. Once the union strikes, management is free to bargain individually with any worker it can get to accept employment. Bact-to-work movements thus threaten the strike, strikers' jobs, and even collective bargaining itself.

ways of imposing costs have been discovered. One primary cost of disagreement may simply be the refusal of one party to cooperate in the daily tasks of production. Such lack of cooperation has sometimes taken on organized aspects in the form of slowdowns or "working to rules." One industrial relations manager described how on-the-job pressure may create a cost of disagreement that brings results. He relates the experience he and his New York electrical company had in trying to get workers to accept new work methods and new wage rates:

> We needed the changes if our control panels were going to be competitive. In recent years other firms had caught up with our sales and it was a question whether we could stay in this part of the business. No serious opposition to the new standards developed until we got to the panel-wiring department. As soon as we put in the new standards the production from all fifty men dropped from a third to a half. Now they knew the old standards were too loose and they knew we had to raise them. . . .
>
> We'd raised them 25 units and we might have been off 5 units either way, maybe. But they accused us of making it too tight and wanted us to cut back 10 or 12 units. On the average the wirers had been making from [97 to 104 percent of rate] and a few of the fast ones made as much as [118 percent]. Now they were making only [60 to 67 percent]. For five months they refused to work overtime too. That was allowable under the contract unfortunately. Well, I can tell you, our production schedules were really being hurt. They finally gave up the overtime ban but kept on with the slowdown for another five months. We couldn't fire them because they're too skilled and replacements are hard to get. Besides we needed that production. Finally we gave in and dropped 12 points to get out of our tight production corner.

Noncooperation as a cost of disagreement need not always assume an organized form, however. Resentment over management failure to concede some point that employees deem of little moment to management but of considerable significance to themselves may result in unpremeditated holding back. Even such a little matter as refusing employees the right to open windows on pleasant days, when no safety or efficiency reason for refusal appears to exist, may create a resentment that workers express in early quitting, lingering in the washroom, or any of a number of outlets for private aggression. The failure of agreement between unions and management, both across the bargaining table and at the place of work, can produce a lack of cooperation and engender a latent hostility that increases the difficulties and costs of reaching future agreements.

The threat to management of a loss of cooperation in production loses much of its potency as a cost of disagreement if management believes that its employees have already developed an antagonism leading to loss of on-the-job cooperation. The loss becomes a "sunk" cost, so to speak; something once lost cannot be lost again. Only if management is made to believe that cooperation can effectively be reestablished by conceding its terms does the loss add to employee's bargaining power. Loss of cooperation may be a strong bargaining card for the union before it is played, but once played it has much less effect because further disaffection will add only marginal future costs of disagreement to management.

MANAGEMENT TACTICS AND THE COSTS OF DISAGREEING

The discussion so far has run in terms of the union's power to make disagreement with its terms costly to management. It is here that the dramatic actions of industrial relations are encountered. But managements and employers, too, are able to make costly the workers' disagreement with their terms. In the past, their methods of achieving this often bore a more precise resemblance to those of the union than at present. The so-called La Follette hearings in the United States Senate in the period from 1937 to 1939 on the violation of free speech and the rights of labor by companies and employers' associations resulted in thousands of pages of printed testimony on the use of violence and intimidation in opposing employee organization for collective bargaining. The boycott was matched by the blacklist and sabotage by the *agent provocateur.* These forms of pressure were rendered illegal by various legislative acts, but the decisions of the National Labor Relations Board continue to reveal actions by some managements designed to render the unions' disagreement with them costly. They have included actions such as discharge for union activity and encouragement of rival unions.

Plant Closures

In recessions or periods of economic readjustment, hard-pressed companies have threatened plant closure if their unions did not accept proposed changes in their agreements. For example, in 1981 striking brewers, bottlers, and drivers rejected an agreement, 207 to 111, that had been negotiated by their union leaders. The managers of the Pittsburgh Brewing Company then ordered "all necessary action to commence closing" the plant. They pointed out the company had not paid a dividend on its common stock in nine years and that competition from national brands of beer had seriously cut into the sales of their main product, Iron City Beer. Within two days the union members reversed their vote, 254 to 32, and accepted the once rejected agreement; the board of directors rescinded the order to close.[27] Such a threat is so powerful that unions have protested in the courts the unilateral decision of management to close plants. The Supreme Court decided, however, that a company could shut down a part of its operations without having to bargain over the decision. The managers must bargain over the effect of the closure, though, settling the matters of severance pay, layoffs, and transfers.[28]

Stockpiling

The most common method by which management can increase the cost to the union of disagreeing with its terms is by withholding employment except on terms agreeable to management. Management, expecting a strike, may attempt

---

[27]See *The Wall Street Journal,* May 18, 1981.
[28]*First National Maintenance v. NLRB,* 452 U.S. 666 (1981).

to lessen its own costs by encouraging customers to stockpile before the agreement terminates. While sales stop during a work stoppage, the expanded sales prior to it may average out revenues. Thus in the 1977 Miners' strike, major coal buyers stockpiled the fuel in anticipation of a two-month-long interruption of production. Volkswagen, for example, had purchased double its normal store of coal; Koppers, the Pittsburgh-based producer of coke and chemicals, among many other products, prepared for "a strike of relatively short duration, say a month or two, [which] wouldn't cause us any great problems;"[29] Cincinnati Gas & Electric Co. had increased its normal 85-day supply of coal to a 100-day store; and U.S. Steel indicated that before the strike it had been running its mines at full production even though the steel mills were operating at a low rate. A spokesperson explained, "we haven't been chewing up coal at a normal rate, so, as a result, supplies are more than adequate at the mill level [for a long work stoppage]."[30]

Strike Insurance

In several industries—newspaper publishing, air and rail transportation, rubber, California fruit and vegetables, Hawaiian sugarcane, and major league baseball—managements have developed and used strike insurance. Its purpose is to provide financial assistance to firms involved in labor disputes and to increase their bargaining power. The airlines have conducted the longest and largest experiments with strike insurance. Six of the largest trunk carriers—American, Capitol, Eastern, Pan American, Trans World, and United—initiated a Mutual Aid Agreement in late 1958. The Civil Aeronautics Board gave approval the next year. Four of the smaller lines joined a year later. Over the years, some companies left and others joined.

Studies of the effects of strike insurance indicate that the airline managements' hopes of winning increased bargaining power were probably not realized. The most authoritative analysis concluded that:

> . . . airline strike insurance, which the Mutual Aid Agreement supplies, appears to have provided escalated costs and benefits and longer strikes, but little else. It is an illustration of the adverse consequences of strengthening the weapons of industrial warfare without any evidence of counterbalancing benefits.[31]

Although the insurance payments may have increased the unions' costs of disagreeing with management terms, the unions apparently were able to increase their members' strike benefits or generate increased membership support so that at the same time they raised management's costs of disagreeing with their terms, canceling out a gain for either.

[29] *The Wall Street Journal,* Oct. 4, 1977.
[30] Ibid.
[31] S. Herbert Unterberger and Edward C. Koziara, "The Demise of Airline Strike Insurance," *Industrial and Labor Relations Review,* vol. 34, October 1980, p. 89; and "Airline Strike Insurance: A Study in Escalation," *Industrial and Labor Relations Review,* vol. 29, Oct. 1975, pp. 26–45.

The baseball owners' reliance upon strike insurance (more accurately "business interruption" insurance) in 1981 appears to have had the same effect that the airlines' use of it produced—a longer strike. The twenty-six big-league clubs raised a strike fund of $15 to $20 million by levying a 2-percent fee on gross revenues over two years. In addition, they bought their insurance through Lloyds of London with a $2 million premium. After 150 scheduled games had not been played, each club received $100,000 for each further game not played until the insurance had paid out $50 million. As the insurance ran out, by August 5, the club owners and the Major League Baseball Players Association resumed negotiations and speedily reached a settlement.

The Lockout

The lockout, as presently practiced, is not an action distinct from the union's strike; rather, it constitutes a way of looking at the same action from another point of view. When it is time to renew an agreement, management insists upon changes in provisions of the agreement, as in the case of the baseball dispute, or a reduction in wages. The union rejects this demand, and management withholds agreement on any other basis. The union calls out its members rather than accept management's terms. Thus the initiative in setting off the action rests with one or the other, but the resulting action involves simultaneously a withholding of labor and a withholding of employment. The relative cost to each of disagreeing with the other will depend upon a variety of conditions, including the economic and political circumstances in which the parties find themselves. But the costs are relative—the dollar loss of income to the workers cannot be laid alongside the dollar loss of income to the company because a dollar of income has a different value in each case.

Moreover, the cost to the employees may be more than simply temporary loss of income. It may involve an actual loss of job, through replacement either by other workers or by machines. And the cost to the union as an organization may be loss of members and even of bargaining rights. Such costs fell upon the Professional Air Traffic Controllers Organization when it called its illegal strike against the FAA, a federal office under the Department of Transportation. The FAA fired the striking members, first for violating signed pledges not to strike and second for acting contrary to law; it then sought decertification of the union as bargaining agent since few of its members then worked for the agency.

Public Relations

Finally, each party may resort to public opinion and political pressure to add to the other's discomfiture. By picketing,[32] newspaper advertising, press

---

[32]On occasion an employer may use picketing to advantage. When a grocer in Burbank, California opened a new store in the summer of 1981, Local 770 of the United Food and Commercial Workers picketed his nonunion establishment. With customers staying away, he hired his own pickets who carried signs advertising special price reductions on common food items. Many cus-

releases, or radio speeches, each may try to arouse the public to express disapproval of the other's course of conduct, in the hope that the pressure of government officials, social disapproval, and loss of public favor will constitute a further disadvantage that the other will be unwilling to incur. The uncertainty and diffuseness of public response and the difficulty of making social pressure articulate render such tactics of questionable value, however, except under unusual circumstances, such as when the public's own welfare or convenience is involved or when a particular controversy is converted into a question of general principle (whether PATCO is more powerful than the United States government, for example).[33]

Public support is most effective when aroused through public leadership. If government officials can be persuaded that it is in their own best interests to intervene in a labor dispute, whether because of concern for general welfare or because of political debt to one of the bargaining parties, the result may be to focus sentiment that previously was diffused. Pressures upon one or the other of the parties will be multiplied as fellow employers or fellow unionists fear that public disfavor, as expressed through elected officials, will lead to greater costs to themselves. If an intransigent employer is publicly castigated by the president or a governor, there may be concern generally among employers that a political climate unfavorable to management is being created. If a recalcitrant union is condemned by a state or local officials, other unionists may worry that legislators may be moved to introduce bills designed to control strikes affecting public health, safety, or comfort. Thus the cost of disagreement can become generalized, spreading from the particular parties in dispute to others more remote. Nevertheless, government pressure may involve costs specific to one or the other of the bargaining parties—perhaps a loss of government contracts to a company or an injunction against the union.

These are relatively intangible costs, but they are of the sort that have become important to both employers and unions. The size of bargaining units, the intractability of settlement, and the serious consequences of strikes in our interdependent economy have encouraged governments—local and federal— to intervene in disputes in order to protect public welfare. The effects of such intervention ultimately make themselves felt in the political sphere, in the kind of government elected and the kind of social legislation which it sponsors. These are matters vital to the future strength of the respective interest groups.

Labor union leaders, for example, were quick to perceive the indirect, far-reaching costs to them of President Reagan's decisive action in the firing of the striking air traffic controllers in 1981. Thomas R. Donahue, secretary-treasurer

---

tomers thought it was an advertising gimmick, crossed the line, and tripled the store's business. The union withdrew its pickets soon thereafter. (*The Wall Street Journal,* Aug. 6, 1981.)

[33]The public response to the air traffic controllers' strike in 1981 was mixed. The Harris poll found that 51 percent of respondents opposed the strike and 40 percent approved; 63 percent thought the strikers must have had legitimate reasons to sacrifice their jobs, but 68 percent thought that the strike should not have been called because of its impact on air transportation and the economy. (*The New York Times,* Aug. 21, 1981.)

of the AFL-CIO, asked a question about the nature of those costs and gave his answer:

> Breathes there a city manager with soul so dead that he will not want to look like a hero when he sees the President of the United States being applauded for being tough and closing every door to a settlement in defiance of all civilized rules of collective bargaining? I don't think there is.[34]

He and many labor scholars agreed that the president's stand would have the effect of stiffening government bargaining positions at all levels. Some feared it would also encourage municipal authorities to seek changes in local labor laws to further restrict strikes and their effects.

BARGAINING POWER AND THE COSTS OF AGREEING

Our discussion is by no means intended to be an exhaustive analysis of the costs to one of the bargaining parties of disagreeing with the other, upon which relative bargaining powers partly rest. It does indicate, however, the way in which the strength of one party is in part dependent upon the cost to the other of disagreeing on its terms. The further determinant of one's bargaining strength is the cost to the other of *agreeing* with it on its terms. As we have seen, it is the relative cost to the bargaining opponent of agreement and disagreement on one's terms that establishes one's bargaining power. Let us turn next, then, to a brief consideration of some of the costs of agreement. This is a matter no less complex than the costs of disagreement. For convenience we shall dissect it into three subcategories: (1) direct costs of concessions, (2) secondary costs of concessions, and (3) nonmarket costs of concessions.

Bargaining Power Inversely Related to Cost of Demand

From the definition of bargaining power used here, it is evident that the higher the monetary demands, the higher the costs of agreement to the party on whom the demands are made and the weaker the bargaining power of the demanding party (with some modification that will be noted shortly). The definition thus stresses that bargaining power is relative to what is being bargained for. A group's bargaining power may be weak relative to one set of demands, whereas the *same group's* bargaining power may be strong relative to a different set of demands. Since the different demands affect the other party's costs of disagreement and agreement differently, bargaining power varies with the demands.

The direct costs of agreement will generally be tied up with specific monetary costs. How much will a wage demand increase the wage bill, or how much will be added by a more liberal vacation plan or group insurance program? Here the amount directly added to the year's budget will be the most pertinent consideration. In addition to the amount of the direct costs, the duration of the increases and additions will also be pertinent. If a company believed that a wage increase once granted would extend for only one year or if a union

---

[34]A. H. Raskin, "The Air Strike is Ominous for Labor ," *The New York Times,* Aug. 16, 1981.

believed that a wage cut once instituted would be withdrawn at the end of the year, there would be less resistance than one usually finds to wage changes. Experience has convinced managements that once a pay increase is granted or a union's demand gets written into the collective agreement, it is usually there to stay.[35]

In recent years unions have agreed to cut wages, but they did so reluctantly and under pressure of continuing high unemployment and, often, plant closings. Union leaders fear that something lost in such a backward step can be regained only by repeating the struggles they have once gone through.[36] For either bargainer, then, the cost of agreement may be the monetary loss not simply for the period over which the agreement extends, but for some indefinite period beyond. If the wage cost of agreement is limited to a definite time, it will be because one of the bargainers is willing to accept at a later date the costs of forcing a readjustment. These future costs, properly discounted, must be added to the cost of the present agreement.

In the case of retroactive agreements, not only current and future direct costs, but also past costs may need to be computed. This is particularly important in the case of pension agreements. Under them, employees now at advanced ages may become eligible for minimum pensions within perhaps as little as five years, without any fund having been set aside in the past for that purpose. It becomes necessary to establish such a fund at the present time, as though the pension system had already been operating over a period of years. These are not, of course, past costs in any literal sense, since payments must be made in the present or future. Part of the cost of agreement is these liabilities incurred in prior years that were not calculated or provided for earlier. The experience of big automobile firms in 1979 well illustrates the size and importance of such costs. In negotiating agreements with the United Automobile Workers, the firms improved pension benefits. Unfunded vested benefits rose 56 percent at General Motors to $6.1 billion, increasing that obligation to 32 percent of net worth, up from 22 percent. The improvement at Ford Motor

---

[35]Arthur Okun pointed out that nonunion as well as unionized firms make wage commitments from which they cannot easily escape. He wrote, "While nonunion firms do make commitments that are morally, and even legally, binding for a year ahead on wage rates (and for some salaried employees, on total earnings), they generally opt for implicit rather than explicit contracts beyond that period. . . . To develop an effective implicit contract, the employer must try to promote favorable expectations and yet curb the likelihood of subsequent disappointments." (*Prices & Quantities,* Washington, D.C.: The Brookings Institution, 1981, pp. 89–90.)

[36]An effective statement and examination of the rationale of this position are to be found in Professor Henry C. Emery's article of years ago, "Hard Times and the Standard Wage," *Yale Review,* vol. 17, 1908, pp. 251–267. Speaking of the unionists, Emery concluded (pp. 266–267): "What they dread most of all is a reduction of wages, not so much because they unreasonably refuse to make sacrifices when the whole community is suffering, but because they believe, and they think they know from experience, that a reduction of wages once made is very difficult to restore. . . . When the manufacturer cannot pay standard wages and run full time at a profit, let him curtail his production, let some men be discharged, but let the level of wages continue intact. Then, when the readjustment comes, there will be no need of a fight, but, automatically, as the demand for products increases, the capitalist's self-interest will send him again in search of more labor." The primary difference in this respect between the time when Emery was writing and today is that unions now are less inclined to await the readjustment, but rather tend to compel it.

Company increased its unfunded vested benefits by 64 percent, up to more than 18 percent of net worth. A 9 percent increase at Chrysler Corporation raised the company's liability to almost 66 percent of net worth, up from 38 percent.[37]

Problems in Calculating Direct Costs

Direct costs may not be easy to compute. In some instances nothing but guess-work is possible. What will be the cost in relaxed incentive or morale and authority if greater control over discipline is granted the union or if straight seniority is recognized in layoffs and promotions? What will be the cost in reduced output if union stewards are given the right to challenge time studies? What will be the cost of a severance pay plan? The number of jobs regularly available depends upon the state of technology and the level of general business activity. The former cannot be accurately forecast for more than short periods, and the government's changeable willingness to push and maintain full-employment measures determines the latter. The acceptance of such costs *may* be nothing more than an exercise in optimism and their rejection a reflection of pessimism. One needs to examine the terms of agreement realistically; they may promise gain as well as cost, and both ought to be evaluated. Disciplinary systems in which unions participate can improve morale. Employee representation in time studies sometimes facilitates their acceptance. To the extent that such results are possible, the cost of agreement may be restrained and even reduced.

Real but Hard-To-Define Indirect Costs

The secondary costs to one party of agreeing to the other's terms present problems of a somewhat different nature. If more than one union exists in the company, the concessions won by one of them are likely to provide precedents that the others will insist on following. No management is likely to grant a wage increase to one union while denying it to others in the same plant. The invidious comparisons would provoke discontent or worse among the employees. Similarly, when a union negotiates with a number of competing firms, it is often obligated to grant to all firms whatever concessions it may grant to any individual firm; any firm left out would be at a competitive disadvantage and strenuously insist upon the same terms received by the others. This is the so-called most favored nations arrangement, to borrow a term from international tariff agreements, under which the most favorable terms conceded to one buyer must be generalized to all. Even without the formality of such a clause, a union cannot easily offer concessions to one firm without expecting to have to offer them to competitors. Other unions in the industry may also be pressed to accept the concessions. In 1981 the Air Line Pilots Association made sizable

[37]"Pension Survey: Unfunded Liabilities Continue to Grow," *Business Week,* Aug. 25, 1980, pp. 94–95.

concessions to United Airlines, as noted above, increasing scheduled and flight hours, agreeing to two instead of three pilots on the large planes and giving up night and overtime bonuses. The chairman of the union's executive council acknowledged that the union had been under intense pressure from other airline labor groups; they accused the United pilots of "taking a giant step backward" and "giving up the store."[38]

In such a case, the direct cost of the pilots agreeing to changed work rules at United may offer secondary gains to competing airlines that seek changes. In addition, other unions, such as the Clerks, Stewardesses, and Machinists, may also find their costs of agreeing to management's terms increased—they will have to accept the costs of work-rule changes proposed by United and the other lines since the pilots have weakened the union positions generally.

A secondary cost to management of any improved terms for those in the bargaining unit is likely to be their extension to those outside the bargaining unit. If the pay or vacation plan or pension system of rank-and-file production workers is improved, such conditions must also be improved for supervisors and higher levels of management, entailing further costs. Some companies make a practice of retaining percentage pay differentials between levels of authority, with first-line supervisors receiving a specified differential over their highest-paid workers, second-line managers receiving a stated differential over the supervisors, and so on up the ladder. In such situations it has sometimes become a standing joke that the union wins pay increases for management. Thus secondary costs of agreeing with the union must be added to the direct costs of such agreement.

The change in production costs as a result of wage adjustments, the change in prices, and the resulting changes in product demand constitute what is unquestionably the most important secondary cost. These changes should perhaps be considered direct costs, since their calculation is necessary before one can even determine changes in the total wage bill. The degree of slack in management's cost structure and the degree of competition in its product market will be highly relevant considerations to both parties in determining the cost of agreement on the other's terms. If added costs can be absorbed without affecting price or if reduced labor costs are simply compensatory and do not lower price, secondary effects on demand for the product can be ignored. If, however, price changes result from changes in labor cost, then the more competitive the product market, the more significant will be the secondary results. The greater the elasticity of demand facing the individual seller, the more marked will be the response to any price changes, either up or down.

Nonmarket Costs of Agreeing

Lastly, there are nonmarket costs of agreeing to the other's proposals. These are factors not associated with the cost-price relationship but which generally

---

[38]John Curley, "United Air Pilots Clear Pact Granting Carrier Job-Rule Concessions," *The Wall Street Journal*, Aug. 14, 1981.

involve long-term interests and matters of principle. One example concerns the union's status. On the one hand, if management entertains some objection to the very presence of a union in its plant and conceives of it as being inimical and undesirable from either a personal interest or a social point of view, the cost of agreement with the union will be perceived as very high indeed. Such recognition of unions has been and appears to be yet, one of the costs of agreement that American employers generally have been most reluctant to assume. On the other hand, to a union seeking support and adherence of employees in a given plant the cost of agreeing on management's terms may be to brand it as ineffectual and even venal. "Selling out" to management is a phrase of opprobrium sometimes applied literally as well as figuratively (note the other unions' accusation of the Air Line Pilots, above); the result may be that hard-won members or employees on the verge of signing up with a union will fall away, and the organization will collapse.

Another matter of principle over which unions and management contest with vigor is the union shop. Managers express their opposition to it because it limits employees' individual freedom to join or not to join a union. This is not the only reason for opposing it, however. Compulsory membership under a union shop ensures the union a larger and steadier flow of dues income than if employees joined and paid dues voluntarily. The hard-to-measure effect of a union's bargaining power is real and significant, according to many managers. The spokesman for a large aircraft company stated that his firm's objection to compulsory union membership was that it increases the strength, the resources, and the striking power of the union. The vice president of industrial relations for a large electrical manufacturer provided a similar reason for his company's refusal to agree to a union shop: "We don't want that money from nonmembers going into the union treasury."[39]

There is also a tactical cost of agreement that the negotiators of both parties calculate carefully. This cost is associated with the principle of the opening wedge. A union or management may object less to the direct or secondary costs of some particular proposal than to the possibility of its being used as a springboard for some future demand which they are totally unwilling to consider. Unions have been opposed to grievances over expulsions from the union that also entail discharge from employment under a union security agreement. They oppose such reviews not because of a fear of having a few employees reinstated to their jobs against the wishes of the union, but because of a much deeper fear that this will establish a precedent for outside intervention in union affairs, thereby threatening the union's bargaining power.

In some instances, managements have been hesitant about agreeing to the participation of unions in the description and classification of jobs, contemplating the danger that this might lead to the union's insistence on discussion and agreement prior to any reassignment of duties among employees and open the possibility of establishing "job jurisdictions" as binding as craft jurisdic-

---

[39]James W. Kuhn, "Right-to-Work: Symbol or Substance?" *Industrial and Labor Relations Review,* vol. 14, 1961, pp. 587–594.

tions. Such examples might be multiplied. Here the cost of agreement includes an admission of interest by the one party in an area in which the other seeks to retain exclusive discretion.

There are indeed certain principles to which unions and managements may adhere so firmly that they constitute creeds with deep ethical or moral roots, the compromise of which will scarcely be considered. In some such instances the cost of agreement may be viewed as infinite. Some managements have closed down their plants rather than give in to the union, and some unions have allowed their organizations to disintegrate during a protracted strike rather than agree on management's terms. In these situations the cost of agreement on the other's conditions is set so high that presumably the cost of disagreement on those same conditions could not be raised to top it. The cost to management of agreeing on the union's terms, for example, would be regarded as so great that the union would be unable to make the cost of disagreement any greater. In such a situation the union's bargaining power would be weak relative to its demands.

CONCLUSION

When bargaining power is viewed in this manner, it follows that it may be altered in one of two ways: (1) by changing the cost to the other party of agreement on one's terms, or (2) by changing the cost of disagreement. Generally speaking, a union may increase its bargaining power either by *increasing* the cost to management of *disagreeing* on the union's terms or by *reducing* the cost to management of *agreeing* on the union's terms. This conclusion is subject to an important modification, however. A union or management may not always be able to alter one of these determinants of its bargaining power independently of any effect on the other determinant. One cannot always assume that a union will automatically increase its bargaining power by reducing the cost to management of agreeing on the union's conditions. Bargaining power and its two components are relative to particular proposals.

If a union were to reduce its wage demands from $1.32 to $1.08, for instance, such action would tend to lessen the cost to management of agreeing with the union; hence it would seem to increase the union's bargaining power relative to the new demand. But before one could arrive at such a conclusion, it would be necessary to observe the effect of this action upon the union's membership. By reducing the prize to be gained, the union may have weakened the desire of its members to fight for it. Whereas the employees might have been willing to strike for an increase of $1.32 an hour, they may decide that $1.08 an hour is not worth fighting for. In any event, if management believed such to be the effect, it would conclude that the cost of disagreeing with the union even on the latter's reduced demands would have been substantially lessened. The union's bargaining power relative to the revised terms it was seeking would depend upon management's revised estimates of the costs of both agreement and disagreement. The result might be weaker as easily as stronger bargaining power for the union.[40]

Can Legislation Equalize Bargaining Power?

Our analysis of bargaining power reveals the fallacy of attempting to equalize bargaining power by legislation. Bargaining power is dependent at least as much upon what each party is seeking as upon each party's coercive ability, and what the parties seek is largely beyond the control of legislation, except with respect to specific issues. Indeed, as we have seen, coercive power—the imposing of costs of disagreement—is only relative to the objective being sought.

One cannot conclude, however, that legislative control over bargaining power is not feasible or desirable. Legal rights and restrictions certainly affect the broad reaches of bargaining power; legislators trimmed management's power when they outlawed the use of the blacklist and restricted injunctions. They also reduced some unions' bargaining power when under the Labor-Management Relations Act of 1947, they limited use of the secondary boycott in interstate commerce. Through Title VII of the Labor-Management Reporting and Disclosure Act of 1959, Congress attempted to curb the bargaining power of the Teamsters prohibiting hot cargo boycotts and to limit the power of the building-trades unions in using organizational picketing. The public widely questions unions' privilege to strike under any circumstances. Some states have banned strikes in public utilities. In disputes that involve the railroads or shipping, where the president determines that national health and welfare are involved, unions and management may have to observe a waiting period before a strike is permissible. In these instances legislative action has reduced the power of one or the other of the parties to make disagreements with its terms costly to the other. Furthermore, most state governments and the federal government prohibit strikes by public employees. Even the eight states allowing strikes limit their use in various ways.[41]

Evaluating the Costs of Agreeing and Disagreeing

The view one takes of the bargaining process itself will in part determine what limitations are considered acceptable in either private or public employment.

---

[40]At the same time, even should management conclude that the workers would be unwilling to strike for the $1.08 increase, its careful appraisal of the situation might lead it to believe that its refusal to grant even this "measly" pay raise (as the workers might regard it) would involve intangible costs of disagreement in the form of distrust, hatred, or noncooperation, rendering disagreement more expensive than agreement. An astute union leadership would point out such a possibility, but regardless of whether or not it did, as long as management recognized this element it would enter into a calculation of the union's bargaining power. Of course, if neither group considered this possibility, it would not enter at all into determination of the union's bargaining power. *Bargaining power is a subjective concept*—and a complex one.

[41]David Lewin, "Public Sector Collective Bargaining and the Right to Strike," *Public Sector Labor Relations: Analysis and Readings,* Thomas Horton & Daughters, 1977, p. 246.

On the one hand, those who regard collective bargaining as a marketing procedure involving the sale of labor services may uphold the strike and lockout, for example, as necessary to a freedom not to contract, as an alternative to a forced sale or purchase. To protect that freedom one might oppose limitations in principle. On the other hand, those who look upon the bargaining process as the basis of a group government or as an industrial relations system might conclude that the strike and lockout as instruments of bargaining power are unnecessary in principle even if unavoidable at present. Possibly the bargaining parties might develop more refined methods of giving unions power to make managerial disagreement with them costly, and vice versa; one hopes that these methods may be more in keeping with functional group governments or the operational requirements of the economy. If the end purpose of the bargaining process is an agreement, voluntarily accepted by those who are party to it, this objective may be as effectively accomplished, at least in certain situations, by means other than the strike or lockout and without any greater degree of compulsion. It is a question of whether our ingenuity is sufficient for the task.

Strikes and lockouts as exercises in bargaining power may be looked at in another way. They are means of making one party's disagreement with the other more costly, thus increasing bargaining power. But as we have seen, bargaining power may also be increased by reducing the cost to the other party of agreeing.

A cost reduction may be accomplished by methods other than simply lowering the demands made. Two unions may make the same wage demands, for example, but where one is satisfied to leave the problem of meeting them up to management, but the other may offer its cooperation to help make the wage concession less costly. As our analysis indicates, agreement will come when the costs of agreement are less than those entailed by disagreement. If it is possible systematically to reduce the costs of agreement by improved methods of collective bargaining, it may follow that such methods of making disagreement costly as the strike and lockout will simply find less frequent use. Without being banned, they would thus disappear as a major problem. Occasional resort to them would be acceptable as that measure of tolerance for private group disagreement and breakdown which seems unavoidable in a democratic society. There is much to recommend this view, and we shall explore its possibilities in considerably greater detail later in Chapter 15.

Throughout this chapter mention has been made of costs to the union and management. A moment's reflection will reveal, however, that since "union" and "management" are simply entities, in this context collections of individuals, costs will be estimated differently depending upon the influences that bear upon those doing the estimating. This is a question that involves the political structure of each union and company. In Chapter 7 we shall examine how the political factor enters into the bargaining process.

COLLECTIVE BARGAINING AND ITS POLITICS: THE UNION

The union is a political[1] system, and the aggregate of interests represented by management constitutes another political system. The decisions reached in the bargaining process are in part dependent upon the political characteristics of union and management. It will prove fruitful to center discussion around two essential ingredients of any political system, the issues of authority and responsibility. We shall be concerned with the derivation of the authority of the leaders and the nature of their responsibilities. Let us turn first to the union.

DEMOCRACY IN UNION ELECTIONS

The union as a political system offers opportunities for careerists. In most unions, an official position carries with it the promise of advancement and a respectability and prestige worth striving for. In national organizations, shop stewards do not have to limit their aspirations to a local presidency; they can look forward to state or regional offices or special staff functions, from which a successful campaign may take them to the general executive board. The higher offices are assignments rewarding in their importance, if not in their pecuniary return; they customarily involve supervision over some vital aspect of the union's affairs and collaboration in the formation of central policy. The presidency of the national union may even come within reach. Thus the stew-

---

[1]It will be readily observed that the word "political" is loosely used in Chapters 7 and 8 to include phenomena not strictly embraced by that term. "Political" as used here refers to the non-economic influences—organizational forces and governing rules found among those who make up unions and managements.

ard working in the shop may entertain the hope of eventually gaining one of the influential offices of our contemporary society. Union offices sometimes lead to political positions in local and state governments and occasionally are an avenue to federal appointment, though seldom to elective federal positions. It is not surprising, in view of the status now attached to union officeholding, that there should be some workers who aspire to union office and seek their preferment within that organization rather than through business advancement.

Since a union office is commonly won through election, the would-be officer must first become a candidate and campaign for votes. Though sometimes unopposed, a candidate usually has to defeat a rival. Once elected, officers must retain their support or add to it if they expect to be returned to their positions. To accomplish these results, they must convince fellow workers of their capacity to do things for the union membership. The obvious vote catchers are pay increases, reduced hours, and better working conditions. These become campaign promises to attract support, and elected candidates will feel some compulsion to try to make good on their promises in collective bargaining negotiations. In some instances the promises are impossible to achieve, and the result is likely to be a disillusioned electorate or a leader who fights to get as much of the impossible as is possible.

Furthermore, in line with American custom, unions do not require members to vote. Abstentions are usually numerous, and to have a minority of the electorate carry an election is far from uncommon. Those most sure to vote are the members who are against a candidate—voting "agin" rather than "for" also being a common American practice. Aggrieved bloc voting and abstentions make candidates particularly vulnerable to any group displeased with either their promises or their accomplishments. Both practices also foster volatile changes in voting, of which local union officers are constantly aware. These facts of political life have long been familiar to Americans.

The political nature of unions thus leads to a rather continuous importunacy, affecting what the union will demand in collective bargaining as well as what it is satisfied to accept. The standard method by which union leaders evidence their responsibility to their constituencies is by seeking from management general gains for all in the bargaining unit or specific benefits for particular members. Thus appeals for votes customarily identify workers' interests and promise to satisfy them if the candidates are elected.

The success of such election appeals is indicative of the members' preferences and strongly influences union proposals. One local candidate may run on a platform pledged to support the national officers in demands for pensions and retraining benefits, for example, while an opponent might urge that the union demand a straight 30-percent increase. Although the election of one of the candidates would not settle the nature of the bargaining demands actually made, it would provide a measure of members' expectations. Such contests for membership support on the basis of self-interest occur at all levels of authority within the union. Note the appeal for votes in this handbill circulated by an employee who was campaigning for the job of local union president:

Members of Local 440, I.U.E.!

Election of officers will be this Friday. If you want leadership and ability vote for Joe Pucci. If Local 440 is to meet the challenge of the new management we need a strong, experienced president. The Admiral [company president] says he's going to cut costs and raise efficiency—Joe Pucci will see to it that he doesn't cut jobs and raise hell with our hard-won standards.

Joe Pucci knows how to win for the workers—he is an experienced Chief Steward in the Fabricating Department, the plant's largest.

1 [Over the last three years] he won over [$146,000] in back pay through grievances he initiated or handled. In the last six months alone he has won [$117,000] in back pay.

2 Of the 12 cases he has taken to arbitration he has won 10. No other department has so high a proportion of wins.

3 The Fabricating Department has filed more grievances against management trying to take away our contractual rights than any other department.

Joe's philosophy is:

1 To tell those in his department what the facts are. He has regularly distributed grievance reports to all stewards in his department and interested members.

2 He does not trade off grievances and would fight any steward who tried to.

3 He is not afraid of telling a man if he is wrong, but if he is right, and his case is just, Joe Pucci will sit on the door of the I. R. Department until the grievance is settled.

4 He doesn't let technicalities entangle him—he is out to solve problems, not to be a contract lawyer—and he does solve grievances—he does serve the members.

His Record Proves It!

His stand on out-of-classification work is this: As long as the company is willing to pay regular rates to first grade wiremen to work on relay adjustments we should allow it.

1 Second grade wirers have nothing to fear. Under the government contract overtime will be unlimited and nobody will lose any work.

2 No second grade wirers will lose jobs because of layoff. The government wants and needs as much of the work as F.T.C. [the company] can provide.

3 If F.T.C. does not do the work, it will have to be subcontracted to Kellog. Joe is in favor of our people getting the work and the pay.

4 He will fight to keep all of the AK-10 Relay work [with the loose piece rates] here in any case.

Vote for Experience, Ability, and Your Best Interest—Joe Pucci.

(Vote against dare-devil contract finishes, bumbling arbitration, and weak leadership.)

THE ELECTORATE'S INFLUENCE ON BARGAINING

Political campaigning may affect bargaining conferences and negotiations as well as union demands. Intraunion factionalism based on rival candidacies may raise antagonisms among the representatives at the bargaining table and lead to splits or at least a lack of cohesion in pursuing bargaining strategy. A management official in the New England leather industry observed: "Internal union politics creates dissension in the union negotiating committee frequently during a discussion of the merits of an employer's counter-proposal. . . . The followers of the union political adversaries are unwilling to be placed on the spot, so to speak, and subjected to criticism on the floor of the union meeting if either group takes a stand contrary to the views of the other."

Decisions and actions that affect various work groups or workers with special interests in different ways can cause serious political troubles within a union. Professor Leonard Sayles was one of the first to point out how different seniority plans can cause dissension within a union and serious political problems for local leadership.[2] In a large midwestern plant, a local union secured the right to have its officers sit with management representatives on the skill classification board. The board determined what jobs were to be classified as skilled. The classification was a desired one because it protected workers from being bumped by semiskilled workers in layoffs. Every group with even a faint claim of being skilled clamored for that rating, rocking the union with intrigue and dissension. The local officers found the political pressures unbearable, being able to satisfy only a few work groups and having to make many unhappy. Within eighteen months the local renegotiated the agreement and withdrew from the classification board. Thereafter the officers involved themselves in the more politically appealing work of grieving management's "impossible and unreasonable" classifications.

The fact that the membership ultimately holds within its power the giving of union office means that at times it can force its leaders to conform to its wishes, even when the leaders are opposed in principle. Officials have sometimes admitted pushing for agreements that they believed to be unfair to the employing organization because they felt themselves too weak politically to oppose their members and rivals for office. Managers report, and union leaders will sometimes confirm, that during informal negotiations preceding actual bargaining, union representatives have readily agreed that wage demands were beyond reason. The representatives may then point out that their members would nonetheless ask for increases, inquiring of the employer representatives; "What are we going to do about it?" In 1981, the president of the Professional Air Traffic Controllers Organization faced such a situation openly and formally. Initially he accepted terms he characterized as fair, but he warned government officials that his members would not accept them, as indeed they did not. In a membership vote the terms were overwhelmingly rejected.

---

[2]Leonard Sayles, "Seniority: An Internal Union Problem," *Harvard Business Review,* vol. 30, 1952, pp. 55–61.

Member Approval of Agreements

Managers have good reason to take such warnings seriously, for agreements are not usually completed until members approve them. Experience indicates that approval is by no means automatic. William E. Simkin, an experienced arbitrator, pointed out that it is in the mutual interests of both union and management negotiators to offer a package that will win membership acceptance. Rejection is a repudiation of the union leadership if it truly supported the package.

Unions with at least 40 percent of total union membership require ratification votes (this estimate is based on a study of national union constitutions); many local unions may also require such votes, but only an examination of their bylaws would reveal the number.[3] The ratification votes are not pro forma and cannot be taken for granted by managers or union leaders. A study of votes some years ago indicated that members reject 10 to 15 percent of agreements submitted to them.[4] More recent data indicate about the same outcomes.[5] Rejection causes problems for managers, too, Simkin pointed out:

> Most important, a dangerous precedent may have been established for future negotiations. [On the one hand,] employees understandably may get the idea that a way to get more is to reject the initial agreement. On the other hand, if the company stands firm, a strike is quite likely to occur.[6]

Several examples of settlement rejections by union members will illustrate the problem. One of the most complex was the vote by the skilled members of the United Automobile Workers against an agreement between the union negotiators and Ford Motor Company in 1973. The skilled members had long been dissatisfied with their limited influence in a union dominated by semi-skilled workers. By 1966 another union, the International Society of Skilled Trades, was eagerly courting the UAW's skilled members, promising autonomy and full attention to their problems. In response the UAW approved a constitutional provision allowing skilled members the right to vote separately on ratifications of agreements. Most of the skilled members believed they had gained a veto of terms and provisions they did not like.

When the union's executive board submitted the tentative agreement negotiated with Ford in late 1973, the overall vote to approve was 2 to 1. However, more than three-quarters of the 28,000 skilled members voted against ratification. The skilled workers objected particularly to a clause that allowed Ford to substitute unskilled part-time help or outside contractors for skilled workers doing overtime hours if large numbers of skilled workers declined to bid for

---

[3]Herbert J. Lahn, "Union Contract Ratification Procedures," *Monthly Labor Review,* vol. 91, May 1968, pp. 7–10.

[4]William E. Simkin, *Mediation and The Dynamics of Collective Bargaining,* Washington, D.C.: Bureau of National Affairs, 1971, p. 145.

[5]Federal Mediation and Conciliation Service, *Thirty-Second Annual Report 1979,* Washington: Federal Mediation and Conciliation Service, 1980, p. 19.

[6]Ibid., p. 145.

voluntary overtime. Despite the rejection by skilled workers, the executive board declared the agreement accepted by a majority of the members; it also ordered the overtime clause renegotiated, seeking a local option.

Many of the skilled workers were angry with their union leaders. Some of the traditional-minded dissidents filed suit in the Wayne County Circuit Court, but the more important action was an appeal to the union's Public Review Board, a "court" of outside neutral experts established by the union to resolve internal union disputes. After hearings it found for the executive board in a split decision. The dissent gradually quieted, but the potential problems lurking in ratification votes, arising from political differences within the organization, continue to worry union leaders and company officials.

After the difficulties of ratification by the UAW members, a presidential National Commission for Industrial Peace addressed the broad issues involved. It asked whether the public should consider how much democracy should be encouraged in unions. The one agreement in eight that is rejected by members creates serious issues for management. Union members of the commission argued that union dissidents had used the votes to hinder effective collective bargaining. They pointed out that leaders whose efforts were rejected by members "tended to become shy and have not exercised the leadership and general responsibility necessary in this controversial area. This made it possible for minorities 'to impose their wills on majorities' and for relatively small numbers of dissidents 'to prevent settlements and cause unwarranted turmoil'."[7]

However union leaders and business managers may view the democratic practice of ratification votes, there is little or no public support to limit it. Democratic participation through free and open elections is a valued part of American ideals and thus will undoubtedly continue. In 1979 United Airlines' ground-service employees twice rejected agreements negotiated by their union, the International Association of Machinists (IAM). The terms included generous wage increases, but members believed they should have received more. Settlement was reached only after a 55-day strike. Members do not always reject agreements because of too small a wage increase. Other items may become touchy political issues, as in the 1981 negotiations between the miners and the mine operators. The union members decisively rejected the first agreement reached by union and management negotiators, as described in Chapter 3. They objected to provisions that they argued would allow "scab coal" and "scab workers." Such terms carry powerful emotional content and dissident union leaders made the most of them. The rejection was a serious political setback to the new president of the union (labeled "Sell-out Sam" by his opponents and critics) and cost management more than nine weeks of lost production. Furthermore, management had to improve the nonwage terms to which the members had strongly objected.

National officers are not the only union leaders who may find ratification

---

[7]"Democracy's Impact On Union Bargaining," *Business Week,* May 18, 1974, p. 27.

troublesome. Local officers sometimes find themselves in untenable positions. With help from the national union representatives they may be able to recover with little loss of face. An official of one of the railroad unions explained the possible procedure: If the general chairperson, who is the local negotiator and an elected official, realizes that it would be wise to give ground on certain union demands but finds it difficult to do so without loss of prestige, the national office could "advise" yielding. This would provide an out; the local official would have stood firm, but would have been overruled by the national office. In other cases local officers may be in a position to demand and secure support from their national officers, even though the latter disapprove of the cause. A high officer of the United Automobile Workers admitted that strikes by powerful locals were sometimes approved by the national office only because it was known that they would be called anyway. Disapproval would discredit the national's authority and diminish the prestige of its officers. The intricacies of local-regional-national politics in large unions cannot be explored here; they do, however, have their bearing upon the bargaining process.

Special Interest Groups within the Union

The existence of special interest groups within the union, usually of an occupational or regional nature, further complicates the political life of union officers. Leaders deal with such groups according to their political power. Union officers must balance interests if they can, seeking compromises where possible, or in extreme political situations sacrifice some blocs of votes to win others. Particularly in an industrial union, a number of grades and varieties of skills may be represented, and some of these occupational groups seek preferment over others. One textile company official writes of "the attempts of various groups such as spinners and engineers to secure higher wage increases and preferred working conditions over that of common laborers or female employees engaged in the production process."

At least as difficult to resolve are the conflicting interests of workers in separate plants who are covered by the same agreement. Union leadership, pursuant to a policy of wiping out regional wage differentials, may make a concerted effort to establish a standard rate over a wider area, only to find the groups that had previously enjoyed a higher rate pressing the following year for the restoration of the traditional differential. Business firms in one area may be in a position to make a more liberal agreement than those in another area; locals in the more prosperous section of the industry may then become embittered at union leaders who allow themselves to be guided by the financial condition of a representative firm. Union leaders, whose jobs rest on votes, are necessarily sensitive to such considerations.

In view of the occupational and sectional blocs within unions, one writer suggested: "An important aspect of the leadership function is reasonably to ensure that every interest group which can exercise effective political pressure is represented in the bargaining process. In a multi-craft union, the important crafts will be represented; in a multi-industrial union, the different branches of the trade; and in regional or national negotiations, the various geographical units of the organization."[8] Methods for achieving an integration of special interest groups within the union for purposes of collective bargaining are varied. They include allowing interest groups' representatives to sit on the policy committee that drafts the union's proposals, as when delegates from all the big auto company locals come together in conference; provision for representation on the negotiating committee, as when an Amalgamated Clothing and Textile Workers' Union joint board chooses a bargaining committee including members from each of the four main crafts—cutters, tailors, pressers, and finishers; or opportunity for special interest representatives to approve the tentative agreement before the negotiating committee accepts it, as when representatives from all the plants of a glass-manufacturing firm (who have been present at negotiations, while leaving the actual bargaining to their national officials) must consent to the drafted agreement before it goes to their membership for final approval. In all these procedures the need for understanding and reconciling divergent interests and points of view is readily apparent. The political process becomes part and parcel of the bargaining process.

There is, then, between the union electorate and its elected officials a relationship that contributes to the bidding up of demands upon the company. A candidate for office or an officeholder must match the promises of rivals; the candidate must not get too far ahead or fall too far behind the promises of others. A candidate may even eliminate rivals by outpromising them and by demanding and getting more and more. Responsibility to the membership is gauged primarily in such terms, and it is on this relationship that elected officials' authority largely rests.

POLITICAL THREATS FROM OUTSIDE THE UNION

In addition to the candidate-electorate bond, there is a second relationship which intensifies the bidding-up effect—the union-membership relation. To win new members, to hold the interest of members once they have joined, and to stave off the raids of rival unions, it is incumbent upon the union officers to persuade employees not only that continuing benefits are to be secured through membership but also that the benefits of this union are relatively greater than could be secured through some other union. It thus becomes an additional responsibility of union leaders to maintain and if possible to expand the membership and strength of the organization they have inherited. This too is largely a matter of making promises and of seeking to make good on promises once made.

The capacity of union officials to make sweeping promises to employees during organizing drives has been the occasion for wry comment by many members of management. As the National Labor Relations Board long ago

---

[8]Arthur M. Ross, *Trade Union Wage Policy,* Berkeley, Calif.: University of California Press, 1948, p. 33.

observed: "Where groups are to be organized and moved into action it is not unusual for the leaders to promise more than can be secured or to indulge in some exaggeration."[9]

But once organized, unions may find that they must work to hold their members by warding off the efforts of rival unions to win them away. The United Mine Workers, for example, sought for some time to win away U.S. Steel employees who worked in the iron mines. They were already members of the United Steelworkers but the miner's organizers argued they would win better terms of employment.

"No-raiding" provisions within the AFL-CIO have diminished to some extent the political significance of the union-membership relationship. Respect by each union for every other union's existing jurisdiction would seem to eliminate much of the pressure to satisfy members that their union is doing as well as another, since the other is no longer a potential rival. This is true only within limits, however. For one thing, there are rival unions outside the AFL-CIO federation that do not respect its jurisdiction—notably the Teamsters. For another, good performance in one's present bargaining units, compared with the performance of other unions even within the AFL-CIO, is necessary for effective organizing of new units.

The union officer's responsibility to maintain the strength of the union can be enforced at local levels by pressure from national officials; but at the national level, who is there to determine whether officers have been duly responsible to the organization? This check is provided, if at all, by the close tie between the leaders' responsibility to the present membership and their responsibility to the continuing organization. It is difficult indeed to press for advantages for present constituents if the organization is crumbling away, and conversely an expanding organization finds it easier to win concessions on their behalf. "Trade unions need power in order to materialize their most immediate daily objectives."[10] To some extent, then, the membership will itself seek to make officers responsible not only for the achievement of immediate gains but also for the strengthening of the organization, by which future gains can be better assured.

There are thus two major pressures focused on union leaders. As candidates for union office they must match the claims of rival candidates, and as representatives of the union organization they must match the performance of other unions. These pressures are felt at all levels of union authority. Both local and national officers must protect their own positions and at the same time ensure that another organization does not wean away present or potential members. But if such pressures exist, what determines their content? Why are some appeals powerful and others weak? What is it in a given situation that causes

---

[9]*In the Matter of Rabhor Rubber Company, Inc.* vol. I NLRB, 1936, p. 470.

[10]J. B. S. Hardman, *American Labor Dynamics,* New York: Harcourt, Brace & World, Inc., 1928, p. 104. Hardman was himself active in the union movement for many years. He continues on this same page: "Generally and objectively speaking, trade unionism is a sustained, systematic effort at power accumulation, and this function of trade unionism is also its driving force."

an electorate to respond, a membership to fall away, or an occupational group or local union to push for special treatment? What influences members' notion of their union's responsibility to them? What justifies their grant of authority to their leaders?

Invidious Comparisons: Increasing Members' Expectations

The answers appear to lie largely in workers' comparison of their situation to that of others. Discontent leading to membership demands arises because groups are treated differently when they expect to be treated similarly or when they are treated similarly when they expect to be treated differently. Members of the same union working at the same job but in different plants may be paid different rates, creating a pressure on the union leadership to raise the rates of the "underpaid" group. Skilled workers may become upset because of an insufficient differential between their own wages and the wages of unskilled labor. The skilled autoworkers forced the UAW to give special recognition to their claims and to provide special bargaining procedures, as noted above. Such discontent does not necessarily arise spontaneously. Rank-and-file leaders and rival candidates for office often look for differences that lend themselves to political exploitation, differences useful for arousing and intensifying discontent.

Even without any political leadership, invidious comparisons stimulate discontent. Groups working together or in close proximity to each other may perceive differences or similarities in their work that give rise to invidious and political rivalries. An example is the difficulty that arose when District Council 37 of the American Federation of State, County and Municipal Workers, in New York City, agreed to the appointment of civilian clerks as police administrative aides (PAAs) who were to be ready to work on all shifts on all days. As the city freed police of clerical chores, it needed additional PAAs in the scattered precinct houses and other police offices open twenty-four hours a day, but too few applicants appeared to fill the positions available. It became clear that the uncertain hours and shifts made the PAA positions less desirable than those with regular working times; to compensate for the possible inconvenience of the work shift, the city agreed to a base pay above that for regular clerks who worked only day shifts from 8 A.M. to 4 P.M.

Trouble arose when regular clerks discovered that in some locations police supervisors were using PAAs regularly on the 8-to-4 shift. The PAAs argued that since they were ready and willing to work night shifts and odd hours, even though not asked to do so, they deserved the higher pay. With reluctance the union's grievance representatives became involved. After negotiations the Police Department agreed to use PAAs only in offices that were open around the clock. The regular clerks agreed not to grieve if, in such offices, some PAAs worked the regular day shift.

But no sooner was this internal union dispute settled than a new one arose:

the PAAs complained that the union was discriminating against them. They asked to be allowed to take the promotional exam for advancement to administrative assistant, a level up from the position of regular clerk. The union officers faced a serious problem in this demand, for promotion opportunities to assistant were all too few in any case and if the younger, better-schooled PAAs competed for them, they would win an undue portion of them. The clerks would be doubly aggrieved, having their few promotion slots filled by others who enjoyed higher pay all along. The union leaders sought to resolve the matter by persuading the city to establish a separate promotion ladder for the PAAs, with a new title, *senior* PAA. As might be expected, the solution only created a further problem. Regular clerks then argued they should be allowed to seek promotion through the new ladder as well as their old one. The PAAs strongly objected. The leader of District Council 37 finally separated the regular clerks and the PAAs into two locals, but the conflict and rivalry continued.

Workers on their own may also compare their situation with that of members of other unions, and this influences the pressures they apply to their leaders. When one union can point to significantly larger wage gains than another, workers may be tempted to leave the one and join the other. The Teamsters, the country's largest union, has often recruited members with the boast that it gets more for workers. Invidious comparisons are not wholly responsible for the political pressures upon officers and the group pressures with which union leaders must contend, but they are important determinants of those pressures and interest. The pressures of invidious comparisons are, of course, not unique to union members. Senior electronics engineers may be well satisfied with their salaries until they note that junior engineers are being hired at almost as high a salary. The bank vice president in charge of loans may be exceedingly pleased with a raise until discovering that the vice president for foreign accounts received an even larger increase.

The problems of comparative pressures within unions, among unions, and between union and nonunion workers has probably increased as media coverage has widened. Union proposals and collective bargaining provides news for radio, television, newspapers, and magazines. Union activities in one part of the country are quickly known in other parts, suggesting achievements to be copied or developments to be avoided. Both union leaders and managers have learned the value of explaining their activities to the public. Public relations and educational staffs of both companies and unions seek to keep union members, nonunion workers, and the public informed about conditions of work.

The wide publicity usually given to labor negotiations undoubtedly stimulates comparisons between groups and helps to generate compulsions that the union leaders cannot resist. They are spurred to action by interest blocs whose members express concern about an "unfair" situation compared to others. Such pressure can be termed "equitable comparison," since it is based on a sense of what is fair or just—what one group is due in light of what has been done for some other group or groups. Another term that might be used is "coercive comparison." It connotes a contrast that induces a peculiar urgency and a stimulus to action. It suggests a relationship that requires correction or an imbalance between groups that calls for immediate adjustment.

It is possible, of course, that comparison may provide cause for complacency or satisfaction—"We are doing as well as the next person"—or even for self-congratulation—"We made out better than the others," But the comparison must still be made in order for one to arrive at that conclusion. There is a compulsion in the social environment requiring the comparison—invidious though it may be—before people can determine whether they should be satisfied or not. It is this equitable comparison or coercive comparison, then, which drives union leaders to frame demands on employers in order to satisfy their constituents and retain their votes and their membership.

Decreasing Members' Expectations

The comparisons do not necessarily push in only one direction, toward higher wages or better terms of work. Under adverse economic conditions, concessions by a union in one location or industry may push unions elsewhere and in related industries toward moderation in bargaining, if not outright wage cuts. In 1981 a number of industries found competitive forces adversely affecting their sales, and managements turned to cost cutting as a remedy. General Tire and Rubber Company, for example, won from Local 466 of the United Rubber Workers significant wage cuts at its Marion, Indiana, plant early in the year. The members accepted a 17-percent cut in hourly pay, a suspension of the cost-of-living adjustment, and cancellation of the supplemental unemployment benefit. The following month Local 186 at Firestone's Memphis, Tennessee, tire plant agreed to cost concessions, and by June the members of the United Rubber Workers employed by General Tire in Logansport, Indiana, also agreed to wage concessions.

The United Rubber Workers were responding not only to the wage cuts taken by fellow members but also to the concessions made by workers in other industries. Chrysler workers, threatened by the company's bankruptcy, had reluctantly agreed to reduce wages and benefits by $622 million over three years. They had done so at the insistence of Congress, which approved an aid package for the ailing company. But workers across the country realized that wage cuts were both possible and publically acceptable. At the same time the United Food and Commercial Workers accepted cuts in pay for members employed in a number of supermarket chains in the east; the steelworkers at Ford and at the Mesta Machine Company in Pennsylvania also gave up benefits. Even the Operating Engineers in northern California, one of the more powerful unions among the building trades, had accepted a wage reduction. Each additional concession by a union made it easier and more likely for other unions to accept similar concessions or at least to moderate their expectations of gains.

COERCIVE COMPARISONS AMONG WORKERS

What is the basis for one group's comparing itself with another? Would operating engineers be inclined to compare themselves with semiskilled lathe operators? Would building trades workers compare themselves with automobile mechanics? Are common laborers concerned with how well they have faired relative to die cutters? Are there "noncomparison groups" as a modern version of Cairnes's "noncompeting groups"?[11]

Economists tend to approach comparisons within the theoretical framework in which they consider labor markets. They compare the wages and working conditions of workers in a given occupation with those of workers in the same occupation in another location. If a single wage does not prevail or if wage differentials between similar workers cannot be explained on the grounds that they equalize different working conditions so that the packages of wages and working conditions are equal, then economists would expect coercive comparison to bring about either a change in terms or a movement of workers. As a matter of fact, however, students of labor have come to appreciate that the "labor market" belies its name; there is no geographical area within which wages tend toward equality, even for workers of similar skills. Differentials continue over long periods of time.[12]

Wage surveys show that different firms even within a fairly restricted region offer wages that vary widely for the same occupational level. In the late seventies in New York City, for example, the highest-paid janitors received more than 3.33 times more in straight-time hourly earnings than did the lowest-paid. Maintenance electricians, most of whom are organized, showed a considerably smaller differential of 2.2 times. White-collar workers such as stenographers, clerks, and industrial nurses reported intermediate differentials, the highest earnings being from 2.5 times to almost 3 times the lowest.[13] When occupational wages are classified by experience, seniority, or skill or level, they also reveal considerable dispersion; and the lower the rank, the wider the variation.[14]

---

[11]John E. Cairnes, *Some Leading Principles of Political Economy Newly Expounded,* New York: Harper & Brothers, 1984, pp. 70–73. Cairnes assumed that there were "industrial layers" within which competition for jobs took place but that workers in one layer did not compete for jobs with workers in other layers. For comment on Cairnes, the reader is referred to H. J. Davenport, "Noncompeting Groups," *Quarterly Journal of Economics,* vol. 40, 1926, pp. 52–81.

[12]This matter has been discussed by Lloyd Reynolds in his article, "Wage Differences in Local Labor Markets," *American Economics Review,* vol. 36, 1946, pp. 366–375; and by Robert L. Raimon, "The Indeterminateness of Wages of Semi-skilled Workers," *Industrial and Labor Relations Review,* vol. 6, 1956, pp. 180–194. A later, more extensive exploration of long-continuing differentials is found in Peter B. Derringer and Michael J. Piore, *Internal Labor Markets and Manpower Analysis,* Lexington, Mass.: D. C. Heath and Company, 1971.

[13]The U.S. Department of Labor Statistics regularly issues reports on *Wages in New York City* and for other cities too.

[14]See Lloyd G. Reynolds, *The Structure of Labor Markets,* New York: Harper & Row, Publishers, Incorporated, 1951, pp. 157–158; and J. W. F. Rowe, *Wages in Practice and Theory,* London: Routledge & Kegan Paul, Ltd., 1928, p. 111.

The absence of an equality of occupational wages within a geographic area does not itself support the conclusion that local comparisons are of no importance. Research in both the United States and Great Britain indicates that workers accept differences in wage levels of neighboring firms if they have existed so long that everyone regards them as customary. Practice and tradition powerfully influence acceptance of differentials that are rooted in little else and may indeed make it difficult to modify existing wage relationships.[15]

Even though comparisons may not drive occupational rates to equality within a community or region, they may serve to keep rates among the companies in that area in line with each other according to traditional relationships. If the hourly rate for maintenance electricians goes up by 10 percent in the dominant firm in a locality, other firms may have to make adjustments of the same amount, even though the rates in the different companies cover a considerable range. Similarly, if the telephone company or electrical utility raises its typists or secretaries by $18 a week, other employers in the community may have to approximate that adjustment, perhaps with lag, or face greater difficulty in recruiting replacements when its present secretaries leave.

Workers are not uninformed about wage changes and differentials in their areas, though blue-collar employees rely more upon informal sources—friends and relatives—than upon newspapers or agencies for their information. The informal network that provides workers with wage and job data is not necessarily inefficient. Since wage rates vary greatly according to company, location, occupation, and travel time, workers need a lot of other information. Thus, word of mouth may very ably keep workers up to date on jobs and their changing characteristics.[16]

A Standard Wage for Comparison

Another likely basis for wage comparison is some standard wage scale or wage change within a region, industry, or occupation which is significant to employees. Workers may measure their own wage against changes in the scale set by a large employer in the community or against the gains of a prominant union. Both are apt to be publicized by the press and widely known by workers directly involved. Even if the workers' own employer is not included in the bargaining unit or operates in a different industry, they reasonably entertain an expectation that *changes,* if not absolute magnitudes, may move in some rough relationship. Even in the absence of large-scale bargaining units, many national unions have sought standardized wage scales over the area within which the products of their members are competitive. Local unions are expected to conform in order to prevent one local from undercutting the wage rates of other locals, thereby permitting price-cutting by employers and leading to a shift of work from higher-wage to lower-wage shops.

---

[15]See Albert Reese and George P. Shultz, *Workers and Wages in an Urban Labor Market,* Chicago: The University of Chicago Press, 1970.
[16]Ibid.

Where locals conduct most of the negotiations, as in construction, the rivalries between them, even if they belong to different building-trades unions, can exert a powerful upward force on wages. Collective bargaining is conducted in an extraordinarily complex way in construction, with considerable variation by branch of industry, region, location, and craft. There were more than a dozen major unions and over 400,000 employing contractors in the mid-1970s. Employees and unions have in force at any one time about 6000 construction agreements, most covering only a local area; and one-third to one-half of them are renegotiated every year. Because members of various crafts work together on projects and building sites and there is great worker mobility, union members are well aware of the wage scales won in settlement. The many contractors face stiff competition in bidding for work and are especially vulnerable once they are in the midst of a project. The many craft·locals vie with others to secure a better wage. The result is a strike-prone, high-wage-scale industry.

During the early seventies, for example, construction, with about 5 percent of total employment, contributed almost a quarter of all strikes and a fifth of all workdays lost to strikes. Furthermore, the rivalry that provoked the strikes paid off for a long time. Average hourly earnings in construction increased much faster than did those in manufacturing: in 1947 they were 28 percent higher and by the early seventies they had risen to 59 percent higher.[17] One can conclude that for a quarter of a century the fragmented construction unions pursued a leapfrogging standard wage, each local rivaling the others in their attempt to secure a higher wage. The result was a significant recent growth of nonunion construction, particularly in private home building. As a result of such competition as well as adverse economic conditions for construction, wage differentials have shrunk to levels of twenty years ago.

The standard wage, as we have previously seen, was designed to prevent the use of wages for such competitive purposes. Some union leaders, moreover, have given up the attempt to draw any geographical lines bounding the area of competition. They have come to the conclusion that such boundaries cannot be fixed. Since they are constantly shifting and subject to breakdown, the only feasible method of accomplishing the objectives of the standard-wage program is to standardize the wage scale throughout the entire jurisdiction of the union. Thus there have emerged from union headquarters *national* wage policies for the benefit of the entire membership, deviation from which must be explained by the local union. That numerous deviations from such a national standard customarily have been permitted does not belie the fact that the standard remains the basis for comparison.[18] With the growth of multinational corporations and increasing competition across national borders, unions now are

[17]About one-fifth of the strikes in construction arise over jurisdiction disputes. They are usually of short duration, so they do not often come to public attention.

[18]The existence of a national standard or pattern does not necessarily mean that all bargains will conform to it or that deviations from it are necessarily a challenge to its validity. The standard is only the basis for comparison, from which deviations must be justified. It is even possible that patterns of deviation may develop.

faced with the issue of an international standard wage. So far political and social difficulties have limited the efforts devoted to the matter.

Particularly when members receive their union newspapers, they are confronted with what other workers in the industry have won on the same kind of job. Week by week, reports continue of settlements in one shop or another. Members begin to develop an expectancy of a certain kind of settlement of the standard union demands. If the standard demands are pared down in their own local negotiations to less than what they have come to expect, union leaders are likely to have a hard time selling an agreement unless their explanations are unusually persuasive. The national union office is also under some pressure to support local unions having difficulty in winning the standard package. When a national representative is sent in to assist local negotiators—a frequent practice—there is likely to be some pressure upon the representative to fight for a bargain at least as good as those won by other locals in the area.

Industry standards are thus another—and significant—determinant of equitable comparisons within the union, along with the community rate structures, but the question remains of how industry standards become established. Certainly they are not static. What compulsion or what coercive comparison is involved that leads the officials of one national union to determine that last year's goal was an increase of 10 percent, whereas this year's objective will be profit sharing or sabbatical vacations?

Which Standard Is Chosen?

There are in reality two questions here. The first concerns the nature of the union demand—whether a profit-sharing plan, unemployment benefits, severance pay, or a promotion program. The particular demands are in the long run decided by the social and institutional influences bearing upon the basic objectives of workers. These objectives may be such things as security, a desire for greater participation in determining their own conditions, and the enhancement of self-respect. When the attainment of these objectives is blocked or threatened in the work environment, workers have an incentive to remedy the situation. But no matter how desirable the attainment of these immediate goals, there remains the second question of feasibility: To what extent is it possible to achieve them? For when demands entail costs, workers may have to sacrifice severance pay for a pension plan or accept a pension plan offering admittedly insufficient payments rather than no plan at all, hoping that increases may be won later.

On the one hand, a union negotiator will frame any current demand with reference to what the union is likely to get from the variety of employers within the industry (though the exaggeration of demands for purely tactical purposes at times makes this a rather unimportant consideration). Now, what constitutes an acceptable settlement will be based partly on a calculation of what the variety of employers with whom the union bargains can afford to grant. To the extent that ability to pay is taken into account, it may act as restraining influence on the negotiators. On the other hand, as we have seen, the political necessity of satisfying the constituency and holding the members' allegiance serves as an upward pressure on demands and acceptable settlements. Will the membership be disaffected if the concessions won are less than those previously received and widely publicized by a rival union? What if a comparable union is able to win greater gains elsewhere after this agreement is signed? Considerations of this nature lead union officials to anticipate what other unions are likely to ask for and win; they are encouraged to seek to match or surpass these anticipated gains in order to make their own positions and that of their union secure.

Interunion comparison is thus a force of some significance—a comparision may cross community and industry lines. The concern over what other unions have done or are likely to do is not due solely to the fact that other unions may become rivals for members. In some instances relationships become established, inviting comparison even though there is little likelihood of the members seeking to transfer from one union to the other. Those comparisons must be respected by union leaders if they expect to maintain their authority within their union.

In other instances one union may be dominant in the community, perhaps because of the presence of a large manufacturing plant or cluster of plants employing its members. Advances made by it are then likely to constitute something of a standard by which other unions in that area will guage their own success. These interunion comparisons thus at times involve community standards, and at other times they are unrelated to standards existing in a particular community.

Interunion comparisons become more urgent when unions are competing for the same groups of workers. Greater success may provide a rival with a springboard for an organizing campaign in the heart of another's actual or potential membership. Unions seeking to extend their sphere of influence will thus make unusual efforts to do better than other unions working the same territory.

Interunion Rivalry

If the Teamsters' leadership decides to expand its membership by enlisting workers in a variety of fields totally unrelated to trucking, it must make a dramatic demonstration of the superiority of its bargaining power by winning concessions beyond those achieved by the unions whose jurisdictions it is raiding. The Communication Workers, the United Food and Commercial Workers, or the State, County, and Municipal Employees must respond to such inducement by providing similar or equivalent benefits if their members are being lured. If they cannot win any benefits immediately, they must at least present a show of activity—special committees appointed to study the problem and render reports on demands made, even if they are presently without hope of fulfillment, in order to "prepare" management for the eventual concession.

Such union rivalries acquire an intensity that truly renders their respective collective bargaining agreements subject to coercive comparison.

The danger of unfavorable comparison in part explains the tenacity with which unions conduct some strikes. Failure to win a favorable settlement may be a threat to survival only in a degree less real than failure to win an agreement at all. If a rival union has settled its dispute at another plant, nothing less than the terms it won can be accepted—at least without a fight. Under these circumstances small differences loom large because they become potent symbols of other values; then equal or like gains become the sine qua non of industrial peace. A sixty-day strike over a few cents per hour may be economically irrational, but politically it may have all the logic of survival.

Rivalry continues between unions, particularly between the large conglomerate unions such as the Teamsters, the Machinists, and the Electrical Brotherhood and the smaller unions that have recruited members from a narrower industrial or occupational base. Industries change with advancing technologies, merging old skills and jobs into new or hybrid kinds of work. Firms organized by one union branch out into different areas of manufacturing where another union may dominate; or companies change the method of work, contracting out maintenance and new construction or installation work, for example. Should the shop union be allowed to supply or organize the workers brought in by the contractor, or should they be allowed traditional craft-union representation? The question is one of importance to unions when, as at present, membership is declining and none can afford any losses.

Since the mid-fifties unions have been defensively maintaining membership and expanding only marginally into new areas of the private sector. Under such circumstances, coercive comparisons among them have probably been somewhat moderated. Each has had to concentrate on its own affairs and eschew expansionary policies apt to dramatize its standing vis-à-vis other unions. Nevertheless, concern over prestige and status among unions and union leaders and the contests of interest groups within unions will—indeed, inescapably must—continue to create internal political pressures affecting the course of collective bargaining.

CONCLUSION

Members have available to them a variety of democratic procedures through which they can express their dissatisfactions with their leaders. First, they may vote in a certification election when a particular union is chosen; and last, they may vote in a decertification election when a union may be removed as a representative of the work force. Many unions also require members or a representative delegate body to approve any settlement. Typically members elect their shop stewards and local union officers, though in some unions, such as those in the building trades, higher officials appoint local representatives at the place of work. Elected delegates to national conventions usually must approve changes in dues and adjustments in officers' salaries.

Most unions enroll workers in a variety of occupations. Even within the same occupation, members possess a range of skills and carry out their jobs in many different circumstances. The result is that in most unions, members belong to one or several interest groups that often vie with each other for benefits and status. The diverse interest groups use democratic procedures to pursue their goals, generating a lively, continuous political milieu within unions, though seldom does one find so formal a system as in civil government with its political parties.

Union leaders can seldom ignore the wishes and will of their members. Any leader who allows union policy and goals to drift from those acceptable to a majority risks rejection of a negotiated agreement, a rival candidate for the office at the next election, or in extreme cases a membership vote to decertify. Thus union officers conduct their bargaining, at whatever level, with a wary eye upon the likely response of the membership to the possible outcome. They must continually test the political winds, and if they do not take their guidance from the members, they nevertheless must take into account members' attitudes and sentiments. Until union negotiators are sure of members' support or until they have crafted a settlement proposal acceptable to a majority of the members (or the interest groups formed by the members), they are not apt to be able to negotiate effectively with managers across the bargaining table. The negotiations which must go on within the union are often as important as, and may take more time, effort, and skill than, the negotiations with management.

COLLECTIVE BARGAINING AND ITS POLITICS: MANAGEMENT

Organization managers do not approach collective bargaining merely as rational, objective decision makers who carefully order preferences on the basis of cost-benefit calculations. They must also approach it at the same time politically in any organization, whether public or private, profit or nonprofit, whose members are numerous enough to sustain divergent interests and sufficiently cohesive to form groups seeking power, influence, and status. Professor Charles Merriam pointed out nearly forty years ago the similarity of business corporations and government agencies:

> All of these organizations have their own rules and regulations. All have their own personnel. All have their own plans and programs, formal and informal. All have their own codes, common understanding, and expectancies, as to courses of action. Many of them have their own bureaucracies, their own factions or parties, their own leaders and demagogues, their own politics—petty or noble. There have been "parties" of a sort in the College of Cardinals.[1]

Managers seldom can order their preferences in a simple hierarchy but rather must choose among competing goals and the demands of various groups or interests. The choices involve complex trade-offs of gains and losses. Once the choices are made, they must be accepted by or enforced for everyone involved; either implies the acquisition and use of power. The necessity of securing and maintaining power may often persuade managers to sacrifice effi-

---

[1]From Charles E. Merriam, *Public and Private Government,* New Haven, Conn.: Yale University Press, 1944, reprinted in Sanford A. Lakoff and Daniel Rich (eds.), *Private Government,* Glenview, Ill.: Scott, Foresman and Company, 1973, p. 12.

ciency, simply defined. Added complications also arise because uncertainty blurs analysis and the indeterminacy of human response may confound even modest hopes and expectations.

Managerial authority may be remarkably concentrated, as in an owner-directed business firm, or widely diffused, as in an agency of local government. In both types of management, as well as for those in between, the politics of managing involves vertical and horizontal dimensions. The interactions of superiors and subordinates understandably involve political issues of rights, legitimacy, control, and response, and so do the relationships of managers at different levels with various constituencies, such as stockholders, customers, employees, and union leaders.

MANAGERS AS GOVERNORS OF POLITICS

Though managers in both private and public organizations are involved in organizational politics, the involvement is undoubtedly more clearly recognized in the case of public managers. We will first examine some of the features of politics in governmental organizations and then consider the effects of politics in large private firms.

Public Managers: Diffused Authority and Fractionated Responsibility

The contending factions seeking to influence the policy that public managers administer are usually public and thus obvious. The external political interests play upon government organizations continually, adding to and complicating the internal politics that arise in any organization. External political considerations play a particularly important role in defining managers' authority and limiting their control and responses. They not only complicate managers' organizational politics but also enmesh their responsibilities in confusion and ambiguity.

The American constitutional system of checks and balances, or separation of powers into legislative, executive, and judicial branches, begins the diffusion of managerial authority, but other practices and customs extend it further. The executive functions may be legally shared at state, county, and local levels between separately elected officers, such as a governor and a secretary of state or a county clerk and a sheriff. Legislative functions may be divided between state assemblies and city councils, each of which may in turn delegate rule-making activities to various agencies, either appointed or elected, such as school boards, health departments, and public works commissions.

Diffusion of authority and divided managerial functions in government make coordination of work effort and efficient delivery of services difficult to achieve. The extent to which government authority can be divided was illustrated in New York State in the early 1970s. A study group found 1606 general-purpose local governments, 5111 dependent special town districts, 80 county districts, more than 762 school districts, and 813 fire districts. In addition there existed almost 300 other authorities and agencies. All these units of governments were established and their basic powers defined by more than 6000 pages of state laws embodied in 11 statutes scattered through 13 volumes.[2] Local and city governments as well as states are managerial puzzles with much overlapping of jurisdiction and duplication of efforts. New York City, for example, in 1978 listed 900 subsidiary units, including 170 major, citywide agencies.[3]

In such circumstances managers can seldom operate effectively. The division of government creates such diffusion of authority that workers may find themselves subject to no effective authority. They may simply follow traditional routines and devise for themselves such work rules as they believe appropriate. In the parks department of New York City, for example, five different managers exercised field supervision and held inspection responsibilities for the same geographical area. One commentator observed, "Consequently, the probability of no one doing a job is as great as having five people do it."[4]

In a single suburban county courtroom in New Jersey, one can find four government employees, each appointed by different authorities, with no one exercising close managerial authority over the employees' activities. The governor appoints the judge, with the advice and consent of the state senate, and the senior assignment judge assigns the cases. The county board of supervisors must pay the salaries and expense of the court. The court clerk is a civil service appointee of the elected county clerk but is paid by the board of supervisors and works under the direction of the judge. To whom the clerk is responsible, and for what, is not always clear to any of the parties involved. The third employee is the court reporter, a civil servant, assigned from a pool through the state's court administrative office. The reporter can take on extra pay for extra work, serving those who need special transcripts or reports. The fourth employee is the court police officer, sometimes known as the sergeant-at-arms, who is a civil service appointee of the elected sheriff. The sheriff may assign officers not in court to guard duty at the county children's shelter or county hospitals. Officers can also pick up extra pay, as can police from anywhere in the county, by working on their days off for other jurisdictions that need additional police forces.

Personnel and industrial relations managers in many local governments complain that the courtroom situation is all too typical of diffused managerial authority and confused, ineffective management. Particularly affected is the decision-making power over issues traditionally raised by unions in collective

---

[2]New York State, Report of the Temporary State Commission on the Powers of Local Government, "The Capacity for Change," *Strengthening Local Government in New York,* part I, Mar. 1973, pp. 11–12.

[3]Robert Shrank and Jack Bigel, *Improving Productivity in Municipal Agencies, A Labor-Management Approach,* New York: 1975, p. 4.

[4]Ibid.

bargaining.[5] A number of different appointing authorities may hire and be formally responsible for employees who work in wide and overlapping ranges of
their job titles. Some may work in the same office or institution with people
who have identical job titles but discover that they work a different number of
hours for the same pay. Health technicians at a county hospital, for example,
may work the regular eight-hour day of all hospital workers while they com-
mingle with and work alongside county health department technicians who
work a six-and-one-half-hour day.

Problems and Opportunities for Negotiators

The diffusion of authority among governmental managers provides opportunity for community interest groups to become involved in collective bargaining and the issues with which it deals, increasing managers' political difficulties. Milton Derber has pointed out that:

> In some instances . . . [groups] may desire representation on management's bargain-
> ing team, in others the right to attend the bargaining sessions, in still others the
> opportunity to present their views to the bargaining team or to the legislative body
> prior to the approval of collective agreement. Illustrations of such interest-groups'
> desires are found in laws in Montana, Oregon, and Florida requiring student repre-
> sentation in University negotiations and in the court petition of a Parents' Union to
> obtain the right to participate in negotiations during the 1972–1973 Philadelphia
> teachers' strike.[6]

Astute political bosses or elected officials are sometimes able to pull the
diverse managerial functions and activities into coherence by means of political machines or party influence. Unfortunately, the coherent operations that
further the interests of the officials (or of the machine or party) seldom increase
efficiency or improve delivery of services. As Alan K. Campbell, former dean
of the Maxwell School at Syracuse University and director of the U.S. Office
of Personnel Management (formerly the Civil Service Commission), pointed
out: "One of the major problems is that we don't seem to have a system [within
government] to go about accomplishing productivity increase. There is no
built-in mechanism within the public sector for the maintenance of a wage system which is simultaneously tied to productivity increases. . . ."[7] Most local
governments do not even collect information on program costs, fringe benefits
of employees, unit costs, and workloads. Such information, however, must be

[5]Thomas Kochan, "A Theory of Multilateral Bargaining in City Government," *Industrial and
Labor Relations Review,* vol. 27, July 1974, p. 526.
[6]Milton Derber, "Management Organization For Collective Bargaining in the Public Sector,"
in Benjamin Aaron, Joseph R. Grodin, and James L. Stern (eds.), *Public Sector Bargaining,* Washington, D.C.: Bureau of National Affairs, Industrial Relations Research Association Series, 1979,
p. 83.
[7]New York State, "The Capacity for Change," p. 71.

available at the operating level before managers can attempt crude measures of output, quality, and productivity.

Another consequence of the diffusion of authority in government that injects complicating politics into collective bargaining is the separation of revenues from services. Taxpayers must supply the revenues, lawfully levied, whether or not they receive the services funded by the revenues. Furthermore, those responsible for raising taxes may have but indirect relationship to and control over the appointing authorities, who may be independently elected officials. To compound difficulties, as noted above, the appointing authorities may not carry out the function of overseeing and directing the work force or service personnel.

The politics with which public managers must be concerned—for their authority is diffused, their responsibilities are shared, and their goals are multiplied, even as they are held accountable to elected governmental officials responsive to a variety of interest groups—does not allow them to operate along neat, well-defined paths or to pursue efficiency as an economist might define it. Organizational politics thus may generate both conflicting and common interests. The separation of responsibility for raising taxes from the management of services can lead to conflicts, initiated by either those who levy taxes or those who spend them. On the one hand, union negotiators may take advantage of fragmented authority to play off one against another. If a police association cannot win a desired pension program from a city government, it may appeal to the state legislature and succeed in such an "end run." Or a teachers' union may help elect its friends to office and expect them to push its demands and favor its interests. On the other hand, government officials directly answerable to the taxpayers' electorate but only distantly responsible for managing local facilities or service may refuse to fund increased wages or even customary rates and benefits. When this is joined with a willingness to use armed forces to break strikes—a willingness increasingly manifest through the seventies—collective bargaining contends with serious difficulties.[8]

The diffusion of authority and fragmentation of responsibility can also foster common interests between government managers and their employees. A large wage bill and a high level of activity, even in the absence of increased or useful services, can often serve agency managers very well. The higher the bill, the larger the agency budget and thus possibly the greater the influence and importance of the manager. (Managers' own pay and perquisites often vary directly with agency budgets.) A higher bill offers an argument as well for more funds and employees the next year, or at least a smaller cut than otherwise might be contemplated.

Public managers can also find that union leaders and union procedures help

---

[8]James B. Jacobs, "The Role of Military Forces in Public Sector Labor Relations," *Industrial and Labor Relations Review,* vol. 35, Jan. 1982, p. 163. Government authorities called up the National Guard in public sector disputes forty-seven times from 1970 through August 1981; twenty-seven of the call-ups occurred after 1977.

them grapple with the problems of diffused managerial authority. Decentralized control not infrequently prevents managers from acting in situations where it would be to their advantage. Managers in one agency simply may not know enough about the variety of problems in all the various related or affected agencies to be able to formulate and pursue policies affecting such matters as transfers, promotions, merit pay, educational benefits, leaves, overtime, and absences. If a single union represents public workers in many or all of the relevant agencies, its representatives and officers can at times coordinate policies, iron out conflicts, and in general resolve contradictions in policies and inequities in their execution. They may become useful adjuncts of the managers, contributing to a cooperative relationship.

The policies of management in government can on the one hand, contribute both to conflict in industrial relations and to cooperation through collective bargaining. On the other hand, in some governments dealing with a multiplicity of worker organizations having divergent interests, conflict may be more likely to break out in and between negotiations. There is no reason that either condition should dominate, and the most likely outcomes are mixtures of both, with various combinations of conflict and cooperation. The diversity of relationships between public employees' unions and public managers is probably as great as that between unions and managements of private organizations.

Private Managers: Coordinators of Multiple Interests

By convention, managers of nongovernment organizations are called "private" managers. When they head and direct sizable aggregates of people who pursue various specialties and carry out a variety of activities in a more or less cooperative, coordinated effort, their positions are nearly as public as those of government officials. They are almost as involved in politics, as well, having to concern themselves with issues of power, accountability, and control. Richard Eells suggests that the conventional image of private organizations markedly and increasingly diverges from corporate reality; the result is an accumulation of stressful tensions.

> One example is the debate about the respective positions of share-owners and managers in the control of large enterprises where stockholding is widely dispersed: the so-called separation of ownership and control. Another example is the touchy question of social responsibility—the problem of the general public's share in the authority structure of large enterprises, since obviously responsibility and authority must somehow be linked together. A further example is the unresolved problem of union power vis-à-vis corporate managers: the encroachment of organized workers on managerial authority and the drive by labor unions to enjoy a "fair share" of the fruits of enterprise. Then there are the growing concerns about human relations in industry, the sensitivity of managers to the personality requirements of people in the work force, the nature of authority at the workplace, and the right of discipline . . . One of the most important problems confronting the managers of the modern cor-

poration is whether the basic pattern of authority relationships—internal and external to the organization—is functionally appropriate in view of contemporary corporate objectives and the organizational requirements for achieving these objectives.[9]

The most prestigeful and among the most thoughtful business managers recognize that there are widely shared public expectations that they and their firms should serve the public interest as well as private profit. The members of the influential Business Roundtable, avoiding any explanation of how they might weight the two values, simply declared that:

> Corporations operate within a web of complex, often competing relationships which demand the attention of corporate managers. The decision-making process requires an understanding of the corporation's many constituencies and their various expectations. Key among these are the following: Customers . . . Employees . . . Communities . . . Society at Large . . . Suppliers . . . [and] Shareholders . . . Carefully weighing the impacts of decisions and balancing different constituent interests—in the context of both near-term and long-term effects—must be an integral part of the corporations decision-making and management process. Resolving the differences involves compromise and trade-off. It is important that all sides be heard but impossible to assume that all will be satisfied because competing claims may be mutually exclusive.[10]

The Roundtable members illustrated their point with a contemporary problem about which employees, union spokespersons, and community leaders have shown great concern: the closure of plants. Managers may believe that a closing will allow more efficient use of resources, better products, and improved competition. But workers and the affected community may have much to lose—jobs and economic health, which in turn affect stability of families, the viability of schools, the existence of small service businesses, and the programs of churches. The members assert that one of the fundamental problems confronting corporate management is "balancing the shareholder's expectations of maximum return against other priorities." They further indicate that some, though not all, believe that "by giving enlightened consideration to balancing the legitimate claims of all its constituents, a corporation will best serve the interest of its shareholders.[11]

Constituencies may welcome such a conception of enlarged managerial responsibilities, but they are apt to remain wary for it offers them only dependent position and role. The Roundtable members imply that if conflicts arise or responsibilities need to be assigned, the managers themselves should be left free to choose the appropriate solution. Moreover, the conception fails to encompass the prickly fact that managers seek their own independent objec-

---

[9]From Richard Eells, *The Government of Corporations,* New York: Glencoe Press, The MacMillan Company, 1962, reprinted in Lakoff and Rich, *Private Government,* pp. 62–63.

[10]*Statement on Corporate Responsibility,* New York: The Business Roundtable, Oct. 1981, pp. 5–8.

[11]Ibid, p. 9.

tives and are not simply passive mediators or coordinators of the interest of others.[12] Nevertheless, it indicates that modern managers recognize the social nature of private enterprise. It is suggestive in its recognition that stockholder interests are now no longer exclusive in the large corporations but must accommodate other interests. There is no denial of stockholder welfare as an objective, but it becomes one of several. The freeing of managers from the stockholders' legal leash permits others to claim consideration.

Reconciling Conflicts among Interests

Managers who accept multiple responsibilities must accommodate the variety of interests within the processes of the corporate political system. They are subject to several different pressures and the groups that apply them will not necessarily measure their demands by the same values or seek compatible goals. Relative profits to stockholders, relative status and prestige to management itself, relative wages and welfare to employees, and relative prices to consumers—those considerations are *all* coercive with respect to management. Managers have to reconcile these matters in some manner if they are to meet their various responsibilites.

In law and tradition, managers place first their obligation to protect stockholder interest. As the Business Roundtable explained: "Shareholders have a special relationship to the corporation. As providers of risk capital [they] make the corporation possible." Even if profit maximization can no longer be assumed to be the sole motivation, the profit-making ability of the firm remains for managers a major constraint, if not a primary objective. In fact, changes in the way in which Americans hold stock and exercise the power that inheres in it has made managers even more concerned with profits—particularly short-term profits—than in the past. The Business Roundtable pointed out that:

> At one time most shareholders were long-term, personally-involved individual investors. Now a high proportion of them is made up of institutionally-grouped and often unidentified shorter-term buyers most interested in near-term gain. This has affected their role among business constituencies. The expectation of near-term gain can exert pressure to subordinate long-run objectives to more immediate profit consideration.[13]

The increasing concentration of stockholder power in banks, trusts, pension funds, and investment houses hardly strengthens managers' claim that they can appropriately coordinate and fully represent the multiple interests of their varied constituencies. Of course, managers by law must continue to act as the representatives of their stockholders. They meet unions at the negotiating table

[12]Harvey Leibenstein, *Beyond Economic Man: A New Foundation for Microeconomics,* Cambridge, Mass.: Harvard University Press, 1976, chap. 10; and Albert O. Hirschman, *Exit, Voice and Loyalty,* Cambridge, Mass.: Harvard University Press, 1970.

[13]*Statement on Corporate Responsibility,* pp. 7–8.

to bargain over ways of accommodating workers' interests as their representatives define them. Managers thus claim to be best situated to represent all
the interest groups, including the employees. This implies a lofty and privileged position for managers. It suggests that managers, better than any other
group, can perceive and acknowledge the various interests with due reward,
whereas union negotiators occupy a parochial position and represent *only* the
workers.

The conflict is most evident, consequently, in collective bargaining, for of
all the groups that managers have had to recognize, employees are usually the
most effectively organized. Though they enjoy no control over the selection of
their managers, through their unions employees can, in a sense, grant or withhold authority to those managers who continue in office. Collective bargaining
is a method of defining management's responsibility to the employees as one
interest group in the business; the signing and ratification of a labor agreement
confers or reaffirms managerial authority as far as the union and its members
are concerned. The strength of the union thus acts to reinforce the obligation
to the employees that some managements have voluntarily assumed.

There are some who question managers' good faith when they announce the
enlargement of their responsibilities. Even if the stockholder interest was less
concentrated and insistent than at present, some critics maintain that management is not apt to show much concern for its employees. The questions and
skepticism may have some base, but it is noteworthy that unions in the private
sector have not increased their membership in recent decades and have not
recruited many white-collar workers to their ranks. Apparently large-scale
organization has not eliminated white-collar suspicions of unions; it may not
have altogether destroyed whatever bonds have existed between worker and
managers, even when the manager is no longer the owner. The relationship has
become more formalized, the stockholder interests are as strong as or stronger
than ever.

Several reasons for such concern may be suggested. First, the very size of
the corporation has made managers aware that they have a political relationship with their employees and that their authority over the work force must be
accompanied by some responsibility to it. Second, public opinion, sometimes
expressed through governmental actions, has required managers to respond to
the needs of their workers. And third, the development of industrial psychology has made managers increasingly conscious of their control over personnel
through their ability to win a response. Industrial psychology has stressed that
leadership involves eliciting cooperation that cannot be won if the interests of
those whose cooperation is desired are given insufficient consideration. Even
in the absence of unions there is reason to believe that managers' decisions
would be at least in part guided by considerations of employee welfare. The
union serves to stimulate that consideration further.

We do not intend to overstress an aspect of employee-management relations
sometimes understressed. That some managerial decisions are made with a
regard for employee interests does not imply that conflicts of interest are absent

or avoided. For one thing, some managements have insisted on determining unilaterally just where the employees' interests lie. Attitudes of paternalism have not been wholly shaken. There is sometimes a reluctance to give up the belief that responsibility to employees can best be served by informed decision as to what conduces to their interest—the notion that management knows best. Thus management sometimes feels obliged to resist the union for the employees' own welfare. A challenge to this authority may at times be looked upon in the same manner that a father would view his children's questioning of his decisions. This paternalistic attitude may prompt resistance to employees' attempts to form an independent organization.

Unions an Indication of Managers' Failure

The union's very existence constitutes for some managers an unwelcome suggestion that management has failed in discharging its responsibilities to its employees, a suggestion which can be rebutted if the union is considered to be not truly representative, but the work of hotbloods and an imposition upon loyal employees by self-servers. Such opinions permit managers to assert, in the words of one corporate official, "We are admittedly antiunion, but we like our workers." In making an overall assessment of management's attitudes toward trade unions, Professor D. Quinn Mills summarized as follows:

> Unions exist as a reflection of management failures. Unions are able to organize only where an employer is insensitive to the needs and desires of the workforce. Where managers are insensitive, the workers will vote for a union, and the managers deserve it. Where managers are alert and sensitive, employees will not want a third party (that is a union) in the relationship between the company and the employees. Furthermore, where managers are sensitive, employees have no need for a union.[14]

Embedded in these antiunion attitudes is a moral judgement about management's relationship to its employees. Managers—at least some managers—admit they have responsibilities that go beyond those that may be imposed by the labor market or that in the short run can be profitably evaded. For them, the very existence of unions and worker support for them is an indication of their own failings. Whether one agrees or not with the attitudes and their morality, their ethical concern cannot be lightly dismissed as fictitious or deceiving. It reveals that many managers are guided in employee relations, to a degree they define for themselves, by a concern for workers' interest as they—the managers—conceive them. There is thus an indication that at least a number of corporate leaders are motivated in the area of relevant business decisions by a consideration held in common with the union, even though the means are vastly different.

Workers, through their union relationship, influence the actions of their

---

[14]D. Quinn Mills, "Management Performance," in Jack Stieber, Robert B. McKersie, and D. Quinn Mills (eds.), *U.S. Industrial Relations 1950–1980: A Critical Assessment,* Madison, Wis.: Industrial Relations Research Association, 1981, p. 112.

union leaders. Through their employee relationship, they influence the actions of their managers. Thus workers are an influential element in the political structures of both organizations. Their political significance in the corporation has perhaps been obscured in the past by the legal tradition of stockholder rights, by managerial opposition to independent forms of employee representation, and by union-management conflict. These factors are all important, of course, but they do not negate the political role that employees play in the corporation. Managers, like union leaders, are interested in their support and loyalty. They cannot concern themselves with only worker interest, as the union does. They must retain the support and loyalty of other groups as well, some of whom have interests conflicting with those of employees.

This conclusion suggest two corollaries. To some extent managers' concern for workers is competitive with that of the union leaders. They aspire to win the primary loyalty of the same group of employees. But in some degree, the element of common interest in employee welfare may serve as the very basis for agreement, since the work force is a constituency common to both management and union organizations. In part, it is controlled by both union and management; in part, it controls both.

INTEREST GROUPS WITHIN MANAGEMENT

So far in this chapter we have treated management as a single interest group pursuing an agreed set of goals. In fact, it is made up of a number of various and sometimes contending groups who may understand and emphasize organizational objectives in different ways and urge conflicting priorities in the pursuit of overall goals. Seen from the inside, private management may appear as fractious and diffused as public management. This situation is encouraged because specialized departments and divisions of a company and professional staffs are expected to concentrate upon their own responsibilities: by devoting their attention to one area of corporate activities, they give less to other areas and tend to become partisans in company councils for their particular interests.

In a study of departmental power and perspective among large firms, Charles Perrow found that members of a department tend to develop a narrow perspective of their role and contributions:

> With only a couple of minor exceptions, [sub]groups minimize the overall power they have, maximize the amount they should have, see their middle and lower management groups as more powerful than others see them, and minimize the extent to which they should be justly criticized . . . [p]erspectives are quite self-serving; each group magnifies its ventures, its resources (if we can treat middle and lower management power as such), its needs, and the injustice of its position.[15]

---

[15]Charles Perrow, "Departmental Power and Perspectives In Industrial Firms," in Mayer M. Zald (ed.), *Power In Organization,* Nashville: Vanderbilt University Press, 1970, p. 78.

Consider the possible reaction of managers in various company departments to a union demand for extended vacations of three months every five years for senior workers. The finance department may oppose the demand, seeing in it a costly increase in labor expenses for the present and an indefinite commitment for the future, as the length of service of the labor force increases. The production department may object too, arguing that the agreement will put the company at a competitive disadvantage in labor costs; more than half of the company's workers already have over fifteen years of seniority, while only one-third of the work force of a major competitor have as much as fifteen years. The marketing department might argue that acceptance of the demand would be preferable to a strike or any interference with production since sales are rising and a comprehensive advertising campaign has just reached its climax. The engineering department may favor the union demand for two reasons. First, it hopes to see established in the company a precedent for long leaves with pay so that its people may press such a program for its engineers. With sabbaticals available for its members, the engineering department could keep its expensive talent up to date and also have an extra attraction to offer when bidding for new engineers. Second, the extended-vacation demand of the union would raise labor costs sufficiently to justify company investment in a new mechanization process the department proposes to develop. The public relations department may point out that acceptance of the union demand could win the company much favorable publicity for having made a responsible and imaginative attack upon the present serious unemployment. The managers of the industrial relations department may also favor the extended-vacation plan, believing that should the company reject it outright it would lead to a strike or at least seriously disturb union-management relations, painfully built up after the bitter strike of five years earlier. Out of the differing judgments and varied concerns, a single company approach and policy have to be fashioned.

Unions' Use of Managerial Differences

Union negotiators, aware of the differences of opinion within management, may make use of their knowledge—and any intelligence data or information they may secure—to strengthen those who incline favorably toward their proposal and weaken those opposed. For example, they may "concede" that only the senior third of the work force should receive the extended vacation, thus answering the objection of those in the production department. Then, with only the finance department still opposed, the balance within the company may swing toward acceptance of the plan.

At the employee level, the differences between management groups are easily discernible. Supervisors often feel conflicting pressures from different groups. Their immediate line superiors may call for increased production to meet an important schedule. Inducing workers to cooperate in meeting the schedule may involve them in concessions forbidden by the industrial relations people. The workers may agree to raise the work limit they have customarily imposed and to allow supervisory trainees to perform production work in return for ten more minutes of washup time and assignment of helpers to pick up scrap. Both concessions can easily become "past practices," if continued, and precedents for similar concessions elsewhere in the plant. In time the provisions of the agreement regulating washup time and the assigning of helpers can be subverted, to the embarrassment of industrial relations. (The union leaders may be upset, too, to discover that their carefully negotiated provisions against supervisors working have been weakened by shop concession to management.)

Many of the pressures on managerial decisions that appear to arise outside the business are effective influences only because they coincide with the independent motives of particular management groups. Managers and employers live in the society of other managers and employers, and it is to be expected that they court one another's friendship and regard. This in part explains why one of the cardinal sins of business conduct is to offer a wage rate or a wage increase that proves embarrassing to other employers. Managers and employers live in a climate of public opinion which induces them to behave in a socially acceptable manner, that is, one which encourages their social acceptance.

Not all managers occupy top positions, for any large organization establishes various levels of authority. Some managers enjoy operational authorities over, and are assigned responsibilities to, other members of management. In the organization there are usually departmental, office, or plant interests that must be accommodated, just as in the case of unions there are occupational and sectional interests requiring recognition. A companywide policy cannot be set without considering its impact on the component units, and similarly, policy must take into account the possibility that as precedent it may affect all parts of the organization. Upon this possibility industrial relations managers build their power and extend their influence within organizations. They claim to perceive the "big picture" and to be able to coordinate the approach of all divisions and departments. Although the union may be perceived as an outside threat and nominal antagonist, it is also the source of power for industrial relations. The managers are not unaware of their ambivalent relationship to unions. One explicitly recognized it in reporting to a researcher. "As I told one of the [other industrial relations] group who was damning unions—Don't bite the hand that feeds you."[16]

Opportunities for Industrial Relations Managers

The need for a uniform, consistent policy in dealing with the union has persuaded most top managers to centralize industrial relations. A very high pro-

---

[16]Fred H. Goldner, "The Division of Labor: Process and Power," in Zald, *Power in Organizations*, p. 105.

portion of large private business firms centralize responsibility for industrial relations policy at the head corporate level. The top labor relations officer assumes the responsibility in 60 percent of 668 firms surveyed in 1979, and the chief executive officer has that responsibility in another 32 percent.[17] As government regulations of labor, job safety, and discrimination have increased in recent years, the centralization has probably increased in the last decade and a half, but the data are too sketchy to draw firm conclusions.[18] What is clear is that top managers of large private organizations perceive labor relations and collective bargaining as matters of highest importance. The policies followed and the negotiations carried out receive their close attention. The only aspects of labor relations decentralized to plant or division levels are the administration of the agreement, grievance processing, and settlement of employee complaints.

The concentration at the top has also produced a high degree of specialization and encouraged professionalism among industrial relations staffs. The staffs are not small, averaging one staff member per 200 to 400 union-represented employees, and most top industrial relations or personnel managers— fully four out of five—have spent their whole careers within their function.[19] They are the experts upon whom the chief operating officers rely for most technical and operational advice on labor policy; however, they play a secondary role in deciding bargaining strategy and in the development of broad labor policy. In dealing with these latter matters the chief operating officers apparently believe their position better allows them, in the words of the Business Roundtable, "to weigh employee benefits in the light of competition around the world and the fundamental necessity to produce profits to support the continuing existence of the enterprise."[20]

[17]Audrey Freeman, *Managing Labor Relations,* New York: The Conference Board, 1979, p. 27.

[18]Scholars have found evidence that collective bargaining has encouraged some centralization in government. Studies conducted in the late sixties revealed that in cities, authority for personnel issues shifted to the executive at the expense of the legislative branch and the civil service system. See John F. Burton, Jr., "Local Government Bargaining and Management Structure," *Industrial Relations,* vol. 11, May 1972, p. 124. Later studies in the mid-seventies of state governments also showed a "thrust toward increasing centralization" in response to collective bargaining. See Ralph T. Jones, *Public Management's Internal Organizational Response to the Demands of Collective Bargaining,* draft final report proposed by Contract Research Corp., Belmont, Mass., for Labor-Management Services Administration, contract no. L-74-207, updated, p. 27. (Mimeographed.)

Whatever the trend toward centralization, it is not overwhelming and it will be long before industrial relations functions are as centralized in the public sector as in the private sector. Other investigations indicate that centralization is hardly inevitable and that the diffusion of managerial authority remains a powerful block to its realization. Even when formal centralization appears, the informal reality of decentralization, the end run, and powerful municipal unions' own managerial role may prevail. See Raymond D. Horton, David Lewin, and James W. Kuhn, "Some Impacts of Collective Bargaining on Local Government," *Administration and Society,* vol. 7, Feb. 1976, p. 509; and David Lewin, "Local Government Labor Relations in Transition: The Case of Los Angeles," *Labor History,* vol. 17, Spring 1976, p. 191.

[19]Freeman, *Managing Labor Relations,* p. 29. Union staffs do not appear to have grown in numbers or specialization nearly as much as their managerial counterparts. Apparently slow union growth or declines have persuaded union leaders that they can not afford the skills necessary to assure at least technical bargaining parity with management.

[20]*Statement on Corporate Responsibility,* p. 6.

This must end a rather summary survey of the separate political pressures within the corporation that have a bearing on management: stockholders; employees; interlocking business groups; and management itself, including all its operational subdivisions such as plants, offices, and divisions. It is evident that business firms, governments, and their agencies are all political systems, as is the union. Interest groups within each of them, as well as the ongoing nature of the system itself, generate compulsions and differences among themselves. The resulting pressures and jostling for advantage or priority affect managerial decisions and influence collective bargaining relationships. As in the case of the union, then, we shall have to inquire what determines the pressures that arise within the organization to produce the results they do. How do managers reconcile the conflicting comparisons, which severally may coerce the separate interest groups but which finally and in total are all coercive of the managers?

This problem, as stated, is too broad for investigation here. We must reduce it to dimensions that permit brief but meaningful exploration. Within the context of collective bargaining, the most fruitful approach is to consider how managers look at the issue of wages.

THE COERCIVE COMPARISON OF WAGES

The Scylla and Charybdis between which managers must steer to avoid disaster are costs and revenues. Costs determine the organization's ability to stay within its budget limitations. It cannot long satisfy its various constituencies if it runs over the limits. (The federal government, of course, can and does incur large deficits and so pushes beyond its budget limits quite regularly. It does so, however, at the risk of generating adverse economic and political reactions.) From the point of view of private managers, reducing existing costs allows greater flexibility within the budget limits, more managerial discretion, and perhaps even greater net profits. But a large portion of the costs (those arising from value added by the firm and therefore not including material and supply costs) are the incomes of participating groups: wages; managers' salaries; interest; and even dividends, if seen as charges and not residuals. Each group is willing to have management cut costs, but only if its own income is not thereby adversely affected.

In fact, each group not only defends its income, but if possible, tries to enlarge it. Employment for even one group, however, let alone all groups, pushes against budget limits if productivity remains the same. Approval of higher pay in such a situation would require managers in a private firm to try to increase their budget by raising prices; public managers would have to appeal to the taxing and appropriation—"ways and means"—authority for increased revenues. In either case unwanted consequences may be generated. Higher prices for privately supplied goods or services may mean a reduction of sales and revenues; higher taxes levied by public authorities may mean a loss of votes for elected officials in future elections. There is, of course, no precise or fixed relationship between wages and dividends, interest or rent. The connections between costs and revenues may be indirect and offset by many economic variables. Nevertheless, cost-revenue linkages are thus among the principle sources of coercive comparison affecting managerial decisions. We have already considered comparison regarded as coercive by employees and their union leaders. We are interested now in how managers settle upon a wage policy in light of the multiple interests they represent and the comparisons considered equitable or coercive by each and all of them.

Public Management

In the public sector, wages as costs are only loosely linked to revenues through taxes. The employing agency is usually quite separate from the taxing authority; furthermore, governments seldom offer their services in a competitive market; thus the pressure to cut or hold down costs is reduced. Yet overall budget restraints require that some kind of limit be imposed upon wage costs, particularly if, as is true of many local governments, they must balance their budgets or cannot easily increase their borrowing. Almost all governments have sought a fair standard to use as a limit and found it in "comparable pay" or the "prevailing wage." The Federal Salary Reform Act of 1962, for example, mandates federal pay rates "comparable with private enterprise pay rates for the same levels of work." A typical local government in Los Angeles, which requires salaries and wages "at least equal to the prevailing salary or wage for the same quality of service rendered to private employers."

A comparable wage standard appears to be both simple and economically sound. It should be acceptable to the workers involved, since it guarantees them pay as good as they could typically earn elsewhere. Thus it should assure public managers an adequate supply of employees and a turnover no higher than the average in whatever area or industries furnished the standard. It should not unduly affect local labor markets and wage levels since it tracks rather than leads changes and adjustments. In practice the comparable standard is not at all simple and its economic merit is far more questionable than appears at first glance.

Setting the wage on the basis of the standard is subject to manipulation, of course, by the involved and contending interests groups. It is a detailed, technical activity whose effect will be most closely examined and best understood by those who are most directly affected. It is hardly surprising, therefore, that governments' comparable standards, as applied, often show a considerable upward bias. Usually wage data are sought not within a labor market, but over a broad geographical area within the government's jurisdiction. Prevailing wage data are usually sampled only from medium-sized and large firms, which typically pay higher wages than small firms. Small firms would be more difficult to survey, of course, but the prevailing wage calculated from a wider survey would be lower than the rate based only on large firms. Wage rates for government workers might be significantly reduced.

Other equity issues arise in setting government wages, even when prevailing or comparable standards are applied. Federal as well as state and local legislatures have proved themselves reluctant to set the salaries for top appointed officials at rates higher than their own or at least as high as those paid to managers and professionals in private service. They tend to hold down their own pay in response to general electorate criticism of increases they vote for themselves. Consequently, salaries for top government officials are also held down and usually lag considerably behind those paid to comparable corporate managers or professionals. (Union officers face the same criticism from their members when they seek higher salaries. The result is that the higher-paid union leaders receive salaries far lower than business executives and more in line with those of top government officials.) In practice, then, governments tend to overpay at the lower ranks and underpay at the top.[21] Despite grumbling by high government officials and a probably higher-than-desirable turnover among top officers, the public does not appear to be much concerned. It seems to find the resulting egalitarian pay structure appropriate to government. It may not be the most economically efficient structure, but it reflects an acceptable—at least a tolerable—compromise of the various interest groups concerned and involved.

Private Managers

Managers in the private sector have not found as clear-cut a formal standard for determining wages as have public managers. They use a variety of wage standards, emphasizing one or the other or combinations of them as may best suit their purposes when they attempt to balance the demand of their constituents. Comparable wage standards are powerfully compelling, though they are finally circular, self-referenced. They are subject to such a variety of definitions and measurements and managers are so pressed by market forces that the wage standards serve as only a very general guide to wage setting. Even when managers may look to the local labor market for wage comparison ("keeping up with the area"), they do not necessarily seek equality of rates with other firms. Some may set their wage structures higher and others lower, being concerned with their relative positions, not the absolute level of their wages.

Managers use area wage comparisons for reasons not easily explained by economic theory. Competitors for labor in a local market are a consideration, of course, but many managers are also concerned with what they, workers, and people in the community perceive as equitable treatment. They may use the comparisons as a gauge of their wage position compared with neighboring firms. If they have not been leaders in the past, managers may not wish to

---

[21]Walter Fogel and David Lewin, "Wage Determination in the Public Sector," *Industrial and Labor Relations Review,* vol. 27, April 1974, p. 410; Daniel J. B. Mitchell, "The Impact of Collective Bargaining on Compensation in the Public Sector," in Aaron, Grodin, and Stern, *Public Sector Bargaining,* pp. 118–149.

become leaders inadvertently, surprising managers in other firms and forcing them to act when they are not ready or willing to act. The respect of fellow managers may be an important objective, not readily sacrificed by making wage adjustment that embarrass those managers.

Managers of nonunion firms show themselves to be acutely sensitive to their wage position in an area hierarchy. They usually wish to keep their workers from organizing and therefore, as a study of a sample of large nonunion firms found, often pay "as liberally or more liberally than their unionized competitors." The study also indicated other common features of their compensation plans:

> First, management usually set wages for production and maintenance workers according to local labor markets rather than adopting a national standard as is sometimes the basis of union wage scales. Second, the companies closely monitored union settlements in order to maintain equal or superior compensation. Third, these companies communicated their pay and benefit policies well. . . .[22]

Comparisons between Areas and Occupations

Even a simple examination of area data provides suggestions of wage patterns among local labor markets. It appears that unionized workers in large automobile plants, concentrated in a particular market area, are able to command high wages. The Detroit metropolitan area is such a high-wage area; and furthermore, through the 1960s and 1970s union and management negotiations steadily increased the autoworkers' pay differentials above the average pay in all durable manufacturing. It rose from about 15 percent in 1961 to 24 percent in 1971 and to 29 percent in 1975. Such a rise is surprising since American producers were steadily losing auto sales to foreign competitors; it shows how little impressed those in the industry—union leaders or managers—were with their industry's increasing relative costs.

A look at occupational pay in three areas—Detroit; Toledo, Ohio, 60 miles to the south; and Muskegon, Michigan, 180 miles to the northwest—appears to show a patterning effect of the sizable and widening differential in auto wages. In Toledo the average pay for office clerks and for skilled and unskilled workers in manufacturing was about 10 percent lower than in Detroit, but Toledo's differential over national averages increased steadily over the same period, paralleling that of Detroit. In Muskegon, much farther from Detroit and its heavy industrial manufacturing, pay averaged 10 to 18 percent lower than in Detroit, and the pattern of widening auto wage differentials is but dimly reflected.

Insofar as wage levels in Toledo or even Muskegon were pulled up by the local labor market effects—the historical or traditional area wage differential—of Detroit, firms were hampered in keeping labor costs down to meet the larger

---

[22]Fred K. Foulkes, "Large Non-unionized Employers," in Stieber, McKensie, and Mills, *U.S. Industrial Relations 1950–1980: A Critical Assessment,* p. 149.

and larger inflow of competitive goods from abroad. Until auto wages, and thus Detroit's, fell relative to those elsewhere, these firms lost wage advantages to the south. Occupational wages in Atlanta and Dallas, for example, had no historical area ties to Detroit and not only maintained much lower absolute wage levels but revealed no increasing differential over the period.

Thus may be explained the harsh employment effect of the depression in the early 1980s upon firms and industries closest to, and most affected by, the exceedingly generous wage gains of the autoworkers from 1961 to 1978: The affected firms could not adjust their wage differentials fast enough to stay competitive. Many closed their doors, transferring production and jobs to the south or west and sometimes allowing foreign imports to take the place of their production. Such wage behavior, displayed by both unionized and nonunion firms alike, strongly indicate managers' responsiveness to local labor markets. They appear to give more weight to community comparison than the unions do.

Even though workers may not know the specific rates of a local company, they probably are aware of its comparative ranking as a wage payer, even in such rough terms as "a good payer," "above the average," or "tight." If this is the case, the very roughness of the community standard is conducive to a simultaneous accommodation of the industry standard, for discrepancies between the two can be tolerated as long as they have no radical effects on a company's placement in the local wage structure. A company may thus open or close the gap between its rates and those of another local company with which it is being compared without exciting apprehension from either employees or employers, as long as the change is not so great as to drop it out of its customary wage class and suggest comparison with a company or companies in a different class, thus upsetting established expectations.

Since an area wage can be more ambiguous and variable than governments' upwardly biased prevailing wage, private managers enjoy considerable latitude in making wage adjustments. Moreover, wage rates cover ranges both inside their organization and outside, allowing opportunity for fairly easy managerial changes in the community's wage hierarchy. Where in the hierarchy a firm places itself depends in part upon the type and quality of worker required. If the jobs can be filled by transient, unskilled laborers, the firm may choose a low position in the hierarchy; if a sizable portion of the jobs require specialized skills and a stable work force, managers would probably seek a high position in the hierarchy. In both cases the wages may be quite satisfactory to the various constituents—workers, stockholders, and other employers in the area.

Thus community and industry standards for a particular company define a *range* within which wages may be set, not so much on economic considerations as on the political basis of equitable comparisons. The placement of wages somewhere *between* community and industry levels (whichever may be the upper or the lower limit) thus in itself constitutes the wage-setting problem. It may not be necessary to accept one or the other limit as controlling; but recognizing that equity resides in part with each, management may mediate the settlement.

Finally, there may be a movement from an earlier acceptance of one standard to a more general acceptance of another. There does indeed appear to have been a greater tendency in the past for managers of nationwide firms to compare wages on a local basis than is the case today. The continuing demand by unions for a wage pattern throughout an industry has had its effect on managers' thinking. Employees, through their unions, have insisted upon the comparison considered more equitable by them; to some extent managers have been willing to go along, and to some extent they have been forced to go along.

Pushed by some of the larger industrywide unions, industry comparisons have come to be recognized as legitimate. Managers of many large unionized firms that operate a number of plants in many different communities have decided that intraindustry comparisons are worth considering. Unions have certainly pushed toward industrywide wage setting, arguing that equity requires equal rates for equal work, particularly when the same price is charged for the products turned out by the workers. Gearing a company's wage rates to industry standards, however, does not imply a policy of equating them with an industry average of dominant rate structure. As with an area standard, some firms may prefer a higher or lower wage. The managers of those that pay more may believe the added costs are offset by improved employer morale, better union relations, and good public relations.

Although different industries manifest what appear to be particular wage standards—that is, a pattern and range of wage structure peculiar to themselves—the apparent standards may be artifacts of other industry characteristics. Firms in the same industry may well hire essentially the same skilled mixes in the same technology, employ work forces of similar demographic characteristics, and bargain with the same union or group of unions. The wage standard thus may be industrywide in scope because the varied forces and influences affecting and determining wages are essentially the same throughout the industry, not because the parties chose a wage and applied it industrywide.

Whatever the sources of industry patterns, managers keep as informed about industry wage patterns as they can. Companies regularly exchange wage data, and trade associations collect wage information. Managers want to know the wage situation fully in their industry to reduce the possibility of invidious comparisons, either by their employees on their own or by unions bargaining for the workers. Such comparisons clearly exert a coercive force; wages below others in the industry may well increase the resistance of the affected employees and the union to an agreement on the firm's terms. Wages at least equal to the average or above it should reduce the costs of agreement, increasing management's bargaining strength.

Many large firms operate in more than one industry and many unions organize workers in a number of industries.[23] Coercive wage comparisons, which

---

[23]"Union membership exhibits a remarkable degree on industry dispersion. Excluding unions representing only government employees, 97 unions, or 55 percent of the total, have 80 percent or more of their membership in a single industry. . . . The highest degree of industry dispersion was

may be made across industry boundaries because of these cross-industry ties, will tend to blur industry wage structure and standards. The degree to which such comparisons are made and the influence they have on union or management wage policies is not known. Daniel Mitchell believes that wage patterns can still be found on an industry basis but that they exert influence on wage settlement beyond them. He suggested that the influence may be transmitted through large, national unions seeking settlements as much like the pattern-setter as they can win.[24] Industry patterns, if such they are, appear usually when a major firm settles first with its union or group of unions. Either General Motors or Ford usually establishes the automobile industry pattern with the United Auto Workers; and either General Electric or Westinghouse (most often the former) provides wage leadership in the electrical equipment industry.

Comparison of Wage Increases with Profit Gains

In addition to area and industry comparisons, there is another comparison of more uncertain standing that may influence managerial wage policy—the comparison of profits (or dividends) and wages. There is also, perhaps to a lesser degree, the comparison of these two returns with the price charged to customers. It would be surprising, in view of managers' professed responsibility to these three groups, if there were not some sort of comparison of the relative advancement of their interests. Managers are not apt to raise wages willingly when dividends have slumped to low levels. And some sense of obligation to the buying public might restrain wage and profit increases if these contributed to soaring prices.

Though this sense of obligation does not appear to be strong, it can be used to help moderate price increases, with government encouragement. Studies by the Council on Wage and Price Stability and the Council of Economic Advisers estimated that annual wage increases were 1 to 1½ percentage points lower during 1979 than they would have been if the government had *not* publicized its voluntary pay and price standards.[25]

Traditionally, managers have strongly argued that wage setting, in which unions participate, is not to be mixed with pricing policy or directly related to profitability. In the difficult negotiations over terms for autoworkers at the end of World War II, Walter Reuther of the United Automobile Workers explicitly linked wages and prices. He demanded of General Motors a 30 percent

---

found in manufacturing. For example, in the chemicals and allied products industry, no union reported more than 80 percent of its membership in that industry. Unlike 26 of the 29 unions in that industry had less than 20 percent of their membership in that field." [*Directory of National Unions and Employee Associations, 1977,* Bureau of Labor Statistics Bulletin 2044, 1979, p. 72.]

[24]Daniel J. B. Mitchell, *Unions, Wages, and Inflation,* Washington, D.C.: The Brookings Institution, 1980, pp. 190–197.

[25]See *Economic Report of the President, 1981,* p. 59.

increase in wages without any increase in automobile prices, challenging management to open its books to prove its contention that it could not meet his demand. Company negotiators dismissed the demand as "socialist dreams." Until 1982 they continued their dismissive attitude, though the union regularly insisted in every negotiation on the relevance of pricing to wage setting and the need for the books to be opened.

In 1982 General Motors and the whole American automobile industry were suffering from intense foreign competition, the lowest sales in a generation, and large deficits. In reopening the agreement six months before its expiration date, the company and union presidents announced they had already agreed in principle to link wage and benefit concessions by the union to lower prices for automobiles. They even agreed that they would jointly select an independent accounting firm to examine company records to make sure that all savings on labor costs were passed on to consumers. General Motors' chairman told the public that the agreement "could usher in a new era of labor-management cooperation because it addresses the heart of the problem in our industry today—noncompetitive labor costs and inflated car and truck prices."[26] Though the parties did not reach an agreement on the terms proposed, both recognized an explicit linkage of prices and wages. The proposal legitimated for the union at least an indirect voice in determining prices and access to company books; it was a dramatic and significant change of position by the management of the nation's largest manufacturing firm.

Managers had long found it useful to compare relative rates of increases in wages and profits as a rejoinder to union demands for price cuts. General Motors officials had pointed out before 1982 that shareholders had already made sacrifices; in 1980 they had had to cut quarterly dividends by 48 percent. Of course, this and other managerial comparisons may be viewed simply as expedient arguments rather than equitable comparisons. Managers have usually pointed to profits when they are low but refused to consider them relevant when they are high. Yet to ignore such internal comparisons as having no significance would be unwise. The economic pressures upon many large American manufacturers in the late seventies and early eighties made such comparisons increasingly important. The equity of claims by the constituents of business corporations appears to be more widely recognized than ever before.

PROBLEMS IN MULTIEMPLOYER BARGAINING

In formulating a wage policy, managers may have to resolve seeming conflict between the local and industry wage standards. The reconciliation of such conflicts would indeed appear to be a prerequisite to concerted bargaining by employers in different localities. Even where all accept the same standard, its impact on the firms will differ, requiring a reconciliation of interests. It is

[26]Douglas R. Sease and Robert L. Simison, "GM to Cut Prices of Cars if UAW Grants Savings," *The Wall Street Journal,* Jan. 13, 1982.

appropriate, then, for us to consider at this point the political problems peculiar to employers negotiating through associations when divergent interests on their own side of the bargaining table must be harmonized before agreement can be sought with the union.

The reasons leading employers to bargain jointly have previously been suggested. Primarily they involve the effort of the companies to avoid being "whipsawed," a gaming expression meaning to be worsted in two ways at the same time. It is relevant to bargaining insofar as unions try to raise one employer's rates above that of the others, which, in addition to constituting a victory in itself, permits a second victory by allowing the union to insist that other employers' rates be brought into line—an example of the use of comparison to achieve a desired objective. The nature of employer's associations varies markedly, ranging from those whose decisions are automatically binding upon all members to those whose decisions are advisory only.

The authority of the association leadership stems from the member firms, and its responsibility is for their collective interests. When a union and an association bargain they must face the problem of treating different member firms in the same way. Any common application of wages or working conditions may well affect each quite differently. Thus resolution of those differences among association members may be as difficult as resolution of issues in dispute between the association and the union. Because of variation in the size, profitability, or efficiency of association members, some will be more willing to make concessions to the union than others.

Differences in personal or business philosophy, geographical location, and traditions and precedents may also lead to divergent views. Conflicts within an association become most apparent when certain members must face the prospect of prolongation of a strike because other members have prevented their preference in granting the union's demands.

The Example of Trucking

The internal political difficulties of an employer's association are well illustrated in the trucking industry. The national employer's associations include a wide diversity of firms—common, contract, and private carriers; long-haul, short-haul, and local cartage; big and small firms; and the financially strong as well as the economically marginal. The generally applied wage and working conditions have different effects upon the various firms, particularly marked between long- and short-haul firms. First, the labor costs of the former arise primarily from on-line drivers, whereas labor costs for the latter are mostly generated in local operations—pickup and delivery at the end of each run. Furthermore, road drivers earn mileage rates and local drivers are paid on an hourly basis. In addition, productivity gains in recent years have generally favored long-haul firms. Trade-offs between hourly and mileage wage increases thus can have a sizable differential effect upon firms.

A second source of conflict is the differing impacts of work rules upon different types of carriers. Fixed starting times can be very costly to short-haul carriers and much less costly in long-hauling. Any rule that limits the efficiency or raises the cost of pickups and delivery, of course, hits harder at short-hauling. Finally, the large long-haul firms are usually financially stronger than their short-haul associates and are also more profitable.[27]

Where employers' associations have had more experience and have learned to respect and live with the costs of settlement, they have been able to avoid impasses. They engage in the familiar political process of "log rolling" with interest groups within the association, or there is a philosophical acceptance by the weaker (or by the minority) of the decisions of the stronger members (or of the majority). In some cases the divergence of interests between certain groups within the association is frankly recognized, and provision is made for differential treatment by permitting separate group negotiations on certain phases of the agreement, such as wages, though the results must sometimes be approved by the full negotiating committee.

CONCLUSION

By now it should be evident that in discussing wages it becomes difficult to distinguish which influences are political and which economic. For economists, who in considering the influences on prices have been concerned almost exclusively with the coercive comparisons in the relevant markets, must now admit other, nonmarket comparisons of a coercive nature which nonetheless affect prices. If economics is concerned only with prices in competitive markets (in which political influences presumably may be disregarded), its concern is narrowed to virtual nothingness. If it admits concern with prices and other economic relationships in noncompetitive markets, then it must inevitably admit coercive comparisons arising out of nonmarket influences of the sort discussed in this chapter and Chapter 7. The political factor becomes an economic phenomenon.

The emphasis here has been upon how standards of wage action in some degree reflect the responsibilities of those in authority, those who are in a position to determine policy. The political responsibility to particular interest groups that compose the organization and to the organization as a whole is the basis for those comparisons the participants feel should be equitable. The comparisons that cannot be escaped—the coercive comparisons—help to define the meaning of responsibility in wage setting. There is nothing cut and dried, nothing definitive, nothing precise in terms of revealing what standards will be chosen and how they will affect outcome. There remain to be reconciled the conflicts between the standards deemed equitable by managers and those viewed as coercive by union leaders. There is the possibility that standards and comparisons may be manipulated for particular advantage. These problems

---

[27]Levinson, "Trucking," in Somers, *Collective Bargaining: Contemporary American Experience,* p. 140.

inhere in the political systems within which managers, union leaders, and employers operate. As their concepts of corporate and union responsibility change, we may expect the determination of wages and the whole of collective bargaining to change. Such change is evident today in the hard-pressed manufacturing sector as all the participants react to the challenge of changing competition and a swiftly adjusting economy.

In Chapter 9 we shall examine the manner in which authority and responsibility in union-management relations have been molded and modified over the years by the developments of the law.

COLLECTIVE BARGAINING AND PUBLIC POLICY

The rhetoric of union leaders, and of the managers who negotiate with them, is filled with praises of "free" collective bargaining. Spokespersons from both sides regularly defend the system as it is, commending it for concentrating on general procedures and not on outcomes. Free collective bargaining may be more historical than a present reality, however. No other major industrial nation has erected such comprehensive laws affecting unions' internal activities and such pervasive regulations as unions' organizing efforts, representational rights, and obligations. The National Labor Relations Board and the courts have also elaborated a long list of rules specifying matters that must be bargained and matters that cannot legally be negotiated.

Some informed observers and scholars believe that Americans need a more efficient, coherent, and useful national labor policy than the melange of rules, regulations, and laws under which collective bargaining must be conducted at present. Derek Bok, president of Harvard University and a former professor of labor law, complained:

> [A]fter a dozen years of teaching labor law . . . I would argue that large areas of the law . . . rest so heavily on sheer guesswork that no one can be confident that our rules actually serve the public interest. . . . [M]ore than half the work of the National Labor Relations Board is devoted to defining the proper employee unit in which to hold elections and enforcing an intricate body of rules governing the electioneering behavior of unions and employers. Unit determination often consists of fine-spun applications of vague, even contradictory, principles with no convincing demonstration of how the public interest is served. One can argue that these decisions cause little harm, especially if the size of the election unit is unimportant. But they do cost inordinate amounts of money, time and energy . . . the law grinds on in an unceasing

effort to build a consistent body of rules from what are often unproven or unrealistic premises.[1]

Earlier, Professor John Dunlop, a former secretary of labor, had also protested the shortcomings of American labor laws. He found them all too rigid in application, when in a decentralized collective bargaining system flexibility and versatility were needed. The complex appeals procedure and adversarial hearings before both the NLRB and the courts provide slow adjudication of disputes and make enforcement a difficult and lengthy process, as in the case of J.P. Stevens described in Chapter 1. He also argues that the plethora of rules and regulations encourage both union and management to engage in legal gamesmanship: since the rules are useful to one party or the other at different times, neither is willing to abandon them out of fear of suffering a disadvantage.[2]

Both criticisms are well taken. Chapters 9 through 11 detail some of the complexity of national labor policy, particularly as it directly affects collective bargaining. You will note that many complex provisions arise when policy makers seek to reconcile conflicting goals. They want to encourage workers to join unions and to bargain collectively, but they want at the same time to allow workers to choose union representation freely and to bargain individually. Legislators and judges do not want to set standards for wages, hours, and working conditions (though they recognize a need for minimums); but neither do they want unions or managements to be able to use any bargaining tactic to secure such demands as they may choose to pursue. The public interest needs to be recognized and protected.

Complicating the making of national labor policy have been the limits reached by overall union growth and the narrow reach of collective bargaining. At its greatest extent, union membership covered less than a third of the labor force. If legislators wished to attack discrimination in hiring and promotion, improve safety and health conditions at the place of work, assist in training workers, help workers displaced by plant closings and imports, or provide retirement pensions and medical benefits, they could not look to collective bargaining as a vehicle for their policies. Its already too limited coverage was actually shrinking in the manufacturing sector. Thus they had to devise new, nonunion national labor policies. These have sometimes conflicted with collective bargaining (as when affirmative action supercedes seniority) or overlap and duplicate labor-management procedures (safety complaints can be processed through the Occupational Safety and Health Administration as well as through grievance channels). Sometimes, as in the case of unemployment insurance and social security programs, the national policies provided a basis on which collective bargaining could build; the former supplied a base for sup-

[1]Derek C. Bok, "A Flawed System," *Harvard Magazine,* vol. 85, May–June 1983, p. 40.
[2]John T. Dunlop, "The Limits of Legal Compulsion," *Labor Law Journal,* vol. 27, Feb. 1976, pp. 68–72.

plementary unemployment benefits (SUB) and the latter encouraged private, company, and industry pensions.

Chapters 9 through 11 explore the legal history of collective bargaining. It is a story of attempts to reconcile conflicting goals and of the interactions of legal and economic influences on these reconciliation attempts. We will consider how policy makers can improve public policies to help unions and management lessen the burdens and cut the costs that Bok and Dunlop describe.

THE BARGAINING UNIT

The term "bargaining unit" (or "negotiating unit") is often used loosely to refer to two different groupings. Very generally it identifies the jobs or occupations of those to whom the term of a collective agreement apply. However, it may also refer to the employees, designated by the National Labor Relations Board, whose majority vote authorizes a union's exclusive representation. These employees make up an "election district." Negotiating units and election districts do not necessarily coincide and often bear little resemblance to each other. As workers, union leaders, and managers pursue their complementary and conflicting interests, they frequently find the dimensions of the legal bargaining unit (the election district) either too confining or too broad to serve some purposes they pursue in ad hoc negotiating units.

THE DIMENSIONS OF THE BARGAINING UNIT

Since a bargaining unit identifies those to whom the terms of an agreement apply, its two major dimensions are the groupings of employees and of employers. The former may be conveniently called the "type" of bargaining unit and the latter the "area." An examination of the various types and areas reveals the numerous possible configurations that bargaining units may take.

There are two basic types of units: craft and comprehensive. The pure craft unit includes only those workers who possess a specialized skill or perform a particularized function. It is usually only a part of a larger body of employees. Examples of such craft units are the 8500 members of the Screen Actors Guild in Los Angeles, who negotiate with the Association of Motion Picture and

Television Producers; the more than 10,000 employees of the Seattle Professional Engineering Employees Association, who bargain with the Boeing Company; or the Signalmen, who work for the major railroads. Comprehensive units include a mixture of several occupations, skills, or functions within a given organization or industry. Unions such as the United Automobile Workers and United Steelworkers, for example, typically negotiate for both skilled and semiskilled workers; some of their units are so comprehensive that they also include not only blue-collar, but also clerical, professional, and technical occupations. Among the large electrical and gas utility units, over 40 percent of the workers are covered by agreements that include professional and clerical employees along with those in blue-collar production occupations. Only 3 percent of the large chemicals units are so comprehensive.[1]

The craft or occupational members may unite around their common work interests, setting themselves apart from other employees even when they share the same location or company. They seek to advance their self-interest by gaining special consideration for their skills. Members of comprehensive units tend to emphasize common employment interests that transcend skill, occupational, or functional differences. They use the organized power of their broad grouping to press for benefits that all may enjoy. Either kind of unit may be appropriate and effective, depending upon particular circumstances.

If we set up polar definitions, we might define a pure craft unit as one that includes only those workers performing a precise function for which they require special skill and training. No other workers in the particular labor force would perform the function or possess the same skill and training. A pure comprehensive unit would include all employees on a particular payroll, whether they were involved in professional, clerical, maintenance, or production work or in subsidiary operations such as cafeteria work or trucking. One can find very few such polar units. In practice, most bargaining units fall into an intermediate category blending elements of both pure craft and pure comprehensive units.

Most units resemble one type more than the other, though, so we commonly categorize them as either craft or comprehensive. Craft units, according to the Supreme Court, may be simply groups of employees "which normally have the necessary cohesiveness and special interests to distinguish them from the generality of production and maintenance employees.[2] The NLRB has suggested that a craft unit may be made out of a "distinct and homogeneous groups of skilled journeymen craftsmen, performing the functions of their craft on a nonrepetitive basis, or of employees constituting a functionally distinct department working in trades or occupations for which a tradition of separate representation exists.[3] The most frequently encountered comprehensive units are

[1]*Characteristics of Major Collective Bargaining Agreements, January 1, 1980,* Bureau of Labor Statistics Bulletin 2095, 1981, table 1-9, p. 2.
[2]*Mallinckrodt Chemical Works,* 162 NLRB 387 (1966), quoted in Douglas L. Leslie, *Cases and Materials on Labor Law: Process and Policy,* Boston: Little, Brown and Company, 1979, p. 96.
[3]Ibid., p. 97.

those comprised of all production workers or of production and maintenance workers. Such units make up more than four-fifths of the agreements among large bargaining units in manufacturing. They are not quite as common in non-manufacturing but still they predominate.

The area of bargaining units—that is, the employer dimension—is also variable. It may be only a single department or plant of a small employer, or it may include all the plants of a large corporation. Some bargaining units contain a single employer, and others contain most of the employers in an entire industry. Whatever the area, its *type* of unit may be either craft or comprehensive.

Examples of Various Units

The number of possible different combinations of types and area of bargaining units is large. For example, the USW when negotiating with U.S. Steel, negotiates a master agreement for all its members, whatever their occupations, in all the company's plants across the country. At the other extreme, the American Federation of Teachers typically bargains only for its craft members—teachers—in the school or schools of a particular school district.

In the case of General Motors, each plant local of the UAW is a bargaining unit *for certain subjects only,* such as relief time. However, for most matters, including wages, pensions, and health benefits, the bargaining unit includes the UAW members in all the company's automotive plants, scattered from New Jersey to California. Both the popular press and the negotiators refer to the master agreement as companywide, although it does not cover workers in non-automotive plants. (In 1982, for example, General Motors not only negotiated with the UAW for approximately 400,000 employees but also negotiated with the International Union of Electrical Workers for some 23,000 nonautomotive employees in New York, New Jersey, and Ohio.)

In contrast to General Motors, Western Electric negotiates on a plant-by-plant basis. At most of its larger operations it deals with the International Brotherhood of Electrical Workers; but at its Dallas, Kansas City, and Merrimack Valley plants it negotiates with the Communications Workers of America. Like General Motors and Western Electric, almost every large corporation bargains with many unions, sometimes dozens of them in a variety of bargaining units; most represent small groups of workers whose history and occupation have differentiated them from the bulk of the company work force. Some may have organized in plants or division that once were independent companies or attracted members who enjoyed special skills or a distinct occupation.

A local union may be identified with more than one employer, as is the practice of locals of the International Typographical Union (ITU). In New York City it enrolls as local members those who work for the three large daily papers, yet it signs separate agreements with the publishers. Negotiations have been conducted sometimes jointly and sometimes separately, depending upon the issues involved and the competitive pressures upon the publishers. A single

ITU local is thus identified with several legally defined bargaining units and different employers.

Other unions, such as those in the building trades, the Service Employees International Union (representing building service workers), and the Hotel and Restaurant Employees Union, typically negotiate with formal employers' associations, their agreements covering all the association's members. But in other cases the unions may deal with groups of employers who have not formally banded together into an association. Such is the case in Chicago, where a number of independent meat stores negotiate together with the United Food and Commercial Workers and sign a single agreement, but are not formally associated. A similar case is the agreements the Upholsters negotiate with several firms producing picture frames in the Chicago area. The managers negotiate together but they have not formed an association.

Multiemployer units are often complex groups and display characteristics not found in single-employer units. They vary in geographical extent—city or metropolitan, regional or national. An example of the first is the Laborers' International Union bargaining unit of about 3000 employees who work for the member firms of the Association of General Contractors in Baltimore, Maryland. An example of a regional unit is the 1200 workers covered by the agreement the Graphic Arts union negotiates with the Graphic Arts Association of the Delaware Valley, Pennsylvania. The truly national multiemployer unit, comparatively rare, is exemplified by the 4800 employees for whom the Teamsters negotiate agreements with the National Master Automobile Transporters association.

If employers have come together because they produce a similar product or supply a similar service, they may be said to be engaged in industrywide bargaining.[4] An example is the Steel Companies Coordinating Committee, representing nine major steel firms. Employers may also join with one another for negotiating because of the similarities of their demand for labor. An example might be construction firms in an urban area conducting what has been called "labor-market bargaining" with the building-trades unions.

Not all the employers in an industry or labor market who bargain with a union do so jointly. Some may act independently, avoiding both association and joint bargaining, as small garmentmakers and coal-mine operators often do. Where a formal association does not exist, an employer may refuse to go along with the majority, making a settlement on other terms; for example, Rupert Murdock, publisher of the *New York Post,* refused to join the other

---

[4]The term "industry" is subject to confusion in labor relations writings because it is the root word for two different concepts. *Industrial* unionism and *industrial* bargaining units have been so called because they embrace all or most workers in the industry, cutting across craft lines (as distinguished from craft unions, which cut across industry lines). In this discussion the term "comprehensive bargaining" has been used for this case, and "industrywide bargaining" has been used to designate the grouping of employers along industry lines. Sometimes "industrywide" is used in the sense of the entire industry (nationwide), as when one refers to "the iron and steel industry." But at other times it is used simply to designate the association of employers on the basis of the industry attachment in any given area.

New York publishers in 1978. Even in formal associations, not all employers necessarily participate in negotiations; but the terms of the agreement apply to all.

Hierarchies of Negotiating Units

We have seen how the area of the bargaining unit may be limited to a single department of a single plant or may range up to a multiemployer unit that includes most of the companies in an entire industry on a nationwide scale. We must now take into account the formal and informal bargaining units subsidiary to these primary units. Even within a single department, an individual employee constitutes something of a unit in bargaining for whatever special terms can be secured without conflicting with the terms of the more general unit in which the worker is included.[5]

More likely is the development of work groups as informal bargaining units. As they are only a fraction of the explicitly recognized unit, their negotiations have been called fractional bargaining. Informally negotiating through a shop steward with the first-line supervisors and shop time-study personnel, work groups often arrive at understandings that supplement and at times even contravene the agreement covering the wider unit. More formally, local union leaders typically negotiate with plant officials provisions supplementary to the companywide or industrywide agreement. Occasionally local arrangements will be worked out which run counter to the master agreement negotiated at the company, regional, or industry level, on a sub-rosa, unpublicized basis.

A whole hierarchy of bargaining units may thus be established, each level having its own field of special competency. The bituminous coal industry provides an example of such a system. Here the union negotiates with the Bituminous Coal Operators Association, thereby covering most of the large underground mines. The agreements set forth the basic rates of pay, hours of work, and other conditions of employment. Under these master agreements, each district of the United Mine Workers negotiates supplementary agreements with district operators' associations. The district agreements are concerned principally with the preparation and cleaning of coal, disciplinary rules and penalties, and other factors involved in the day-to-day operation of the mines.

Such district agreements, however, cannot provide for all conditions peculiar to the individual mines, and local unions come together with local associations or individual companies to negotiate agreements supplementary to the district agreement. Difficult work such as the undercutting of coal involves

---

[5]Section 9(a) of the *National Labor Relations Act* asserts the right of any individual employee or a group of employees "at any time to present grievances to their employer and to have such grievances adjusted, without the intervention of the bargaining representative, as long as the adjustment is not consistent with the terms of a collective-bargaining contract or agreement then in effect." This provision of the law is probably unenforceable. Nevertheless, it recognizes the fact that individual workers or work groups may want to—and on occasion do—bargain for themselves.

questions of wages and working conditions that can best be settled by reference to actual situations. Then, within each mine, groups of miners may try to resolve problems peculiar to their immediate job situation. They must bargain to change, adjust, or preserve work practices to their benefit, and they may even engage in slowdowns and wildcat strikes to support their demands. Operators and the union refuse to recognize this form of subordinate-unit (more accurately, insubordinate-unit) bargaining, and they discourage it, but sometimes it receives the support of a provision of the agreement that validates existing local practices.

The hierarchy of bargaining units described above is of a vertical nature, following the organizational lines of both management and the unions. Another kind of hierarchy is possible that might be said to be horizontal in nature. In this, a single master agreement setting forth general terms is supplemented by a series of separate craft or occupational agreements which provide for the preculiar interests of groups and employees. As in the vertical hierarchy, still narrower work groups at the job level may add supplementary and informal rules and provisions to the craft provisions. The subsidiary unit in a horizontal hierarchy might be conceived as a number of craft or craftlike units within a comprehensive unit. A number of unions that enroll a comprehensive membership have given special attention to various skilled groups. Both the autoworkers and the rubber workers, for example, established skilled-trade departments through which skilled workers could seek more effective craft influence and representation in bargaining.

Industry Dispersion of Negotiating Units

The available data on bargaining units indicate that bargaining units vary greatly in their dimensions and that in some unions the units are widely dispersed across industries. Union boundaries often do not match the standarized industrial categories specified by census data. An examination of large bargaining units (which cover about one-third of union workers) indicates that the largest unions are the most widely dispersed (see Table 12). Were data available on the tens of thousands of smaller bargaining units, the dispersion would be greater than for only the large units. The Teamsters have units in more industries than any other union, some of them seemingly far removed from the core union occupation of truck driving. The Teamsters have organized a large group of Honeywell employees in Minneapolis, thus accounting for the unit in "instruments," and they have a unit of 1450 workers at the Owens-Corning Fiberglass Corporation in Aiken, South Carolina. More clearly related to their typical members' occupations are the dispersed industry units of the Machinists and the United Automobile Workers. The UAW organized a unit of over 1000 distribution employees at International Harvester's Depot and Distribution division—an easy extension into wholesale trade from the union's organization of Harvester's production workers. The Machinists have a multiemployer unit of about 1000 auto repair workers in the San Mateo–

TABLE 12
SELECTED UNIONS WITH LARGE BARGAINING UNITS* IN VARIOUS INDUSTRIES, 1980 TO 1982

Industry	Union†								
	Team-sters	USW	IBEW	UAW	IAM	Carpen-ters	Ser-vice	UFCW	CWA
Electrical, electronic	X	X	X	X	X	X			X
Fabricated metals	X	X	X	X	X	X			
Transportation equipment	X	X	X	X	X	X			
Construction	X	X	X			X			
Primary metals	X	X	X	X	X				
Retail trade	X			X	X			X	
Machinery		X	X	X	X				
Services	X		X		X		X		
Utilites	X	X	X		X		X		
Furniture		X		X		X			
Communications	X		X						X
Mining	X	X						X	X
Food	X						X		
Chemicals	X	X							
Instruments	X			X					
Surface transportation‡	X	X		X	X				
Wholesale trade	X			X					
Apparel								X	
Lumber						X			
Paper			X						
Printing, publishing	X								
Stone, clay, glass	X								
Air transportation					X				
Real estate							X		
Hotels, restaurants							X		

*Units including 1000 or more employees.
†USW = United Steelworkers; IBEW = International Brotherhood of Electrical Workers; UAW = United Automobile Workers; IAM = International Association of Machinists; Service = Service Employees International Union; UFCW = United Food and Commercial Workers; CWA = Communications Workers of America; Carpenters = United Brotherhood of Carpenters.
‡Except railroads.
Source: *Bargaining Calendars*, Bureau of Labor Statistics, various years.

Santa Clara, California area, whose skills are similar to those of its members in the aircraft, auto, and machinery industries.

THE PATTERN OF BARGAINING UNITS

We shall now consider the dimensions of bargaining units from a broader perspective in order to observe any typical patterns that emerge when all units are viewed together. We possess no complete or accurate information about all bargaining units because no census of them has ever been made. However, every two years the Bureau of Labor Statistics estimates the number of collective bargaining agreements, which corresponds roughly to the number of bargaining units. The bureau also furnishes data on the number of units by industry and kind of area—single plants, multiple plants of single employers, and multiemployer units. From this information we can draw some conclusions about the kinds of units found in the United States.

First, the distribution of bargaining units more or less parallels the distribution of business firms by size (see Tables 13 and 14).

Only a little more than an eighth of the business corporations—the largest ones—account for 90 percent of the total receipts, while almost a quarter of the corporations take in a miniscule share of receipts, about one-tenth of one percent. The ten largest unions, about 6 percent of the total, negotiate more than three-fifths of all the agreements and thus may be presumed to account for about the same share of all bargaining units. And 61 percent of the unions (106 of the total) negotiate fewer than 3 percent of 180,000 agreements.

If one assumes that in general the larger corporate receipts, the larger the number of employees, the parallel data suggest that bargaining is typically on a firm-by-firm basis; unions have generally followed industrial organization in establishing bargaining units. Other data appear to support this conclusion. Sixty percent of all large units (over 1000 employees) are single-employer; we

TABLE 13
DISTRIBUTION OF NATIONAL UNIONS BY SHARE OF
BASIC COLLECTIVE BARGAINING AGREEMENTS, 1978

Number of agreements	Percentage of all unions	Percentage of all agreements
Under 200	60.8	2.6
200 to 499	11.7	3.2
500 to 999	8.0	5.1
1000 to 1999	8.6	11.0
2000 to 2999	1.7	4.0
3000 to 4999	3.4	12.5
5000 and over	5.7	61.6

Source: Directory of National Unions and Employee Associations, Bureau of Labor Statistics Bulletin 2079, Sept. 1980, table 21, p. 75.

TABLE 14
DISTRIBUTION OF CORPORATE BUSINESS FIRMS
BY SHARE OF TOTAL RECEIPTS, 1977

Size class of receipts	Percentage of business corporations	Percentage of total receipts
Under $25,000	20.6	0.1
$25,000 to $49,999	8.6	0.1
$50,000 to $99,999	12.0	0.5
$100,000 to $199,999 ⎱ $200,000 to $499,999 ⎰	34.3	⎱ 4.7 ⎰
$500,000 to $999,999	9.5	3.8
$1,000,000 and over	14.0	90.9

Source: Statistical Abstract of the United States, 1981, table 897, p. 534.

may presume that as high a proportion of the smaller units, whose average size is under 100, are also single-employer units.

Trends in Types of Units

The overall share of large multiemployer units has been fairly steady since 1961, but the stability results from contrasting trends in manufacturing and nonmanufacturing (see Table 15). In manufacturing, multiemployer units have declined significantly both in number and in worker coverage. The decline has been general throughout almost all the various manufacturing industries. Multiemployer units are most dominant in nonmanufacturing (see Table 16) and it is this sector that multiemployer units have increased, both in coverage of employees and number. In several industries—trucking, trade, and hotels and

TABLE 15
SHARE OF MULTIEMPLOYER UNITS FROM 1961 TO 1980,
BY AGREEMENT AND NUMBER OF WORKERS COVERED*

	Agreements (%)		Workers (%)	
	1961	1980	1961	1980
Total	35.9	40.4	41.2	43.0
Manufacturing	12.4	6.8	13.0	6.7
Nonmanufacturing	23.5	33.6	28.2	36.3

*For all units of 1000 employees or more (excluding railroads and airlines).
Source: "Major Union Contracts in the United States," *Monthly Labor Review*, vol. 85, Oct. 1962, table 1, p. 1137; and *Characteristics of Major Collective Bargaining Agreements, Jan. 1, 1980*, Bureau of Labor Statistics, table 1-8, p. 19.

TABLE 16

PERCENTAGE OF EMPLOYEES COVERED UNDER
COLLECTIVE BARGAINING AGREEMENTS* BY INDUSTRY AND AREA OF UNIT, 1980

				Single employer		
Multiemployer			**Single plant**		**Multiplant**	
Construction	99.7		Chemicals	87.4	Communications	98.9
Wholesale trade	95.6		Paper	70.4	Rubber, plastics	85.0
Hotels, restaurants	95.4		Electrical machinery	67.1	Primary metals	80.1
Apparel	92.3		Fabricated metals	44.7	Stone, clay, glass	75.9
Mining	96.4		Petroleum refining	44.1	Utilities (gas, electric)	68.2
Transportation†	84.9		Tobacco	43.6	Instruments	67.3
Services	78.6		Transportation		Transportation	
Publishing, printing	77.8		equipment	32.7	equipment	64.9
					Nonelectrical	
					equipment	58.4

*Units with more than 1000 employees.
†Except railroads and airlines.
Source: Characteristics of Major Collective Bargaining Agreements, January 1, 1980, Bureau of Labor
Statistics, Bulletin 2095, May 1981, table 1.8, p. 19.

restaurants—the absolute number of multiemployer units declined slightly
even as the number of workers covered increased. Membership growth appears
to have taken place not in the number of units but within the units. In construction, however, the number of multiemployer units almost doubled, going
from 168 to 324, while the number of workers covered increased by nearly 50
percent. Here the unions appear to have grown by adding new units.

In European countries where labor unions are significant organizations, single-employer bargaining has been until recent years more the exception than
the rule. The unions typically bargain with industry associations for minimum
terms; and in some countries, such as West Germany, the government extends
those terms to cover all workers and employers in an industry, even if they are
not represented in the negotiations.[6] European unions most commonly have
tended to bargain with a collectivity of employers over the wages and conditions of whole industries. In times of prosperity, they often find it possible and
desirable to negotiate supplementary agreements with individual firms, gaining
benefits above the industrywide minimums. To the extent that such bargaining
is less typical here, American bargaining confronts the union with differently
organized industrial power and business decision making. The less extensive
range of bargaining of most American unions tends to dilute the wider political

[6]The American government, through the secretary of labor, often makes the same kind of extension with regard to wages, hours, and working conditions for workers employed on government
contracts. The Walsh-Healy and Davis-Bacon Acts permit the extension by allowing the secretary
considerable latitude in setting the minimums at those prevailing in the industry. The secretary
usually decides that union standards are the minimums prevailing. With the great number of government contracts and the huge government expenditure of recent years, the impact of extending
prevailing standards to these workers may be significant.

and economic responsibilities of union and management negotiators, since the impact of the terms of the agreements—or of failures to agree—upon the economy is of lesser scope.

Different industries show quite distinct patterns of units. We have noted that multiemployer units predominate in nonmanufacturing industries. The predominance probably is a function of the large numbers of small firms in that sector. For the same reason, apparel and publishing and printing also have many multiemployer units, though they are manufacturing industries.

Explanations of the dominance of single or multiplant units among various industries are not easy to find, however. That single-plant units should predominate in chemicals, but multiplant units in rubber and plastics, appears to be a characteristic best explained by the history of initial union-organizing strategy and employer response. Two-thirds of electrical machinery units are in single plants even though more than 40 percent of the industry's employers work for only four large firms—General Electric, Western Electric, Westinghouse, and RCA. About the same share of bargaining units in gas and utilities, 68 percent, are multiplant units, but utilities are scattered widely across the country and even the largest has no more than 6 percent as many employees as General Electric. The stone, clay, glass industry shares many of the characteristics of the industries that have many multiemployer units. Small firms are common, and yet three-quarters of the units are multiplant.

The area pattern of bargaining units is reasonably clear at any one time, but it is always in the process of changing. Mergers, bankruptcies, and growth of firms may shift their units from single-employer, single-plant to single-employer, multiplant—or from the latter to the former. Various forces play upon unions and employers both, leading them to work toward a narrowing or broadening of the bargaining unit. They may experiment with multiemployer bargaining for some time before formalizing the arrangement, for example. Subsequently they may become dissatisfied with the experience and return to their former bargaining units. Units that started out as multiemployer may dissolve into narrower units by a process of slow erosion. There are more changes and shifts among bargaining units than appear in the record. An examination of the forces that play upon the structure of bargaining units can throw light upon the changing dimensions of the units and make more understandable the existing patterns of collective bargaining in the United States.

THE LEGAL FORCES SHAPING BARGAINING UNITS

The dominant influence in the shaping of bargaining units appears at first glance to be the government, acting through several agencies regulating labor relations, the most visible of which is the National Labor Relations Board. Our labor laws require the agencies to define the election district—that is, the workers who can determine by majority vote whether they want union representation of their interests and if so, which union they want to represent them. The National Labor Relations Act charges the board, for example, to "decide . . .

whether . . . the unit appropriate for the purposes of collective bargaining shall be the employer unit, craft unit, plant unit, or subdivision thereof."[7] Note that the board does not have to designate the *most* appropriate unit, but only one that it can reasonably defend as appropriate.[8]

Thus the legal identification of those workers to be exclusively represented by a union is a matter of public policy and political debate. Thus, too, discussion of bargaining units tends to focus upon the formal, legal determinants of the bargaining unit as an election district rather than the less formal but nonetheless important organizational, social, and economic determinants of the negotiating unit. Board policies primarily reflect a concern for stability in collective bargaining, expressed explicitly in a 1966 decision not to sever a craft group from a well-established unit:

> [There] is the need to balance the interest of the employer and the total employee complement in maintaining the industrial stability and resulting benefits of an historical plantwide bargaining unit. . . . [The board considers] the interests of all employees in continuing to bargain together in order to maintain their collective strength, as well as the public interest and the interests of the employer and the plant union in maintaining overall plant stability in labor relations and uninterrupted operation of integrated industrial or commercial facilities.[9]

The parties themselves often appear less interested in long-term stability than in the immediate purpose of winning a representational election. A rival union may petition for a change in the bargaining unit in the belief it thereby has a better chance of ousting the currently incumbent union. Each seeks to persuade the NLRB to include or exclude particular groups of workers in the election district in order to serve its own interests in winning the election. A union may argue that personal secretaries be excluded, for example, if the organizers believe they are apt to vote against union representation for the nonprofessional staff of a private college; the college officials, in turn, may seek the secretaries' inclusion, believing that their "no" vote will tip the election against the union. Neither party uses such pragmatic—even cynical—arguments before the NLRB, however. The board seeks to base its determinations of the appropriate election unit on the more objective characteristics of the work, occupational, and organizational structure.

The board rejected bargaining power as a consideration of the appropriate unit. It argued that:

> The application of a power test would bring economic warfare to the forefront of collective bargaining, instead of keeping it in the background where it belongs. . . .

---

[7]Sec. 9(b).

[8]See *Morand Beverage Co.,* 91 NLRB 409 (1950).

[9]*Mallinckrodt Chemical Works,* 162 NLRB 387 (1966), reprinted in A. Howard Myers and David P. Twomey, *Labor Law and Legsilation,* 5th ed., Cincinnati, Ohio: Southwestern Publishing Co., 1975, pp. 166–167.

The Board would be faced with an impossible administrative problem in trying to decide when equality of bargaining power does not exist.[10]

Its second reason is more compelling than its first. Economic warfare and the influence of economic forces powerfully condition collective bargaining, whether the board explicitly recognizes it or not. But bargaining power, as we have seen in Chapter 6, is so multidimensional and changeable that the board could hardly use it as a sensible criterion for unit determination.

Lacking any clear or helpful guides from Congress, the NLRB has determined the appropriate bargaining unit on a case-by-case basis. Generally, its decisions have been guided largely by the desires and practices of unions and employers. If the two parties agree upon a particular unit, the board usually confirms it, though if it believes the interests of the employees may not be well served, the Board has sometimes established units contrary to the wishes of both. Where the parties disagree about the definition of a unit, the board gives particular weight to any substantial bargaining history of the group. In many cases, of course, there is no history of bargaining, and the board then relies upon a number of other criteria, using them flexibly. It may consider such factors as the arrangements followed in other plants of the same employer or in plants of other employers in the same industry. It may also look for the similarities of employment interests among the workers involved and consider the expressed desires of groups of employees and of the employers, the composition of the petitioning union, and the employer's administative organization.

Special Treatment for Craft Workers and Professional Employees

Under the Labor-Management Relations Act of 1947, Congress instructed the NLRB not to take the bargaining history into account when considering the appropriateness of craft units.[11] Congress apparently meant to make a bit easier, than under the original labor law of 1935, the separation of craft groups from comprehensive bargaining units, if the craft workers so desired. The NLRB responded minimally, usually concluding that separating a craft from a more inclusive unit would be a threat to industrial stability. The result has been that craft workers included within larger established units have, for the most part, had to seek their interests through internal union politics rather than through their own separate organizations.

The Taft-Hartley amendments to the National Labor Relations Act also made special provision for professional employees. The NLRB may not set up a bargaining unit that includes both professionals and nonprofessionals unless the professionals agree by majority vote. Though Congress defined "profes-

---

[10]*Continental Baking Company,* 99 NLRB 123 (1952), p. 777, as reported in *Seventeenth Annual Report of the National Labor Relations Board* (1953).

[11]Sec. 9(b)(2).

sional" at some length,[12] the board has not found simple any application of the definition to the blurred and confusing categories of employment situations. For example, it classified as professionals non-college-trained plant engineers of a telephone company, but found accounting employees making cost analyses for a window-glass company to be nonprofessionals. The board declared that the character of the work rather than the individual qualifications of employees determined professional status. Thus it found editorial employees of a newspaper as well as radio announcers, singers, and continuity writers to be nonprofessionals.[13]

Guards and Supervisors

Decisions by the National Labor Relations Board about craft workers and professionals affect the kind of bargaining unit available to them, thereby making organizing easier or more difficult and enhancing or lessening bargaining power. But they do not deny to either group the protection of the labor law. Other Taft-Hartley amendments have denied full collective bargaining rights to two kinds of employees—guards or security personnel and supervisors.[14] Guards may organize for the purposes of bargaining collectively, but they cannot be a part of or affiliated with any organization that includes other workers. Under NLRB rulings even guards are excluded from regular units if more than half their time is spent on security work. As separate units, unaffiliated to any other labor unions, organizations of plant guards and company security employees have not been able to provide much bargaining strength. The result is that guard unions have not attracted many members. Their collective bargaining rights are, as the Supreme Court pointed out, "distinctly second class."[15]

Supervisors are excluded from all rights to join a union or bargain collectively; employers may lawfully discharge or otherwise discipline supervisory personnel for union activities. In 1974 the Supreme Court extended this exclusion to *all managerial employees,* even if they do not have the authority to formulate or carry out an employer's labor relations policy.[16] More recently the effect of the exclusion has been significantly increased by the Supreme Court's ruling that full-time faculty members of private nonprofit institutions of higher

---

[12]Sec. 2(12)(a), and (b).

[13]See Benjamin J. Taylor and Fred Witney, *Labor Relations Law,* 2d ed., Englewood Cliffs, N.J., 1975, pp. 308–309.

[14]Section 2(11): "The term 'supervisor' means any individual having authority, in the interest of the employer, to hire, transfer, suspend, lay off, recall, promote, discharge, assign, reward, or discipline other employees, or responsibility to direct them, or to adjust their grievances, or effectively to recommend such action, if in connection with the foregoing the exercise of such authority is not merely routine or clerical nature, but requires the use of independent judgment."

[15]Taylor and Witney, *Labor Relations Law,* p. 307.

[16]*NLRB v. Bell Aerospace Co.* 416 U.S. 267 (1974).

education are managerial employees. They do not enjoy the rights of employees under the National Labor Relations Act.[17]

The independence required of plant guards' unions and the exclusion of supervisors (as originally defined by law, and of managerial employees as defined by the Court) have denied effective unions and the benefits of collective bargaining to a sizable number of those in the labor force who have indicated a desire for both. The Taft-Hartley amendments affecting supervisors effectively undermined the Foreman's Association of America in the late forties. Its membership declined sharply as employers refused to recognize it, and it dwindled away, impotent without legal support. In removing the faculty of private colleges from the protection of the labor law, the Court also threatened bargaining agents in some eighty-five institutions in which they had already secured recognition. Seventy had even secured agreements. The removal has created an anomaly: employees in public institutions possess greater bargaining rights under state laws than employees in private institutions have under either state or federal law. More than 560 state colleges and universities recognized faculty bargaining units and had already negotiated agreements by 1980.[18]

Other such anomalies between public and private bargaining can develop in states in which the right of collective bargaining is through agencies whose legal mandates are often different from that of the NLRB. Some states have not passed any enabling collective bargaining statutes and thus have no agencies to determine bargaining units. In states that do have statutes, most exclude managerial and confidential employees from membership in educational bargaining units, for example, but they show little consistency in the exclusion of school principals and vice principals.[19] Under state laws the organization of hospitals proceeded with a fragmentation of bargaining units. Hospital administrators sometimes found themselves dealing with many small units whose jurisdictional quarrels and barriers to flexible staffing created severe problems.

In Minnesota, for example, as an outgrowth of the policies followed by the state's labor relations agency, multiple bargaining units became the norm for many of the hospitals. Among those certified were units for pharmacists, radiologic technicians, LPNs, RNs, stationary engineers, maintenance employees, clerical workers, and unskilled nonprofessionals. New York State, in another example, sought initially to limit bargaining units to five occupations, but eventually accepted as many as 12, including a unit of supervisors.[20]

[17]See *NLRB v. Yeshiva,* 100 Supreme Court Reporter 856 (1980).
[18]"Supreme Court's Yeshiva Decision Produces Uncertainty, Disappointment," *Chronicle of Higher Education,* Mar. 3, 1980.
[19]Robert E. Doherty, "Public Education," in Somers, *Collective Bargaining: Contemporary American Experience,* pp. 521–522.
[20]Richard U. Miller, "Hospitals," in Somers, *Collective Bargaining: Contemporary American Experience,* p. 410.

Health-Care Employees

Congress had explicitly exempted nonprofit private hospitals from NLRB jurisdiction in 1947, but it became increasingly concerned with strikes and disruptions in the delivery of health care as unions struggled to organize workers and to conduct bargaining under state laws—or in their absence. In 1974 Congress brought nonprivate hospitals under the federal labor law, instructing the NLRB to avoid a proliferation of bargaining units. Almost a year later the board established standards for five basic units—registered nurses, other health-care professionals, technicians, service and maintenance employees, and business office clericals. Later it recognized a sixth employee unit—physicians.[21]

Hospital managers accused the NLRB of disregarding Congress's instructions; they favored fewer, more inclusive units. The controversy over the board's bargaining unit policy for hospital employees in the seventies was an ironic reversal of the controversy over its policy in the forties and early fifties. In the earlier period, critics feared that the NLRB was encouraging units to be too large and comprehensive. These enlarged units, it was argued, would produce industrywide bargaining. The consequences would be a growth of monopoly power, intensification of strike effects, and denial of full expression to special groups of workers. The evidence—first that industrywide bargaining was increasing, and second that it produced the predicted adverse results—has turned out to be much less convincing than the charges at the time were emphatic.

Coordinated and Coalition Bargaining

Nevertheless, managerial and business concern about large bargaining units continues to be expressed. When a group of eight major unions[22] undertook to coordinate their 1966 negotiations with General Electric and Westinghouse, the managers of General Electric refused to meet with the "coalition," as they termed the arrangement. The unions appealed to the NLRB, which upheld the coordinated bargaining; the second circuit court of appeals confirmed the board's decision.[23] Management feared that coordinated bargaining was a means of forcing upon it a wider, more powerful negotiating unit than it liked. To support its dislike of such a unit, General Electric management argued that coalition bargaining[24] would escalate disputes into industry-crippling strikes and reduce the authority of locally elected union representatives.[25]

[21]Ibid., pp. 386–387.

[22]By 1982 thirteen unions were represented in the Coordinated Bargaining Committee for General Electric and Westinghouse.

[23]U.S. Court of Appeals (2d Cir., 1969) 412 F. 2d 512.

[24]The unions carefully used the term "coordinated bargaining," which suggested a looser grouping and more independence for the constituent members than "coalition bargaining."

[25]See William N. Chernish, *Coalition Bargaining,* Philadelphia: University of Pennsylvania Press, 1969, for a study that generally accepts management's views and judgments. A later empir-

Although coordinated bargaining has been helpful to the electrical workers' unions in their negotiations with General Electric, it has not been so successful in their dealings with Westinghouse. In 1966 the International Brotherhood of Electrical Workers broke with the other unions to conduct, by itself, a two-week strike before agreeing to terms not significantly different from those gained by the other unions. In the 1979 bargaining, the three major unions of the coordinating group struck Westinghouse; the IBEW settled 10 days before the United Electrical Workers and International Union of Electrical Workers did. Even with government approval of a negotiating unit wider than their election districts and more inclusive of a company's workers than their historically separate negotiating units, the coordinating unions have run into practical difficulties and confront organizational rivalries that inhibit widespread acceptance of coordinated bargaining units.

Coordinated bargaining may sometimes serve management as well as unions. In the construction industry many employers have concluded that the multiplicity of bargaining units contributes to employer weakness in bargaining and works to a general industrial instability, grossly inflated costs, and labor inefficiencies. Congress has considered but not yet approved proposals to amend the National Labor Relations Act in ways that would allow local contractor associations exclusive representation rights. These rights would prevent individual contractors from leaving the bargaining unit to negotiate special agreements with the building-trades unions, allowing them to work through local strikes. Contractors who make such agreements can seriously weaken the employers who need to make a united stand in the face of union demands if they are not to be whipsawed.[26]

If coordinated bargaining should be required by law in the construction industry—making a multiemployer group the exclusive representative of a number of independent, private employers—public policy would face a number of equity issues with which multiemployer units have so far dealt voluntarily. How would the member employers decide group policies? Could the group negotiate against the wishes of a member employer when the settlement vitally affects costs and ability to continue in business? Would all contractors in a given area have to join the designated group? How could the group deal with free riders who accept its benefits but choose not to share the costs?

However Congress resolves the issue of coordinated bargaining in the construction industry and whatever rules the NLRB applies in defining bargaining units (as election districts), the law is but one force shaping bargaining units. Once the board defines a bargaining unit for the purposes of conducting a rep-

---

ical study rejected management's assertion: see Robert A. McLean, "Coalition Bargaining and Strike Activity in the Electrical Equipment Industry, 1950–1974," *Industrial and Labor Relations Review,* vol. 30, Apr. 1977, pp. 354–363.

[26]For a detailed study of the problems of appropriate bargaining units in construction see Donald Cullen and Louis Feinberg, *The Bargaining Structure in Construction: Problem and Prospects,* Labor-Management Services Administration, 1980.

resentational election and certifying a particular union, the parties may either expand or reduce the unit for which they negotiate agreements. The NLRB does not forbid unions and management from voluntarily adjusting the unit size and coverage to meet their useful and practical purposes.

The board determination is not, however, without significance. When the NLRB certifies a unit, it creates a basic legal legitimacy for the unit and the basis for a kind of union sovereignty over it. A union that wins an election is entitled to exclusive representation of the workers in that unit, whether or not they are union members. The negotiated terms apply to everyone in the unit. This right of exclusive representation contributes to the maintenance of the union and also to the stability of industrial relations for the firm.

THE ECONOMIC FORCES SHAPING BARGAINING UNITS

In forming unions to negotiate with employers, workers join together in an alliance to increase their bargaining power. The higher the proportion of those who ally within any given jurisdiction, the stronger the union, since it can more effectively impose a cost upon employers who disagree with its terms. Also, the stronger the bargaining position of each member, the stronger the bargaining power of the union.

The Labor Market

The strength gained from numbers would seem to indicate that unions should enroll as many as they can; it would seem, too, that the strength gained from enrolling workers who command strategic positions would lead unions to include as many of these workers as possible. The goal of improving bargaining power thus leads unions to seek to represent all workers who might otherwise compete among themselves and thereby undermine wages and working standards. The objective is to achieve terms that are more or less standard over the area within which workers are potential threats to one another. They must also cover that area within which employers threaten one another by competitively cutting labor (or, more generally, production) costs. The threat to workers is direct, affecting their wages and working conditions, whereas the threat to employers' profit margins is indirect. Willingness on the part of any group of workers to accept a lower wage endangers the wages of all workers in the market; pressure by any competitive company to secure a lower wage also potentially endangers the profits of all other companies. Both unions and companies have reason, therefore, at least to maintain and probably to extend the coverage of the agreement to all competitors.

When a number of competitors are all bidding for the same type of labor, they may initiate a labor-market threat or provide the union with an opportunity to bid up wages. If one or more employers can force down the going wage rates in individual negotiations with the union, there is likely to be an irresistible pressure from other producers to receive the same favorable terms.

A generally lower wage scale will thus have been introduced by individual concessions. Fear of such a result explains why in some instances unions have withstood making special concessions to even a hard-pressed firm. At times unions have countenanced the closing of a company rather than grant special favors which might endanger wage rates in other plants.

The Product Market

The threat to wages may be initiated in the product market, where businesses of lesser degrees of efficiency may be driven to cut costs (including wages) in order to meet the price competition of more efficient competitors. Such cutting can set up a chain reaction as other firms seek to retain their relative competitive positions. Such was the situation among American automobile producers in the early 1980s. In 1980 the UAW made sizable wage and fringe concessions to Chrysler Corporation when it was faced with bankruptcy. As a condition of continued government assistance to the company, the UAW had to agree to additional pay cuts the following year. Union leaders declared that they would not renegotiate other major agreements, however. As sales of new automobiles plunged and Japanese competition became increasingly severe, the other producers also asked for wage concessions six months before the then current agreements expired in 1982. With reluctance the union gave in first to Ford, then to General Motors, and finally to American Motors.

The concessions granted to the major firms then applied wage pressure to the parts suppliers. The major firms found it less costly to manufacture their own parts than to purchase them from outside; the suppliers felt compelled to seek givebacks from the union that allowed them at least to maintain their economic position. Threats from the product market are interrelated, of course, with threats in the labor market. Wage cutting may lead to price-cutting, and General Motors, in a first bid for concessions in early 1982, promised a cut in automobile prices if it won the wage cuts. In a more competitive, less oligopolistic industry such as clothing, price-cutting might precede the attempts at wage cutting.

Economists have long recognized the importance of competitive pressures in forcing unions and employers to extend the area of their bargaining. Over seventy years ago, Professor John R. Commons incisively analyzed the way in which an expanding product market intensified competitive pressures on wages and forced unions to extend their organization and to seek national bargaining.[27] He and other observers of the labor scene found convincing evidence that the extension of the product market threatened the financial positions of those firms unable to secure the same wage concessions as their competitors. The Industrial Commission, established by President McKinley, declared in

---

[27]John R. Commons, "American Shoemakers: A Sketch of Industrial Evolution, 1648–1895," *Quarterly Journal of Economics,* vol. 24, 1910, pp. 39–84; reproduced in Commons et al., *Documentary History of American Industrial Society,* vol. 3, pp. 18–58.

1902, for example: "The great advantage which is claimed for wide-reaching collective bargaining in trades where there is competition in the general market, is the equalizing of cost of production and of the conditions of labor, in such a way that manufacturers in no one locality can secure an advantage over those elsewhere by cutting wages or otherwise granting less favorable conditions to their employees."[28]

In the face of union weakness in the late nineteenth and early twentieth centuries, employers in a number of industries pushed for national bargaining. In the pottery, bituminous coal, stove, glass, and Great Lakes longshoring industries, employers saw national bargaining not just as a device to establish uniform wages and stabilize costs but also as a means of helping to regulate output and maintain prices. They were as anxious to protect themselves from the intensified competition of the rapidly expanding markets as were the workers.[29]

Competitive pressures in labor and product markets are still at work, causing unions and management to alter their bargaining units. Although they may lead to an expansion of the area of bargaining units, such is not always the case. The decline in the number and coverage of large multiemployer units in manufacturing since 1961 indicates that contraction of the area may be typical in many subindustries. Other forces, such as technological and product changes, administrative efficiency, and internal union politics, may divert the thrust of competitive pressures—or in some situations intensify them.

Competition may be so directed or redirected that smaller units become more desirable. For example, through the fifties and sixties the airlines attempted to form a multiemployer unit to negotiate with the various unions in the industry, actually carrying out joint bargaining with the Machinists in 1953 and in 1966. But the union found no virtue in the arrangements, and the great diversity in the carriers' operating and economic characteristics impeded cooperation. The carriers could not even sustain a successful, helpful coordinating group to facilitate the sharing of ideas about labor relations and the distribution of information. After trying out various modes of bargaining and coordinating, the twenty-two-member board of the Airline Industrial Relations Conference disbanded in late 1978 and settled for a two-person agency to collect and distribute collective bargaining data to the various carriers. The narrower, single-company negotiating units were accepted as the only likely ones in the industry.[30]

Technological Change

A technological change, such as improved transportation, may exert both an expansionary and a narrowing force upon bargaining units, depending upon

---

[28]*Final Report of the Industrial Commission,* pp. 840–841.

[29]For a discussion of these examples, see Lloyd Ulman, *The Rise of the National Trade Union,* Cambridge, Mass.: Harvard University Press, 1955, pp. 519–535.

[30]Mark L. Kahn, "Airlines," in Somers, *Collective Bargaining: Contemporary American Experience,* pp. 354–355.

the other forces and influences at work. The continued improvement in the highway system over the last twenty years increased the geographic mobility of construction workers, widening the effective labor market. Both union leaders and contractors believed worker mobility increased particularly in the crowded northeast. At the same time, and perhaps because of the widening labor markets, individual national contractors and the unions increasingly negotiated agreements for ever-broader units. But the wider coverage of these agreements and the broader negotiating units that strengthened the big employers in their dealing with the unions sometimes adversely affected smaller contractors in more local bargaining units. Those with national agreements are permitted to "work through" local strikes, providing jobs for the striking workers and putting competitive pressure on the local contractors who may be attempting to hold the wage line. Such results do not commend wider agreements and negotiating units to many local contractors, of course. Even in the absence of national agreements, outside contractors who do not feel much loyalty to the local contractors' association may either break ranks during strikes or in other ways be a weak spot in the local contractors' front. Thus even as the industry develops wider units, many contractors are not anxious to see them prevail.[31] Increased mobility has produced moves to expand bargaining units but also activated counteracting forces in the industry. Most observers and participants see the present structure of bargaining units as unsatisfactory, but there is little agreement about how satisfaction may be gained.

Improved transportation has contributed to small-plant bargaining units in the chemical industry. Transportation is not the only factor involved, since raw materials are widespread and the products are sold in a number of different markets. Nevertheless, the flexibility and availability of fast motor freight have encouraged geographic dispersion of the industry. No single city, state, or region is the dominant site of chemical production, and thus unions are forced to spread out their organizing efforts. Bargaining in the larger units remains largely on a plant-by-plant basis even though the five largest firms employ more than a third of all chemical workers. In 1961 single-employer, multiplant units accounted for 43 percent of the total in the industry, but by 1980 they made up only 13 percent; in neither year were there any larger, multiemployer units. The geographic dispersion is so great and the product markets are so divergent that the local labor market becomes the most relevant arena in bargaining.

Improved transportation, changing technologies, and diversified product markets have allowed firms in a number of industries in addition to chemicals to move their plants to the suburbs and rural areas. These forces may thereby have contributed in manufacturing generally, as in chemicals, to the increasing prominence of narrow-area units, particularly units of single plants.

Technological developments may change not only the area but also the type

---

[31]Cullen and Feinberg, *The Bargaining Structure in Construction: Problems and Prospects,* pp. 12–13.

of bargaining units, since skill requirements are often affected. Technological changes may sometimes reduce the skill required of workers. If machine methods of production make less necessary skills that require highly specialized training and experience, a larger number of workers with simple mechanical proficiency can enter the labor market. A larger pool is available to the employing companies, and the competitive pressures on the workers are increased. The new technology may create more jobs, but there are also more workers available to fill them. Reduction of skills means greater ease of replacement. This type of development in the food-processing and retailing industries probably helped convince the Meatcutters, for example, to merge, first with the United Packinghouse, Food and Allied Workers in 1968 and second with the Retail Clerks in 1979, to form a new union, the United Food and Commercial Workers. The shift of meat processing from large urban centers to slaughter houses and packing plants near feed lots dispersed those involved in meat processing, requiring broader units. Changes in distribution also allowed the shipment of boxed beef, already cut into pieces, which altered the skill requirements at the retail level. With the decline of butcher shops and the rise of supermarkets, the skilled meatcutters discovered more and more a community of interest with the unskilled supermarket clerks. They were encouraged to eschew craft units and to seek the benefits of comprehensive bargaining units that would include them both.

Technological changes can eliminate a narrow grouping of workers and force them to broaden the type of bargaining unit to include other skills if the union is to survive at all. The decline of the railroads, for example, forced the various crafts to join together. The firemen, no longer required on diesels, were particularly at hazard. In 1969 the Firemen and Enginemen, Trainmen, Conductors and Brakemen, and Switchmen formed the United Transport Union (UTU). Even more consolidation of bargaining units was needed, however, and in 1973 the UTU, Maintenance of Way Employees, and Railway Clerks agreed to coordinate bargaining in their group negotiations with the major carriers. By 1978 a number of the smaller crafts, long hard-pressed by employment cutbacks—the Sleeping Car Porters, Freight Handlers, and Express and Station Employees—merged with the Railway Clerks; craft units negotiating separately with individual carriers had almost disappeared from the industry.

Technological change may just as often increase skill requirements, of course, as reduce them. In so doing it may bring about the formation of new craft units. Modern technologies require large numbers of technicians and engineers; where many of these employees have been grouped together, as in aircraft plants and electronics firms, some have organized and sought separate bargaining units for themselves. The development of hospitals as community centers for health care has provided employment for increasing numbers of professional and craft occupations, such as registered nurses, therapists, dietitians, laboratory technicians, and health aides. When they have organized for the purpose of bargaining collectively, many have sought craft unions, wishing to preserve their identity and to control their work interests without the complications of other occupational groups. The pressure upon employing hospital management to recognize narrow occuaptional groups has been intense. In New York State, government labor agencies initially sought to limit the kinds of units to five but eventually accepted as many as twelve.[32]

Industrial Organization

The structure of industrial organization significantly affects the structuring of bargaining units. The growth in the size of the business unit quite naturally led to a growth in the size of bargaining units. The large corporation has its roots in the nineteenth century and before, but its primary growth has been during the twentieth century. Its organizational development has been both horizontal and vertical. Firms have spread their control over a greater proportion of a particular production process or product market, and they have also integrated under a centralized authority the supply of raw materials, their conversion into finished products, and their marketing. Large corporations have given birth to subsidiary corporations which themselves might grow to vast sizes. A single plant of one such subsidiary corporation might have more than 10,000 workers on its payroll.

Even though the bargaining unit was confined to a single plant, in terms of numbers of workers and processes covered it meant a tremendous expansion of the scope of the agreement compared with the days of individual enterprise, partnerships, and early corporations. The units need not and have not been confined to single plants, however, and centralized corporate control certainly has stimulated companywide units in such industries as steel, automobiles, rubber, and retail trade.

In those industries in which individual plants are located in relatively isolated labor markets or produce for markets different from those of the companies' other plants, single-plant bargaining has flourished. Such is the case in the chemical industry, as mentioned above, and in many of the large nationwide food processors such as dairies and baking companies; single-plant unions have become more prominent in the food industry since 1961. Nevertheless, centralized financial control works toward widening the coverage of the unit to include not only the plant but also the company. In retail trade, for example, the share of multiplant units has increased from 31 percent in 1961 to 41 percent in 1980.

As unions negotiate for and companies agree to pension, insurance, and welfare programs, companywide bargaining can offer advantages. Actuarial considerations and considerations of efficiency in administration may make a broad unit of coverage somewhat more desirable. The location of authority for making agreements on particular subjects is therefore affected by the form of industrial and union organization. Large centralized organizations encompass-

---

[32]Miller, "Hospitals," in Somers, *Collective Bargaining: Contemporary American Experience,* p. 410.

ing many plants may require broad bargaining units for companywide matters such as supplemental unemployment insurance, but they may need small units for handling other issues such as working rules, piece-rate changes, and layoff procedures.

Changing Economic Conditions

Changing economic conditions may change the locus of decision making, though, inducing both managers and union leaders to move local issues out of the local plant unit to the companywide unit. In the automobile industry, work rules, long matters of local concern, began to receive attention of those at companywide bargaining tables in the 1982 negotiations. Plant efficiency and local productivity had become a major focus of top managers' attention. The UAW's national leaders pledged themselves to be responsive to innovative job assignments in the plants, and when local negotiations cannot reach agreement over work-rule changes after sixty days, national union representatives and company officials may step in and assist them in resolving disputes.[33]

In other cases employers may run into difficulty when they try to bargain with locals controlled by policy pronouncements of the national union. Some national unions draft form contracts that the local is powerless to alter without approval, leaving to local decision only certain terms that cannot be determined nationally. For example, wage deviations from the standard may be permitted, whereas policies with respect to union security, seniority, hours, and grievance procedures are predetermined for the local. If an agreement is reached at all, then in these particulars it is reached on the terms of the national union. Employers might never meet the national officials, and yet they will have to submit to their terms.

It will be recalled from an earlier examination of the procedures of collective bargaining that most national unions require local unions to submit local agreements for approval. Here again there is the chance for the national headquarters to determine local policy by refusing to sanction what has been agreed to locally. Thus employers may find themselves bargaining with a local group that is powerless really to exercise discretion in negotiating some issue.

This problem of reaching the source of authority and responsibility may confront the union as well as management. If a bargaining unit consists of only a single plant of a company, the local union may find that the plant management is powerless to override company policy on certain controversial issues. This situation may also arise when a subsidiary of a parent company is involved. Spokespersons for the Communications Workers of America have asserted that the union's negotiations with the individual Bell telephone companies were at times meaningless because policies were controlled by the par-

---

[33]See "Can GM Change Its Work Rules?" *Business Week,* Apr. 26, 1982, p. 116; and William Serrin, "Shrinking U.A.W. Tries to Steer a Steady Course," *The New York Times,* June 22, 1982, p. 117.

ent American Telephone and Telegraph Company (AT&T). No changes could be made by the managers of subsidiary companies until AT&T officials gave their approval. The effect of such frustrations was continued efforts by union leaders over the years to expand the bargaining unit to include the principle policy makers. Finally in 1974 AT&T agreed to negotiate with each of the major unions on a national basis. Ironically, after the long union struggle to win a broad, companywide negotiating unit, the court-initiated split of AT&T in the early 1980s confronts the unions with a number of smaller, regional companies. Negotiating may have to return to its historical pattern.

IS THERE A PREFERRED TYPE OF UNIT?

A union or management may prefer a particular kind of bargaining unit at one time and disapprove it at another time. Both parties may change positions on the desirability of a particular unit, and not infrequently they use each other's previous arguments. A union that once argued for a multiemployer unit now borrows management's earlier case for employer-by-employer bargaining, while management uses the union's former rationalization to argue in favor of multiemployer bargaining. An example is provided in the experience of the unions attempting to organize the California farm workers. When the United Farm Workers under the leadership of Cesar Chavez began to organize farm workers beyond those employed by winegrowers in the early 1970s, a number of threatened growers signed agreements with the Teamsters. In accepting the Teamsters, they also had to accept multiemployer bargaining, a form well suited to Teamster experience and liking. The growers asserted that they preferred the Teamsters, nevertheless, because it was a businesslike and efficient organization. Furthermore, its union leaders did not raise issues about control of the work force and social issues.

The passage of the California Agricultural Labor Relations Act in 1975 ended the existing multiemployer units, for it allowed certification only of single-employer bargaining units. The unit was defined for representational elections, though multiemployer negotiating units could be established voluntarily. The growers insisted upon the single-employer unit as a way of making collective bargaining more difficult for the UFW and because some of the large, corporate growers did not want to get involved in the labor problems of other growers. The UFW eventually came to favor multiemployer bargaining, for it permits a far more efficient form of negotiation. The union became the defender of cost-effective bargaining and industrial stability, a defense that formerly had been attractive to growers who wanted to justify their agreements with the Teamsters.[34]

At the time of the Taft-Hartley amendments to the National Labor Relations Act (1947), an observer of the labor scene could easily have gained the

---

[34]Karen S. Koziara, "Agriculture," in Somers, *Collective Bargaining: Contemporary American Experience*, pp. 263–301.

impression that business managers generally opposed multiemployer units and those other units that covered most of the workers in an industry. The National Association of Manufacturers uncompromisingly denounced industrywide bargaining, and the matter became a matter of public comment and political debate. The popular arguments, both pro and con, tended to simplify the issue of industrywide bargaining to a single dimension: its enhancement of union bargaining power. Management could be expected then to oppose industrywide bargaining, and unionists would naturally favor it. In the complex world of practical affairs, the effects of the kind, size, and type of bargaining unit are not so simply limited, however. Units broader than a single plant may impose costs upon a union as well as increase its bargaining power, and management may find benefits for itself that would offset its relative loss of bargaining power.

Pragmatic Judgments Prevail

Thus it should be no surprise to the reader that in fact and practice there is neither a general management position nor a general union position on bargaining units. Either party may choose, or be willing, to accept units of whatever kind, size, type, or area that fits its pragmatic needs and purposes as well as the requirements of bargaining power.

The scope of the bargaining unit depends upon the pragmatic judgments of the parties as they balance their answers to three questions: (1) Who will gain or lose from changes in the unit? (2) Will the internal authority of the organization support the agreement covering the unit? (3) How will relative bargaining power be affected by narrowing or widening the unit? The balance may be precarious and may change over time. Thus one can find examples of seemingly well-established units that either break up or expand. As the bargaining power of one party increases or decreases, the other party may find it worthwhile to try to change the scope of the unit to improve its position. Such changes may lead to a widening of the unit, but they may also tend to narrow it.

One can sketch out in general terms the trade-offs that managers and union leaders consider in adjusting bargaining units. Since the scope of the unit, after the National Labor Relations Board has determined the election district, is a matter of voluntary and mutual agreement, one or the other party may offer concessions on other issues to secure a particular unit. The scope of the negotiating unit, therefore, is a bargainable issue, even as are wages, hours, and working conditions. To move from a single-plant to a multiplant unit may lower the costs of negotiating to both union and management. There should be economies of scale in the number and time of legal advisors and staff devoted to bargaining.

There could also be offsetting losses and reinforcing gains. Single-plant bargaining allows more autonomy to both plant managers and local union leaders. The value of it to managers depends upon the independence of the plant's production process from the firm's other plants. If each plant carries out a complete production process and quick, flexible response to changing labor and product market forces is required, local plant autonomy may be valued highly. Of course, if the plant is part of a vertically integrated production system, dependent upon another plant for preliminary processing and in its turn contributing to other plants for final producing, autonomy of a single plant unit may penalize the firm, the managers may decide that a multiplant unit is desirable.

Union leaders and members may make a similar kind of calculation. Single-plant units may be more responsive to the demands of the immediately affected workers and thus result in a more unified membership. But if the single-plant unit offers less bargaining power to the union than a multiplant unit, the overall economic gains may be curtailed, provoking member dissatisfaction.

The bargaining structure and bargaining power of both parties interact with each other in a variety of ways. If there are rival unions among the several plants of a firm, single-plant units would help management whipsaw the unions, gaining concessions from the weakest unit. As the unions coordinated their negotiations, or as one won out over the other, multiplant bargaining would become more attractive, for the union or unions could then begin to whipsaw the company, concentrating on the most vulnerable plant. (A vertically integrated firm would suffer more whipsawing than a horizontally integrated firm, as noted above.) In an industry where small firms predominate, management may seek multiemployer units to limit the union's whipsawing tactic, though it loses some autonomy and the union's bargaining power may be considerably enhanced.

Recent empirical studies by labor scholars indicate that the kind of bargaining unit found in a particular industry is predictable; the forces that encourage one or another and that induce the parties to establish particular types of units can be identified. The most detailed and sophisticated study of blue-collar bargaining units in the U.S. manufacturing sector, as it was in 1975, reached three conclusions. First, the smaller the firms and the less concentrated the industry (as in garments and trucking), the greater the probability of association with multifirm bargaining units. Second, among firms with more than one plant, the probability of multiplant or firmwide units increases as industry concentration and plant size rise. Third, union rivalry is associated with decentralized units, and the greater the proportion of the work force in unions, the more centralized the units.[35]

From our examination of these various cases, it would appear that bargaining units change—expand or contract—as one or both parties try to manipu-

---

[35]Wallace E. Hendricks and Lawrence M. Kahn, "The Determinants of Bargaining Structure in U.S. Manufacturing Industries," *Industrial and Labor Relations Review,* vol. 35, Jan. 1982, p. 181. Another study that reports similar findings in Great Britain is D. R. Deaton and P. B. Beaumont, "The Determinants of Bargaining Structure: Some Large Scale Survey Evidence for Britain, *British Journal Of Industrial Relations,* vol. 18, July 1980, p. 202.

late the bargaining unit to improve their bargaining power as economic conditions and industrial structures change. We have examined some of the major forces shaping bargaining units, but in doing so we have given the most attention to those formal arrangements recognized in law or written understanding and official titles. There are also informal arrangements that affect the effective operation of the more formal bargaining unit, and to these we shall now turn.

THE INFORMAL UNITS: FRACTIONAL AND PATTERN BARGAINING

As changeable and varied as the bargaining units are that we have so far discussed, they probably show considerably more stability and less variety than the informal bargaining arrangements made by workers, union leaders, managers, and supervisors as they attempt to take advantage of immediate opportunities and constantly changing situations in the industrial world. In probing the forces that mold bargaining units, we can gain a more complete understanding of them by (1) analyzing the diverse interests of workers and management and the way in which these manifest themselves in fractional bargaining units, and (2) examining the influence of settlements in particular units upon other settlements in other units responsive to any resulting coercive comparisons or economic pressure.

Since fractional bargaining is a common, though not always recognized practice under collective bargaining, it follows that fractional bargaining units are common, though not necessarily recognized parts of broader bargaining units. The sovereignty that a certified union enjoys over a legally determined bargaining unit is hardly absolute; it is limited by the ability of its members to dissent and their willingness to maintain an independent authority. Almost all unions have become more comprehensive in the past three decades, enrolling workers with a variety of skills, occupations, interests, and concerns. The resulting large unions have gained strength from the massing together of such workers; more properly, they have gained strength whenever their comprehensive membership has been united. But by incorporating competitive diversity, they have built in cleavages of interests and lines of weakness not present in more homogeneous organizations. The larger the unit, the more difficult it becomes to find issues on which all will agree, and the more likely it is that various members or groups of members will find their own interests served by bargaining independently for certain demands.

Causes of Fractional Bargaining Units

Fractional bargaining develops not out of a rejection of collective bargaining but out of a dissatisfaction with the all-inclusiveness of it; the fractional unit does not supplant but rather supplements the larger unit of which it is a part. In the same way that unions and companies often negotiate a companywide master agreement specifying settlements on matters common to all plants but allowing local plant negotiators to settle issues peculiar to their circumstances, fractional bargainers negotiate terms applicable and pertinent to the still more parochial interests of work groups in the plants or of special occupational groups in several plants. In Chapter 6 we saw that fractional bargaining is possible largely because of collective bargaining. For the same reason, the fractional unit is dependent upon the broader bargaining units. Without the organizational strength of the broader unit and the union-secured protection from arbitrary discipline, the members of fractional units could not easily pursue their own interests. In fact, if they had no larger unit protecting rights and securing demands common to them and the other members of the wider unit, they would probably be so engaged in a joint effort with those of differing job interests to secure their common interests that they would pay little attention to their divergent interests. Only after the United Automobile Workers were well established, for example, did the skilled workers demand special consideration of their problems. And only after the United Rubber Workers had effectively organized the tire plants did fractional bargaining present a problem to the union and plant managements.

The place and role of the unofficial subordinate bargaining units in the wider, formal unit are clearly demonstrated when unions and managements recognize them. In one industry—rubber tires—a number of agreements allow foremen and shop stewards to make departmental arrangements modifying or changing, within limits, some of the agreement's provisions, as they allow local union officers and plant managers to negotiate supplementary provisions. The supervisors and stewards may be free to negotiate such things as changes in the groupings of workers among whom overtime work is equally distributed, substitution of shorter hours for layoffs during times of reduced work, the conditions under which workers may change shifts, and the trial period for a piecework rate. In the automobile industry the recognition of fractional units took a different form with the UAW's acceptance of the skilled workers as a subsidiary bargaining unit. The skilled groups were granted separate ratification machinery and more effective representation in the various levels of the bargaining process. A convention resolution explained the union's action this way:

> We must find new ways to implement the principle of industrial unionism in order to meet today's problems, to meet the problems common to all the workers in our Union and at the same time to be able to deal satisfactorily with their special problems. No member of our Union has a right to special privilege, but every member of our Union, who may have a special problem because of the nature of his work, has a right to have this special problem dealt with effectively.

The development of fractional units does not indicate the disintegration of the other, broader bargaining units; it does indicate a decentralization of bargaining authority for unions and management. It is a manifestation of the complex relationships between workers and between managers as they daily pursue their various divergent and convergent goals. As workers and managers turn their attention to different interests, they organize themselves into different units, in and through which they hope to further these interests. Interests common to many will generate broad units, whereas specialized, competitive interest will encourage narrow units; however, neither type of interest necessarily excludes the other. If the two conflict, the parties concerned may have to choose between one or the other; or, more likely, they will work out a compromise that preserves some of the gains each unit can attain or they will form some new unit in which the tensions between cooperative and competitive interests can better be accommodated.

The tensions between cooperation and competition arise not only within recognized bargaining units but also among bargaining units. The settlement that the police win in negotiations with a city government is of interest to the firefighters and sanitation workers, in particular, and more generally to the other unions that have organized the city's employees. The UAW's members in the General Motors bargaining unit are affected by and concerned about the concessions their union makes to hard-pressed Chrysler. The outcomes of negotiations in one bargaining unit exert some influence on outcomes in other units; if the influence is significant and regular enough, we may perceive patterns, and we seek to understand their nature and causes.

Pattern Bargaining

During and after World War II, students of collective bargaining noted settlement patterns that were clearly evident within industries and sometimes across industries. The wage settlement reached within a major or at least prominent bargaining unit became a "key bargain," serving as a guide for settlement in other units. They did not indicate, in any strict sense, the establishment of a new bargaining unit; yet for those issues set by the pattern, the bargaining unit was informally extended beyond its original scope. The "pattern unit" was not always easy to define, for the pattern was adjusted and modified in intricate ways by the effects of labor markets, wage rates, product prices, and interunion rivalries. Settlements might conform to the pattern in some details but not in others.

The patterning of wages occurred before collective bargaining was widespread, of course. Wage leadership in steel existed for at least twenty years before 1933, with U.S. Steel usually acting as leader.[36] Wherever there is a dominant firm or union in an industry or wherever there is a small group of large producers, wage leadership is apt to appear. Unions and collective bargaining have undoubtedly helped to reinforce (and enforce) the patterns; they have also helped to spread the patterns further throughout the economy and perhaps faster than before. Union negotiations are not always successful in getting a "wage follower" to agree to the pattern, but the pattern is an understandable, clear-cut basis for beginning the bargaining talks. When the wage pattern is one

---

[36]George Seltzer, "Pattern Bargaining and the United Steelworkers," *Journal of Political Economy,* vol. 59, 1951, p. 322.

of decreases, as it was for automobiles, the airlines, and trucking in the early eighties, management rather than union took the initiative in demanding the pattern.

Managers of large unionized firms have no doubt about the existence of patterns, at least through any one bargaining season or round. A Conference Board survey in 1978 estimated "that the pattern established in their largest bargaining unit affected approximately two and one half times as many employees outside the unit within the firm, and another four times as many employees outside the firm but within the area or industry."[37]

The Bureau of Labor Statistics regularly reports on industry patterns. For example:

> In the last round of negotiations in 1979 a pattern for settlement in the [petroleum refining] industry was set when Gulf Oil Corp., which set the pattern in the two previous contract negotiations, and the OCAW [Oil, Chemical and Atomic Workers] agreed to a 2-year contract.
>
> In the past, bargaining has been conducted separately with each company. The Rubber Workers has selected a "target" from among the "Big Four" for full-scale bargaining. Once an accord has been reached, it has been used as a pattern for subsequent settlements with companies throughout the industry.
>
> Contracts [for meat-products workers] are negotiated with individual companies either on a single plant or company-wide basis. Larger packers, such as Armour, Morrell, Swift, and Wilson, negotiate master agreements. One firm usually signs a pattern-setting agreement, after which similar contracts are negotiated by the others. Variations in contract terms often occur because of differences in plant locations or company practices.[38]

As the Bureau of Labor Statistics suggests in its comment about the meat-products pattern, there are variations between settlements. The pattern is a goal to aim for; it is not always attained. For internal political reasons, union leaders would like to do as well for one group of members as for another. Unless a follower firm can convince union leaders and workers that economic conditions press too hard to allow the pattern, the union will insist on it. The pattern does not by any means cover all the issues negotiated in collective bargaining. Most generally it is thought of in terms of wage changes, but other major issues such as pensions, work rules, flexible assignment of workers, and quality standards have spread in pattern fashion from company to company and from industry to industry. Even these issues have been handled in a variety of ways and adapted to the particular circumstances of different companies and the various industries. Pattern bargaining is more flexible than bargaining in a formal multiemployer unit. The key bargains may not always be made by the same parties, and the application of the pattern may vary considerably from firm to firm in the same industry if different economic conditions impose themselves.

---

[37]Thomas A. Kochan, *Collective Bargaining and Industrial Relations,* p. 113.
[38]*Wage Calendar, 1982,* Bureau of Labor Statistics Bulletin 2127, 1982, pp. 2, 9.

Empirical studies of pattern in bargaining across industries indicate that it was not as noticeable in the 1960s or 1970s as in earlier times. Furthermore, the industries that participate in a national pattern change considerably from one round to the next.[39] Since settlements in one company or industry vary, even within patterns, researchers cannot easily define a pattern; some are strong and others weak, shading from those that can be clearly defined to those that are so indistinct that they may not exist. Pattern bargaining units, like those of fractional bargaining and other single-plant, multiplant, and multiemployer units, are not fixed but are subject to change as management and unions adjust to the varying conditions that influence their negotiations.

The prevalence of single-employer bargaining units in the United States might suggest at once more isolated determination of labor conditions among firms and less diversity of approach to problems within firms than in practice is the case. The boundary lines of bargaining units are not fixed and unchanging, but variable; the parties in collective bargaining adjust them to fit their needs. To focus upon the development of multiemployer units or pattern bargaining and thereby conclude that American collective bargaining is imposing a uniformity upon industrial relations is to overlook the many ways in which diversity is accommodated, if not encouraged. Pattern bargaining can raise serious problems, as does fractional bargaining, and each deserves careful study and attention; but if both are examined as activities carried on within a complicated, changeable structure, the problems may not seem as insoluble or of the same dimension as they would otherwise.

CONCLUSION

The legal and economic influences that shape bargaining units are many and complex. Legal provisions defining permissible bargaining units are primarily directed toward defining appropriate election groups who may then choose an exclusive bargaining representative. Economic influences may later lead the parties to change and adjust the election unit to suit their negotiating needs. Units recently defined and organized reflect the formalities of legal constraints, but well-established units may exist only as formal entities while the informal negotiating units become far more prominent. The parties adjust their negotiating units to fit their ongoing purposes, often transforming the original unit significantly. Nevertheless, the legal constraints continue to shape units—for example, forbidding the parties to join professionals and guards in bargaining units with production workers. Even these constraints may loosen over time if the members of two different units find cooperative or coordinated bargaining desirable. They may simply so arrange their negotiations, pursuing the same goals and using the same strategy, that in effect they bargain as one.

---

[39]Robert J. Flanagan, "Wage Interdependence in Unionized Labor Markets," *Brookings Paper on Economic Activity,* vol. 3, 1976, p. 635; and Daniel J. B. Mitchell, "Union Wage Determination: Policy Implications and Outlook," *Brookings Paper on Economic Activity,* 1978, p. 537.

The resulting pattern of bargaining units reflects in some degree the past history of union organizing but also mirrors the varied history and changing conditions under which collective bargaining continues. The parties pragmatically adjust and change units to suit their needs in an economy continually changing in response to technological development and competitive pressures. Where collective bargaining is well and widely established in a firm or an industry, one finds a hierarchy of bargaining (negotiating) units. At the job or shop level they may be shadowy and informal fractional units. Plant units are usually formally recognized, providing the stage upon which the parties conduct much of the daily administration and application of the terms of the agreement. Companywide units usually serve to coordinate the bargaining for a number of plants scattered over a wide area. Within them the parties set the general terms, particularly wage changes and major benefit provisions, that apply to all unit members. Beyond companywide units, there may be industrywide units. A generation ago many observers presumed that industrywide units would become the norm, but since they gave no consistent advantage to either union or management as industry changed, the parties have used them only now and then, here and there.

CHAPTER 10

THE LAW OF
COLLECTIVE BARGAINING

A key to understanding the law affecting collective bargaining is an appreciation of the problem that unions have posed for a rapidly changing American
society. In the nineteenth century, unions had no legally or socially acceptable
role in the small-scale commerce and trade of a young, basically agrarian
nation. Only in the latter 1930s did manufacturing employment finally surpass
agricultural employment, and as late as 1950 more than 40 percent of the
American population lived in rural areas. The scattered hired farmhands gave
little thought to their own organization, and small merchants joined independent farmers in viewing the organization of the landless urban workers as a
threat to their own values. As long as these groups constituted an effective
majority of the electorate and their political influence was dominant, the law
hindered, limited, and regulated union-organizing efforts.

We shall be less concerned with the doctrines of these formative years—for
at best they are ambiguous—than with the problems they were designed to
meet. Such an approach suggests that the central preoccupation of the courts
has been the legitimate exercise of group power in a democratic society. However much one may agree or disagree with court rulings over the years (restrictive of unions up to the 1930s and more supportive afterwards), the judges
were responding to more than class interests or immediate political pressures.

Right down to the early 1930s (but not precisely coincident with the first
New Deal administration, since the Norris–La Guardia Anti-injunction Act
preceded it by almost a year), the prevailing view of the public as well as of
jurists was that American society was rooted in individual freedom. It could
be threatened as much by powerful private groups as by a powerful government. Court orders and judicial decisions that restrained union power were

thus generally well received, particularly if they protected nonunion employees seeking to escape union control.

The interest of the employer, of course, lay with nonunion workers. They supplied employers with the concept of "outraged individual rights," which could be and was molded by contemporary legal doctrines into a potent weapon against unions. The employers' contest with the unions was thus transformed from a quarrel between private interests into a struggle involving social principle of deep import. That so many cases in American labor law turn on the legality of the closed shop and the propriety of union coercion of workers is no accident. In both situations individuals must conform to group demands; that is, they must join a union in order to work in the first instance and must respond to threats and violence in the second.

INDIVIDUAL FREEDOM, GROUP POWER, AND COMMUNITY WELFARE

The legal concern was not simply for the rights of individual workers but also for the community's welfare, since this too may be subject to abuse by private power.[1] Centuries before the emergence of laissez faire doctrines in economics, English judges had established the common-law principle that private groups were suspect if they were organized for economic purposes. Too easily they could develop restraints on trade and thus unlawfully monopolize a market to exploit the public for private gain. When the late-eighteenth-century enthusiasm for the virtues of free trade was added to the long-standing legal condemnation of private restraints of trade, lawyers and judges could hardly be expected to view with anything but deep suspicion the attempts of workers to organize to raise the price of labor.

In curbing the activities of trade unions, judges were thus expressing a legal doctrine that was predominantly concerned with the freedom of individuals and the welfare of the community. Concern for employers as such was merely incidental. Of course, employers profited from the political and legal doctrine of individualism and the economic doctrine of free trade; they supported those doctrines because they were favorable to their interests, and they unhesitatingly employed them to fight unions because they were effective. It would be fallacious, however, to treat early labor law as though it were only the *product* of special interest.

Those with an unsophisticated view of democratic lawmaking may depict business managers as having the power to create labor law solely for their own benefit and the judiciary as being banefully warped by class considerations. But judges could assert and employers could appeal to individualistic, antiunion legal doctrines because many of the voting public accepted and approved their

---

[1]This belief and its application to unions are spelled out with painful explicitness by Henry Simons, *Economic Policy for a Free Society,* Chicago: The University of Chicago Press, 1948, chap. 6. The date of writing indicates the persistence of this notion.

underlying sociological presuppositions. Even as late as 1930 one out of four employed workers was engaged in agricultural pursuits; the farm experience and rural life did not promote much support for, or appreciation of, union purposes. Not because judges are less class-conscious or employers less concerned with self-interest do we now find labor law and legislation more hospitable to unions than formerly. Rather, the legal change reflects a social change in the places Americans live and the ways they work. There is now a broad recognition of the need for groups to play a larger role than before. Despite our increased acceptance of unions, though, the focal issue in labor law remains a question to which a democratic nation must continually address itself: What are the appropriate roles of individual, group, and state? The answers provided by labor law over time indicate that judges and legislators have weighed the rights and privileges of individuals against those of the group by changing standards. As standards have changed, so has the emphasis upon one set of rights over another.

From Individual Rights to Group Rights

Although it oversimplifies the matter, 1932 may be conveniently taken as the year of demarcation between the legal emphasis upon individual rights in industrial relations and the emphasis upon group rights. Prior to 1932, the doctrines of criminal conspiracy and illegal purposes had cast doubt on the legitimacy of union activities, and the use of injunctions and the application of antitrust legislation to unions had served as restrictions upon group action through collective bargaining. Beginning with the Norris–La Guardia Anti-injunction Act of 1932, however, and continuing with the National Industrial Recovery Act of 1933 and the National Labor Relations Act of 1935, Congress accorded signal importance to group action. In the late thirties and early forties, the Supreme Court reinterpreted the laws of picketing and the antitrust laws in such a way that unions were largely exempted from them. Thus it, too, placed the group above the individual worker for the purpose of bargaining with employers.

Critics of unions enthusiastically supported the Labor-Management Relations Act of 1947 and the Labor-Management Reporting and Disclosure Act of 1959. Both contained provisions meant to further individual rights. The first guaranteed the right of employees to refrain from joining unions and bargaining collectively; the second offered a "bill of rights" to union members. From the perspective of the present, the guarantee and offer did not mark any significant retreat from emphasis on the group. The two sets of amendments confirmed the legitimate role of unions in our society, though they also indicated continuing public concern for individual rights, both outside and within groups.

More recent legislation at both federal and state levels indicates the continuing emphasis on group rights, now for public employees. In 1978 the Civil Service Reform Act legislatively established the right of federal employees to organize and bargain collectively about the conditions of employment.[2] Furthermore, by 1979 all but twelve states had enacted collective bargaining laws, allowing group rights to at least some of their own and local government employees.[3] Like the older acts, the newer legislation reminds us that the issue of respective roles in society of the individual and of the group continues to be pertinent.

UNIONS AS CRIMINAL CONSPIRACIES

In surveying the law of collective bargaining, we first encounter the doctrine of criminal conspiracy, a doctrine still shrouded in uncertainty and controversy. Some authorities maintain that its substance rendered illegal any concerted action by organized workers, whether or not each worker could have legally undertaken the same action alone. According to this argument, the combination tainted the action. Other authorities assert that the doctrine of criminal conspiracy did not outlaw union action as such but merely condemned certain methods of achieving objectives. Condemnation fell primarily upon efforts to enforce the closed shop and upon violence used to prevent the recruiting of strikebreakers.

One can find cases that support both views, but for our purposes there is no need to reexamine the respective arguments. Quite evidently, the basis for either view lay in the impact of the action upon first, the economic independence of the individual worker; and second, the economic security of the community. That employer interests were served in defense of these objectives simply marks, as has already been noted, the assumed coincidence of private and public interests, just as at a later date the public interest expressed by Congress and the courts coincided with private union interests.

The Cordwainers' Case

In the economic and political climate of the early nineteenth century, employer as well as worker combinations stood condemned before the law.[4] Group

---

[2]Public Law 95-454, Title VII. The act confirms rights granted earlier in President Kennedy's Executive Order 10988 in 1962 and President Johnson's Executive Order 11491 in 1969.

[3]Hugh D. Jascourt, "Recent Trends and Developments," in Hugh D. Jascourt (ed.), *Government Labor Relations: Trends and Information for the Future,* Oak Park, Ill.: Moore, 1979, p. 10.

[4]Thus Justice John B. Gibson of the Supreme Court of Pennsylvania held in the case of *Commonwealth ex rel. Chew v. Carlisle,* involving a combination of employers: ". . . a combination of employers to depress the wages of journeymen below what they would be, if there was no recurrence to artificial means by either side, is criminal. There is between the different parts of the body politic a reciprocity of action on each other, which, like the action of antagonizing muscles in the natural body, not only prescribes to each its appropriate state and condition, but regulates the motion of the whole. The effort of an individual to disturb this equilibrium can never be perceptible, nor carry the operation of his interest on that of any other individual, beyond the limits of fair competition; but the increase of power by combination of means, being in geometrical proportion to the number concerned, an association may be able to give an impulse, not only oppressive to individuals, but mischievous to the public at large; and it is the employment of an engine

action came close to being tinged with treason, a manifestation of private authority that was at least a potential threat to the state.[5] Consider the argument of counsel for the prosecution in the case of the Philadelphia cordwainers in 1806:

> Why a combination in such case is criminal, will not be difficult to explain: we live under a government composed of a constitution and laws ... and every man is oblige to obey the constitution, and the laws made under it. When I say he is bound to obe, these, I mean to state the whole extent of his obedience. Do you feel yourselves bound to obey any other laws, enacted by any other legislature, than that of your own choice? Shall these, or any other body of men, associate for the purpose of making new laws, laws not made under the constitutional authority, and compel their fellow citizens to obey them, under the penalty of their existence? This prosecution contravenes no man's right, it is to prevent an infringement of right; it is in favour cf the equal liberty of all men, this is the policy of our laws; but if private associations and clubs, can make constitutions and laws for us ... if they can associate and make by-laws paramount, or inconsistent with the state laws; What, I ask, becomes of the liberty of the people, about which so much is prated; about which the opening counsel made such a flourish!
>
> There is evidence before you that shows, this secret association, this private club, composed of men who have been only a little time in your country, (not that they are the worse for that,) but they ought to submit to the laws of the country, and not attempt to alter them according to their own whim or caprice ... when they associate, combine and conspire, to prevent others from taking what they deem a sufficient compensation for their labour ... and when they undertake to regulate the trade of the city, they undertake to regulate what interferes with your right and mine.[6]

In a similar vein, the prosecution in the 1809 case of the New York Cordwainers declared:

> This conspiracy, unnaturally to force the price of labour beyond its natural measure, is as dangerous as any kind of monopoly, and if it be tolerated, as well may regrating, forestalling, and every other pernicious combination.
>
> Suppose all the bakers in New York were to refuse to bake till they received an exorbitant remuneration. Suppose the butchers should enter into a similar combination, and if there be impunity for these, why shall not all other artisans do like-

---

so powerful and dangerous, that gives criminality to an act that would be perfectly innocent, at least in a legal view, when done by an individual." [Brightly's Report 36 (1821).] Justice Gibson in this decision appears to view rather leniently the combination of capital and excuses the combination's conduct on the ground that it was formed as a defensive move against the union of employees; but the greater sympathy most members of the bench admittedly felt for employers should not blind us to the fact the class interest was justified—in terms of public welfare.

[5]Note the modern expression of this view in Milton Friedman and Rose Friedman, *Free to Choose,* New York: Harcourt Brace Jovanovich, 1970, p. 292: "Both the fragmentation of power and conflicting government policies are rooted in the political realities of a democratic system that operates by enacting detailed and specific legislation. Such a system tends to give undue political power to small groups that have highly concentrated interest . . . a process that sacrifices the general interest to serve special interests, rather than the other way around."

[6]Reprinted by permission of the publishers from Commons et al., *Documentary History of American Industrial Society,* vol. 3, pp. 135–138.

wise? What will become of the poor, whose case the counsel so feelingly takes to heart? The rich will, by their money, find supplies; but what will be the sufferings of the poor classes?

Suppose that some rich speculators, acting upon similar principles, should, in a cold winter, combine to purchase up all the wood, and refuse to sell it but at an extravagant advance, should we have no law to protect the poor against such oppression? And would it be argued, that without an express statute the law could furnish no remedy? As such acts would be against the public good, and immoral in a high degree, they would therefore fall under the animadversions of the general law; and as offences against the whole community, be subject to public prosecution.

There are duties which every man owes to the society of which he enjoys the benefits and protection, which never can be detailed, but must be regulated by acknowledged principles of judicature. A baker, therefore, who lives by the supply of the public, shall not abuse that public by a sudden interested and malicious withholding of his ordinary supplies; but though it were otherwise, and that every individual was permitted, as far as in him lay, to distress his fellow-citizens, yet if he combines with others to do so, he is guilty of a distinct and well defined offense, that of an unlawful conspiracy, for which he is indictable and punishable.[7]

THE DOCTRINE OF ILLEGAL PURPOSE

The case of *Commonwealth v. Hunt*[8] in 1842 has often been cited as marking the end of the doctrine of criminal conspiracy. In his decision, Chief Justice Shaw of the Massachusetts Supreme Court, a man of considerable judicial influence, refused to apply the doctrine to a bootmakers' union accused of seeking to impose the closed shop. What this case did achieve, however, was simply judicial recognition that group action might have justifiable objectives. In the original trial, Judge Thacher had asserted: "The question is not whether the society [members] have used their power to the extent of mischief of which it is capable but whether they have not assumed a power . . . which in the hands of irresponsible persons is liable to great abuse." Chief Justice Shaw, on appeal, in contrast asserted that abuse—whether actual or intended—must be shown if union action was to be considered unlawful. Important as it was, this single decision did not completely deprive the criminal-conspiracy doctrine of vitality, but for the next thirty years there were no significant developments in the law pertaining to collective bargaining.

Then, beginning about 1870, opponents of labor organization began to rely upon civil suits against unions for injunctions and for damages. These almost completely replaced the criminal actions. The old theory of the threat to society by group action was still evident, but in a new format and with Chief Justice Shaw's emendation that the monopoly power of unions did not prima facie indicate abuse. He had declared that it may have justification. The courts were

---

[7]Reprinted by permission of the publishers from Commons et al., *Documentary History of American Industrial Society,* vol. 3, pp. 313–314.
[8]Metc. 111 (Mass.).

ready to tolerate the activities that organized workers designed to advance their own interests, but with severe qualifications.

The activity could not be inimical to public welfare; that is, it had to fit the philosophy of free-market competition. Furthermore, the union could not be involved in the use of force to restrict nonmember workers. Judges quickly enjoined a union or subjected it to claims for damages if its activities did not meet their interpretations of these conditions. Unions dared not damage the employer unless by doing so they furthered their members' immediate advantage; they could not threaten public welfare through what the courts defined as monopoly restraint; and coercing workers to join the union or preventing workers from taking strikers' jobs was forbidden. The new doctrine thus involved little change from the older conspiracy doctrine. It was simply accompanied by different and perhaps more effective judicial remedies.

Unions in the Eyes of Judges

As is apparent, the legality of a union's bargaining activities turned upon the way in which the courts construed the union's purposes. Some judges were more lenient toward workers' organizations than others. The Massachusetts courts, for example, acquired a reputation for severity, at least when compared with those of New York; but on the whole, court decisions were restrictive of union activities.

In deciding whether a union's purpose was legal or illegal, judges were naturally informed by their own background and training, as any person is in making judgments. But the union posed problems that were difficult for even the most disinterested minds who had to work with legal tools of analysis, originally shaped for quite different purposes. It was a relatively novel organization, radical in its challenge to employers and the market.

Since the passage of years has not made the solutions to the same problems any easier—or often any more obvious—to disinterested people, we might temper the criticism of our predecessors with charity. Judges, business managers, and the community at large could hardly be expected to encourage a form of economic and social organization that countered accepted doctrines of individuality and which seemed to threaten society's best interests.

Critics have sometimes charged the courts with preempting the legislators' role, arguing that unions should not have been restricted unless the legislature had so decided. During the nineteenth century, unions posed real social problems and raised novel issues not covered by laws and as yet unexamined by the electorate or their representatives. Until such examination had been made and public policy had been hammered out in free and open debate, the criticism runs, the courts should not have intervened. Since, except in a few state laws of special application, legislatures made virtually no attempt during this period to define the place of unions, it is maintained that the courts should have left unions and employers to their own devices. American government is characterized by a separation of powers, with lawmaking and law interpreting assigned to separate and different bodies. The courts were overstepping their limits when they undertook to rule on the legality of unions' purpose and policy. In so doing, they unwisely strayed into the legislative realm of making law.

This criticism of the courts unhappily begs the issue. It emphasizes the laws passed by legislatures and slights the importance of common law, that judge-made law which has been handed down over the years. As Justice Holmes reminded us in a famous phrase, the common law is responsive to the felt needs of the times; it represents, though admittedly imperfectly, the crystallized sentiments of the community about the behavior which may be expected of its citizens in a variety of familiar situations. The common law comes into existence in the form of court decisions (precedents); frequently used phrases sometimes take on a vitality of their own. Then, in the form of principles or doctrines, judges and lawyers may apply precedents to circumstances quite different from those in which they originated. In some instances such application of doctrine serves well; but unless the underlying social relationships are the same, the fitting may be poor indeed. Judges must decide in each case brought before them whether the facts justify application of particular common-law remedies. Only in the event that common-law doctrine is considered not pertinent to the facts of a case is the issue a proper one for the legislature rather than the courts.

Deciding whether common law applies is seldom any easy matter. The common law, in line with prevailing political and economic doctrine, clearly condemned restraints by any lesser group than the state. An individual was free to infringe upon the rights and limit the interests of another by acting in self-interest through the free, competitive market, but infringements and limitations arising from group action were inadmissible. Thus the courts felt compelled to condemn activities of organized groups of workers that infringed upon the individual rights of persons—other workers, employers, and even corporations, which were persons by virtue of legal fiction. Moreover, group interference with the workings of the market implicitly threatened the community with higher prices through higher wage costs.

Reconciling Individual and Group Rights

Though today we may disavow some particulars of these older beliefs, they once enjoyed, and to some people still enjoy, an apparent reasonableness. The courts undertook, of course, to examine the unions' purposes and procedures in terms of their conceptions of the proper interests of individuals and society as a whole.

Let us take a single example. From the earliest records of legal actions against unions down to our latest labor legislation, the closed shop[9] has been a

---

[9]The closed shop requires employers to hire only workers who are union members. The union shop requires employers in a bargaining unit to join the union within thirty days of hiring. The closed shop gives a union far greater control of the labor market than the union shop, but both subordinate individual to group rights.

thorny issue. Employers have been accused of combating it in order to reduce the effectiveness of the union, and without doubt the charge has considerable justification. But it is also true that the closed shop has been condemned more generally for its alleged infringement on the rights of individual workers who choose not to become members. Many citizens of all shades of political and economic faith subscribe to that condemnation today. One can fairly conclude that when nineteenth-century judges held that the closed shop was illegal and so enjoined strikes designed to achieve it, they were seeking to serve more than their own prejudices. There would appear to be reason to believe in the good faith of such pronouncements as the following:

> We have no desire to put obstacles in the way of employees, who are seeking by combination to obtain better conditions for themselves and their families. We have no doubt that laboring men have derived and may hereafter derive advantages from organization. We only say that, under correct rules of law, and with a proper regard for the rights of individuals, labor unions cannot be permitted to drive men out of employment because they choose to work independently. If disagreements between those who furnish the capital and those who perform the labor employed in industrial enterprises are to be settled only by industrial wars, it would give a great advantage to combinations of employees, if they could be permitted by force, to obtain a monopoly of the labor market.[10]

Since the closed shop poses the issues of the relationship of individual and group in a peculiarly striking way, it frequently occupied the attention of the courts. That they frequently declared it an unlawful objective is not surprising, for Congress has done the same, making the closed shop illegal under the National Labor Relations Act. The act also places restrictions upon the use of the union shop, a modified form of the closed shop. The old problem of the closed shop, now in the form of the union and agency shop, continues to arise before the courts. Then as now, we seek answers to the perennial but immediate problems of the rights of individuals and groups in our society; then as now, we use the courts as a principal instrument for providing us with at least provisional answers.

As courts came to examine the lawfulness of union purposes, they became the arbiters of the demands a union might make and, to some extent, of the tactics it might employ in collective bargaining. In the words of the Supreme Judicial Court of Massachusetts: "Whether the purpose for which a strike is instituted is or is not a legal justification for it, is a question of law to be decided by the court. To justify interference with the rights of others the strikers must in good faith strike for a purpose which the court decides to be a legal justification for such interference."[11]

For an illustration of the application of this principle, which has sometimes been called the "doctrine of illegal purpose," we turn to a case in which the manager of a theater wished to employ an organist; through exercise of bar-

---

[10]*Berry v. Donovan,* 188 Mass. 353, 74 N.E. 603 (1905).
[11]*De Minico v. Craig,* 207 Mass. 593, 94 N.E. 317 (1911).

gaining power the musicians' union sought to induce the employment, instead, of a five-member orchestra. The court's opinion reflects the concern of the judges of a century earlier, when the conspiracy doctrine had flourished. It was for the welfare of society in the face of monopolizing organization:

> If it is legal for a union of musicians to combine for the purpose of forcing a plaintiff (who wants an organist only) to employ an orchestra of several pieces, that is to say, if that indirect purpose of enabling the union musicians to earn more money justifies the adoption of the minimum rule, it is hard to see why it is not legal for a union of carpenters (for example) to refuse to work on a building belonging to the plaintiff unless he uses in the construction of it hand-made doors, window frames and window sashes, in place of doors, window frames and window sashes made by machine. Heretofore it seems to have been assumed that a rule forbidding union members to work on machine-made material in order to get the work of doing it by hand was not a legal combination. . . . There is more money for masons, carpenters and plumbers in building a ten-storey store than there is in building a store of two storeys. If it is legal for musicians to adopt a minimum rule fixing the number of musicians who shall be employed in all the theaters within its jurisdiction, it is hard to see why a minimum rule may not be adopted by the allied trade unions of masons, carpenters and plumbers fixing the number of storeys of which every store to be erected in the business district is to consist. That is to say, masons, carpenters and plumbers may combine to refuse to work on any store less than ten storeys in height even though the owner of the land wishes to erect a store of two storeys only and even though the owner in his judgment cannot without pecuniary loss erect one having more than two storeys. . . . Other illustrations might be put showing the far reaching consequences of a decision upholding the legality of this minimum rule.[12]

Similarly, when another local of the same union brought pressure upon an operatic society to induce it to substitute "live" music for "canned" music, the court reasoned:

> The self-interest of labor, like the self-interest of any other body, received immunity only for those objectives which have a legitimate and reasonable relation to lawful benefits which the union is seeking. When the labor objectives are illegal, the courts must control, otherwise there are bodies within our midst which are free from the provisions of the Penal Law. When doubt arises whether the contemplated objective is within the legal sphere, or without and so illegal, it is for the courts to determine. . . .
>
> For a union to insist that machinery be discarded in order that manual labor may take its place and thus secure additional opportunity of employment is not a lawful labor objective. In essence the case at bar is the same as if a labor union should demand of a printing plant that all machinery for typesetting be discarded because it would furnish more employment if the typesetting were done by hand. We have held that the attempt of a union to coerce the owner of a small business, who was running the same without an employee, to make employment for an employee, was an unlawful objective and that this did not involve a labor dispute. (*Thompson v. Boekhout,* 273 N.Y. 390.) So, too, in a case just unanimously decided, we held that

[12]*Haverhill Strand Theatre, Inc. v. Gillen* 229 Mass. 413, 118 N.E. 671 (1918).

it was an unlawful labor objective to attempt to coerce a peddler employing no employees in his business and making approximately thirty-two dollars a week, to hire an employee at nine dollars a day for one day a week. (*Wohl v. Bakery & Pastry Drivers Union,* 284 N.Y. 788.)[13]

This argument of the courts involved them in a difficulty. As one court pointed out, in a case where the union was being attacked for its adherence to the closed shop, a single individual has the right "to refuse to work for another on any ground that he may regard as sufficient, and the employer has no right to demand a reason for it." The court then continued:

> The same rule applies to a body of men who, having organized for purposes deemed beneficial to themselves, refuse to work. Their reasons may seem inadequate to others but if it seems to be in their interest as members of an organization to refuse longer to work, it is their legal right to stop. The reason may no more be demanded, as a right, of the organization than of an individual, but if they elect to state the reason their right to stop work is not cut off because the reason seems inadequate or selfish to the employer or to organized society. And if the conduct of the members of an organization is legal *in itself,* it does not become illegal because the organization directs one of its members to state the reason for its conduct. [Italics supplied].[14]

According to this view, it is lawful for individuals to cease working for an employer, whether they do so individually or jointly, without explaining why they have done so. No court would find them guilty of any offense for such an action considered by itself. If, while undertaking such lawful action, the workers choose to state why they are doing so, that is their affair and adds nothing to their guilt or innocence. That is to say, motive or purpose is immaterial if the action itself is legal. This doctrine did not in earlier years win, nor has it yet won, unquestioned acceptance, however. It is difficult for courts to ignore the objective behind an action complained of.

The Problems of Adjusting to a Changing Society

The confusion, ambiguities, and inconsistencies surrounding the law of union action throughout this period can perhaps be better understood if we think of the courts as one instrument of society's adjusting to changed social conditions. American industrial society was in the process of rapid and thorough-going change.

From the days of the conspiracy doctrine in the early 1800s until the end of the nineteenth century, many developments caused markets to widen. First turnpikes and canals and then railways opened the country; manufacturers increasingly turned to specialization of production and adopted the use of interchangeable parts; business firms grew enormously in size; technological innovations swept across the nation; the country recklessly exploited its natu-

---

[13]*Opera on Tour v. Weber,* 285 N.Y. 348, 34 N.E. 2d 349 (1941).
[14]*National Protective Association v. Cumming,* 170 N.Y. 315, 63 N.E. 369 (1902).

ral resources; and the population increased sixteenfold. All these changes contributed their own special problems, and each required readjustments in social attitudes and patterns of behavior. One of the most evident aspects of the changes were the spread of "combinations" and group actions. Justice Holmes, speaking in dissent from the Massachusetts Supreme Court, had pointed out in 1896 that "the organization of the world, now going on so fast, means an ever increasing might and scope of combination. It seems to me futile to set our faces against this tendency."[15]

The spread of group action, as a response to altered social and economic conditions, did bring changes in the judgments of the courts and legislatures. Technological, managerial, and financial necessities made the combination of business desirable and perhaps even imperative. With some adjustment of view but little change in values, courts were able to stay within the bounds of their legal and economic concepts by pretending that a corporation was not a group of stockholders but a person. For many years, then, a single worker stood in law the same as a corporation, however vast its resources. Since in the contemplation of the law both a worker and a corporation were persons, the courts saw collective bargaining as a process by which a *group* of persons (the union) confronted a *single* person (the corporation). Formally, the collectivity of workers' groups was more threatening to trade and individual freedom than the collectivity of the corporate person. Until the legislators, and later the courts, recognized and took better into account the group nature of corporations as well as of unions, the activities of organized workers were more severely restricted than those of corporations.

Congress attempted to deal with the reality of which Holmes had spoken: the combination movement in the rapidly changing economic environment. It passed the Sherman Antitrust Act in 1890 and the Clayton Act in 1914. Although the primary stimulus for these laws arose from a widespread public concern over the monopoly powers of business trusts, the courts applied their restrictions chiefly to unions for some time, partly as a result of the formal legal analysis mentioned above. The Supreme Court decisions interpreting the acts were uniformly unfavorable to unions and restrictive of their activities until 1940.

The history of the law of collective bargaining from the cordwainers' case in 1806 to the beginning of the great depression may be summarized briefly by saying that the bargaining process established itself in this country free of any taint of illegality because of its nature. The combination of employees into unions for the purpose of negotiating an agreement with employers and management was not itself unlawful. However, both a union's coercive tactics to strengthen its bargaining positions—strikes, boycotts, or picketing—and its members' purpose in using them could bring it under court scrutiny. The employer against whom the tactics were directed had to complain, of course. Once the case was before the court, the judges would decide whether the tactics

[15] *Vegelahn v. Guntner,* 167 Mass. 92, 44 N.E. 1077 (1896).

were employed to intimidate nonunion workers and whether the purpose was monopolistic, a group infringement of individual rights and a threat to the general interest of society. These concerns, as we have noted, coincided with the special interests of the business community. Until the 1930s, therefore, unions could avail themselves of the bargaining process but they often had to justify before the courts their special use of it and their bargaining tactics.

THE ENTRANCE OF THE FEDERAL GOVERNMENT

The passage of the Norris–La Guardia Anti-injunction Act in 1932[16] brought about a fundamental change in the law of union-management relations. The act removed the power of federal courts to enjoin virtually the whole range of union coercive activity not involving fraud or violence, except under severely limited conditions. The language of section 2 of the act warrants notice:

> Whereas under prevailing economic conditions, developed with the aid of governmental authority for owners of property to organize in the corporate and other forms of ownership association, the individual unorganized worker is commonly helpless to exercise actual liberty of contract and to protect his freedom of labor, and thereby to obtain acceptable terms and conditions of employment, wherefore, though he should be free to decline to associate with his fellows, it is necessary that he have full freedom of association, self-organization, and designation of representatives of his own choosing, to negotiate the terms and conditions of his employment, and that he shall be free from the interference, restraint, or coercion of employers of labor, or their agents, in the designation of such representatives or in self-organization or in other concerted activities for the purpose of collective bargaining or other mutual aid or protection; therefore, the following definitions of, and limitations upon, the jurisdiction and authority of the courts of the United States are hereby enacted.[17]

Note that this legislation placed no obligations upon employers. Although it championed the rights of employees to organize and protected the concerted action of unions in striking, picketing, and boycotting, it did so only by clarifying for the federal judiciary formerly disputed common-law propositions about the role of unions in society. This act was followed by similar legislation in a number of the industrialized states. Where such legislation existed, unions were allowed to employ virtually the full arsenal of their coercive tactics in support of their bargaining demands as long as they avoided fraud and violence.

The National Industrial Recovery Act

The National Industrial Recovery Act (NIRA) of 1933 in its section 7(a) went a step further. It provided that all the so-called codes of fair competition con-

---

[16] Actually the Railway Labor Act of 1926 might be considered an earlier manifestation of this change, but that act applied to only one segment of the labor movement, whereas the later legislation was more comprehensive in its coverage.

[17] 47 Stat. 70 (1932).

tain a clause in which employers guaranteed not to interfere with, restrain, or coerce employees who sought to organize for bargaining purposes. Even when enforced the pledge was relatively ineffective, for the intent was to place collective bargaining on a voluntary basis. Unions were to be free to seek concessions from employers, and employers were to be free to reject union demands. Agreement was to be forthcoming, if at all, as a result of negotiation backed by bargaining power.

The National Labor Relations Act

Of course, under the federal and state anti-injunction acts, unions could use all their bargaining tactics. Notably lacking, however, was any compulsion upon the employer to recognize the union or bargain with it. If employers were strong enough to resist the pressure of unions, they remained free to pursue independent paths, ignoring as best they could the unions' very existence. If they wished, employers might encourage and support the formation of company unions in an effort to distract the interest of their employees from a national union. Unions were entitled to an existence unobstructed by law, but their recognition and advancement were to come through their own efforts. Only later did NIRA labor boards administratively decide that section 7(a) obligated an employer to recognize and bargain with the union. The decisions remained largely unenforceable, though.

Although section 7(a) was regarded by many as radical step forward, the National Labor Relations Act of 1935 marked the complete break with the past. It declared that the policy of the United States was to "[encourage] the practice and procedure of collective bargaining. . . ." It spelled out what the National Industrial Recovery Act was able to suggest only by administrative construction: the obligation of an employer to bargain with a union designated as exclusive representative of the employees in a given unit. The unit was to be defined by the National Labor Relations Board, and the selection of representative was to be accomplished by majority decision of the interested employees. Moreover, the National Labor Relations Act provided the remedial penalties which the NIRA had lacked. The federal courts were to enforce board orders.

This was a sweeping change in the law of collective bargaining. Not more than five years earlier, the attempt by unions to back up bargaining demands by strike, picketing, or boycott was subject to judicial restraint. Judges had had free reign in restraining unions and providing employers with injunction relief if they found union objectives to be inimical to social welfare, as legally construed, or if they regarded union efforts as unduly impinging upon the independence of other workers.

The new legislation made the actions of the majority of workers legally controlling over a minority, specifically sanctioned the closed shop, and placed employers under a legal obligation to recognize and bargain in good faith with certified unions. The earlier Norris–La Guardia Act had severely weakened the injunctive authority of most courts with respect to the tactics employed by unions. Thus, within the space of five years, there had jelled into law the conviction that unions were a desirable social force. Under law, workers were entitled to an organized, protected voice in the determination of the conditions under which they were to work. For the first time in American history, collective bargaining was enforced as a matter of public policy.[18]

We will not review here the social, economic, and political setting that gave rise to the National Labor Relations Act of 1935, but we may recall the impact of the great depression and the popular support of the New Deal reform program as forces that helped bring about a restatement of the law of collective bargaining. The troubling experiences of the 1930s led to a redefinition of the roles of groups and individuals in a society in which the organization and the group rather than the individual seemed controlling. The thesis on which the National Labor Relations Act of 1935 rested was stated in congressional debate by the man by whose name the act is often known: "Caught in the labyrinth of modern industrialism and dwarfed by the size of corporate enterprise, he [the worker] can attain freedom and dignity only by cooperation with others of his group."[19] However, to conclude that such a conception rose suddenly as a vision would be a mistake. It has been in the making for many years. In the courts it has received explicit expression at least as early as Holmes's Massachusetts dissent in *Vegelahn v. Guntner.* The minority view had been growing, and the economic catastrophe of the thirties transformed it into a majority view. After 1932, the laws defining the rights of individual, group, and government had to be changed, and there was a shift of emphasis from individual initiative to group and state initiative. The effect of this realignment remained open to debate, but its reality could scarcely be questioned.

The significance of the National Labor Relations Act of 1935 to the role of unionism and collective bargaining in American society is highlighted by contrasting the requirement concerning employers' conduct under the new law with the permissible scope of their actions toward unions prior to 1932. Whereas unions previously not only could be ignored but also could be fought, their recognition was now required when they represented a majority of employees. Furthermore, intimidatory action by employers was made illegal. Previously employers were under no obligation even to sit down with a union committee; they were now obligated to negotiate in a good-faith attempt to reach an agreement, which had to be put into writing upon request by the union. Previously unions were thrown upon their own resources; union activity was now protected by the federal government. Previously unilateral imposition of disadvantageous terms by one party upon the other had been legal and, as we saw in earlier chapters, was commonly practiced; such unilateral conferring of advantages was now considered unlawful, a denial of good-faith bargaining.

---

[18]The Supreme Court upheld the constitutionality of the National Labor Relations Act in 1935 *NLRB v. Jones & Laughlin Steel Corp.,* 301 U.S. 1 (1937).
[19]Senator Wagner, *Congressional Record,* May 15, 1932, p. 7565.

Problems of First Adjustment

Employers and unionists had difficulty adjusting to the new situation. It is remarkable testimony to the adaptability of American society that so sweeping a change in social relations could have been so successfully accomplished within so short a space of time, despite the resentment of employers and the heady emotions of unionists which it evoked. That specific employers continued to violate the new requirements provides little ground for modifying such a conclusion. In part this represented simply one aspect of adjustment: in some cases an immediate unwillingness to accept the change at its face value or to believe in its permanence, and in other cases a misunderstanding of new obligations.

However successfully the transition was made, it was in many respects a painful one. Zealots on both sides were not averse to using violence. The organizing of strikes in automobiles, steel, rubber, and other large-scale industries precipitated mutual resentment and recrimination that died slowly. Many, if not most, managers regarded the National Labor Relations Act as the worst of the New Deal legislation. The background of violence and melodrama was caught by *Fortune* magazine in an article that sought to present an objective portrait of the act and the board administering it at this time. Illustrative of the conflict between unions and management upon which the peaceful processes of the board had sometimes to be superimposed was this testimony of a witness of a 1937 Michigan labor riot:

> Mr. —— [a member of the general executive board of his union] was attacked by four or five men who kicked him in the general region of his stomach and plugged him from the rear . . . and he was finally forced to the cement over to my left and there a separate individual grabbed him by each foot and by each hand, and his legs were spread apart and his body was twisted over toward the east, and then other men proceeded to kick him in the crotch and groin and left kidneys and around the head and also to gore him with their heels in the abdomen. . . . [And later] . . . the girls were at a loss to know apparently what to do, and then one girl near me was kicked in the stomach and vomited at my feet. . . . I stayed there until practically all the literature had been gathered from the ground and until the girls had been pushed back on the trolley and the trolley had gone and it became very quiet around there and relatively still.[20]

Although violence of this order can scarcely be considered representative, the accompanying bitterness of feeling between the parties was prevalent. It was a period when shifts in social, economic, and political relationships were occurring swiftly and were deeply, sensitively, and quickly felt. The adjustments called for were profound.

For American managers the new labor law and the changes in labor relations it entailed signaled an overturning of the managerial order—an undermining of employer authority. In arguments against the National Labor Relations Act

---

[20]"The G— D—— Labor Board," *Fortune,* Oct. 1938, p. 115.

before the Supreme Court, lawyers for the Jones & Laughlin Steel Corporation asserted that the new impaired basic managerial effectiveness. "[A]bsolutely essential to the efficient management of employer's business" was the right to judge the capability of employees; to have to recognize the union and bargain with it would confer "a kind of . . . [special] status upon union employees, which will inevitably encourage laziness, insolence, and inefficiency. . . . [The Act] is a constant threat to the [company's] normal right to manage its own business."[21]

For many managers, the legal requirement that they admit labor leaders—outsiders and third parties, as they saw them—as *comanagers* in limited but expanding areas was intolerable. Its consequences were to be manifest in both the organization and operation of the firm. Neither manifestation necessarily gave rise to the difficulties about which mangers expressed concern. Some discovered, on the contrary, that bargaining penalized them chiefly if they acted arbitrarily or proceeded with inconsistent policies and that it could reward them if they dealt with the unions to establish regular personnel procedures, follow reasonable rules, and observe due process.

Collective bargaining introduced an element of stability, even possible rigidity, in production processes where change is probable, the unexpected is seldom absent for long, and flexibility is needed for long-term success. It thus called for a higher order of managerial skills than had customarily been assigned to labor and personnel functions. The treatment of workers and the handling of their pay could no longer be matters of local, arbitrary decisions. The firm could be held to published standards and its officers had to defend and account for their actions. They had to regularize procedures, examine the full costs of policies, and seek the most efficient ways of proceeding. Collective bargaining also encouraged top managers to consider carefully the full consequences of their labor policies upon all business functions and the effects of financial, marketing, and production policies upon labor relations.

CHANGING LAWS—OLD CONCERNS

Both the Labor-Management Relations Act of 1947, which amended the National Labor Relations Act of 1935, and the Labor-Management Reporting and Disclosure Act of 1959 reaffirmed the right of most private employees to organize and to bargain collectively through representatives of their own choosing. The right had been assured in the National Labor Relations Act of 1935 and was first recognized by the Norris–La Guardia Anti-injunction Act of 1932 as a necessity in an industrial society. In the historical perspective of government's continuing definition of the rights of individuals, groups, and the public, these enactments declared unions to be essential, given the fact of large

---

[21]*NLRB v. Jones and Laughlin Steel Corporation,* argument for respondent, 301 U.S. 20–21 (1937).

corporate employers; but they also sought to keep unions from unduly imping-ing upon the rights of either individuals or the public.

Passage of the 1947 amendments was a response to the wave of strikes in the year and a half after the ending of World War II. There were a series of industrywide strikes in major industries and even general strikes in two cit-ies—Rochester, New York and Oakland, California. The unprecedented strike exasperated the general public and alarmed many people; they were widely per-ceived as the outcomes of dangerous concentrations of economic power in the hands of a few union leaders. Congress passed the 1959 act in the wake of extended congressional investigations that had revealed a sordid picture of cor-ruption and unethical behavior among some unions and employers. They had also brought to public notice a dismaying lack of democratic procedures within some unions. As had happened twelve years earlier, wide popular sentiment favored legislation that would attempt to protect the rights of individual work-ers and the public; in addition it approved legal provisions to curb the power of union leaders.

Encouragement of Collective Bargaining among Public Employees

Legal support for collective bargaining by *public* employees and legislative encouragement of their organizing have appeared since passage of the Labor-Management Reporting and Disclosure Act of 1959. Writing in 1959, Ida Klaus, a knowledgeable labor lawyer, reported that at no level had any govern-ment established

> a thoroughgoing and systematic code of labor relations at all comparable in funda-mental policy, basic guarantees and rights, and procedures for their enforcement, with those of prevailing labor relations laws in the private sector.[22]

And as early as 1947 the federal government and a number of states had enacted harsh antistrike laws aimed at public employees. Such employees enjoyed a constitutional right to associate, of course, and in a number of places they had formed associations through which they pursued their interests even before 1900. The right to associate did not provide for collective bargaining, however, nor did the associations' leaders receive official recognition as employee representatives. Government officials argued that the public interest could not be served by imitating the private sector. Collective bargaining by public employees would involve them in the lawmaking process, infringing upon the sovereignty of government and countenancing an illegal delegation of authority.

Although legal theory remained the same, employment practice was chang-ing rapidly. In 1947, state and local governments employed a little over 3.5

---

[22]Ida Klaus, "Labor Relations in the Public Sector: Explorations and Experiment," *Syracuse Law Review,* vol. 10, 1959, p. 184.

million people; by 1959, they had increased employment to 5.8 million, an annual increase of more than 4 percent a year. The increase continued at the same pace for another 20 years. By 1975 state and local governments surpassed durable manufacturing in number of employees. Some of the same conditions that had moved industrial workers to organize and demand collective bargaining now pushed public employees. Many found themselves involved in growing bureaucracies where employment relationships were increasingly depersonalized. Civil service procedures for handling grievances proved cumbersome and often unresponsive to the perceived needs of employees and their desire for participation. They began to press for other procedures and sometimes even used the strike to express their dissatisfactions.

In various states, government officials had already begun to grant some limited recognition to their employees. Michigan, Ohio, and Pennsylvania allowed employees to communicate their views on employment conditions. Nebraska created an industrial relations court to hear disputes. Many local governments had to contend with employees' unrest and strikes, and officials often pragmatically decided to work out settlements, offering de facto recognition to unions or associations and ignoring penalties.

Through the 1950s a few states began to experiment with limited forms of public union recognition and the duty to meet and confer, if not to bargain collectively. President Kennedy's Executive Order 10988, in 1962, extended collective bargaining rights to civilian federal employees. It and further executive orders, and even the legislative approval of the Civil Service Reform Act of 1978,[23] did not simply borrow the procedures or processes of collective bargaining from the private sector. The parties could bargain only about matters affecting policy and practices or working conditions, not wages and hours. Any issue affecting an agency's budget or new technology was excluded, and management's right to direct and discipline employees were specifically reserved. Perhaps most important, employees were granted no right to strike.

The federal government's recognition of collective bargaining for its civilian employees and its recognition of unions as the workers' exclusive representatives encouraged state and local governments to follow suit, particularly in the more urbanized areas where professional management is common and civil service is well established. The organization of public employees and government's acceptance of collective bargaining proceeded far more easily than unionizing had in the private sector a generation before. Public debate was relatively muted, and certainly no government agency ever fought unions and resisted collective bargaining with the outraged determination of many private managers. Public employees' unions conducted strikes for improved condi-

---

[23]The Civil Service Reform Act of 1978 protected the right of civilian federal employees to organize and to bargain collectively on conditions of employment. It confirmed and regularized the rights formerly authorized by various executive orders. The Postal Reorganization Act of 1971 made collective bargaining for employees of the U.S. Postal Service subject to the provisions of the National Labor Relations Act, with two major exceptions: a ban on strikes and a ban on the union shop.

tions with increasing frequency, disrupting schools, garbage collection, fire fighting, and even police services and the post office.

Government officials sought to protect the public against the disruption of vital public services while at the same time recognizing the rights of public employees. Most concluded that if public employees were forbidden to strike, "it is elementary justice to assure [them] . . . that they have the right to negotiate collectively."[24] Even when states allowed their employees to strike under some conditions,[25] little protest was made by the public and other criticisms have not been numerous.

Similarities and Differences between Public and Private Sectors

Some legal scholars have warned, though, that collective bargaining by public employees may produce more serious consequences for the public than has collective bargaining in the private sector. Professors Harry H. Wellington and Ralph K. Winter of the Yale Law School have argued that to grant typical collective bargaining rights to public employees "would leave competing groups in the political process at a permanent and substantial disadvantage."[26] They assume that public employees with full rights of collective bargaining, including the right to strike, would enjoy too powerful a position; they could endanger the health and safety of the community. The demand for their services is relatively inelastic, and the electorate is more apt to punish the elected officials than the strikers. Professors Wellington and Winter rest their case upon assumptions that can be tested against the empirical evidence of experience. Until that testing is performed, we cannot reach definite conclusions. But this argument, offered by persons not unfriendly to labor, is weighty enough to convince legislators to move cautiously in granting collective bargaining rights to public employees.

Professor Robert S. Summers, of Cornell University Law School, goes further in his criticism of collective bargaining in the public sector. He asserts that it both conflicts with and diminishes democracy; he would neither borrow from the private sector not have any kind of procedures that limit the decision-making powers of democratically accountable public officials.[27] Even if public employees' unions are not more powerful than other interest groups, Summers finds them inappropriate for dealing with government. The very process of collective bargaining will short-circuit the public voice and frustrate the realiza-

---

[24]New York Governor's (Taylor) Committee on Public Employee Relations, *Final Report,* Mar. 31, 1966, p. 20.

[25]Vermont (1967); Montana (1969); Pennsylvania (1970); Hawaii (1970); Oregon (1973); Alaska (1974); Minnesota (1975); and Wisconsin (1977). See B. V. H. Schneider, "Public-Sector Labor Legislation," *Public-Sector Bargaining,* Grodin and Stern, pp. 201–203.

[26]Harry H. Wellington and Ralph K. Winter, "The Limits of Collective Bargaining in Public Employment," in David Lewin, Peter Feuille, and Thomas A. Kochan (eds.), *Public Sector Labor Relations,* Thomas Horton & Daughters, 1977, p. 28.

[27]Robert S. Summers, *Collective Bargaining and Public Benefit Conferral,* Ithaca, New York: Institute of Public Employment, 1976.

tion of democratic values. Professor Summers apparently projects an idealized form of the democratic process and finds threats to it in the form of a specially recognized interest group, the union. In the world of practical affairs, governmental decision making seldom proceeds as he ideally describes it; agencies are often large, are almost always complex, and have numerous interests vying with each other to influence policy. Decision making is usually fractured and dispersed, subject to many different tugs and pulls; seldom is it a process directly responsive to the electorate or even to those elected. There is little reason to believe that in practice government decisions affecting employees will be less efficient or democratic if collective bargaining helps mold them. In that belief, the federal government and most states have extended recognition to unions and approved collective bargaining, though usually with limits and restrictions. They are gradually learning how they might best balance the interests of the public employees and the public.

CONCLUSION

Americans have found collective bargaining a useful, acceptable method of mediating relationships between employees and employers. The result is not always successful, and changing conditions and the rise of new technologies requires readjustments of rights and claims among the various interested parties. By and large, collective bargaining has served the nation reasonably well, though it will continue to require readjustment.

The procedures, requirements, and rights involved in the resolution of these problems will continue to be examined by legislators and reviewed by judges. One or another group at the bargaining table will gain or lose as a consequence, and it will support or attack, accordingly, any changes made. At times the groups may be influential enough to hold up or hasten the changes, but their special interests are not the only ones influencing our lawmakers. To explain law as nothing but the product of dominant groups is as cynically naive as it is unsophisticatedly optimistic to argue that law always promotes the general welfare. The changes in American labor law reveal more than whether union or management has the upper hand at the moment. They also indicate that if they are to retain their favorable position, dominant groups must recognize and respond to social sentiments.

CHAPTER 11

THE ENCOURAGEMENT AND REGULATION OF COLLECTIVE BARGAINING

When public policy toward unions and collective bargaining moved beyond the laissez faire approach of the Norris–LaGuardia Act of more than fifty years ago, it faced new issues and problems. How were governments to encourage unions and enforce collective bargaining? Except for a short time at the end of World War I, employees and union leaders had been free to engage in and define collective bargaining as they saw fit. Neither legislators nor judges had ever tried positively to define the process or content of collective bargaining, though the courts had certainly intervened.

Before the 1930s intervention had been in the form of negative regulation, a decision on whether the demands and purposes for which unions bargained were lawful. Time and again state judges had held the closed shop to be an unlawful demand that unions could not legitimately seek through collective bargaining. The courts had also limited collective bargaining when unions sought such ends as protection from technological change, maintenance of jurisdiction, the removal of supervisors who discriminated against union members, and penalties for employers who contracted out work that union members had previously performed. The National Labor Relations Act of 1935 made a marked departure from such repressive concern with unions and their activities. It and subsequent labor legislation, both at the federal level and among the states, has been supportive of collective bargaining.

GOVERNMENT INSISTENCE UPON COLLECTIVE BARGAINING

The government had long intervened through its judicial organs in a way that favored employers. Courts had consistently restricted union demands and had granted almost impregnable defenses against unions in the name of property rights. Beginning in 1935 public policy swung sharply in the opposite direction. Henceforth it was to be formally aligned behind collective protection of individual liberty. The preamble to the 1935 act, essentially repeated in the 1947 amendments, clearly indicates that alignment:

> Section 1. The denial by employers of the right of employees to organize and the refusal by employers to accept the procedure of collective bargaining lead to strikes and other forms of industrial strife and unrest, which have the intent or the necessary effect of burdening or obstructing commerce. . . . The inequality of bargaining power between employees who do not possess full freedom of association or actual liberty of contract, and employers who are organized in the corporate or other forms of ownership association substantially burdens and affects the floow of commerce, and tends to aggravate recurrent business depressions by depressing wage rates and the purchasing power of wage earners in industry and by preventing the stabilization of competitive wage rates and working conditions within and between industries.
>
> Experience has proved that protection by law of the right of employees to organize and bargain collectively safeguards commerce from injury, impairment, or interruption, and promotes the flow of commerce by removing certain recognized sources of industrial strife and unrest, by encouraging practices fundamental to the friendly adjustments of industrial disputes arising out of differences as to wages, hours, or other working conditions, and by restoring equality of bargaining power between employers and employees.[1]

In 1935 Congress was preoccupied not with the power of unions but with their weakness; it was not concerned with limits to collective bargaining, but with its survival. Without collective bargaining, economic efficiency was impaired and employment as well as wages were diminished, according to the act; collective bargaining was expected to moderate recurrent business depressions, help wage earners maintain purchasing power, and stabilize competitive wage rates and working conditions. The act benefited unions, of course, but it was not so much an instrument to further the interests of labor as it was a pragmatic response of Congress to the challenge of an urban industrial economy in distress. By the mid-1930s the conditions under which workers might enjoy their rights and the public interest might be served had changed. They were not those of the late nineteenth and early twentieth centuries. Both courts and legislature recognized the changes that had taken place in the economy.

In the 1960s, when the federal government and a number of state and local governments first acted to encourage their own employees to organize and bargain collectively, the nation confronted no economic crisis comparable to the great depression. But the situation of public employees had changed greatly within a generation. The number of federal employees had increased from less than 1 million in 1939 to more than 2¼ million in 1959. Employees in state

---

[1]47 Stat. 449 (1935). Compare the language here with that of the Norris–La Guardia Anti-injunction Act of 1932, quoted in Chapter 10. Here the act promises to encourage and protect; in the 1932 act, Congress sought merely to free unions from limitations imposed by courts.

and local government had begun to increase in number, rising from just over 3 million in 1939 to 5.8 million in 1959. (By 1984 their number had more than doubled to over 13 million, whereas the number of federal employees had increased by less than half a million.) The influence of their numbers was multiplied by their grievances. Work forces were so large that the cumbersome procedures of civil service did not meet their job needs adequately or afford sure and quick due process. Furthermore, public employees' wages and fringe benefits lagged behind those elsewhere. By historical standards, they had slipped below those in the best of the private sector. Many among both the public employees and elected officials concluded that unionism and collective bargaining would better serve not only the public employees but also the public interest.

Government intervention to help unions and public employees as once it had helped business and private employers was a development to be expected in a democratic society. As the impact of group power upon individuals and the public changed, the electorate and legislators changed the law accordingly. Those who supported the intervention certainly believed that the government was serving the public interest in protecting unions' right to exist, even though they may not have anticipated that the government would become so deeply involved in defining and regulating the processes of collective bargaining.

Early Attempts to Gain Voluntary Acceptance

Earlier in the century at least two serious efforts had been made to gain businesses' voluntary acceptance of unions and collective bargaining. Each had failed, making the alternative of government intervention almost inevitable. Under the leadership of Mark Hanna and Samuel Gompers and with such outstanding public representatives as August Belmont, Grover Cleveland, and Charles W. Eliot, the National Civic Association (NCA) attempted at the turn of the century to develop more peaceful industrial relations by promoting collective bargaining agreements and voluntary machinery for mediating and arbitrating labor disputes. Though the NCA had aroused some interest and gained some influence in twenty-two states by 1905, the antiunion attack of the National Association of Manufacturers upon the closed shop and its vigorous promotion of the open shop (really a nonunion closed shop) proved much more congenial to American business managers generally.

In 1919 President Wilson called a tripartite National Industrial Conference to evaluate collective bargaining and union representation as they had been carried on during World War I. The employers would not agree, however, to continue to recognize the right of workers to be represented by independent union leaders, and the conference broke up. Even against the urging of outstanding public-minded business leaders, influential employers rejected any voluntary recognition of or dealings with unions. In the same year, just before the great steel strike, John D. Rockefeller, Jr. had urged Henry Clay Frick and Judge Elbert Gary, the two most influential officers in U.S. Steel, to consider collective bargaining or at least employee representation. They refused, Gary objecting that "representation of any kind . . . is only the entering wedge to the closed shop, which . . . is fatal to business." The following year, Herbert Hoover also called upon a number of business leaders in such citadels of capitalism as Standard Oil of New Jersey, United States Rubber, and General Electric, asking them to consider establishing some liaison with unions and their leaders. The companies gave cool and distant response to the call and, along with the managers of most other large companies, elected to fight unions with the open-shop "American plan."[2]

A dozen years later, business managers still opposed the recognition of unions and the practice of collective bargaining as firmly as ever. With passage of the Norris–La Guardia Anti-injunction Act in 1932, unions were freed from most of the restrictive injunctive powers of the courts; the coercive tactics used to promote worker and union interests were given an equality with the tactics of business managers to limit those same interests. This hands-off approach of the government did not encourage business to accept unions, though. It only fostered increased conflict and more bitter clashes between resisting managers and workers trying to organize. Even section 7(a) of the National Industrial Recovery Act did not persuade American management that it should voluntarily accept collective bargaining with unions of the workers' choice. It did lead to a widespread development of company unionism, which in time conceivably might have led to a voluntary acceptance of independent unions and real collective bargaining, but in the caldron of discontent that was fired by the great depression, social change boiled rather than simmered. In 1935 the government passed new legislation, the National Labor Relations Act, which actually encouraged and protected collective bargaining.

The Enforcement of the Labor Laws

To enforce the new labor law, Congress established the National Labor Relations Board of three members appointed by the President for a term of five years. It was to conduct elections within appropriate bargaining units to determine by a majority vote of the employees, the union that would gain exclusive representational rights. Furthermore, the board was to prevent employers from engaging in unfair labor practices that would interfere with the exercise of those rights. In 1947, the board was given the further responsibility of preventing unions from engaging in unfair labor practices.

In extending to public employees the right to organize and to bargain collectively, the federal and state governments have established agencies to perform functions similar to those of the NLRB. The Civil Service Reform Act of 1978 created a Federal Labor Relations Authority, and most states with labor legislation have analogous boards, commissions, or agencies, "public employee

---

[2]Irving Bernstein, *The Lean Years,* Boston: Houghton Mifflin Company, 1960, p. 147.

relations board" (PERB) being a frequently used name. The more recently formed boards and agencies have been greatly influenced by the decisions and ruling of the NLRB over the years. However, Congress and state legislatures have not allowed public employees as much freedom in bargaining as private employees have, and they have imposed various restrictions upon union organizing that require the new agencies to formulate policies of their own to fit the particular cases coming before them.

One might reasonably assume that much of the work of the NLRB would have become unnecessary as private employers came to accept unions and collective bargaining. Acceptance of unions in one industry has not necessarily induced acceptance in another. Employers who have not bargained with unions still show a tendency to view collective bargaining as an alien and threatening ideology. As noted in Chapter 2, even some employers with long experience in bargaining have difficulty in accepting it as a pragmatic, democratic means of resolving industrial problems. Collective bargaining in those areas in which it is well established has gained a measure of acceptance that may have greatly reduced the need for government encouragement and protection of it—but unionists and their supporters would not agree with this. Employers who have bargained regularly with production workers, for example, greet the organizing of white-collar workers with something less than enthusiasm. They often resist even the organizing of blue-collar workers in new plants. Thus the NLRB still maintains a heavy caseload of representational hearings and elections; both unions and employers continually appeal to it to rule against unfair labor practices. Unions seek protection against employers who may try to limit the scope of bargaining or hamper union organizing. Employers seek to keep unions within the bounds of the law and ask for protection from unions that attempt to impose rather than negotiate provisions of agreements.

The newer federal and state labor agencies may be expected to have an easier time, with fewer demands made upon them. The employers are the governments themselves, and once the legislature has granted recognition to unions and approved collected bargaining, neither of these should be long delayed. Nevertheless, the limits upon the scope of public employees' bargaining and the restrictions upon unions' concerted activities raise many new issues and questions. Both the public employees' unions and public officials who bargain with them may find ample reasons to appeal to their relevant labor agencies to define the specific issues to be bargained, exactly to whom they will apply, and what tactics may be used in pressing for particular terms. As in the case of the NLRB, the work of the federal and state labor agencies may continue unabated over the years.

Thus the original intentions of the legislators have not been realized. They had expected to establish the basic rules for collective bargaining, allowing the parties freedom to determine the scope and nature of collective bargaining within the limits set. In a number of ways both NLRB and the later federal and state agencies for public employees have shaped the scope of bargaining, however, and even influenced the nature of it. Some shaping has been quite direct, some indirect and unintended. To this shaping we now turn.

THE INFLUENCE OF GOVERNMENT UPON COLLECTIVE BARGAINING

In the years immediately after legal encouragement of organizing has been assured, government's indirect influence upon collective bargaining is probably more important than its direct influence. This indirect influence manifests itself through the determination of the appropriate bargaining unit. By including some workers in and excluding others from a bargaining unit, the NLRB and the other labor agencies help determine whether there will be any collective bargaining at all. In some working situations a majority vote for a particular union as exclusive representative of a body of employees might be denied by *excluding* one particular component group, such as a skilled occupation or one whose community of interest or experience had separated it from the rest. While these might have voted for the more comprehensive union, they might prefer their own specialized representation, and subtracting them from the larger unit could leave only a minority of the larger body in favor of union representation. Or a different unit determination might give a union a majority by including a number of strongly prounion groups that would dilute an antiunion sentiment.

Unions and employers, whether private or public, have usually sought that bargaining unit (election district) that would best serve their immediate ends. Unions want a unit that will assure a favorable vote, and beyond that very pragmatic interest they want a unit that will be cohesive enough to sustain maximum bargaining pressure upon the employer. If employers want to avoid collective bargaining, they may desire a unit that denies a majority vote to the union; if they accept collective bargaining, their concern is to establish a unit that will be administratively efficient and convenient to deal with.

In recent years PERBs and similar state agencies have had to wrestle with the issue of the breadth of units—broad or narrow inclusion of workers. This is the same kind of issue that the NLRB confronted in its first decade. The workers included in a unit, of course, influence the kinds of provisions and terms for which unions will bargain and even the kinds of politics and the organizational stability of the union. Consider the case of District Council 37 of the American Federation of State, County and Municipal Employees, in New York City. Within its bargaining unit it has five divisions: (1) professional, technical, and cultural employees; (2) hospital workers, mostly in low-status jobs; (3) blue-collar workers, mostly custodial personnel and laborers; (4) administrative and clerical employees; and (5) school employees such as lunchroom orderlies, aides, and paraprofessionals.

In coordinating the various interests of the heterogeneous membership and conducting collective bargaining for the whole unit, the union leaders and staff must seek provisions and negotiate terms that will win broad and common support across the unit. Although they attempt to meet the special needs and specific demands of particular workers, the negotiators find egalitarian, across-the-board benefits the most politically rewarding. The union has even taken the lead in changing work rules and operations in the interests of administrative efficiency, when such action has helped preserve jobs. Collective bargaining within a narrow occupational unit, such as that of the Patrolmen's Benevolent Association in New York City, contrasts sharply with that of District Council 37. Union leaders are more concerned with protecting work rules and ensuring the status, rights, and prerogatives of their members; they continually challenge managerial changes, such as one-officer patrol cars, the introduction of civilians into station houses, and demand-based assignments related to the frequency of crime.

Collective bargaining is also affected indirectly in these two cases by the influence of the unit upon leadership qualities. The large, complex unit that the officers of District Council 37 represent has been able to assure political stability by providing opportunity for continually adjusting majority coalitions among the different groups. Although they may lose the support of one group opposed to a certain policy, with some give and take they can win the support of another so that there is little or no net loss of support. As a result, leaders stay in office for long periods and become experienced and knowledgeable negotiators, well able to understand and deal with complex issues at the bargaining table. In contrast, the police change their leaders frequently. In internal union debate about collective bargaining issues, the members tend to coalesce around a given position, shifting en masse from one position to another. Almost all members have similar interests; the union is not so much a coalition of various and different interest groups as it is a single interest group itself. Its leaders have little opportunity to negotiate with smaller groups, brokering majorities for one or another program and maintaining stability. When membership support changes, it typically changes throughout the whole union. The result is sharp swings of support from incumbent leaders who did not win all the promised gains to opposition candidates who shrilly repeat the promises and accuse the current leaders of betrayal.

The kind of bargaining unit and type of worker for which a union negotiates no doubt influences bargaining. This is not to say, however, that government determination of the unit greatly changes the history of bargaining thereby. Even if the city of New York had favored a single unit that included the police and other uniform services as well as all other municipal workers, it is not likely that such a single unit would have been viable. The community of interest within the police, firefighters, and sanitation workers was and continues so strong that it could not be denied in bargaining. They had identified themselves as separate groups long before any unit determination took place. Furthermore, as we have seen in Chapter 10, the formal, legal bargaining unit fixed by a government agency is not necessarily the actual unit of bargaining in practice. After unions win representational rights and their leaders and managers explore the problems and opportunities of collective bargaining, the indirect influence of the labor agencies upon the content of the agreements through unit determination tends to wane.

Good-Faith Bargaining

Once workers choose a union as their exclusive representative, the union and management are required to bargain in good faith. Under the National Labor Relations Act, good-faith bargaining must cover wages, hours, and other terms and conditions of employment; public employees in federal service can not bargain over pay and fringe benefits, though, while those in some states, such as teachers in New Jersey, are given an indefinite scope. Whether the duty to bargain is spelled out in detail or only sketchily defined, the parties have appealed for official rulings on the limits or permissiveness of the scope. In the process of setting forth rules, the NLRB in the private sector and the various labor agencies in the public sector have, case by case, described the ambits of collective bargaining.

Particularly in the private sector, the issue of management obligation to negotiate turns upon good-faith conduct. Has it bargained with intent to reach an agreement or have its negotiations been only a smoke screen behind which it seeks to discourage the union? It may have met regularly with the union but conceded nothing, undermining the employees' confidence in the ability of the union to accomplish anything. So presented, as it inevitably must be, the issue reduces to one of subjective attitudes the results *intended* by management.

The NLRB, which is the agency most likely to be asked to answer such a question, can scarcely probe the minds of the managerial negotiators and reach any certain conclusions about intent. States of mind and intentions are not easy to lay bare. Consequently the board has been forced to adopt the approach of using what it refers to as "objective indicia." This means relying upon circumstantial evidence and deciding whether the established facts—the objective evidence—support a judgment that negotiations were conducted in good or bad faith. The subjective factor of intent is inferred by a reasonable examination of the evidence.

The Case of General Electric

The difficulties of judging good-faith bargaining upon influence were well illustrated in a case involving General Electric's former bargaining strategy, popularly known as Boulwarism. The managers prepared what they characterized as a firm, fair offer, in their desire to "do right voluntarily." Prior to and during negotiations the company produced, in the words of a judge who heard the case on appeal, "a veritable avalanche of publicity, reaching awesome proportions . . . to tell its side of the issues to its employees." The company was willing to change its offer if its facts were wrong, but it would not change simply because the union disapproved of the offer. It also denounced the traditional give-and-take of bargaining as "flea-bitten eastern type of cunning and dishonest but pointless haggling."[3] Both the NLRB and the circuit court of appeals found that such bargaining was not in good faith. They accused the company of using a communications and bargaining strategy that in effect precluded bargaining. The board's trial examiner specifically condemned GE's declaration that "a union could obtain no added benefits that it would not otherwise grant."[4]

The findings of the NLRB, upheld by the courts, may have inferred correctly that the company did not bargain in good faith, but reasonable observers might have held a contrary opinion on the grounds that General Electric had negotiated with its unions for many years, dealing with them regularly and fully at the plant level in resolutions of grievances, and had never failed to reach a settlement. It is evident that good-faith bargaining may be variously interpreted; there are no simple or objective criteria to define it. Its definition is made even more difficult because neither party is legally bound to agree to any proposal or required to make a concession.[5]

The Meaning of Good Faith in Bargaining

Despite its refusal to require agreement, Congress declared in 1947 that the parties had to execute a written contract incorporating any agreement reached if so requested.

A onetime board member described the NLRB's role:

> ... the Act thus shows that it is concerned to a great extent with maneuvering the parties to the bargaining table. The Board, under the Act, is constituted as the midwife of the bargaining relationship. It oversees the birth of that bargaining relationship and attempts to prevent any miscarriages. But once the parties have passed the threshold into the bargaining arena, the Board had accomplished much of what it can do. After that threshold is passsd, the Board's further involvement with the collective bargaining process is limited to defining the subjects about which the parties must bargain and to seeing that the bargaining is not simply a charade. Although those are not negligible tasks, they do not compare in importance to the Board's task of getting the parties safely to the table for meaningful bargaining.[6]

The courts have approved this role for the board. The Supreme Court declared that:

> It is implicit in the entire structure of the Act that the Board acts to oversee and referee the process of collective bargaining, leaving the results of the contest to the bargaining strength of the parties. . . . [T]he Act . . . does not contemplate that unions will always be secure and able to achieve agreements even when their economic posi-

---

[3] *NLRB v. General Electric Co.*, 418 F. 2nd 736 (2d. Cir. 1959), *cert. denied,* 397 U.S. 965 (1970), excerpted in Leslie, *Cases and Materials on Labor Law: Process and Policy,* pp. 379–382.
[4] Ibid.
[5] See National Labor Relations Act of 1947, sec. 8(d).
[6] Peter D. Walther, "The Board's Place at the Bargaining Table," *Labor Law Journal,* vol. 28, 1976, p. 131.

tion is weak, or that strikes and lockouts will never result from a bargaining impasse. It cannot be said that the Act forbids an employer or a union to rely ultimately on its economic strength to try to secure what it cannot obtain through bargaining.[7]

In defining good-faith bargaining, the board has ruled that employers may not refuse to meet or negotiate with the workers' duly chosen representatives. They must make a genuine attempt to achieve an understanding of the proposals and counterproposals advanced and must exhaust every avenue and possibility of negotiations before admitting that an impasse exists. Neither party may insist upon meeting at unreasonable times and places. Dilatory tactics indicate bad-faith bargaining, as in the case of a company that failed to make a single bona fide written proposal over a fifteen-month period of negotiations despite the union's submission of at least three drafts of proposed agreements. To make an offer directly to employees, going over the heads of the union officers, on a matter that has been considereedd with a union committee is taken as evidence of bad faith.

Employers may not in good faith take unilateral action on a matter on which the union has a right to be heard. In various decisions the board has declared that employers must, if requested, bargain over arbitration bonuses, checkoff, grievance settlement, seniority, and holiday provisions. Furthermore, it has decided that employers do not bargain in good faith if they refuse to prove or verify claims that they cannot meet wage demands because of an inability to pay.

GOVERNMENT DETERMINATION OF THE CONTENT OF AGREEMENTS

The requirements imposed by the National Labor Relations Act and the decisions of the NLRB were intended not so much to shape the content of collective bargaining as to distinguish between real and apparent bargaining. Employers and managers have often resisted the duty to bargain with considerable ingenuity and stubbornness, requiring the board to define at least the minimum conditions of that duty. That definition does not advance collective bargaining if managers continue to oppose meaningful bargaining. Under the act they do not finally have to agree to union terms and can act unilaterally if no agreement is reached.

Even when management and unions initially agreed on the scope of their bargaining, they sometimes disagreed as unions pushed for broader scope over time. Agreements at first were short and simple, covering general wage provisions and the rudiments of a grievance procedure. Later, they began to include pensions, supplemental unemployment benefits, stock bonuses for employees,

---

[7]*H. K. Porter Co. v. NLRB,* 397 U.S. 99 (1970). Also see a similar declaration by Chief Justice Hughes in the case that determined the constitutionality of the National Labor Relations Act of 1935, *NLRB v. Jones & Laughlin Steel Corp.,* 301 U.S. 1, 45 (1937).

subcontracting, plant relocation, profit sharing, retraining, and the quality of work life.

Some employers have raised questions about the wisdom of bargaining about these issues and a few have refused to bargain over them. They have usually insisted that these involve matters of managerial authority and responsibility, exclusively within the discretion of managers. In such cases, if the union involved has disagreed, the issue has come before the NLRB for a decision. Did the matter fall within the legal scope of good-faith bargaining as defined by the act?

Mandatory Issues

The decisions pose some knotty problems. Is the board intervening directly in the bargaining process and thus interfering with the parties' autonomous shaping of the content and application of collective bargaining? Will the board's determination tend to set the limits—maximums—that union and management may seek from each other? Interference it undoubtedly is, but whether significant and limiting is more difficult to say. With court approval the board has broadly interpreted wages, hours and conditions of work to include all the varieties of pecuniary emoluments involved in cases that disputing unions and employers have brought before it. Thus there appears to be no limitation imposed by government upon this area of bargaining. But in declaring the various pecuniary issues bargainable, the board and courts have emphasized again and again that the parties are under no legal requirement to reach an agreement, no matter what the subjects over which they may have to bargain. Though a company must bargain at union insistence over a stock-purchase plan, it need not agree to union terms or even to a plan at all.

For example, the finding by the NLRB and the Supreme Court in 1964 that subcontracting was a proper subject for mandatory collective bargaining cannot be said to have caused the spread of subcontracting provisions in agreements. It may have been a factor, of course. Strong union interest in limiting subcontracting, coupled with union bargaining power, was necessary to secure such provisions. In apparel and construction almost every agreement covering workers in a large bargaining unit limits subcontracting; the action can be a serious threat to union jobs and union leaders have pressed management to limit it. In the electrical machinery industry, however, fewer than a quarter of the agreements contain provisions limiting subcontracting. Though unions can bargain about the matter, it has not received high priority. The contrast between the spread of subcontracting provisions and the limited acceptance of negotiated stock-purchase plans is sharp. Fifty-seven percent of all large agreements limited subcontracting in 1980, but only two percent include negotiated stock-purchase plans, though they were declared a mandatory bargainable issue in 1956. The contrast suggests that the NLRB plays a marginal, though not wholly insignificant, role in pushing bargaining into new areas.

The board has excluded from mandatory bargaining some issues, largely of a nonpecuniary nature. Employers may not insist upon bargaining over internal union discipline or require a secret-ballot vote of all employees on the employer's final offer. A union may not insist upon bargaining over illegal provisions such as the closed shop, nor may it insist upon a performance bond that would be forfeited upon aaany subbstantial but undefined breach of contract. It may not seek to impose requirements such as local residence on employees outside the bargaining unit. An employer may, but does not have to, bargain about such issues as contributions to an industrywide promotion fund, strike insurance plans, or continuation of free investment counseling for former employees.[8]

Wherever federal and state laws read the same, state labor agencies and state courts usually follow the precedents set by the federal government in determining scope of bargaining. For example, the Supreme Court decided that retirees are not employees within the meaning of the National Labor Relations Act. Therefore an employer does not have to negotiate over a union proposal that retirees' pension benefits be increased.[9] The New York City Office of Collective Bargaining and the state's Public Employment Relations Board then held that the city and state bargaining laws should be similarly construed.[10] Some issues arise in public employment that have no counterpart in the private sector, though, and state agencies must devise their own ruling about the scope of bargaining. With the multiplicity of state and local governments, the rules often differ considerably.

For example, teachers' unions have insisted that they have a professional interest in school matters that go far beyond those included in the usual narrow definition of working conditions. Accordingly they have sought to bargain over the beginning and ending dates for school terms. Officials of school systems in many states objected, arguing that the determination of the school term was a managerial and even legislative function that school boards could not delegate or share. The Wisconsin Employment Relations Commission, upheld by the Wisconsin Supreme Court in 1967, ruled that the school calendar has a direct and intimate relationship to the salaries and working conditions of teachers.[11] Labor agencies in Nebraska in 1971 and in Michigan in 1972 agreed with this ruling. In Maine the court found in 1973 that bargaining over the calendar was excluded because the basic labor act in the state specifically excluded educational policies from the scope of mandatory bargaining. The New Jersey court

---

[8]See Taylor and Witney, *Labor Relations Law,* p. 349. The authors also pointed out that employers did not have to bargain over the prices charged by an in-plant cafeteria. However, in 1979 the Supreme Court declared they were a mandatory bargaining issue. See *Ford Motor Co. v. NLRB* (101 LRRM 2222–2229).

[9]*Allied Chemical & Alkali Workers Local 1 v. Pittsburgh Plate Glass Co.,* 404 U.S. 157 (1971).

[10]*NYC OCB Decision No. B-21-72 (1972* and *Troy Uniformed Firefighters Ass'n and City of Troy,* 9 PERB 3015 N.Y. (1977).

[11]*City of Madison v. Wisconsin Employment Relations Board,* 37 Wisc. 2d 43, 155 N.W. 2d 78, 65 L.R.R.M. 2488 (1967).

ruled in a similar way in a dispute between teachers and a county college; in Connecticut the court also excluded the school calendar from mandatory bargaining because the basic labor act limited bargaining to "salaries and other terms of employment" and did not include the term "hours."[12] Under such various decisions the parties are free to limit their bargaining or to extend it as they see fit. The agencies and board seldom intervene except at the request of one of the parties: Only if one of them disagrees and wishes government support in its stand is there intervention.

Forbidden or Illegal Issues

The government has also influenced the subject matter of collective bargaining in more direct ways. Some issues have simply been legislatively declared to be out of legal bargaining bounds. The National Labor Relations Act prohibits the closed shop, permitting the union shop only under certain conditions that make it not much more than an agency shop, and limits the form of the checkoff. It forbids, though ineptly and in vain, featherbedding provisions; it requires that notification be given sixty days prior to a proposed termination or modification of an agreement; and it limits royalty payments and the applicability, coverage, purpose, and administration of welfare plans. Furthermore, it requires that workers be given the right to present grievances without the intervention of the union.

Both federal and state legislations restrict the scope of bargaining for public employees more than for private employees. Following the lead of the federal government, some states forbid bargaining over certain managerial rights. Minnesota, for example, declares that:

> A public employer is not required to meet and negotiate on matters of inherent managerial policy, which include, but are not limited to, such areas of discretion or policy as the functions and programs of the employer, its overall budget, utilization of technology, the organizational structure and selection and direction and number of personnel.[13]

In some states the restrictions are specific as well as general. New York provides that "[n]o retirement benefits shall be negotiated . . . and any benefits so negotiated shall be void."[14] Hawaii also excludes retirement benefits from the scope of bargaining. But states may also mandate inclusions as well as exclusions. The most common is the requirement for binding arbitration of disputes over the interpretation and application of the agreement. Typical is the Min-

---

[12]See Harry T. Edwards, R. Theodore Clark, Jr., and Charles B. Craver, *Labor Relations in the Public Sector,* New York: The Bobbs-Merrill Company, Inc., 1979, pp. 301–302.

[13]*Minn. Stat. Ann.* ch. 179, sec. 179.66 (1) Supp. 1972). New Hampshire, Hawaii, Kansas, Nevada, Pennsylvania, Vermont, and California have similar exclusions.

[14]*New York Civil Service Law* sec. 201(4) (McKinney Supp. 1978).

nesota law which states, "All contracts shall include a grievance procedure which shall provide compulsory arbitration of grievances."[15]

Who Likes Government Intervention?

Both business managers and union leaders maintain that the less government intervenes in collective bargaining, the better the situation will be. But in practice each party finds that intervention can serve its own purpose on occasion. Furthermore, each can frequently find public support for intervention. Having once established and supported the general framework of collective bargaining, the federal government has had to bear the responsibility—not always deservedly—for any adverse consequences of bargaining. If the incidence of strikes was deemed to be too high, government policy was at fault; if certain provisions of some labor agreements were held to be detrimental to private or public values, those persons adversely affected made government policy the culprit. Since legislation had ultimately encouraged or allowed the abuses to develop, so the argument has run, new and more legislation was the remedy. Thus have the critics of government regulation pressed for the government to intervene in the details of industrial relations and collective bargaining. And usually one or the other of the parties has found it expedient to support that intervention.

The basic labor laws have affected collective bargaining and collective agreements in another significant and indirect way. They have opened wide the doors to court review of the content of collective bargaining; either party may bring suit for violation of an agreement in the courts. Violations under federal laws go to federal courts, of course, and those under state laws to state courts. In evaluating the contested claims before them, courts may inspect not only the authority and scope of the agreement, but in cases of disputes over arbitration and arbitrators' awards, the propriety of this process and its outcomes. Labor law has become a major legal field in the United States, and the courts handle a heavier load of labor disputes than in any other industrial country. Whatever the popular rhetoric about the value of free collective bargaining and the dangers of government intervention, the reality of American collective bargaining is quite different. The legislatures have intervened both to require and forbid a considerable range of provisions, and the courts continually and closely monitor almost every aspect of bargaining.

PROBLEMS OF REGULATING COLLECTIVE BARGAINING

Whether one can judge the explicit and implicit legal restrictions, limitations, and regulations of collective bargaining as good or bad, wise or foolish will not be examined here. Rather, we shall consider the problems confronting the gov-

---

[15]*Minn. Stat. Ann.* ch. 179, sec. 179.70(1) (Supp. 1973).

ernment in its attempt to regulate collective bargaining. First is the application of general rules and overall decisions to a highly diversified industrial experience. Collective bargaining in the United States is conducted by a large number of different kinds of unions and managements, in both the private and public sectors; it is carried on in a great variety of industries located in different sections of the country. Difference in circumstances can bring about erratic and unforeseen consequences for the varieties of industrial relations subjected to the same or similar rules and regulations.

The National Labor Relations Act, for example, prohibits the closed shop under all circumstances; but in some industries the closed shop has long served a useful purpose for workers, employers, and the unions. Legislators restricted the use of the closed shop because they believed that its subjects individual employees to unfair discriminatory treatment. However, they might have been well advised to consider the effects the prohibition would have on the unions and firms in industries long used to and dependent upon it and its quite different effects upon labor organizations that secured it merely for the sake of administrative convenience. Unions in the construction and maritime industries developed the closed shop not only to safeguard their membership and control jobs but also to provide a means of organizing a disorderly labor market so that transient employers could hire experienced workers whenever they were needed. Construction jobs are scattered geographically, different kinds of workers are employed by different employers, and employers bid on jobs in many different areas and do not usually carry their workers from job to job. They expect to be able to hire qualified workers locally. Individual construction workers find that their jobs come and go and that they need a source of information about jobs and a means of finding the employers hiring in their own locality. To meet the practical problems of the workers and employers, the building-trades unions historically served as the industry's employment agency. Under these conditions, abuses could and did exist. Union officers sometimes discriminated among workers unfairly, required kickbacks, and refused membership and thus work to deserving workers. But the institution of the closed shop performed quite legitimate functions, nevertheless. Instead of attacking just the abuses of the closed shop, by flatly prohibiting it as a negotiable provision in collective agreements legislators denied unions and employers any of its benefits.

In some cases in which unions had secured the closed shop merely for additional union security, the prohibition probably did cut out a possibility of abuse with little other serious effect, but in the construction industry (and several other industries) it complicated the operation of the labor market as well. The problem was so severe that employers and unions ignored the law for some time. As first the National Labor Relations Board and then the courts began to grapple with the problem of enforcement of the general ban on the closed shop, they had to concern themselves with the details of collective agreement provisions in the industry. After some years of regulatory attempts, the board finally devised rules that would allow what amounted to a nondiscriminatory union-run employment agency or hiring hall for those industries where such a device was necessary.

Allowing for Industry Variations

Experience having demonstrated the need for differential regulation in different industries, the Labor-Management Reporting and Disclosure Act of 1959 recognized this need by providing special rules for some industries. It treats the construction industries separately, largely incorporating the special rules worked out by the NLRB. Not only does it give exemptions to construction but it also accords the clothing industry immunity from the restrictions on hot-cargo agreements. Congress recognized that the maintenance of stable and successful collective bargaining in this industry would be nearly impossible if the unions could not enforce standards against nonunion employers to whom work was subcontracted.

Congress thus has given explicit recognition to the fact that when it enacts laws regulating collective bargaining and asks the board and courts to apply the same rules to all, the impact of the law can become capricious and harmful to one of the major purposes of that same law—the encouragement of collective bargaining and the development of orderly and peaceful procedures for the settlement of labor disputes. Yet if there are exceptions to the rules, as in fact have been provided, why are not exceptions made for many other situations?

The board's application of the labor law to an increasingly heterogeneous mix of unions and industries becomes more complex and difficult. Special interest groups pressure the NLRB and Congress for more exemptions. Furthermore, there is danger that as the board wrestles with the practical problem of determining the fine line between mandatory and permissible topics of collective bargaining, the parties (particularly the weaker in any given situation) will be tempted to appeal to the board for tactical reasons of harassment, gambling on winning a favorable verdict. The NLRB and courts are flooded and public policy becomes ensnared in detail.

The ability of Congress, the courts, or the NLRB to make sound public policy is seriously impaired as the issues of collective bargaining become confused and lost in details. The dangers of regulating minutiae of collective bargaining are not only the loss of unions' and managements' control over their own affairs but also the loss of the government's ability to effectively and flexibly regulate collective bargaining in the interests of the public and individual workers, the historical concern of the government.

The more details a government agency considers in administering and regulating, the heavier its case load is apt to be. Each additional legal provision calls for its own interpretation, multiplying enormously the chances for uncovering new and unforeseen circumstances that require special application of the general provisions, and increases rapidly the opportunities for disputes and question. The same problems arise in the activities of state and local government labor agencies. If any of them becomes so caught up in regulating the details of bargaining scope, tactics, and processes that it loses its ability to respond alertly and flexibly to public needs, both the bargaining parties and the public will lose. The government labor agencies need to be wary of filling their time and devoting their efforts to endless, diffused issues of minutiae. They would then be able to respond only to pressures and demands, not to effectively initiate or enforce public policy. The immediately concerned and interested parties no doubt prefer the labor agencies to concentrate upon details; it relieves them of resolving their difficulties themselves, but it also tends to put the agencies at their mercy and direction. Only the parties enjoy the specialized interests and command the resources to enable them to master the intricacies of the law and hearing procedures; only they are likely to find ways to use the agencies for their own purposes. Certainly the parties are not likely to advance the public interest, except accidentally and secondarily to their own.

To the extent that the NLRB and state labor agencies turn their attentions to the details and minutiae of special legislative provisions and exceptions, we can expect their regulatory role to suffer. They will be less able to meet their responsibilities to safeguard the public interest and the rights of individual workers in labor affairs. We could expect union and management experts, wise in the bureaucratic labyrinth of the regulatory agencies, to capture effective control of public policy as it affects collective bargaining.

An expectation that disagreements between unions and management in the private sector will usually protect public interest by requiring one or both parties to appeal to government regulatory agencies for support overlooks the community of interests that exists between them in many cases. For example, the public has shown a good deal more impatience with and disapproval of the closed shop than have employers in some industries. As long as they have secured an adequate supply of qualified workers, employers in the printing, maritime, and construction industries have not shown too much concern with the abuses that existed under the closed shop. With good reason we can conclude that since in the past they have not been so much guardians of public interest as protectors of their own, they are not likely to act differently in the future.

THE RIGHTS OF INDIVIDUAL EMPLOYEES AND COLLECTIVE BARGAINING

A basic reason for government to allow unionization and encourage collective bargaining was the vulnerability of individual workers, employed by large, bureaucratic organizations, to arbitrary treatment. They could hardly bargain in the labor market on equal terms, and employees' rights were apt to be only those granted unilaterally and arbitrarily by management. Collective bargaining introduced a measure of industrial democracy, which many legislators and labor supporters believed would assure rights of due process and fair treatment to individual workers. As unions grew large and collective bargaining spread widely throughout the economy in the late thirties and the forties, it became apparent that union interests did not always correspond with those of individual workers. First, union processes and procedures were not always democratic and responsive to the needs of all the workers covered by collective bargaining; and second, even in democratic unions, the leaders and negotiators elected by the majority have to balance individual and collective interests in ways that sometimes subordinate the former to the latter.[16]

Racial Discrimination

The NLRB early recognized that a number of unions practiced racial discrimination, thus denying to workers who might be included in their bargaining units the full protections of collective bargaining. It refused to sanction units determined on the basis of race. In 1943 it declared, "The color or race of employees is an irrelevant consideration in determining in any case the unit for collective bargaining."[17] It also expressed its opinion that unions discriminating against workers because of race could not lawfully enjoy exclusive representational rights. The Supreme Court also declared, in 1944, that under the law, unions had a duty to provide "fair representation" of all employees in a bargaining unit.[18] The NLRB left enforcement of this duty to the courts, however, until 1962, with the exception of racial discrimination. In 1944 the board ruled that a white-run union had to process equally the grievance of a black employee within the bargaining unit.[19] Eighteen years later, the NLRB readied itself to define and enforce fair representational rights:

> Section 7 [of the National Labor Relations Act] . . . gives employees the right to be free from unfair or irrelevant or invidious treatment by their exclusive representative in matters affecting employment.[20]

Employees aggrieved by a union's refusal to process complaints, whether for racial reasons or not, could now appeal their case to the board. Later, in 1967, the Supreme Court also allowed individual employees a limited appeal to the courts if they had exhausted union remedies, except in those cases in which the employer, union, or both had refused to allow the remedies to be used[21] or the union officers had not pursued a case with reasonable diligence.[22]

---

[16]*Alexander v. Gardner-Denver Co.*, 415 U.S. 36,58 n. 19 (1971).
[17]*United States Bedding Company*, 52 NLRB 382 (1943).
[18]*Wallace Corporation v. NLRB*, 323 U.S. 248 (1944).
[19]*Hughes Tool Company*, 566 NLRB 981 (1944).
[20]*Miranda Fuel Company*, 140 NLRB 181 (1962).
[21]*Vaca v. Sipes*, 386 U.S. 171 (1967).
[22]*Hines v. Anchor Motor Freight*, 424 U.S. 554 (1976).

The Widening Protection for Individual Employees

While the National Labor Relations Board and the courts were deciding how far they might intervene in collectively bargained outcomes to protect the rights of individual employees, Congress was extending both the kinds and the range of individual employment rights. Title VII of the Civil Rights Act of 1964 and other similar laws require employers and unions not to discriminate in hiring, firing, or fixing compensation or in the terms, conditions, or privileges of employment on the basis of race, color, religion, sex, national origin, veteran's status, or handicaps. The rights to employment under these laws belong to individuals and may not be negotiated away by union bargainers or denied under labor-management agreements by labor arbitrators. Congress has also passed a variety of laws to protect the environment, enhance product safety, and promote consumer protection. Each has included a standard provision forbidding employers to take reprisal against any employee who complains privately or publicly. The provision allows courts to award damages to employees if warranted.

Apparently Congress found too many individual employees unable to enjoy a number of protections that public interest had come to recognize as needed in a society in which almost all in the labor force were dependent upon employers for job, work, and livelihood. Unions had spread their protection to no more than a third of the work force at the most, and their coverage has actually declined since the mid-1950s. The Supreme Court recognized that the protection of employment rights through collective bargaining and through various administrative agencies and the courts poses problems for public policy. In a 1981 case, members charged their union with unfair representation because it did not pursue their wage grievance to arbitration; they therefore sought court recognition of their claim under the Fair Labor Standards Act (FLSA). The Court pointed out that:

Two aspects of national labor policy are in tension in this case. The first, reflected in statutes governing relationships between employers and unions, encourages the negotiation of terms and conditions of employment through the collective bargaining process. The second, reflected in statutes governing relationships between employers and their individual employees, guarantees covered employees specific substantive rights. A tension arises between these policies when the parties to a collective-bargaining agreement make an employee's entitlement to substantive statutory rights subject to contractual dispute-resolution procedures.

The national policy favoring collective bargaining and industrial self-government was first expressed in the National Labor Relations Act of 1935 . . . Predicated on the assumption that individual workers have little, if any, bargaining power, and that "by pooling their economic strength and acting through a labor organization freely chosen by the majority the employers of an appropriate it have the most effective means of bargaining for improvements in wages, hours, and working conditions." . . . these statutes reflect Congress' determination that to improve the economic well-being of workers, and thus to promote industrial peace, the interest of some employees in a bargaining unit may have to be subordinated to the collective interests of a majority of their co-workers. . . . The rights established through this system of majority rule are thus "protected not for their own sake but as an instrument of the national labor policy of minimizing industrial strife" by encouraging the practice and procedure of collective bargaining.[23]

The majority decision went on, however, to qualify the role of collective bargaining as the protector of individual employee rights.

Not all disputes between an employee and his employer are suited for binding resolution in accordance with the procedures established by collective bargaining. While courts should defer to an arbitral decision where the employee's claim is based on rights arising out of the collective-bargaining agreement, *different considerations apply where the employee's claim is based on rights arising out of a statute designed to provide minimum substantive guarantees to individual workers.* [Italics added.][24]

The majority decision made it clear that the statutory rights of individual employers were not limited to those under the FLSA. It noted that rights under Title VII of the Civil Rights Act were "separate and distinct from the rights created through the 'majoritarian processes' of collective bargaining." Such individual rights should be examined and resolved by the courts de novo.[25] The Court has concluded that Congress meant to accord parallel or overlapping remedies for violations of workers' employment rights, where they enjoy both contractual and statutory bases for them. Increasingly the Court has recognized the statutory rights of individual employees. It is concerned that union leaders

might *validly* permit some employees' statutorily granted wage and hour benefits, [for example,] to be sacrificed if an alternate expenditure of resources would result in increased benefits for workers in the bargaining unit as a whole. [Italics added.][26]

In 1981 the Supreme Court also ruled that a union member did not have to exhaust union grievance appeal procedures before making a legal complaint of unfair representation.[27]

The minority on the Court and some observers fear that the opening of parallel and overlapping procedures for enforcing individual employment rights will unduly burden the courts and undercut collective bargaining. They may do so, pulling complaints out of the grievance system and bypassing arbitrators under the agreements; but they might also encourage collective bargaining. Individual workers find that appeals to administrative agencies take time, money, and some expertise in law and government procedures. Nonunionized

---

[23]*Barrentine et al. v. Arkansas-Best Freight Systems, Inc.,* 79 S. ct. 2006, Apr. 6, 1981, Slip Opinion, pp. 6–7

[24]Ibid., p. 8.

[25]See *U.S. Bulk Carriers, Inc. v. Arguelles,* 400 U.S. 351 (1971).

[26]*Barrentine,* 101 S. Ct. 1146.

[27]*Clayton v. International Union, UAW,* 101 S. Ct. 2088 (1981).

workers who seek to protect their statutory employment rights may find a new and powerful reason to join a union: to secure assistance in presenting their cases.

CONCLUSION

We need not decry government regulation of collective bargaining in private industry because it impinges upon the autonomous determination by unions and management of wages, hours, and conditions of employment. On the one hand, the public and the government have a legitimate concern with collective bargaining and its outcome, and experience has demonstrated that autonomous determination does not always produce felicitous results. On the other hand, government regulation that attempts to remedy too many shortcomings of collective bargaining or abuses that arise under it may become so snarled in its own comprehensiveness that it loses its force in the ever-changing industrial scene.

We may desire to limit the scope of collective bargaining in the public sector by regulating it more closely than in the private sector. Decisions made by government administrators and through collective bargaining with public employees' unions are less constrained by competition and related market pressures than are those in the private sector. Therefore, if unions can use strikes and other concerted activities to support their attempts to win benefits for the workers they represent, legislative restrictions upon bargaining scope may be needed. If government narrows public employees' bargaining to only peripheral issues and nonpecuniary matters, it runs the risk of devitalizing both the unions and their negotiations. The recent adverse economic climate in many of our large cities has stiffened the resistance of local government officials to the demands of public employees' unions; and both the union leaders and members have learned that they bargain within limits, even if the public sector is not as constricted by financial limits as the private sector. It may be better to allow a fair measure of autonomy to the parties, letting them experiment and discover the consequences of broadening or narrowing bargaining. If such autonomy helps to maintain the vitality of collective bargaining, keeping it from slumping into the bureaucratic, unimaginative rigidities of most civil service programs, the costs of some excess may well be worthwhile.

Since in collective bargaining, as in all other social activities of human beings, good and bad consequences usually flow from the same activity, we need to be quite sure in our evaluation that we have weighed both. When attempting to remedy the bad, the effect of the remedial action upon the good ought to be considered. Such careful consideration may well persuade us that the price we pay for a number of the benefits of collective bargaining is the sacrifice of some individual and public rights and the cost of regulating or limiting collective bargaining is the loss of some of the benefits we might have otherwise enjoyed.

Before regulating collective bargaining and labor affairs further, we might look well at the possible gains and losses that would result from such an extension. We need full and open debate upon the probable effects, both good and bad, of any regulation, and we need a clear realization of both the possibilities and the limitations of government action. It may be more worthwhile for the government to maintain and alter only the broad framework of collective bargaining and to put up with some abuses than to try to remedy many minor shortcomings by regulating the details of collective bargaining, thereby running the risk of impairing its ability to perform its primary functions.

In first promoting voluntary associations and encouraging collective bargaining and in then restraining the associations and regulating collective action, legislators have contended with a persisting paradox. Even as they enact laws to regulate unions and to restrain collective bargaining, they reaffirm our national judgment that full freedom of association enhances individual liberty—that collective action is beneficial to individuals and to the public. Eighty years ago, Professor A. V. Dicey described well the paradoxical problem with which we and our governments must wrestle:

> [The right of association which] from one point of view seems to be a necessary extension of individual freedom is, from another point of view, fatal to the individual of which it seems to be a mere extension. . . . This paradox raises a problem which at this moment in all civilized countries perplexes moralists and thinkers no less than legislators and judges: How is the right of association to be reconciled with each man's individual freedom? Curtail the right of association and personal liberty loses half its value. Give the right of association unlimited scope and you destroy, not the mere values, but the existence of personal freedom.[28]

Those who oppose government regulation or curtailment of collective bargaining might well remember that more is at stake than the strengthening or weakening of unions. Those who perceive in unions a curtailment of workers' freedom or a limit on the liberty of whose for whom they bargain ought to remember that more is involved than simple individualism. Our labor legislation and the administration of labor laws spring in part, of course, from special pleading for unions and business—but only in part. They also well up from deep, continuing, and traditional concerns at once broader than these organizations (the public interest) and narrower (the individual worker). However much business and unions plead their interest, we will wisely recognize the partial validity of those arguments and not dismiss them out of hand. The result may be less-than-perfect legislation and court decisions; they may even be as paradoxical as the problems they are designed to solve.

---

[28]A. V. Dicey, "The Combination Laws as Illustrating the Relations between Law and Opinion in England during the Nineteenth Century," *Harvard Law Review,* vol. 17, 1903–1904, pp. 513–514.

THE ECONOMIC REACH OF COLLECTIVE BARGAINING

Government statistics and employer associations collect many data about wages, earnings, hours, and employment. In their analyses of the data, economists can detail such findings as differentials among occupations and industries; they can identify the differences between labor costs to employers and take-home pay for employees; and they can describe earning trends by sex, age, and race. Interpreting the data is not easy, however. Most economists do not possess a very satisfactory wage theory; at least, the data and the available theories do not match well. Economists tend to rely upon one theory to explain a particular aspect of wages and employment but then use quite another theory to interpret a different aspect. Marginal productivity may provide an explanation of wage differentials, for example, but another theory must be used to explain the continuing high and stable level of wages in the presence of considerable unemployment.

Labor clearly is not just another factor of production, with its allocation and earnings to be explained as they are for capital—land, plant, equipment, or inventories. Labor is always literally embodied in a person, the worker or employee; as human beings they bring to the place of work complexities that capital does not. They compare themselves with each other, considering not only their absolute return but also their relative pay, and compare their various working conditions with those of other workers. They are producers, of course, but they are also consumers, as capital is not, and the rewards of consumption may well affect their willingness and ability to produce—their motivation, enjoyment, and interest at work.

The investments that many persons make in work skills are risky ones, not easily transferred or salable. An autoworker with twenty years of experience on the assembly line, confronted with a plant shutdown, can not easily convert his or her skills into those of a computer programmer. Furthermore, workers may develop or possess several skills, but seldom can they find employment that allows them to use all at the same time, switching back and forth in ways that maximize short-term returns. A nurse is not apt to be able to switch quickly to journalism nor the journalist to be able to take up the practice of law. One's investments in human capital cannot usually be split up, as capital stocks can be, and invested in those areas that bring in the highest returns.

As a consequence, an understanding of the economics of wages is not easily grasped. The student confronts several different theories that do not fit well together and in some cases contradict each other. They may even fly in the face of some of the observable facts that data supply for us. The economic effects of collective bargaining are not easily described, either. Chapters 12 through 15 examine the major wage theories and their implications for, and interpretations of, collective bargaining.

The labor market within which collective bargaining operates is large, accounting for more than three-quarters of the national income. The economic importance of labor markets and the influence of unions in them raise public concern about collective bargaining. Peaceful negotiations may raise wages—and perhaps increase unemployment—to levels damaging to others in the economy; through strikes and industrial turmoil, unions and management may disrupt large sections of the economy, hurting those who have no say in the proceedings or the settlements. These public concerns are reflected in opinion surveys. Unions "are the least trusted major institution in American Life. . . ."[1] Yet the surveys also consistently show that the public views unions as essential to a democratic society, doing more good than harm. They are, after all, among the largest mass-membership organizations in the nation. Their size is apparently perceived as carrying with it significant power. The public believes that such power is likely to be used through wage setting and strikes to serve the narrow self-interests of organized workers, not those of a broad public. In Chapter 15 we will consider the measurable dimensions of strikes, their economic effects, and means of settling them.

---

[1] Seymour Martin Lipset and William Schneider, *The Confidence Gap: Business, Labor, and Government in the Public Mind,* New York: The Free Press, 1983, p. 199.

12

THE ECONOMICS OF WAGE SETTING THROUGH COLLECTIVE BARGAINING

Some economists have long been embarrassed or exasperated by unions and their members' demands for collective bargaining. They have seen unionists as well-intentioned but seriously misguided in their efforts. In early-nine-teenth-century England, social reformers such as Joseph Hume, Francis Place, and George White were convinced, on the basis of Ricardian economic theory, that workers could accomplish nothing through unions. They argued that the recently enacted anticombination laws encouraged workers wrongly to believe that unions might help them raise wages. A better public policy, they insisted, would be repeal of the laws forbidding unions; let workers organize and discover from actual practice that unions could not help.

After astute parliamentary maneuvering, they gained their point in 1824. The repealers were confident that unions would not last; any benefits won by them would be temporary. The natural laws of economics would stymie long-term union success and prove their futility to the workers. Any higher wages could not last; they would quickly induce competition for jobs and encourage working families to have more children—more future workers—which would soon restore wages to their lower, natural rates.

To the consternation of the lawmakers, however, workers failed to perceive the futility of their collective efforts and their unions. They conducted strikes far and wide, seeking higher wages and better working conditions. The next year Parliament reimposed some of the old restraints upon unions.

In the succeeding century, workers in the United States as well as in England persisted in trying to form unions and to raise wages, despite governmental restraints and the warnings by economists of disagreeable and even dire consequences. Though later economists examined union wage policies with sophisticated tools, such as marginal analysis, their judgments generally continued to be the same: workers in general could not benefit themselves substantially through collective bargaining. The self-regulating action of the competitive market could not be improved by "artificial" means. At best, any strategically situated group of workers who did succeed in pushing up its wages would reduce the demand for its services and leave some workers, ready and willing to work, with no jobs at all.

Those who could perceive no economic justification for unions have offered a number of explanations for the persistence of unions and of workers' attachment to them. Some argue that workers must have a myopic view of their own interests; short-run gains so entrance them that they fail to perceive the disadvantageous long-run results. Although they might raise their wages, for example, and enjoy better conditions for themselves, they fail to realize that they have simultaneously created a problem of unemployment for those who otherwise would have had work. Unionized workers are motivated by self-interest, as are others in the economy; they are quite willing to benefit themselves at the expense of others if they find the opportunity. The well-organized carpenters, for instance, might be pleased with their high wages and unconcerned that they thereby tend to raise costs and diminish housing sales to the direct and indirect detriment of other workers.

But even those who are skeptical of any general justification of unions admit that in certain situations unions can help workers. They may at times be able to offset the power of employers who are exploiting them. Such a circumstance might arise if an employer were the only buyer of a particular labor service, because of either geographical isolation or occupational specialization. In such cases the employer could offer less than the workers' true productive value, and they would have to accept, enjoying no alternative employment. Collective bargaining might therefore be beneficial, at least to the extent that it counters such exploitation. Beyond that point it has no economic merit. Of course, unions might be justified on other than economic grounds, such as protecting members from discriminatory treatment and harsh discipline.

On the whole, then, the most widely accepted wage theories cast unions in roles that range from the misguided reformer to the selfish, calculating monopolist. Based on the values of an individualistic society or on the assumption that individual action is the norm for market behavior, economic theory tends to cast all collectives in a dubious light. Singularly unable to hide their collectivity behind any legal fiction, as corporations have done, or to be assumed simple profit maximizers, as economists continue to characterize even the largest business corporation, unions present themselves as obvious and dubious anomalies in the free-market system.

THE MARGINAL PRODUCTIVITY THEORY OF DEMAND FOR LABOR AND WAGE DETERMINATION

Orthodox wage theory holds that labor's marginal productivity determines its demand schedule and thus contributes, with the labor-supply schedule, to a particular wage and employment. By examining the way in which marginal productivity affects demand and thus influences wages, we can gain an appreciation of conventional economic analysis of wages; the theory also provides a basis for evaluating wage criteria and the economic consequences of collective bargaining. The marginal productivity theory necessarily rests, as does every theory, on simplifying assumptions:

1 The economy is composed of many firms, none of which is able to exercise a measurable influence on its product or factor markets.

2 The managers of each firm strive to maximize profits, and workers try to realize the maximum monetary worth from their work.

3 Business firms operate under constant or increasing costs of production, so an increase of output does not lower unit costs (i.e., the law of diminishing returns of nonproportional output applies).

4 Unemployment is only low-level and temporary, that is, "frictional."

5 A goodly number of workers possess a high degree of mobility, being able to move from one job to another at little cost to themselves.

6 Methods of production are flexible, so managers can combine labor and capital in different proportions.

7 There is a sufficient homogeneity among workers of a given level of skill to enable managers at negligible cost to substitute one for another.

8 Tastes and technologies do not change within the period of time that it takes for economic influences to make themselves felt.

9 Employers and workers possess a reasonably complete working knowledge of the state of product and factor markets.

The key concept of the theory is the "marginal value product"—the net value to the firm of employing one more unit of labor. (For the sake of convenience, the marginal value product is often referred to as simply though misleadingly, the "marginal product.") The marginal productivity theory of demand for labor, in its simplest version, asserts that for a given supply of labor, workers would *tend* to be distributed among firms and industries in such a manner that the value of workers' marginal product would be equal in all types of work for which they qualify. Since the theory assumes workers of a given skill class to be interchangeable—for most practical purposes one could be substituted for another, given a little time—the wage rate would be the same for all workers of that skill level. When all workers are receiving a wage rate equal to their marginal value product in whatever business they are employed and the wage rates for given services are equal in all lines of production, the labor market is in equilibrium. In that condition there would be no market pressures operating to change wage rates. Only an extraneous influence, such as a new invention or a change in demand for particular products, could upset the equilibrium. The market's reestablishment of it would take a little time as workers and wage rates adjusted to the changes, but eventually a new equilibrium would be reached or at least approached.

Under the law of diminishing returns, the marginal product of a given amount of labor varies inversely with the amount of capital used. On the one hand, the larger the work force that is used with a fixed amount of capital, the smaller is the marginal product and thus the smaller the wage. Even if time is allowed for managers to transform the given amount of capital into equipment more suited to an increased work force (as by reinvestment of depreciation accruals), the output attributable to the "final worker" is smaller than if fewer were used. Given the capital stock, the more workers, the less the value of their marginal product, and thus the smaller the wage.

On the other hand, the greater the amount of capital used with a fixed number of workers, the greater is labor's marginal product, and the higher is the wage. Such an analysis does not consider the possibilities that workers might improve their skills and abilities or that the efficiency of capital might be improved through invention and development. These possibilities are put aside not because they are unrealistic, but in order to simplify the analysis and avoid complexities that can obscure underlying tendencies.

The Normal Wage in an Equilibrium Situation

The equilibrium wage for a skill class in this theoretical approach may be considered normal in that it is the wage which the demand for and supply of that grade of labor tend to establish and maintain over time. Any rate above the marginal product would be a loss to the firm, encouraging managers to lay off workers until the return from the marginal unit of labor equals the wage rate paid. According to the law of diminishing returns, the marginal product would increase as fewer workers used the same amount of capital. Workers who were about to be laid off could avoid that unhappy event only if they offered to work for a lower wage, a wage equal to the value they were contributing to the company. Their offer would force the rest of the employed to accept the same lower wage, too, since all are substitutable for one another. Thus competitive pressure among the workers would bring the wage rate back to (or keep it at) the level of the marginal value product of the original work force. At that rate, and only at that rate, all the workers would be employed.

The same competitive forces would also protect workers from wage level *below* their marginal product. Should a firm attempt to cut wages, its managers would find that other firms would bid away its underpaid workers; those firms could realize additional profit on any wage rates less than labor's marginal product. Competition between them for workers would continue until wage rates were restored to the level of workers' marginal product. The competitive forces that tend to push wages toward an equilibrium level not only safeguard workers' employment but also prevent their exploitation. The attractiveness of such a theory should be readily apparent. Note, as well, that it offers no room for unions or collective bargaining to play a useful role, except in cases of monopolistic employer exploitation.

The theory applies more to *long-run tendencies* than to immediate or short-term wage determination. Wages move toward the value of the marginal product, but only if all the various influences that affect the labor market are free fully to work themselves out.[1] Although wages paid by any particular firm at any one time may not actually equal the marginal productivity of workers, they probably do fluctuate around it, according to those who espouse the theory. The discrepancies between wages and the marginal value product would set up pressures, according to the theory, and in time would bend the wages in the appropriate direction. Thus, though the theory does not predict wages with mathematical precision, it indicates the direction and strength of the major influences that play upon them.[2]

The Realism of the Theory

The marginal productivity theory may have been more valued in the nineteenth century when it was first elaborated than in more recent years. Some of its underlying assumptions were closer to being descriptions of the economic system than they were abstractions of it. The work force at the turn of the century, for example, was occupationally and in schooling far more homogeneous than today's. Many workers could move from one job to another at little cost to their own investment in education and training. Unskilled or less-skilled workers were relatively more numerous and perhaps more easily substitutable for each other. Insofar as employers used them in jobs with minimal skill requirements, they could be dismissed and hired at little cost to the firm.

Even if the assumptions of the theory have become less realistic over the years, economists still use them. Theories are cast aside not because of their weaknesses or limitations but only when a better theory is available—and we have none yet. In addition, the marginal productivity theory is an important part of a wider theory of the *price system,* or, what amounts to the same thing, the theory of *general* economic equilibrium. According to its tenets, wages are but one form of price. Price is not only the payments for purchased goods but also the charge for the services of labor or capital and the use of land or raw materials. Some economists would add the return from the services rendered

---

[1]Albert Rees pointed out that employers do not explicitly calculate the marginal product of their workers, and in their intuitive estimations may only correctly identify an average, leaving room for both higher and lower wage rates at any particular time: "It should not be imagined that employers make explicit estimates of marginal product every time they hire a worker. Of course they do not. Most employers are not familiar with the term "marginal product." Yet they do make judgments about whether or not new employees are likely to be worth as much as they cost, and many describe their decisions in these terms, which comes to very much the same thing. . . . Millions of such decisions are made intuitively every day—fortunately, correctly in the great majority of cases." *The Economics of Work and Pay,* New York: Harper & Row, Publishers, Incorporated, 1973, p. 63.)

[2]Ronald G. Ehrenberg and Robert S. Smith explain: "Whether employers can verbalize the profit-maximization conditions or not, they must instinctively *know* them in order to survive in a competitive environment. Competition will "weed out" employers who are not good at generating profits, just as competition will weed out pool players who do not understand the intricacies of how speed, angles, and spin affect the motion of bodies through space. Yet one could canvas the pool halls of America and probably not find one player who can verbalize Newton's laws of motion!" (*Modern Labor Economics, Theory and Public Policy,* Glenview, Ill.: Scott, Foresman & Company, 1982, p. 56.)

by entrepreneurs as well. Since all these prices interrelate, a change in one leads to a change in others. The process by which prices in one sector of the economy, whether for finished goods or factor services (inputs), are established and maintained is dependent on the action of all other prices.

A simplified version of the relationship of competitive factor pricing to general equilibrium theory can be set forth in a series of propositions:

1 The demand for the factors of production, including labor, is derived, arising from the demand for goods and services. Product prices and factor prices are thus directly related, the latter made possible only by the former.

2 The factors of production are in various degrees effective substitutes for one another, so that the price for one factor, such as labor, cannot be determined independently of another factor, such as capital, which might substitute for it. An example might be employers installing laborsaving machinery because of the high cost of labor—the installation of a computer-controlled robot on the automobile assembly line.

3 Because the factors of production are substitutes for one another, the ratios of all factors' return to their marginal product will be equal in the long run.

4 Allowing the same assumptions used to support the marginal productivity theory, one may generalize about the long-run tendency of the system: Whatever the factor—land, labor, or capital—each unit of a given class will be paid a price equivalent to its marginal product, and that marginal product will be the same in all productive uses.

5 Under the same assumptions, the equilibrating process proceeds more or less automatically. Any deviations from long-run pricing quickly generate correcting counterpressures, arising from the competition for factors of production and from their long-range substitutability. Business will substitute a lower-priced marginal product of one factor for the higher-priced marginal product of another until the prices of all factors are proportional to their marginal products and no further gain is possible.

The Attractiveness of the Theory

The automatic, impersonal way in which wages and other prices are assertedly governed in a competitive price system is attractive to persons who are skeptical of the ability or efficiency of government officials to determine them. Thus there is an ideological component in the ardent defense of the system's theoretical validity. The price system presumably establishes an allocation of the factors of production among industries according to general consumer preference, given the distribution of income; it does so efficiently—at lowest cost—and also avoids control by any dominant social group. Furthermore, it requires little, or at least a minimum of, government intervention. The price system, of which the marginal productivity theory is but one facet, thus appears to achieve the organization of the economy along lines that promote economic efficiency and preserve the western political ideal of individual liberty.

Because the theory so powerfully argues for, and agrees with, values cherished by most Americans, one needs to guard against confusing the theory as an analysis of empirical events with the theory as a prescriptive doctrine. To maintain that the pricing system represents a kind of ideal while at the same time holding that it does not fully represent the forces at work in the society is a logical and consistent approach that quite a few economists take.

If, however, one asserts that the theory is descriptively valid, there is reason to question whether in fact it is, at least in a meaningful way for either public or private policy makers. The highly abstract nature of the theory is readily apparent, but that, in itself, is not sufficient reason for rejecting it. Theories are admittedly generalizations and as such must concentrate upon central tendencies. To say that the assumptions of a theory do not conform precisely to fact is to state only the obvious, not a defect. Legitimate objection may be raised only if there is reason to think that the assumptions stray far from the fact and are unrevealing of central tendencies.

Those economists who find little or nothing to commend in the wage policies of unions make their judgment in the belief that the central tendencies and long-run pressures generated by general equilibrium theories are realities. They conclude that equilibrating forces to bend wages in the direction of marginal productivity, even though it is a moving magnet. And these economists believe that insofar as collective bargaining or employers' personnel policies may distort the wage structure in the short run, they produce counteracting, corrective influences that secure their ultimate defeat. Or economists may consider the process in another way and view collective bargaining and corporate personnel policies as interferences with the equilibrium system, condemning them for their short-run mischief even if these effects are mitigated in time. These views, of course, are generated by the wishful or objectively derived belief that the assumptions of the general equilibrium analysis are tenable, useful characterizations of our society even though they are admittedly imperfect.

HICKS' RESTATEMENT OF THE THEORY

The marginal productivity theory received its first systematic exposition shortly before the turn of the century, though its antecedents may be traced back at least another half century. Fifty years ago, Professor J. R. Hicks introduced a recognizable modification of the theory. After observing the growing role of British labor unions and the rise of state-supported systems of unemployment compensation, he concluded that unions might raise wages above competitive levels with the consequence of lingering unemployment. As we have noted, the original theoretical formulation allowed for the possibility that excessive wage rates would cause unemployment. It went on to assert, though, that the unemployed would search for work and in competing with the employed would drive the wage rate back to normal levels.

To Hicks it was apparent not only that short-run unemployment could emerge, but also that long-run unemployment was a fact not to be ignored. He pointed out that long-run equilibrating forces might not be sufficient to lower wage rates to normal levels, and thus hard-core unemployment would and did present itself.[3] The unemployment would continue, in his opinion, until new inventions and increased capital accumulations raised the competitive wage rates to the level of the bargained rates. Only then would the unemployed be absorbed.

Hicks' restatement abandoned the notion that marginal productivity, with a given supply of labor, determined or regulated wages. Nevertheless, it still suggested a norm for wage settlement. Through marginal productivity the level of wages and the level of employment were functionally related to each other. Whatever the wage, employers would attempt to adjust employment so that the marginal product of labor equaled it. If unions or government—or even personnel managers for peculiar reasons—pushed wages above the competitive level, workers would suffer the unfortunate consequences of otherwise avoidable unemployment. Hicks warned that the worker "endeavors to protect himself, through Trade Unionism and the democratic State. But our examination of the effects of [wage] regulation has shown that this protection can rarely be adequate. Carried through to the end, it can only result in a great destruction of economic wealth."[4]

A Theory of Employment Rather than of Wages

Hicks' restatement (and Keynes' downward wage rigidity) provided for the firm a theory of employment.[5] Though wages may be fixed through collective bargaining, personnel policies, or government laws, employers will vary employment so that they roughly equate wages with workers' marginal productivity. Under some circumstances, adjustments of employment would be slow, whereas in others they would be fast; in either case, however, marginal productivity would guide the process. The more directly and immediately competitive pressures played upon the firm and its product market, the more quickly it would have to respond to the guidance of marginal productivity. A labor union might use its bargaining power to push the wage rate above the

---

[3]"Sticky" wages, that is, wages that displayed a downward rigidity, had long been noted. Neoclassical economists thought that they aggravated recessions and the resulting unemployment. Keynes observed wage rigidity and took it to be an exogenous but basic economic influence, to be accepted. It was for him an empirical generalization, "an institutional characteristic, which neither had nor needed a full theoretical explanation." (Arthur Okun, *Prices and Quantities, A Macroeconomic Analysis,* (Washington, D.C.: The Brookings Institution, 1981, p. 9.) The effect of wage rigidity was to cause unemployment when demand contracted; but Keynes did not believe that flexible wages would eliminate unemployment. Wage cuts could adversely affect expectations, dampening both investment and consumption, further depressing demand. See Richard Kahn, "Some Aspects of the Development of Keynes' Thought," *Journal of Economic Literature,* vol. 16, June 1978, pp. 553–555.

[4]Hicks, *The Theory of Wages,* p. 323.

[5]Albert Rees asserts, "The basic purpose of a theory of the demand for labor is to determine how much labor employers will want to employ at different rates. . . . Where wages are determined in the market . . . it becomes a major component of a theory of wage determination." (*The Economics of Work and Pay,* p. 57.)

competitive level and even to hold it there more or less indefinitely. But the consequence would be to induce the firm to cut back employment and production. Its former marginal return would fall below the new rate, making it unprofitable for it to hire as much labor as it had before. Because of diminishing returns, a smaller work force in combination with the same fixed capital would produce a higher marginal return—one that could be equated to the new, higher wage rate. The personnel office of a regulated firm (an electrical utility, for example) might grant high wages to its employees, but it would use fewer of them than if it operated in a more competitive setting. A union might successfully shield the wage rate from the competition of unorganized workers, but it could not shield all its members from the resulting loss of jobs.

Hicks' restatement makes two assumptions that need to be noted. First, it assumes that any given level of employment is uniquely associated with a particular wage. The relationship of the two variables in thus determinant. A change in one requires a change in the other. If the assumption is not valid, of course, changes in one variable will not bring associated changes in the other; no single wage may be normal for a particular employment. Indeterminateness in the relationship of wages and employment therefore will lessen the usefulness of the theory as an analytical tool. The greater its indeterminateness, the less its value as a norm as well.

The second assumption upon which Hicks' restatement rests is that firms tend to move toward a competitive equilibrium, adjusting wages or employment to marginal productivity in the long run. The effects of marginal productivity are thus likened to those of the sun upon our weather, as it seasonally moves from latitude to latitude. Surely, but almost imperceptibly, the sun brings the warmth of summer with it as it rises from the spring equinox to the solstice, whatever may be the daily and weekly variations.

The Indeterminate Relationship of Wages and Employment

There are good reasons to believe that, in the short run particularly, wages and employment are indeterminately related. For example, on the supply side, employment often appears to be not so much a function of wages as of the number of jobs available. When jobs become scarce, some workers simply leave the labor market and therefore apply no downward pressure upon wages. Younger workers may resume their studies, some workers may go back to unpaid occupations, and older workers may retire earlier than they would otherwise. When more jobs are open, these same kinds of workers may enter the labor market or stay in it, attracted not so much by higher wages as by the availability of work. Such behavior makes it possible for wages to remain the same even though employment changes quite radically.

The number of people who yearly enter and exit from jobs is very large and in some industries makes up a major portion of the labor force. In 1983, for example, of the 91 million full-time workers, 24 million worked only part of the year. Almost 20 percent of full-time construction and lumber workers in

TABLE 17
PERCENTAGE OF EMPLOYED AND UNEMPLOYED
PERSONS BY OCCUPATION, [a] 1950 AND 1980

	1950	1981
White collar		
Employed	37.5 (7.5)*	52.7 (16.4)*
Unemployed	19.4 (3.1)*	26.9 (5.7)*
Blue collar		
Employed	39.1	31.1
Unemployed	54.9	43.6
Service		
Employed	11.0	13.4
Unemployed	13.7	15.8

[a] data for farm workers not shown.
*Professional, technical and kindred workers.
Source: Manpower Report of the President, 1966, and Employment and Training Report of the President, 1982.

1982 were employed from 1 to 26 weeks; more than one out of six full-time entertainment and recreation employees worked less than half a year. Michael J. Piore explained that:

> to get people who are willing to accept the menial, low-wage jobs involved, one has to call upon groups with a marginal attachment to the labor market and these groups tend to have high rates of movement into and out of the labor force. . . . The groups are such that, with relatively little effort on the part of employers, it is possible to induce a large increase in the amount of labor they supply. At the same time, because of the character of the jobs to which they are confined, those members of groups who are already working constitute a reserve of people ready to move up to higher-level jobs. Thus, for practical purposes, there is an infinite supply of labor both for menial and for better-paying jobs. . . . In terms of conventional [wage] theory, which relies on the forces of supply and demand to set wage rates, these rates are indeterminate.[6]

In addition to the short-term indeterminacy on the supply side, there are forces on the demand side that encourage employers to decouple wages as short-term functions of marginal productivity and employment. Employers have shown an increasing tendency to treat more and more of their labor costs as quasi-fixed. They are reluctant to lay off white-collar workers as readily as they do blue-collar workers. The number and relative importance of the former in the labor force has increased greatly over the years and this trend may be expected to continue. (See Table 17.) The increase in employment has been most rapid among professional and technical workers, a group of employees who continues to experience the lowest rates of unemployment and layoffs in

[6]Michael J. Piore, *Unemployment and Inflation, Institutionalist and Structuralist Views*, White Plains, N.Y.: M. E. Sharpe, Inc., 1979, pp. 12–13.

business recessions. Thus the wages earned by such white-collar workers and the number of them employed may have little relationship to their marginal value product. Arthur Okun explained:

> [There] is a good reason for employers to operate with *lower* quit rates in a weak labor market, as they do in fact—rather than to trim wages enough to increase quit rates. . . . The firm may optimize by adopting a principle of keeping [its wage] . . . at its "normal" level (or path) in the face of disappointments in product demand that it views as temporary.
>
> Under these circumstances the firm may also find it optimal to keep workers on the job and keep paying them during a period of slack, even when the wage exceeds the current marginal revenue product of the workers. If the slack period is confidently expected by the firm to be very short in duration and if the goods produced by the firm are readily storable at low cost, these workers may be used to build up inventories in slack periods. But if there is considerable uncertainty about the possible duration of the slack and high costs of storage (including the impossibility of storing outputs that are services), output may be reduced. The firms may be able to assign the workers maintenance tasks like cleaning, repairing, and painting, or it may really keep them in a state of "on-the-job underemployment." . . . Many firms during slack periods will operate "off" their production function—with more workers than are technologically required to produce their output. On-the-job underemployment is therefore often optimal for the firm, and it is the source of the dent in productivity during recession and slack time.[7]

Contributing to the short-term indeterminate relationship of wages and employment to marginal productivity is the ambiguity of our concepts of wages and labor. The wage to which workers respond, for example, may be one thing (take-home pay), but the wage to which employers adjust employment may be quite different (labor costs, including training program; subsidized cafeterias; and work clothes). Changes in the demand and supply of labor are not easily related to any common wage unit in such a situation. Furthermore, the supply of labor in terms of productive units may change with no variations in wage rates. Workers may increase or decrease their productivity by considerable amounts, irrespective of wages, because of changes in morale, interests, or incentives. Whether their productivity in a particular firm is stable over time or only averages out over time is a poorly explored matter.

Competition is the force that drives wages and employment to adjust to marginal productivity. In the American economy, though, whole industries have been able to shelter themselves for long periods of time, with foreign imports of little consequence until recent years. Others, such as utilities, shipping, trucking, airlines, and telecommunications, long enjoyed regulation protecting them against the rigor of competition. Management in all those industries paid relatively high wages and may have employed fewer people than they might have under competitive conditions. Certainly when government deregulated trucking and airlines in the early 1980s, as competition increased in tele-

---

[7]Okun, *Prices and Quantities, A Macroeconomic Analysis*, p. 57.

communications with the breakup of AT&T, and when foreign imports took away significant portions of the auto and steel markets, compounding the recession losses, managements began to trim employment sharply. Many also sought—and won—concessions in wages and work rules. The forces of marginal productivity were present and effective once competitive influence began to outweigh the counterforces. Note, however, that those influences, and thus easily measured or predictable marginal productivity effects, had been kept at bay a long time.

Although the concept of the long run may give a usefulness to the marginal productivity theory, it does so by raising further doubts about the theory's relevance to many public policy issues and collective bargaining outcomes. One may point out not only that "in the long run we are all dead," as Keynes did, but more pertinently that in a dynamic, growing economy in which war expenditures, antidepression programs, and innovating industries continually introduce new economic forces and alter established institutions, the concept of the long run may be elusive and not particularly helpful. We may require a series of short-term adjustments to continually new or fluctuating situations. Marginal productivity may not produce any sure and predictable effects because its influence upon wages or employment may be continuously dissipated or transformed over time. It does not necessarily act with the sureness and unalterable purpose of the sun in its annual peregrinations back and forth across the equator. The long-run effects of marginal productivity can be known only as an extrapolation of the present into a future that may never arrive. Always moving off at a tangent from the expected long-run world, the real world may long postpone the consequences predicted by marginal theory—though, of course, it can produce new and unexpected problems.

For example, consider the various ways in which the Bureau of Labor Statistics reports wage changes. (See Tables 18 and 19.) Managers and unionists, employers and workers may respond to quite different "wages." Hourly earnings increased proportionately more than weekly earnings, but both are con-

TABLE 18
PERCENTAGE WAGE CHANGES, 1979 TO 1983
(PRIVATE, NONFARM SECTOR, PRODUCTION WORKERS)

	1979–80	1980–81	1981–82	1982–83
Average hourly earnings				
Current $	8.1	8.9	5.9	4.4
1977 $	−4.9	−1.2	0.0	1.4
Average weekly earnings				
Current $	6.9	8.5	4.7	5.0
1977 $	−5.8	−1.5	−1.2	1.9
Hourly earnings index				
Current $	9.0	9.1	13.7	4.6
1977 $	−4.0	−1.0	0.9	1.5

Source: Current Wage Developments, Bureau of Labor Statistics, November 1984, Table 1, p. 28.

TABLE 19
AVERAGE PERCENTAGE CHANGE IN WAGES PROVIDED
BY MAJOR COLLECTIVE BARGAINING SETTLEMENTS, ALL
INDUSTRIES, 1980 TO 1983

Compensation and wage adjustments	1980	1981	1982	1983
Compensation				
First year	10.4	10.2	3.2	3.4
Over life of contract	7.1	8.3	2.8	3.0
Wage				
First year	9.5	9.8	3.8	2.6
With COLA	8.0	8.0	2.2	1.9
Without COLA	11.7	10.6	7.0	3.3
Overlife of contract	7.1	7.9	3.6	2.8
With COLA	5.0	5.5	2.1	2.0
Without COLA	10.3	8.8	6.6	3.7

Source: Current Wage Development, Bureau of Labor Statistics, November 1984, table 15, p.40.

siderably below spendable weekly earnings, a variant of take-home pay. And when they are corrected for inflation and presented in constant dollars, workers' earnings are seen to have declined, not increased. Were there data on wage rates rather than just *earnings,*—which include overtime premiums, shift differentials, and incentives—there would be another set of wage figures to add uncertainty about which wage the various parties consider.

HUMAN CAPITAL AND JOB SEARCH: CHANGING THE ASSUMPTIONS OF THE THEORY

Economists have given up any attempt to explain short-run wages or unemployment in terms of marginal productivity (at a given supply), and thus they have abandoned a most critical and perhaps a decisive area of wage determination. They continue to recognize, though, that productivity is a broad and pervasive ingredient of wage changes for the whole economy. Increases in productivity allow wage setting to be a positive-sum game, one in which both producer and workers can gain; and perhaps even consumers may gain if prices drop and/or quality improves. Without productivity increases, some wages can rise (in real terms) only if others decline. But such recognition does not help economists predict or explain short-term wage changes and does not shed much light even on long-term wage determinations. The marginal productivity theory has simplified too much the process by which managers make business decisions and workers make job choices. It also assumes more rigorous economic constraints upon the demand for labor and simpler influences upon the supply of workers than the world of experience justifies.

In recent years economists have examined labor markets closely and concluded that two of the assumptions originally undergirding the marginal productivity theory of demand of labor so simplify that they distort and mislead. First, workers, even within a given skill class, are not nearly as homogeneous and substitutable as assumed; second, neither employers nor workers possess a knowledge of job rates and employment opportunities as complete and full as assumed.

Professors Theodore W. Schultz and Gary S. Becker called attention to the human capital investments that workers make in themselves (and that are made in them through the public educational system) and that employers make in them by way of both formal and informal on-the-job training.[8] (Human capital may also be improved through better health care or given increased value through migration, but we will not explore these here.) Once labor market analysis recognizes human capital investments in workers, it admits variation among workers and the cost to employers of selecting the particular workers needed.[9] In Okun's phrase, at least some managers wish "to buy quality of work rather than merely time on the job spent by interchangeable people."[10] They thus establish a variety of personnel practices, screening applicants, testing recruits with a tryout and training period, and rewarding employees who stay on.[11] They carry out such activities and maintain such programs at no small cost to their firms, thereby imposing a "toll" when they hire workers, thus accumulating an investment in those who stay on the job. Such a toll and investment help explain a good many features of typical wage systems of large corporate businesses. Furthermore, they provide a rationale for many personnel practices and wage payments that advocates of the original marginal productivity theory implied would appear only under union pressure, because of governmental demand, or in monopoly situations.

If managers find that by raising wages they can lower their quit rate and thereby reduce their toll costs and training investment expenses, they will be encouraged to do so, in proportion to those costs. The higher wages will also attract a larger supply of applicants than would otherwise be the case. Employers can economize on labor costs, however, if they pay a lower wage to entering workers than to those with more experience; and a lower wage, with a *believable* promise of higher wages later, can induce a self-selection of workers who are most likely to stay with the job and form a stable work force.

Such workers will reduce the toll costs and losses of the firm's investments

[8]T. W. Schultz, "Investment in Human Capital," *American Economic Review,* vol. 51, March 1961, pp. 1–17; Gary S. Becker, *Human Capital: A Theoretical and Empirical Analysis, with Special Reference to Education,* New York: National Bureau of Economic Research, 1964.

[9]A survey in 1964 found that 60 percent of American workers acquired all of their job skills through informal, casual on-the-job training. Two-thirds of college graduates reported that they had acquired their job skills in the same manner, with only 12 percent reporting formal training and special education as most helpful in acquiring skills. See *Formal Occupational Training of Adult Workers,* U.S. Department of Labor, Manpower Automation Research Monograph No. 2, 1964, pp. 3, 18, 20, 43.

[10]Okun, *Prices and Quantities, A Macroeconomic Analysis,* p. 62.

[11]Becker pointed out that in the traditional theory of labor demand, employers would be as willing to hire the same workers day after day as they would be to hire a different set of workers each day. Clearly, most large, complex firms could not operate with the casual labor force implied by the second option. See Becker, *Human Capital,* p. 21.

in trained workers. In the attempt to lower quit rates, reducing costs and losses, and yet attract an acceptable quantity and quality of applicants, managers must look to their firms' long-term reputation for providing steady, full-time employment. Managers may offer seniority rights and a variety of other fringe benefits that make long-term employment attractive to productive workers. Even without a union, such a strategy would make economic sense, given the toll costs of selection, hiring, and promotion, as well as the on-the-job training costs. As Okun pointed out, firms will also maintain wage rates in a time of depressed product demand and will delay layoffs (or proceed with them in inverse order of seniority). The economics of their human capital investments will induce them to pay careful attention to their reputations. Cutting wage rates whenever the labor market loosens up is not a wise or sure way to secure an able, productive labor force. Managers and employers must deal with the real problems of a nonhomogeneous work force and of job applicants who come with very different levels of abilities, skills, and tastes. Solutions to those problems often require wage policies quite far removed from those implied by the original marginal productivity theory.

Lack of Full Knowledge in Job Search

The second assumption of the original theory also often has little validity in fact; job applicants and workers looking for new employment do not always possess full knowledge of the labor market and its job rates. Even in exceedingly casual markets—for farm laborers (fruit pickers or weed pullers), for example, or dishwashers in restaurants of a large city—job applicants are not apt to know about all the jobs that are open and the pay they offer. Workers usually search for jobs and find them one at a time, sequentially having to make a decision to accept or reject. They must use such knowledge as they may have gleaned from the search, from friends and acquaintances, and from any public sources of information. They must temper their job knowledge with their guesses about the probability of future alternative opportunities and wages. The search model implies that equally qualified workers receive different rates of pay in equally pleasant jobs. Otherwise, no search would be needed; workers could with assurance take the first job that is offered. Thus at any one time wages tend to be dispersed, even if other characteristics are similar. The realities of the labor market allow for—indeed, present to both workers and employers—so many variables that wage setting leaves much room for indeterminacy.

Competition among Interdependent Groups

Arthur Okun analyzed the problematic and contingent influences that play upon the labor market and concluded:

> The world of employer-worker attachment creates a complex optimization problem for the firm's personnel management. The firm is not only required to minimize the wage costs of a given employment but also to develop effective mechanisms to pro-

mote and assess productivity, and to build a reputation that will both enhance the supply of willing applicants and hold down quit rates. Job seekers, in turn, must assess the relative attractiveness of job offers that differ in many dimensions. . . . The toll introduces enormous complications in reaching efficient solutions within the framework of the employment relationship.[12]

The current state of wage theory is hardly satisfactory, for it does not incorporate enough of the complexities with which both managers and workers must deal. Even relaxing the assumptions about homogeneity and the costs of information, as the human capital and search models do, only makes a start toward introducing into the theory the realities of modern social organization and wage-determining institutions.

The neoclassical economic system from which the theory of marginal productivity is derived is founded upon competitive individualism. Society is asserted to be merely a collection of individuals (or families, at most), each assiduously maximizing its own welfare. The overwhelming reality of modern industrial society, of course, is something quite different: Society is composed of large numbers of groups—firms, agencies, businesses, corporations, and unions—that both cooperate and contend with each other in many different ways. The members of the groups also cooperate and contend with each other in a multitude of various patterns. We perceive the various groups as individuals and fit them into our traditional theories at the danger of misleading ourselves. Large institutions rarely are but the shadow of an individual; centralized direction may be more apparent than real; and the harmony of interest among group members may be but an artifact of fierce struggle, tough negotiations, and barely gained compromises.

To focus upon the shadow and appearance may lead us to ignore the larger issues and the basic causal relationships. The fact is that our most interesting and significant problems involve the making of decisions where conflicts of interest must first be reconciled. Where two groups are interdependent, so that neither is functionally complete without the other, conflicting interests must be accommodated in making business decisions that affect both. Without accommodation, a decision reached by one is meaningless because it will not evoke from the other the cooperation necessary to carry on the business of the enterprise.[13]

DISCRETION IN WAGE DETERMINATION

In Chapters 7 and 8 we suggested that collective bargaining involves political (organizational) as well as economic activities. It involves two different polit-

---

[12]Okun, *Prices and Quantities, A Macroeconomic Analysis,* pp. 81, 83–84.

[13]After examining the current state of wage and employment theory, Arthur Okun concluded that economists had to look beyond simple economic relationships to explain, let alone predict, what goes on. Both firms and workers have incentives to develop and maintain relationships that lessen or overcome distrust. If they do not, they necessarily will forego productivity gains in which both can share.

ical systems—unions and management—in a common decision-making process. When two such groups are joined in a single enterprise, it is unlikely that they can accommodate their various interests by any simple, textbook equating marginal product and wages even in the long run. If they do equate them, the process will have been a complicated and indirect one. First, neither party realizes marginal productivity as an immediate reality in its own right. The parties do not measure it, record its changes, or analyze it, except as it may influence the variables of prices, profits, wages, outputs, and inputs about which they collect information. Second, each party must incorporate in its decisions the manifold noneconomic considerations that demand some form of expression. In collective bargaining the parties are not simply making a contract in the sense that an agreement may *or may not* be reached or that mutual accommodation may *or may not* be forthcoming. Functional interdependence assures that some decision *must* be jointly reached if the business of production is to go forward at all.

If intergroup processes such as collective bargaining are admitted as ways through which business decisions are made, at least in part, then it is likely that the personification of either the union or the firm and the assignment of unified personal interests to either will have misleading results. The collective method of wage determination would appear to invalidate or at least modify the conclusions of a theory that rests on the assumption that an individual employer enters into a personal contractual relationship with individual workers, with either party free to seek a better contract elsewhere. The principle of marginalism *may* have its impact on one or the other party to the joint decision-making machinery, depending upon the validity of the maximizing principle, but this is something quite removed from a general theory of wages.

Collective bargaining cannot produce decisions different from those achieved through individual bargaining if economic forces allow no discretion. If the economic system is competitive enough to compel unions and management to conform to its requirements on pain of reduced profits, unemployment, or both, collective bargaining and individual bargaining are equally constrained. Insofar as competition is not wholly limiting, however, and the economic environment contains areas of permissiveness, the parties to collective bargaining enjoy some discretion of making their decisions. They are free to abide by standards other than those of the rigorously competitive market. They may secure special advantage for themselves, finding that in their situation wages and employment have no unique relationship. As noted, the value of the division and specialization of labor and of other economies of scale in production, financing, and risk pooling create enormous problems for both workers and managers trying to secure the greatest efficiencies in production. Working together and with trust, unions and managers may be able to solve many of them, but seldom in straightforward or easily predictable ways. Economists have also long pointed out that oligopoly, product differentiation, and price leadership provide situations of economic indeterminateness favorable to the political play of collective bargaining.

Unionist Dislike of Market Competition

Despite American unions' formal support of antimonopoly policies, unions have not favored increased competition in business. When relieved of inexorable market pressures, businesses are in a position to make concessions in collective negotiations that otherwise they might not be able to make. Unions can enter into a bargaining relationship with management on many matters that otherwise would be beyond the control of either, only because systematic competition does not compel a certain kind of decision. Unions often help develop monopolistic arrangements among businesses unable to secure them alone. Every metropolitan area has its organizations of building-trades contractors, dry cleaners, laundries, trucking firms, barbers, and so on, supported by the labor unions, who realize the damaging effect on wage and working standards of excessive competition from those who compose the local industry. Unionists want to avoid any competition that would lead to price-cutting and which might, by chain reaction, spread throughout the trade and ultimately threaten a general reduction in union wage standards.

When unions have organized employers on a market-area basis, they can then negotiate with associated employers terms that otherwise would have been impossible. Each employer may now accept the terms because all other employers accept them. In some instances unions have undertaken to police their agreements by refusing to provide workers for those who cut prices as well as those who cut wages, insisting on conformity to some general scale of prices that is sufficient to keep average employers in business and permit them to adhere to union standards of wages and working conditions.

Where individual firms are partially freed from the constraint of market pressures, the union can play a greater role in the making of business decisions. Where individual firms are strongly competitive, the union can play its role only by first organizing the industry so that it may bargain as a unit. The possibility of bargaining indicates an area of discretion. The degree of competition in the product market is inversely related to the elasticity of demand for the product. A high degree of elasticity in the demand for a product indicates the availability of excellent substitutes; perfect elasticity indicates the availability of perfect substitutes—identical products. To the degree that price competition recedes and discretion over price enters, there is an increasing inelasticity of demand for the product. Where such inelasticity exists, higher wages can, if necessary, be accommodated by higher prices. Monopolistic elements such as the differentiation of products, the oligopolizing of competition, and the welding of competitive units into an industry organization all contribute to a reduced availability of substitutes, an increased inelasticity of demand for the product, and a greater degree of control over price.

Union leaders who represent members in regulated industries certainly believe that they and their members can do better for themselves when competition is restrained by government regulation. As Congress moved to deregulate the airlines, trucking, bus transportation, and railroads in the late seventies and early eighties and looked forward to deregulating communications, banking, insurance, health care, and utilities, the affected unions joined with the immediately concerned industry management to protest strongly. Whether regulation allows higher wages—at the expense of consumers—or permits other nonwage benefits such as stability and reduction of risk for both management and unions is not clear. It may result in both. In some cases unionized workers may well win gains greater than those in comparable nonunion firms or occupations; in other cases they appear not to win more.[14] The less union leaders and managers must contend with the impersonal, economic forces of competition, the better they seem to like the situation. The relative insulation of those from organizational influence and political manipulation may limit managers' and union leaders' sense of control and narrow their range of discretion, making their decisions more difficult and limiting the trade-offs available to them. It is hardly surprising that the UAW strongly supports any government policy that limits the importation and competition of Japanese automobiles. It supports quotas on imports, has lobbied hard for a "local content" act (autos sold in the United States would have to have a certain percentage of American-made parts), and favors Japanese investments in U.S. production facilities. The auto manufacturers join the union in favoring the first two protective measures.

But insofar as the self-equilibrating economic forces do not fully determine wages, set prices, or allocate the factors of production and to the degree that government attempts to channel such forces, discretionary decision making is admitted. The decision makers and bargainers, then, need some other standards or guides. If we cannot, or do not choose to, rely upon competitive market forces to provide those guides, we must establish alternatives of a kind compatible with a democratic society.

Many economists are skeptical that market processes and standards can be relied upon to provide socially viable wages and employment. Their observations and experiences of discrimination for reasons of race, sex, age, religion, physical handicap, or sexual preference persuade them that economic variables simply do not relate to each other in unambiguous ways and certainly not in ways that assure the most productive, efficient use of workers. Although prices and wages continue as important forces in our society, not all people are satisfied that the price *system* satisfies our needs as a community; its means of economic control constrains some arbitrarily and it excludes too many from its full benefits. They argue that in our evolving culture, many economic relationships come into existence and are perpetuated or are allowed to disintegrate for reasons other than price. The forces operating in the economy are many; they are not all traceable to the market. Which forces are to be encouraged, sublimated, or subdued, by whom, using what methods? These are matters of fierce public debate and agonizing private decision.

---

[14]Econometric studies have come up with varying answers, but their analyses have examined different variables, making conclusions difficult. See Ronald G. Ehrenberg, *The Regulatory Process and Labor Earnings,* New York: Academic Press, Inc., 1979, chap. 1, pp. 1–34, for a recent survey of a number of the studies.

THE VALUES UNDERLYING WAGE STANDARDS

Let us probe deeper into the problem of standards of wage determination and for the allocation of scarce resources (another problem of traditional and continuing concern to economists). How can laborers, workers, and employees—all key factors of production—distribute themselves among the variety of occupations, industries, and locations in ways that generally satisfy them and are socially accepted? In liberal western society, economists have usually assumed that the standard of distribution (allocation) should be informed by the effective demand of the consuming public. That standard should both allow and encourage people to produce the goods and services that consumers effectively choose in the marketplace. Goods from computers to motorbikes and services from psychiatric counseling to televised situation comedies should be provided in the proportions that consumers wish, given their distribution of income. As tastes change, the relative supplies of goods and services should likewise change, requiring a transfer of workers from one line of production to another. Economists have thus seen the allocation problem as one of making changes or transfers of the factors of production in accordance with the market-effective desires of the consuming public.

In the neoclassical theoretical system, change could and should take place largely in accordance with the principle of marginal productivity, examined above. If that principle were followed throughout the economy, workers would shift themselves between occupations, industries, and regions in a manner ultimately determined by consumer preferences in products. An increased demand for a particular product would raise the price of that product, permitting the payment of higher wages to attract more workers so that output could be increased. As more workers competed for the favored jobs and as output rose (lowering the marginal value product), both the price of the product and the wages of those producing it would recede from their temporary high levels. Meanwhile, since demand had shifted away from other products, their prices would tend to decline, lowering the marginal value product. If wages were maintained, the employers would have to cut back employment and output. With a smaller output to satisfy existing demand, prices would tend to rise to their former levels, raising the marginal value product, allowing firms to increase employment and output.

With increased employment, workers would be attracted to the firms rather than given an incentive to look for work elsewhere. Movement of workers away from those industries where demand had lessened to those where it had increased would go on as long as consumers continued to shift their demand and thus change the marginal value product. In this way, consumers' choice would have effected a shift in the allocation of resources; changing demand leads to price changes. The price changes affect producers' outputs, which in turn affect their need for labor. Changes in the demand for labor influence the supply of workers, attracting some to other occupations and pushing others away from jobs once held.

Note that this analysis of market-driven allocation presumes a good deal of price and wage flexibility; a rapid response by producers who are able to raise and lower output; and a mobile, informed, and responsive work force. Employers and employees are assumed to be able and willing to shift people in jobs and occupations and adjust wages up or down with no untoward effects upon organizational arrangements, long-term commitments, or personal motivations; more likely, the theory assumes there is no structure of relationships to be seriously distorted. It analyzes a world of individuals, not corporate organizations. Workers, producers, and consumers are conceived as people with no fixed relationships, whose primary interests are in quickly adjusting to the impersonal tides and currents of the marketplace, pursuing only those values that they can express through it.

Individual Freedom and Efficiency

Economists generally recognize two values well served by the market: individual freedom and efficiency in allocation of resources and production.[15] Efficiency is the value upon which most economists rest their case.[16] Efficient allocation, in accordance with consumer preference, can be assumed only if market forces remain beyond the control of any producer or consumer. The power of any group to control markets is a form of monopoly, capable of distorting prices and inducing consumers to alter their buying in line with the new, distorted prices. Production then no longer conforms to the originally

---

[15]Individual freedom in the market is greatly affected by one's income, of course. Thus the level and distribution of income as well as the market are significant determinants of it. Milton Friedman asserts that the liberalism of a capitalistic economy emphasizes "freedom as the ultimate goal"(*Capitalism and Freedom,* Chicago: The University of Chicago Press, 1962, p. 5); and appears to favor at least a minimal income guarantee for all or a reasonably equitable distribution of income. Arthur Okun is much less sure that capitalism is based on or assures freedom. The primary value it allows is efficiency. (Okun, *Equality and Efficiency,* Washington, D.C.: The Brookings Institution, 1975, pp. 35–61).

[16]See Thomas C. Schelling, "Economic Reasoning and the Ethics of Policy," *The Public Interest,* Summer 1981, pp. 37–61. He argues that economists can contribute best to policy by offering efficient solutions to problems, allowing policy makers to devise additional solutions that promote other values. He assumes that policy makers will allow economists first opportunity to identify the problem and to devise their solution, around which the other solutions will be crafted. Frank H. Knight, the eminent economic philosopher, long ago warned, however, that "it is impossible to form any concept of 'social efficiency' in the absence of some general measure of value. Even in physics and engineering, 'efficiency' is strictly a value category; there is no such thing as mechnical efficiency. It follows from the fundamental laws of the indestructibility of matter and of energy that whatever goes into any apparatus or process comes out *in some form.* In purely mechanical terms, all efficiencies would be equal to one hundred per cent. . . . When more than one form of useful output (or costly input) is involved, the necessity arises for having a measure of usefulness, of value, *before* efficiency can be discussed." [Second italics added.] (Frank H. Knight, "The Ethics of Competition," *Quarterly Journal of Economics,* vol. 37, 1923, pp. 579, 580). Thus economists who espouse the efficiences the competitive market system tout a derived value and may rest their case upon an almost simpleminded original value, as Okun does explicitly: "more is better, insofar as the 'more' consists of items that people want to buy." (Okun, *Prices and Quantities, A Macroeconomic Analysis,* p. 2.)

given consumer preferences, for they are now bent by monopolistic influences. The principle of efficient allocation of resources, the basis for maximum consumer satisfaction, is violated.

Discretion in setting wages (and prices), whether because of varying degrees of monopolistic power, government regulation, or indeterminacy in the relationship of wages and marginal product, may well deny the distribution of labor judged optimum by the standards of the competitive market. We know, however, that in one way or another producers in almost every industry seek, and most enjoy, such discretion.[17] We are less concerned here with the general business aspects of the matter, though, than with the activities of unions and corporate personnel departments. The assiduous, omnipresent efforts of business managers as well as unionists to gain some form of protection against the risks, uncertainties, and constant change of the competitive marketplace suggest that both hold to values other than efficiency and judge their efforts by standards different from those of the market. Customarily, economists have tended to characterize unions as invidious wielders of monopolistic power, pushing up wages rates, disturbing the structure of competitive market prices, and doing violence to the principle that workers, like all factors of production, should allocate themselves among jobs on the basis of what society, in its consumer capacity, most wishes—that is, efficiently. The characterization also applies, in large part, to many large employing corporations. After all, they maintain wage rates and establish conditions of work not markedly different from those sought by union negotiators. Economists have been laggard in recognizing the extent to which managers use and enjoy discretionary wage setting, even under nonunion conditions. As noted earlier, however, they have long recognized the prevalence of wage rigidity, an economic feature not easily correlated with, or limited to, unionized firms.

A sense of realism requires us to accept the elements of market control and the presence of indeterminacy in wage setting, which allow both managers and unionists to bring to bear upon their decision making values and standards not encompassed by market theory. They cannot rely upon competitive pricing to set a precise wage or even to secure an exact allocation of resources according to the economists' standard. The development and use by corporate managers

---

[17]Consider what an expert in job evaluation and in company pay policies concludes: "Markets do play a significant role in establishing job pay rates and in allocating employees to jobs where needed. At the same time, however, markets operate imperfectly, or at least the operation of the market is not well communicated to the participants. Constraints on both employers and employees exist so that markets provide little direct information about appropriate wage levels and differentials for many jobs. As a result, administrative decisions are also a significant part of wage determination (though not just at the discretion of the employer, since unions and government also share authority regarding pay setting).... The market operates less efficiently even for key jobs [directly related to and affected by market forces] than one might predict given a theoretical perspective.... Employees weigh many factors besides wages in their decision to join, and especially their decision to leave, organizations.... As a consequence, the relationship between wage levels and employment is often tenuous." [Donald P. Schwab, "Job Evaluation and Pay Setting: Concepts and Practices," in E. Robert Livernash (ed.), *Comparable Worth, Issues and Alternatives,* Washington, D.C.: Equal Employment Advisory Council, 1980, pp. 54–55.]

of their complex personnel policies, job evaluations, and wage structures, as well as public acceptance of unions and their use of collective bargaining in helping to set wages, imply at least a partial abandonment of the economic standard of allocating economic resources by reference to consumer wants. While economists may continue to hold out the standard of market contingency as a norm or as a measure of the trade-off costs of the application of other standards, it is not often perceived as an operational standard, one by which labor allocations are made or wages set.

What standards are available to either managers or union negotiators? Are there none upon which the parties can agree? Must both wages and employment be subject to the chance decision of bargaining power, whim or expediency? Or are commonly recognized and accepted standards available to the parties to guide them within market constraints? If we are to answer these questions, we must understand why they arise in the first place. The appearance of large employing organizations with complex internal relationships, along with the development of human capital investments through training and schooling, have created labor markets considerably removed from the individualistic, flexible, competitive markets postulated by economic theory. This may be the immediate answer.

The Search for Justice

Modern industrial societies certainly have created large organizations in pursuit of market efficiency, and they may have encouraged specialization by expanding training and school opportunities for similar reasons. But it is doubtful that the pursuit of efficiency alone explains either action. Both managers and employees respond to other values as they go about determining wages and filling job openings.

A competitive market may be efficient, but it offers no sense of justice. "According to Friedrick von Hayek [Nobel laureate economist] (and others) 'it is meaningless to describe the manner in which the market distributes the good things of this world among particular people as just or unjust.' "[18] Traditionally, economists have been content to imply that the production of market value was morally meritorious. John Bates Clark, a leading American economist at the turn of the century, argued that the free, competitive market offered "a certain rough justice"; but justice has not been assured, and it has been all too rough to be accepted by most Americans. They have usually sought to introduce a sense of equity and fairness—forms of justice—and thus modify

---

[18]Quoted in Ernest van den Haag, "Economics Is Not Enough—Notes on the Anticapitalist Spirit," *The Public Interest,* Fall 1976, p. 109. Elsewhere Von Hayek has written, "in a free society, it is neither desirable nor practicable that material rewards should be made generally to correspond to what men recognize as merit and . . . it is an essential characteristic of a free society that an individual's position should not necessarily depend on the view that his fellows hold about the merit he has acquired. . . . " (Quoted by Irving Kristol, " 'When virtue loses all her loveliness'— some reflections on capitalism and 'the free society,' " *The Public Interest,* Fall 1970, p. 6.)

competitive outcomes. Laborers have not been alone in this seeking. Small business proprietors strongly supported fair-trade laws in the thirties to protect their interests, for example, and only in recent years have the courts struck them down. The major steel producers maintain, as Bethelem Steel did, that:

> America's system of free enterprise is based on the concept of *fair* competition. That's what free enterprise is all about. Based on fair competition and independent action, it affords any group of investors the opportunity to succeed, or to fail.[19]

In the producers' view, fair competition would allow American firms to continue usual production and sales without having to meet the lower prices of imported steel from foreign companies whose technology surpassed theirs.

Many and perhaps most American business managers would agree with Bethlehem that free enterprise is indeed based on *fair,* not free, competition. Although the efficiency of the market is a desirable value and a goal worth striving for, it is not the only value at stake but one goal of several worth pursuing. In supporting fair trade or fair competition, neither small retailers nor the giant steel firms argued for market efficiency. Indeed they could not, for the fairness they promote promises higher prices for consumers. They sought to maintain their position, status, and continued existence despite competitive pressures and the demands of consumers; they sought protection from the pressure of the competitive market toward greater efficiency and lower prices. Seeking such protection does not mean that they necessarily will secure it. It does indicate, though, that managers' motivations may well be more complex than those regularly assumed by economic theory. That American business managers defend their interests and appeal to fairness as a standard of judgment is no more surprising than the same defense made by workers and union leaders of their interests. People are not apt to legitimate any system, whether a whole economy or a company organization, if it is perceived as unjust. No matter how productive or efficient it may be, it will be unacceptable if power, privilege, and rights are not sanctioned by morally meaningful criteria.

In exploring the matter of values that underlie wage standards, it is necessary to take specific cognizance of two basic assumptions of those who advocate competitive pricing. First, in economic affairs efficient allocation is the primary goal of the parties involved and the best outcome; second, alternative goals are not only secondary but also inferior. Pursuit of them results in a less productive, therefore less desirable, outcome than pursuing efficiency. In analyzing labor issues, economists usually assume that workers will be motivated to change jobs and locations if there are possibilities of improving their wages and other economic compensation; differences in wage levels will stimulate worker movement. They also assume that unions have come into existence to exploit their and the workers' position in the market, gaining special advantage for themselves even at the expense of general market or firm efficiency. It is because these two assumptions are unsatisfactory *as generalizations* that the matter of wage standards remains problematic.

---

[19]From an advertisement in *The New York Times,* Aug. 27, 1980, p. D3.

Economists never imagined, of course, that individuals in the market system should be guided exclusively by a concern for efficiency. It has been regarded as a value of relative importance, but its primary and normative use are vital in, and characteristic of, a capitalistic society. Despite some qualifications, efficiency undergirds economic theory *as though* it were the only value by which activities and policies can be measured. The justification for such an approach is that it permits a more precise and conclusive system of deductive theory and, at the same time, can be supported as an approximation to reality in the market-enterprise countries of the world.

Perhaps because the possibility of making determinate economic analyses seems dependent upon a system with a single value and a dominant objective, there has been reluctance among economists to incorporate into their theory the multiple values people bring to the marketplace and the variety of objectives they seek. Such incorporation would present an indeterminate theory, one with several answers and various standards by which one could judge economic activities. In fact people do bring to work and jobs various values, objectives, and standards, which complement, reinforce, and conflict with each other in bewildering ways. They are not at all easy to sort out, of course, but attempts to do so probably bring us closer to understanding and appreciating the reality with which managers, unionists, and public policy makers must deal than the traditional, simplifying assumptions of economics.

The Inadequacy of Market Standards for Both Managers and Employees

It is significant that managers as well as employees and union representatives regularly appeal to wage standards and values other than those offered by the market or recognized by economists in their theoretical formulations. Donald P. Schwab, a student of personnel practices, argues that market forces simply do not reach all jobs and positions in large modern corporations, and thus managers must extrapolate wages and other conditions of work from those that are reached. Their extrapolation is carried out with the realization that:

> Organizations have multiple pay objectives. Not only do they seek to attract, but also to maintain, motivate, and satisfy their work force. Since these objectives often have low interrelationships, a variety of pay policies and procedures are developed.[20]

He had argued that:

> It is not surprising, therefore, that organizations develop and implement a variety of pay procedures to help accomplish these multiple objectives. Merit raises, fringe benefits, job evaluation, payment for seniority and wage surveys are illustrative. Some are designed to encourage participation, while others are aimed at motivating performance. Still others are expected to satisfy employees. Some have a direct impact on jobs and hence apply to all employees on those jobs; others have their major

---

[20]Schwab, "Job Evaluation and Pay Setting: Concepts and Practices," in Livernash, *Comparable Worth, Issues and Alternatives,* p. 74.

impact on individuals, independent of jobs. These varied policies are implemented within a political as well as an economic environment.[21]

In addition to judging wages and compensation by the market standard of efficiency, personnel and industrial relations managers evaluate their policies and practices for consistency, orderliness, understandability, and acceptability. Such standards reflect a concern for, and attention to, the value of fairness, equity, and other such variants of justice.

Arthur Okun, in attempting to explain worker and manager behavior that affects the movements of wages and employments, concluded that both are invoked in a relationship more complex than can be explained by the simplified assumptions of traditional economic theory. He explained:

> Firms and workers have incentives to establish and to maintain [their] . . . relationships by mechanisms that overcome distrust. If neither explicit nor implicit contracts could be developed that curbed the role of distrust, firms would be obliged to pursue the strategy of hiring casual workers; in that event, they and the whole society would forego productivity increments that come from screening, trying out, training, and rewarding. The development of rules and conventions for fair play become an essential element in the pursuit of efficiency. In this dimension, equity and efficiency are tied together rather than traded off against each other.[22]

Since Okun believes that managers of nonunion firms are as likely as are union leaders, workers, and managers of union firms to be interested in fair play and equity, they are values and objectives that can be rationally entertained. While Okun recognized elsewhere the possibility of trade-offs between forms of equity and efficiency, he reminds us not to forget that there exists the possibility of complementarity between them. The realization of that possibility will require approaches to wage setting and analyses of industrial relations that go considerably beyond the ambits of conventional economic theory and its standards of value.

UNIONS AND WAGE STANDARDS

Efficient allocation of resources in accordance with consumer demand is a key assumption of economic theory. We may conclude, however, that as a description of the values held by those in the market or as a representation of their activities, it is subject to challenge. We have indicated that managers, speaking for their organizations, espouse values and pursue objectives more complex than those postulated by economics. It seems reasonable that union leaders, acting on behalf of their organizations, would hold values and seek goals at least as mixed as those of managers. We now seek to examine directly the equity values that unions express and the ways in which they attempt to rec-

[21]Ibid., p. 71.
[22]Okun, *Prices and Quantities, A Macroeconomic Analysis,* pp. 84–85.

oncile the sometimes conflicting and at other times complementing goals of efficiency and fairness.

In recalling the subject matter of collective bargaining, already examined in Chapter 4, we note that matters discussed at the negotiating table deal with more than wages and the returns of productivity. Many of them appear to be concerned with equity between workers and fairness in apportioning rights. In particular, the unions' high regard for protective rules is clear; dismissal, temporary loss of job, recall, and promotion must follow set procedures, avoiding arbitrary action and surprise. *Due process* is held to be important in and of itself, a form of justice. The desire to dispose of grievances in an orderly and fair manner, appealing for settlement to those not immediately involved in the dispute, is certainly rooted in a sense of justice as well. The workers' insistence that employers explicitly recognize their union representatives and that they be treated as equals indicates their interests in dignity.

Equity as a Standard

Even when workers seek through their unions what appear to be purely economic gains—wage increases and adjustments to pay—they usually are striving for equitable benefits as well. Work groups and union shopleaders frequently set production (and earning) limits to protect older members from too fast a work pace. In the eyes of the workers, such a limit may also contribute to their job security by avoiding high inventories that might induce layoffs. Union leaders often seek piece-rate adjustments, not just because workers want higher earnings or a more easily achieved base rate, but also because they seek a fair and comparable rate. The slogan "equal pay for equal work," given legal force and pertinency in the Equal Pay Act of 1963,[23] was not merely a demand for higher pay, but a cry against employers' discriminatory administration of wages and against favoritism. However opportunistically both parties use the standards of equity, fairness, and comparability, each finds them appealing and significant. Especially important, as Okun noted, is the use of them by employers who *do not* bargain with unions. Managers sometimes use them with success to resist rate improvements and sometimes to argue for pay cuts. For such reasons one may conclude that workers organize unions and use collective bargaining to gain more than the largest economic gain. As with the members individually and with employers, a complex of motivating factors appear to lie behind unions' behavior.

Why Workers Join Unions

A second approach to explain union organization and its goals draws on theories that have been advanced by students of labor unions in the United States. Here we present but the briefest of summary statements.

---

[23]*Fair Labor Standards Act,* 29 U.S.C. Sec. 206(d).

John R. Commons set forth the thesis that unions were responses to changes in economic conditions, not to class needs or psychological pressures. In this country they were a response to the widening of product markets. That widening led to a separation of interests between journeymen and employers.[24] In local community markets, the interests of the two were nearly parallel. They usually worked side by side; they experienced the same satisfactions in a quality product; immediately felt social pressures served to maintain a reasonable standard for both prices and wages; and journeymen had grounds for entertaining the expectation of graduating to employer status. As markets expanded so that an enterprise sold not only locally but also within a region and then in the national market, however, the financial and employing functions became separated; and competition for sales pressed downward on prices, with lower prices made possible through downward pressure on wages. Employees were thus forced to organize as a group with interests opposed to those of their employer, that is, as an anticompetitive force.

Selig Perlman explained the rise of the labor movement on the ground that workers were motivated by a "scarcity consciousness"—an awareness of the scarcity of the economic goods of life and of the scarcity of jobs making possible the purchase of those goods.[25] They banded together in unions to secure a kind of job control, allowing them a greater sense of security in the midst of scarcity.

Carleton Parker, following a different line of analysis, concluded that worker organization arose as an aggressive reaction to the frustration of deep-rooted instincts that was brought about by modern industrial methods.[26]

Robert Hoxie denied any single causal explanation of the formation of unions but maintained that the whole complex of environmental and personal influences in a particular setting provided the formative forces. Such influences varied from situation to situation.[27]

The historian Frank Tannenbaum emphasized worker reaction to the atomism of society characterizing the nineteenth century. The extreme individualistic philosophy, he wrote, looked upon every worker as a discrete economic unit, unrelated to fellow workers in any significant way. It disregarded the fundamental social grouping of people around their work, which trade unions came into existence to protect.[28]

These capsule summaries, although they do an injustice to the careful elaboration of the scholars and do not permit an examination of the possibility of the integration of their ideas, serve to suggest that unions have appeared in this

---

[24]Commons, "American Shoemakers: A Sketch of Industrial Evolution, 1648–1895," pp. 39–84; reproduced in Commons et al., *Documentary History of American Industrial Society,* vol. 3, pp. 18–58.

[25]Perlman, *A Theory of the Labor Movement.*

[26]Carleton Parker, *The Casual Laborer,* New York: Harcourt, Brace & World, Inc., 1920.

[27]Hoxie, *Trade Unionism in the United States.*

[28]Frank Tannenbaum, *The Labor Movement: Its Conservative Functions and Social Consequences,* New York: G. P. Putnam's Sons, 1921. He restated his thesis in "The Social Function of Trade Unionism," *Political Science Quarterly,* vol. 62, 1947, pp. 161–182.

country as responses to both economic and noneconomic values and goals of their members. There appears to be little basis for believing that an economic motive has been singled out of the whole range of human and worker values and that unions have operated on that level alone. Moreover, in those theories that stressed market activities, as Commons' did, organization is said to have arisen not from an intent to make the most of them but rather from a desire to ameliorate their effects. When economists argue that unions have no purpose but to gain economically from a favored position in the market, they are stating one of the basic assumptions of competitive pricing theory rather than a conclusion based on obtainable evidence.[29]

Mixed Values as Standards

We are now prepared to gather together the fruits of this digression on worker and organizational values. The evidence strongly suggests that both employees and the unions they form are significantly responsive to other than economic values and goals. Also important is the drive to ensure a sense of legitimacy— of fairness and equity—between workers and their jobs, between workers and each other, and between workers and management in their industrial societies.

Economists consider fundamental the values assumed in the competitive model because its efficient operation assures the satisfaction of consumer wants, which was the very reason for the economy's existence. Consumer wants are viewed as unlimited. In an exchange economy, the degree of their satisfaction is dependent on purchasing power, which in turn is dependent upon the payments to the factors—wages, in the case of workers. The desire for wages is therefore presumed to be directly related to the desire for consumer satisfaction. Since the latter was considered to be unlimited, the former was viewed in the same light. The desire for economic gain out of an efficient and efficiency-directed system is thus thought to be dominant.

The classical concept of real costs had taught that work was the price that must be paid for the real utilities that came with consumption. Values were thus derived not from the productive process but from consuming the fruits of that process. The more efficient production was, the more there was to be consumed. Efficiency thus was not merely a prime, but the primary value of economics. Consumption became the end; it was the only good. The system allocated factors according to the principle of obtaining maximum consumer satisfaction. The means by which labor was to be allocated was the money wage, which derived its motivating power from its exchange value.

What we discover, however, is that the system is partial and incomplete in resting on the premise that consumption is the only purpose of the economy.

---

[29]Indeed, only one of the above-mentioned theories of the American labor movement suggests that an effort to satisfy the pecuniary drive through systematic exploitation has been a motive for union organization. Hoxie, who believed that unions must be explained individually and not as a movement, recognized that from time to time in isolated unions such exploitative efforts might dominate, though by no means did he consider this representative of unions as a whole.

Workers and union leaders, even as employers and business managers, serve other purposes as well. They are not solely interested in satisfying consumer wants; they find satisfaction beyond efficiency gains in the process of production and in enjoyment of the job and the worker society. These, as well as consuming, are important parts of living. The workers' interests and values as producers must therefore be considered along with their interests as consumers.[30]

CONCLUSION

When the problem is put in this way, it becomes clearer why it is impossible to specify a particular value as the basis for wage setting. Several pertinent values are not only used by unions and expressed by workers but also honored by employers. All the parties attempt to balance the expression of the various values—economic or market efficiency, equity, fairness, or others—trading them off if they have to, or preferably expressing them in ways that allow complementarities. The attempts are many and various, often dependent upon the changeable circumstances of particular times and places.

Our knowledge of the complex of values expressed and pursued by all the parties should bring us to an important conclusion, however. The notion that unions have interfered with the optimum allocation of labor, in the traditional sense, is valid only if one assumes that consumer interests should be paramount. If one is prepared to grant that people may legitimately be concerned with their productive lives and with the kind of society in which they work, even if their views in such respects differ from the views of others, then one can only conclude that the standard of optimum allocation is faulty. *Maximum* consumer satisfaction ceases to become the basis for determining what is the best distribution of resources among competing uses. The generalization that unions are exploitative, the judgment that unions disrupt economic organization, and the dictum that unions ignore consumer interests are to some extent based on a criterion that a great many Americans do not accept as the only one. Failure to recognize this fact sometimes leads people to take paradoxical position, praising unions for forcing reluctant managers to pay more attention to workers' needs while condemning them for upsetting the competitive price mechanism.

What can be said, then, in specific answer to our question about the standards used to guide the determination of wages and the allocation of labor

---

[30]Even classical and neoclassical writers admitted this in employing a concept known as "psychic income," which was sometimes used to explain wage differentials. It was said that the enjoyment workers derived from their employment might lead them to accept a smaller wage than they could receive elsewhere. So little impact did this concept make on the body of doctrine, however, that it constituted little more than an interesting footnote to the mainstream of thought. There was no appreciation that here they were touching on the phenomenon of worker interest, a matter of such importance that it was to threaten—in our day—the system which excluded it.

among productive employments? Managers—who are increasingly responsible for large organizational entities, corporate enterprises that manifest the complications and problems of complete societies—through personnel practices indicate their implicit agreement with unions' and workers' findings that the traditional economic standard of efficiency is too limited. At least, it cannot sensibly be used as an exclusive standard. The values that legitimize organizational distributions of authority and justify regular, established relationships between people of varying interests and abilities must receive careful attention and respect.

Moreover, we may conclude that the basic problem has not been created by unions. The problem has arisen because of a failure on the part of many in society to appreciate the narrow philosophy that emphasized a single value: efficiency. Though our society may be individualistic in its consumption, and as consumers we prefer "more" to "less," we are far removed from individualism in our productive endeavors. Most people in the labor force are employees. Many of them work in vast corporate communities, public and private, where they need and recognize values that modulate their producing relationships into satisfying, legitimate patterns. This not to say, of course, that unions may not take actions that many in the community would find unwarranted. Union leaders, no less than others in society, have sought for themselves and their members equity, freedom, and fairness in ways that denied them to others or may have grossly impaired efficiency. Nevertheless, unions play an important institutional role in reminding us all that there are values to be respected other than that of efficient serving of consumers. Industrial and corporate communities cannot thrive and prosper or maintain their necessary cooperative spirit and legitimacy unless they respect those other values.

The Use of More than One Standard

Another way of phrasing this general conclusion is to say that optimum allocation, defined in the old sense of the distribution of the factors of production most condusive to consumer satisfaction, is not now, if it ever has been, the dominant economic problem. It remains important, but as one of several major concerns of economic study. The improvement of consumer satisfaction through more and efficient production is an objective worth pursuing, butalong with other objectives such as the assuring of equity within the corporation, the promotion of fairness in dealings with workers, and the advancement of producer satisfaction—that is, the satisfactions derived from the work process itself.

Some sort of compromise may be necessary in reconciling such simultaneously held objectives. Trade-offs may have to be made. Providing equity and fairness on the job and in the employing organization may impair producers' efficiency and reduce the capacity to satisfy consumer interests as fully as would otherwise be the case. But we need not assume that there can be no reconciliation. We noted that Arthur Okun believed that the mutual trust between employers and workers that was fostered by the promotion of values such as fairness and equity might well work to enhance productiveness and to increase efficiency. Other, more recent studies have also suggested that through collective bargaining unions may have contributed to such reconciliation.[31] It is a subject that deserves more and careful consideration.

[31]Charles Brown and James Medoff, "Trade Unions in the Production Process," *Journal of Political Science,* vol. 86, June 1978, pp. 355–378; Kim B. Clark, "The Impact of Unionization on Productivity: A Case Study," *Industrial and Labor Relations Review,* vol. 33, July 1980, pp 451–469; and Richard B. Freeman and James L. Medoff, *What Do Unions Do?* New York: Basic Books, Inc., 1984, pp. 78–93.

CHAPTER 13

THE ECONOMICS OF COLLECTIVE BARGAINING: EFFECTS ON NATIONAL INCOME LEVEL

The marginal productivity theory does not enable one to determine wages, even if the supply of labor is assumed, though it may indicate the tendency of employment to decline if wages rise or to rise if wages drop, other things remaining the same. In Chapter 12, we concluded that in many situations market forces, even in the short run, impose only broad limits, within which group decision making may allocate factors of production and distribute income. The market's influence affects both the allocation and distribution, but usually in a general way. Specific wages and relative earnings typically are more immediately determined by institutional imperatives and in light of equity considerations. We pointed out that the question of who gets how much is answered by agreement between groups in various functional roles; in most situations the groups possess a certain latitude of discretion within the more or less competitive marketplace. These decisions made locally—decentralized and at various times, of course—have an impact on the national economy: their summation affects the size of the national income and its distribution.

WAGE POLICIES AND NATIONAL INCOME

By encouraging consumption and investment within the economy, wage policies can contribute to an increase in the national dividend. By discouraging either or both, they may help produce a smaller dividend. The fact that managers and union leaders have some discretion in determining wage policies does not mean that they will use that discretion wisely. We have concluded that economic theory explains only in part the relationship of particular wage rates to one another and to profits. We should be careful, however, not to slip into the error of believing that the distribution of national income has no effect upon output. Through its impact on employment or on productivity, it may indeed raise or lower output. But recognizing the existence of some relationship between wages, employment, productivity, and output and variations in productivity are parts of economic dynamics, and to examine them one must consider the process of income creation.

For a long time economists assumed that at a given level of real national income, employment would vary inversely with real wages. Thus before the great depression of the 1930s most economists argued that rising unemployment indicated inflexible wages, rates held at too high a level. They espoused a policy of cutting wages in a time of depression to stimulate employment.

John Maynard Keynes, in *The General Theory of Employment, Interest and Money* in 1936, cast doubt upon the wisdom of such a policy. A reduction of wages in the midst of a depression, he maintained, would force the affected workers to cut back their consumption expenditures and thus erode aggregate demand. With overall demand weakening, consumers could well expect further wage cuts to cut aggregate demand still further; this persuaded them to postpone expenditures on durable goods. Producers might generate similar expectations, aggravating the depression. Consequently wage cuts were not likely to increase employment at all.[1]

The Problem of Sticky Downward Wages

In Chapter 12 we noted that many employers, as well as unions, resist wage cuts. Their resistance has been and is founded upon sound personnel policies designed to encourage the loyalty, maintain the trust, and promote the efficient use of long-term employees. Employers had contributed to downwardly inflexible wages before unions were a significant influence in the economy. Professor Mitchell has pointed out that "at the onset of the Great Depression, [when union membership was exceedingly small] wages did fall in nominal terms. However, what is remarkable is the resistance of real wages to the decline in business activity. An hour of manufacturing labor in real terms cost almost 14 percent more in 1933—the trough of the depression—than it did in 1929. Compensation per full-time employee in the entire domestic economy fell in real terms by less than 1 percent in 1929–33."[2] It is hardly surprising that downwardly rigid wages should have also been found as unions grew in number and as collective bargaining spread across industry.

THE UNEMPLOYMENT-INFLATION TRADE-OFF

Over the two decades after World War II, most economists, and probably the public, were still concerned with the dangers of recession and depression. They

---

[1] J. M. Keynes, *The General Theory of Employment, Interest and Money,* New York: Harcourt, Brace & World, Inc., 1936, chap. 19.
[2] Mitchell, *Unions, Wages, and Inflation,* pp. 157–158.

tended to agree with Keynes that downwardly rigid wages were a protection against a spiraling decline of aggregate demand. Inflation had been but an occasional problem: first, at the end of World War II when Congress abruptly ended wage and price controls, allowing pent-up demand to express itself; and second, during the Korean war, when government military spending over-stimulated the economy from 1950 to 1953. By the mid-sixties, however, the threat of inflation appeared increasingly important; Keynesian explanations and policies were not sufficient to deal with the problems that loomed over the economy. Defense expenditures during the Vietnamese war contributed to the inflation, but it continued through the 1970s even as military spending fell. Moreover, the inflation continued at historically high rates as unemployment rose.

Economists had long been willing to grant the fact that the general level of wages did not readily fall in response to unemployment. They continued to believe, though, that it rose in response to excess aggregate demand, through tightening labor markets. Professor A. W. Phillips formalized the relationship between money wages and unemployment in an article published in 1958.[3] He examined the changes in the two variables in the United Kingdom over a period of almost a century and concluded that there was a high inverse correlation between the level of unemployment and money wages.

Prominent economists seized upon the relationship as a guide to national policy and dubbed it the "Phillips curve." Through appropriate use of monetary and fiscal policy, they suggested, policy makers could choose a desired combination of unemployment and price inflation indicated by the curve. A few economists were so bold as to indicate the nature of the choices available: 8 percent unemployment with no wage increases, unemployment in the 5 to 6 percent range with wage increases of 2 to 3 percent, or 3 percent unemployment with rises in wages of 7 percent.[4] Unfortunately, economists could not find in the United States stable relationships between wage increases and the unemployment rate. They found, indeed, that unemployment sometimes rose along with wages. To explain the lack of stability, some argued that the relationship was not fixed along a single curve but changed over time. The curve shifted so that any given wage increase could be associated with a number of different rates of unemployment. Policy options were then realized to be more complex—and probably considerably more difficult to achieve—than first presumed. Beyond the adjustment of monetary and fiscal policy, their exercise also required the use of active manpower programs to lower unemployment and perhaps even wage and price controls of one kind or another to limit increases directly. Economists were interested in discovering, and policy makers needed to know, more about how wages related to levels of employment and output.

[3]A. W. Phillips, "The Return Between Unemployment and the Rates of Change of Money Wage Rates in the United Kingdom, 1862–1957," *Economica,* vol. 25, Nov. 1958, pp. 283–299.

[4]Paul Samuelson and Robert M. Solow, "Our Menu of Policy Choices," in Arthur M. Okun (ed.), *The Battle Against Unemployment,* New York: W. W. Norton & Company, Inc., 1965, pp. 66–71.

Union Influence on Wage Levels

In the past twenty years, researchers have examined the effects of unions and collective bargaining in some detail, using many different data sources and methodologies. They have revealed a number of interesting and suggestive correlations; but since these do not necessarily prove causal connections, it is possible that unionism is not so much a causal force of particular wage levels, differentials, and structures as it is a result. It is clear, nevertheless, that there is a strong positive association between the rates of unionization and either wage levels or rates of wage increases. Various studies also indicate that over the last thirty years, the differentials between union and nonunion wages have grown. They may have been about 10 to 15 percent in the fifties and rose to 20 to 30 percent by the mid-seventies.[5]

The differentials between union and nonunion wages vary not only over time but also by occupation and industry. The lower the skill level, for example, the greater the differential, ranging from 42 percent for laborers to less than 1 percent for professionals and −4 percent for sales workers.[6] An industry study found that in 1975 unionized white male blue-collar workers received a wage differential over comparable nonunion workers of 43 percent in construction; 16 percent in transportation, communications, and utilities; 12 percent in nondurable manufacturing; and 9 percent in durable manufacturing.[7]

If we assume that through collective bargaining unions win better wages or fringe benefits than do nonunion workers, what could we expect the effect to be upon investments? The benefits might encourage greater investment in laborsaving devices but might equally discourage their introduction in low-wage areas by raising the cost of the devices. Aside from the wage-cost factor, union intervention into matters over which managers have formerly assumed sole discretion might dampen managerial expectations. The result could be the discouragement of new enterprise or of the expansion of existing firms. Yet the improved wages and other benefits may either cut turnover, thus lowering labor costs, and/or encourage workers to increase their contributions to productivity.[8] There thus appears to be nothing inherent in unionism to permit conclusive analysis of its likely effect on the level of income.

One aspect of this problem deserves special attention; a person may reach fallacious conclusions by generalizing from particulars. A wage policy that is advantageous to the individual union or firm may disadvantageously affect the whole economy if it is generalized. A wage boost in a single local company can benefit the immediately affected employees without detectable effect upon the economy. Should the company be not a local firm but a large corporation— General Motors, for example—the results may be quite different. So large a

[5]Mitchell, *Unions, Wages, and Inflation,* chap. 3.
[6]Farrel E. Bloch and Mark S. Kuskin, "Wage Determination in the Union and Nonunion Sectors," *Industrial and Labor Relations Review,* vol. 31, Jan. 1978, pp. 183–192.
[7]Orley Ashenfelter, "Union Relative Wage Effects: New Evidence and a Survey of their Implications for Wage Inflation," (unpublished manuscript, Princeton University, 1976).
[8]Richard B. Freeman and James L. Medoff, *What Do Unions Do?* New York: Basic Books, Inc., 1984, pp. 94–110.

company can set a pattern for the automobile industry, and via coercive comparisons among workers and rivalries among union leaders it may influence settlements in the rubber, steel, aerospace, and farm implement industries; indirectly it may affect wage settlements in nonunion industries quite far removed from the automotive industry and its suppliers. We can no longer be sure that a policy benefiting General Motors' employees will not have repercussions on the economy as a whole, such as an inflationary impetus. The same caveat can be made about wage settlements approved or made by managers in a particular industry, whether unionized or not. If followed in other industries on a large scale, the action may prove of no benefit to others and conceivably of some harm.

UNIONS AND NATIONAL WAGE POLICIES

We have here touched on a problem that looms as a major one for collective bargaining and for policy makers who hope to influence national wage outcomes. In negotiating agreements, unions and management usually act independently of others in the industry. Nonunion firms also make their decisions in their separate councils. Within the decentralized authority structure of the nation, both union leaders and managers determine their wage policy *as though* that policy has no bearing upon the actions of other unions or firms.

Problems of Decentralized Wage Setting

Suppose, for example, that the leaders of the United Steelworkers had decided in the mid-seventies that they would not seek a wage increase in basic steel, even though they believed they could win sizable gains. They might have reasoned that a large wage gain granted them throughout the economy would only feed inflation and thus reduce or eliminate any real increase. Moreover, by raising costs of American steel the union could expect to encourage greater imports of Japanese and German steel, contributing to further unemployment. (In 1975 the unemployment rate averaged 11.3 percent for durable manufacturing, almost triple the rate two years earlier.) Since steel wages and the steel wage settlement were prominent in the economy and other unions would likely attempt to follow the Steelworkers' lead, the union might wisely have foregone a wage increase. The leaders could have argued that their members would lose little or nothing and perhaps their forebearance might benefit the economy as a whole.

If the Steelworkers' leaders ever considered such a possibility, the realities of internal union politics, workers' expectations, and coercive comparisons with other large unions quickly eliminated it. Aggressive challenges from rank-and-file leaders threatened the national leaders more than they had for many years; inflation continued at a pace that significantly cut into members' wages (the consumer price index jumped over 20 percent from 1973 to 1975), making members uneasy about further sacrifice; and what if, contrary to their expectations, the leaders found that the United Automobile Workers had not followed the Steelworkers' example? The UAW might have sought and won a large wage increase. For political reasons, both internal and external, the steel union leaders no doubt felt they occupied too exposed a position to ask their members to forego wage increases. To avoid weakening themselves they decided to make demands for sizable wage increases.

They were in no position to consider the effect of their policy upon the economy as a whole. Thus, insofar as there existed wage leadership, pattern setting, or wage imitation, the steel union and industry negotiators set afoot national wage movements that probably did not well serve either their or the economy's long-term best interests. Neither was in a position to consider only what would happen to itself. They dared not assume responsibility beyond their own immediate concerns. And thus *national* wage policies can be influenced or set in motion informally, in the guise of *individual* union and company adjustments.

The fact is, then, that we cannot be sure of the effects a given wage policy will have on employment; the effects will depend upon circumstances peculiar to a given time and place, which must be elucidated before even approximate prediction is feasible. Furthermore, the effects of a wage policy in a particular firm or industry are likely to be quite different from the effects of that same policy applied to the nation at large. Because of the way the collective bargaining process has developed in this country, union and business leaders formulate wage policies *as though* they were intended for only a particular firm or industry; however, because of economic interdependence, the policies of the largest unions and companies become rough precedents. Smaller unions and firms spread their effects to important segments of the economy and perhaps to the whole.

National Spillovers from Local Wage Determinations

Most economists and labor students believe that spillover effects from union to nonunion wages occur, particularly from those firms that are large and prominent and produce basic goods such as steel and autos. They perceive patterns in bargaining outcomes that appear to be the results of wage imitation— the terms and conditions determined by one group of negotiators are followed in varying but still recognizable degree by other groups. The ability to recognize meaningful patterns is a human ability that surpasses and may confound mathematical analysis; that empirical evidence of pattern bargaining is mixed, at best, should occasion no surprise. Agreements cover so many detailed and varied fringe items and set the terms of pay under so many contingent situations—such as overtime, travel, craft and skill use, machine breakdown, shifts, work rules, holidays, safety procedures, cleanup, and sickness— that settlements cannot easily by copied, nor can researchers easily compare them. Detected settlement patterns and recognized wage imitations may therefore be subtle and perhaps even imagined.

When government has attempted to control wages, its tribunals have been eager to find patterns that would help them to rationalize their efforts at control and to ease the burdens of applying rules. If they can regulate the wages of a whole sector or large portion of the economy by influencing a patterned relationship, they save enormously over case-by-case regulation. Unions and firms may also find pattern determination in their interests when appealing to the wage tribunals. By "finding" patterns that they had not before perceived, they may provide themselves with arguments for or against wage and fringes not yet established.[9] Nevertheless, there is wide agreement that at least some of the largest unionized industries and their unions do establish wage patterns and show certain degrees of wage imitation. Three of the most likely industries are steel, automobiles, and national trucking. Beyond industry boundaries, even among these three, patterns tend to fade, but key settlements and the rationales used by the parties to support them influence negotiations to some extent in other and wider areas.

Federal Attempts to Regulate Wage Levels

In times of government wage control, settlements in these large industries receive special public attention and their influence is greatly extended. Since World War II the federal government has taken a keen interest in a national wage policy during three periods. The first was during the Korean war, from 1950 to 1952; the second was during the Kennedy and Johnson administrations, from 1962 to 1968; and the third was during the administrations of Nixon and Ford, from 1971 to 1974. In each, government policy makers were concerned that union leaders and managers through particular settlements would initiate wage changes adversely affecting general wage levels.

The standards used by bargainers in their negotiations become matters of public as well as private interest whenever their influence extends widely beyond their own area of coverage, but especially in times of government intervention. Insofar as unions and management enjoy discretionary power in fixing wages, they usually appeal to such standards as will popularly justify their wage policies. The same is true of public bodies—wage stabilization boards or pay boards—that need to generate wide support for, and acceptance of, their wage policies. In the heat of negotiations, union and management bargainers have not always recognized or appealed to any easily defined standards; they argue for or reject adjustments opportunistically as fortune and bargaining power favor. With experience, and especially through government's attempt at defining national wage policies, all involved have learned the value of sophisticated standards by which wage changes may be justified to the parties' own constituents and also to the public.

One or the other of the negotiating parties often tries to mobilize public sentiment in support of its position, unions arguing that a living wage requires the rejection of a wage cut while prices are generally rising, employers that poor earnings (a lack of ability to pay) necessitate a wage cut. Union members

---

[9]See M. W. Reder, "The Theory of Union Wage Policy," *Review of Economics and Statistics,* vol. 34, Feb. 1952, p. 40, note 24, for comments on such "findings" in the fifties.

are usually sympathetic to wage appeals that argue the justice of wage changes moving with a rising price level; such an appeal may also weaken managers' resolve to avoid a wage increase. Or by favorably comparing company pay scales to those elsewhere in the area or industry, managers may help persuade their workers and the union leaders with whom they are negotiating that the initial wage requests are not realistic.

Just because unions and managements—or government wage agencies— appeal to a particular standard one time is no guarantee that they will agree to accept or to use that standard another time. All parties use wage standards expediently, rejecting one formerly used because it now does not support a desired change and pushing another that had been discarded earlier. Despite this expedient behavior, certain wage standards appear to have something particularly compelling or appealing about them.

Comparability is the standard most commonly used, for example, not only by the parties and government regulators but also by private arbitrators. (There are no clear definitions of comparisons, however, either of how to proceed with them or of what wage elements are to be compared.) After comparability perhaps come cost-of-living changes and a firm's ability to pay. Less popular standards are the living wage and firm or industry productivity. Not used in the United States are such possible standards as the size of the family or the unemployment rate.

THE POPULAR WAGE STANDARDS: COMPARABILITY, ABILITY TO PAY, AND COST OF LIVING

Since individual settlements can influence national wage levels and thus the economy, we might well examine why unions and managements use the standards they do. The consequences of following various standards may be quite different, and thus national interest may be served better if some are used at one time and others at another time. Confronted with rapid inflation, economic crises, or emergency strikes, agencies of the federal government have long wrestled with the problem of finding relevant and meaningful wage criteria. They have relied primarily upon those criteria most commonly used by the immediately involved parties, and they have discovered that none has been without flaws.

Comparability

The popularity of comparability as a wage criterion is not hard to understand.[10] It can usually provide negotiators with a dollars-and-cents figure, it has an aura

[10]Comparability here is not the same standard as that used in recent years by advocates of compable worth. The term "comparable worth" refers to the inherent similarity of worth of jobs or positions that may not require the same skill, effort, or responsibility and may not even be performed under similar working conditions. Collective bargaining negotiators have not yet gone beyond the obvious and objective job characteristics in determining comparability.

of fairness, and often it is in accord with the economic forces pressing upon managers and the political pressures felt by union leaders. That workers performing the same work side by side should be paid the same wage is a standard that was widely recognized long before unions and collective bargaining were significant. By extension, the standard has been applied to the wages of workers performing the same work in different plants in the same area or even in distant locations. When any important feature of work in one location resembles that of work performed elsewhere, workers or managers are tempted to use the resemblance as the basis for an adjustment in the wage rate. Each may argue that the rates ought to be as comparable (or incomparable) as the work.

The further removed workers are from each other in distance and job content, the more obscure the basis for comparison becomes and the less useful is the standard. It offers no solution to the problem of relative pay for dissimilar workers dissimilarly situated. How should the pay scales for the West Virginia coal miners compare with those for the Carolina textile workers; the timber workers of Oregon; the electronic workers in "Silicon Valley," California; or the lab technicians and nurses in New York City hospitals? Even when job duties appear to be much the same for different workers, the conditions under which the duties are carried out may be quite different and the work thus not easily comparable. Maintenance electricians employed by a university, for example, may bring to their work the same mechanical skills that electricians hired by construction firms bring to their work. The former will be steadily employed at a single location the year round, in good times and bad, with opportunity to build up vacation and pension benefits; the latter will have to seek work throughout a wide area wherever construction is carried on, moving from employer to employer as each job is completed. They may experience fairly long periods of unemployment when construction slumps, or during booms they may find that overtime pay is an important part of the wage. While apparently each performs the same kind of work, the conditions of employment are quite different, and no doubt a higher *hourly* wage is justified for the irregularly employed construction electricians.

Negotiators may claim that there is a historical dimension to comparability as well as a spatial or job-content dimension. A group of workers may seek a wage increase comparable with that of a more highly skilled group, for example, claiming as justification the historical differential between the two. Although their work and wage rates are not comparable with those of skilled workers, they compare the differential pay of the two skill levels in the past with the present differential pay. Of course, should the less skilled group successfully invoke the historical comparison and restore the earlier relationship, the skilled group could then argue that it has now lost its hard-won gains of the past. To maintain *its* historical position, it would have to secure a new wage adjustment. Such flexibility in a wage standard commends it to those who wish a tactical argument to justify whatever demand they may have. With ingenuity and selective use of data, one may make out a case for almost any wage change.

Yet despite the variability of the standard, it usually measures economic and social pressures to which managers, union leaders, and workers are responsive. For all the opportunism with which comparability is used by negotiators to support their wage demands and offers, it appeals to a standard that is easily recognized and widely understood. If in the same labor market wages go up for workers in some plants, pressures will soon develop for a comparable rise in the wages of workers in neighboring plants. First, management will not as easily be able to attract a steady flow of adequately skilled workers if its firm's wages lag behind; second, workers will begin to grow restive if their wages do not follow those of workers in other plants whom they know or hear about. Their morale and work performance may be impaired, and a few may even leave for better pay elsewhere. Third, union officers will find their leadership positions endangered if they do not push for benefits at least as great as those secured by workers in comparable plants and unions.

These pressures are more apt to develop among the follower firms and industries than among those which make the key bargains[11] for industries and the nation. Many smaller firms and nonbasic industries seldom initiate significant wage changes or pioneer in new pay programs; rather, they follow, closely or from afar, the direction of wage changes made by the key bargainers. Although the followers may look to the settlements of others for guidance, the key bargainers cannot. To do so would involve them in fruitless circularity. Thus the key bargainers must look to other wage criteria to guide their demands and wage decisions. They must seek other wage standards.

The Difficulties of Ignoring Comparability

The difficulty in finding and using other criteria for national wage standards is well illustrated in the experience of the federal Pay Board under the Economic Stabilization Act from 1971 to 1973. It proposed, and adopted over the objection of its labor members, a general pay standard of 5.5 percent, ignoring at first the effects upon wage structures within plants and firms and within and between industries. That figure was implicitly based on a long-term, historical average increase in national productivity, adjusted upward somewhat to recognize the continuing inflation. The labor members particularly objected to

---

[11]Professor Daniel Mitchell distinguishes two variations in the way key bargains may influence wages: "In one version, units look at each other's wages and attempt to achieve target wage differentials. A world of mutual interaction in which everyone is watching everyone is potentially unstable; there may be no consensus on what the long-term wage differentials should be. This version suggests that an external spark such as a sudden increase in labor demand could set off a wage explosion like that in the construction industry in the late 1960's and early 1970's. Certainly, explaining the behavior of construction wages during that period would require reference to [such a version]. . . . A second version involves one-way causal flows. In this version they are "key" wage determination units that set patterns for other units. The model can be based either on adaptive attempts to maintain wage differentials by follower units or solely on the wage increments. Either view suggests that the cause of wage determination can be easily affected throughout the economy by manipulating a few wage setting units." (Mitchell, *Unions, Wages, and Inflation*, p. 215.)

inclusion of fringe benefits within the single percentage increase, particularly health, welfare, and pension programs. Labor unions found a ready business ally in the insurance industry, whose interests paralleled their own. Both successfully lobbied Congress to amend the basic legislation and exclude fringes from coverage by the general limit. The Pay Board defined the pay it could legally review as broadly as possible, adopting a "base compensation rate" that involved not only straight-time hourly earnings (excluding incentive plans) but also employer costs for such items as shift differentials, overtime premiums, vacations, holiday and sick leaves, bonuses, severance pay, pension plans, and health and welfare plans. It calculated this rate for the hours worked. Thus it was able indirectly to bring within its control the costs of the excluded fringes.

The board almost immediately realized that it would have to grant exceptional increases above the 5.5 percent. A number of them involved comparable standards. Where an employee unit had received an increase in tandem with— equal and directly related to the increases of—another unit, whose wages were set first, for at least five years, the increase could be as large as 7 percent. The Pay Board also approved increases above the 5.5 percent figure and up to the limit of 7 percent if the parties could demonstrate wage and salary inequities arising from changed technology. It also gave special consideration to workers whose increases over the previous three years had seriously lagged behind those of the industry. The Pay Board recognized that labor shortages might make higher-than-usual wage increases necessary. If an employer had not been able to fill positions for at least three months despite intensive recruiting, the wage might be raised to the limit of 7 percent. The board also discovered that it had to make special allowance for well-established escalator formulas upon which general increments depended. The wage increases and cost-of-living adjustments were so intertwined that they could not easily be separated. In addition, the Pay Board made exceptions for merit increases, provided they had been adopted before the stabilization program began; Congress also mandated the exclusion of already established productivity and incentive plans. Though the general allowable increase of 5.5 percent reflected the productivity gains of merit or incentive plans, simple equity and fairness seemed to call for special consideration to be given to employees who improved their output.

Professor D. Quinn Mills well pointed out the difficulties involved when the government attempts to establish national wage policy on the basis of a single criterion, as did the Pay Board:

> Those who propose a single standard appear to believe that it will be effective because it is not only simple but unambiguous. However, a thorough familiarity with the process of wage determination suggests that no single figure can be applied unambiguously (even conceptually) to all situations. Let us offer a very common example of the difficulty of applying a single standard. In the course of a two-year period in a single plant, variations will occur in the timing of wage increments and in the distribution of increases among job classifications (accompanied, inevitably, by changes in distributions of workers among classifications). These variations will result in differences of opinion as to the correct application of any established criterion. What is

the appropriate base from which to measure the new increase? How should one treat expected changes in employment among wage classifications? Thus, a general standard involving a stated percentage increase over existing wage rates (or earnings) is not unambiguous but, in fact, often quite confusing, unless it can be applied on a case-by-case basis by stabilization authorities. There is therefore no substitute for a review process to determine the applicability of the single-percentage standard in individual situations.[12]

Ability to Pay

On its face, ability to pay appears to be a helpful wage standard. Under fully competitive conditions it should indicate the direction wages might take. A declining industry losing its markets because of changing tastes, for example, might not be in a position to pay average wages, whereas a new, expanding industry might be able to pay above-average wages. Lower wages in the declining industry would lead to a desired pressure upon workers to leave; higher wages in the expanding industry would attract needed workers. Considering the quasi-monopolistic nature of most product markets and the consequent semidiscretionary control over prices enjoyed by management, union leaders are skeptical of any wage conclusions based on competitive assumptions. Furthermore, they are generally committed to "taking wages out of competition." They feel that to agree to lower wages in a declining firm or industry may only increase wage pressures in industries with more successful, growing firms.

If workers are convinced that they have to choose between present or lower wages and loss of jobs, they may well prefer a settlement that saves their jobs. Only in special circumstances, however, can both union and management bargainers agree that such a choice confronts them; out of thousands of contract settlements over the period from 1979 to early 1982, a period of rising unemployment and business recession, one scholar could find only forty-six examples of concession settlements.[13] Of these, twenty-one involved wage cuts, thirteen wage freezes, and eleven relaxation of work rules. One of the more publicized settlements involved the Chrysler Corporation, which survived only because of government bailout. The terms involved concessions by the union; by late 1982, when their agreement came up for renegotiation, Chrysler workers earned about $2.68 less per hour than their counterparts at General Motors and Ford. In the months before the negotiations, Chrysler's chief executive officer, Lee A. Iacocca, had tried to bolster the corporation's image in the financial community by emphasizing its $1 billion cash reserve and downplaying its $145 million loss during the first half of the year. But workers saw in the large reserve an ability to pay greater than the company negotiators acknowledged or the union bargainers believed existed. By a 2 to 1 vote, the workers rejected an agreement that allowed only a modest wage improvement.

[12]D. Quinn Mills, *Government, Labor, and Inflation,* Chicago: The University of Chicago Press, 1975, pp. 156–157.

[13]Daniel J. B. Mitchell, "Recent Union Contract Concessions," *Brookings Papers on Economic Activity,* vol. 1, 1982, p. 168.

Should all agree that a firm faces bankruptcy or a shutdown unless wages are cut, union officials may still doubt the wisdom of accepting lower wages or foregoing a wage increase. First, wage benefits may become more difficult to secure from other, healthier firms, for they will seize on the comparability standard and point to the lower rate as good reason to keep their own down. Second, there is no assurance that the faltering firm will be saved by the workers' sacrifice. For example, in the late seventies and early eighties the United Rubber Workers authorized concessions in a number of companies in an attempt to save plants from closing. Nevertheless, about two dozen rubber industry facilities closed down. One of the local presidents observed, "if things are really bad, once you've asked to make concessions it's usually too late to save the plant."[14]

Although managers usually appeal to ability to pay only when their firms are in a shaky financial condition or when they are regulated by government bodies,[15] unions look to it as a standard wherever management has discretion over price, whether the firm is expanding or declining. If the firm is operating in a monopolistic product market, its management exercises some degree of control over the factors which determine the size of the net revenue available for distribution. Unions find profits a convenient and easily recognized measure of the available revenue and thus of the firm's ability to pay. Of course, profits can be interpreted in many ways, and the wisdom of different distributions of net revenue—whether for new research efforts, new plant and equipment, extra dividends, *or* wages—can be debated at great length with reasonable arguments.

Many managers refuse explicitly to recognize ability to pay as a proper wage standard or even as a matter for discussion in negotiations; they usually refuse to discuss it on the grounds that it involves financial matters that are of legitimate concern only to stockholders and management. They are not anxious to open their books to union leaders and they decidedly reject the union's involvement in pricing and investment policies a issues outside the scope of union responsibility and competency. Despite its rejection by many managers, union leaders continue to use the standard in a loose and opportunistic way. Workers, or certainly union leaders, as well as stockholders watch the profit positions of firms.

Although union leaders are seldom willing to forgo any adjustment in wages just because a firm is unprofitable, they realize that with higher profits wage increases are more easily won and are often larger. When business is good and profits are high, not only do union members expect wage increases, but managers feel freer to agree to them. Management is less willing to engage in a production-stopping strike when sales are booming and earnings are high.

---

[14]Robert S. Greenberger, "More Workers Resist Employers' Demand for Pay Concessions," *The Wall Street Journal,* Oct. 13, 1982, p. 16.

[15]Public utility companies have used the argument that their ability to pay wage increases is limited by their fixed and regulated rates, passing on wage pressures and bargaining demands to public regulatory commissions or government-controlled agencies. See Ehrenberg, *The Regulatory Process and Labor Earnings,* chap. 4.

Unionists know as well as managers that at such a time higher labor costs can be passed on through prices or absorbed in an improved productivity. They also known that in times of poor sales and declining profits, wage increases will be difficult to secure.

Although ability to pay undoubtedly influences wage decisions under collective bargaining and in extreme cases of financial distress may provide a specific guide for settlement, it is not a particularly helpful standard in most situations. The lack of agreement over the relevance of specific data and their meaning can cause such controversy that ability-to-pay arguments complicate rather than help wage determination. Bargainers ordinarily prefer a standard that is more easily understood, more objective, and simpler to use. The cost-of-living standard as measured by the government's consumer price index (CPI) achieved great popularity because it apparently provides those characteristics lacking in ability to pay.

Cost of Living: Maintaining Real Wages

The CPI has the merit of providing precise figures, objectively collected and reported; nevertheless, when used as a cost-of-living criterion for wage adjustment, it is imprecise and often misleading. The prices of goods measured by the CPI are averages that may or may not be representative for any particular group of workers. Members of a union who work in a firm with plants in the four corners of the country may find that the kinds of goods they buy and the price movements of the items they purchase display great diversity from one area to another. Automobile employees, for example, live in the San Francisco area, Detroit, Buffalo, New York, and near Atlanta. Living costs are not the same in these widely separated cities and changes in the prices of even the same consumer products probably affect workers in various locations differently. In mid–1984 the CPI was 9 percent higher in San Francisco–Oakland than in Buffalo, and over the preceding twelve months it had increased by 5.2 percent in the former and by 2.9 percent in the latter. However, a rise in heating-fuel prices would probably affect workers in cold and snowy Buffalo more than those in the temperate Bay Area of California. Thus if a true cost-of-living adjustment were to be made, it would require a multiplicity of wage changes and levels for comparable jobs.[16]

Furthermore, if changes in cost of living were the only guide for wage deter-

---

[16]The CPI is based on prices for a fixed "market basket" of goods, chosen in a certain base year. Of course, consumers do not buy a fixed array of goods but adjust purchases as relative prices change; if the price of beef goes up and chicken stays the same or declines they can be expected to buy less beef and more chicken. Also, because of quality changes, people may receive as much or more value even while using less of any item—an electronically controlled television set or a more potent drug, for example. Because of these changes, some economists argue that a better measure of cost-of-living than the CPI would be the deflator for personal consumption expenditures (PCE). It is a measure of the price changes for those goods and services consumers actually buy. In the later seventies and early eighties, as interest rates and housing costs rose faster than other items in the CIP, the difference between the CPI and PCE widened appreciably. The PCE, reflecting actual buying patterns, lagged the CPI.

mination, they would do no more than assure the maintenance of real wage levels. In a sense the process would hardly be one of determining wages but merely one of adjusting money rates to stabilize the welfare content of workers' paychecks. And the adjustment would be a lagging one, bringing money rates into line with the preceding period's price changes. There would be no opportunity for reallocating labor by changing relative wages of work groups or industries, and workers would have no means of sharing the economy's productivity gains.

To commend it, the cost-of-living standard has, first of all, expediency. It is easy to comprehend, and its apparent precision makes it simple to apply. It is particularly attractive to workers and union leaders in times of inflation, because it provides a sure and reasonable argument for wage increases. As CPI figures are widely available and publicized, they can be expected to be used. Professor Mills found that negotiators seldom refer to the official statistics on employment and unemployment during bargaining sessions, but they frequently use CPI data,[17] at least during the period of price rise. When prices remain stable or actually decline, workers find the cost-of-living standard considerably less appealing and tend to drop it. The popularity of cost-of-living adjustments in union-management agreements diminished in the mid-1950s as inflation slowed after the Korean war. In such industries as steel, metal cans, and railroads the parties dropped the clauses entirely. When inflation again appeared in the 1970s several industries reintroduced them, and they were adopted for the first time in the telephone industry in 1971, in coal mining in 1974, and in the rubber tire industry in 1976.

Despite its shortcomings as a wage standard and the fact that it is used primarily in times of rising prices, management and unions find the CPI serviceable, as well as expedient. A rising price level tends to upset workers' income expectations; it destroys the expectations that wage increases are a net gain. Daily and weekly shopping allows workers and their families continually to monitor price changes and to recognize the erosion of their paychecks. If wages do not soon follow prices, workers are provoked to make known their dissatisfactions. Union leaders discover political merit in seeking to restore to their members the wage losses inflicted by inflation; they may suffer political defeat if they do nothing to help workers maintain at least a parity between wages and prices.

Managers, too, are responsive to the demand for wage increases to offset consumer price rises. Like the workers, they seem to appreciate the unarticulated ethical notion that employees should not suffer a real loss of income through price movements beyond their control. However, though managers also like the convenience of cost-of-living adjustments, they recognize the need to predict and protect their labor costs. If prices move faster than expected, a COLA rigidly tied to the CPI could prove troublesome, pulling wages up far faster than a company may easily be able to accommodate. Therefore, most

---

[17]D. Quinn Mills, *Employment and Unemployment Statistics in Collective Bargaining*, National Commission on Employment and Unemployment Statistics ground paper no. 10, 1979.

firms insist upon limits or caps upon the COLA increases. One study found, for example, that COLAs typically allow a wage increase of 0.57 percent for each 1 percent rise in the CPI.[18] Some firms require a certain minimum increase before wages are adjusted as well as a limit on the total adjustment permitted. Professor Mitchell has concluded that, "Artful negotiators can play an astounding variety of games with escalators [COLA clauses] so that union leaders can claim victory in obtaining such clauses while management limits the risks of tying wages to uncertain future price developments."[19]

PRODUCTIVITY

Public fear that unions and management will reach inflationary wage settlements, to the detriment of the economy, has prompted some economists and government officials to offer productivity as a standard for wage determination. In times of full or near-full employment, wage increases greater than productivity gains must either squeeze nonwage income or push prices upward. Many nonwage sources of income are not easily squeezed, however. For example, if dividends are held down, interest is apt to rise. Thus from 1972 to 1982, personal interest payments increased more than half again as fast as dividends while employee compensation increased less than either. Thus wage rises greater than productivity increases will transmit most of their impact to prices. Insofar as such wage gains push up prices generally, workers gain in real wages only the amount of their increased productivity. The conclusion is clear: The only *effective* means by which workers as a group may improve their real income is through increasing productivity. If wage settlements in periods of full employment are to benefit workers generally and are not to contribute to inflation, they need to be in line with increasing productivity.

As a criterion for wage determination, productivity appears to have considerable merit; it would tend to guard the public against inflationary settlements and at the same time emphasize to workers and managers the best source of further and continued improvements in real wages. Surprisingly, then, we find that productivity is not a popular wage standard. Though the management of General Motors as early as 1948 persuaded a skeptical UAW to accept an annual improvement factor related to a productivity increase, few other managers elsewhere have sought to tie general wage levels to productivity. Of all the common wage criteria, productivity has been probably the least used in collective bargaining negotiations.[20]

---

[18]Victor J. Scheifer, "Collective Bargaining and the CPI: Escalation vs. Catch-Up," *Proceedings of the 31st Annual Meeting,* Madison, Wis.: Industrial Relations Research Association, 1979, p. 261.

[19]Mitchell, *Unions, Wages, and Inflation,* pp. 49–50.

[20]In the 1970s productivity bargaining became a popular activity in the unionized public sector; and in a few private sector industries—automobiles, steel, construction, retail food, meat-packing, railroads, printing, and longshoring—the parties attempted with varying degrees of success to enhance productivity and shere the gains with workers. The recession in the early 1980s dampened enthusiasm for such bargaining and turned attention to other, more pressing problems. See Joseph Goldberg et al., *Collective Bargaining and Productivity,* Madison, Wis.: Industrial Relations Research Association, 1975.

The Difficulties of Applying a Productivity Standard

The productivity standard's lack of favor among managers and union leaders and its rare use by arbitrators may be due to first, the difficulty of defining the relevant productivity data; and second, the difficulty of applying the standard in wage determination. If the rate of growth of productivity is to serve as a benchmark for a national wage policy, there must be agreement about the appropriate methods for measuring the trends, either for industries in general or specific ones. The government provides productivity data for the private business section (and nonfarm business sector) but it does not regularly and on a timely basis supply specific industry figures.

Over a period of years productivity varies considerably; for the nonfarm business sector from 1948 to 1981, the change in output per worker-hour reached a high of 6.0 percent in 1949–50 and a low of −2.4 percent in 1973–1974. Even grouping the data and taking average changes over several years still shows wide fluctuations (see Table 20); it also indicates a fairly steady decline since the immediate post-World War II era. Very short time intervals may give excessive weight to business cycle movements in productivity and indicate more wage variation than either employers or workers find acceptable. Yet very long intervals may hide significant breaks in trends; for example, it would be inappropriate to set wages in the 1980s on the basis of productivity gains made in the 1960s.

A National Wage Standard?

The Council of Economic Advisers (CEA) in 1962 suggested a productivity standard for a national wage policy, though through the rest of the decade it was merely a guidepost indicating a preferred target for settlement rather than a requirement to which settlements were held. It clearly influenced the Pay

TABLE 20
PRODUCTIVITY CHANGES IN
THE NONFARM BUSINESS SECTOR,
1948 TO 1983

	Average changes/year (percent)
1948 to 1949	3.2
1950 to 1954	2.6
1955 to 1959	2.3
1960 to 1964	2.9
1965 to 1969	2.1
1970 to 1974	1.5
1975 to 1979	1.3
1980 to 1983	1.1

Source: *Economic Report of the President, 1983*, table B-41, p. 209, and *Monthly Labor Review*, vol. 107 (October 1984) p. 84.

Board in the 1970s, however, when it established a single-figure increase against which all settlements were judged during the economic stabilization program of 1971 to 1973. During recessionary intervals no such standard was required to avoid inflationary wage increases, but with the reappearance of inflation the productivity standard will undoubtedly be considered again. The noninflationary standard put forward by the CEA was based on the behavior of wages and prices in a smoothly functioning competitive economy operating near full employment. It assumed no changes in the relative shares of labor and nonlabor incomes. The rate of increase in wage rates, including fringe benefits, in each industry was to equal the trend rate of overall productivity increase.

One should note that the standard included guides for noninflationary price behavior as well as for wages. Prices were to be reduced if the industry's rate of productivity increase exceeded the overall rate—for that would mean declining unit labor costs. There was to be an increase in price if the opposite relationship prevailed. Prices should remain stable if the industry's and overall productivity changes were the same.

The CEA standards were offered with the realization that considerations of equity and efficiency would require modifications and adaptations to the needs and conditions of particular circumstances. The council pointed out four important qualifications and concluded by noting how difficult the application of any standard is to the nation's large and diverse industrial scene.

1 Wage rate increases would exceed the general guide rate in an industry which would otherwise be unable to attract sufficient labor; or in which wage rates are exceptionally low compared with the range of wages earned elsewhere by similar labor, because the bargaining position of workers has been weak in particular local labor markets.

2 Wage rate increases would fall short of the general guide rate in an industry which could not provide jobs for its entire labor force even in times of generally full employment; or in which wage rates are exceptionally high compared with the range of wages earned elsewhere by similar labor, because the bargaining position of workers has been especially strong.

3 Prices would rise more rapidly, or fall more slowly, than indicated by the general guide rate in an industry in which the level of profits was insufficient to attract the capital required to finance a needed expansion in capacity; or in which costs other than labor costs had risen.

4 Prices would rise more slowly, or fall more rapidly, than indicated by the general guide in an industry in which the relation of productive capacity to full employment demand shows the desirability of an outflow of capital from the industry; or in which costs other than labor costs have fallen; or in which excessive market power has resulted in rates of profit substantially higher than those earned elsewhere on investments of comparable risk.

It is a measure of the difficulty of the problem that even these complex guideposts leave out of account several important considerations. Although output per man-hour rises mainly in response to improvements in the quantity and quality of capital goods with which employees are equipped, within their own control. It is obviously in the public interest that incentives be preserved which would reward employees for such efforts.

Also, in connection with the use of measures of overall productivity gain as benchmarks for wage increases, it must be borne in mind that average hourly labor costs often change through the process of up- or down-grading, shifts between wage and salaried employment, and other forces. Such changes may either add to or subtract from the increment which is available for wage increases under the overall productivity guide.

Finally, it must be reiterated that collective bargaining within an industry over the division of the proceeds between labor and nonlabor income is not necessarily disruptive of over-all price stability. The relative shares can change within the bounds of noninflationary price behavior. But when a disagreement between management and labor is resolved by passing the bill to the rest of the economy, the bill is paid in depreciated currency to the ultimate advantage of no one.[21]

With such limitations and qualifications as those described, a productivity standard would appear to provide little help to union leaders and managers concerned with determining wages in specific situations. A number of officials in both unions and business organizations rejected the council's suggestion that productivity be a guide for appraising wage behavior; the rejection appears to have stemmed as much from the fear that government would interfere in collective bargaining as from doubts about the usefulness of the guideposts themselves. The shortcomings of productivity as a wage criterion are no greater than those of the other criteria, and it would not require more careful use. None of the criteria provides clear, unambiguous guidance in wage determination, and they are all subject to opportunistic use and manipulation. Productivity's lack of popularity among negotiators may not stem from its limitations as a wage standard but rather from its abstract nature.

Productivity changes, as such, do not produce any direct effects that managers, workers, and union leaders recognize as social and economic pressures. It is not recorded as any of the normal accounting variables that business managers watch. Of course it has an influence upon profitability and costs and eventually upon prices and wages, but the relationship is not direct, and not easily known or defined. Its changes are almost unnoticeable even to managers, for only sophisticated analysis reveals it. In contrast, a comparison of wages can develop direct and immediately perceived coercive pressures upon employers and workers; observation of profit levels can also excite both employers and workers to demand changes in wages. All can directly and easily understand the meaning of price change in consumer goods. Whereas comparability, ability-to-pay, and cost-of-living and living-wage standards are based upon data and knowledge that are a part of the common daily experience of those concerned with labor agreements, productivity is a figure devised by economists from unfamiliar, if not arcane, sources.

---

[21] *Economic Report of the President, 1962.*

Can Productivity Be Made Relevant to Collective Bargaining?

If managers and union leaders are to be persuaded to consider productivity regularly and seriously in their wage negotiations, they must see the relevance of it to their deliberations and feel the force of some necessity to measure their settlements by it. Since productivity changes do not manifest themselves directly and clearly through the usual mechanisms of the market and the political procedures of unions and companies, we need other means of impressing the parties with the importance of productivity. Government officials have long stressed the desirability of noninflationary wage increases, urging public condemnation of settlements larger than those justified by productivity gains. But as yet neither government agencies nor private sources have provided industry leaders and union negotiators with data about productivity and productivity studies that were appropriate, timely, and detailed enough to make them both useful and reliable.

Use of a productivity standard in wage determination will hardly end disputes over the kind and size of wage adjustments, nor will productivity supplant other wage standards. It can help protect the economy against inflationary wage settlements, and more important, it may emphasize for those engaged in the productive process the value of increasing productivity. Serious consideration of productivity and an understanding of its implications suggest that wage determination need not be merely a matter of distributing income but can also be an effort to increase income.

The Importance of Productivity in the Economy

Improved productivity is likely to result in increased income to the firm in which it occurs. The imperfections of competition allow an individual firm some discretionary control over price and production policy and thus make possible the appropriation of a share, though usually not all, of the productivity gains. Through lower prices or better service, a firm may pass along to its customers some of the gains. The source of the gains may be the more efficient use of materials by avoiding waste and scrap, so that costs are cut without reducing the need for labor in the firm; or it may be the more efficient handling of new business with the same work force, thus increasing revenues but keeping costs stable. The use of new and more efficient machines, technologies, or work methods *may* reduce the number of workers, or it may not. Depending upon the elasticity of demand, an improvement in the product or service, a lowering of price, or both may increase sales. Any increases in production to meet sales will tend to increase employment and will thus offset any reduction in the number of workers.

Insofar as revenues increase because of lower costs or higher sales, productivity can provide added benefits for workers and management. The particular distribution of the benefits and the effects upon employment will be subject in some degree to the bargaining process. Workers may prefer to take some of their benefits in the form of higher wages, fringe benefits, a reduced workweek, more holidays, or longer vacations.

Not only is productivity the decisive influence in improving workers' real incomes in the long run, but it also provides them with the opportunity to increase incomes in the short run, if their representatives and their managers can agree upon ways to promote productivity and to share in its bounty. Workers and their union have an interest in productivity in other firms as well as in their own. Higher productivity elsewhere is likely to lead to price declines, to act as a drag on prices, or to provide improved products; either higher wages from productivity gains in their own firm or lower-priced products from other firms raise real incomes. Increased productivity would seem to be an attractive goal for union leaders and managers to pursue through collective bargaining, but despite the benefits that productivity increases promise, unions and managements have joined together only occasionally, under rare circumstances, explicitly to raise productivity.

COLLECTIVE BARGAINING AND THE PROMOTION OF PRODUCTIVITY

The countinuing decline in national productivity over the last two decades have convinced many managers, union leaders, and government officials that all involved need more imaginative and persistent joint efforts than ever before. Even a person who reads only a local newspaper is probably aware of the productivity problem in the American economy. Industry conferences, union meetings, government symposia, university studies, and foundation publications in recent years have examined, considered, and celebrated ways in which productivity may be increased. The secretary of labor declared that:

> The key to a better economic future for America is the workplace . . . and making it a more productive environment is the real challenge of the day.[22]

He suggested what that workplace might be like:

> [One] that will resolve tensions, not create them; a nourishing environment characterized by institutional loyalty with managers who listen to their workers and view them as valuable partners, too important for quick-fix layoffs. Workers, in turn, should be encouraged to see their own success as inseparable from the firm's success and to recognize that further improvements in their wages and other conditions of work cannot be met without increased productivity.[23]

These words were addressed to labor and management representatives at a time when recession and unemployment seriously threatened. Forty years earlier, during World War II, the government also encouraged union leaders and

---

[22]*Report on the Secretary of Labor's Symposium on Cooperative Labor Management Programs,* U.S. Department of Labor, Labor-Management Services Administration, 1982, p. 4.
[23]Ibid.

managers to work together to raise productivity. It was a matter of clear national interest, and joint committees appeared to be a way of furthering it. Thousands of such committees were formed but many did not function; a few hundred were able to operate well enough to produce noticeable results, and only a handful were able to maintain themselves after the war.[24] Nevertheless, through the decades after the war, many people kept alive the idea that increased cooperation at the place of work would significantly increase productivity and also enhance the quality of work life.

Experiments to Increase Productivity

During the 1960s, some unions and firms experimented with productivity bargains and cooperative arrangements designed to help both management and workers adjust to technological change.[25] In the 1970s a number of companies and unions entered into cooperative programs that were to improve the quality of work life and also enhance productivity. Between 1975 and 1979, for example, General Motors introduced semiautonomous work groups in sixteen plants, all nonunion. After agreeing to a Procedure for Preferential Consideration for Hiring at Specific Plants in the fall of 1978, which encouraged union members to move from existing plants in the north to new southern plants, the union became a participant in the activities of work groups in several of the plants. As the company extended use of the work groups to new plants, both north and south, since 1979, the union has almost always been involved.

Union-management efforts to increase productivity and improve the quality of working life also received wide public notice and detailed scholarly study in the Bolivar, Tennessee, project and the Rushton, Pennsylvania, experiment. The former was a collaborative effort begun in 1972 by Harman International Industries and the United Automobile Workers. It appeared to have gained considerable early success, though a more than twofold increase in sales might have made any program look good. The recession of 1980 and 1981 required layoffs of one-third to one-half of the work force, and union and management leadership changed considerably over the course of the project. Although some of the changes instituted survived, the project in retrospect did not look as promising a model as it had before.

The experiment by the Rushton Mining Company in Osceola, Pennsylvania, and the United Mine Workers was stimulated by a training program at Pennsylvania State University in early 1973. It involved only a part of the workers. Productivity may have increased slightly, job safety improved, and quality of work life may have otherwise improved somewhat. The experiment was not expanded to all the workers, and the tensions among the work force

[24]Dorethea de Schweinitz, *Labor and Management in a Common Enterprise,* Cambridge, Mass.: Harvard University Press, 1949.
[25]James J. Healy (ed.), *Creative Collective Bargaining,* Englewood Cliffs, N.J.: Prentice-Hall, Inc., 1965.

over the high pay only for those involved caused internal union problems. Although it was initially successful, like many other earlier experiments, projects, and programs it was not sustained.[26]

The occasional efforts made during more than a generation of union leaders' and managers' careers and the varied projects attempted in both large and small plants indicate that cooperative efforts specifically directed toward increasing productivity and improving the quality of work life are not regular parts of collective bargaining. They are at present innovations that may not find wide acceptance. There is little indication that they will become important in the near future unless both government policies and general economic conditions are able to offer larger inducements and stronger incentives than are now present. One should not judge such a conclusion as disappointingly pessimistic. After all, the cooperative experiments already conducted and the new ones being tried are attempting to add to an already high level of productivity. The parties are trying to improve what is in general extraordinary cooperation. The enormous production flow of American factories, mines, offices, and organizations requires a vast, complex web of cooperative behavior from all those participating. To find new ways to improve the existing cooperation and to raise productivity to even a slightly higher level requires high degrees of imagination and involves managerial and employee responses to the subtlest motivation and personal interactions. That we do not quickly or easily find and make better and more effective responses is not so much because of a failure of our attempts as a measure of the existing difficulties and problems encountered.

The Reality of Productivity to Employees

As already suggested, the abstractness of productivity is a major obstacle to its use by any of the parties in collective bargaining. However important it may be to the real level of wages, productivity does not directly impinge upon anyone's experiences. Unlike changes in prices, wages in comparable occupations, and corporate profits, productivity changes produce no effects easily identifiable with them. In fact, a significant change in productivity may not be noticed at all. Gains in labor productivity and profits are *not* well correlated, for example, and in a market economy managers must act on the basis of the latter, not the former.[27] Understandably, workers may feel betrayed if they cooperate to increase productivity and then, despite any gains, managers lay them off because of sliding profits.

The lack of relationship between productivity and profits reflects in part a difference between *productivity* and *production*. Workers sometimes assume

---

[26]For a review of the more prominently reported productivity programs see Robert Zager and Michael P. Rosow (eds.), *The Innovative Organization,* New York: Pergamon Press, 1982.

[27]Paul S. Adler, "The Productivity Puzzle: Numbers Alone Won't Solve It," *Monthly Labor Review,* vol. 105, Oct. 1982, p. 15.

that higher production means higher productivity. This is not necessarily true, particularly if the increased production is gained by using aging and obsolete machines, inexperienced workers, and inefficient plants. Total output may be raised, but the increased flow of goods or services may well be below the former average output per employee. Manufacturing experienced the reverse situation in the early 1980s. As sales declined and profits slumped in the period from 1979 to 1981, managers of many large manufacturing firms closed old plants, laid off workers, and cut back production. Overall manufacturing production fell by 4.5 percent in 1979–80 and more than twice as fast, by 9.8 percent, in 1980–81. However, productivity rose in manufacturing as managers concentrated their smaller production in efficient plants and used their much reduced work forces more effectively. (Employment declined by 1.16 million, an 18 percent decline in twenty-four months.) This kind of productivity gain, accompanying large-scale layoffs in a time of recession and depression, probably does not commend itself to workers as an attractive standard of any kind.

Workers have other reasons for viewing a productivity standard with skepticism. Not infrequently, managements of both private and public organizations have promised higher pay for greater productivity through their participation in an incentive wage system. To the workers, the higher pay may seem to come only from harder work, not from a true increase in productivity. (That would be an increased output for the *same* input, or the same output for a smaller input.) They find themselves asked to produce more units and though they gain a higher total wage, they must expend more effort. Such "productivity" reflects the common confusion of increased production with productivity gains, noted above. That workers view productivity plans with some suspicion is understandable.

Union-Management Cooperation and Productivity

Nevertheless, many observers urge managers to make greater efforts than they have in recent decades to pursue productivity gains by enlisting union help and hiring workers' participation.[28] Since productivity increases, the results of increased efficiency, are of fundamental importance to general wage settlement, they argue that managers should persistently and urgently seek union-worker cooperation to that end. While managers have often sought to improve worker productivity, they seldom encourage the use of genuinely cooperative methods. Managers traditionally have considered improvement a matter of their initiative, one solely of their direction and administration. They have generally assumed that workers respond only to managerially devised rewards and penalties, contributing when their interests are harnessed and to the extent that their motives are exploited.

---

[28]See, for example, Jerome Rosow (ed.), *Productivity: Prospects for Growth,* New York: Van Nostrand Reinhold, Work in America Series, 1981; and Vernon M. Buehler and Krishna Shetty (eds.), *Productivity Improvements: Case Studies of Proven Practice,* New York: AMACOM, American Management Associations, Inc., 1981.

One may safely generalize that on the one hand, managers have placed heavy reliance on incentive wage systems—piecework, bonuses, and rating plans—to elicit greater worker response. Industrial managers have long used so-called scientific or modern personnel policies that encourage the use of incentive wage plans as means to achieve volume production at low cost. On the other hand, there is among American managers a widespread belief in the efficacy of contingent punishment—the loss of a job for poor work performance, insubordination, or personality characteristics inimical to maintaining order or morale in the workplace. Managers thus continue to rely primarily upon pecuniary incentives to motivate employees: extra pay for improved performance and loss of pay or job for a disobedient or poor worker.

Not only managers, but also arbitrators indicate their approval of the use of such discipline. Professor Ivar Berg has even found a trend of their increasing acceptance of the managerial approach just described. After a study of arbitrators' awards from the early 1950s to the early 1970s he concluded that:

> arbitrators tend increasingly to focus upon worker obedience. The essential trend over the period examined, then, clearly illustrates an increase in concern about the maintenance of relationships of superordination and subordination between workers and managers in the most literal of the senses implied in the treatment of the subject by Max Weber [i.e. bureaucratic organization] ... neither managers nor arbitrators, so far as we can determine from extensive clinical evidence, are even slightly less concerned about worker responsiveness *and obedience* today then over the past twenty-year period. [Italics added.][29]

American managers have almost always defined and instituted industrial incentives very much as they might specify and install more efficient, effective machines. That workers might respond to motives and pursue interests unrecognized by the usual incentive systems has been largely ignored in practice. The systems rest on the assumption that workers seek, above all else, more income. Managers using these systems assume perhaps too easily that workers' consumer wants are unlimited, dominating other possible motives. To the extent that workers are interested in satisfying wants of a different nature—increased enjoyment in work and a greater control over work environment, for example—a range of worker aspirations remain unrelated to the job. The potential satisfactions that might be gained are not harnessed as driving forces for improved, more productive performance.

Close examinations of the assumptions of the usual incentive systems and of the typical manager-employee relationships reveal that workers are not merely passive participants in the production process; they are not interested in a job simply for pay with which they can buy enjoyment in the consumers' market. They have demonstrated again and again that they are not instruments to be manipulated in the pursuit of managerially defined goals. They show themselves to be active participants in the production process who, as coop-

[29]Ivar Berg, Marcia Freedman, and Michael Freedman, *Managers and Work Reform: A Limited Engagement,* New York: The Free Press, 1978, pp. 180, 183.

erative partners, can benefit themselves and management or who, as antagonistic subordinates, can restrict and hamper the achievement of industrial goals.

Why then have managers not more typically and more insistently than they have to date sought worker cooperation and union participation in the enhancing of productivity? Workers apparently have much to contribute and both parties have much to gain. Given the rewards for overcoming the obstacles mentioned above, one might think that a drift or trend toward more cooperative, productive relationships would be more visible than appears to be the case. Such thinking no doubt assumes that the key to the development of such a trend inheres in the motives of workers, union representatives, and managers. The assumption misleads if it causes one to ignore the difficult commitant requirements to change the complex web of structures within which all parties operate or if it leads one to overlook the complications that arise in adjusting institutional roles and modifying organizational values. The transformation of structural arrangements, the development of new roles, and the acceptance of values different from the traditional demand leadership skills of a high order. Ordinary managers and union leaders, trained and experienced in the maintanance of stably predictable relationships, may find the logic of change that promises greater cooperation and participation too threatening or too difficult. It may threaten the position and power of those involved and it may attempt to impose impossible conditions upon the larger unit—that is, the large corporate entity, the relevant labor market, or the national union.

Problems of Cooperating to Gain Productivity

Professor Richard Walton identified the major problems that arose in a number of productivity experiments he examined. Managers failed to follow through in ways that met the heightened expectation of workers; some managers were simply willing to reduce their own supervisory role and admit worker participation; and turnover remained too high, so that continuity of the experiment was undermined. Not only was worker turnover a problem, but promotions for managers, who were thus lost to the experiment, plagued the most successful experiments. The chances for the operation to expand, given its increased efficiency, were limited by overall corporate balance; production and investment decisions were made on other bases in distant headquarters.[30] Walton points out that reforming the workplace to gain increased productivity appears to meet even limited success only under quite special conditiions: small-town environment, small work force, new plants, geographic separation of the experimental unit from a firm's other facilities, use of outside consul-

---

[30]See Richard Walton, "Innovative Restructuring of Work," in Jerome M. Rosnow (ed.), *The Worker and the Job: Coping with Changes,* Englewood Cliffs, N.J.: Prentice-Hall, Inc., 1974, pp. 145–176.

TABLE 21
SCHOOLING OF THE CIVILIAN LABOR FORCE

Education	1959		1983	
	Number (millions)	Percentage of total labor force	Number (millions)	Percentage of total labor force
Less than 4 yrs high school	33.1	50.3	14.9	17.8
High school graduate	20.2	30.7	33.4	39.9
Some college	6.1	9.3	15.2	18.1
College graduate	6.3	9.6	20.2	24.2

Source: Handbook of Labor Statistics, Bureau of Labor Statistics Bulletin 2070, table 69, p. 140; *Educational Attainment of Workers, March 1982–83*, Bureau of Labor Statistics Bulletin 2191, table 1, p. 2.

tants, long lead times, and no unions or a positive union-management relationship.

One may conclude that innovative union-management cooperation and productivity programs are not likely to become important aspects of industrial relations. Too many variables are beyond the immediate control of either business executives or union leaders. Furthermore, neither workers and union representatives on the one side nor managers on the other can afford to give up the rights, privileges, and rewards to which they believe themselves entitled. They may call armistices, but no permanent treaty is ever negotiated. As long as a sizable portion of American managers dislike collective bargaining and seek to escape it, or, more important, prevent its spread, unions will only warily join in efforts to improve productivity.[31] In organized plants, union leaders will certainly continue to protect their members against changes to which they have not been a party. In such situations all such changes must be negotiated, and therefore are not apt to bring fundamental reforms speedily.

Higher levels of education, as well as unions, have impaired managers' age-old habit of manipulating workers. If we assume that those in the labor force with some college schooling can not be as easily driven or enticed as those with little schooling, we may see considerable change in future worker-manager relationships. (See Table 21.) The better-schooled work force, whether unionized or not, is not apt to respond as tolerantly as did the earlier workers to demeaning managerial treatment. They know themselves to be people as rational as managers. They are as concerned with their self-interest as their organizational superiors are with theirs; and they are as aware of the wider community values, changing legal standards, and general protections and rights employees can expect to enjoy.

Experience suggests that both union members and well-schooled employees

---

[31]Fred Foulkes, *Personnel Policies in Large Nonunion Companies,* Englewood Cliffs, N.J.: Prentice-Hall, Inc., 1980.

will join with employers to increase productivity if managers meet them as people whose interests and values are to be taken seriously and given due respect. Managers will have to involve themselves in ways deeper and more personal than simply introducing new machines, improving fringe benefits, or negotiating new participatory and consultative procedures. They will have to explore with workers and union representatives the values that all can share while contributing to the enhancement of productive cooperation. That exploration will require some change than the limited experiments have so far involved. Philip Selznick's comments of 1957 remain valid:

> [I]t involves transforming men [and women] and groups from neutral, technical units into participants who have a particular stamp, sensitivity, and commitment. This is ultimately an educational process . . . [it] is the art of institution building, the reworking of human and technological materials to fashion an organism that embodies new and enduring values. . . . to institutionalize is to *infuse with value* beyond the technical requirements of the task at hand. The prizing of social machinery beyond its technical role as largely a reflection of the unique way it fulfills personal or group needs. Whenever individuals become attached to an organization or a way of doing things as persons rather than as technicans, the result is a prizing of the device for its own sake. From the standpoint of the committed person, the organization is changed from an expendable tool into a valued source of personal satisfaction . . . The institutional leader, then, *is primarily an expert in the promotion and protection of values.*[32]

CONCLUSION

The matter of incentives and their relationships to productivity has been dwelt on here at considerable length because of its importance. Often treated as primarily a psychological problem, it is no less an organizational and an economic problem. It constitutes a challenge of great promise to both our intellectual and moral capacities—as individuals and as a society. If managers, union leaders, and member workers could join together more wholeheartedly than at present to increase productive efficiency—without being driven or coerced, but by responding to a wider range of interests within which to deal with continuing conflicts and differences—such problems as the encouragement of investment, adjustment to economic change, and flexible use of the work force will allow easier solutions.

Union participation can then be an asset, as valuable in securing capital funds and calling forth investments as the reputation of the product itself. The relationship between union and management could be a favorable characteristic of a firm's operations, whereas it is regarded unfavorably in some industries at present.

If unions and management are to realize their potential for increasing pro-

---

[32]Philip Selznick, *Leadership In Administration: A Sociological Interpretation,* New York: Harper & Row, Publishers, Incorporated, 1957, pp. 17, 28, 149–150, 152–153.

ductivity beyond present limits, union leaders and members as well as managers will have to respond to the challenge. It is not solely a matter of society's recognizing the legitimate aspirations and needs of workers, but of unionists and managers recognizing the expectations and needs of the broader community of which they are a part. The recognition will involve a social responsibility that will grapple not only with individual motivation and values but also with procedural, organizational, and institutional arrangements.

CHAPTER 14

THE ECONOMICS OF COLLECTIVE BARGAINING: UNIONS, FIRMS, AND MARKET CONTROL

We are now in a position to return to the issue discussed at the end of Chapter 12. There we suggested that producer interests can be fairly accomodated along with consumer interests only if market forces operate with less than full freedom. Those who protect themselves from those forces, sheltering themselves from the unrelenting pressures and uncertainty of competitive markets, exert, in varying degrees, monopolistic power; if their protection is sufficiently great they may enjoy a position permitting exploitation of other groups. In Chapter 13 we observed that the effects of general wage changes are not easily predictable or fully known. But wage increases *unaccompanied by productivity gains* will have adverse effects, either through squeezing the other shares of income or by pushing up prices and "taxing" consumers. Strategically located unions and some firms in oligopolistic industries may enjoy such economic power that they can raise wages, irrespective of productivity, and injure others. Many observers believe that the political necessity of every union to keep up with rival unions drives it to use power in exactly that way.

We observed in Chapter 13 that for the economy at large and even for workers as a whole, an increase in productivity is the only effective source of real income gains. Yet this is but a formal truth of theory and of little significance as a determinant of wage policy in either an employing organization or a union. In moving from the general to the particular—from society at large to the single enterprise—we find this fact, of which all managers and union leaders are well aware: The same benefits arising from a *productivity* gain (that is, from a larger output with the same or lower costs) may also be secured from *higher prices* with the same costs (if demand is not so elastic that total revenues actually decline). Unionists' interest would appear to be the same in either case. Both provide a larger kitty out of which to bargain for wage increases for members. Thus, although workers *as a whole* can gain benefits for their members substantially only through increased productivity, *individual* unions can equally well obtain increases by exercising market control sufficient to require a rise in prices. If the exercise of this control is easier than helping to improve productivity, will not unionists and managers be tempted to resort to it for their gains?[1]

First, let us restate the questions we have posed:

1 By admitting that some control over market forces by both parties to collective bargaining may be desirable, do we not run the risk of licensing strong groups to exploit weaker ones, allowing the stronger to distort the structure of relative wage rates to its own advantage?

2 Although we clearly cannot say that upward wage changes are *always* desirable, under *any* given conditions, does not union market power, coupled with union political dynamics, perpetually push union wages upward, with detrimental effects upon productivity, employment, and output?

MARKET POWER AND ABILITY TO PAY

Our approach to these problems can perhaps best be made by referring again to the principle of ability to pay. In one sense, it can be regarded as the productivity principle modified for application to situations of imperfect competition. In this sense, a firm's ability to pay—its capacity to sustain a particular cost structure—is measured partly by productivity changes and partly by the effects of discretionary control over price. Higher wages may be supported not only by greater output from a given input (lower labor cost per unit) but also by the exploitation of the firm's advantages in the product markets. A union may thus improve its wage bargaining position not only by cooperation in improving productivity but also by cooperating in exploiting any market advantages. The union label has long constituted one form of product differentiation that seeks to take the products of favored companies out of competition with other companies. Unions have also used both primary and secondary boycotts in support of market restrictions against would-be competitors. Multiemployer bargaining may lead to interfirm price agreements to which a union may or may not be party but from which it seeks benefit for its members.

The ability-to-pay principle has another, less sinister connotation, though. It can be regarded simply as the union's recognition that net value productivity—a firm's ability to earn income—is the source of its members' wage receipts and that moreover, within limits, most firms can affect their relative earning capacity. They may expand it by careful, efficient management or contract it through neglect. The economic limits to a union's interest in managerial

---

[1]Some scholars argue strongly that the temptation is so widespread and union leaders and managers so prone to fall into it that such behavior is a major obstacle to economic growth. See Mancur Olson, *The Rise and Decline of Nations,* New Haven, Conn.: Yale University Press, 1982, p. 62.

efficiency were once thought to be imposed by market forces that determined wage rates independently of the individual manager. Market forces are not always dominant, however, and thus a union may press for wage increases to the limit of the ability of the business to provide them. That ability is directly dependent upon the total operation of the business, in which a large element of discretion exists. All the aspects of a business operation obviously relate to a company's success as a revenue-receiving (and consequently a revenue-paying) institution. A union may therefore improve its chances for a better wage bargain not only by increasing worker efficiency but also by insisting upon improved performance in any and all aspects of a firm's operations; both measures enhance the firm's ability to pay.

The possibility of wage gains from management efficiencies provides unions with a reason to become interested in aspects of business operation traditionally conceived as the sole concern of management. Does accounting procedure understate the amount of revenue available for distribution? Is the marketing policy weak, so that the plant constantly operates at a disadvantageous level of output? Are sales spotty, reducing revenue available for distribution? Does an inept financial management impose an unwarranted charge against the firm's finances? Does lack of interest in research and development jeopardize the company's future profitability? Depending upon the quality of its leadership, a union might easily conclude that factors like these affect its ability to bargain for wage increases. It then might seek ways to assure improvements in managerial efficiency. The approach to the wage question thus becomes entangled with the question of the appropriate subject matter of collective bargaining.

The ability-to-pay principle does not assume the wage-paying capacity of the business to be limited by market forces; within limits it can be expanded. Such expansion of wage-paying capacity may be effected by (1) exploiting a firm's market advantages; or (2) improving business performance, increasing not only labor but also managerial productivity.

Union Response to Ability to Pay

Unions sometimes appear to deny the principle of ability to pay by their adoption of a policy of standard wages. In pursuit of such a policy, unions seek to raise the wage rates of competitive producers simultaneously and equally, without respect for individual profitability. They seem to establish some standard external to the firm as a substitute for the ability-to-pay principle, which is concerned with only the individual firm itself. This conclusion is more apparent than real. First, in the very setting of their standard wage demands, unions concern themselves with the relative abilities to pay of all the firms with which they deal. They cannot ask for a wage that only the most efficient producer can afford to pay, for then they would prove unable to enforce their demands on the majority. Nor can they set the standard where it will be satisfactory to the least efficient producer, for then they would deny possible wage increases to the majority of their members. The standard must be set somewhere between the most and the least efficient.

Usually union negotiations do not simply ignore the problems of struggling firms; to demand that they keep pace and maintain the wage levels of the standard firm may inflict unemployment upon members who work for them. Yet sometimes, as in construction or garments, union officials will demand a standard rate above the level that marginal firms can afford. In the garment industry, the leaders hope that the demand will force out such firms to the long-run benefit of the industry. In construction, such a demand is more apt to push marginal firms into nonunion work or at least send work into nonunion firms. The continuing and employed members, of course, benefit by receiving their higher pay.[2] More frequently, though, union leaders are willing to modify the ability-to-pay principle by granting concessions to weaker firms. Particularly during recessions, when marginal firms find themselves hard-pressed, they have sought concessions and unions have reluctantly granted them.[3] Because such concessions appear in episodes and are responses to economic distress, they are usually but temporary movements away from the unions' common rate, in line with wider-than-usual variations in the ability to pay.

In multiemployer bargaining units, increasingly found in the nonmanufacturing sector, a union may be able to make its demands upon an entire market, allowing it to evaluate the ability to pay of a whole industry. A union might try to increase productivity, for example, by encouraging the general modernization of machinery and plant or the undertaking of market and industrial research; but it may also try to exploit its market power by keeping out competitors or refusing to supply labor or needed materials of firms not adhering to a price policy that permits the demanded wages. Both productivity and ability-to-pay wage standards thus may become entangled with the question of the comprehensiveness of the bargaining unit, since multiemployer units may permit wage benefits not feasible in a smaller unit.

In examining wage bargaining, the fundamental distinction already made between the productivity and ability-to-pay standards should be kept in mind: Productivity necessarily involves a larger revenue-paying capacity, not only for the individual business, but for the economy as a whole. Not only do workers benefit in the particular firm or industry in which productivity increases, but, as consumers, other workers also benefit to the extent that prices decline. Even should the product price remain stable, with the whole benefit accruing to the particular workers involved, other workers are at least not adversely affected. The wage rates set in accordance with the ability-to-pay principle do not necessarily give the same result. They may reflect the rewards of market power as well as of productivity. Insofar as the wage increases come from that power,

---

[2]Researchers have found good evidence that in construction through the 1970s, unions' labor markets were so fragmented that they were able to keep wages high, even at the cost of considerable unemployment and loss of unionized jobs to nonunion workers. See David.E. Shulenburger, Robert A. McLean, and Sara B. Rasch, "Union-Nonunion Wage Differentials: A Replication and Extension," *Industrial Relations,* vol. 21, Spring 1982, p. 248.

[3]Mitchell, "Recent Union Contract Concessions," pp. 165–204, examines periods of concession bargaining from the 1950s to the 1980s.

the nation as a whole gains no return, and other workers may suffer through higher prices of the products they purchase. Only members of the particular union gain, and at the expense of everyone else. This may not be a result consciously pursued by the union, it is true, but simply the consequence of demands for higher wages made without respect for productivity increases in firms possessing wide discretionary pricing powers.

To the extent that business operates in imperfectly competitive product and factor markets,[4] then, wages are set on the basis of relative bargaining power, in which ability to pay enters as an important consideration of union, management, or both. Whether consideration of ability to pay is helpful or harmful to the consuming public as a whole will depend upon the relative stress placed on its components of productivity and price control.

Union and Management Exploitation of Consumers

The issue implicit in the ability-to-pay approach may be phrased in various ways, some of which have already been mentioned. How can we accommodate producer interests through organizations possessing market power without at the same time permitting their excessive use of that power to exploit others? Can we render compatible the need for organizations which by their very nature possess market power and the need for restraining the use of that power? To some it is a question of the extent to which companies or unions can be allowed to restrict competitive forces. To others it is a question of the extent to which security aims, achieved through exploitation of market power, are warranted. It might also be regarded as a question of the extent to which unions shall be allowed to improve their conditions by joining with employers to improve methods of production.

It may be that managers' and workers' legitimate organizational interests in job satisfaction, including a degree of job security, require something less than rigorous price competition. Yet some continuing competition may be useful to avoid stagnation and to help avoid a situation in which workers and employer exploit a protected position at the expense of consumers and other unorganized groups.[5] Where can and should we try to strike the balance? How much competition is too much, and how much is not enough?

Let us first put the question with specific reference to relative wage rates.

---

[4]If the product market is perfectly competitive, short-run prices will be set without respect to wages; if the labor market is perfectly competitive, short-run wages will be set without respect to product prices. When both markets are imperfect, the result is unpredictable, but it does appear that there is a more direct relationship between wages and prices: Price discretion permits wage discretion.

[5]See Thomas Gale Moore, "The Beneficiaries of Trucking Regulation," *Journal of Law and Economics,* vol. 21, 1978, p. 327. Moore concluded that "three-quarters or more of the cost to shippers and ultimately consumers of trucking regulations take the form of income transfers to labor and capital involved in trucking." Moshe Kim confirmed the conclusions in a similar study of Canadian trucking, "The Beneficiaries of Trucking Regulation, Revisited," *Journal of Law and Economics,* vol. 27, 1984, p. 227.

Consider the situation in the basic steel industry through the 1970s. Starting with an average hourly wage about 17 percent larger than for manufacturing generally, steelworkers won wage increases that pushed their differential to 34 percent by 1980. Over the same period they also improved their fringe benefits substantially, gaining additional vacation time and holidays, improved severance pay, supplemental unemployment benefits, insurance, and pension contributions. One may guess that such gains could be achieved only because the United Steelworkers bargained with substantially all steel employers and secured uniform terms with the major producers. Those producers continued to act as if they enjoyed—and would continue to enjoy—an oligopolistic market relatively safe from foreign competition. With no significant amount of steel production from unorganized mills, the danger of domestic competition produced at lower labor cost was virtually eliminated. Foreign competition appeared to industry leaders to be only marginal, unable to threaten their core markets. The cost of employer concessions to the union could thus be passed along to consumers through price increases, a tactic that the industry had relied upon for decades.

On what grounds can we judge whether steelworkers were entitled to benefits that were made possible only by the steel consumers' paying higher prices than otherwise would have been the case? Steelworkers' jobs are demanding and often require heavy physical labor, and these workers may well have deserved their benefits and amelioration of their lot. The question remains, however, what balance of interest should be struck between the steelworkers and other workers who, as consumers, purchase goods made of steel? Were some of the consumers as deserving of benefits, and were their conditions of work as much in need of improvement? On average over the ten-year span, steelworkers' hourly earnings increased each year at the rate of 5.7 percent; autoworkers' earnings rose more slowly at about 3 percent a year; and in electrical and electronic equipment workers' earnings increased at slightly over 1 percent a year. Apparel workers' earnings actually declined about 0.9 percent annually. Were the workers in these other industries less deserving than those in steel?

Should such a group of workers, in collaboration with its managers, be entitled to extract from consumers whatever its strategic position permits? Shall grocers, dentists, schoolteachers, and construction workers, in turn, charge the steelworkers whatever they can get away with? Shall our distributive standard be nothing more than bare economic power—the exploitation of whatever market advantage one possesses and can defend from dilution?

Shall each group of workers be permitted or encouraged to determine its own rates, depending upon its bargaining power vis-à-vis its employer and the particular industry's bargaining power vis-à-vis the public, based largely on the elasticity of demand for its product? If our answer is "yes," for want of any alternative, are we not simply acceding to the exploitation of the weaker, less strategically situated groups, allowing the makers of products with a low elasticity of demand to gain at the expense of those whose products have available substitutes? The former raise their wages by raising the prices of their products; the latter must pay the higher prices but cannot themselves take similar action for fear of an adverse effect on the demand for their products. Should the only restraint imposed on unions, then, be the elasticity of the demand curve facing their company or industry?

Those favorably disposed toward unions have generally in the past met such arguments with the contention that as unions mature they will develop a sense of social responsibility and moderation. The steelworkers' example over nearly a half century suggests that either the argument is not well founded or unions have not yet matured. Any sense of social responsibility rests upon mere self-restraint. To rely upon so weak a force to constrain private interests may not be wise public policy. If the power of a union to satisfy the income wants of its members rests upon the ability to pay of the firms with which it deals, and if that ability to pay can be augmented not only through the increasing of physical productivity but equally through the more effective exploitation of market advantages, will not human nature take the union along the latter course of action? With such an easy alternative, what reason do we have for assuming that notions of social responsibility will deflect unions to the difficult and problematic methods of increasing technological efficiency?

Is there no restraint other than that which unions may themselves impose? It seems clear that there is; few unions, however strong, can immunize themselves indefinitely from the forces of a rugged kind of competition. Market exploitation, whether by unions or management, cannot be so firmly entrenched as to be forever free from competitive threat. The problems appear at first so insoluble because we are accustomed to view their immediate effects. By widening our time horizons somewhat, we put the problem into a proper perspective. So steelworkers and managers discovered in the rapid slide of production and employment in the recession of the early 1980s.

COMPETITION THROUGH INNOVATIONS

Professor Joseph A. Schumpeter pointed out that the problem of power is one with which economists have stubbornly wrestled for years, without satisfactory result.[6] Their classic economic models assumed business units so small that they were incapable of exerting any influence on the market. Their competition led to an optimum allocation of resources in accordance with consumer wants and a distribution of income that accorded with each individual's contribution to the economic system. Although their normative judgments seemed conclusive, their assumptions were not. Business units grew ever larger, and with the growth of the large corporation came widening control over the market—discretionary powers over prices and production. But, mirabile dictu, despite the

---

[6]The argument is set forth in Joseph A. Schumpeter, *Capitalism, Socialism and Democracy*, 3d ed., New York: Harper & Row, Publishers, Incorporated, 1950.

increase of market power, the consumer's position improved. Prices of goods declined over the years, the quality of products improved, and the standard of living advanced. Market powers did not seem to bring with them the evils which economists had foreseen.

The reason for this seeming paradox, declared Professor Schumpeter, was that economists had been worrying about the wrong kind of competition. They had been concerned about price competition among small units, whereas the more significant price movements were long-run declines caused by innovation and technological change. Small units could not avail themselves of such technical developments since these were feasible only with large aggregations of capital equipment. Business managers would not undertake the risky investments of capital, though, unless they could reasonably expect some measure of financial protection derived from that market power condemned by economists. The corporate leaders who sank large sums of money into fixed capital did not do so unless they were reasonably sure that their innovation, perhaps protected by patents and trade secrets, would offer protection against immediate and competitive price competition, thus providing an adequate return on their investments. The prerequisite condition for the investment of large sums in mass-production techniques was thus some degree of market control. Economic theory was turned on its head; monopoly was the instrument through which the prices of goods were reduced to the consuming public. Paradoxically, market power carried with it benefits to the public. It provided a degree of security necessary to foster business actions that in the long run favored consumers.

Schumpeter did not concede, however, that the investing innovators were immune to all forms of competition. If they had been, there would have been nothing to force a lowering of product prices as costs of production declined through improved techniques. There was a dynamic competition at work, different from the simple price competition of orthodox economic theory, said Schumpeter. No business, however large or strategically situated and however great its market power, could preserve itself forever from the competition that came with innovations—new products and new technologies. Innovations might come from other firms within an industry; they might equally well come from other industries. Their introduction could be tentatively delayed by collusion, agreement, or suppression, but such practices were not likely to be effective indefinitely. Inventiveness, ingenuity, and initiative in one quarter or another almost certainly assures us that although market power may provide a necessary short-run protection to large capital investments, it cannot give permanent protection against competitive products or technologies.

Many large firms maintain extensive research departments, Schumpeter observed, because they are a necessary condition of business survival. If firms were not constantly looking for new techniques and products, they would lose sales to some new and better product or to a similar product sold at a lower price because of improved methods of production. Competition forces business managers to anticipate such eventualities, and this innovative competition, argued Schumpeter, is infinitely more effective than the simple theory of price competition.

Technological Innovation as a Check on Union and Management

We may seem to have digressed from a discussion of the market powers of unions. Yet Schumpeter's argument should suggest a relevant question: If unions' wage objectives are limited by the ability to pay of the firms with which they bargain, will they seek to expand that ability to pay by helping the firm to protect its market from competion or through improving productivity? We can expect unions to seek whatever protections they can win, politically or economically, and in the short run they may gain in varying degrees. However, we cannot expect a union to be able to maintain an exploitable industry position any better than an industry's firms can on their own. In the late 1970s and early 1980s it was notable that as Congress deregulated both airlines and trucking, the unions associated with those industries responded to the increased competition by moderating their wage demands and even agreeing to concessions and givebacks.[7] It has also long been a commonly observed fact that low wages are associated with competitive industries; usually the more competitive, the lower the wages.

Unions that push up wages unmindful of their impact on prices may in time be brought up short by the development of new products replacing the ones up-on which their members are dependent or by the introduction of new production techniques that drastically affect employment. Union market power often is exerted only through business units, and thus the presence of that power depends upon the market power of the business units. Unions in some competitive industries, such as garments, printing, or trucking, may provide a means to cartelize them, controlling or extinguishing competition, to the benefit of both their members and the firms involved. In both situations, insofar as the businesses or industries are subject to dynamic Schumpeterian competition, so are the unions subject to the same restraint.

This may not be so strong a protection for consumers as we would wish. That it nevertheless constitutes an important bulwark seems undeniable. The power of the Steelworkers was used to exploit their former strategic advantage, encouraging firms to raise prices and wages; but low-cost foreign competition, substitute materials such as glass, plastics, and aluminum, and new and more automated technologies may have made that victory a temporary one. In this way, the once-proud position of the coal miners has been seriously weakened by coal substitutes for both heat and power. Thus neither the Steelworkers nor

---

[7]"The Teamsters concessions [in 1982] were negotiated against a background of federal deregulation of the trucking industry, a structured change that permitted entry of nonunion competition. During the final year of the old agreement it was widely reported that many trucking employers were paying less than contractural wages with apparent acquiesence from Teamsters locals. Mitchell, "'Recent Union Contract Concessions," pp. 170–171.

the United Mine Workers have been immune to the effects of their own policies, any more than steel producers and mine operators have been. The exploitation of their advantage probably has hastened the arrival of products and processes competitive with both steel and coal, for the competition was of a kind not wholly within the power of the union to control.

It appears, then, that there are two chief limitations upon the power of an organized group of workers to raise wage rates relative to the rates of other workers: (1) in the short run, the elasticity of demand for their product;[8] and (2) in the long run, the competitive restraint of new products and new techniques of production.

Let us now turn to the question of whether these two checks operate with equal effectiveness when unions bargain with single companies and when they bargain on an industry basis. The first of these limitations, the elasticity of demand for the product, is more effective if bargaining proceeds on a firm-by-firm basis. If the union at Ford raises its rates higher than the union at General Motors, adversely affecting costs of production and prices of Ford cars, a shift in demand from Fords to Chevrolets will act as a brake on its actions. It is possible, however, that the union will recognize the disadvantage of firm-by-firm bargaining and seek industrywide bargaining or some form of pattern bargaining that would accomplish the same purpose. In such a situation will not any restraint normally supplied by interfirm competition, with differential labor costs an important competitive factor, be substantially reduced? Since all firms similarly situated are granting roughly equivalent increases, will not managements more willingly grant wage demands, with the consequence that rates in that industry in the short run will rise without much limitation? There is a lighter check on union pressure since the elasticity of demand for an industry product is considerably less than that for any particular output of a firm in the industry.

There is a measure of truth in this argument, but it is overstated. The fact that the wage rates of all competitors in an industry rise simultaneously does not mean that all will be affected to the same degree. The more efficient firms may be able to accommodate such an increase without any impact on prices whatsoever. Other firms may be able to meet the increases by improving the efficiency of their organizations. But some firms are likely to face the prospect of accepting losses in operation or forcing an increase in prices, which may reduce the demand for the products of the less efficient firms. The union may well concern itself with the problems of these struggling firms and seek to improve their efficiency, as the UAW did when it made special concessions to a Chrysler faced with bankruptcy. Firms that gain no concessions are not always pleased with their settlements, of course, and union leaders can not make concessions easily or casually.

---

[8]This involves both simple price elasticity and cross-elasticity of demand, that is, the effect of a change in price on the quantities demanded of that product and also of other products (the substitution effect).

The reader will recall the kind of problem introduced on the management side of the bargaining table in resolving conflicting interests among management representatives when bargaining is conducted on a multiemployer basis. The differential impact of wage increases on the business positions of the various firms will act as something of a restraint on the unions, solidifying managerial opposition to rates that work undue hardships on certain of their number. The bargaining power of those for whom the cost of agreeing to the union's terms is greatest rises relative to that of both other members of the employers' association and the union. Multiemployer or industrywide bargaining may relax somewhat the restraint provided by the elasticity of demand for the product, but it certainly does not lift the lid and permit "easy pickings" for the union.[9]

Moreover, industrywide and multiemployer bargaining does not affect Schumpeterian competition insofar as firms within an industry remain competitive among themselves on all except wage rates. Each will continue to strive to improve its product offerings and to better its methods of production. Research into new products and technologies will still serve to limit the power of unions to push rates upward. Wages in the innovating firms may be raised, but in other firms that feel the competitive pressure of the innovation, wage and price ceilings will exist. It must be remembered that such "dynamic" competition occurs between industries no less than within a particular industry, as the cases of steel and coal remind us.

With respect to the effect of union market power on relative wage rates, then, we can say that our major restraints are the elasticity of demand for the product and the differential impact of wage changes on profits, in the short run, and the competition of new goods and new productive methods in the long run. These restraints operate not only among whole industries but also among individual companies within an industry, as long as effective product competition remains. This latter proviso is one which we shall have occasion to explore more fully later.

IS THE PUBLIC SECTOR A SPECIAL CASE?

Many economists and labor scholars have argued that unions of public employees enjoy special advantages in bargaining with government officials. Professors Henry H. Wellington and Ralph K. Winter, of the Yale Law School, put the case well:

> [T]he social costs of collective bargaining in the private sector are principally economic and seem inherently limited by market forces. In the public sector, however, the costs seem economic only in a very narrow sense and are on the whole political. It further seems that, to the extent union power is delimited by market or other forces

---

[9]This is not to say that under such bargaining in an industry characterized by oligopoly or price leadership a wage increase may not lead to uniform price action, but only that the differential impact of the wage increase on the firms in that industry will act as a limitation on the size of the increase.

in the public sector, these constraints do not come into play nearly as quickly as in the private . . . Government does not generally sell a product the demand for which is closely related to price. There usually are not close substitutes for the products and services provided by government and the demand for them is relatively inelastic. . . . Because much government activity is, and must be, a monopoly, product competition, nonunion or otherwise, does not exert a downward pressure on prices and wages. Nor will the existence of a pool of labor ready to work for a wage below union scale attract new capital and create a new, and competitively less expensive, governmental enterprise.[10]

They conclude that the inelasticity of demand for government services and the slight possibility of competitive entrants into the market supplied by government typically put public employees' unions in stronger bargaining positions than private sector unions.

Empirical studies of the wage effects of public employees' unions indicate that collective bargaining has brought substantial wage and fringe benefit gains[11] above those secured by unorganized public workers. They did not shed light, however, on any special power that the unions might have wielded. Some studies and anecdotal evidence suggest that as state and local governments began to experience fiscal difficulties from the mid-1970s into the early 1980s, public employees' unions agreed to lesser settlements than they had gained earlier. One study found that when a local government confronted tight fiscal conditions "the money settlements . . . were more modest than in the favorable fiscal situations, particularly with respect to fringe benefits, in which virtually no improvements were made."[12] In New York City, 1975, the public employees' unions moved toward coalition bargaining when a fiscal crisis befell the municipal government. They also agreed to eliminate a number of fringe benefits. Perhaps more significantly, they were more ready to accept massive layoffs than to negotiate wage reductions.[13]

It appears that unions in both private and public sectors moderate their gains and even offer concessions in the face of economic adversity. Further studies may be able to determine whether public employees' unions protect themselves and their members *relatively* better than those in the private sector.

---

[10]Wellington and Winter, "The Limits of Collective Bargaining in Public Employment," in Lewin, Feuille, and Kochan, *Public Sector Labor Relations* pp. 25, 27.

[11]See the various articles under the title, "Wage Impacts of Unionism," in Lewin, Feuille, and Kochan, *Public Sector Labor Relations,* pp. 397–405, provides a brief review and summary of twenty-one studies from 1961 to 1976. Also see Linda N. Edwards and Franklin R. Edwards, "Wellington-Winter Revisited: The Case of Municipal Sanitation Collection," *Industrial and Labor Relations Review,* vol. 35, Apr. 1982, pp. 307–318. The authors of the latter article warn, as we note later in this chapter, that the correlation of public unions and their members' favorable wage differential over similar, nonunion employees may not signify undue market power. Until the relative productivity of the two groups of workers can be measured and compared, we do not know whether the costs of the higher wages are borne by the taxpayers (or consumers) or covered by more efficient production and work.

[12]Milton Derber and Martin Wager, "Public Sector Bargaining and Budget Making under Fiscal Adversity," in Lewin, Feuille, and Kochan, *Public Sector Labor Relations,* p. 396.

[13]David Lewin and Mary McCormick, "Coalition Bargaining in Municipal Government: The New York City Experience," in Lewin, Feuille, and Kochan, *Public Sector Labor Relations,* p. 137.

Until the evidence is in, we can neither confirm nor disprove the Winter and Wellington thesis.

THE IMPACT OF UNION MARKET POWER ON PRODUCTIVITY, EMPLOYMENT, AND OUTPUT

Let us turn now to the second aspect of union market power that we shall consider here: Its impact on productivity, employment, and output. Economists have sometimes argued that unions adversely affect employment if they have organized all employees in a region or industry and negotiate "excessive" rates. Then fewer employees will be hired than at lower, "competitive" rates. Unemployed persons would like to work and would be willing to work at the rates being paid, but to hire them at existing union rates would be unprofitable to employers. Some of the unemployed would be willing to work even for lower rates, but the union through its hold on the employer will not permit their effective competition with its members on the job. The presence of pools of unemployed workers may thus be blamed directly on the unions.

Moreover, it is said, the strength of unions and the pressures of coercive comparison, based on union rivalries, provide an almost irresistible and persistent upward pressure on wages. It may be that the effects of any given wage increase can be predicted only in light of circumstances existing at the moment, but it seems a fairly safe prediction that continuous wages increases must certainly lead to recurring unemployment. If union bargaining power, based on special market position, establishes ever-higher wages levels, surely from time to time under a particular combination of circumstances the level of rates will serve as a bar to the employment of idle but willing workers. Union power will adversely affect not only employment but also productivity and output whenever it is used merely exploitatively rather than to help increase productive efficiency and share in it. As wages rates rise over the years without relation to increases in productivity, the argument goes, there appears a double phenomenon: pockets of unemployment and pockets of inflation.

The validity of this argument rests on the assumption that union power is not likely to meet effective resistance, so organized workers are allowed to push rates up to excessive levels. We have already seen, however, that union power is rarely irresistible and that effective restraints on its exercise do exist. There is no need to repeat here anything but our previous conclusion that the elasticities of demand for particular products and the development of new substitute products and techniques are, in general, important checks to union pressures, though they are often ignored or underrated. In particular instances where these general restraints prove ineffective, they require strengthening or supplementing.

There is no reason to assume that management's bargaining strength is likely to wither away over time. Managers have powers of resistance of which the unionists are acutely aware, even if the public is not. Their motive in resisting union demands is to preserve their competitive status vis-à-vis other firms not only in their own industry but also in other industries. If the price of their industry's product rises, they are likely to find that consumers will begin to divert their incomes to other uses. The wage policies of particular unions with a strong bargaining position may cause unemployment here or there and may exert some inflationary pressure in one area or another, but the union strength that can produce these consequences is not apt to persist without the appearance of an effective check.

Employment and wages manifest an inverse relationship that should not escape our examination. Are there conditions under which these checks on union power may be undependable? If there is a continuous high demand for all labor throughout the economy, will not at least some unions be placed in a position where they can boost their rates with reduced employer resistance, since the scarcity of labor will cause employer to compete against employer and industry against industry? Will not union leaders and members discount any adverse effects on employment due to rising costs and prices if those workers who lose their jobs can count on quickly finding others? A period of prosperity brings with it a competitive bidding for labor and a strong demand for products, which make possible the easy payment of higher wages. Managers try to avoid strikes that interrupt profitable production and threaten the loss of hard-to-get workers. The union's strategic position is improved therefore at the very time that the employer's will to resist is weakest. Wage increases can be compensated by prices increases with little injury to demand. The cost to the employer of agreeing on the union's terms declines, and the cost of disagreement on those terms increases.

Empirical Evidence of Union Influence

Empirical evidence of the effects of unions and collective bargaining indicate that they are more varied and less easily demonstrated than theory or speculation suggest. First, unions' effects on wages vary over time and particularly with the waxing and waning of the economy; they also differ according to the occupations and industries examined. It is quite clear that wages in strongly unionized industries and occupations are higher than in those unorganized or with few union members.[14] Of course, the higher wages may be *caused* by other forces and influences, including those that also induce workers to join unions; it may even be possible that the level of wages may be at least a partial cause of unionism.[15] The difficulty is in specifying what nonunion wages

---

[14]Mitchell, *Union, Wages, and Inflation,* pp. 81, 89.

[15]Professor Barry Hirsch examined the relationship between unionism and earnings dispersion within both manufacturing and nonmanufacturing industries for 1970. He concluded that the more homogeneous the work force in its benefit preferences and jobs interests as well as skill and occupational characteristics, the more responsive it will be to unionism. "For any package of services a union can offer close to the preference of the median voter, support for the union will be greater the more highly concentrated are preferences around the median. Stated differently, for a given level of demand for union services, a union can more easily construct a package that will satisfy a majority the less dispersed are preferences around the median. Thus unionization should be more likely, more effective, and more stable politically the more homogeneous are a group of workers." ("The Interindustry Structure of Unionism, Earnings and Earnings Dispersion," *Industrial Relations and Labor Review,* vol. 36, Oct. 1982, pp. 24–25.)

would be without unions; when both coexist in different firms at the same time, there is bound to be interaction between them, greatly complicating any analysis.[16]

The earliest studies of union effects on wages concluded that they were greatest during the depression years of the 1930s, with a differential of 28 percent or more; they declined during the post-World War II period to a 5 percent differential; and then they gradually rose again to a difference of 10 to 20 percent[17] up through the 1970s. Union wage effects appear to be greatest in construction, where there is up to a 43 percent differential. The effects are much less in transportation, communications, and utilities, with a 16 percent differential; in nondurable manufacturing, 12 percent; and in durable manufacturing, 9 percent.[18]

Both upward and downward wage effects *associated* with unions, which may not be entirely *caused* by unions, are probably greater than studies have usually indicated. Professor Richard Freeman has found that union settings are associated with a higher level of fringes than nonunion settings: unions are found particularly to favor pensions, vacation pay, and life, accident, and health insurance, probably indicating union response to their older, longer-tenured members. He concluded that the union fringe effect exceeds, in percentage terms, the union wage effect, probably averaging about 36 percent.[19]

However, one cannot conclude that unions simply benefit themselves, in a monopolistic way, at the expense of nonunion workers. Were unions simply using market power to benefit their own members, one would have expected them to develop a differential between union and nonunion employees in their period of fast and early growth and then to maintain it. That the empirical evidence does not support so simple a monopoly model indicates at least that it is misleading and perhaps that it is simply wrong. Not only do unions affect wage differentials between union and nonunion workers, but they also help determine the differentials *among unionized* workers in business establishments and throughout the industries they organize. Again Professor Freeman has examined the union effect upon wage dispersion, the ranges between high and low wages. He found that unions consistently seek a wage system that

---

[16]Some union-nonunion wage differentials may be the consequence of quite different job characteristics that may not be readily identifiable. One study, for example, finds that unionized blue-collar jobs are more hazardous than nonunionized blue-collar jobs. J. Paul Leigh, "Are Unionized Blue Collar Jobs More Hazardous than Nonunionized Blue Collar Jobs?" *Journal of Labor Research,* vol. 3, Summer 1982, p. 349.

[17]H. G. Lewis, *Unionism and Relative Wages in the United States: An Empirical Inquiry,* Chicago: The University of Chicago Press, 1963; and Albert Rees, *The Economics of Trade Unions,* rev. ed., Chicago: The University of Chicago Press, 1977.

[18]Bloch and Kuskin, "Wage Determination in the Union and Nonunion Sectors," pp. 183–192; and Orley Ashenfelter and George E. Johnson, "Unionism, Relative Wages, and Labor Quality in U.S. Manufacturing Industries," *International Economic Review,* vol. 13, Oct. 1972, pp. 477–508.

[19]Richard B. Freeman, "The Effects of Unionism on Fringe Benefits," *Industrial and Labor Relations Review,* vol. 34, July 1981, pp. 489–509.

favors redistribution in favor of the lower-paid.[20] The result is that union wage policies encourage standardized rates within and across establishments, significantly reducing within firms the wage dispersions among blue-collar workers and also narrowing the white-collar/blue-collar differential. These "flattening" effects of union wage policies may dominate the more widely studied industry wage effect, so that on net unions may reduce rather than increase wage inequality.

The existence of union wage differentials does not, however, necessarily indicate that employer costs are thereby raised; that consumers are exploited through higher prices; or that other, nonunion workers suffer through lower wages elsewhere. Both the introduction of unions and the continuing operation of collective bargaining entail fundamental changes in management, the work force, and the workplace. These changes may produce substantial and positive productivity effects that can offset all or a large part of such wage and fringe differentials enjoyed by unionized employees.[21] Managers may select workers with more training or experience; worker turnover and absenteeism[22] may be reduced, with resulting productivity gains. Collective bargaining may also lower the need for a significant portion of supervisory costs. Of course, a number of union provisions—seniority, restrictions on flexible assignment, and limits on discipline—may adversely affect productivity. The effects of collective bargaining depend upon a complex variety of adjustments, and until they are carefully sorted out and gains weighed against losses, judgments might wisely be made with caution.

The Bounded Nature of Union Influence

Analyses of unions' wage effects indicate that unions probably influence wage levels and certainly influence the form of compensation, particularly the kinds of fringe benefits. But they also suggest that unions cannot—or do not, at any rate—set wages without let or hindrance, particularly if the benefits won raise production costs significantly. In some industries they may gain more than in others, and under some adverse economic conditions they may win less than under more favorable circumstances. Though the federal Employment Act of 1946 made full employment the nation's primary economic goal, that goal has not been pursued with consistency; periods of recession and rising unemploy-

---

[20]"In a simple median voter model of union behavior, the 50+ percent of members who earn less than the mean would favor a policy of greater gains for the lower paid. Union opposition to personal rates probably also reflects worker solidarity and preference for objective standards as opposed to the subjective decisions of foremen. It is difficult to see how the union would be able to maintain its organizational strength and monopolistic prices, in fact, with significant personal differentials within firms." Richard Freeman, "Unionism and the Dispersion of Wages," *Industrial and Labor Relations Review,* vol. 34, Oct. 1980, pp. 5–6.

[21]See Kim B. Clark, "The Impact of Unionism on Productivity," *Industrial and Labor Relations Review,* vol. 33, July 1980, p. 451.

[22]Steven G. Allen, "Compensation, Safety, and Absenteeism: Evidence from the Paper Industry," *Industrial and Labor Relations Review,* vol. 34, Jan. 1981, p. 207.

ment appear often enough to require unions to moderate their wage claims and bargaining expectations. In the recession of 1974–75, unemployment rose as high as 9 percent and the industrial production index dropped by 17 percent from its peak-to-trough. Unemployment rose higher and production dropped even more in the 1980–82 depression. In both periods unions made wage and fringe concessions, sometimes actually cutting wages and giving up fringe benefits as well as forgoing increases. Most unionized employers, along with national lobbying groups, favor and work for antiinflationary government policies. The state of the economy is not just an autonomous influence upon collective bargaining but is actively shaped, to some degree, by managements and unions.

Even should the government manage the economy more ably to keep it consistently closer to a full-employment condition, it does not follow that unions, through collective bargaining, would inevitably win wage increases that would thereby push up prices in an inflationary spiral. During the early 1960s, when prices rose quite slowly (under 2 percent annually) and unions' size and influence were close to their peaks, collective bargaining and price stability appeared to be quite compatible.

It appears that in a full-employment economy the stage is set for inflation. It is a stage that unionists prefer and bend their lobbying efforts to achieve. They consistently favor government social programs, easy-money policies, and increases rather than cuts in public expenditures. Collective bargaining gains can be won more easily under such conditions than in more restrictive, deflationary, and frugal times. When price rises come and wages begin to move upward, it is not *solely because of* union action, but also because of the possibilities the stage provides for *all* groups in society to seek advantage. Business managers, professionals and farmers no less than labor believe they can push up prices and cost with little fear of consequences. Full employment moderates the forces of both short- and long-term competition. Power that leads to either a creeping or galloping inflation is not unique to labor unions. Neither that power nor the inflationary outcomes will be deflected simply by attempts to restrain unions. Full employment under nonunion conditions will still generate pressures from the business sectors of the economy. Inflation thus is not a unique problem of union market power at all, but rather one to which all sectors contribute; it is transmitted through all economic transactions.

Once inflation begins in the United States, because of monetary and fiscal policies or because of shocks such as the rapid rise in petroleum prices in the 1970s, the processes of wage determination in both union and nonunion firms help to explain its perpetuation. The spiraling of wages and prices, each chasing the other, is a troublesome reality with which public policy makers must grapple. Union and management negotiators tend to extrapolate from the past into the future, projecting forward, through their multiyear agreements, the price increases already experienced. Even in nonunion situations, managers set next year's wages by taking into account current and expected price changes. The continuation of inflationary pressures is complicated not so much by unions' market power as by the sensitivity of both employees and employers to the equity of at least maintaining real wages.

Casual and popular observers can easily be persuaded to overstate the market power of unions. There exists the possibility of strong groups exploiting the weak—unionists gaining high wages at the expense of unorganized workers—but that exploitation exists only in particular situations, not generally. Union wage gains differentials may be substantially—or entirely—offset by union-induced productivity gains. Where they are not, and union gains represent simple exploitation of market power, there are effective eventual limits in the form of price, product, and technological competition. These restraints are more effective where business firms actively compete. The effects of union wage setting upon productivity and output may be beneficial; or they can be adverse in particular firms or industries, causing unemployment and lowering production. In the adverse cases the remedies are almost always the previously enumerated competitive forces. They usually operate to bring home to the responsible parties the costs and consequences of exploitative behavior. The danger that continuing high employment will divert the attention of unionists from improving productivity as a basis for wage increases is not one that inheres only or particularly in collective bargaining. In an inflationary period or in times of high employment, all economic groups may attempt to get ahead of others or at least to keep up. Controlling inflation and improving productivity require broad-gauged policies that affect many or all groups, employers and employees alike.

These are greater restraints upon unions' exercise of market power than is popularly assumed, and the market power of unions is hardly as looming as many believed in the heyday of union growth in the 1940s and 1950s. There may be some excessive and restrictive practices that public policy might wisely proscribe, particularly those that limit product competition or attempt to hinder the introduction of new techniques and machines. Both regular price competition and Schumpeterian innovation impose limits on the aggrandizement of economic power. What remain to be questioned are the methods by which innovations are encouraged and the policies that allow them to flourish. In exploring these questions, public authorities may want to examine carefully the deregulation of industries smothered in noncompetitive procedures, the uses of antitrust action, and the facilitating of new industrial and business development. There is no reason why public policy should not be directed to breaking down or reducing the market powers of either unions or business firms.

Implications for Public Policy

The conclusion that unions are subject to substantial market restraints is an important guide to public policy. We can accept unions for the desirable role that they play in giving security to their members and in allowing workers a measure of participation in the production process; and that acceptance does not necessarily, and certainly does not always, subject consumers to exploitation by the unions. One may want to examine the effects of specific union policies, just as one examines the specifics of business practices; if they are found to be peculiarly immune to competitive restraint or particularly adverse in their impacts upon important groups of the public, one may urge special government action. But to the extent that the economy can rely upon competition—price, product, and technological—it can secure the social advantages of unionism and escape the bleak choices of submitting to union domination, repressing unions, or accepting a government that would set wages and prices authoritatively.

We have thus found that both competition and various degrees of market control exist in the economy, with both contributing to social well-being. Competition drives the economy toward an efficient allocation of resources and helps ensure effective service for consumers; some market control by producers and unions allows them a degree of stability and protection in an otherwise uncertain, changing, and variable economy. The question next posed is: How much competition and how much private control—what shall be the blend or mix of these two? This, we submit, cannot be answered once and for all. The answer will change with social needs and perceptions over time. It will probably involve more of an ad hoc approach that price theory suggests. The theory presumes a timelessness in its teachings that probably does not exist. We may begin, for example, simply by drawing up lists of restrictive control tactics that appear to us to pass beyond a reasonable regard for other private group interests to exploitation. We may think of these as unfair labor practices, of either unions or management, that adversely affect consumers.[23]

The banning of offensive, wasteful practices will presumably leave unions and managements a sufficient degree of control to permit them to protect their interests as creative producers and yet leave them subject to competitive forces sufficient to protect the public that looks to them for the satisfaction of consumer needs. We shall encounter the same problem of achieving a workable balance again, in other contexts. So pragmatic an approach may fail to please those who insist upon rigorous solutions, but it appears capable of meeting present issues. The neat, systematic solution has not yet disclosed itself, and if it should ever arrive, events will probably have already begun to outmode it. In the meantime, we can at least read the signs and discover the general direction in which we should move to reach the desired objective.

---

[23]The reader will find it a rewarding exercise to draw up a tentative list articulating the reasons for including certain practices but excluding others. Consider how important a particular practice is to both the producers and consumers involved. For example, in the introduction of new machines or production techniques, should the union have veto rights? If not, should displaced workers be given special placement and seniority rights, or if no other jobs are available, extra severance pay? What would be the consequences upon the employing firm, consumers, the community, and taxpayers in the place where the workers live?

CONCLUSION

Market powers of unions exist and cannot be denied; they are necessary to the very existence and functions of unions. That their exercise will not be intolerable seems likely as long as they are balanced by competitive restraints. The large union, like the large corporation, has become a continuing part of our society. Those who mold and make public policy need to understand its limitations and weaknesses as well as its strength. It should not be uncritically accepted or unreasonably feared. Americans accept the market power (or control) of the large corporation and should be able to accept the power wielded by the large union. They broadly approve of the purposes both serve. And just as in the case of the large corporation, they must be assured that such control is not used in ways and for purposes that show themselves to be inconsistent over time with other broad social objectives.

We may now pause to survey the territory over which we have passed in Chapters 12 through 14. We set out to examine some of the major economic problems introduced by collective bargaining. In doing so, we found it advisable to inspect the widely held theory of wages—the marginal productivity theory—as a possible basis for evaluating union wage actions. The theory is not strictly a wage theory, however, but rather a theory of employment at given supply levels. Few employers or unions operate in an auction market where wages are continually adjusting to the hourly or daily supplies and demands for labor. Actual business and union decisions are made in, through, and by means of organizations whose interests demand more stability, certainty, and trust in the employment relationship than the theory originally recognized. Wherever unions join managers in setting wages, they become participants in the process, assuming in part a managerial role. Moreover, the marginal productivity theory proceeds from the premise that the appropriate standard of resource allocation is to maximize consumer satisfaction. Economists increasingly recognize that such maximizing does not exclude a need for stability and trust in the employment relationship. Such a need requires employers also to concern themselves with workers' job satisfaction and loyalty. Employers thus move on their own toward policies very much like those sought by unions.

The marginal productivity theory is highly abstracted from reality and fails to offer us a normative guide to wages. We can not even be sure whether the unemployment that may arise is the result of an unwise or deliberate exercise of union market power or the consequence of a large firm pursuing labor policies meant to engender employee trust and loyalties in its pursuit of long-term competitive efficiency. The simpler versions of the marginal productive theory may have been applicable to another kind of society, more individualistic than twentieth-century western society, in which autonomous groups negotiate with one another to effect important economic relationships. We find that collective bargaining, as one of those intergroup relationships, has brought with it this problem: If earlier standards for determining the acceptability of wage rates cannot be applied, are new standards available?

Unionism, with its collective bargaining program, inescapably confronts us with the fact that the wage standards suitable to an individualistic society are inapplicable where autonomous groups negotiate economic agreements. They are inapplicable where competing groups must accommodate one another's interests in a common discretionary decision-making process in order for production to take place at all. This conclusion can hardly be surprising. Economic standards in a democracy must largely be couched in terms of procedures. Where action and decision are left to private individuals and groups, we normally judge by the methods they employ rather than by the decisions they reach. However much we may disagree with the price policy of a firm or the wage policy of a union, we are inclined to grant the firm or the union the privilege of making its own decision, provided we believe it is operating within the rules of the game as they may be defined at a particular time. Only in emergencies or distress situations or in cases that do not lend themselves to prevailing procedures do we impose standards in the form of substantive decisions—wartime price control, minimum wage laws, or public utility regulations, for example.

The competitive system did not base the justice of its arrangements upon the particular price or wage that emerged from it. There was no substantive standard by which actual prices could be judged. There was no fair wage of so many cents per hour for grade A labor and no fair price of so many cents for a particular product of a given quality. Such standards had been used in earlier days, it will be recalled, when the state regulated prices and wages and, through guilds, guarded quality and performance. The competitive process was adopted, however, and used as a procedural standard: Whatever wages and prices emerged from a market that was beyond the influence of any group and in which buyers and sellers had knowledge of the alternatives offered and were free to take advantage of any such offers were fair and just simply because the process generated them.

Conflicts between Wage Standards: The Need for Trade-offs

Having departed irrevocably from such competitive arrangements, we live now in a society where large corporations can devise their wage and production policies, large unions can frame their own policies on the same matters, and decisions come by negotiated agreement between the two. We tend to turn to substantive standards for help in determining the acceptability of specific wage values. None has proven to be entirely satisfactory; none can be expected to be satisfactory in the way the competitive standard was, for substantive standards are not apt to provide the same service that the procedural one did. The most-used standards are those of comparability and cost of living; they reflect the market influences intimately known by workers and managers. Their use suggests that we can expect acceptance of other standards only if they, too, are meaningful and relevant to workers, union leaders, and managers. Productivity, a standard that is to be commended if for no other reason than because it emphasizes the source of improvement for the general income level, seldom makes itself felt directly or meaningfully. We suggested in Chapter 13 that the meaning and implications of productivity could be made clearer and that workers as well as managers need to understand clearly the fundamental importance of increased productivity to real wage increases. Employees are not persuaded to step up production by any psychological sleight of hand. They respond as managers do—or as anyone else does—when they receive meaningful recognition of their interests in the total productive effort and of their ability to contribute creatively to production.

There has been considerable exhortation to the unions to use their efforts to improve efficiency. But the problems of productivity and market power are joined in the principle of ability to pay. A union's wage objectives can be met, in a particular firm or industry, by either increased productivity or exploitation of monopoly advantage. The route to wage increases through exercise of market power is generally so much easier than the productivity method that we might reasonably expect most unions to follow it.

Accepting the suggestion that Schumpeter made with respect to the restrictive practices of business, we concluded that the competition which comes, over time, from the introduction of new products and new technologies is likely to prevent any long-run exploitation of consumers as a whole by special producer interests (both union and business). Short-run exploitations may emerge—first on the part of one group, then on the part of another—but even these will be somewhat checked by the effect of differing price, elasticities of demand for products, and the differential effects of wages on the profit positions of individual firms. As for harmful effects on employment, these can indeed emerge. Our protection against such effects lies in the same price, product, and technological competition to prevent any group from perpetuating an undue short-run advantage. The related problem of whether full-employment conditions give an unacceptable support to union power we found to rest largely on a misconception. The threat of inflation under such circumstances is not a union phenomenon.

Our conclusion was that we need some kind of workable compromise between the power of private groups to control their own affairs and markets and the competitive process, which limits the extent of such control. For producer satisfactions, we require a measure of limits on competition; for consumer interests, we require a measure of competition. It is a blend of these which is needed. In general and as a first approximation, the blend that has resulted from union practices does not appear to place excessive power in the unions' hands. By taking action to curtail specific practices that appear to be more destructive of consumer interests than their benefit to producer interests warrants, we can proceed on a tentative basis to assure the needed balance. This is admittedly a pragmatic rather than a systematic approach.

CHAPTER 15

STRIKES AND COLLECTIVE BARGAINING

Those whose knowledge of industrial relations is based only upon news reports very likely believe that strikes and collective bargaining inevitably go together. They may assume that, like love and marriage (and a horse and carriage) in the old song, "you can't have one without the other." In fact, most collective bargaining occurs, and the parties reach settlements in a large share of cases, with no strike. There are no available data on the share of negotiations over the terms of agreements that end in strikes. An estimate can be made on the basis of the notices of contract expirations that unions report to the Federal Mediation and Conciliation Service. In the late 1970s strikes followed contract expiration in only a little more than 4 percent of these cases. The chances of negotiations breaking down and a strike resulting thus appears to be slight, one out of twenty-five.[1]

Of course most of these bargaining units are very small, typically with only a few hundred workers; strikes in most of them would rate news only in local newspapers. Strikes in larger units, those covering 1000 or more workers, are both more probable and more noticeable. In a study of negotiations in large manufacturing units from 1954 to 1975, it was found that on average one out of every six or seven negotiations resulted in a strike. In some years from a quarter to nearly a third resulted in strike, and in others the probability of a strike was as low as one in twenty.[2] No data are available for large nonmanufacturing units, but a reasonable guess is that the probability of strikes for them is higher than for all units, small as well as large.

Whatever the total strike probabilities may be, some unions and manage-

---

[1]See U.S. Federal Mediation and Conciliation Service, *Annual Report,* various years.

[2]See Bruce E. Kaufman, "The Propensity to Strike in American Manufacturing," *Industrial Relations Research Association Proceedings, 1978,* Madison, Wis., p. 423.

ments go for years, even decades, without strikes. The United Steelworkers and the eight largest steel companies have not experienced an industrywide strike since 1959–60. Actors' Equity has gone as long with no strike in the theater. The International Ladies' Garment Workers Union has bargained with the major New York City employers' association since 1958 without resort to a major walkout. The United Automobile Workers and General Motors have bargained together since 1970 with no companywide strike.

The last-named collective bargaining relationship, peaceful as it has been for over a decade, reveals, however, the way in which the possibility of a strike is an ever-present consideration in the strategy and approach of both parties. Though strikes do not inevitably accompany bargaining, they are usually available as a means for the parties to impose costs upon each other. They thus continue as a positive, constructive influence upon negotiators, pushing them toward compromise of initial expectations and into settlement. For example, despite the good record of no companywide strikes at General Motors involving the UAW after 1970, the leaders of both organizations were acutely sensitive to the union's nine-day strike at Chrysler in 1973 and its sixty-eight-day strike against Ford in 1976. Furthermore, they had to cope with a "ministrike" of twelve-hours at General Motors in 1976, and a year later nearly 13,000 workers at the Delco-Remy Division of General Motors struck for two weeks in a dispute over local issues.

The possibility of a strike is high enough, even in times of good relations, that it is probably an ever-present part of every negotiator's calculations. Both parties know that they will reach agreement when acceptance of the terms proposed by one party is judged by the other party to be more advantageous than disagreement on those terms. Since a strike hurts management by stopping production and pinches workers by cutting off their wages, neither party is apt without serious consideration to reject terms proposed by the other. Acceding to the proposals or demands of the other party usually involves a cost, but so does a strike, which may be brought on by refusing to accede. The two costs must be balanced.

As long as a strike threatens greater loss than does agreement to at least one of the parties, there is reason for them to settle. Without such a threat they may continue to disagree indefinitely and never bargain seriously, each simply refusing to give ground in an effort to reach a settlement acceptable to both. The right of management to disagree with union terms in the face of strikes or strike threats is quite as important as the right of unions to use strikes and the threat of them to gain concessions. Thus, though collective bargaining need not and does not always result in strikes, the possibility or ultimate threat of strikes is a necessary condition for collective bargaining.

THE PUBLIC REGULATION OF STRIKES

For many years, however, the public—and even unionists—had good reason to believe that strikes themselves were an intimate, inevitable part of bargaining. In the early days of unions, both parties attempted to impose terms unilaterally, and the strike quite overshadowed any other aspect of collective bargaining. Even after more stable bargaining relationships had been established in some industries, such as that in the stove industry following 1881, the strike continued to dominate the collective bargaining arena. Employers generally opposed unions and bargained with such fierceness that they contributed to, and provoked a good deal of, violence in strikes. Since strikes disrupted the orderly industrial process that delivered goods and services to the public, they caused popular concern in the first place; when violence, accompanied by damage to property and injury to persons, was added, a large part of the articulate public expressed outrigh hostility to strikes, and many people rejected strikes as a suitable activity under any conditions.

The Cost of Strikes to the Public

Even after 1842, when state courts began to recognize unions as legitimate organizations in themselves, not restraints of trades per se, these courts insisted that unions could use the strike only within limits. A common means of limiting strikes was for courts to decide that a strike was for an illegal purpose and thus unlawful. The judge, of course, decided for what purposes the workers could strike. All too often the judge failed to perceive any legitimate worker purpose but easily recognized—and condemned—the injury caused by a strike. Justice Holmes, on the Massachusetts court, argued in 1896 that strikes were but a manifestation of competition and should be no more limited than competition among businesses:

> [A new company may drive established rivals to ruin, but the courts do not call this unlawful.] The reason, of course, is that the doctrine generally has been accepted that free competition is worth more to society than it costs, and that on this ground the infliction of the damage is privileged [as long as] . . . the damage is done not for its own sake, but as an instrumentality in reaching the end of victory in the battle of trade. . . . [If] the conflict between employers and employed is not [seen as] competition . . . if the policy on which our law is founded is too narrowly expressed in the term free competition, we may substitute free struggle for life. Certainly the policy is not limited to struggles between persons of the same class competing for the same end. It applies to all conflicts of temporal interests.[3]

Holmes's "less popular view," as he called it, was not accepted as a basis for public policy until the enactment of the Norris–La Guardia Act in 1932. The delay in acceptance is understandable, as is the steady movement away from his view since. Although one may properly understand union-represented workers and their employers as being competitors, the analogy of their competition with that of business rivals is imperfect. A strike may injure the parties and also inconvenience consumers who depend upon the stopped production;

---

[3]*Vegelahn v. Guntner,* 167 Mass. 92, 106–107 (1896).

normal market competition may destroy a firm's business, but the public is presumably not thereby injured. The successful competitor justifies the injury to a business rival not merely by any interest and gain but also by presumed better service to consumers.

Now, certainly the public generally may benefit from strikes if workers secure better wages and working conditions, but only if one assumes that the benefits won outweigh strike costs and that the benefits are not offset by losses of stockholders or others. Consumer expenditures may be thereby stimulated, and the health and welfare of the workers and their families may be improved. But if these benefits do accrue, they are indirect and diffused; judges—and the public—have found it difficult to evaluate and compare them with the perceived losses suffered as a result of strikes. Whatever the benefits, they have usually been obscured by the immediacy and dramatic quality of strikes.

How effectively the injunction served the purpose of restraining strikes is questionable. The record of strikes that did occur sheds no light upon what the record might have been had the injunction not been used. Neither the number of strikes nor the number of strikers showed any noticeable change between 1890 and 1905 that might be attributable to use of injunctions. The relative number of strikes and strikers did decline significantly from the highs of World War I to new lows around 1930, but economic conditions were as likely a cause as legal action. Even as they declined during the twenties, however, strikes continued to plague industry and the public.

Encouraging Collective Bargaining to Avoid Strikes

The most bitterly fought strikes prior to World War II were usually the result of worker attempts to organize and to secure recognition. Once the union was recognized and in a position to negotiate collective agreements, the business-minded leaders of unions of the American Federation of Labor (AFL) made clear their desire to avoid strikes and to reach peaceful settlements. They turned to the strike with reluctance and as a last resort. An obvious way to control strikes, so it appeared then, was to encourage unionization and collective bargaining. Assured of the opportunity to bargain, unions would use the strike sparingly, and organizing strikes could be virtually eliminated. Proponents of the National Labor Relations (Wagner) Act of 1935 had other and broader aims than lessening the incidence of strikes, but clearly this was an important one. In the Labor-Management Relations (Taft-Hartley) Act of 1947 was this declaration of policy, repeating essentially the declaration of the earlier Wagner Act and thus since 1935 a part of our basic natural labor policy:

> Industrial strife which interferes with the normal flow of commerce and with the full production of articles and commodities for commerce, can be avoided or substantially minimized if employers, employees, and labor organizations each recognize under law one another's legitimate rights in their relations with each other, and above all recognize under law that neither party has any right in its relations with

any other to engage in acts or practices which jeopardize the public health, safety or interest.[4]

The period of the National Labor Relations Act, 1935 to 1947, was exceptional in the history of government control and regulation of strikes. Both legislatures and courts allowed nearly free rein to unions to engage in strikes. As long as strikers avoided violence, almost any concerted activity was permissable. The act imposed no restriction upon jurisdictional strikes, secondary boycotts, or strikes of any kind. By 1940 the Supreme Court had gone so far as virtually to enshrine picketing as a form of free speech under the Fifth Amendment,[5] and in the following year it interpreted the Norris–La Guardia Act in such a way as to exempt most union activities from antitrust proceedings.[6] The government did not allow such freedom simply because strikes had become more acceptable instruments; rather, it did so to effect a better balance of power between unions and management and thus ultimately to lessen the incidence of strikes. Such as expectation assumed a great deal. The reluctance with which management accepted collective bargaining, the irresponsibility of some union leaders, and the inexperience of many union members were certainly not conducive to a restrained use of the strike.

Already angered by the coal strikes of World War II and the many wildcat strikes that increased in frequency as the end of the war came nearer, many citizens and an overwhelming majority of Congress lost all patience with the wave of strikes that occurred in the year immediately following the end of the war. One great industry after another was shut down. Workers walked out of coal mines, steel mills, and automobile and meat-packing plants; they closed most of the electrical manufacturing firms, the ports, and the textile mills. Even the railroads were stopped for nearly two days. In the following year the Labor-Management Relations Act imposed explicit strike restrictions, the most dramatic of which were the provisions for handling strikes considered to be national emergencies.

The act recognizes that the right to strike is essential to free collective bargaining, but it seeks to curtail strikes whose benefits to the parties are judged too small to justify their costs and injury to the public. Dissatisfaction with our strike experience and the legal restrictions that our legislators have imposed upon strikes do not indicate a lack of confidence in collective bargaining or a desire to ban strikes. They do reflect, however, a belief that this weapon must be used with full regard for its impact on others and only after all other reasonable efforts to achieve agreement have been exhausted. Many legislators, and presumably many citizens, would have agreed with a distinguished group of labor students who declared that "the importance of the right to strike (or

---

[4]Labor Management Relations Act, 1947, Section 1(b).
[5]*Thornhill v. Alabama,* 310 U.S. 88 (1940).
[6]*United States v. Hutcheson,* 312 U.S. 219 (1941).

to take a strike) does not mean . . . that a strike is alwys the right course of action for parties in disagreement to follow."[7]

The federal government has formally encouraged collective bargaining for nearly half a century, partly in the hope that the burden of strikes and their accompanying losses might be lessened. The public has shown a willingness to bear the costs of strikes insofar as these may be part of the necessary price of decentralized decision making in economic matters. Even today the articulate public, at least, expresses its impatience with strikes that affect whole industries or that disrupt indispensable local services such as transportation, food delivery, garbage collection, and hospital care. It wants assurances that the price paid in any strike is not merely a cost of inefficient negotiations or willful actions by stubborn or emotional negotations.

THE TREND OF STRIKES

An examination of the statistical record of strikes indicates that unions (in contrast to unorganized workers) have successfully asserted their control over major strikes in this country. Between 1890 and 1900, unorganized workers were responsible for one-half to one-third of all strikes. In the years immediately after the turn of the century, from 1900 to 1905, unions were already demonstrating their growing control: more than three-quarters were union strikes. (The union strikes involved more workers on average and so they accounted for more than four-fifths of all the strikers.) Through the 1920s and 1930s unions conducted roughly nine out of ten strikes, and by World War II almost all strikes arose out of union negotiations. (In recent years fewer than 200 strikes out of 3000 to 5000 annually have not involved a labor agreement and thus a union in some way.)[8]

The thousand of strikes that occur each year appear to have disappointed the hopes of Congress and the public, expressed originally in the National Labor Relations Act. Up to the passage of the act most strikes were used primarily to organize workers, to force employer recognition, and to establish collective bargaining. In providing election procedures to decide recognition and in legally protecting rights to organize, legislators might reasonably have hoped to have made the strike less needed. But the record suggests that industrial strife still abounds, and if it has been substantially minimized one must examine the data carefully to detect this. The spread of unions and the presumed maturing of industrial relations has been accompanied by a long-term increase in both the absolute numbers of strikes and of workers involved. In the years

[7]Committee for Economic Development, *The Public Interest in National Labor Policy,* 1961, p. 86.
[8]Florence Peterson, *Strikes in the United States, 1880–1936,* Bureau of Labor Statistics Bulletin 651, 1938; and *Analysis of Work Stoppages,* Bureau of Labor Statistics, various years. For a discussion of union attempts to gain control of strikes before World War I, see Ulman, *The Rise of the National Trade Union,* chaps. 6, 12, 14.

from 1933 to 1940 there were an average of about 2500 strikes annually, with roughly 1.1 million workers involved; forty years later, from 1973 to 1980, the economy averaged over 5000 strikes a year, with about 2 million workers involved. Of course, the increase may be due to forces and influences other than those of industrial relations. The labor force has doubled in size and union membership has increased even more. With many more workers organized and enjoying the availability of bargaining and the possibility of effective strikes, it is likely that the use of strikes would increase even if basic industrial relations had improved. Such appears to be the case, for if one measures the frequency of strikes and the number of workers involved against the number of union members (what may be called the strike rate and the participation rate), a long-term decline in both is evident. (See Table 22 and Figure 3.)

TABLE 22
TREND OF STRIKES IN THE UNITED STATES, 1930 TO 1980

Year	Fre-quency*	Participation rate†	Year	Fre-quency	Participation rate
1930	1.87	5.4	1956	2.19	10.9
1931	2.45	10.3	1957	2.11	8.0
1932	2.76	10.6	1958	2.17	12.1
1933	6.30	43.5	1959	2.17	11.0
1934	6.01	47.6	1960	1.95	7.7
1935	5.62	31.3	1961	2.07	8.9
1936	5.44	19.8	1962	2.18	7.4
1937	6.77	26.6	1963	2.03	5.7
1938	3.45	8.6	1964	2.17	9.7
1939	2.98	13.4	1965	2.29	9.0
1940	2.88	6.6	1966	2.46	10.9
1941	4.20	23.1	1967	2.50	15.6
1942	2.86	8.1	1968	2.67	14.0
1943	2.84	15.0	1969	2.99	13.0
1944	3.50	15.0	1970	2.69	15.6
1945	3.32	24.2	1971	2.41	15.4
1946	3.46	32.0	1972	2.31	7.9
1947	2.50	14.7	1973	2.40	10.1
1948	2.39	13.7	1974	2.66	12.2
1949	2.52	21.2	1975	2.25	7.8
1950	3.39	16.9	1976	2.49	10.7
1951	2.97	13.9	1977	2.45	9.1
1952	3.22	22.3	1978	1.86	7.1
1953	3.00	14.2	1979	2.14	7.6
1954	2.04	9.0	1980	1.74	6.1
1955	2.54	15.8			

*Number of strikes per 10,000 union members.
†Workers involved in work stoppages, as percentage of union membership.
Source: For union membership, 1930 to 1969, *Analysis of Work Stoppages, 1980,* Bureau of Labor Statistics Bulletin 2120, table 1, p. 8; and *Handbook of Labor Statistics,* Bureau of Labor Statistics Bulletin 2070, table 165, p. 412. For union membership, 1970 to 1980, Gifford, *Directory of U.S. Labor Organizations,* table 2, p. 1.

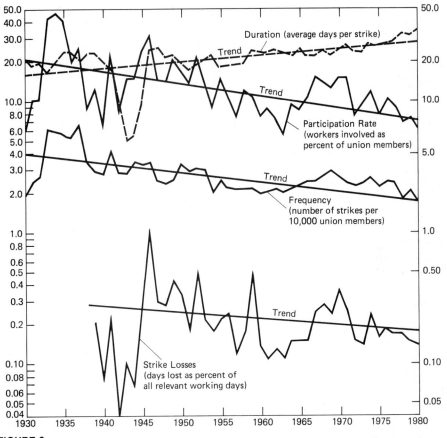

FIGURE 3
Measures of strikes, 1930–1980. (*Source:* Bureau of Labor Statistics, *Analysis of Strikes.*)

Fewer but Longer Strikes

The downward trend over the time series is unmistakable, with the strike and participation rates of each succeeding cyclical peak lower than those before it. A newspaper reader or a person whose knowledge of strikes is gleaned from television news reports would not gain such an impression. Of course, strikes show great fluctuation from year to year, so at any one time no trend is easily perceived. Strikes also appear at first glance to display great irregularity. However, one can identify both institutional and political influences as well as business cycle conditions that may explain in a general way much of the changes. Their complex interaction is not easy to unravel, however.

Periods of rapid inflation have resulted in strike surges—after World Wars I and II, during the Korean war, and through the years of the Vietnamese war and the following high inflation period. Government's lifting of wage and price controls in 1919, 1946, and 1974 led to decided increases in strikes. On the one

TABLE 23
STRIKE TRENDS BY MAJOR INDUSTRIAL SECTORS, 1969 TO 1980

	Manufacturing		Nonmanufacturing			
			Number of strikes		Workers involved*	
Year	Number of strikes	Workers involved*	All	(Government)	All	(Government)
1969	2822	1308.0	2893	(411)	1174.0	(160.0)
1970	2481	1128.1	3240	(412)	2177.1	(333.5)
1971	2391	862.7	2762	(329)	2416.8	(152.6)
1972	2056	645.9	2954	(375)	1067.7	(142.1)
1973	2282	962.4	3072	(387)	1287.3	(195.9)
1974	2823	1145.3	3253	(384)	1632.4	(160.7)
1975	1897	463.8	3134	(478)	1281.8	(318.5)
1976	2245	974.5	3406	(378)	1445.5	(180.7)
1977	2537	787.7	2970	(413)	1252.3	(170.2)
1978	2121	567.8	2110	(481)	1054.8	(193.7)
1979	2296	680.6	2536	(593)	1046.5	(254.1)
1980	1809	354.0	2080	(536)	913.0	(223.6)

*In thousands.
Source: *Handbook of Labor Statistics* (1980), Bureau of Labor Statistics Bulletin 2070, table 171, pp. 429–437; and *Analysis of Work Stoppages,* Bureau of Labor Statistics, various years.

hand, the enactment of the National Labor Relations Act in 1935 almost surely contributed to both the organizing drives and the high strike activity of the late 1930s. On the other hand, the public alarm over strikes at the end of World War II and the passage of the Labor-Management Relations Act in 1947 probably helped dampen strikes during the late 1940s. The low level of strikes in the late 1950s and early 1960s may reflect in part the stable price levels that the economy then enjoyed.

Professor Bruce Kaufman argues that the political and institutional influences on collective bargaining have been more stable over the past thirty years than were those of the previous thirty, and thus the economic variables are now relatively more important in determining the ups and downs of strikes.[9] His conclusion may be accurate for the whole record, but as we have seen in earlier chapters, manufacturing unions have lost members relative to those in nonmanufacturing. Their share of strikes has declined as well. Most of the absolute increase in strikes through the 1970s has come in the nonmanufacturing sector, and growing numbers of organized public employees accounted for only a portion of that increase (see Table 23). Unions in manufacturing have seen employment drop so rapidly and so far that many of them, particularly in autos and steel, may well have to modify their collective bargaining policies and practices. Professor Everett Kassalow asks, "[up]on whom [will] the mantle of bargaining leadership . . . fall[?] The very scale and concentrated character of steel and auto bargaining has made them almost unique. The new,

[9]Bruce E. Kaufman, "The Determinants of Strikes in the United States, 1900–1977," *Industrial and Labor Relations Review,* vol. 35, July 1982, p. 473.

more promising industries such as electronics, for example, are structured around smaller companies and plants. No such bargaining leadership is likely to occur there . . . More union size is no substitute for the pace-setting role hitherto enjoyed by auto, steel and a few related unions."[10]

Although a decline in the strike rate is not easily apparent and is even apt to be overshadowed by the secular increase in the absolute number of strikes, managements and unions do appear to be moving toward more careful, less frequent use of the strike. Certainly collective bargaining may receive credit for having lessened the violence of strikes. Seldom do labor unions and management engage in strikes with the bitterness and vehemence that often characterized strikes of the thirties and before. Once collective bargaining is established, it entails a continued working relationship from which neither party is able to escape. No matter how long a strike lasts or how deep a disagreement may temporarily separate union and management, they must eventually come together, reach some conclusion, and continue the day-to-day administration of their agreement. Unless one or both parties reject collective bargaining, they realize that the injection of bitterness and the rancor of violence inflicts not only a present wound but also a lasting injury. Thus past experience in bargaining with each other and the expectation of doing so in the future usually persuade labor leaders and managers of the wisdom of avoiding violence.

Strikes: Unplanned but Carefully Considered

Although negotiators do not often plan strikes, they seldom find themselves involved in a strike for which they have not prepared; they understand well the costs to be borne and the interests pursued. The marked seasonal variation in the number of strikes indicates that winter is not a favored time to strike, and particularly the month of December. For workers to strike during December would mean threatening their holiday season with no pay; and the likely bad weather is unpleasant for pickets, unsuitable for painting the house, and not good for hunting. Strikes are more than three times as likely to occur in May as in December. Good weather reduces the cost of strikes to workers, allowing them opportunity to catch up on house repairs and to enjoy some inexpensive recreation. Moreover, family expenses are low, with heating needs down, no special holidays to shop for, and school expenses at a minimum.

Union leaders and managers approach strikes in a businesslike manner as well, recognizing that they will resume their cooperation after the strike. Neither has reason to cause lasting damage to equipment, the office or the plant, or their productive efficiency. In steel, the furnaces are carefully banked to minimize damage; in the automobile industry, passes are issued to nonstrikers and supervisors, allowing them to enter and leave the plants and to take care of essential maintenance; in electrical equipment, at least one company allows

[10]Everett M. Kassalow, "Concession Bargaining, Something Old, But Also Something Quite New," *Industrial Relations Research Association Proceedings of Thirty-Fifty Annual Meeting, 1982,* edited by Barbara D. Dennis, Madison, Wis.: IRRA, 1983, pp. 372–382.

striking employees to draw vacation and other special pay, and it even grants pay advances to strikers upon their return to work. Most strikes are kept under sufficient control, so that however unpleasant their consequences or inconvenient their effects, they can hardly be called primitive. At least they are no more primitive than the campaign charges, angry countercharges, half-truths, parades, emotional rallies, and general folderol of political rivals for public office. The simplified, obscurant arguments advertised in the news media by some unions and managements, the frantic appeals to the public, and the grandstanding requests for government investigation are no worse than what is used in unfriendly corporate takeover fights. Striking pickets seldom march with more fervor than that displayed by members of a right-to-life group marching in front of an abortion clinic or a women's group picketing pornographic stores.

Here and there, violence in strikes flares up—in a mill town in the south or in a strike of hospital workers in Warren, Ohio. In such disputes pickets have marched in massed rank, and occasionally disgruntled workers have even overturned cars, slashed tires, or sabotaged plants.[11] In a few places one may discover that a long-fought strike has destroyed a well-established union-management relationship and local unions have been weakened beyond repair. Even today in some locations where unions are rare, organizers have been run out of town and harrassed. These are, however, occasional incidents, as atypical of today's industrial relations as bloody battles between strikers and strikebreakers were common at an earlier time when employers could refuse even to contemplate union recognition, let alone engage in a continuing process of bargaining. The violence and damage that once accompanied encounters between unions and employers created doubts in the minds of many observers about the desirability and feasibility of collective bargaining as a process, but the peaceful strikes that now typically accompany barganing only raise questions about its efficiency and effectiveness.

The declining incidence and increasing average duration of strikes suggest that the parties increasingly have learned to calculate their strike strategies, using the strike only when the prospective benefits may be expected to outweigh the probable losses. Such careful calculation may well reduce the number of casual and "accidental" strikes, but it appears to have increased the number of strikes in which the parties are well prepared to endure a serious test of strength. One would expect a decline in the number of short, small strikes in which local leaders, out of frustration or inexperience, get involved in work stoppages; but there may be an increase in long strikes. One would expect unions over time to use fewer overall strikes but to be well prepared for those they do conduct.

---

[11]The violence in the nationwide "strike" of independent truck drivers in early 1982, which included at least one killing and many shootings, was *not* a union activity. Those who engaged in the strike were individual proprietors, truck owners who also drove. The Teamsters, representing organized, employed truck drivers, disapproved of the strike and did not participate in it.

The Decline of Short and Wildcat Strikes

Strike data show, first, that in the long term the number of strikes and their participation rates have fallen irregularly since the 1930s and 1940s. Even during the most recent strike upturn of 1967 to 1972, neither measure reached the high peaks of earlier cycles. Second, strike losses (worker-days idle as a percentage of working time) continued their long-term decline; and third, the average duration of strikes increased rapidly through the 1970s. (See Table 24.) Relative to their membership, unions have called fewer strikes and involved fewer strikers, but once having begun their strikes, they appear to have carried them on for a longer time. From 1967 to 1970 strikes averaged a mean duration about 9 percent above that in the period from 1957 to 1960, but from 1977 to 1980 they lasted about 50 percent longer.

A complementary explanation is that throughout the 1970s, unions and managements succeeded in cutting back on short strikes, which often are wild-

TABLE 24
DURATION OF STRIKES, 1930 TO 1980, AND STRIKE LOSSES, 1930 TO 1980

Year	Duration*	Losses†	Year	Duration	Losses
1930	22.3	n.a.	1956	18.9	.24
1931	18.8	n.a.	1957	19.2	.12
1932	19.6	n.a.	1958	19.7	.18
1933	16.9	n.a.	1959	24.6	.50
1934	19.5	n.a.	1960	23.4	.14
1935	23.8	n.a.	1961	23.7	.11
1936	23.3	n.a.	1962	24.6	.13
1937	20.3	n.a.	1963	23.0	.11
1938	23.6	n.a.	1964	22.9	.15
1939	23.4	.21	1965	25.0	.15
1940	20.9	.08	1966	22.2	.15
1941	18.3	.23	1967	22.8	.25
1942	11.7	.04	1968	24.5	.28
1943	5.0	.10	1969	22.5	.24
1944	5.6	.07	1970	25.0	.37
1945	9.9	.31	1971	27.0	.26
1946	24.2	1.04	1972	24.0	.15
1947	25.6	.30	1973	24.0	.14
1948	21.8	.28	1974	27.1	.24
1949	22.5	.44	1975	26.8	.16
1950	19.2	.33	1976	28.0	.19
1951	17.4	.18	1977	29.3	.17
1952	19.6	.48	1978	33.2	.17
1953	20.3	.22	1979	32.1	.15
1954	22.5	.18	1980	35.4	.14
1955	18.5	.22			

*Mean duration in days.
†Days idle during year as percentage of estimated total working time.
Source: Analysis of Work Stoppages, Bureau of Labor Statistics Bulletin 2120, table 1, p. 8.

cat stoppages, out of control of the local union as well as local plant managers.[12] In the early part of the decade strikes of less than three days in length accounted for a quarter to a third of all strikes and workers involved; by the end of the decade they accounted for less than a fifth. Such a reduction in short strikes would help raise the median duration particularly, which in fact went up from about ten days at the beginning of the decade to nearly sixteen days at the end. Whether by bringing short strikes under control or by having fewer but longer strikes, it appears that union leaders are increasingly managing strikes. A consequence is that the total incidence of strikes may be decreasing, but once strikes are called they are harder than ever to settle.

Strike-prone Industries

We may find encouragement, however, in the fact that strikes do not plague all sectors of the economy or raise serious problems in all industries. Overall figures are often misleading, and those of strikes certainly are. Strikes have been particularly concentrated in a few industries, thus limiting the scope of the problem with which public policy must deal. Four industries—construction, mining, transportation, and communications—accounted for 38 percent of all time lost through strike in the ten years from 1969 to 1979. Construction, with its fragmented bargaining structure and decentralized, local industry structure, is especially prone to strikes. Employing fewer than one out of twenty nonagricultural employees, construction accounted for more than one out of six days lost through strikes from 1969 to 1979. Mining, with fewer than one out of one hundred employees, accounted for one out of thirteen days lost over the same period. Note that manufacturing is not included among these four strike-prone industries.

The incidence of strikes changes significantly among industries over time, both in those that have long experienced a high rate of strikes and in those where strikes have traditionally been rare. Consider the changes in mining and in government, both of which experienced a decided increase from the 1950s to the 1970s (see Table 25). In the earlier period strike losses in mining had fallen to very low levels, 4 percent of the national totals from 1954 to 1957. The United Mine Workers were still under the strong leadership of John L. Lewis, production was strong, and competition from open-pit mines was not a serious problem. Twenty years later strike losses in mining were up to 10 percent of national totals, and the absolute number of days lost had increased by more than four times. Over those same two decades government employees had organized themselves, and by the 1970s they were not only bargaining col-

---

[12]The quality of management can have a significant effect upon the number of wildcat strikes. Such was the finding of Jeanne M. Brett and Stephen B. Goldberg, "Wildcat Strikes in Bituminous Coal Mining," *Industrial and Labor Relations Review,* vol. 32, July 1979, p. 465.

TABLE 25
STRIKES IN SELECTED INDUSTRIES AS PERCENTAGE OF TOTALS,
1954 TO 1957 AND 1977 TO 1980

Industry	Number of strikes		Workers involved		Workdays idle	
	1954–1957	1977–1980	1954–1957	1977–1980	1954–1957	1977–1980
Mining	9.2	10.9	6.0	15.5	4.0	14.2
Government	0.6	11.0	0.1	12.5	0.04	6.3
Construction	25.3	7.8	18.3	12.3	16.2	8.5

Source: *Analysis of Work Stoppages*, Bureau of Labor Statistics, various years.

lectively but also using the strike in many state and local government jurisdictions; the number of strikes and the days lost through strikes increased by many times. It may have been the case that both government officials and union leaders negotiating on behalf of public employees were learning the hard way the costs and limits of their newly practiced bargaining skills. In another twenty years we might find considerably lower strike losses in government, if industrial relations matures as it has in such industries as apparel and steel.

The concentration of strikes in a few industries at any one time suggests why the public expresses its concern, even though the total losses of worker-days are relatively small. Through the 1970s, a time of relatively high strike incidence, the yearly losses averaged 0.2 percent of total working time, or about three and one-half to four hours for each employee involved. On-the-job accidents in 1978 caused about half again as great a loss, and absenteeism probably inflicted even heavier losses upon production. But a strike usually brings the production of goods and services to a complete stop, or at least threatens the output of affected plants, factories, or offices. It has a far more noticeable impact than the continual, scattered losses of accidents and employee illnesses. Furthermore, the public can be annoyed, inconvenienced, and alarmed by strikes if, as may seem to be the case, they disappear from one sector only to develop in another.

Strike Losses

As noticeable and inconvenient as strikes may be in their impact, the public's economic losses due to strikes are usually more apparent than real, according to industrial relations experts.[13] Stockpiling, postponable demand, and substitute supplies or services lessen the effect upon both consumers and producers;

---

[13]See, for example, John A. Ackermann, "The Impact of the Coal Strike of 1977–78," *Industrial and Labor Relations Review,* vol. 32, Jan. 1979, p. 175. He found "that employer predictions of strike effects proved to be consistently exaggerated, whose effects probably never constituted an actual emergency."

prestrike anticipation, poststrike makeup work, and cyclical or seasonal variations in production and employment can also whittle away strike losses for the workers and companies involved. An economy with a variety of transportation systems—trucking, airlines, and water and rail shipping—allows the slack created by a strike in any one of them to be picked up by the others. If local newspapers are closed down by a local strike, the public still receives news by radio, television, and national publications. Should phone workers or those in oil refineries and chemical plants strike, supervisors and managers can usually keep the automated machinery operating at close to full capacity for months. A walkout in local grocery or department stores may inconvenience patrons, but with our well-developed transportation system and private autos, most will simply travel a bit further to shop for the duration. Workers in rubber, steel, and autos who have gone on strike have discovered that consumers can and will buy foreign imports if strikes cut off their regular supplies. The general recognition that strike losses may hurt the immediately negotiating parties more than consumers and the public may have contributed to a marked lessening of governmental concern about emergency strikes. At the end of World War II, when the explosion of strikes occurred in 1946, such strikes were perceived as a most pressing concern. Today, few consider them likely and in any case they are so rare as not to present a pressing problem for public policy.

WHY IS THE PUBLIC CONCERNED ABOUT STRIKES?

Is the public then wrong in its concern over strikes? It would appear that the situation is well expressed in the limerick:

There once was a faith healer from Deal
Who said, "I know pain isn't real
But when I puncture my skin
With the point of a pin
I dislike what I fancy I feel."

Though the experts assure us that the pain of strikes is not real, the public continues to object to it. Perhaps, then, the economic pain of strikes that the experts assure us is greatly exaggerated may not be what most concerns the public.

First, newspapers play up potential losses of strikes much more than they report the after-the-fact actual losses. The public may thus become more exercised about possibilities than the facts justify. A week's strike by a major city's sanitation workers may not cause a health hazard, but a month's strike could. If the work stoppage should continue, the public can expect a real and rapidly spreading injury. Should the public remain calm and unworried until the potential injury materialized, pressures for settlement would not be exerted upon the parties until the time when real losses could mount rapidly and disastrously. For the public to await the full force of an emergency before showing much concern for the strike that caused it would be like not consulting a doctor until one was sure an illness was indeed serious, if not fatal. If the parties are not subjected to the thrust of popular criticism and the rough-and-ready judgment of the public, will they display much regard for the public interests? Granted that the daily headlines of strike losses and the cumulative effect of constant reporting magnify the real effects of strikes, do they not also serve the purpose of alerting the public to the potential dangers of the strike and of warning union and management that more is at stake than just their own interests?

We need not and should not, of course, disregard the analyses of strike losses made by the experts. They give us reason to believe that even in emergency strikes immediate settlement on *any* terms seldom needs to take precedence over careful consideration of the terms of settlement. There is time to make the most of all the techniques for reaching an understanding among the parties. The knowledge that measurable economic losses of past strikes have seldom been judged to be excessive may warn us to avoid hysterical evaluation of a future strike. It would be unfortunate, though, if it persuaded people to display any less determination to impress the parties with the public's concern and willingness to help both resolve their disputes peacefully.

The second public concern provoked by strikes and not measured by mere economic loss is the overt, dramatic exercise of power by those who are not responsible or necessarily responsive to all those affected. When union members empower their leaders to call a strike, they grant them the authority to close down a plant, hospital, or office and the power to stop a flow of goods and services to consumers, to shut down suppliers and retailers, and to affect the business and income of those who depend upon the purchases and expenditures of the strikers. A strike may have only limited adverse effects if it closes down a small portion of an industry. In such a case people not directly involved can probably turn to other sources for the production now stopped or find other outlets for the goods they would otherwise well to the struck firm. Small strikes, though annoying and costly to some in the community, are usually too limited to arouse much concern or to have a significant impact upon public welfare. In such a case the power wielded either by union leaders in calling the strike or by managers in taking the strike is not overweening.

STRIKES AND THE PUBLIC INTEREST

The strikes that most clearly demonstrate the power to affect the public interest by leaders not responsible to the public are those which close down whole industries, stop vital services, or touch the economic life and welfare of a wide community. The former, the closing of industries by strike, has become increasingly rare in recent years, though examples can be found. The Oil, Chemical and Atomic Workers conducted a 186-day nationwide strike against petroleum companies in 1980. Several unions, led by the Steelworkers, struck the copper mining and refining producers in 1980, closing them down for 146 days; the United Mine Workers struck the underground coal producers in 1977, first closing mines for over a month in Ohio, Pennsylvania, and West Virginia and three months later conducting a three-month strike in all the eastern mining states. The United Rubber Workers called out members nationwide in 1976, closing down the four largest tire producers for 141 days. Such actions are an undoubted demonstration of great power.

Strikes by the American Federation of State, County and Municipal Workers called out over 13,000 of New York City's health and hospital employees in 1976; 21,000 of Massachusetts' employees in the same year; and more than 10,000 employees of the state of Wisconsin in 1977. These impose at least a burden of inconvenience upon those communities. A strike by more than 17,000 public employees in Philadelphia in 1978 interfered with the work and activities of over 4 million people in the metropolitan area. The eighty-two-day strike by the clerks of the Norfolk & Western Railway in 1978 disrupted the usual distribution and transportation schedule for hundreds, if not thousands, of firms in a wide region of the country. To no public official and to no government body does our nation entrust such power without regular, formal accountability to those affected by the decisions made. Even the governor and the legislatures of the states may not tax or otherwise penalize their populations without answering to them. Nevertheless, there is no formal, regular procedure for calling union leaders and managers to public account for their actions, for the injury they may inflict upon great numbers of people and communities. Any public responsibility shown by either party is self-assumed, not imposed, and thus subject to neglect when contradicted by private organizational responsibilities.

The Responsibility of Union Leaders and Managers

Whatever the ramified effects of a strike may be and however many people may be affected, union leaders may well deny that in leading their striking members they are exercising power. They explain that they act simply as they have to act, responding to the force of circumstances largely beyond their control. The rise in the cost of living, increased wage benefits received by workers in other industries, and the threat of technological unemployment excite among their members and local leaders demands for improvements. If they did not respond to these demands and bargain with all the skill and force available to secure the best possible terms, they would find their positions threatened and perhaps even lose office. Moreover, they neither call nor conduct a strike on their own authority. The union members must agree to it, and unless they support it, it will not be maintained. As they contemplate the restrictions and necessities to which they must conform their actions, union leaders can conclude that they have little choice and thus little real power; they see themselves as merely responding to demands and pressures. They do not consider themselves the initiators. They feel caught between the demands of an electorate to whom they are accountable and a management deaf to negotiating arguments; strikes are forced upon them. Whatever its effects, union leaders reason that the strike is consequence not of their particular actions but rather of a whole set of conditions over which they enjoy, at best, but partial control.

Before questioning this attitude toward union responsibility for strikes, we should remember that the power to stop production and thereby affect the well-being of many people and whole communities is not uniquely displayed in strikes. Firms, offices, and industries may run far below their capacity because of slack or inefficient management.[14] Although the impact of the resulting unemployment and lowered incomes in the immediate community is less drastic and spreads its detrimental effects in other communities less dramatically than that of the strike, the final losses and effects may be as great or greater. In recessions managers may also adversely affect communities as they seek improved profits. For example, steel companies closed one plant after another in the early 1980s as they reduced their capacity, ending jobs and sources of livelihood for tens of thousands of workers. The cities affected, such as Youngstown, Ohio; Birmingham, Alabama; and Lackawana, New York, were hard hit. Those adversely affected, but with no say in the decisions, protested, demanding laws to restrain such "arbitrary" and unilateral action. The protests and demands paralleled those made by public critics of unions' use of strikes.

Both union leaders and managers are involved in decisions and activities whose spreading consequences affect people far removed from the immediate concern of company or union. The larger the organizations through which they transmit their decisions, the greater and more significant the effect will be. Managers and labor leaders who can influence the performance of a few huge organizations or agencies in key sectors, public or private, may impinge upon the welfare and well-being of a sizable portion of our nation. Yet neither union leaders nor business managers have any legal responsibility to the people they influence, nor is there any direct or regular process by which those affected might hold the leaders accountable for their decisions. Managers of government agencies are usually indirectly responsible to the people whose lives they affect, but accountability is often minimal and unsatisfactory. Thus the complaints of swollen and insensitive bureaucracies.

Like labor leaders, business managers may well deny that they exercise power when cutting back production or services and ordering layoffs. They argue that they do not act out of choice but rather conform to the implacable demands of economic realities. When demand slacks off, they would be foolish indeed to maintain production. They must respond to the market for goods and services, setting production at the most effective level; to produce more than is demanded will bring losses and, in private firms, a decline in profits. Such results would endanger their reputations and jeopardize their positions. If the losses continued, the managers would undoubtedly be replaced. Thus, like labor leaders, they argue that whatever the unpleasant consequences of their particular actions, they stem from a set of circumstances over which managers have little, if any, control.

Anyone who understands the working of the market system and the nature of economic requirements appreciates the coercive influences to which managers respond. Were producing units as small as those postulated by the theory of perfect competition (where the activity of any one firm has no significant effect upon the market and all prices are given to the firm), managers could

---

[14]Hirschman, *Exit, Voice and Loyalty,* Cambridge: Harvard University Press, 1970.

correctly plead that they are only responders to, not exercisers of, power. When producing units are large, as many are today, and share oligopolistic markets (or enjoy even monopolistic positions in the case of public agencies), managers enjoy some opportunity to affect, and perhaps even to change, the conditions under which they sell goods or deliver services. They can influence the demand for their product; in private firms, they can adjust prices and differentiate their products. They need not necessarily take supply prices as given where, because of ownership or dominant size, they may be able to secure price modifications. One can reasonably conclude that on the one hand, managers are not as passive and as lacking in control over their market circumstances as they may like to assume when discussing public responsibility. On the other hand, neither are they as free of coercive market pressures as their critics may assume.

Since the large labor union is a much newer institution than the large firm and is less easily fit into the market system (a union's successes and failures, like those of public agencies, cannot be summed up meaningfully in a statement of profit or loss), it may be more difficult to appreciate the coercive influences to which union leaders respond. Though the external market as well as internal politics subject both firms and unions to pressures, the generally more democratic form of government among unions emphasizes the political, just as in governmental agencies. Since political affairs appear to be more amenable to personal direction than the market, people tend to believe that unions are more influenced by arbitrary, personal decisions than firms.

When popular commentators explain a union's demands as if they were those of the union's president, they greatly oversimplify the forces that influence unions; the actual position of union officers in making policy is not unlike that of business managers. They are both subject to coercive political realities that limit their ability to gain benefits for their organizations. Union leaders have opportunities to affect and perhaps even to change the political situation within which they operate, of course. They can help mold their members' demands and seek techniques that mitigate contention within the union and between the union and management. Yet, although they have some freedom to maneuver and can play an active role in their organizations, they are not as free to determine union policy or to order strikes or make or break agreements as union critics may like to assume.[15]

The Legitimacy of Public Concern

Both union and business leaders often act as they do in given circumstances because the penalties are too great if they act otherwise. Assigned certain

---

[15]The limits of power of union presidents were well illustrated in the early 1980s. The president of the UAW recommended to Chrysler workers that they accept a concessionary agreement that he and his negotiators had worked out with the company in late 1982. The Canadian members rejected the agreement and after a strike forced the president and the company to renegotiate somewhat better terms, not only for themselves but also for the American workers. The episode hardly demonstrated strength of leadership. In the same year the president of the Steelworkers found that the 633 members of the union's Basic Steel Industry Conference (ratifying body) would not accept the concessions to which he had just agreed. To reduce the chances that such an embarrassing rejection might again occur, the executive board reduced the number of local officials who could vote on the future agreements.

responsibilities by law to members of their own organizations and held accountable through various procedures to individuals or groups who seek their own private interests, the leaders are not always in a position to display a lively concern for public interest, even should they recognize it. Since the great organizations of which they are a part can and do seriously affect the public interest, a question of responsible use of power arises. We presume that public officials negotiating with union representatives can be held accountable through regular election procedures. But how can the agents of mighty corporations and strategically located unions best be made to consider the public interest as well as private, parochial interests in their decisions?

The question arises in specific form when we consider the pricing policy of industries such as steel and construction, but it arises more dramatically, insistently, and unforgettably when we feel the effects of a strike or contemplate the potential damage of a continuing work stoppage.[16] Thus the public concern over strikes—and the results of collective bargaining—does not grow just out of prejudices against unions, though they may be involved. Public anger and anxiety over strikes arise from a wider concern with the private exercise of great organizational power in a highly interdependent, urbanized, industrial society. The public has good reason to feel that the leaders of such large and powerful parts of the national polity as business firms and unions should increasingly display a growing sense of responsibility to an ever-wider community.

Our brief consideration of the influences that play upon union and management warns us that not by easy or simple ways may we encourage or require a wider responsibility on the part of these organizations in the use of the strike. Unions and management meet in an encounter where vital interests, rights, and claimed prerogatives are at stake. Incessant demands of stockholders, customers, and suppliers press upon corporate managers, and the constant necessities of democratic politics limit union officers. These leaders can afford to respond to public interest as they bargain with one another only if the cost of *not* doing so is great enough to impress them. And the public can safeguard its interests only if it is willing to bear the cost of impressing its will. Admonishment by newspaper editors and exhortation by public officials are not apt to accomplish much unless they have behind them the threat of unwelcome penalties. Unions and management must have reason to withstand the private coercive pressures that play upon them if such a stand is in the public interest; they need to be at least allowed, if not required, to consider the public's as well as their own private interests in collective bargaining.

In spite of the difficulties of grappling with so basic and thorny an issue as the social responsibility of private organizations, public concern over strikes and the power they display makes necessary a search for new, and a reappraisal

---

[16]The public displays the same kind of sensitivity to the dramatic in accidents. More concern is expressed by public spokespersons at the news of the death of 150 airline passengers in a single commercial plane crash than is expressed over the news that approximately 46,300 people were killed in automobile accidents in 1982. Such a response does not necessarily indicate a greater concern over air safety, but clearly it receives more headlines.

of old, approaches to collective bargaining. Such a search and reappraisal may be especially needed in those few industries that contribute a disproportionate share of strikes. The union leaders and business managers should be wary of confusing private advantages with democratic liberties; indeed both may need to contemplate the implication of Justice Brandeis's words that in industrial relations "all rights are derived from the purposes of the society in which they exist."[17]

Public Responsibility for Peaceful Settlement

Despite the risk of complicating the process of private collective bargaining by further public involvement, the offer or requirement of more outside aid to union and management negotiators can be defended for a reason other than public concern. In the United States, state and federal legislatures have shown an inability or reluctance to act boldly in establishing labor standards, developing social welfare, and helping industry and labor adjust to technological change. Government has usually set minimum wages, pensions, unemployment pay, and medical benefits at levels lower than many industries could afford and unions could secure. The result has been to thrust upon collective bargaining the task of pushing for higher and better provisions than those guaranteed by legislation. Labor made its gains through use of economic power. There should be little surprise that the conflict can become sharp indeed and that public interests do not dominate in the resolutions of issues.

In the late forties, pensions to supplement minimal social security benefits became a bargaining issue over which a number of serious strikes occurred. Later, supplemental unemployment insurance arose as an issue as workers sought more protection from recurring depressions than state and federal governments would provide. Pensions and social insurance benefits were the major issues in disputes that contributed almost one-fourth of the losses resulting from strikes that involved 10,000 or more workers from 1947 to 1959.[18] In the last decade the states and Congress have shown but slight interest in major comprehensive programs to help workers meet the problem of technological change and plant closings. Convinced that they must look to their own devices and protection of the status quo to defend themselves against change, workers in mining, construction, transportation, and government have resorted to strikes. Some of these strikes have been lengthy, indicating in part the depth of feeling of workers in an unstable, insecure work world; they also indicate the poverty of aid extended by the community to them and to management. As long as the nation does not see fit to provide adequate protection against economic insecurity, particularly industrial decline and change, there is a rea-

---

[17]Quoted by David L. Cole, "Government in the Bargaining Process: The Role of Mediation," *The Annals of the American Academy of Political and Social Science,* vol. 333, 1961, p. 52.

[18]*The Dimensions of Major Work Stoppages, 1947–1959,* Bueau of Labor Statistics Bulletin 1298, 1961, p. 9.

son, and perhaps a duty, to offer more aid to the collective bargaining process, helping the parties to use that process as efficiently and effectively as possible.[19]

PROCEDURES TO AID PEACEFUL SETTLEMENT

No single procedure is applicable or useful in all bargaining situations. The issues in dispute and the importance to the community of services jeopardized by a possible strike may vary greatly from dispute to dispute. A procedure that might successfully contribute to settlement of a dispute involving a public utility might be most inappropriate in a construction dispute, and still another procedure might be necessary to produce a settlement of a strike involving nurses in a public hospital. Effective aid to peaceful settlement is apt to be forthcoming only if a number of procedures are available. Reliance upon any one method has obvious shortcomings. If it is sufficiently innocuous to be used frequently, the government may overuse it and the parties learn to calculate its possible effects. Once the procedure becomes a part of their calculations, each party will maneuver its negotiations and plot bargaining strategy to minimize the impact of the procedure upon goals. In such a case the procedure may not aid settlement but discourage it. Apparently, the fixed process for dealing with national emergency strikes under the Labor-Management Relations Act of 1947 has had this effect.[20] One side or the other may resist settlement, feeling sure that no economic pressures will develop during the eighty-day injunction period or that the situation may turn more in its favor in the meantime.

There are a variety of possible substitutes for the strike or for means of averting strikes. Some have had extensive use, and labor students have had time to examine their strengths and shortcomings; others have seen little use; and some are but speculative suggestions. Nevertheless, whether they have been used or only suggested, even a brief examination of the procedures reveals that there is available a range of approaches to peaceful settlement. To seek to avoid strikes by using only one technique is to deny industrial relations the full range of possibilities for peaceful resolution of conflict.

Supporters of collective bargaining have long argued that in a democracy the prohibition of strikes will not encourage unions to develop responsible bargaining. With the spread of unions among public employees and the wide acceptance of collective bargaining in government, one can argue that the prohibition is not apt to be very significant if it is not backed by legal force. Thirty-

---

[19]At the federal level Congress has provided only piecemeal legislative protection to protect the jobs and incomes of workers adversely affected by government actions. Among those receiving some assistance in recent years have been railroad workers; local transit workers, when private systems have been converted to public or have received public subsidies; employees displaced by foreign imports resulting from tariff changes; workers displaced by the expansion of national parks; and those private workers displaced by the closing of defense bases, merger of air carriers, and changes in programs affecting the disabled.

[20]W. Willard Wirtz, "The 'Choice-of-Procedure' Approach to National Emergecy Disputes," in I. Bernstein, H. L. Enarson, and R. W. Fleming (eds.), *Emergency Disputes and National Policy,* New York: Harper & Brothers, Publisher, 1955, p. 147.

one states prohibit strikes by employees of local governments and political subdivisions such as counties, towns, and cities; only eight explicitly allow strikes—Alaska, Hawaii, Minnesota, Montana, Oregon, Pennsylvania, Vermont, and Wyoming. The others make no provision or do not allow collective bargaining of state employees. Prohibiting strikes is but a gesture if it is not enforced, and seldom do states impose the statutorily mandated penalties upon illegal strikers.

The Public Sector

Strikes by government employees typically number in the hundreds in recent years, with few legal reprisals ever taken. When governments impose penalties upon illegally striking public employees, the results can seriously impair industrial relations for those immediately involved. An example was New York's response when in 1979 approximately 7000 prison guards walked off their jobs for seventeen days at thirty-three penal facilities. The state's Taylor law prescribes penalties for striking public employees, the loss of two days' salary for every day on strike, and for sanctions against the union as well, a loss of dues checkoff. Toward the end of the second week workers began to trickle back, for they were losing an average of about $126 a day. In addition, the state obtained a temporary restraining order. When the union leaders did not end the strike, the court fined the union $450,000 plus $100,000 per shift as long as the strike continued. It also sent the union's executive director to jail for thirty days.[21] After the strike the employees were split into hostile and angry groups. Those who had walked out had suffered large wage losses with no gains to show for them, and those who had stayed on the job took home almost $2000 in extra overtime pay. "One local union leader, interviewed a year after the strike said that he still would not talk to any of the 'scabs' or give union cards to any of the trainees who worked during the strike."[22]

Heavy penalties no doubt have a chilling effect on public employees' strike behavior when they know that officials will and have imposed them. In New York they will not quickly forget the prison guards' experience. It is likely also that federal employees will consider carefully before any of them again defy the ban on strikes. President Reagan's swift and uncompromising actions to penalize the air traffic controllers who walked out in 1981 taught a powerful lesson. The strikers lost their jobs permanently and their union its certification and then its existence. To avoid clear and blatant violation of strike prohibitions, workers call in sick or work by the rules, slowing or impairing operations.

If public employees cannot strike, however, they need alternative means by which they may resolve their disputes with management. State legislators have

---

[21]The contempt fine finally totaled $2,550,000, but the union secured a reduction after the strike to $1,220,000, which was still a heavy penalty.

[22]Lynn Zimmer and James B. Jacobs, "Challenging the Taylor Law: Prison Guards on Strike," *Industrial and Labor Relations Review,* vol. 34, July 1981, p. 542.

put their faith in various procedures designed to entice and encourage peaceful settlement or to induce the parties to end walkouts quickly, returning to negotiations or accepting arbitrated awards. Like the federal government confronting national emergency strikes, the states seek procedures that first, encourage settlement without reliance upon outside authority, and second, will maintain public service with little or no interference.

"SOFT" APPROACHES

The softest approach of all is found in the procedure of admonition. It has long been used by presidents and governors as well as majors and other local officials: they express official and public dissatisfaction with the threat or occurrence of strikes. Sometimes government officials will admonish union leaders and managers privately, but taking their concern to the public is apt to be more effective. Typically they deplore the intransigence of either side or both (a mayor or local official does not ordinarily complain of the local government's intransigence, of course), express concern over the consequences of particular settlements, or warn the parties involved that they will resolve the matters in ways that protect the public.

Governmental definition and verbal assertion of the public interest are not in themselves strong pressures for peaceful settlement, but they do encourage union leaders and managers to define publicly the particular interests they represent in terms that at least appear consonant with a wider interest. Also, insofar as government pronouncements help to create a climate of opinion unfavorable to strikes and to strengthen public conviction that peaceful settlement should be possible, the risk of further intervention or sanctions is increased if negotiations break down. Admonitions exert the greatest influence if they are not used excessively and if they carry with them an implied threat of stronger action. The smaller the unit within which the dispute takes place, the less likely admonition is apt to work. The interest in a small strike is not apt to be widespread enough to generate any public force.

Public Exhortation

Encouragement of peaceful settlement of labor disputes by exhortation is probably the easiest method to use but the most difficult with which to succeed, even under the best of circumstances. Its ease of use recommends it, but its limited effectiveness cautions against placing much reliance on it. If labor and management discover that they can safely ignore official admonitions because they are merely high-placed opinions supported by no threat of forceful action, these will have slight effect upon bargaining. Should admonitions be followed by stronger government action, though, high government officers must consider carefully the consequences of becoming directly involved in particular disputes and bargaining issues. Involvement in disputes can be politically embarrassing if it is not successful. It can also complicate settlement. As the federal government increasingly finds itself concerned with the problems of economic growth, productive efficiency, inflation, avoidance of depression, the country's competitive position in world markets, and the problems of unemployment, its officials will no doubt increasingly feel a responsibility to define the national interest and assert it. To assert it successfully, however, they may have to do more than admonish. They may have to provide some explicit, understandable guidelines for nationally powerful unions and management—standards by which the public can judge the reasonableness of their actions.

Mediation

A second procedure for encouraging peaceful settlement without the use of sanctions is mediation. It is one of the simplest and most frequently exercised methods of strike prevention; twenty-four of the states make it available for disputes involving state and local employees. The Federal Mediation and Conciliation Service closes out 20,000 to 26,000 mediation cases a year. Paradoxically, it is the most used yet the least effective of all the procedures. Mediation helps unions and management resolve differences and conclude agreements in thousands of negotiations year after year. It contributes to settlements between large, powerful protagonists who have to resolve difficult issues and it also helps small, relatively inexperienced bargainers negotiate routine agreements. There is nothing in mediation that compels agreement, however, and its voluntary nature makes it ineffective when the parties in collective bargaining prove intransigent and the issues intractable. When a strike is very likely, then mediation—at least routine mediation—fails or is at its weakest.[23]

Just because mediation sometimes fails, it does not follow that it must be viewed as a weak instrument. The Federal Conciliation and Mediation Service, along with state and local mediation bodies, has developed a cadre of experts skilled in exposing the areas of basic disagreement and in discovering opportunities for agreement. These experts know how best to encourage the parties to display an additional bit of flexibility that fits demands and concessions together into an acceptable agreement. They are usually knowledgeable about the economics and technologies of industries and are able to understand the peculiar problems and to speak the special language of those with whom they deal. People from outside the mediation services sometimes serve as mediators. Public officials, community leaders, and university teachers may be called to assist in some local disputes, but increasingly mediation has become a job for professionals. In graver national situations, however, there has more recently developed a practice of calling in a special ad hoc mediation panel consisting of prominent individuals whose judgments cannot lightly be ignored.

---

[23]See Thomas A. Kochan and Todd Jick, "The Public Sector Mediation Process: A Theory and Empirical Examination," *The Journal of Conflict Resolution,* vol. 22, June 1978, p. 21.

Mediation may take place before negotiators reach an impass or a strike occurs. In such a case of preventive mediation, the mediator may join the bargainers in their early sessions, becoming familiar with the background of the negotiations and gaining an inside knowledge of the issues and their implications for the parties. Should the mediator's active services be needed later, the mediator will already be well informed. Also, the presence of an outsider may be useful in reminding the parties that public interests are involved and should not be disregarded. Since negotiators often move from one critical stage to another rather than progressing toward one overall crisis, a mediator may be able to offer suggestions or perform services during the course of negotiating that help reach a final agreement. Perhaps more often the parties themselves request a mediator when they have deadlocked. In some situations, such as those involving public employees and some local public utilities, legislation prescribes mediation before a strike can be carried out. The parties are usually compelled to accept only the mediator's services, not any decisions or suggestions.

Even where mediation is compulsory, any resulting agreement is still voluntary.[24] In fact, it is the noncompulsory nature of mediation that encourages its use. It may help the parties reach an agreement, but it cannot endanger any essential principle or interest of either. Thus it does not threaten to interfere with free collective bargaining, nor does it threaten any penalties or control if that bargaining results in strikes harmful to the public.

Voluntary Tripartite Study and Informed Neutrals

In a few situations over the years unions and management have experimented with the procedures of "voluntary tripartite study" or the use of "informed neutrals." An appropriate term might be "consultation," though not all the functions performed by informed neutrals help the parties define and solve difficult joint problems. It resembles mediation, but unlike that procedure it can be applied to problems before they reach a bargaining stalemate or crisis. Preferably consultation would be used before an issue has come to the bargaining table. The informed consultants would deal with anticipated problems and with those that have existed for a long time but can be well handled apart from current negotiations. As a guide, adviser, and conscience to both parties, in anticipation of identifiable, incipient problems, the informed consultant might be able to help both parties approach each other as problem solvers and not merely as negotiators. Since the proceedings are divorced from immediate pressure to reach an agreement, they are probably most usefully applied to problems involving long-term relationships. By shifting emphasis from present terms and pending issues to longer-term, lasting problems, the parties may be

---

[24]Fourteen states require public employees to submit disputes to arbitration if they do not reach settlement after mediation. The necessary alternative of arbitration may well chill any positive effect of mediation, should one party or the other believe its chances are better with arbitration.

able to exercise a greater degree of foresight and imagination and thus raise the process of collective bargaining to a more constructive level.

In the late 1950s and early 1960s a number of unions and managements tried such use of consultation,[25] but it has not spread or even continued where it worked well for a time. In some cases it did not resolve intractable underlying issues, as in the railroad industry, and strikes eventually occurred. Consultation can be an effective means of avoiding or settling disputes only if both union and management can and will contemplate long-term planning of their relationships. Both must be sophisticated in their approach to business planning and control; managers must be willing to admit to their confidence both union leaders and the neutral consultant, while the union must be responsible to that trust. Furthermore, this three-way confidence is difficult to achieve because both union and management are usually fearful that a consultant's recommendations may be unacceptable to one of them while handing to the other a bargaining weapon of considerable value. This procedure is thus no guarantee of peaceful settlement of disputes and control of strikes.

Fact-Finding

A third technique that can help to avert strikes is fact-finding. The term is an anomalous one, since the finding of facts is its least important aspect. The problem is one of interpreting the facts. Labor experts mean by fact-finding a way of securing proposed terms of settlement that will secure wide public backing and require the parties to give careful, serious attention to them. The terms may be formulated by an expert or panel, which presumably enjoys such prestige by virtue of the appointing authorities and the arrayed expertise that its advisory proposals command respect. It is a common form of dispute resolution. The Railway Labor Act (RLA) has called for fact-finding in serious disputes for more than fifty years, and the Labor-Management Relations Act of 1947 still requires fact-finding as part of its national emergency strike provisions. Furthermore, twenty states have included it in their alternatives to strikes by nonuniformed employees of local governments.[26]

Thus, though it is the most common procedure available for dispute resolution, few researchers or practioners regard mediation well. Professors Peter Feuille and Hoyt Wheeler condemn it for its

deadly mixture of high expectations and low performance. Settlement expectations are high because the procedure appears quasi-adjudicative (with its hearing room, formally anointed factfinder, witnesses, exhibits, and written report which often con-

---

[25]George H. Hildebrand, "The Use of Tripartite Bodies to Supplement Collective Bargaining," *Proceedings of the Industrial Relations Research Association, 1961,* p. 657.

[26]Fact-finding often does not apply to firefighters and police because it is commonly recognized to be an inconclusive method of resolving disputes, and also because the two groups of workers have been politically powerful enough to win arbitration from state legislators. Arbitration is a more conclusive way to end disputes, even if members are not satisfied by the outcomes. Arbitration at least provides an authoritative figure to blame, excusing the union leaders.

tains settlement recommendations), yet performance may be low because either party is free to reject the fact-finder's report.[27]

A number of studies of fact-finding under the RLA and in recent public employees' disputes have shown its scant success. Many of the disputes were left unresolved and sometimes the parties were actually left farther apart than before the fact-finding hearings! The record has been so unsatisfactory that several states have eliminated fact-finding as a *final* dispute procedure, replacing it with compulsory arbitration.

Soft-approach procedures can contribute to peaceful settlement of disputes, but only in certain circumstances and only as one of a number of available procedures that public authorities may invoke to prevent or conclude strikes that threaten the public welfare. Even the full realization of the potential for resolution in fact-finding, mediation, consultation, or admonition will not provide a solution for all disputes. Their effective use can help considerably in many cases; their efficient, wise use probably helps prevent stalemates and a resort to strikes. But we must realize that some encounters involving interests and rights viewed by the parties as vital may be too sharp, too intractable, and too difficult to be resolved by reason or moral suasion. In these cases the governing authorities may have to apply sanctions and levy penalties before the parties will foreshorten or forego strikes that threaten injury to the public. A "hard approach" may then be necessary.

"HARD" APPROACHES

In taking a hard approach, the government may either provide a settlement that the parties reject on pain of penalties or penalize one or both sides until an agreement is worked out. The oldest procedure for limiting strikes is that of the injunction. As a short-run means of preventing a strike, it is without equal, though as an instrument for settling the dispute that gives rise to the strike, it is nearly useless. Historically the injunction was not used or intended as a means of settling disputes. Legally it is an order of the courts by which an action is forestalled. It is granted upon petition and proof of an appellant that otherwise irreparable injury will be inflicted. Under the Labor-Management Relations Act, a finding that a strike threatens national health or safety substitutes for a finding of irreparable injury. Its effectiveness depends upon the severe penalties a court may impose if an injunctive order is not obeyed. Disobedience of an order puts one in contempt of court, for which a judge may inflict whatever fines or jail sentences are found appropriate. Federal judges have under the national labor law levied fines of millions of dollars, and state judges have jailed local strike leaders for refusing to order members back to work in the midst of an enjoined and illegal strike.

---

[27]Peter Feuille and Hoyt Wheeler, "Will the Real Industrial Conflict Please Stand Up?" *U.S. Industrial Relations 1950–1980: A Critical Assessment,* Madison, Wis.: Industrial Relations Research Association, 1981, p. 270.

Though it may solve the immediate problem of a strike, the injunction is hardly suitable for long-run control of strikes. It is basically inequitable, favoring whichever party has the most to gain from preservation of the status quo and injuring the party seeking change. Since unions usually have been the initiators of change in industrial relations, they have felt that they had the most to lose from injunctions. For this reason and also because of their atavistic remembrance of the easy use (and misuse) of the injunction before 1932, unions have heartily condemned the national emergency injunctive procedure.

The favoritism inherent in the use of the injunction tends to block rather than speed settlement of disputes. Whichever party is favored will probably relax its efforts to reach an agreement as long as the injunction is in force. Under the national emergency procedures, an injunction must be lifted after a maximum of eighty days, and experience shows a mixed record. Sometimes the parties have settled during these cooling-off periods and in other cases the strikes have resumed.[28] Even if a later settlement is retroactive to the beginning of an injunction, there may still be gains to be secured by waiting. Production cycles may change to the advantage of one or the other party, and workers' enthusiasms and hopes may fluctuate, so that whatever settlement is ultimately worked out reflects a shift in relative bargaining strengths from those existing at the time the injunction was imposed.

Despite its limitations, the injunction already has a useful role to play in dispute settlement—not as a prime lever to achieve the settlement but rather as a powerful means of protecting the public from the detrimental effects of a strike. Certain disputes that involve particularly vital services or that threaten widely perceived public interests create irresistable political pressures to settle them peacefully. Used wisely and with caution, injunctive relief is a valuable tool. It is one that federal government officials have learned to use sparingly. Since 1972 the national emergency procedures have been used only once, during the nation's longest coal strike in 1978.

Government Seizure

A second forceful procedure, more powerful but also more politically dangerous to the user than the injunction, is governmental seizure and operation of a plant, firm, or industry involved in, or threatened by, a strike. With few exceptions, the government has used seizure only in wartime because of the constitutional protection of private property. In the years between Presidents Lincoln and Truman there were seventy-one seizures or attempts to seize.[29] Since the Supreme Court's emphatic judgment against Truman's seizure of the major steel producers in 1952, however, no president has intervened in a seri-

---

[28]Donald Cullen, *National Emergency Strikes,* ILR paperback no. 7, Ithaca: New York State School of Industrial and Labor Relations, Cornell University, 1976.

[29]John L. Blackman, *Presidential Seizure in Labor Disputes,* Cambridge, Mass.: Harvard University Press, 1967.

ous labor dispute with this tactic. A few states have provided for seizure in strike-control legislation, but governors also use it with reluctance.

Though it has not been used for more than three decades, seizure offers opportunities that may commend it to a future Congress under some circumstances. It can have the same result as the injunction, maintenance of the *status quo,* unless the government is authorized to make reasonable changes in the terms and conditions of work. Furthermore, the government may be compensated for its managerial contribution, receiving at least its costs or perhaps a percentage of the profits. Under seizure, the government's purpose is to make both parties less than satisfied with its performance. The union should receive less than its leaders and members hoped to win from management, and the managers should lose more than they would have under an agreement with the union. The hoped-for result is to drive the parties to settle their dispute and allow the government to remove itself from the scene.

There are obvious dangers in the government's use of seizure. It could degenerate into a cumbersome and awkward form of compulsory arbitration. Since special boards would be needed to determine just compensation for the owners and workers during the period of government operations, their proceedings and court appeals therefrom could snarl the whole procedure into an unworkable political and legal tangle. Another danger is that the government inadvertently (or out of political favoritism) might establish terms or conditions quite satisfactory to one party or the other. If that were to happen, there would be little pressure upon the party to compromise its stand, and settlement of the dispute would be frustrated. Finally, if seizure were made the only instrument available to the government for dealing with strikes, it would not help in most strike situations. Seizure is so drastic a step that it is a last-resort means of handling a strike and in any case would be used but rarely. Until Congress passes legislation authorizing presidential use of it, however, it remains only a possible, though in appropriate circumstances a promising, procedure.

Compulsory Arbitration

A third procedure, relying upon "the persuasion of power rather than the power of persuasion", is compulsory arbitration. It is a much simpler process than seizure, and unlike the injunction it provides a settlement. If the parties are unable to reach an agreement, an outside authority examines the claims and arguments of each and then fixes the terms of a settlement which must be accepted.

Both union leaders and managers in private industry have strongly opposed government-imposed compulsory arbitration as a threat to free, voluntary collective bargaining. They fear that it would not be limited to rights already negotiated under an agreement but would include the resolution of disputes over interests, matters on which no agreement yet exists. Paradoxically their opposition to it enhances its value as a possible means of settling disputes or stopping strikes. Even the possibility of its use should exert pressure upon the parties to reach an agreement on their own. If the government were empowered to intervene in true emergency disputes with compulsory arbitration, even though it seldom chose to exercise that power, the parties might be encouraged to submit their differences to voluntary arbitration. It thus would be an instrument of last resort, serving mainly as a prod to bestir the parties to approach voluntary dispute settlement more creatively than they had up to that time.

The main criticism of compulsory arbitration is that it undermines voluntary collective bargaining; it allows the parties to avoid the often unpleasant confrontation of their own difficulties, creating a dependency upon public authority. The criticism is valid if we judge the experience of a country such as Australia, where compulsory arbitration has long been used to handle all disputes. But if the government were to use compulsory arbitration in the private sector infrequently, as only one of several means of handling large, disruptive strikes, the criticism would lose much of its force.

Compulsory arbitration is more readily accepted and practiced in the public sector as an alternative to strikes of public employees. As state and local governments have found softer approaches failing to avoid strikes, they have turned to compulsory arbitration, often experimenting with different forms of it. Conventional arbitration allows an arbitrator (or panel of arbitrators) to hear both parties and render an award.

Final-Offer Arbitration

Professor Carl M. Stevens proposed in 1966 a variation: final-offer arbitration.[30] Each party submits a final offer acceptable to it; the arbitrator picks one of the two. The procedure, he argued, would encourage each party to converge upon a settlement that will be close to the other's and thus acceptable to the arbitrator. A number of states have adopted the procedure, particularly for police and firefighters. A few states include among the possible settlements from which the arbitrator chooses a fact-finder's recommendation in addition to the final offer of each party. Final-offer arbitration appears to work reasonably well, but it poses problems. The definition of a final offer is not as clear-cut in practice as it might seem to be in theory. The parties may find it necessary to redefine their "final" offer again and again, even as the arbitrator is attempting to choose between them. Furthermore, in some cases neither party's final offer, as a whole, may be reasonable, and the arbitrator may wish to choose selected items from each offer, constructing a new package.

With the development and wide use of compulsory arbitration in the public sector, researchers have studied the experience in the various states. Unfortunately, none has been able to provide many sure conclusions. Professor John Anderson, after a comprehensive examination of the studies to date, suggested

---

[30]Carl M. Stevens, "Is Compulsory Arbitration Compatible with Bargaining?" *Industrial Relations,* vol. 5, May 1966, p. 38.

that the effectiveness of compulsory arbitration remains unknown.[31] If compulsory arbitration becomes a regular part of negotiations, it may weaken voluntary efforts at settlement, particularly if one party or the other perceives gains through arbitration that it would not otherwise win. This "chilling" effecton free collective bargaining has long been recognized as a weakness of compulsory arbitration, a weakness that final-offer arbitration might overcome. Arbitration regularly used, however, may discourage either or both parties from innovatively approaching their problems, attempting to resolve on their own the new and changing issues that time, technology, and a cyclical economy continuously create. Compulsory arbitration, used in many of the states as an alternative to strikes, is likely to produce mixed outcomes, depending upon many different influences; moreover, it is not apt to promise enough flexibility or to impose harsh enough penalties to eliminate all strikes. It might best be conceived and used as an alternative to strikes in extreme situations, but not as an effective substitute on a regular basis. Other procedures might wisely be made available and used by public authorities.

Legislative Action

A fifth procedure for dealing with strikes and aiding peaceful dispute settlement is referral to the appropriate legislature. Most labor experts agree that except in the most unusual circumstances a legislature is a completely inappropriate body for adjudicating specific labor disputes. Yet the emergency strike procedures under the Labor-Management Relations Act of 1947 end with the unresolved dispute presented to Congress for its action. The fear of complicating an already difficult dispute with uninformed partisan politics may have contributed to the settlement of some emergency disputes. Though the occasion would doubtless be rare, referral of a dispute to a legislature might be helpful if a single important and easily grasped issue involving principle were in dispute. The effectiveness of the more possibility or threat of referral to the legislature is, however, the better argument for the procedure. In either case, we might expect its use to be extremely limited.

The Statutory Strike

One further suggested procedure for protecting the public from the injuries of a strike and inducing the parties to reach an agreement is the statutory strike.[32] During such a strike the employees would continue their work at the direction of the government unless, as individuals, they chose to resign. The government would also direct management to continue production. The interest of the public would thus be preserved insofar as it would continue to enjoy the goods and

---

[31]John C. Anderson, "The Impact of Arbitration: A Methodological Assessment," *Industrial Relations,* vol. 20, spring 1981, p. 144.

[32]Neil W. Chamberlain, *Social Responsibility and Strikes,* New York: Harper & Row, Publishers, Incorporated, 1953, pp. 279–286; and David B. McCalmont, "The Semi-strike," *Industrial and Labor Relations Review,* vol. 15, 1962, pp. 191–208.

services usually supplied by the parties in dispute. To encourage the parties to reach an agreement and to permit them to impose upon each other the same kind of penalties levied by a strike, the government would limit the earnings of each to less than would normally be received. Since by threatening or calling a strike each party indicates a willingness to take a loss itself in order to impose a loss upon the other, they should, at least in logic, have no objection to the statutory strike. It could even be made a desirable alternative by penalizing the parties only a portion of the loss that would result from a regular strike. The workers would forfeit some fixed proportion of their usual wages, and the company would give up a proportionate share of earnings. Both would thus sustain losses and be under pressure to reach an agreement, but the public would not be affected by the dispute. The contest of economic endurance would continue until the parties worked out concessions or arrived at some compromise acceptable to both. Once they reached a settlement, the government would end the statutory strike, and the parties would again receive their full earnings.

An obvious difficulty with this procedure is in adjusting the penalties so that the relative bargaining power of the parties is not greatly changed. If the penalties under a statutory strike hit one party harder than would those of a regular strike, the government is influencing the outcome of the dispute and the kind of settlement. Nevertheless, as one of a number of possible procedures which might be invoked in a critical situation, the statutory strike would appear to have enough merit to warrant serious consideration. To date, though, it has received little attention and almost no use.

There is thus available such an array of procedures for promoting and inducing peaceful settlement of disputes and for avoiding strikes that the high incidence of strikes in the United States compared with other free countries seems unnecessary. The potential threat of strikes and their display of great power wielded privately for private interests suggest that the public, through its representatives, might wisely urge the government to encourage, if not demand, that labor and management resolve their difficulties with a greater sense of responsibility to those outside their own organizations.

CONCLUSION

Since so large an incidence of strike falls upon a few industries, special public attention and assistance might be given to their industrial relations with the purpose of reducing our total industrial conflict. To repeat a thought expressed earlier in the chapter, some strikes are a necessary price we pay for private decision making in a pluralistic, open society, and for that reason we should not be misled into too ready a condemnation of all strikes. However, some of the nation's strikes may be simply a price exacted from the public for less efficient and less responsible negotiations than it has a right to expect. Suitable governmental action may prod unions and managements to give more attention to improving their social as well as their technological machinery.

THE FUTURE OF
COLLECTIVE BARGAINING

Throughout American industrial history the parties to collective bargaining have more often assumed formal adversarial stances than cooperative ones. Such a posture accords well with the striving, competitive ethos of the marketplace. It also emmulates the traditional ways in which Americans handle both politics and legal issues. Yet the public evaluates the resulting contention and conflict ambivalently. It apparently hopes for something more from industrial relations.

If unionists and managers treat each other only as adversaries, they may provoke deep anxiety among many Americans for two reasons. First, such treatment accords all too well with the Marxist notion of contending economic classes. The notion is often perceived as alien and undesirable, as is behavior that appears to validate it. Second, strife and conflict at the place of work appear to threaten industrial cooperation. Threats to the pervasive cooperative efforts of workers and employers are treated more seriously than the actual losses they may imply because Americans assume that cooperation is a basic, necessary aspect of economic success. It provides the matrix within which the economy's productivity is won. Nevertheless, public opinion surveys show that Americans strongly support collective bargaining, believing that unions benefit their members. They remain anxious, though, about the economic power of unions and the strikes that may result from collective bargaining. Their feelings express themselves as distrust of unions as organizations and of union leaders.

In a review of various public opinion surveys between 1966 and 1981, Seymour Martin Lipset and William Schneider found that unions are the least trusted major institution in American life, despite the fact that they have the largest mass membership of any organization in this country. Americans [show] . . . approval of their function accompanied by condemnation of their behavior.[1]

They also conclude from the twenty-four surveys examined that public "antagonism toward labor leaders is greater than that towards unions." The opinion sampled characterizes unions and their leaders as powerful and essentially self-serving. They are seen as people who give low priority to the public interest or the good of the whole society. In addition those sampled believe union leaders to be exceptionally corrupt and unethical among the leaders of major institutions.

Despite the low ratings the public gives to unions, it approves of the services they render to their members–that is, collective bargaining—and their political activities. In a Harris survey for *Business Week,* more than 80 percent of those polled agreed that workers should have the right to union. Furthermore:

> Some 88% of Americans—virtually the same proportion as in 1975—subscribe to the proposition that "most unions in the U.S. have been good forces" in promoting government response to social needs. More than half the public still believes that unions are a defense against employer exploitation, and two-thirds believe that employers would hire and fire unfairly if it were not for unions. Only on the assertion that unions guarantee a hearing for grievances has agreement dwindled—from 92% to 82%. . . . Asked whether a young person who got a job as an hourly worker would be made better or worse off in terms of wages, security, and conditions by union membership, 73% said "better" if the job was in an industrial plant; 55% replied "better" if the job was in an office.[2]

The public's dislike of unions accompanied by its favorable judgment of collective bargaining may reflect a fundamental ambivalence that most Americans, at once both consumers and employees, feel about the contending economic forces that play upon them in their dual roles. As consumers they desire increasing productivity that will bring lower-priced and higher-quality goods and services to the market; as employees they want protection of their wages, hours, and conditions of employment at the place of work. Collective bargaining provides the latter, but the public blames powerful unions and their leaders for impairing the former. Unions are perceived as agents for pushing up costs and thereby raising prices, and their leaders are presumed to be responsible for the disliked strikes and restrictive work rules that seem to destroy cooperation on the job and interfere with productivity.

The dominant feature of industrial life in the United States has long been the vast, pervasive voluntary cooperation at the place of work. Without the cooperative efforts of employees at all levels of the various organizations in which they work, national production could not sustain its high level and increasing productivity could not as easily be achieved. The cooperation is so

---

[1]Lipset and Schneider, *The Confidence Gap: Business, Labor, and Government in the Public Mind,* p. 199.

[2]"Still No Confidence In Labor Leaders," *Business Week,* Apr. 16, 1984, p. 16.

much a part of the usual and regular work relationships that almost everyone takes it for granted. Industrial cooperation is to American workers as water is to fish. Cooperation is simply a part of the environment within which they move. Strikes and conflict on the job are especially disturbing exactly because they are unusual—exceptions to normal expectations.

Despite apparent public dislike of strikes, by the standards of other nations the United States has a high incidence of work stoppages, particularly those of long duration. (Even so, the amount of working time lost to work stoppages is a small fraction of 1 percent, averaging only 0.23 percent over the period from 1939 to 1980. These losses are probably smaller than those caused by the common cold.) Both employers and employees have been able to afford the relatively high strike losses, but the public is uneasy about the loss, small as it is, because it seems to arise from an inability of unions and management to cooperate as much as is socially desirable.

As noted in Chapter 15, the level of overt conflict involving union members in strikes has trended downward over half a century. But the world has changed significantly during this period, so that even a lessening of strikes may not be sufficient for the public. The United States has lost the world economic dominance that it enjoyed in the immediate decades after World War II; foreign competition has increased sharply, particularly in manufactured goods where unions and collective bargaining have been most prominent. The deregulation of trucking, airlines, and railroads over the past decade has imposed competitive pressures on unions in these industries, confronting them with economic strictures never before experienced. As a result of the rapidly changing economic scene and the growing competition from abroad, the public recognizes a need for more cooperation between employers and employees than either party has shown in the past. Their improved record of strikes may not be sufficient, given the new situation the economy faces. Many thoughtful citizens believe that only further and more cooperation between unions and managers will enable the nation to respond to present-day challenges.

Developing different and more cooperative forms of collective bargaining will not be easy. The problems involved must be faced squarely. Solving them will undoubtedly require unwelcomed limitations on managerial authority and displeasing restrictions on union leaders. Public authorities may also have to change their largely hands-off approach to collective bargaining. The economic forces now at work are forcing reconsideration of existing procedures and ways of bargaining in any case. Cooperation between labor and management may commend itself to the parties, as well as to the public, more than at any time since the critical years of wartime production, more than forty years ago.

16

FROM CONJUNCTIVE BARGAINING TO COOPERATIVE BARGAINING?

Collective bargaining has changed considerably since the early ninteenth century. Workers and managers have adapted it to meet their new needs and altered circumstances and will continue to do so. At first unions existed in the shadow of illegality; judges were suspicious of their activities and employers were actively hostile toward them. Unionists responded with tactics and strategies that they found appropriate. Consulting among themselves, they formulated their final terms, to be imposed unilaterally upon employers if and when the economic or political tides pulled in their direction. With the turning of the tides, however, the bargaining initiative passed back to the employers, who would respond in a like manner, unilaterally imposing their terms upon the workers.

This seesaw approach to wage setting developed little mutuality and emphasized conflict. As the century wore on, a small but significant number of union leaders and employers began to appreciate the need for better ways of dealing with each other. They sought methods that would resolve, not intensify, their conflicting interests. Where unions were likely to be a continued presence and employers needed the organized workers to carry on their business, the parties found it sensible to establish procedures and work through processes that helped rather then hindered their dealings. They began to experiment with joint discussion of the terms of employment rather than leaving the formulation and imposition to the temporarily stronger party. By the end of the 1800s joint negotiations of the terms of agreement had become an important and regular part of collective bargaining.

Meeting jointly to discuss their expectations and to explore their offers was no small advance. The two parties threshed out issues between themselves, contributing in some degree to the knowledge and information of each other. They often learned that what was important to one may not have been as obviously important to the other. They also gained some sense of participation in the resulting decisions, giving both a stake in the terms of the agreement; there also developed a commitment to accept the terms for a given period rather than to throw them over at an opportune moment.

The benefits of joint bargaining compared to unilateral imposition were noticeable. As the economy grew, the range of business activities multiplied; organizations grew apace in size and complexity, becoming increasingly important in the conduct of both private and public affairs. More and more individuals had to deal with groups, finding themselves members of still other groups. Where joint efforts were necessary, as they were in all economic, social, and political life, joint group decisions had to be reached. The alternatives were authoritative compulsion by the state or by a dominant group, both of which went against the vague but strong democratic impulses of the American people. Collective bargaining thus filled a pressing and immediate need of the industrializing economy, according well with the values and traditions of the society.

Although the establishment of collective bargaining was an important advance for workers and employers, one should not credit it unduly. There is no reason to believe that collective bargaining as it has evolved to date is, in itself, the only or best means of adjusting interests among different industrial groups or of making decisions that affect the operations of an industrial society. Just as unilateral procedures of determining the terms of employment gave way to joint negotiations, we can expect the unions and management to modify and adjust present-day collective bargaining to the needs of new social forces and changed economic conditions. The continuing process of adjustment found throughout our society is not likely to bypass collective bargaining. Of course, wholesale remaking of union-management relations is neither likely nor desired by many people. The public, through the law, and the parties themselves, through their own efforts, are at present examing advances in new directions that promise better results than now accrue to employees and managers and to the society at large.

MUTAL DEPENDENCE VERSUS CONTRACT

In examining collective bargaining, one should be careful not to regard it as the same as the negotiation of a contract between two individuals. In some very small bargaining units, such an analogy may still be applicable; and over considerable periods of time, as new plants are built and operations are shifted[1]

---

[1]In 1981 the Supreme Court ruled that an employer could unilaterally decide to move a business, sell it, or subcontract work and install laborsaving machinery, since these actions involve the basic scope and nature of the enterprise. See *First National Maintenance Corporation v. National Labor Relations Board,* 452 US 666 (1981). This decision made "escape" from unions and collective bargaining easier than before.

or mills closed,[2] the relationship between employer and union are sometimes ended as relationships may be terminated in the case of individual contracts. For most units of the size of the modern business enterprise or government agency, however, the comparison is invalid. Once workers have chosen a union as their representative, it is unlikely, though not impossible, that they will revert to an unrepresented status.

Two examples illustrate the difficulties of ending a collective bargaining relationship. The first, that of Louisiana-Pacific Corporation, indicates that the costs can be high indeed; and the second, that of United Motors, indicates that the social and political pressures can make it impossible. In mid-1983 a strike by 1700 unionized employees of Louisiana-Pacific, members of the United Brotherhood of Carpenters, hit seventeen lumber plants in the Pacific northwest. Management refused to settle without substantial concession. The strike dragged on. By the end of the year the company had restaffed fifteen of the plants with 650 new hires and 550 union members who returned to work. The union began a boycott of company products and also a campaign to enlist the assistance of major stockholders and lenders. After a year, the workers who had replaced the strikers petitioned for decertification of the union, and in nine of the plants they secured it. Elections were expected at most of the other plants with the same probable outcome.

Thus Louisiana-Pacific, which also operates twenty-two nonunion mills, ended its relationship with the union that had organized its workers. It did so at considerable cost, however. Industry observers guessed that the strike had cost the company more than $4 million and the pain and trauma of a violent strike. Competitors liked the wage and work-rule concessions that the company won but were not sure that they wanted to secure them in the same way.[3]

United Motors Manufacturing Inc. appeared to be better positioned to escape dealing with a union. It is the joint venture of Toyota and General Motors in Fremont, California. The new company produces in the refurbished GM Fremont plant that had been closed for some years. The new company has no formal ties to GM as an employer and certainly had no legal responsibility to deal with the union or to hire back the laid-off GM workers. There were reasons why the new company managers were not anxious to deal with the union or the former employees. The plant had recorded a miserable industrial relations record. *Fortune* described the situation:

> The old UAW work force, and the GM management it did battle with, together gave the Fremont plant one of the worst disciplinary records in the GM system. . . . The

---

[2]In 1984 the Supreme Court held that an employer may disregard the terms of a collective bargaining agreement after filing a bankruptcy petition. See *National Labor Relations Board v. Bildisco & Bildisco,* 115 LRRM 2805 (1984). Whether a bankrupt firm can simply end all its dealings with a union is not clear. The majority decision declared that although the firm "remains obligated to bargain in good faith under NLRA ss8 (a) (5) over the terms and conditions of a possible new contract, it is not guilty of unfair labor practice by unilaterally breaching a collective-bargaining agreement before formal Bankruptcy Court action." Slip Opinion, p. 19.

[3]"A New Wage Pattern in Lumber as a Union Gets the Ax," *Business Week,* July 9, 1984, p. 32.

shutdown [in March 1982] left more than 800 grievances outstanding, including over 60 contested firings, and an orphaned local union bitterly at odds with both GM and the regional UAW leadership.[4]

Despite the initial and understandable refusal of Toyota's Japanese managers to consider opening the Fremont plant with a unionized workforce, they changed their minds. The union simply would not allow so heavy a blow to its prestige, and unionists expected wide support among the public already concerned about foreign ownership of American industry. The union threatened that it would block the joint venture unless its laid-off members had first shot at the jobs. The managers of the new company concluded that the UAW probably possessed enough political clout to thwart the plan in Washington. The plant opened with a unionized workforce, though with very different industrial relations, as we shall see later. The example indicates that even with a change in owner and a new management, the ties between workers and those who manage at a given location are not easily broken. They are certainly not broken with the facility that individuals enjoy. Individuals can go their separate ways after having met the terms of any contract into which they may have entered and need not have any relationship with each other again.

The most characteristic aspect of contract in western society—its voluntary nature, which we subsume in the phrase "freedom of contract"—requires the possibility of alternatives. Freedom to contract is dependent upon freedom *not* to contract, which in turn depends upon the opportunity to make another choice. For individuals, such freedom not to contract is frequently available. On a collective basis, it is available only under special conditions and probably at considerable cost. There is little chance for a body of employees, refusing the terms offered by their employer, to find alternative employment collectively as a body. Over a period of time, of course, many individual employees may be able to find other jobs.[5] Only somewhat less forcefully, the same result is encountered by management. There is little chance for an employer of hundreds or thousands of workers to replace them all with another working force if managers cannot reach an agreement with the union representatives.[6]

---

[4]Michael Brody, "Toyota Meets U.S. Auto Workers," *Fortune,* July 9, 1984, p. 54.

[5]In the case of many large enterprises, it would not even be feasible for a body of employees to find alternative employment individually. For all employees of any company employing 2000 workers, for example, there is only one job prospect—the company where they are employed. If a few of that number were laid off, they might be absorbed by other companies; but all 2000 were dismissed, only the relief rolls would ensure sustenance for many of their members. Such situations developed again and again in the early 1980s as steel mills and auto assembly plants closed across the country; a few workers found employment elsewhere, typically in trade or service industries; some retired early on social security and company pensions; but many were still looking for work months later.

[6]Under special conditions an employer may be able to replace even thousands of workers when an agreement fails to be reached. President Reagan, for example, agreed to the federal government's firing of more than 10,000 air traffic controllers, members of the Professional Air Traffic Controllers Organization. Union leaders refused to recommend that their members return to work after calling a strike on August 3, 1981. Their replacement was possible because first, the strikers were government employees and were acting illegally. Second, because roughly a third of those

As long as the system of collective bargaining is preserved, there is no alternative for most employers and groups of employees other than coming to terms with their immediate bargaining partner on the other side of the table.

Collective bargaining in most instances today thus requires that the parties reach some agreement. However prolonged strikes to settle disputes over divergent interests, some agreement must ultimately be forthcoming; since the parties can not disengage from each other, their collective bargaining relationship continues. Neither party is independent; neither can perform its function without the other. Only by ridding itself of collective bargaining, which allows workers to participate in negotiations and to resist managerial demands, can management gain an independence of operation. When the parties accept collective bargaining their respective organizations remain separate from each other, but they also become mutually dependent. For each, the achievement of its own function depends upon a working relationship with the other. Under a system of collective bargaining, neither management alone nor the union alone has any industrial relations significance; rather, they acquire significance only in relation to each other.

The fact of mutual dependence cannot be overstressed, for it is perhaps the most fundamental aspect of modern industrial society.[7] Among labor scholars and the public there is a lack of an adequate terminology with which to discuss this dependency. The term "collective bargaining" is most frequently used to mean any form of agreed association between union and management, but such blanket use necessitates resort to other terms if we wish to differentiate between kinds of association. To describe simply the relationship where union and management come to agreement through sheer functional necessity, let us use the term "conjunctive bargaining."

CONJUNCTIVE BARGAINING

In the sense used here, conjunctive bargaining does not arise out of one party's sympathetic regard for the other; nor does it arise because of its voluntary choice of the other as partner. It develops from the usual requirement that some agreement—any agreement—be reached so that the operations on which

---

employed either stayed at work or returned to their jobs within forty-eight hours after the President warned them of imminent dismissal. They provided a skeleton work force that was able to provide at least minimal service. Third, the Federal Aviation Administration, as sole provider of air traffic control services, was able and ready to impose a new, semiautomated landing procedure upon air carriers. These changes sharply reduced needs for air traffic control personnel. Air traffic was slowed and the total number of flights was reduced, to the inconvenience of the flying public, but the FAA, with strong backing from the president, continued its labor-saving procedures for months until it could train and hire new controllers. Fourth, the federal government had at its disposal many qualified military controllers who were temporarily assigned to the FAA.

[7]Mutual dependence does not hinge on a system of private propery. It exists also under public ownership or control, if some form of employee representation is maintained. Note the relationship of government managers and public employees in collective bargaining arrangements.

both depend may continue. Conjunctive bargaining represents the stage in a working relationship at which each party agrees, explicitly or implicitly, to provide certain requisite services, to recognize certain loci of authority, and to accept certain responsibilities in respect to the other. Without such an agreement, there could be no operation. Such bargaining may therefore be thought of as the minimum basis for continuation of the organization and union in a going concern.

Neither party can secure its objectives without a joint working relationship. Reciprocally, the terms of that relationship define the extent to which each attains its objectives, given its relative bargaining power, when dealing with matters of divergent interests. Coercion is the principal ingredient of conjunctive bargaining power. The resolution of divergent interests through conjunctive bargaining provides a basis for carrying out the activities of the organization—and nothing more. With whatever coercive powers that are at its disposal, each party wrests the maximum advantage possible, without much regard for the effect of this on the other.[8] The bargaining relationship comes into being because it is all but inescapable, and neither party grants more than is necessary. It is probable that conjunctive bargaining is still the most common form of bargaining relationship in the United States, half a century after widespread unionization first appeared.

Conjunctive bargaining has produced benefits as well as problems for both employers and managers, despite its limitations. It has challenged company officials and employers to manage rationally and to examine policies carefully and objectively. As union negotiators have pushed managers for costly benefits, management has had to seek increased efficiencies. Several outstanding students of labor concluded a detailed examination of collective bargaining more than two decades ago with this comment:

> The challenge that unions presented to management has, if viewed broadly, created superior and better balanced management, even though some exceptions must be recognized. . . . If one single statement were sought to describe the effects of unions on policy-making, it would be: "they have encouraged investigation and reflections."[9]

Sometimes managers will even explicitly admit as much. The head of a medium-sized wholesale food company, for example, said,

> This will sound funny, but by virtue of the fact that they [the union] cause us to pay higher wages, they force us to find ways to improve productivity, which in the long run is good.[10]

---

[8]This may still be compatible with not pressing a maximum short-run bargaining advantage because of a belief that certain restraint will prove beneficial in the long run. The tactical possibilities are varied. In conjunctive bargaining, however, the emphasis is on a coercive and competitive relationship.

[9]Sumner H. Slichter, E. Robert Livernash, and James J. Healy, *The Impact of Collective Bargaining on Management,* Washington, D.C.: The Brookings Institution, 1960, pp. 951–952.

[10]Quoted by Frank Allen, "Bosses Say Unions Do More Bad Than Good," *The Wall Street Journal,* December 11, 1980.

In a recent study, Richard B. Freeman and James L. Medoff have also concluded that the managerial response to the union challenge probably contributes to productivity and overall efficiency. Through collective bargaining, employees enjoy a range of choices when dissatisfied with their jobs or their working conditions; they have options for voice and redress through the grievance process. Instead of simply leaving an unsatisfactory situation, they can negotiate solutions. They find that:

> [Collective bargaining] changes the employment relationship from a casual dating game, in which people look elsewhere at the first serious problem to a more permanent "marriage," in which they seek to resolve disputes through discussion and negotiation.[11]

Conjunctive bargaining may have benefited the public as well. According to Freeman and Medoff, through collective bargaining unions reduce income inequalities, even allowing for the admitted monopoly effects. If the public believes greater equality is a good, it should find that collective bargaining makes at least a small contribution toward it.

Conjunctive bargaining appears to have benefited workers who have come under its coverage. It provides protection against arbitrary management demands, offering a system of industrial jurisprudence whereby employer and employees settle disputes under the agreement both rationally and peacefully. As noted above by Freeman and Medoff, it also enables employees to present their views, giving them a voice in some of the decisions that vitally affect their work lives. As Justice Brandeis pointed out when unionism was still in its infancy:

> Men are not free if dependent industrially upon the arbitrary will of another. Industrial liberty on the part of the worker cannot, therefore, exist if there be overweening industrial power. Some curb must be placed upon capitalist combination. Nor will even this curb be effective unless the workers cooperate as in trade unions. Control and cooperation are both essential to industrial liberty.[12]

Because unions and managements all too often have not been able to move beyond conjunctive bargaining and mix cooperation with control, they have inflicted costs upon themselves and the public that might well have been avoided. The rigidities of conjunctive bargaining lead unions and managements to cling to established procedures and processes simply because they have the power to do so; and such bargaining can encourage strikes whose impacts and effects spread beyond the parties. Both rigidities and strikes tend to reduce the benefits of conjunctive bargaining. More important, if unions and

---

[11]Richard B. Freeman and James L. Medoff, *What Do Unions Do?* New York: Basic Books Inc., Publishers, 1984, p. 94.

[12]From his address, "True Americanism," quoted by William Feldesman, solicitor, National Labor Relations Board, in a speech before the Graduate School of Business Administration, University of Virginia, Charlottesville, Va., Oct. 18, 1963, p. 3. (Mimeographed.) Brandeis limited his need for liberty to those employed in private, profit-making firms, but today the same need can be perceived in public and nonprofit organizations, as well.

management do not progress beyond conjunctive bargaining, they forgo opportunities from which both might benefit.

In a joint relationship that is based on necessity, the extent to which either or both parties can attain objectives is dependent on the organizations' performance. That performance is measured by the total rewards to all involved, less their total costs. Both rewards and costs should include more than pecuniary considerations, of course. The status of the organization in its field and the prestige of a quality product or service might be included, so that for a private business firm more than profit is included. Similarly, monotonous and routinized operations, disadvantageous location, or health hazards might be viewed as costs, along with the outlays for materials and services obtained outside the organization.

The performance evaluation that attaches to the organization as a whole defines what the parties will divide between them, both costs as well as rewards. Managers and union leaders have thus fought not only over the distribution of pecuniary gain but also over who shall take credit for good performance in other respects, such as the quality of the product, the welfare of the employees, and increased productivity. In addition there is also contention about who shall take the blame for poor performance in such matters as unsafe conditions of work, restrictionist policies, and strikes. No matter how strong the bargaining power of one relative to the other, the advantages that each can derive or the costs each seeks to shrug off arise from the total performance of the organization. At the extreme, organizational failure (bankruptcy in a private firm or voter rejection in a public agency) means its complete incapacity to satisfy the objectives of both managers and union member employees.

Numerous factors determine performance, among them all the forces impinging on the demand for the product or services and the supply costs of production. There is one factor of peculiar interest to us in the present context. We have just noted that under a system of collective bargaining, some joint action of the parties is essential to the very operation of the organization. It may now also be added that how well the parties act jointly will determine, in large measure, how well they operate at all. Performance is in part dependent on the nature of the relationship between the parties; that nature fixes the boundaries within which each party can achieve its objectives, but is itself limited by the relationship existing between those parties.

Conjunctive bargaining, through which the parties agree to terms as a result of mutual coercion and arrive at a truce only because they are indispensable to each other, is but one kind of relationship between them. It provides no incentive for the parties to do more than carry out the minimum terms of the agreement that temporarily resolves their divergent interests. The obligations that each assumes in the conduct of the business and the advantages from the consequent performance that each has wrested from the other are fixed. For one party to give a superior performance by cooperating more effectively with the other is not likely to win it any further concession because concessions are predetermined. Conjunctive bargaining allows the minimum required cooperation of each with the other; it tends to become the maximum actual cooperation as well.

Indeed, there sometimes arises a fixed determination on the part of managers or union members not to meet their obligations in any greater degree than the other party can exact. The result sometimes takes the form of "getting away" with as much as possible. Unions have charged managements with denying members the full rights of the collective agreement. In the words of one labor official who was speaking of a supervisory training program: "So far as we can see all the company is trying to teach its foremen through the program is how to be diplomatic in chiseling the workers." Managers have indicted unions for encouraging relaxed effort on the job. One industrial relations manager reported that he was convinced that in his plant, employees were literally subjecting themselves to greater fatigue through their efforts to delay work and slow down production.

Because of its emphasis on minimum obligation, conjunctive bargaining limits and restricts organizational performance. It imposes limits on the ability of each to secure its objectives, regardless of its relative bargaining power. If a better working relationship can be established between the parties, so that they recognize something more than a minimum of mutual obligations, performance can usually be improved. The potentialities of the organization for satisfying the objectives of the parties will thus be more effectively realized.

COOPERATIVE BARGAINING

Neither union leaders nor managers feel free to establish a more fruitful bargaining relationship unless they believe that they will gain something from the added benefits. This amounts to saying that neither will gain additional advantages unless the other gains too. Neither party will expect the other to give up something for nothing. Realistically, we may expect that the efforts of one party to best the other will never be abandoned. Such efforts do not rule out the possibility that intelligent managers and union leaders will discover that their mutual relationship can be improved, to the advantage of each, by holding out the promise of benefit to the other party. This appears to be a prima facie case for cooperation based on selfish benefit rather than altruism or adherence to the Golden Rule, however valuable those approaches may be.[13]

The basis for cooperative bargaining is the dependence of each party upon the other. As a matter of fact, each can achieve its objectives more effectively if it wins the support of the other. This means that when one party is seeking a change the better to secure some objective, it is more likely to succeed in its design if it anticipates the objections that may be raised by the other party, on

---

[13]Cooperation with the other party because motivated by moral principle is not to be slighted. The argument here is simply that cooperation is not dependent on a spiritual conversion or religious or ethical belief; it can be supported on the basis of advantage to each party. "Advantage" should be defined in broader terms than pecuniary return, of course.

whose cooperation its own success depends. The objections raise issues of divergent interests, and unless these are resolved, it will prove impossible to define an area of common interest in which cooperation can be established. In order to win the necessary cooperation, the initiating party may have to make concessions—greater perhaps than it considers fair or just and despite the fact that such concessions may be unnecessary as a matter of traditional authority. They are made because, on their granting, a joint effort is forthcoming that produces a greater advantage to the initiating party than would have been possible without them.

The distinction between the divergent interests and the common interests of unions and management may appear to be a simple one, but it is actually quite subtle. Where interests are accepted as common rather than divergent, the notion that the agreement sums up what had to be given up or all that could be gained fades; the parties approach bargaining with the realization that the better the performance of each, the better the joint performance. Furthermore, each understands that the better the joint performance, the greater the advantage for both.

Cooperation is not an unheard-of activity of unions and management in the United States, but traditionally it comes in the form of a joint protection of industry interests from competitors or a joint demand for special concessions from government. Thus it has not been unusual for unions and industry spokespersons to join together to lobby for public subsidies and special legislation. The United Mine Workers and the Bituminous Coal Operators Association have politicked against federal government support for fuels that compete with coal. The Amalgamated Clothing and Textile Workers Union has campaigned for restrictions on textile imports. The Teamsters and Trucking associations jointly opposed the deregulation of the trucking industry. The United Automobile Workers show themselves as eager as the automobile company managers to limit Japanese imports. The maritime unions have backed industry representatives as they sought to preserve the legal barriers against foreign flagship operations in domestic trade, and organized teachers jointly lobby with local school authorities for larger state appropriations and together seek to prevent federal budget cutbacks of educational programs.

Not at all uncommon has been the joint cooperative effort of union leaders and managers to persuade consumers to buy the products or services with which they are chiefly concerned. The cigar makers' and hatmakers' unions long conducted advertising campaigns to persuade the public to buy more of their products. Unions such as the United Rubber Workers have from time to time urged consumers to buy goods produced by companies with whom they negotiate, publishing the names of the companies and their products in their monthly papers. Locals of the UAW have mounted publicity campaigns for American-made autos and against Japanese-made cars. The whole effort of the AFL-CIO's union-label department has been directed toward improving sales of goods produced by organized companies. The garment unions particularly have supported the union-label program with television and radio advertisements.

A few unions have cooperatively dealt with employers to help them cut costs and improve efficiencies by supplying technical experts and engineering advice. This kind of special help is usually needed immediately after a unit is organized so that it can produce efficiently enough to pay the new, higher wage rates and yet survive. Unions have from time to time cooperated with management to implement programs of cost cutting, explaining the details and persuading the workers to accept them. Such cooperation is usually of a limited nature, restricted in both time and comprehensiveness.

Since the 1970s union leaders and managers have increasingly recognized the need to give more attention to safety on the job and health at the place of work. By 1980 more than half of all the large bargaining units[14] in manufacturing (about 60 percent of the workers covered) had established joint committees on safety. In steel 94 percent and in transportation almost 70 percent of the workers had such committees. Cooperative efforts were also common in areas involving apprenticeship training and the administration of benefit plans. Many employing firms and unions had also established joint programs to deal with drug abuse, alcoholism rehabilitation, and preretirement counseling.

Public officials and leading citizens have called for an increase in cooperation between unions and management. They are particularly interested in programs to increase productivity and improve the economy's competitive position in the world. For example, Paul Tsongas, Democratic senator from Massachusetts, called for a new unionism that was "leaner, more flexible, more innovative; concerned about efficiency and productivity, and intolerant of featherbedding."[15] Peter Drucker, well-known business consultant, has suggested that unions will become irrelevant if they do not turn their attention to capital formation and productivity issues.[16] Abe Raskin, longtime labor editor of *The New York Times* and associate director of the National News Council, has written that:

> the need and the opportunity have never been greater for chipping away the antagonisms of the past and establishing a fruitful new relationship built on cooperation by management and labor. The key lies in restructuring the lines of command in the workplace to make workers full-fledged partners in shaping the decisions that directly affect their jobs.[17]

Despite encouragement from outside, few unions and managements have attempted cooperation on productivity. Joint committees and programs to serve such a purpose are much less common than those involved with health and safety issues. In 1980 only one out of twenty agreements (covering one out of six workers) in large bargaining units had established labor-management

---

[14]That is, with 1000 or more workers.

[15]Paul Tsongas, *The Road From Here: Liberalism and Realities in the 1980s,* New York: Random House, 1982, p. 148.

[16]Peter Drucker, "Are Unions Becoming Irrelevant?" *The Wall Street Journal,* Sep. 22, 1982.

[17]"Can Labor and Management Form a More Successful Partnership?" (quoted in an advertisement by The LTV Corporation), *The Wall Street Journal,* Aug. 3, 1982.

committees on productivity. They were a bit more numerous in manufacturing; about 8 percent of the agreements and roughly 28 percent of the workers were covered. In large trucking and transportation units 44 percent of the workers had such committees, but in construction fewer than 2 percent of workers had them available.

The record of cooperative programs is thus not impressive, though a few industries show a modest commitment. Furthermore, an examination of cooperative experiments over the years reveals that there is seldom an expansion of whatever processes were used and developed, even if they continue. Under economic duress or in the throes of technological upheaval, managers and union leaders have, from time to time, joined in imaginative and successful cooperative programs. The negotiations of the Pacific Maritime Association and the International Longshoreman's and Warehousemen's Union in the mid- to late-1960s are one example. The two parties worked out peaceful ways to change work rules and introduce mechanization that greatly increased productivity and lowered costs. Relations between the two parties have continued relatively peacefully since, but they have not built upon their earlier cooperative efforts or introduced further programs of cooperation.

Another example was the attempt of the Packinghouse Workers and Meatworkers with Armour Company in the early 1960s to grapple with pressing problems of automation in a rapidly changing industry. They tried some innovative programs of cooperation, but the structure of the industry changed so radically that most became irrelevant and fell into disuse. In more recent years, a few union leaders and managers in the automobile industry have tried to improve both productivity and industrial relations with cooperative quality-of-work-life programs. One example is General Motors' assembly plant in Tarrytown, New York. By 1982, it had involved close to 4000 people in the plant, and costs for special training had totaled over $1.5 million.

The program began with the 1973 national agreement between GM and the UAW, when both parties commited themselves to explorations of the quality of work life. It was the first explicit commitment to such an a program in any major American industrial relations agreement. The local union president explained his attitude:

> We as a union knew that our primary job was to protect the worker and improve his economic life. But times had changed and we began to realize we had a broader obligation, which was to help the workers become more involved in decisions affecting their jobs, to get their ideas, and to help them to improve the whole quality of life at work beyond the paycheck.[18]

Both company and union carried out careful and extensive training sessions to prepare supervisors, shop stewards, and workers for new ways of interacting, dealing with each other, and communicating. They required initial help, train-

---

[18]Zager and Rosow, *The Innovative Organization,* p. 93. This book also reviews a number of other cooperative experiments between unions and management over the last decade. Some failed, some enjoyed limited success, and a few may prove of long-term worth.

ing, and encouragement; they also required continuing support. By 1981 further experimental processes were tried out in a few likely departments, expanding the involvement of workers in shop decisions and speeding up problem solving on the job. Grievances dropped to a low level. Furthermore, the parties decided that each gained from the program, even though the program had experienced marked ups and downs. Model changes and falling sales had forced large layoffs upon them, which often removed leaders and broke up the on-the-job quality-centered work groups. Despite the setbacks, or perhaps because the new program helped both parties to cope with the added economic difficulties better than in earlier times, there was general agreement that the program was worth continuing.

At Tarrytown, workers were offered extensive participation in work decisions and increased responsibility for quality work. The generally favorable response of those involved may commend their introduction elsewhere. It may well be that the relative success of the Tarrytown program convinced UAW leaders and GM officials that they should experiment with the management of the joint venture of GM and Toyota, United Motors, in a completely new form of industrial relations. *Fortune* commented:

> the company and the union have been putting together a labor relations system so dependent upon cooperation rather than confrontation that the very line between union and management has blurred.[19]

The parties announced an interim agreement more than a year before production was to get underway. In the meantime union leaders and managers worked together, "not formally negotiating across a bargaining table, but kicking around ideas for contract provisions that would mutually benefit the work force and the company."[20] *Fortune* pointed out that such an approach has allowed the parties to make an important "breakthrough in scrapping traditional union work rules, the primary impediment to achieving Japan-like efficiency—and quality—in U.S. plants."[21]

The lessons and reward of such experiments as those at Tarrytown and Fremont are of special interest to workers and managers in industries exposed to new forms and pressures of competition. The changing economic scene may encourage wider adoption of cooperative approaches than history would lead one to expect. We cannot yet predict what other attempts will be made to develop cooperative bargaining, as in the automobile industry, and there is no assurance that even the ones now established will survive the test of time.

BARRIERS TO COOPERATIVE BARGAINING

One of the highest barriers to cooperative bargaining is a widespread skepticism, particularly among union leaders, that change is imminent. In a survey

---

[19]Brody, "Toyota Meets U.S. Auto Workers," p. 56.
[20]Ibid.
[21]Ibid.

of national opinion leaders in 1982, the Opinion Research Corporation found that seven out of ten favored an improved change in the relationship of labor and management. Eighty-six percent of union leaders and seventy-six percent of business managers endorsed such a change. Furthermore, almost all agreed that the change was needed to secure increased productivity. However, the conviction that the change would be soon in coming was held more often by business managers than by union leaders, academics or public interest leaders. Almost three-quarters of the managers indicated that the changes could be expected within five years; 60 percent thought that the change would be coming within two years. More than half the labor leaders thought it would take longer, an opinion shared by leaders in the other groups.[22]

Even if the parties overcome their skepticism of the possibility of change in the near future, reaching and maintaining cooperative agreements is no easy task. Neither party is apt to want to concede more than is necessary to win the required cooperation. Negotiations have to continue; each must "feel out" the other party and measure the relative bargaining powers. The possibility of a breakdown in negotiations is always present, of course. But in striving for cooperation, they negotiate and bargain within a different context since the objective has changed. Recognition of the benefits of cooperation increases the chances of resolving divergent interests and also modifies the measure of bargaining power, even if it does not eliminate the possibility of impasse.

The divergent interest over which an impasse in negotiations is most likely to develop between parties seeking to cooperate is not wages or any other money item. Even though money is often a thorny issue, parties that can appreciate the benefits of a cooperative relationship can reasonably make the appropriate estimates of the advantage of an agreement. Even if an agreement does not bring everything each party has wished for, it may still be attractive enough to conclude. If a money advantage is sought to the point of disrupting a cooperative association, much more is lost than simply the cost of the strike or lockout. The cost also may include the return to conjunctive bargaining, one that falls upon both parties.

A real barrier to a cooperative agreement on divergent interests is, paradoxically, a fear of cooperation itself. Although one may be able to establish a prima facie case for the preferability of cooperative to conjunctive bargaining, there is a prevalent fear on the part of manager, union leaders, and employees that its potential benefits are outweighed by its potential dangers. The parties for the most part have been willing to accept the limitations on business performance imposed by conjunctive bargaining rather than subject themselves to the dangers that they foresee in a more advanced relationship.

What are the dangers that union leaders and managers envisage in a joint program of cooperation? For managers, it is a loss of their presumed prerogatives; for union leaders, it is a loss of function, rendering their role and office

---

[22]"Can labor and management form a more successful partnership?" (advertisement by The LTV Corporation).

unnecessary; for employees, it is a fear of insecurity caused by improved efficiency and reduction of jobs. Let us examine these fears more carefully.

Management Barriers to Cooperation

In Chapter 4 we considered the issue of the appropriate subject matter of collective bargaining, and we encountered the opinion generally expressed by managers that the union's right to seek agreements should be confined to certain matters. All other matters are subject to the sole discretion of those who are legally appointed to exercise authority in business operation. Corporate law recognizes the right of owners (stockholders) to designate through elected boards of directors certain officials (management) to act in their interests. To permit unions to have a voice in business decisions, according to this opinion, would dilute the powers of owners and the rights of property. To recognize a union's interest in production problems would simply widen its area of control within the company, leaving management without its highly prized right to make the decisions necessary for the long-run welfare of the company as a whole. Cooperation thus carries an implicit threat to the structure of authority within the enterprise.[23] As might be expected, managers are much more concerned about this threat than are union leaders. The poll of opinion leaders conducted by the Opinion Research Corporation in 1982, for example, showed that only 25 percent of business managers favored worker participation in decision making affecting jobs; almost two-thirds of the labor leaders *strongly* favored such participation.

Managers' attitudes, expressed in the poll, assure one that the issue cannot be lightly disregarded. No doubt a union run by officials who are ideologically opposed to managerial interests may pursue a disruptive course, damaging the organization as cooperative programs enlarge their sphere of influence. But this is only to say that cooperation is not possible with union leaders who do not accept cooperation in good faith. If good faith is present on both sides, the basis for managerial fears is probably a failure to distinguish between matters of divergent and common interest. If divergent interests are involved in production, for example, in the form of speed of operations or downtime allowances, they will in time find their way to the bargaining table for resolution in any event. We have already observed the increasing scope of union interest in management decisions, which over the years has caused managers to negotiate with unions on issues that they earlier had refused to discuss. By refusing cooperation for fear that it will widen the union's area of participation in decision making, managers will not gain any long-run protection from the dilution of their authority, and they will lose the fruits of cooperation.

---

[23]Some scholars argue that government officials, like managers in private organizations, cannot permit their employees to participate in decision making. To allow such participation would infringe upon the sovereignty of government, not merely the prerogatives of managers. Cooperation in this case, they point out, restricts the legimate exercise of democratic power.

Managers' fear that cooperation will threaten their authority arises more from ideology than it does reality. Decision making is widely shared in fact and practice; many people and groups within an organization make decisions, whether they possess the authority—the legitimacy—to do so or not. Managers are always trying to strengthen the role of decisions made with authority and to weaken those that are made without authority. They are only partly successful, however, often sharing decision making despite themselves. What they must preserve, and can protect more easily for it involves great talent and a continuous flow of information and communications, is the unique role that only managers can play: the coordination and reconciliation of all the decisions affecting the organization. Whoever fills this role *is* in fact managing. These persons must finally reconcile the allocation of resources, matching outflows with inflows in a way that preserves and enhances the integrity of the organization. Unions leaders are not apt to assume the burdens of managerial coordination, for their leaders would then find themselves managers, confronting the dilemmas and difficult trade-offs that make up work-a-day managerial life. They would be hard-pressed to command a flow of information that would allow them to make informed moves, and the trade-offs would endanger their political positions within their unions.

Another of the largest barriers to cooperative bargaining does involve the authority of lower managers, the supervisors who work most closely and immediately with employees. If cooperation is to become a reality, their real authority will have to be greatly strengthened and supported by upper management. Donald N. Scobel, an expert in labor relations, director of the Creative Worklife Center and formerly with Eaton Corporation, points out that:

> Often the most difficult part of union-management cooperation comes with a major change in the role of first-level supervisors. Usually, for the new system to work, some middle levels of responsibility must pass down in the organization in a show of good faith. In fact, this change addresses one of the prime complaints of employees: "Let's face it, we've been unofficially autonomous for years. We don't want to officialize the autonomy; we want some real leadership." This leadership can come from those who supervise employees directly.[24]

It is the policy that the new Fremont operations of United Motors appears to have adopted.

> The differences at Fremont begin with a shrunken white-collar population. In old-style U.S. plants, swarms of middle managers preoccupy themselves with problems that crop up on the factory floor. At Fremont, most day-to-day problems will be solved on the floor by work team members. Anything the teams can't handle will be taken by group leaders—salaried foremen who supervise the work of five to seven teams—directly to the line managers of their departments, such as welding, painting, assembly, and so forth. In all, the plant will have five layers of management—only

---

[24]"Business and Labor—From Adversaries to Allies," *Harvard Business Review,* Nov.-Dec. 1982, pp. 132–133.

one or two fewer than the typical U.S. plant—but there will be fewer managers at each level.[25]

Cooperative bargaining need not erode managerial authority, though it will change its locus. It will require the substitution of good supervisor-employee relations for rules. It will require of management a recognition that employees today can be treated as adults with worthwhile ideas about improving the job and raising product quality. They need not be seen—wisely they will not be perceived—as children in constant need of direction. It is neither visionary nor impractical, but the essence of teamwork, which the Japanese recognized to their advantage before Americans have.

Union Barriers to Cooperation

To the extent that cooperative bargaining is successful, unionists may fear the possibility of a withering away of union functions. This threat is premised on a widely circulated belief that if managers understood workers and satisfied their needs, there would be no place for a union. In that event, the withering away would mean the loss of position and influence for all its officers and staff. Can they be expected to sacrifice their own interests, especially when these can be realistically viewed as coinciding with their members' interests? There can be no doubt that historically managers have resisted unions and shown them much hostility. If harmony of interest between employee and employer can be stressed and if managers are careful to give employees some share in the benefits of harmony (say participating in shop production decisions), will not this rob union members of their militancy and even their desire to maintain a separate organization responsive to their peculiar interests?

Once again, it is evident that this is an issue that cannot be brushed aside. Many managers in fact regard independent unions as unnecessary and undesirable; they would welcome their passing from the scene. Where there is such lack of good faith, cooperation is not feasible. Where good faith exists and continues, however, the fears of unionists, like those of managers, appear excessive. Divergent interests between employees and employer will always remain. Indeed, cooperative bargaining in any meaningful sense cannot succeed until employees have become convinced that their special interests have been fully considered. This conviction cannot be sustained unless workers are represented by organizations which, because they are independent, can present workers' problems adequately and press for their recognition in the agreement. The element of bargaining power is not ruled out by cooperation, even though its coercive expression may be reduced, and organization is essential to such power.

Finally, employees sometimes fear that worker acceptance of cooperative bargaining may make the union little more than an adjunct of management,

[25]Brody, "Toyota Meets U.S. Auto Workers," p. 60.

stressing efficiency to the detriment of employee welfare. Joseph Scanlon, who pioneered in the introduction of cooperative programs, pointed out that cost reduction, improved production methods, and the installation of new equipment are associated in the minds of workers with layoff and wage reduction. Their drive for job security develops a resistance to this kind of program.[26] If the union becomes a partner in such activities, on what can the workers depend for protection?

The union's protective role will be lost only if the union becomes responsible primarily to an authority other than its membership. To the extent that the members retain control over the organization, there is a reasonable safeguard against its perversion. Moreover, as Scanlon suggested, cost-reduction programs with their attendant threat to worker security will be sought by managers whether unions cooperate or not, and the workers' greatest protection will come through participation in their introduction.

Thus there appear to be solid grounds for believing that where good faith exists between the parties, the dangers of cooperative bargaining to each have been overstated. Where good faith is present, the benefits of a well-planned program would appear to overbalance the disadvantages. But even if this conclusion is valid, the development of cooperation raises other problems and dangers that should not be ignored. First, a cooperative effort has usually been sustained most readily on the basis of face-to-face relationships and intimate, personal involvement and participation. Providing such a basis for cooperative bargaining is not easy in an economy of large-scale organizations and sprawling bargaining units.

COOPERATIVE BARGAINING AND SMALL GROUPS

The importance of face-to-face relationships in establishing the morale upon which cooperative efforts must build does not make cooperation impossible among employees of large organizations, but for maximum effectiveness it may require a reorganization not only of supervision and management at the place of work, as United Motors is carrying out, but also of the production process. To the extent that collective bargaining is carried on in large units—multiplant, marketwide, or industrywide—cooperation would seem to be less feasible than among smaller units. However cooperatively conducted, can bargaining in such large units successfully establish the local conditions necessary for a truly effective program? Will the settlement of issues of divergent interests by a method that requires consideration of the needs of many differently situ-

---

[26]Joseph N. Scanlon, *Labor's Philosophy Concerning Cost Reduction Programs,* production series, no. 160, American Management Association, 1945, pp. 33–39. See also Douglas McGregor's evaluation, "The Scanlon Plan through a Psychologist's Eyes," in F. G. Lesieur (ed.), *The Scanlon Plan: A Frontier in Labor-Management Cooperation,* New York: John Wiley & Sons, Inc., 1958. For a more recent description of the Scanlon approach, see D. F. Frost, J. H. Wakely, and R. H. Ruh, *The Scanlon Plan for Organization Development,* East Lansing, Mich.: The Michigan State University Press, 1974.

ated plants or firms permit agreement on matters of common interest in the single plant or smaller department?

The answer can be "yes" if union negotiators and managers continue to develop and encourage a "federal" system of bargaining units by a process that links plant and company and even industry. Some problems are so comprehensive that small groups cannot exert any meaningful control over them; they involve relationships and interests that transcend the parochial concerns of local groups. But other problems affect only the smaller group or have but slight spillover influence upon other groups. The officers of the large, more comprehensive group are appropriately involved in the first kind of decision but are unneeded in the latter. Similarly, local competencies are more apt to be satisfactory, or at least satisfying, for local problems than the expertise of the larger groups, but they are out of their depth on more general issues. Cooperation is more effective when decisions are reached in the units most appropriate to the subject involved. No less than in other social organizations, however, there is a need in industrial relations for decision-making units of varying size.

In fact, if the technique of cooperation, which appears to offer much promise, is to be promoted, there are important reasons for retaining in the local jurisdiction as much of the bargaining and negotiations as can be left there. Local resolution of divergent interests permits a better framework for the identification of areas of common interest; excessive control from above can frustrate local initiative. Instances are not wanting where local unions have quietly disregarded the instructions of national officers and where local plant managers have violated the limits of their discretion because they recognized that their successful relationships depended on terms differing from those which had been prescribed for them by higher authorities within their respective organizations.

This operation by unions and management within a system of bargaining units parallels the frame-within-frame approach by which management proceeds in any organization. Each operational level or frame of management prescribes the limits within which managers at the next-lower level must operate. But the limits allow an area of discretion—as wide an area as can be permitted and still ensure the accomplishment of the objective of those in the superior frame. Similarly, in a system of bargaining units, the decisions in the larger unit prescribe only so much as is needful to ensure the objectives sought, objectives that are themselves limited to those that cannot adequately be secured in a jurisdiction of lesser scope. Directive authority—embodied in the agreement—does not attempt to eliminate discretion in the administrative ranks below it but is concerned only with stating standards for the guidance of administrative authority within a framework conducive to the primary objectives sought.

Thus a bargaining agreement on a wide-unit basis does not rule out the possibility of differential terms or conditions between units, firms, plants, or departments. The wider agreement prescribes the standards that must be observed by all component units and the programs that are operated on a pooled basis, such as pensions. Supplementary agreements at the level of the individual firm or plant cover other matters of local interest not in conflict with the general terms. Cooperative bargaining may thus be established in both types of units with respect to the relevant issues. Local members and officials become involved in a responsible way.

American labor and management have already gone far toward establishing the basis for a federal system conducive to cooperative bargaining through the grievance process, which involves those in shop and office as well as at head-quarters in continuous, daily collective bargaining. On the job in the shop or office, workers, managers, and union officials have plenty of opportunity to learn the wisdom of respecting one another's interests and to learn to appreciate the mutual benefits to be gained by bargaining cooperatively. Here, where supervisors, workers, and shop stewards must confront each other daily and join together to produce effectively and efficiently, an appreciation of quid pro quo bargaining is strong. From long practical experience they have learned to base their cooperation on a realistic appreciation of each other's desire to protect their own interest. And there is available to them the device of the grievance process, through which they may openly discuss their demands, protect their interests, and arrange mutually satisfactory settlements.

The strength of American unions in the shop and the prevalence of the grievance process have already helped to produce a good deal of lower-level cooperative bargaining that has helped in the introduction of technological change. Grievance bargaining is not always cooperative, but the common practice of discussing work rules and writing them down makes them explicit and easier to deal with than if they were merely tacit arrangements protected by tradition. They are on view and can be bargained about and often traded off. If managers are willing to offer value for value and not merely insist upon a sacrifice of valuable rules by workers, changes can be secured without stubborn resistance.

Professor Ivar Berg, after an extensive examination of work reform projects and cooperative efforts by labor and management in the United States, concluded:

> In the case of unionized organization, worker participation schemes may augment, but are more likely to compete with, those structural arrangements. Where they do not compete disadvantageously with collective bargaining (and the grievance machinery that generally accompanies bargaining), these schemes will soon be merged with those standing arrangements that have long aided managers and workers to reconcile their interests satisfactorily.
>
> A random sampling of contract agreements and of work rules in accordance with which workers and managers live in most industries will show that work enlargement, work enrichment, and work restructuring take place in the ordinary, daily bargaining process and on a regular basis without the help of interventionist consultants. We see no evidence that the work rules generated in collective bargaining procedures

[of the traditional kind,] explicit or implicit, are less to be admired than those insti-gated by third-party change agents.[27]

CONCLUSION

Cooperation alone does not necessarily foster increased productivity, though, and it may not bring benefits to the community. If unions and employers can evade the strictures of competition, they may well cooperate to protect them-selves from change, or they may even cooperate to restrict competition by lob-bying for government aid to protect their position, as we have noted above. Some cooperation may be at public expense.

A balance between cooperation and competition thus seems important to the future of constructive collective bargaining. The expansive hopes that cooperation and association will solve all problems no less than dangers of excessive reliance on competition will not provide a sound basis for collective bargaining. The conclusion seems inescapable that for a healthy economy, we require a proper admixture of the two.

Competition between groups with divergent interests, whether between two companies or between union and management, has the advantage of avoiding collusion at public expense. Each keeps the other "on its toes." But carried to excess, competition can break down a system of social order—just as cutthroat competition is alleged to do in product markets, or industrial strife in labor-management relations.

Cooperation between groups with common interests has the advantage of encouraging fuller exploitation of the special contribution that each can make to an improved joint performance. They pull together. But carried to excess, cooperation can be a means of massing economic power to exploit third par-ties, as when unions sometimes cooperate to impose a secondary boycott on a neutral employer or when companies form a cartel or rig prices. It is in soci-ety's interests for its economic agents to promote cooperation, as long as they face competition from others, and to compete, as long as they do not engage in economic warfare.

Conjunctive bargaining fails to extract the full advantage that cooperation between unions and managements can bring to society. It probably cannot make contributions as great as cooperative bargaining is capable of making. Cooperative bargaining appears to be at least a stage higher in the evolutionary hierarchy of industrial relations. But for cooperative bargaining to avoid the evils of union-management collusion at the expense of the public, it must func-tion within an economy that subjects the union and management partners to effective competition from others.

If the requirements of effective cooperation and effective competition are not met, the result is rather predictable. First will come public exhortation for

[27]Berg, Freedman, and Freedman, *Managers and Work Reform: A Limited Engagement, p. 219.*

the parties to behave like good citizens and refrain from injuring the public by competing against each other with crippling strikes or by too readily increasing wages and profits through higher prices. If such admonitions are ineffective, as they are likely to be, the next step will certainly be regulation and strike controls on the one hand and wage-price controls on the other.

If unions leaders and managers wish to retain private, discretionary decision-making authority, they must continue to improve the processes of collective bargaining by experimenting with the devices that induce cooperation, and at the same time they must provide some mechanism, perhaps a form of arbitration, for resolving competitive differences between them. If they are to retain freedom of action, they cannot deny the need for institutions to render unnecessary—or at least less necessary—government intervention to preserve the reasonable interests of third parties and the public.

INDEX

INDEX